NINETEENTH-CENTURY NATION BUILDING

AND THE

LATIN AMERICAN INTELLECTUAL TRADITION

A Reader

NINETEENTH-CENTURY NATION BUILDING

AND THE

LATIN AMERICAN INTELLECTUAL TRADITION

A Reader

Edited and Translated by
JANET BURKE
and
TED HUMPHREY

Hackett Publishing Company, Inc.
Indianapolis/Cambridge

For our grandchildren,
Brennan, Grace, Kohl, Madeline, and those to come
that they and their generation might better understand
those with whom they share the Americas.

Copyright © 2007 by Hackett Publishing Company, Inc.

All rights reserved

Printed in the United States of America

10 09 08 07   1 2 3 4 5 6 7

For further information, please address

Hackett Publishing Company, Inc.
P.O. Box 44937
Indianapolis, IN 46244-0937

www.hackettpublishing.com

Cover design by Abigail Coyle
Interior design by Elizabeth Wilson
Composition by William Hartman
Printed at Edwards Brothers, Inc.

Library of Congress Cataloging-in-Publication Data

Nineteenth-century nation building and the Latin American intellectual tradition : a
reader / edited and translated by Janet Burke and Ted Humphrey.
     p. cm.
   Includes bibliographical references.
   ISBN-13: 978-0-87220-837-7 (pbk.)
   ISBN-13: 978-0-87220-838-4 (cloth)
   1. National characteristics, Latin American. 2. Latin America—History—
19th century—Sources. I. Burke, Janet, 1943–   II. Humphrey, Ted, 1941–
   F1408.3.N56 2007
   980.03'1—dc22

                                                                    2006031185

CONTENTS

EDITOR-TRANSLATORS' NOTE

A number of principles govern the selection and translation of the readings in this volume. First and foremost, the selections represent the broad spectrum of opinion regarding the challenges of nation building that nineteenth-century Latin Americans faced as they prepared for lives as citizens of republics. We want those who desire to understand this process to encounter the perceptions and thought of Latin Americans themselves. Doing so is a necessary condition for comprehending Latin America's various political, social, and economic cultures. We have tried to let these Latin American writers and thinkers speak for themselves in their own voices, without proscribing their expression beyond choosing the writers, selecting the work to represent them, and executing the translations. For this reason, our introductions to the authors tend to be more factual than interpretive and evaluative.

More than ninety percent of the translations for this volume are new. Twelve of the authors, so far as we are aware, have never had any of their work previously translated into English. By itself, that fact speaks volumes. In assembling this reader, we have focused on nineteenth-century nation building and the Latin American intellectual tradition, as our title indicates. In the translations, then, we have attempted to render conceptually significant terms consistently. We have also attempted to preserve the distinctive voice of each author, even when doing so might, at first glance, prevent the most fluid English phrasing. Further, we are aware that instructors will use the reader in college classrooms, and we have paid attention both to level of vocabulary and to each author's references, many of which are not well known. We have used these translations in a variety of class settings, and students have found them accessible and stimulating. Finally, we have tried to anticipate the variety of uses to which instructors might put the volume, from supporting survey courses with primary source material to serving as a stand-alone text in philosophy and intellectual history courses. The table of Contents and Guide to Themes will facilitate varied uses. We have attempted to provide a rigorous, challenging set of selections, revelatory of the best Latin American thinking and writing on issues that still plague humanity, selections that will meet a variety of pedagogical needs.

ACKNOWLEDGMENTS

A project of this kind does not come to fruition without untold—and often unre-membered—support from family, friends, students, and colleagues. The original idea and need for this volume developed over six years, and for that reason alone we cannot now recall all those who have contributed to the effort. Having discovered that undergraduates interested in Latin American intellectual history have few English language resources to which they can turn, we began to plot a volume to meet what we estimated would be basic needs. A single volume, extending from times prior to the *encuentro* (first encounter between the indigenous of the Americas and the Europeans) through, say, the middle of the twentieth century, would be both overwhelmingly large and unrealizable in a reasonable amount of time. To begin, then, we have focused on the period we know best and believe will immediately immerse students in the intellectual foment of Latin America—the century following the rise of the Spanish American movement toward independence.

As we began editing and translating the texts, our colleagues at Arizona State University, particularly Professors David William Foster, Joel Gereboff, Elizabeth Horan, K. Lynn Stoner, Tod Swanson, and Michael J. White, provided advice and help at what seemed like a moment's notice. We thank them for their enormous generosity, as we do Professor Karen Melvin of Bates College. The Latin American subject matter specialist at the ASU libraries, Claude Potts, provided support throughout the project. Elizabeth Dreeland provided research support for developing footnotes. Students in our course, Latin American Intellectual History II, provided important responses to and insight into our initial public showing of the translations. Hackett Publishing Company has enthusiastically supported the project from the moment we initially approached the press; we cannot adequately thank them for the confidence they showed in our ability to bring these prodigious minds to the attention of undergraduates. Nor can we thank them sufficiently for finding the two readers who provided invaluable commentary on our translations, Timothy J. Henderson and David Frye. Both helped us see more clearly the context and intent of our selections. Professor Henderson made valuable comments on tightening and clarifying our texts. Professor Frye read and commented in fine-grained detail on eighty percent of the text and provided invaluable footnotes. His comments helped us avoid a number of translations that might have missed the mark and provided innumerable alternatives to our suggested wording. In those instances where we chose to retain our original wording, his suggestions still helped us think through and better understand our decisions. For all this, we can only thank both readers.

Finally, we want to thank our families for their understanding of the time and dedication a project of this kind requires.

JANET BURKE
TED HUMPHREY

GENERAL INTRODUCTION

This reader presents an extended, transcontinental discussion among some of the most creative, engaged, and articulate thinkers of the nineteenth century. Their voices resonate with a mix of profound learning, cool logic, biting humor, passion, even anger. All direct themselves to one overarching and pressing question—now that we are independent of colonial rule, how do we best constitute our new nations to guarantee their success? Alternatively, how do we fashion citizens from subjects and colonized peoples? These *pensadores,* public philosophers, come at these great issues from a number of different backgrounds and perspectives, with the understanding that the key to resolving them lies in different aspects of the Latin American experience. Thus, the discussion takes up such challenges as how to create republican forms of government out of the vestiges of a three-centuries-old monarchical tradition; what to do about the Catholic Church, dominant everywhere; and where to find the appropriate principles on which to build the new educational systems so critical to forming republican citizenries. And what about the indigenous, what about women, what about the Spaniards still living in Latin America? What role do they play in the new societies? How do large countries like Brazil and Argentina secure the population they need to fill in the empty spaces and generate a progressive spirit? What to do about the United States, a nation both admired and feared?

The English-speaking world has for some time had access to well-translated Latin American literature, as the popularity in the United States of the work of Gabriel García Márquez, Carlos Fuentes, Elena Poniatowski, Gabriela Mistral, and Jorge Amado among many others bears witness. These translations have made the literary genius of Latin America concrete for English speakers. Unfortunately, we have not had the same access to the more abstract intellectual work of Latin America's *pensadores,* who throughout the region's history have been engaged in cultural analysis, social formation, and nation building. This volume partially fills that gap in our resources for understanding Latin America by providing a representative selection of readings from some of its most seminal thinkers. They are but the tip of an iceberg, however, only indicating the range and depth of concern for Latin America's future that its peoples felt during the critical stage of building post-independence societies and governments. The figures one meets in this anthology are not only thinkers of enormous power, they are also agents of change who sought to create social good with their writing as well as by accepting positions of great public responsibility. Because their names tend to be unfamiliar among English speakers, we can indicate their importance only by comparing them to such English-language thinkers and writers as Alexander Hamilton, James Madison, Thomas Jefferson, Abraham Lincoln, Jeremy Bentham, James Mill, and John Stuart Mill. The authors in this volume were presidents of nations, founders of universities, holders of elective and appointive office, and military leaders. Many also paid the price of exile for expressing sharp criticism of existing institutions and promoting incisive ideas regarding the nature of government appropriate to the Americas. Nonetheless, in Latin America today, those who were exiled are as well known and honored as those thinkers who were able to remain in their countries. Both are Latin America's cultural heroes and idols, and we can better understand cultures by knowing their heroes.

The reader contains writers from all major regions of Latin America and represents the many strands of its nineteenth-century thinking. Despite the great land mass from which these writings come, they exhibit remarkable continuity and coherence of concern—a conversation in which people separated by thousands of miles contribute almost as if they were in the same city or room. Much of this focus stems from the authors' shared cultural heritage and language, a language they deeply value. The linguistic exception, of course, is found in Brazil, which shared Latin America's monarchical and Catholic past but not its language. Moreover, Brazil did not become a republic until the late-nineteenth century and thus did not confront issues of democracy and republicanism until much later than the majority of the Spanish-speaking nations. On the other hand, Brazil does share concerns and challenges that justify its representation in this collection.

As the Latin American *pensadores* confronted and sought resolutions to their great issues, they found inspiration in the political thinking and institutions of Ancient Greece and Rome, the French Revolution, the French philosophers of the seventeenth through the mid-nineteenth centuries, particularly Baron Montesquieu, Jean-Jacques Rousseau, Auguste Comte, Pierre Leroux, Ernst Renan, Edgar Quinet, Félicité Lammenais, and Hippolyte Taine, and various expressions of republicanism and what they perceived as the rapid political and economic rise of the United States, a nation they both admired and feared. In the natural and social sciences, they were particularly taken with Charles Darwin and Herbert Spencer, whose Social Darwinism coupled with Comte's positivism led them to think about race and culture in ways we no longer find acceptable. Although individual thinkers focused on different issues, the issues were interrelated and, in the end, most authors had to consider some aspect of each of them. This gives one kind of conceptual unity to the selections in this anthology. The great issues with which they grappled include the following:

- **The colonial past.** For these writers the Latin American experience is defined by three centuries of monarchical rule, which followed centuries of an indigenous past, and yet their aspirations and models are largely republican, given their intellectual encounters with non-Spanish, non-Portuguese intellectual life, particularly that of France and Germany, and the reality of democracy in the United States.

- **Federalism versus political unitarianism.** Which unique constitutional forms are relevant to Latin America? Should they, as Simón Bolívar believed, be monolithic and centralized, or should they assume a shared power form, with the weight of authority vested in the states or provinces?

- **The religious tradition.** What ought the role of the institutional Catholic Church be in the new republics? This is the most heated topic of debate, with some arguing that the Catholic past must be honored and the Church exclusive of other faiths (e.g., Lucas Alamán), and others that the Church must be abolished (e.g., Francisco Bilbao), and still others that the health of the Latin American republics requires full acceptance of other Christian traditions (e.g., Juan Bautista Alberdi).

- **Sociability.** The discussion of the fitness of Latin American peoples for social existence, deemed essential to the development of culture and political life, is the most nuanced topic of discussion. At the poles of this debate are José Victorino Lastarria and Bilbao, who argue that the Spanish past constitutes a barrier to social existence that must be overthrown, and Alamán, who argues that the very foundation of Latin American sociability lies in its Spanish past. In between are such writers as Domingo Faustino Sarmiento and Euclides da Cunha, who decry the huge gulf between coastal residents and residents of the interior in their vast countries, Argentina and Brazil, and José Martí and Bolívar, who look ahead to the emergence of the "new American man."

- **Foreign relations.** Consistently, these thinkers are concerned with how their nations will become part of the greater international community. In particular, how will their countries relate to and be recognized by European nations, with whom they must interact if they are to improve their economic situation? And how will they relate to the United States, admired for its achievement but feared because of its perceived economic, cultural, and territorial aggressiveness in a postcolonial world? In general, these thinkers are less trusting of the United States the nearer they are to the Río Bravo.

- **The indigenous.** Are the indigenous peoples a social, political, and economic asset? How are they to be integrated into the new societies and governments? On the one hand, Martí argues that they constitute the single greatest social asset of the newly emerging nations, and on the other hand, Alcides Arguedas and Alberdi regard their existence as challenges to creating viable societies.

- **The role of women in the new societies.** During the nineteenth century, women are not much in evidence among the public philosophers in Latin America, but their role is a matter of importance to various thinkers who either want to carve out a distinctive space for them or see them as a source of salvation for the backward state of Latin America. This reader includes essays by two women, Clorinda Matto de Turner and Soledad Acosta de Samper, who speak about their role in society, and at least one educator, Eugenio María de Hostos, who believes that the proper education of women is critical to successful nation building.

- **Education for citizenship and economic development.** The nature and role of education in a republic is the touchstone to which all of the writers turn as they think their way through the foregoing challenges. At one end of the spectrum, Juan Montalvo contends that education in the European past, particularly that of Greece and Rome, is necessary to the moral and political formation of the citizenry, and at the other, Martí argues that education in the uniquely American past must come before any education derived from Europe. In between is the entire range of views on education, all emphasizing that it is fundamental to citizenship, that is, to human existence as and in a republic.

- **The nature and uses of history.** One of the purest philosophical discussions among these writers involves the nature of history, but even here, the concern for history ultimately has an application—the use of its lessons. One of the most revealing dialogues on this topic occurs between student and teacher, José Victorino Lastarria and Andrés Bello, who disagree significantly but who also deeply value the opportunity to air the issues and think through the consequences of their views. Overall, however, Latin Americans regard themselves as essentially historical persons and nations whose very existence constitutes one of the turning points in human history.

As the editors and translators of the selections in this reader, we intend it first and foremost to be the occasion for a voyage of intellectual discovery and encounter. The majority of the *pensadores* presented here have had either very limited or no previous exposure in the English-speaking world. Every comparable collection of French, German, or Italian writers and thinkers has been available to readers of English not simply in one translation but often in several. These Latin American authors are, the reader will discover, extraordinary writers of incisive argument and persuasive prose as well as highly educated intellectuals fully engaged with the world and the betterment of the human condition. Moreover, they represent the broadest possible spectrum of distinctive voices, using language in creative ways to analyze crucial theoretical and practical puzzles and illuminate the human spirit.

Finally, we understand that any anthology invariably falls short both in the authors it includes or excludes and in the selections used to represent those authors. We believe, nevertheless, that the authors and writings included here will provide a foundation for a deeper understanding and appreciation of the intellectual work that the Latin American *pensadores* undertook in the nineteenth century, as well as a basis for further exploration of the rich intellectual traditions found in Latin America. We hope that this encounter will inspire students to continue the work only just begun here.

Simón Bolívar
(Venezuela/Colombia)

Simón José Antonio de la Santísima Trinidad Bolívar y Ponte Palacios y Blanco (1783–1830), universally denominated *"El Libertador,"* The Liberator, of South America, is as interesting for his contributions to the intellectual life and imagination of South America as he was instrumental to securing its independence from Spain. Bolívar was to become the founding father of five South American republics. He was born in Caracas, Venezuela, the youngest of the four children of Juan Vicente Bolívar y Ponte, a wealthy creole planter and militia colonel, and the aristocratic María de la Concepción Palacios y Blanco. He received his early education from family members, but at age twelve he spent some months at the home of Simón Rodríguez, headmaster of an elementary school in Caracas, who became a lifelong mentor and friend. Over time, a number of others taught and influenced Bolívar, most notably Andrés Bello, with whom he studied history, literature, and geography. At fourteen, he entered the militia in the Aragua Valley in Venezuela and was promoted to second lieutenant within a year. During this time, he studied mathematics, topography, and physics at an academy in his own home. In 1799, he traveled to Spain to continue his studies, which were designed to prepare him for leadership. While there he fell desperately in love with and married María Teresa Rodríguez del Toro, daughter of one of Caracas's most distinguished families. She died in Venezuela within a year of their marriage, and Bolívar never remarried.

While in Europe, Bolívar became interested in Spanish American independence, and when Napoleon invaded Spain, Bolívar took part in the revolutionary activities arising at that time in Venezuela. On April 19, 1810, revolutionaries in Caracas deposed the Spanish captain general and established a governing junta, which named Bolívar commissioner to London to seek British support for the new regime. The new Venezuelan congress proclaimed independence from Spain July 5, 1811. Bolívar thereupon entered military service and rose rapidly to the rank of colonel, being called on immediately to suppress a counterrevolutionary outbreak at Valencia.

He wrote his first major political statement, "Memoria dirigida a los ciudadanos de la Nueva Granada por un Caraqueño" (translated as "The Cartegena Manifesto: Memorial addressed to the Citizens of New Granada by a Citizen of Caracas") in 1812, a statement of the fundamental political principles that would guide his future decisions and actions. Among his other significant writings are the 1815 "Carta a un caballero que tomaba gran interés en la causa republicana de la América del Sur" (translated as "The Jamaica Letter") and his 1816 decree, "A los habitantes de Río Caribe, Carupano y Cariaco" (translated as "Decree for the Emancipation of the Slaves"). During this period, Bolívar was deeply involved in the politics of the "Second Republic," in which he held, lost, and retook civil and military power.

The foundational document of Bolívar's political ideology is contained in a speech he delivered to the Second Venezuelan Congress, convened at his behest in Angostura in 1819 and at which he also submitted a draft of his proposed constitution. Two years later, the Colombian constituent congress adopted a constitution and elected Bolívar the first president to serve under it. This state, created by the Liberator, comprised the later republics of Venezuela, Colombia, Ecuador, and Panama. In 1823, at the invitation of the Peruvian leadership, Bolívar also assumed military leadership of the struggle for independence in Peru. Within two years, the former territory of upper Peru took the name Bolivia and invited Bolívar to write its constitution, whose central feature is a lifetime presidency.

Bolívar's dream of what has commonly come to be called "Gran Colombia" came to grief between 1827 and 1830. Faced with the secession of Venezuela from the Colombian union and the opposition of New Granadan liberals, he resigned the presidency in 1830 and died seven months later.

Influenced by Enlightenment contract theories of the state and by romantic liberalism, Bolívar's thought exhibits a firm grasp of the political realities of and challenges involved in the formation of independent republics among peoples who had known only monarchical government. Even though two of his principal ideas for political stability among such peoples—namely, a lifetime presidency and a league of Spanish American republics—were ultimately rejected, they have had a continuing influence on Latin American political discourse.

The selections that follow are from Bolívar's "Discurso pronunciado por el Libertador ante el Congreso de Angostura el 15 de febrero de 1819, día de su instalación" ("Address to the Angostura Congress, February 15, 1819, the Day of its Installation") and his "Discurso del Libertador al Congreso constituyente de Bolivia" ("Address to the Constituent Congress of Bolivia").

Further Reading

Acosta Saignes, Miguel. *Dialéctica del libertador.* Caracas: Universidad Central de Venezuela, Ediciones de la Biblioteca EBUC, 2002.

Bolívar, Simón. *Obras completas.* Edited by Vicente Lecuna. 3 vols. Havana: Editorial Lex, 1950.

Brading, David. *Classical Republicanism and Creole Patriotism: Simón Bolívar (1783–1830) and the Spanish American Revolution.* Cambridge: Cambridge University Press, 1983.

Bushnell, David. *Simón Bolívar: hombre de Caracas, proyecto de América: Una biografía.* Buenos Aires: Editorial Biblos, 2002.

———. *Simón Bolívar: Liberation and Disillusion.* New York: Pearson Longman, 2004.

Collier, Simon. "Nationality, Nationalism, and Supranationalism in the Writings of Simón Bolívar." *The Hispanic American Historical Review* 63, no. 1 (1983): 37–64.

Cussen, Antonio. *Bello and Bolívar: Poetry and Politics in the Spanish American Revolution.* Cambridge [England]; New York: Cambridge University Press, 1992.

García Hamilton, José Ignacio. *Simón: vida de Bolívar.* Buenos Aires: Editorial Sudamericana, 2004.

Lynch, John. *Simón Bolívar: A Life.* New Haven: Yale University Press, 2006.

Slatta, Richard W. *Simón Bolívar's Quest for Glory.* College Station, Tex.: Texas A&M University Press, 2003.

Address to the Angostura Congress, February 15, 1819, the Day of Its Installation

Sir:

Happy the citizen who, under the coat of arms of his command, has convened the representatives of national sovereignty to exercise its absolute will! I, then, count myself among Divine Providence's most favored beings, for I have had the honor of bringing together the representatives of the people of Venezuela in this august Congress, wellspring of the legitimate authority, repository of the sovereign will, and arbiter of the nation's destiny.

In transferring to the people's representatives the supreme power that had been entrusted to me, I fulfill my heart's desires, those of my fellow citizens, and those of our future generations, who expect everything from your wisdom, honesty, and prudence. In complying with this pleasant obligation I free myself of the immense authority that has overwhelmed me and the unlimited responsibility that weighed heavily on my weak strengths. Only an unavoidable necessity, together with the imperious will of the people, would have made me take on the terrible and dangerous responsibility of *Chief, Supreme Dictator of the Republic.* But now I breathe a sigh of relief, returning to you this authority that, with so much risk, difficulty, and pain, I have managed to maintain in the midst of the most horrifying tribulations that can afflict a social body!

The era of the republic, over which I have presided, has not been a mere political tempest, nor a bloody war, nor a popular anarchy; but it has certainly been the gathering of all disruptive elements—it has been the inundation of an infernal torrent that has overwhelmed the land of Venezuela. One man— and a man such as I!—what dikes could he put up against the momentum of these devastations? In the midst of this sea of torments, I have been nothing more than a lowly plaything of the revolutionary hurricane that carried me away like a feeble straw. I have been able to do neither good nor evil—irresistible forces have directed the course of our events. To attribute them to me would not be just and would give me an importance I do not deserve. Do you want to know the authors of the past events and present situation? Consult the annals of Spain, of America, of Venezuela; examine the Laws of the Indies, the system of the former leaders, the influence of religion and foreign domination; observe the first acts of the republican government, the ferocity of our enemies, and the national character. Do not ask me about the effects of these upheavals, forever unfortunate—one can hardly think of me as even a simple instrument of the great movements that have been at work in Venezuela—nonetheless, my life, my conduct, all my public and private actions are subject to the censure of the people. Representatives! You are the ones who must judge them. I submit the history of my command to your impartial verdict; I will add nothing to excuse it; I have already said all I can to defend myself. If I deserve your approval, I will have gained the sublime title of good citizen, preferable to me than *Liberator,* which Venezuela gave me, or *Peace Maker,* which Cundinamarca[1] gave me, and any others that the whole world might choose to give me.

Legislators! I place in your hands the supreme command of Venezuela. The august duty of dedicating yourselves to the republic's happiness is now yours; the balance of our destinies, the measure of our glory, is in your hands—your hands will seal the decrees that will secure our *liberty.* As of this moment the Supreme Leader of the Republic is nothing more than a simple citizen, and so he desires to remain until death. I will nonetheless serve in the profession of arms so long as there may be enemies in Venezuela. The fatherland has many worthy sons capable of leading it—talents, virtues, experience, everything required to govern free men, are the patrimony of many of those here who represent the people; and beyond this sovereign body there are citizens who, in every era, have shown bravery in confronting dangers, prudence in avoiding them and, finally, the art of governing themselves and governing others. These illustrious great men will certainly earn the votes of Congress, and to them will be entrusted the government that I so warmly and sincerely have just given up forever.

The continuation of authority by the same individual has frequently meant the end of democratic governments. Regular elections are essential in popular systems, because nothing is so dangerous as leaving power with a single citizen for a long time. The people become accustomed to obeying him, and he becomes accustomed to commanding them, from which situation usurpation and tyranny originate. An appropriate zeal is the guarantee of republican liberty, and our citizens should fear with reason that the same magistrate who has governed them for a long time will govern them indefinitely.

Inasmuch, then, as by this act of my support for the liberty of Venezuela I can aspire to the glory of being counted among Venezuela's most faithful admirers, permit me, gentlemen, to explain with the frankness of a true republican my respectful opinion of this *Plan for a Constitution,* which I take the liberty of offering you as evidence of the sincerity and candor of my feelings. As it has to do with everyone's well-being, I dare to believe that I have the right to be heard

---

1. A former province of colonial New Granada and today a state in central Colombia.

by the people's representatives. I know full well that your wisdom has no need of advice; and I know also that my plan will perhaps seem wrong-headed, impractical to you. But, gentlemen, kindly accept this work, more the tribute of my sincere submission to Congress than the result of presumptuous caprice. On the other hand, your function being the creation of a body politic, and, it could even be said, the creation of an entire society, complete with all the difficulties that so singular and difficult a situation presents, perhaps the cry of a citizen can warn you of the presence of a hidden or unknown danger.

Casting a glance over the past, we will see what constitutes the foundation of the Republic of Venezuela.

America, having freed itself from the Spanish monarchy, has found itself in a situation similar to that of the Roman Empire when that enormous mass fell to pieces amidst the ancient world. Every dismembered piece then formed an independent nation in accordance with its situation or interests, but with the difference that those pieces returned to reestablish their original associations. We do not even retain the vestiges of what existed in former times—we are not Europeans, we are not Indians, but rather a race midway between the aborigines and the Spanish. Americans by birth and Europeans by rights, we find ourselves in the dilemma of disputing rights of possession with the natives and of sustaining ourselves in the country of our birth against the opposition of the invaders; thus our case is most extraordinary and complex. There is still more—our fate has always been purely passive, our political existence has always been non-existent, and the more we were put in a status inferior to servitude, the more difficulty we experienced in attaining liberty, because we were not only robbed of liberty but also an active and domestic tyranny. Permit me to explain this paradox. In absolute regimes, the authorized power does not acknowledge limits. The will of the despot is the supreme law, carried out arbitrarily by subordinates who participate in organized oppression by reason of the authority they enjoy. They are placed in charge of all civil, political, military, and religious functions; but in the end, the satraps of Persia are Persians, the pashas of the Great Lord are Turks, the sultans of Tatary are Tatars. China did not search for mandarins in the birthplace of Genghis Khan, who conquered China. On the other hand, America received everything from Spain, which actually had deprived America of the pleasure and exercise of active tyranny, not permitting us tyranny's functions in our domestic affairs and interior administration. This deprivation made it impossible for us to learn the course of public business; neither did we enjoy the personal regard that the glory of power inspires in the eyes of the multitude and that is so important in great revolutions. I will say it once and for all—we were kept separate, apart from the universe, to the degree that it was relative to the science of government.

We American people, under the triple yoke of ignorance, tyranny, and vice, have been able to acquire neither knowledge, nor power, nor virtue. Disciples of such pernicious masters, the lessons we have received and the examples we have studied are entirely destructive. We have been dominated more by deceit than by force; and we have been degraded more by vice than by superstition. Slavery is the daughter of darkness; an ignorant people is a blind instrument of its own destruction—ambition, intrigue, take advantage of the credulity and the inexperience of men ignorant of all political, economic, or civil knowledge. These men adopt pure illusions as realities; they take license for liberty, treason for patriotism, vengeance for justice. They resemble a robust blind man who, urged on by his false sense of strength, marches with the assurance of the most keen-sighted man, and, stumbling on every obstacle, cannot right his course. A corrupted people, if it obtains its liberty, very soon loses it again; because one will strive in vain to demonstrate to the people that happiness consists in the practice of virtue; that the rule of law is more powerful than the rule of tyrants, because law is more inflexible, and everything must yield to its beneficent rigor; that good practices, and not force, are the pillars of the law; that the exercise of justice is the exercise of liberty. Thus, Legislators, your undertaking becomes all the more arduous the more you have to form men corrupted by the illusions of error and by harmful inducements. Liberty, says Rousseau, is a succulent food but difficult to digest. Our weak fellow citizens will have to strengthen their spirit long before they will be able to digest liberty's healthy nutritiousness. Their limbs numbed by chains, their vision weakened in the shadows of dungeons, and they themselves emaciated from the pestilence of servitude, will they be capable of marching with firm step toward the august temple of liberty? Will they be capable of admiring its splendid rays of light close up and of breathing without oppression the pure ether that prevails there?

Contemplate your choice carefully, Legislators. Do not forget that you are going to lay the foundations for a nascent people who will be able to raise themselves to the greatness that nature has determined for them if you provide them a base proportionate to the lofty eminence that awaits them. If your choice is not governed by the tutelary spirit of Venezuela, which should inspire in you good judgment in choosing the nature and form of government you are going to adopt for the happiness of the people; if you do not get it just right, I repeat, slavery will be the result of our transformation.

The annals of past times will present you with thousands of governments. Reflect on the nations that have stood out brilliantly on earth, and you will see, distressed, that almost all the earth has been, and still is, the victim of its governments. You will observe many systems for managing men, but all to oppress them; and if the habit of seeing the human race being led by shepherds of people did not diminish the horror of such a shocking spectacle, we would be stunned to see our docile species grazing the surface of the globe like lowly flocks destined to provide food for their cruel shepherds. At birth, nature truly endows us with the longing for liberty; but, be it from laziness, be it from an inherent tendency of humanity, the certainty is that humanity remains complacent even while hindered by the hobbles placed on it. In contemplating humanity in this state of prostitution, it seems we are justified in convincing ourselves that the majority of men believe that humiliating maxim, namely, that it costs more to maintain the balance of liberty than to support the weight of tyranny. Would that this maxim, contrary to natural morality, be false! Would that this maxim were not sanctioned by men's indolence relative to their most sacred rights!

Many ancient and modern nations have shaken off oppression, but very rare are those that have known how to enjoy a few precious moments of liberty. Too soon they have fallen back into their old political vices, because the people, much more than the governments, drag tyranny along behind them. The habit of domination makes them unaware of the charms of honor and of national prosperity; and they view with indifference the glory of living in the movement toward liberty under the tutelage of laws dictated by their own will. The annals of the world proclaim this dreadful truth.

Only democracy, from my point of view, is capable of an absolute liberty; but what democratic government has ever assembled power, prosperity, and permanence at the same time? And on the contrary, have we not seen aristocracy, monarchy, establish great and powerful empires for centuries and centuries? What government is more ancient than China's? What republic has exceeded in duration that of Sparta, that of Venice? Did not the Roman Empire conquer the world? Did not France have fourteen centuries of monarchy? Who is greater than England? These nations, nonetheless, have been or are aristocratic and monarchical.

Despite such cruel reflections, I feel myself seized by joy because of the tremendous strides our republic has taken in embarking on its noble course. Loving what is most useful, enlivened by what is most just, and aspiring to what is most perfect, Venezuela has, in separating itself from the Spanish nation, recovered its independence, its liberty, its equality, its national sovereignty. Constituting itself as a democratic republic, it proscribed monarchy, distinctions, nobility, special rights, privileges—it declared the rights of man, the freedom of work, of thought, of speech, and of writing. These acts, eminently liberal, can never be admired enough for the purity that has decreed them. Placing its seal on the social act most capable of creating the happiness of a nation, the first Congress of Venezuela has written in the annals of our legislation with indelible characters the majesty of the people worthily expressed. I must summon all my strength to experience with all the passion of which I am capable the supreme good that is contained in this immortal code of our rights and our laws. But how will I dare say it! Will I dare to profane the sacred table of our laws with my criticism . . . ? There are feelings that cannot be contained in the heart of a lover of the fatherland; they overflow, stirred by their own impetus, and despite the one who holds them, an urgent force releases them. I am fully convinced by the idea that the government of Venezuela must be reformed, and that even though many illustrious citizens think as I do, not all have the boldness necessary to profess publicly the adoption of new principles. This consideration urges me to take the initiative in a matter of the greatest seriousness, one that shows excessive audacity in giving advice to the people's counselors.

The more I admire the excellence of the federal constitution of Venezuela, the more I am persuaded of the impossibility of its application to our situation. And, according to my way of seeing, it is a wonder that its model in North America continues to exist so successfully and is not turned upside down at the first appearance of an impediment or danger. Although that people is a singular model of political virtue and moral enlightenment, notwithstanding that liberty has been their cradle, that they have been raised in liberty, and that they are nourished by pure liberty—in sum, even though in many respects that people is unique in the history of the human race—it is a wonder, I repeat, that such a weak and complex system as federalism has been able to govern it in such difficult and delicate situations as those of its past. But be that government as it may be with respect to the North American nation, I must say that it has never remotely entered into my mind to compare the situation and nature of states so different as the English American and the Spanish American. Would it not be very difficult to apply England's code of political, civil, and religious liberty to Spain? Then it is even more difficult to adapt in Venezuela the laws of North America. Does not *The Spirit of the Laws* say that these laws must be appropriate for the people for whom they are made?[2] That it is a great coincidence when the laws of one nation prove suitable for another? That the laws must be relative to the physical appearance of the country, to the climate, to the quality of the terrain, to its location, to its size, to the way of life of the peoples? That they reflect the degree of liberty the constitution can permit, the religion of the inhabitants, their tendencies, their wealth, their number, their commerce, their habits, their manners? Here we have the code we must consult, not that of Washington!!!

The Venezuelan constitution, despite having taken its foundations from the most perfect constitution with respect to the correctness of its principles and the beneficent effects of its administration, differed essentially from the American in one cardinal point, certainly the most important one. The Congress of Venezuela, like the American, distributes some of the jurisdictions of the executive power. We, moreover, subdivide that branch, having granted it to a collective body, thereby subjecting it to the inconvenience of rendering the government periodic, suspending it, and dissolving it whenever its members disband. Our triumvirate lacks, so to speak, unity, continuity, and individual responsibility; it is incapable of prompt action, continuous life, real uniformity, immediate responsibility; and a government that does not possess what constitutes moral authority must be deemed null and void.

Although the powers of the president of the United States are limited by excessive restrictions, he alone exercises all the governing functions that the constitution grants to him, and his administration must necessarily be more uniform, constant, and truly autonomous than the administration of a power disseminated among various individuals, whose composite cannot be less than monstrous.

Venezuela's judicial power is like the American, indefinite in duration, temporary, and not for life; it enjoys all the independence that befits the judiciary.

In its federal constitution, the first Congress looked more to the spirit of the provinces than to the solid idea of forming one indivisible and centralized

---

2. *De l'esprit des lois* (1748), the great treatise by Charles-Louis de Secondat, Baron de la Brèd et de Montesquieu (known simply as Montesquieu) (1689–1755), one of the great French Enlightenment political philosophers.

republic. Here our legislators yielded to the impetuous insistence of those provincials seduced by the dazzling sparkle of the American people's happiness, thinking that the blessings they enjoy are due exclusively to the form of government and not to the character and habits of the citizens. And, indeed, the example of the United States, by its singular prosperity, was too alluring not to be followed. Who can resist the victorious attraction of full and absolute enjoyment of sovereignty, of independence, of liberty? Who can resist the love that is inspired by an intelligent government that simultaneously links individual rights to general rights, that forms the supreme law of the individual will from the common will? Who can resist the rule of a benevolent government, which, with a skillful, active, and powerful hand, directs always and everywhere all its resources toward social perfection, the sole end of human institutions?

But however attractive this magnificent federative system might seem, and might actually be, it was not conceivable for Venezuelans to enjoy it suddenly just as we emerged from chains. We were not prepared for so much good; good, like evil, leads to death when it is sudden and excessive. Our moral constitution did not yet have the strength necessary to receive the benefit of a completely representative government, so sublime that it could well be adapted to a republic of saints.

Representatives of the people! You are called to confirm or suppress whatever seems to you worthy of being preserved, reformed, or rejected in our social contract. To you belongs the correction of the work of our first legislators; I meant to say that it falls to you to cover over a part of the beauty that our political code contains, because not all hearts are created to love everything beautiful, nor are all eyes capable of bearing the heavenly light of perfection. The book of the apostles, the morality of Jesus, the divine work that Providence has sent to us to improve men—so sublime, so holy—would be an all-consuming flame in Constantinople, and all Asia would be ablaze if this book of peace were suddenly imposed on them as a code of religion, laws, and customs.

Permit me to call the attention of Congress to a subject that may be of vital importance. Let us keep in mind that our people is not European, nor North American, that it is more a composite of Africa and America than an emanation of Europe, because even Spain itself is not quite European because of its African blood, its institutions, and its character. It is impossible to determine with complete precision to which human family we belong. The majority of the indigenous has been annihilated, the European has mixed with the American and the African, and the African has mixed with the Indian and the European. All born of the womb of the same mother, our fathers, different in origin and in blood, are foreigners, and all of them differ visibly in their epidermis; this dissimilarity carries an obligation of atonement of the greatest significance.

The citizens of Venezuela all enjoy a perfect political equality through the constitution, interpreter of nature. Although such equality may not have been a doctrine in Athens, France, and America, we ourselves would have had to confirm it to correct the difference that apparently exists. My opinion is, Legislators, that the fundamental principle of our system depends directly and exclusively on equality as established and practiced in Venezuela. That all men are born with equal rights to society's goods is a notion sanctioned by the majority of learned people, as also is the notion that not all men are born equally capable of obtaining every social status—for all should practice virtue and not all practice it; all should be courageous and not all are; all should possess talents and not all possess them. From this derives the effective difference observed among individuals of even the most liberally established society. If the principle of political equality is generally recognized, no less so is that of physical and moral inequality. Nature makes men unequal in ability, temperament, strengths, and character. The laws correct this difference, because they place the individual in society so that education, industry, the arts, the services, the virtues might give him an artificially constructed equality, properly called political and social equality. The merging of all classes into one state, in which diversity increases by virtue of the propagation of the species, is an eminently beneficial inspiration. By this single step, cruel disharmony has been pulled up by the roots. How many jealousies, rivalries, and hatreds have been avoided!

Having dealt with our obligation to justice, to humanity, let us now fulfill our obligation to politics, to society, smoothing over the difficulties that hinder a system so simple and natural, but so weak that the slightest misfortune disturbs it, destroys it. The diversity of origin requires an infinitely steady hand and an infinitely delicate touch to guide this heterogeneous society, whose complex contrivance is dislocated, is divided, is dissolved at the slightest disturbance.

The most perfect system of government is the one that produces the greatest possible amount of happiness, the greatest amount of social security, and the greatest amount of political stability. By the laws that the first Congress decreed, we have the right to expect that happiness will be Venezuela's portion; and by your laws, we should flatter ourselves that security and stability will make that happiness eternal. It falls to you to resolve the problem. How, after having broken all the shackles of our former oppression, can we do the marvelous work of preventing the remains of our iron chains from being transformed into arms that will be liberty killers? The relics of Spanish domination will remain a long time before we manage to destroy them; the contagion of despotism permeates our atmosphere, and neither the fire of war nor the medicine of our wholesome laws has purified the air we breathe. Our hands are now free, and our hearts still suffer from the sorrows of servitude. In losing his liberty, Homer said, man loses half his spirit.

The government of Venezuela has been, is, and must be a republic; its foundations must be the sovereignty of the people—the division of power, civil liberty, proscription of slavery, abolition of monarchy and privileges. We need equality in order to recast as a whole—so to speak—the race of men, political opinions, and public practices. Then, extending our view over the vast field that remains for us to traverse, let us fix our attention on the dangers we must avoid. Let history serve us as guide down this path. Athens first gives us the most brilliant example of an absolute democracy, and at the same time Athens offers us the most melancholy example of the extreme weakness of this type of government. The wisest legislator of Greece did not see his republic last ten years, and he suffered the humiliation of recognizing the inadequacy of absolute democracy for ruling any type of society, even the most cultured, restrained, and limited, because it only shines with flashes of liberty. Let us recognize, then, that Solon[3] has opened the eyes of the world and has taught it how difficult it is to govern men by laws alone.

The Republic of Sparta, which seemed to be a chimerical invention, produced more actual results than Solon's ingenious work. Glory, virtue, morality, and, therefore, national happiness, were the result of Lycurgus's legislation.[4] Although two kings in a state are two monsters to devour it, Sparta had little to regret from its double throne—while Athens promised the more splendid fate, with an absolute sovereignty, free election of magistrates frequently renewed, mild, wise, and politic laws. Peisistratus,[5] usurper and tyrant, was more useful for Athens than its laws; and Pericles,[6] although also a usurper, was the most useful citizen. The Republic of Thebes did not outlast the lives of Pelopidas[7] and Epaminondas,[8] because sometimes it is men, not principles, that form governments. The codes, the systems, the statutes, wise though they may be, are dead works that influence societies little. Virtuous men, patriotic men, enlightened men constitute republics!

The Roman constitution produced more power and fortune than that of any other people of the world; there, there was no exact distribution of powers. The consuls, the Senate, the people—now legislators, now magistrates, now judges—each participated in all the powers. The executive, composed of two consuls, suffered the same inconvenience as that of Sparta. Despite its deformity, the republic did not suffer the disastrous discord that all foresight would have supposed inseparable from a magistracy composed of two individuals, equally authorized with the powers of a monarch. A government whose sole tendency was conquest did not seem intended to lay the foundations for its nation's happiness. A monstrous and purely warlike government elevated Rome to the highest splendor of virtue and glory, and it turned the world into a Roman domain, to show men of how much political virtues are capable and how insignificant institutions usually are.

And passing from ancient times to modern, we will find England and France attracting the attention of all nations and giving them eloquent lessons of all

---

3. Solon (c. 638–558 BC), Athenian lawmaker who rewrote the Athenian constitution.

4. Lycurgus (700–630 BC), ancient and possibly legendary lawgiver of Sparta.

5. Peisistratus (607–528 BC), Greek statesman who became the tyrant of Athens following a coup.

6. Pericles (495–429 BC), influential and important leader of Athens during the Athenian Golden Age, often known as the Age of Pericles.

7. Pelopidas (d. 364 BC), Theban statesman and general.

8. Epaminondas (418–362 BC), Theban general and statesman who transformed Thebes, freeing it from Spartan domination and bringing it into a preeminent position in Greek geopolitics.

types on the subject of government. The revolution of these two great peoples, like a radiant meteor, has flooded the world with such a profusion of political enlightenment that now all thinking beings have learned what the rights of man are and what his duties, in what the excellence of governments consists and of what their vices consist. Everyone knows how to appreciate the intrinsic value of the speculative theories of modern philosophers and legislators. Finally, this star, in its luminous course, has even set ablaze the hearts of the apathetic Spaniards, who also have hurled themselves into the political whirlwind; they have made their ephemeral trials of liberty, have recognized their incapacity to live under the sweet rule of laws, and have returned to bury themselves in their time-honored prisons and bonfires.

Here is the place to repeat to you, Legislators, what the eloquent Volney[9] says to you, in the dedication of his *Ruins of Palmyra:* "To the nascent peoples of the Castilian Indies, to the generous leaders who guide them to liberty—may the errors and misfortunes of the ancient world inform the wisdom and happiness of the new world." May the lessons of experience not be lost, then; and may the consequences of Greece, Rome, France, England, and America instruct us in the difficult science of creating and preserving nations with appropriate, just, legitimate, and, above all, useful laws. Never forget that the excellence of a government does not consist in its theory, in its form, nor in its mechanism, but rather in its being appropriate to the nature and character of the nation for which it is being established.

Rome and Great Britain are the nations that have most distinguished themselves among the ancients and moderns. Both were born to govern and be free, but both were constituted not on brilliant forms of liberty, but rather on top of solid foundations. Thus, then, I recommend to you, Representatives, the study of the British constitution, which is the one that seems destined to bring about the greatest good possible to the peoples who adopt it; but perfect as it may be, I am very far from proposing to you its servile imitation. When I speak of the British government, I am referring only to its republican aspects, and truly, can we call a system a pure monarchy when it recognizes popular sovereignty, the division and balance of powers, civil liberty, freedom of conscience, of press, and all that is sublime in politics? Can there be more liberty in any type of republic? And can we expect more from the social order? I recommend this constitution to you as the most worthy of serving as a model to all who aspire to the enjoyment of the rights of man and to all political happiness compatible with our fragile nature.

We would not alter our fundamental laws at all if we adopted a legislative power similar to the British Parliament. Like the Americans, we have divided national representation into two chambers—the House of Representatives and the Senate. The first is composed very wisely, enjoys all the authority appropriate to it, and is not in need of an essential reform, because the constitution has given

---

9. Constantin François de Chasseboeuf, Comte de Volney (1757–1820), French scholar and politician. His most famous work was *The Ruins, or a Survey of the Revolutions of Empires* (1791). The dedication cited is to the Spanish translation, titled *Las Ruinas de Palmira.*

it the origin, the form, and the powers that the will of the people requires in order to be legitimately and competently represented. If, instead of being elected, the Senate were hereditary, in my opinion it would be the foundation, the bond, the soul of our republic. In political tempests this body would fend off thunderbolts from the government and repulse popular waves. Dedicated to the government by a legitimate interest in its own preservation, it would always oppose the attempted invasions by the people against the jurisdiction and authority of their magistrates. We must admit it—most men are ignorant of their true interests and constantly try to attack them in the hands of their trust-ees—the individual fights against the masses, and the masses against the author-ities. Therefore, it is necessary that in all governments a neutral body exist that can put itself always on the side of the offended and disarm the offender. This neutral body, so that it be neutral, should not owe its origin to election by the government nor by the people, so that it might enjoy a complete independence that neither fears nor expects anything from these sources of authority. The hereditary senate, as part of the people, participates in their interests, in their feelings, and in their spirit. For this reason no one should presume that a hered-itary senate will be detached from popular interests nor forget its legislative duties. The senators in Rome and the Lords in London have been the most solid pillars on which the edifice of political and civil liberty has been based.

These senators will be elected the first time by the Congress. Their successors in the Senate are the priority of the government, which should educate them in a special college designed to instruct those guardians, future legislators of the fatherland. They would learn arts, science, and letters, which grace the spirit of a public man. From their childhood they would know to which career Providence has destined them, and from a very tender age they would lift their souls to the dignity that awaits them.

In no way would the creation of a hereditary senate be a violation of political equality; I am not attempting to establish a nobility, because, as a famous repub-lican has said, to do so would be to destroy equality and liberty at one stroke. It is an office for which the candidates must be prepared, and it is an office that demands much knowledge and the means sufficient to acquire this instruction. Not everything should be left to the chance and luck of elections—the people are more easily deceived than nature perfected by art; and although it is true that these senators would not emerge from the bosom of the virtues, it is also true that they would emerge from the bosom of an enlightened education. On the other hand, the liberators of Venezuela deserve always to occupy a high rank in the republic that owes them its existence. I believe that our posterity would view with regret the obliteration of the illustrious names of its first benefactors. I say more—it is a matter of public interest, it is a matter of Venezuela's gratitude, it is a matter of national honor to preserve with glory, for all time, a race of virtuous, prudent, and brave men who, overcoming all obstacles, have founded the repub-lic at the cost of the most heroic sacrifices. And if the people of Venezuela do not applaud the elevation of their benefactors, they are unworthy of being free and never will be.

A hereditary senate, I repeat, will be the fundamental base of the legislative branch and consequently will be the base of the entire government. Furthermore, it will serve as a counterweight to the government and to the people; it will be an intermediate power that softens the blows that these eternal rivals throw at one another. In all struggles, the calm of a third party comes to be the instrument of reconciliation; thus, the Senate of Venezuela will be the restraining bolt in this structure so delicate and so susceptible to violent influences—it will be the Iris that will calm the tempest and maintain harmony among the limbs and head of this body politic.

No stimulus will be able to corrupt a legislative body endowed with the highest honors, dependent on itself alone, fearing nothing from the people, expecting nothing from the government, a body that has no other objective than curbing every principle of evil and propagating every principle of good, and that is vitally interested in the existence of a society whose unfortunate or favorable outcomes it shares. It has been said with great reason that the upper house of England is valuable to the nation because it offers a bulwark of liberty; and I add, Venezuela's senate would not only be a bulwark of liberty but also a support for perpetuating the republic.

The British executive power is imbued with all the pertinent sovereign authority, but he is also encircled by a triple line of dikes, barriers, and stockades. He is the leader of the government, but his ministers and subordinates depend more on laws than on his authority, because they have personal responsibility, and not even the very commands of royal authority exempt them from this responsibility. He is the supreme commander of the army and the navy; he makes peace and declares war; but it is Parliament that annually decrees the amounts these military forces must be paid. Although the tribunals and judges depend on him, the laws emanate from the Parliament that enacts them. With the goal of neutralizing his power, the person of the king is inviolable and sacred; and while his head remains free, the hands with which he must work are bound. The English sovereign has three formidable rivals—his cabinet, which must answer to the people and to Parliament; the upper house, which defends the interests of the people as representative of the nobility of which it is composed; and the House of Commons, which serves as organ and tribune for the British people. Moreover, as judges are responsible for compliance with the laws, they do not depart from them, and the administrators of the public treasury, being prosecuted not only for their own infractions but even for those infractions that the government itself commits, are careful not to misappropriate public funds. However much one examines the nature of the executive power in England, one can find nothing that would keep one from concluding that it is the most perfect model, be it for a kingdom, be it for an aristocracy, be it for a democracy. Let us apply this executive power to Venezuela in the person of a president, whether named by the people or by its representatives, and we will have taken a great step toward national happiness.

Whichever citizen fulfills these functions, he will find himself aided by the constitution. Authorized to do the good, he will not be able to do evil, because whenever he subordinates himself to the laws, his ministers will cooperate with him; if, on the contrary, he attempts to contravene the laws, his own ministers will leave him isolated in the midst of the republic and will even bring charges against him before the Senate. The ministers, as the ones responsible for transgressions committed, are the ones who govern, because they are the ones who pay for those transgressions. Not the least advantage of this system is the obligation it places on the functionaries closest to the executive power to take the most interested and active role in the government's deliberations and to consider their particular departments as their own. It may happen that the president is not a man of great talents nor great virtues, yet despite the lack of these essential qualities, the president will carry out his duties in a satisfactory way, for in such cases the ministry, operating on its own, carries the burden of state.

As exorbitant as the authority of England's executive power might seem, perhaps it is not excessive for the Venezuelan republic. Here Congress has tied the hands and even the heads of the magistrates. This deliberative body has assumed part of the executive functions, against the principle of Montesquieu, who says that a representative body must not make any active resolutions—it must make laws and see whether those it makes are carried out.[10] Nothing is so contrary to harmony among the branches of government as their conflation. Nothing is so dangerous regarding the people as weakness in the executive, and if in a kingdom it has been judged necessary to concede so many powers to the executive, in a republic these powers are infinitely more indispensable.

Let us focus our attention on this difference, and we will find that the balance of powers must be distributed in two ways. In republics the executive must be stronger because everything conspires against it, while in monarchies the legislative must be strongest, because everything conspires in the monarch's favor. The veneration peoples express for the royal magistracy is a fascination that has the powerful effect of increasing the superstitious respect rendered to that authority. The splendor of the throne, of the crown, of the purple; the formidable support the nobility lends it; the immense riches entire generations accumulate in one single dynasty; the fraternal protection all the kings receive from each other, are very considerable advantages favoring royal authority and making it almost limitless. These same advantages are, consequently, the ones that confirm the need to grant greater authority to a republican magistrate than a constitutional prince possesses.

A republican magistrate is an individual isolated within a society charged with containing the tendency of the people toward license and the propensity of judges and administrators toward abusing the laws. He is directly subject to the legislative body, to the Senate, to the people; he is a man resisting the combined attack of the opinions, of the interests, and of the passions of the social state, who, as Carnot[11] says, does nothing more than struggle continually with the

---

10. Montesquieu, *The Spirit of the Laws*, book XI, chapter 6.

11. Lazare Nicolas Marguerite Carnot (1753–1823), French statesman, general, military engineer, and administrator in successive governments of the French Revolution.

desire to rule and the desire to avoid being ruled. He is, finally, an athlete thrown against a multitude of other athletes.

Only one thing can serve to correct this weakness, namely, well-founded vigor of the executive power more proportionate to the resistance with which the legislative branch, the judiciary, and the people of a republic will necessarily oppose him. If one does not put at the executive's disposal all the means that reasonably pertain to him, he will inevitably fall into worthlessness or abuse—that is, into the death of the government, whose heirs are anarchy, usurpation, and tyranny. There is a desire to restrain the executive with restrictions and hobbles—nothing could be more reasonable—but we should be careful that the bonds intended to restrain are strong, certainly, but not constricting.

Let the entire system of government, then, become strengthened, and let balance be established in such a way that it will not be lost and in such a way that its own fragility will not cause its decline. For the very reason that no other form of government is so weak as democracy, its structure must be of the greatest soundness, and its institutions must be evaluated for stability. If it is not, we can count on having established an experiment in government and not a permanent system; we can count on an ungovernable, tumultuous, and anarchic society, not on a social establishment where happiness, peace, and justice rule.

Let us not be presumptuous, Legislators; let us be moderate in our aspirations. It is improbable that we will attain what the human race has not achieved, what the greatest and wisest nations have not achieved—unlimited liberty, absolute democracy, are the reefs on which all republican hopes have foundered. Take a look at ancient republics, modern republics, nascent republics; almost all have attempted to establish themselves as absolute democracies, and almost all have been frustrated in their honorable aspirations. Men who yearn for legitimate institutions and social perfection are certainly laudable; but who has told men that they already possess all the wisdom, that they already practice every virtue, that they absolutely need to link power to justice? Only angels, not men, can exist free, tranquil, and happy, exercising all sovereign power!

The people of Venezuela already enjoy the rights that they can legitimately and readily enjoy; now let us check the momentum of excessive aspirations that, perhaps, might be raised by a form of government unfit for them. Let us abandon federal structures that do not suit us; let us abandon the triumvirate in the executive power; and, concentrating this power in one president, let us entrust to him sufficient authority to keep struggling against the difficulties resulting from our recent situation, the state of war from which we suffer, and the type of external and domestic enemies against whom we will have to fight for a long time. Let the legislative branch divest itself of all functions appropriate to the executive, all the while acquiring new coherence and new influence in the balance of powers. Let the tribunals be reinforced by judicial stability and independence, by the establishment of juries, by civil and criminal codes not dictated by antiquity, nor by conquering kings, but by the voice of nature, by the cry for justice, and by the spirit of wisdom.

My desire is that all parts of government and administration acquire the degree of vigor that alone can maintain balance, not only among the members making up the government, but also among the different parts making up our society. It would not matter that the mainspring of a political system loosens up because of its weaknesses if this loosening up did not involve the social body's dissolution and its members' ruin. The screams of the human race on battlefields or fields of tumult cry out to the heavens against inconsiderate and blind legislators who believed they could with impunity experiment in wildly unrealistic institutions. All the world's peoples have sought liberty, some by arms, others by laws, passing alternately from anarchy to despotism, or from despotism to anarchy—they are very few who have been content with moderate aspirations, constituting themselves in a way that conforms to their means, their spirit, and their circumstances.

Let us not aspire to the impossible, lest by raising ourselves above the region of liberty, we fall to that of tyranny. From absolute liberty one always descends to absolute power, and the mean between those two extremes is supreme social liberty. Abstract theories produce the pernicious idea of unlimited liberty. Let us constrain public power within the limits that reason and interest prescribe. Let us constrain the national will within the limits that a reasonable power indicates for it. Let civil and criminal legislation, analogous to our current constitution, rule imperiously over judicial power, and then there will be balance, not a clash that impedes the state's progress, and not the kind of complexity that hobbles rather than binds society.

The foundation of a national spirit is required to form a stable government, a national spirit that has as its objective a consistent tendency toward two main points, namely, to moderate the general will and to limit public authority. The boundaries that theoretically fix these two points are difficult to define, but one can imagine that the rule directing them must be reciprocal restriction and concentration so as to minimize, to the degree possible, friction between the general will and legitimate public authority. This knowledge is acquired imperceptibly through practice and study. The progress of enlightenment is what broadens the progress of practice, and rectitude of spirit is what broadens the progress of enlightenment.

Love of fatherland, love of law, love of the magistrates, are the noble passions that must exclusively absorb the republican soul. Venezuelans love the fatherland, but they do not love its laws, because the laws have been toxic and were sources of evil; neither have they been able to love their magistrates, because the former ones were unjust and the new ones are hardly known, because they have just begun their careers. If there is not sacred respect for the fatherland, for the laws, and for the authorities, society is a jumble, an abyss—it is individual conflict between man and man, between group and group.

All our moral strengths will not be enough to extract our nascent republic from this chaos if we do not fuse the mass of people into a whole, the makeup of the government into a whole, the legislation into a whole, and the national spirit into a whole. Our slogan must be "unity, unity, unity." The blood of our citizens is various, let us mix it to unify it; our constitution has divided the branches of government, let us connect them to unify them; our laws are terrible relics of all ancient and modern despotisms, may this monstrous edifice be demolished, fall down, and even its ruins break apart, and let us raise a temple to justice; and under the auspices of justice's holy inspiration, let us issue a Venezuelan code of laws. If we wish to consult monuments and models of legislation, Great Britain, France, and North America offer admirable ones.

Popular education must be the firstborn concern of the Congress's paternal love. Morality and enlightenment are a republic's polar points, morality and enlightenment are our first necessities. Let us take from Athens its Areopagus,[12] and the guardians from its customs and laws; let us take from Rome its censors and domestic tribunals; and making a holy alliance of these moral institutions, let us reestablish in the world the idea of a people that does not content itself with being free and strong, but wishes instead to be virtuous. Let us take from Sparta its austere foundations; and making of these three springs a fountain of virtue, let us give to our republic a fourth power, whose domain shall be the childhoods and hearts of men, public spirit, good practices, and republican morality. Let us constitute this Aeropagus so it watches over the education of children, over national instruction, so it purifies what in the republic has been corrupted, denouncing ingratitude, egoism, coldness in love of the fatherland, laziness, and citizen negligence; let it pass judgment on the principles of corruption, on pernicious examples, correcting habits with moral penalties, just as laws punish crimes with painful penalties—not only what offends them, but also what mocks them; not only what attacks them, but also what weakens them; not only what violates the constitution, but also what violates public respect. This truly holy tribunal's jurisdiction must be absolute with respect to education and instruction, only advisory regarding penalties and punishments. But the annals or registers in which it will record its acts and deliberations, the moral principles and the actions of citizens, will be books of virtue and vice. These will be books that the people will consult for their elections, magistrates for their resolutions, and judges for their verdicts. For all that it might be fanciful, an institution of this kind is infinitely more feasible than others that some ancient and modern legislators have established with less utility to the human race.

Legislators! In the constitutional plan that I reverently submit to your wisdom, you will observe the spirit that has dictated it. In proposing to you the division of citizens into active and passive, I have tried to encourage national prosperity with the two great levers of industry—work and knowledge. Stimulating these two powerful mainsprings of society, what for men is most difficult comes within reach, making them honorable and happy. By placing reasonable and prudent restrictions on the primary and electoral assemblies, we set up the first dike against popular license, avoiding the tumultuous and blind crowd that in all times has imprinted error on elections and has as a consequence tied that

---

12. The "Hill of Ares" in Athens was the site of the Council of the Areopagus (4th century BC), which served as an important legal institution under Athenian democracy.

error to magistrates and the course of government, for this primordial act is the generative act of a people's liberty or of its slavery.

Adding to the weight of Congress in the balance of powers by the number of legislators and the nature of the Senate, I have tried to give a fixed foundation to this first body of the nation and imbue it with the regard so very important for the success of its sovereign functions.

Separating executive from legislative jurisdiction by very well-defined limits, I have not tried to divide but rather to bind—with bonds of harmony born of independence—these supreme powers whose prolonged clash has always destroyed one of the contenders. Although I seek to confer upon the executive a greater number of powers than the ones it enjoyed earlier, I have not wished to authorize a despot to tyrannize the republic, but rather to prevent the despotism under deliberation from becoming an immediate cause of a cycle of despotic vicissitudes in which, alternatively, anarchy is followed by oligarchy and by monarchy. In requesting the stability of judges, creation of juries, and a new legal code, I have requested from Congress the guarantee of civil liberty—the most precious, the most just, the most necessary, in a word, the only liberty, because without it the rest are null. I have requested correction of the most lamentable abuses from which our judiciary suffers because of its defective origin in that ocean of Spanish legislation, which, like time, includes works from all ages and from all men—works of lunacy as well as of talent, sensible productions as well as extravagant ones, monuments of genius as well as monuments of caprice. This judicial encyclopedia, monster with ten thousand heads, which until now has been the scourge of the Spanish peoples, is the most refined torture that heaven's anger has permitted to rain down on this unfortunate empire.

Reflecting on how effectively to regenerate the character and practices that war and tyranny have given us, I have felt myself so bold as to invent a moral branch of government, drawn from the obscure depths of antiquity and from those forgotten laws that once sustained virtue among Greeks and Romans. It might well be regarded as a naïve delirium, but it is not impossible, and I flatter myself that you will not scorn entirely a thought that, improved by experience and enlightenment, might prove very effective.

Horrified by the disagreement that has reigned and must reign among us because of the subtle spirit that characterizes the federalist government, I have been compelled to beg you to adopt centralism and the unification of all the states of Venezuela into a single, indivisible republic. This measure—urgent, vital, redeeming, in my opinion—is of such a nature that, without it, the fruit of our regeneration will be death.

My duty, Legislators, is to present you with a detailed and faithful picture of my political, civil, and military administration, but to do this now would be to exhaust your important attention too much and deprive you of time, as precious as it is urgent. Consequently, the secretaries of state will give to Congress an account of their various departments, providing at the same time the documents and archives that will by illustration give an exact understanding of the republic's actual and positive state.

I would not speak to you of the most notable acts of my command if these were not of concern to the majority of Venezuelans. It is a matter, gentlemen, of the most important resolutions of this most recent period.

Atrocious and impious slavery covered the land of Venezuela with its black mantle, and our sky was filled with stormy clouds that threatened a flood of fire. I implored the protection of the God of humanity, and then redemption dispersed the storms. Slavery broke its shackles, and Venezuela has seen itself with new sons, grateful sons who have converted the instruments of their captivity into weapons of liberty. Certainly, those who before were slaves are now free; those who before were enemies of a stepmother are defenders of a fatherland. To commend to you the justice, necessity, and charity of this measure is superfluous when you know the history of the Helots, of Spartacus, and of Haiti,[13] when you know that one cannot be free and enslaved at the same time without at the same time violating natural, political, and civil laws. I leave the reform or revocation of all my statutes and decrees to your sovereign decision; but I plead for the confirmation of the absolute liberty of the slaves as I would plead for my life and the life of the republic.

To present you with the military history of Venezuela would be to remind you of the history of republican heroism among the ancients; it would be to tell you that Venezuela has entered into the grand scene of sacrifices made on the altar of liberty. Nothing other than the sublime honors offered to the benefactors of the human race could fill the noble hearts of our generous warriors. Not fighting for power nor for fortune, nor even for glory, but only for liberty, the title of Liberators of the Republic is their well-deserved reward. I, then, founding a sacred society with these illustrious young men, have instituted the Order of Liberators of Venezuela. Legislators! To you belongs the power to grant honors and decorations; yours is the duty of exercising this august act of national gratitude.

Men who, as the result of their virtue and talents, have divested themselves of all enjoyments, of all the goods that they previously possessed; men who have experienced how cruel a horrible war is, suffering the most painful deprivations and the harshest torments; men worthy of the fatherland have come to deserve the government's attention. As a consequence, I have ordered them compensated with the nation's revenues. If on the part of the people I have acquired any type of merit, I beg its representatives to hear my supplications as the reward for my unworthy services. Let Congress order the distribution of national revenues in accord with the law that I have decreed in the name of the republic for the benefit of the Venezuelan soldiers.

---

13. Helots were Peloponnesian Greeks who became state-owned serfs in ancient Sparta. Spartacus (d. 71 BC), was a Thracian soldier who was captured by the Romans, sold as a slave to be made a gladiator, and who then led a slave revolt. The former French colony of Saint Domingue, once the largest sugar plantation in the Caribbean, became Haiti, the second independent country in the Americas after the only successful large-scale slave revolt in modern history (1791–1804).

Inasmuch as through numerous triumphs we have managed to overcome the Spanish armies, the court of Madrid, desperate, has tried in vain to take by surprise the consciences of the generous sovereigns who just extirpated usurpation and tyranny in Europe and who should be the protectors of the legitimacy and justice of the American cause. Incapable of attaining our submission with their arms, Spain reverts to her insidious policy; unable to conquer us, she has resorted to suspicious cunning. Fernando has humiliated himself to the point of confessing that he has need of foreign protection to return us to his ignominious yoke, to a yoke that all power is incapable of imposing on us! Venezuela, assured that she possesses forces sufficient to repel her oppressors, has pronounced through the instrument of government her firmest resolution to fight to the finish, to defend her political life, not only against Spain, but against all men, if all men were so degraded that they embraced the defense of an all-consuming government whose only moving parts are an exterminating sword and the flames of the Inquisition—a government that no longer wants dominions, but deserts; not cities, but ruins; not vassals, but tombs. The declaration of the Republic of Venezuela is the most glorious, most heroic, most worthy act of a free people; it is the act that, already sanctioned by the unanimous expression of the people of Venezuela, and with the greatest satisfaction, I have the honor of offering to Congress.

Since the second era of the republic our army has lacked military resources. It has always been without arms. It has always lacked ammunition. It has always been poorly equipped. Now the defending soldiers of independence are not only armed with justice, but also with force. Our troops can compare themselves favorably with the most select of Europe, inasmuch as there is no longer inequality in the means of destruction. We owe these great advantages to the limitless liberality of a few generous foreigners who have seen humanity moan and the cause of reason perish, and who have not viewed it as quiet spectators, but have flown with their protective assistance and have lent to the republic whatever it needed to make its philanthropic principles triumph. These friends of humanity are America's guardian spirits, and to them we owe an eternal debt of gratitude, and we also owe them a religious fulfillment of the sacred obligations that we have incurred with them. The national debt, Legislators, is the repository of the faith, the honor, and the gratitude of Venezuela. Respect it like the Holy Ark that contains not so much the rights of our benefactors, as the glory of our faithfulness. Let us sooner die than break a pledge that saved the fatherland and the lives of our children.

The unification of New Granada and Venezuela into a great state has been the uniform wish of the peoples and governments of these republics. The fortune of war has verified this union so yearned for by all Colombians;[14] we are, in fact, united. These fraternal peoples have already entrusted to you their interests,

---

14. Colombians: Bolívar is referring to all the inhabitants of "Gran Colombia," which included the modern countries of Venezuela, Colombia, Ecuador, and Panama, the latter three comprising the colonial jurisdiction of New Granada. Colombia in its modern sense, as a separate nation and identity, was not created until 1830.

their rights, their destinies. In contemplating the unification of this immense region, my soul soars to the height demanded by the colossal perspective that such an astonishing scene offers. Flying through the coming ages, my imagination fixes on future centuries, and observing from there with admiration and wonder the prosperity, the splendor, the life that this vast region has received, I feel moved, and it seems to me that I already see this region in the heart of the universe, overspilling its vast shores, between those oceans that nature has separated and that our fatherland joins with lengthy and wide canals. Now I see it serving as link, center, emporium for the human family. Now I see it sending to all areas of the earth the treasures of silver and gold that its mountains harbor. Now I see it distributing through its divine plants health and life to the ailing men of the Old World. Now I see it communicating its precious secrets to the learned men who are unaware of how much greater is the amount of enlightenment than the amount of riches with which nature has lavishly endowed it. Now I see it seated on the throne of liberty, gripping the scepter of justice, crowned by glory, showing the Old World the majesty of the modern world.

Deign, Legislators, to accept with indulgence the profession of my political conscience, the final wishes of my heart, and the fervent prayers that in the name of the people I dare address to you. Deign to concede to Venezuela an eminently popular, eminently just, eminently moral government that enchains oppression, anarchy, and guilt—a government that allows innocence, humanity, and peace to reign; a government that lets equality and liberty triumph under the rule of inexorable laws.

Gentlemen, take up your duties—I have ended mine.

Address to the Constituent Congress of Bolivia (1826)[15]

Legislators! I will mention an article that, following my conscience, I have had to omit. In a political constitution a religious declaration must not be prescribed, because according to the best doctrines regarding constitutional laws, these are the guarantees of political and civil rights. As religion touches none of these rights, it is by nature indefinable in the social order and belongs to intellectual morality. Religion governs man in the house, in the study, inside himself—only religion has the right to examine man's intimate conscience. Laws, on the contrary, view the surface of things; they govern only outside the citizen's house. Applying these considerations, can a state ever rule its subjects' consciences, keep

---

15. The territory formerly known as the Audiencia of Charcas, or Upper Peru, was the last mainland Spanish possession to gain independence, after a battle led by Bolívar and his Venezuelan compatriot, José Antonio de Sucre, on April 1, 1825.

watch over their fulfillment of religious laws, and give reward or punishment when the tribunals are in heaven and when God is the judge? Only the Inquisition could be capable of replacing them in this world. Will, then, the Inquisition return with its fiery torches?

Religion is the law of conscience. Every law about religion annuls it, because imposing necessity on duty takes merit away from faith, which is the basis of religion. Sacred precepts and dogmas are useful, luminous, and metaphysically evident; we should all profess them, but this duty is moral, not political. On the other hand, what are the rights of man in this world with regard to religion? Those rights are in heaven; there the tribunal rewards merit and makes justice according to the code that the legislator has issued. All of this being of divine jurisdiction, it seems to me at first glance sacrilegious and profane to mix our laws with the commandments of the Lord. To prescribe religion, then, does not fall to the legislator, because the legislator must designate penalties for infractions of the laws so that the laws are not mere counsels. Without temporal punishments or judges who apply them, law ceases to be law.

Man's moral development is the legislator's first purpose; after this development has been achieved, man bases his morality on revealed truths, and in fact professes his religion, which is the more effective the more he has acquired it though his own investigations. Moreover, fathers of families cannot disregard their religious duty toward their children. Spiritual pastors are obliged to teach the knowledge of heaven—the example of the true disciples of Jesus is the most eloquent teacher of his divine morality; but morality cannot be imposed, nor is he who imposes it a teacher, nor should force be employed in giving counsel. God and his ministers are the authorities on religion, which works through exclusively spiritual means and instruments but never through the national body, which guides the public power to purely temporal ends.

José María Luis Mora
(Mexico)

José María Luis Mora (1794–1850) is generally regarded as the greatest liberal thinker—perhaps the greatest of all Mexican thinkers—during the immediate post-independence period in Mexico. Although Mora believed in rule by the propertied classes, he also saw democratic rule as the best system for maintaining order—he disliked the violence and chaos of revolution as much as he had disliked Spanish domination. In economics, he was influenced by the liberalism of the British theorists Adam Smith and Jeremy Bentham and by French political philosophers Montesquieu and Benjamin Constant. Mora was a politician, historian, priest, writer, educator, newspaper editor, lawyer, and reformer.

A creole, Mora was the son of wealthy parents, José Ramón Servín de la Mora and María Ana Díaz de Lamadrid. He was born in Guanajuato and studied at the well-known Jesuit Colegio de San Ildefonso in Mexico City. Although his family was forced to turn over its wealth in the 1810 Hidalgo uprising, Mora continued with his studies, earning diplomas in philosophy in 1812 and theology in 1818, his bachelor's degree in theology in 1819, and a Doctor of Theology degree in 1820.

He began his career as a liberal political journalist in 1821, writing for the periodical *Semanario Político y Literario,* and continued his political writings later in two others, the *Observador de la República Mexicana* (1828–1830) and the *Indicador de la Federación Mexicana* (1833–1834). But Mora's focus throughout his public life was on educational reform—he was a devoted educator. During the 1820s, he maintained his connection with San Ildefonso, becoming a teacher of philosophy there in 1824. At San Ildefonso, he established the first course in political economics, and in 1824 he was named to the Academia Mexicana de Economía Política. In 1833, Mexican President Valentín Gómez Farías appointed him to the Dirección General de Instrucción, the office of public instruction, and as director of the Colegio de Estudios Ideológicos y de Humanidades. In these roles, Mora led a movement for educational reform that he called the "revolution of 1833." If these reforms had been fully implemented, higher education in Mexico would have been completely reorganized, and the government would have appointed all professors and administrators. In his writings, Mora, although a priest himself, joined with other liberals in an attack on the "monastic" education in the schools, urging schools to concentrate less on religious subjects and holidays and more on subjects such as political economy, commerce, and agriculture. Unfortunately for Mora, the reforms died when Gómez Farías was forced to leave the presidency in 1834.

Mora began his active political career in 1820 as an electoral delegate from the parish of El Sagrario in Mexico City, and, the next year, as a member of the provincial deputation of Mexico. In this role, he worked on issues as varied as educational reform and the problem of Mexico City drainage. When the Constituent Congress of the State of Mexico began its deliberations in 1824, Mora was a deputy; he became president of the Constituent Congress after 1825. In helping draft Mexico's first constitution, he was active in the effort to develop it as a federalist constitution; as a constituent, he later helped restore federalism after President Antonio de Santa Anna abolished it. Mora served as a deputy to the General Congress for Guanajuato in 1832, and he was a minister in the cabinet of President Gómez Farías. In November, 1834, when Mora left for permanent residence in France, his early form of liberalism died out as a productive force in Mexican political life. When Gómez Farías returned briefly to the presidency in 1846, he named Mora minister to England, a post from which Mora tried to convince the British government to intervene on Mexico's behalf against the expansionist moves of the United States. He also worked actively to promote European immigration to Mexico, hoping to stave off another U.S. takeover of parts of Mexico.

Mora's liberal political ideals are contained in his well-known works, which include the "Catecismo política de la Federación Mexicana" (1831), "Disertación sobre la naturaleza y aplicación de las rentas y bienes eclesiásticos" (translated as "On Ecclesiastical Wealth") (1831), *México y sus revoluciones* (1836), and the *Obras sueltas* (2 volumes, 1837). The selections in this volume are taken from the *Obras sueltas* and address two of his persistent themes, ecclesiastical wealth and the rights of Spaniards remaining in Latin America. The essay on ecclesiastical wealth first appeared in the *Revista Política,* and the essay on the expulsion of the Spaniards first appeared in the *Observador de la República Mexicana.*

Further Reading

Escobar Valenzuela, Gustavo Alberto. *El liberalismo ilustrado del Dr. José María Luis Mora.* Mexico, D.F.: Universidad Nacional Autónoma de México, 1974.

González Navarro, Moisés. *José María Luis Mora: La formación de la conciencia burguesa en México.* Mexico, D.F.: Universidad Nacional Autónoma de México, Dirección General de Difusión Cultural, Dirección Editorial, 1984.

Hale, Charles A. "José María Luis Mora and the Structure of Mexican Liberalism," *The Hispanic American Historical Revue* 45, no. 2 (1965): 196–227.

———. *Mexican Liberalism in the Age of Mora, 1821–1853.* New Haven, Conn.: Yale University Press, 1968.

Lira, Andres, ed. *Espejo de discordias: La sociedad mexicana vista por Lorenzo de Zavala, José María Luis Mora y Lucas Alamán.* Mexico, D.F.: Secretaría de Educación Pública, 1984.

Mora, José María Luis. *Obras completas.* Edited by Lillian Briseño Senosiain, Laura Solares Robles and Laura Suárez de la Torre, Mexico D.F.: Secretaría de Educación Pública: Instituto de Investigaciones Dr. JML Mora, 1986–1988.

———. *Obras Sueltas.* Mexico, D.F.: Editorial Porrúa, 1963.

Velázquez, Gustavo G. *El Dr. José María Luis Mora y la erección del Estado de México*. Toluca, Mexico: Gobierno del Estado de México, Dirección del Patrimonio Cultural, 1976.

On the Expulsion of the Natives and Citizens of This Republic Born in Spain (1827)[1]

Aeneas, in order to conciliate the minds of the Aborigines to meet the terror of so serious a war, called both nations Latins, so that they might all be not only under the same laws, but also the same name. Nor after that did the Aborigines yield to the Trojans in zeal and fidelity towards their king, Aeneas.
—Livy, *History of Rome*, Book I[2]

Never would we have touched the clamorous question of the *Spaniards* were we not obliged to do so because of the difficult circumstances in which the cruel persecutors of these unfortunate men have put the nation.[3] Now is the time to come to the defense of all these innocent victims of most unjust persecution; of all the unfortunate Mexican families for whom abandonment, orphanhood, and misery are being prepared in utter cold blood; of all those who owe their livelihood to the capital resources invested by the ones being persecuted; and finally, of all inhabitants of the republic, which can only succumb and bury all its children beneath its ruins if an extraordinary and vigorous effort is not made

---

1. In this essay, Mora uses five terms, *nativo, natural, ciudadano, extranjero,* and *español,* in his discussion of the status of Mexico's inhabitants. *Nativo* and *natura* both refer to a person who was born in a given place. Mora uses *nativo* to designate those who were "native-born" in Mexico; in a striking rhetorical turn, he uses *natural* for all those who have the rights of legal "natives," including naturalized residents born in Spain. He differentiates between *españoles,* Spaniards living in Mexico, and *extranjeros,* foreigners. *Ciudadano* refers to both native-born and naturalized citizens of Mexico.

2. According to Livy's legendary history of Rome, the ancient Latins arose from the intermingling of the indigenous people of the area with the Trojan intruders—a parable, in Mora's view, for the mixing of Spaniards and indigenous peoples to create the Mexican nation. Mora quotes the epigram in Latin. D. Spillan translation.

3. A wave of anti-Spanish hysteria swept Mexico in the mid-1820s, fanned by justifiable fears that Spain wished to retake its former colony, as well as by commercial rivalry between Mexican and Spanish merchants. Proposals to expel every Spanish-born male from Mexico became a winning political formula for the *yorkinos* (the York Rite Masons, a precursor of the Liberal party), and were opposed by the *escoceses* (Scottish Rite Masons, a precursor of the Conservative party). Decrees of expulsion were issued by *yorkino* national governments in late 1827, 1829, and 1833; the resident Spanish population of the country was reduced from perhaps 7,000 to about 2,200 over this period.

to subdue and silence all these contemptible demagogues and all these agitators, malcontents, and disturbers of public peace.

The eternal principles of justice, the nation's honor, the good faith of its agreements, treaties, and guarantees, and the well-being of the republic imperiously demand prompt and repressive measures to put an end to all these ills and to encourage public confidence, which is the soul of societies, the origin and mainstay of national prosperity, and the vital principle that animates and strengthens the body politic.

We are sure that we defend a national cause and that the fate of our country is so intimately tied to the promises made to those who were born in old Spain by the stipulations of Iguala and Córdoba[4] and so necessarily dependent on their effective, punctual, and conscientious fulfillment, that we consider it impossible to proceed otherwise, unless we do so either from a total lack of reason or from sheer perversity and malice.

Only men lacking foresight—men whose view does not extend beyond the objects that surround them or the day in which they live—can disregard the pernicious results of this lack of public good faith; and only an enemy of the fatherland can persist in carrying out measures he knows to be disastrous and contrary to national happiness. This kind of man is, then, one who promotes the expulsion of those who are unfairly called Spaniards. The Bravos, Victorias, Mieres, Teráns, and Rayóns,[5] who suffered every kind of evil and persecution for Mexican independence, are certainly not among this group; among this group are . . . but why name them? Everyone knows who they are, and knows beyond a shadow of a doubt that the most faithful servants of the government of the metropolis—those who only took sides after Independence was already won and their influence not needed, those who for ten years shed torrents of their brothers' blood—now boast of being patriots, seek to confuse the case of Spain with that of Spaniards, and attempt to render hateful those persons who would have caused no harm had they been limited to their own strength by taking away the support that those who now call themselves patriots once lent them.

These visible injustices, these palpable inconsistencies, make us take up our pen to help the inhabitants of our republic face the facts of so important a matter.

---

4. The Plan of Iguala, formulated by royalist general Agustín Iturbide and rebel leader Vicente Guerrero and proclaimed on February 24, 1821, was the statement of principles under which Mexico achieved independence. The third of its "three guarantees" was a promise of equality between Mexicans born in Spain and those born in Mexico. Spaniards who accepted the terms of the plan were guaranteed that they would retain their property and even their positions in the government and church. The Treaty of Córdoba, the Spanish capitulation to Iturbide's independence forces that ended royalist resistance in August, 1821, incorporated the provisions of the Plan of Iguala and made them the law of the new-born country.

5. Nicolás Bravo (1786–1854), Guadalupe Victoria (1786–1842), Manuel Mier y Terán (1789–1832), and Ignacio Rayón (1773–1832) were leaders in the war for Mexican independence and were active in national politics in the late 1820s; Bravo and Victoria served as presidents of Mexico.

It is impossible that an entire nation would let itself be seduced to the point that it would proceed in direct opposition to the principles of justice and public harmony and would persist in carrying out what is manifestly impossible; those who make up the nation cannot be fatuous or perverse in their totality and majority. The nation's masses are not deceived when, in open discussion, they are presented with truths they can neither disregard nor have an interest in opposing. The expulsion of the Mexicans who are commonly and unfairly called Spaniards is just such an instance. We will show by every last bit of evidence that such a measure is contrary to justice and public harmony.

The nation that parts ways with the principles of justice can count on nothing but a precarious and short-lived existence; men naturally conspire together, without deliberation and as if by machine-like impulse, against all who tread upon rights that they have secured, and such is the rectitude of the human heart and so positively does it take an interest in the victims of persecution that nothing can distract it from the obligation it undertakes to destroy all instruments of oppression and tyranny, especially when practiced on helpless persons who have no other support than their innocence, which such oppression feigns not to recognize, and their weeping, which no one wants to hear. This is the present fate of those born in Spain and the dangerous state of our republic. Their rights are disregarded, and the republic stands at the edge of the precipice. But, we will be asked, what are their rights? And we will unhesitatingly respond—those of every Mexican.

Read the history of our independence; recall the promises of General Iturbide,[6] confirmed by the National Congress before and after his fall; open the general legal code of the Union and the individual codes of the states, and this truth will be confirmed most authoritatively. The national will and the votes of the public are expressly and tacitly recorded in these, our legislators' venerable monuments. In all of them, the rules of naturalization and citizenship established for the inhabitants of the Mexican Republic cover those Spaniards they are now attempting to expel, and by those rules the Spaniards have acquired a right to live among us, freely enjoy the fruit of their work and industry, participate in all prerogatives of our natives and citizens, in a word, be true Mexicans—a right they cannot lose from the mere fact of having been born in Spain. Who, then, could doubt that it is the greatest of injustices to outlaw this useful and honored class of citizens, requiring them to leave Mexican territory in manifest and obvious infraction of established laws, in contempt of the most solemn promises and all social guarantees? A point so important warrants careful examination.

The persons we are discussing, under the general principles of justice and under current law, have acquired a right to live among us, which they cannot lose except by voluntary renunciation or by being convicted of a crime.

Those who have lived in a country for many years with absolutely no opposition and who have cultivated or contributed to its growth with the fruit of their

---

6. General Agustín de Iturbide (1783–1824), became president of the provisional regency, then constitutional emperor. He abdicated less than a year later and was executed in 1824.

labor; those who have invested their capital resources, giving work to many who need it, contributing to all the public levies; those who have contracted marriage, procreated, and educated their children, establishing relations with the persons around them and providing services to their fellow citizens; all of them, say the experts on public law, acquire an indisputable right, called residency, to live in the country, and no one can deprive them of it except in an instance of personal culpability. And who could doubt that the Spaniards are covered by these precepts? No one, certainly. They, like all other Mexicans, have contributed to every public levy, they have created national wealth and prosperity with their industry and capital resources, and, above all, they have provided distinguished service with their influence and financial expenditures for the sacred cause of the independence and liberty of the fatherland.

These incontestable facts would be enough in themselves to give them the right of settlement or naturalization in our republic. What should we say, then, when definitive laws, solemn promises, and assurances offered by the entire nation, by its leaders and *caudillos,* by its political bodies, and—to put it plainly—by all classes of society, not only have considered them natives, but also have extended to them the precious and inestimable privilege of citizenship and the power to exert both active and passive influence in all public affairs?

The Plan of Iguala and the agreements of Córdoba declare that they will be deemed and considered to be Mexican citizens; the first Congress of the nation, in the name and with the authority of the whole nation, solemnly ratified these promises; and succeeding legislatures have been so far from renouncing them that, by the federal constitution, the persons under discussion can occupy every public post except those of president and vice president, ministers or members of the Supreme Court of Justice of the republic. The same is true in the various state constitutions. According to them, Spaniards are granted the rights not only to live and reside within the territory of each state, but also to influence public affairs with their vote, and, with very few exceptions, to hold all offices. One cannot doubt that these unfortunate men enjoy their natural rights throughout Mexican territory, that is to say, they enjoy the security of *not being disturbed in their persons, rights, and properties,* and of equality before the law to be treated like the rest of the republic's natives.

Well now, all these rights are being violated by *their expulsion.* Hardly can one be *free* to think, much less to work and write, in a country where one is forbidden to live. It would be the height of ridiculousness to maintain that someone's person and wealth are *secure and free of all disturbance* when he is violently forced to change residence and domicile, and much less can it be said that those for whom one wants to pass *special laws* of banishment are *equal before the law* with all other Mexicans.

Nor should it be said to us that they can enjoy these rights in some other place, because the nation has guaranteed them these rights in its own territory by declaring them its natives. The native and the foreigner enjoy these same rights, and the only difference between them consists in the fact that the foreigner can be expelled with neither the process nor the form of justice when one believes his separation appropriate, because society has not assumed any obligation or commitment to foreigners; while the native, as he cannot be deprived of his right except through personal culpability, cannot, by parity of reason, be exiled except when this culpability is legally recorded. In effect, if there is any difference between the natives of a country and the foreigners in it, as one cannot doubt, that difference can only be what has been specifically set forth here. Both should enjoy the rights we have just expounded and that we call natural; nonetheless, there is no obligation to allow the foreigner to remain in the territory, while the native may not be parted from it.

That the Spaniards are naturalized in our republic is a demonstrated truth, clearer than the midday sun. That the native cannot be expelled without just cause from the nation to which he belongs, we have just proven. Let us see then if the persons we are discussing have given cause for such a procedure and which authority has jurisdiction to decide this matter.

The Spanish are accused of two things, namely, their opposition to independence and their ill will toward it after it was attained. The first charge is so vague, so common and general, that it appears, for that very reason, absolutely contemptible. If we restrict ourselves to the first cry of independence raised at Dolores,[7] not only the Spaniards, but also many Mexicans opposed it, armed themselves against its perpetrators, and fought for the cause of the Peninsula. Why, then, do we not charge these people or try to banish them by a line of reasoning that, if it is a crime for Spaniards, it is the more so for Mexicans? Why are Generals Pedraza, Bustamante, Cortazár,[8] etc., not exiled, when they worked on behalf of the metropolis and against their fatherland much more than the great majority of the sons of Spain currently living among us?

Those generals took up arms and defeated armies of patriots, while the Spaniards were in their homes and contributed, at most, with their money. What would have become of the cause of the Peninsula if Mexican troops, leaders, and officials had not supported it for ten consecutive years? If, even with the support of the country's native-born it could never repress the movement of the revolution nor extinguish the sacred fire of liberty, what resistance could seventy thousand Spaniards, scattered across an immense territory and without available troops, have offered against six million Mexicans defending their rights? None, certainly. Limited to their own numbers, they would necessarily have succumbed, as came to pass in 1821, and the nation would have had no reason to

---

7. The *grito* or cry raised by the parish priest Miguel Hidalgo y Costilla in the northern Bajío town of Dolores on September 16, 1810, marked the beginning of the uprising for Mexican independence.

8. General Manuel Gómez Pedraza (1789–1859), General Anastasio Bustamante (1780–1853), and General Luis Cortazár Rábago were Mexican-born military officers who fought on the royalist side at the outset of the war of independence. Each became active in Conservative politics after Mexican independence; both Gómez Pedraza and Bustamante served as president in the 1830s.

mourn as many losses as it did, losses which its own sons perpetrated as much as did those of the Peninsula.

And are not the ones who caused so many disasters and shed so much blood the very ones who now dare raise their voice and the standard of persecution against persons who, without them, would have caused no harm and who were their blind and passive instruments? Let us be just and agree that, if memories of the past were to be taken into account, many Mexicans should be punished; forgetfulness has been decreed, and justice as much as public harmony urgently demand that forgetfulness be honored.

As for the second proclamation of independence,[9] it is a serious and genuine calumny to assert that the Spanish we are discussing resisted it; many of them participated in our armies and contributed effectively to their victories, such as Generals Echávarri and Negrete;[10] others helped with their influence and wealth; some, almost all of whom have left the republic, resisted it as members of expeditionary forces, but the majority remained quiet and ensconced in their homes. Where, then, is that exaggerated opposition other than in the minds of the fatuous and the hearts of the perverse?

Their alleged hostility toward the national cause is entirely unfounded; no facts are cited that substantiate it, and the conjectures used in an effort to support this accusation are so weak and ridiculous that they would not be worth the trouble of countering if one were to act frankly and in good faith. What can these persecuted men expect from Spain? Nothing. What ties unite them with her? None. Where is everything they most love and with whom are they are most tightly and intimately linked? In Mexico and with Mexicans. In effect, the Spaniards can expect nothing from their country of birth in the miserable state into which the despot who governs it has led it;[11] he cannot help anyone nor promote business of any kind, much less bear the extreme costs of a futile reconquest; he is in the process of seizing the property of all who set foot on his territory and of treating as traitors, or at least as suspects, those who live among us. The many who have emigrated from our republic are so fully aware of this that only a few have returned to Spain, the rest settling in England or France. The opposite happens to them with respect to us; the social ties, the ties of friendship, and above

---

9. Iturbide's proclamation of the Plan of Iguala in 1821.

10. Generals José Antonio Echávarri and Pedro Celestino Negrete were Spanish-born royalist officers who joined forces with Iturbide in support of the Plan of Iguala. Both turned against Iturbide when he crowned himself emperor of Mexico, and Negrete served as interim president after Iturbide's downfall. A conspiracy headed by Echávarri and Negrete against President Guadalupe Victoria in 1827 led to the first wave of anti-Spanish sentiment in Mexico; both men were among the first forced into exile.

11. Fernando VII (1784–1833), king of Spain from 1808–1833, spent the first six years of his reign imprisoned in France during the Napoleonic occupation of Spain. Upon his restoration in 1814 he abolished the liberal constitution enacted in his absence. His reactionary rule provoked a liberal coup in 1820, leading indirectly to the independence of Mexico; restored to the throne for a second time in 1823, Fernando ruled with an iron hand to the end of his life.

all the ties of family, possessions, and capital resources divided between employment and business, unite them with indissoluble ties to the country and to our government.

If love of the fatherland is subjected to minute analysis, in the end it is nothing other than the desire for one's own well-being; and inasmuch as the people we are discussing cannot satisfy this inclination except among us, it is clear that they cannot be hostile to us. To claim that birth binds them more tightly than family and social ties is the greatest of absurdities. To venture such a claim, one would have to disregard totally these inclinations of the human heart. Moreover, any presumption, no matter how well-founded it might seem, must yield to factual evidence, which is that they have lived among us, submitting themselves to our government, having fulfilled faithfully and legally the obligations that this government imposes on them and having satisfied all social obligations.

But let us suppose for a moment that all of them are actually disaffected; that not one of them has a good opinion of independence, that it offends them all, and that they wish to see Mexico returned to the rule of the metropolis—it seems that nothing more could be conceded—yet, even given these unfounded concessions, their enemies have not improved their case. The reason is very simple. They were neither required, nor did they promise, to renounce their opinions and desires in order to remain among us. The contract into which they entered with the nation was that they would not act against the independence and liberty of the fatherland and that they would submit themselves to any responsibilities and obligations that might be imposed on the republic's natives and citizens. If they have complied with this, as cannot be doubted, nothing more can be exacted from them, nor should they be disturbed.

Where would we ever end up and what would become of nations if opinions and desires were turned into crimes? Does any even moderately enlightened government or nation go hunting for opinions or words uttered in the corner of the home or make much of things that absolutely do not warrant it? Such concerns are more appropriate for those who feed on gossip than for persons to whom have been entrusted the fortunes of the fatherland and who understand its dignity and rights. One certainly marvels to see famous preachers of religious tolerance—who every day complain of the clergy, and rightly so, for being the enemy of religious tolerance—provoke with such determination and efficacy the civil intolerance that is infinitely more hurtful than the other could ever be.

One denounces the clergy because its members oppose letting each individual think as suits himself in matters of religion—and then a charge is brought against the Spaniards for supposedly holding opinions against independence? What a strange way to think! But very much in keeping with the factions that stop at nothing to disrupt public tranquility. Unhappy is that nation in which everyone is supposed to think like the government! Liberty will flee aghast from a soil contaminated by all the crimes; hatred and persecution will take the place of civic virtues; and all nations will have an obligation to destroy a people unworthy of the name "people," comparable only to a pride of tigers that has as its sole concern mutually devouring and destroying each other.

From the foregoing, it follows that no well-founded charge can be brought against those of Spanish origin to deprive them of their acquired rights. The nation, and only the nation, is under the strictest obligation to preserve for them the possession of what they enjoy. In effect, the individual states lack the power to decide this point, and the general government[12] has justly denounced the states' excessive use of authority before the legislative Houses of the Union. Clearly the nation, and not each individual state, was the one obligated by contract to maintain and guarantee the rights of the Spaniards; no fraction of the territory was party to this commitment; General Iturbide and, afterwards, the representatives of the Mexican people, by unanimous vote, ratified this promise, as solemn as it is just and necessary.

The federation that arose could not exempt the highest authorities from so general an obligation as public credit and debt, the treaties with Colombia, and others. How, then, can the states, lacking jurisdiction in the matter, proceed to suggest measures that render null and void the credit of the republic and compromise its peace and security? Must, then, the entire nation suffer all the woes consequent to the failure of public trust, simply because the congress of one individual state feigns terrors in which no one believes, and which are not for the states, but rather the highest authorities, to remedy?

No one can doubt that the states should ensure their own internal security and are empowered to do so; but not all the means for doing so are necessarily at their disposal, and for many of those means they must await the decision of the general authorities. Otherwise, the individual states could maintain regular soldiers, incur obligations with foreign nations, declare war on them, keep warships, and do many other things that are prohibited them but which nonetheless contribute to their security. An independent and absolutely free nation is limited in its actions only by justice; but that is not so with our states, which, although they are declared sovereign in some things, are subordinate in others and consequently are subject to higher decisions.

But, could the general Congress revoke the rights and guarantees accorded to the Spaniards? Could it banish them from the territory by decrees or legislative decisions? In no way. Such behavior is entirely beyond the powers of the legislative body, nor can a decision of this type be called a "law" except by abusing words and wrenching them from their true and original meaning. Congress can prescribe general rules for acquisition or loss of the rights of naturalization and citizenship, but never should it decide that certain persons, who belong to this or that party, who have been born in this or that place, should be deprived of them. Such an act is judicial by its very nature, and in no case should it have classes of people as an object, but rather it should be strictly limited to individual persons. Either the Spaniards are offenders or they are not. If the former, they should be delivered to tribunals for processing and punishment; but if they

---

12. Mora avoids the terms "federal government" and "central authorities," perhaps to sidestep the polemics between Centralists and Federalists in early independent Mexico, and instead refers to "the general government," "the highest authorities," and so on.

are found innocent, no authority in the land can deprive them of the rights acquired by the nature of covenants and guaranteed by law.

More clearly, the nation on the one hand and the Spaniards on the other entered into a contract the moment independence became a reality. The former required the latter to submit to all the obligations, responsibilities, and duties of the natives and citizens of the republic, promising them in return the same benefits and privileges that citizens enjoy; the latter agreed, and the contract was consummated. Well now, everyone knows that such obligations can only be rescinded by mutual consent of the contracting parties or because some of the parties fail to comply with the covenant. The first requisite is missing in our case; as for the second, because the question is about the fulfillment of contractual obligations, it falls to the judicial power to pronounce judgment on it, especially because it concerns the imposition of a punishment as severe as banishment or exile.

Neither should it be said that this is a political measure rather than a judicial one and, therefore, is not beyond the powers of the legislative body. Things do not change their nature according to the names that are given them. Everywhere these political measures have been nothing but acts of banishment, in which a thousand unfortunate victims of despotism, who were found bothersome and who were not easy to get rid of by other means, have been condemned to enormous suffering, without their defenses being heard, because it was feared they would be found innocent.

The expulsion, then, of the Spaniards from the territory of the Mexican Republic, however one may view it, has the character of injustice and bears the indelible mark of the most hateful arbitrariness. The expulsion would be a stain that the nation could never wash out and one which it would necessarily come to regret, sooner or later, because of its disastrous results and pernicious consequences, for, beyond being contrary to justice, it is equally contrary to public harmony.

Hatred and rancor, passions as base as impetuous, blind men so completely and lead them to act so rashly that, as long as they can harm those they consider their enemy, they pay no attention to the injuries they cause themselves and others, and reach the point where they completely deny those injuries. This is precisely the situation in which we find ourselves with respect to the Spaniards; men who have contributed little or nothing to the independence of the nation have sworn eternal hatred for them and are resolved to exterminate them, albeit at the cost of ruining the fatherland. So we must put a stop to their hammering and oppose their ill-advised actions if we truly desire the unification of the system, the well-being and prosperity of the republic, and the guarantee of national credit.

No government, especially among those of recent times, has managed to guarantee its security or establish itself on a solid footing through persecutions; toleration and winning converts are all that can compensate for the lack of strength and prestige inherent in a newly created authority, which should never provoke enemies that might attack it but should instead seek backing to sustain itself. We must conform to these principles; yesterday we entered blindly and without experience onto the political path; our authorities lack the prestige of longevity, so necessary for finding respect and obedience. Spain has maintained, in its official notes to foreign ministries, that we are not capable of *fulfilling our promises* or unifying any government, asserting that among us the disorganizing spirit of Jacobinism reigns. What is it, then, that we are going to accomplish by expelling the Spaniards? Destroy ourselves, and whoever reflects even a little will not fail to recognize this fact.

When the republic finds itself divided and subdivided into innumerable factions and parties, when all social ties have unraveled and all the resources of government have lost their power, we are going to create a very considerable number of enemies and disaffected persons. The Spaniards have children, wives, parents, friends, and dependents, all of whom are interested in living here, and all of whom have to regard expulsion with displeasure and unhappiness. The ties that unite citizens with the government, however strong one might suppose them to be, always are less close than those they have to their relatives, parents, and intimate friends. Family society is natural, civil society exists by convention; thus, then, the moment the interests of the two become opposed and come into conflict, the former will overpower the latter, men will abandon their government and will unite with their family. Without doubt it is the most reckless thing imaginable to put private interests in opposition to the public interest, and this is exactly the inevitable result of the rejection of the Spaniards.

We deprive ourselves of the support that these men could give us with their persons and assets, and we earn for ourselves their enmity and ill will and that of their relatives and friends. Could there, then, be anyone who still dares to maintain that this is a means of unifying the system? It would be nonsense to think so and the height of audacity to say so.

The true enemies of the system are not the peaceful Spaniards, who, ensconced in their houses and occupied with their businesses, neither offend nor hurt anyone; but rather, the true enemies are the seditious and wicked people who leave no stone unturned to give truth to the predictions of the Madrid government, which, when it speaks to foreigners, alleges that we are in anarchy and paints us in the blackest colors.

National prosperity necessarily depends on population and wealth; any step, then, taken toward diminishing either one, will certainly destroy it. And who would dare deny that the expulsion of the Spaniards is such a step? The absence of ten or twelve thousand families in a nation so vast in territory and so sparse in population can be nothing less than a deadly blow that weakens it considerably. Spain, which in the sixteenth century was more populated and had more resources than we do at present, has not been able in three hundred years to recover from the decline into which it fell because of the imprudent expulsion of *Moriscos* and Jews,[13] nor to fill the vacuum that their absence left.

---

13. In 1492, following the conquest of the kingdom of Granada by the Catholic Spanish rulers, Fernando and Isabel decreed the expulsion from Spain of all Jews who would not convert to Catholicism. The *Moriscos* (Spanish Moors) who remained in Spain were expelled, despite nominal conversion to Christianity, in 1609, but the two expulsions are often imagined as one. The vacuum of talent and business resulting from these expulsions wreaked havoc on the Spanish society and economy.

There has not been a discerning writer, either Spanish or foreign, who has not condemned that measure and who has not attributed Spain's decline to it, despite the fact that the reasons they had in mind for carrying it out were much more plausible than those we can give for expelling the Spaniards. And can anyone suppose that we are correct in pushing it forward? Can we perhaps give as reasons the difference of religion, dress, language, habits, and practices that Fernando the Catholic had in mind with the banishment of those others? Certainly not. We have everything in common with the Spaniards, and we have no other motives for disturbing them and dealing such an unfortunate blow to the national population than the genuine hatred and feigned fears that certain people profess toward them.

That public wealth will diminish considerably and may be ruined completely with the projected measure is so obvious that it is not necessary to take time to prove it. A country's wealth is proportional to its employment of capital resources; through them, raw materials acquire value and the industry and the hard work of man find employment; their beneficial influence makes the lands productive and supports commerce. A nation lacking capital resources can proceed down the path of prosperity only very slowly, however abundant and substantial its productions might seem, for without the work of man and the capital to pay him, they will not attain their potential value for quite a long time.

Now, then, with the expulsion of the Spaniards, almost all the capital resources are going to leave us—their own, because it is certainly right and natural that they pick up and take their resources with them; those of foreigners, because they will be able to establish themselves in business only with the greatest difficulty. Among us, that is to say, among the native-born of the republic, businesses are just now beginning to take hold and wealth to be distributed; but, always in the shadow of those who have something, and with the help of their credit, the Spaniards are rather more well off, and foreigners make up the rich and powerful families that animate and enliven the republic with their great businesses in all branches of industry, agriculture, and commerce. If both the former and the latter leave, we would be reduced to very little and would be incapable of repaying the public debt as happened in the last days of the Empire; and there is no doubt but that they will leave us if we insist on the planned measure.

Wholesale merchants, like the English, French, etc., cannot devote themselves to retail sales, both because they would thus waste the time they could usefully employ on other things, and because they do not know the language, the prices, the uses, practices, and a thousand other things necessary for this kind of business—in a word, because they lack the experience necessary for the purpose. They need, then, to find persons who have that experience and who, through their credit and capital resources, offer some guarantee for the fulfillment of their pledges and obligations; in the Spaniards they find all this, at least for now, and if they were suddenly to lose the Spaniards, as would be the case with an abrupt expulsion, all their business would stop and they would sustain losses from which they will not be able to recover except very slowly and with great difficulty. This state of affairs would eliminate their inclination and desire for new imports, and all trade would be paralyzed; tax revenues, which are dependent on sales, imports, and exports, would be destroyed within a few days; the government would be forced to commit a thousand outrages to meet its obligations, and the exasperated people would rebel against it. These evils are not in the future; they make themselves felt well enough at present, and their origin is not and cannot be anything other than the spirit of discord and persecution that we see among ourselves.

If political revolutions—or, better stated, the symptoms of disorder and anarchy—destroy public prosperity, it is equally true that they ruin the nation's credit. This credit cannot be sustained except by faithfulness in fulfilling promises, the upholding of stipulated guarantees, and the punctual and conscientious satisfaction of pledges made. And how will our republic be able to satisfy such important duties given the expulsion that has been planned? With this expulsion, the most solemn promises are violated, the most sacred guarantees are trampled, and we render ourselves absolutely powerless to satisfy our debts. Who will want to deal with us in the future or trust a nation that has shamelessly defaulted on pacts confirmed a thousand times, pacts that constitute one of the foundations of its independence? The national flag, with one of its colors,[14] will make clear our infidelity to all the nations of the earth, and it will be a monument of confusion and shame that will transmit our ignominy to the most distant posterity.

On Ecclesiastical Wealth (1831)

1. The matter of ecclesiastical revenue, simple enough for those who try to deal with it using the genuine and solid principles of the Gospel and civil law, becomes a chaos of obscurities and doubts for those who move away from such principles, taking issues out of context and spreading over them the darkness and confusion that have always been the inevitable result of ideas gone astray. As often happens when great and powerful interests hang on the resolution of certain issues, the spirit of partisanship has become mixed up in the current issue to such a degree that, when writers deal with it, one cannot read the pros and cons of their works without experiencing the most unpleasant feelings of irritation.

2. If one were to believe the clergy, the temporal wealth it enjoys is of divine origin, and the clergy possesses it by that very right; the clergy can acquire it without authorization from, without the consent of, and even in the face of indisputable opposition from civil governments; once it has made that wealth its own, that wealth cannot legally be alienated nor lost, and it must remain in the clergy's

---

14. The three colors of the Mexican flag originally stood for the "three guarantees" of Iturbide's Plan of Iguala: green for independence, white for Catholicism, and red for the union of Mexicans and Spaniards.

power forever, exempt from civil jurisdiction in its administration and investment. Such strange claims are counterbalanced by other claims that are no less strange, although they come from the opposite direction. The enemies of the clergy (understanding by this phrase those who wish there to be neither religion nor worship) claim that the clergy must neither possess anything nor have anything on which to live, for, appraising its ministry as unnecessary and pernicious to nations, they see in those who practice it nothing but a heavy burden for the public and a gathering of impostors, suitable only for keeping people in the brutishness and slavery that carry with them superstition and fanaticism. As both parties have taken up positions at the extremes, their writings are filled with gross errors, vague declamations, and ridiculous claims elevated to the level of excess and extravagance.

3. The struggle between impiety and superstition, caused in large part by the clergy's excesses, existed in Europe from the beginning of the Reformation but remained hidden until the French Revolution, when it came into the open; since then, the impious and the fanatics have everywhere made the harshest war on each other, being at different times victors and vanquished, the triumph of either of these sects always causing enormous injuries to society and to religion. Now Mexico's turn has come to be a battlefield where these detestable parties have competed for victory; the fanatics were in a completely commanding position from the establishment of the colony until the end of the last century, when the philosophers first appeared to fight for the dominion that the fanatics had held for so long. It was easy for the philosophers to show that the clergy's claims lacked foundation; because the clergy's claims were excessive, they could not keep up the appearance of reason with which they were furiously battered; and, moreover, because the residents of Mexico had been led to believe that the fundamental bases of the religion and the claims of the clergy were one and the same, once the claims of the clergy became discredited, the fundamental bases of the religion could not sustain themselves and toppled, impiety then taking great strides forward until, in a short time, it had the opportunity not only to defend itself but to fight to its advantage and bring down the enemy. But this defeat was not only a defeat of superstition, something that certainly would have been a great good for the country, but it also destroyed religious principles among a large part of the population, a very grave injury to public order.

4. Any Mexican, a true lover of the religion of Jesus Christ and the well-being of his fatherland, must be deeply interested in maintaining both. With neither religion nor worship, it is impossible to have society or public morality among civilized people; but religion can neither be nor be loved when it becomes confused with the abuses of superstition, with the ambition and greed of the ministers of the altar. So separating religion from all this does a service to religion itself, letting it appear in its inherent brilliance and splendor. Inasmuch as what has principally given the impious pretext to discredit religion has been the enormous abuse of ecclesiastical wealth and the exorbitant claims of the clergy in this matter, whoever shows that religion has no part of any of this leaves its enemies almost completely disarmed and, at the same time, establishes solidly the civil rights of nations and governments, and with those rights, public well-being. The

present essay attempts to provide this service and to this end will examine, first, what is the nature and origin of ecclesiastical wealth? Second, to which authority does management of its acquisition, administration, and investment belong? Third, what authority can determine the expenses of worship and the means of covering them? The analysis of these three principal questions and the subordinate questions they include will contribute to the ability of the public to make up its own mind on such an important matter, rejecting equally the errors of the impious and the extravagant claims of the clergy. In this way the interests of religion will remain unharmed, those interests maliciously confused with the abuse that has been made of religion—abuse by the clergy to honor its claims with so respectable a name, and abuse by the impious to make religion hateful, attributing to it all the evils that are necessary to make it seem so.

5. Ecclesiastical wealth is nothing more than the sum total of the holdings set aside for the expenses of worship and the sustenance of its ministers. These holdings are by their essence and nature temporal and by their use they are called ecclesiastical. Money, lands, their fruits, and everything designated to maintain churches are essentially material, and it is not possible for anyone to make them change their nature because of the end to which they are or can be put; for everybody knows that the essence of things is absolutely independent of the will or caprice of the agents who make use of them. Thus it is that ecclesiastical wealth, if it is by its nature temporal, can never cease being so under any possible assumption. These notions are common and popular and are in perfect accord with the Gospel of Jesus Christ as well as with the doctrines of the most celebrated Fathers of the Church. When the Pharisees asked Jesus Christ if it would be lawful to pay tribute to Caesar, he asked for a coin, which is the representative symbol of all types of temporal wealth, income, or riches, and, having examined it, he said to them, *Whose likeness is this?* They answered him, *Caesar's.* Then he confounded them with this admirable sentence: *Then render unto Caesar what is Caesar's and unto God what is God's.*[15] It is clear that, in a lesson with the sole objective of distinguishing temporal from spiritual things, Jesus Christ numbered among the first the coin that, by its material nature, represents all wealth; and, because wealth designated for worship is of this type, it is equally true that, according to the doctrine of the divine author of the Gospel, it is, by its essence and nature, temporal.

6. All the Fathers of the Church agree in giving the same interpretation to this text and passage of the Bible; it would be pointless and tedious to copy their teachings word for word, given that they are popular and well-known, so we will only cite the explication that St. John Chrysostom,[16] the principal Doctor of the Greek Church, makes of this passage of St. Matthew, expounding its text. "The

---

15. Matthew 22: 19–21.

16. St. John Chrysostom (c. 349–407), Patriarch of Constantinople, Father and Doctor of the Church, wrote explication of Christian scripture following the historico-grammatical method of the School of Antioch.

Pharisees," he says, "having been asked by Jesus Christ, *Whose likeness is this?* And, having received as an answer, *Caesar's,* Jesus said to them, *Then render unto Caesar what is Caesar's and render unto God what is God's.* This is not to give, but to give back what was obvious from the image and inscription. Then, so that they would not say, *You are subjecting us to men,* He added, *and that which is of God, render unto God,* because it is just to give back to men what is from men and give to God what men themselves received from Him. That is why St. Paul says, *Give to each his due; to him who is owed tribute, tribute; to him who is owed tax, tax; to him who is owed fear, fear; to him who is owed honor, honor.* [17] So it is that when you hear, 'Give to Caesar what is Caesar's,' you must understand this as indicating only those things that do not offend piety, for if they did offend piety, neither tax nor tribute would be for Caesar, but rather for the devil." [18]

7. Whoever reads this passage carefully and many others of the Fathers that we omit will come to understand that the wealth called ecclesiastical because of its use is by nature civil and temporal, for all of it consists of coin or its equivalent; nonetheless, this use of the term "ecclesiastical" has been the foundation of the claims of the clergy, who have attempted to SPIRITUALIZE what reason, the Gospel, and the Fathers of the Church believe is material. Indeed, the clergy have introduced a question that, while it seems purely speculative, is not; from the word *ecclesiastical* applied to wealth designated for worship, they have attempted to imply that the wealth was *spiritualized,* and from this very transformation the clergy derives their independence from civil authority, and even their divine right to possess wealth, administer it, and acquire it without any intervention by secular government. So, when the defenders of these claims find themselves hemmed in by reason, the Gospel, and the authorities, all of which show convincingly that the wealth with which we are dealing is temporal by its nature, they appeal to the absurdity of saying that as soon as it passed to the dominion of the Church, its nature changed and consequently ceased to be temporal. To dislodge them, then, from this last redoubt, it will be sufficient simply to examine what it is they mean when they assert that such wealth has been *spiritualized.* The simple analysis of the concept that corresponds to this word will be sufficient to show that, when the defenders of these claims use the word, they are mouthing either a palpable absurdity or something that cannot support them in any way; because, if the word applied to wealth that has as its object the preservation of worship means that the wealth has changed its nature, leaving its former temporal nature behind and acquiring a new spiritual one, this is an absurdity that neither merits nor necessitates a response; besides the impossibility that a concept so monstrous in itself involves—a concept that supposes a change in the essence of things—if, although impossible, it were in fact brought about, that is to say, if the wealth with which we are dealing had indeed lost its

---

17. Romans 13:7.

18. St. John Chrysostom. *Homilies on Matthew,* Homily 70. [Mora's note. The note in the original indicates 70–71.]

temporal nature and acquired a new spiritual one, in this very way the wealth would cease to be useful for sustaining ministers and preserving worship, both of which are material by their nature. And who will be able to doubt this analysis when it is abundantly evident that such a change in the nature of this wealth has not been observed, because it always remains the same after its application to the expenses of worship as it was before? It remains, then, that when the defenders of the claims of the clergy assert that their wealth has been spiritualized, they mean only that it has been designated for purposes directed toward spiritual things, and so they add nothing to what everyone knows and from which nothing that favors their arguments can be deduced, except the right common to all civil corporations that are authorized to acquire temporal wealth.

8. The Church can be considered in two ways, either as a mystical body or as a political association; viewed in the first way, it is the work of Jesus Christ, eternal and unfailing, eternally independent of temporal power; in the second way, it is the work of civil governments, it can be altered and modified, and the privileges it owes to the social order can even be abolished, like those of any other political community. The truth of these notions should be clear to anyone who considers and knows how to distinguish between the two most notable epochs that the Church has gone through, which are well differentiated in its history; the first, before Constantine, and the second, after this prince made a public profession of Christianity. In the first, there existed only the mystical body of the Church; the divine word was preached, the sacraments were administered, questions of faith and morals were decided, the confirmed heretic was separated from the communion of the Church, and everything pertaining to the method and form with which the Supreme Being should be worshiped was regulated. This, and only this, was what the Church did in that epoch when it existed only as a mystical body. When Constantine converted to Christianity, the Church emerged as a political community; then its ministers began to acquire wealth, to have an external court system and coercive jurisdiction, to enjoy the right of imposing on its subjects certain temporal punishments and compelling them by force to submit to those punishments; then, finally, they acquired the civil comforts, honors, and distinctions that they enjoy at present.

9. From the foregoing one can deduce that the only rights that belong unfailingly to the ministers of the Church are those they enjoyed in the first epoch, when the Church existed only as a mystical body; and, with no detriment whatsoever to religion, ministers of the Church can lose those rights that the Church as a type of political community acquired in the second—for, when Jesus Christ promised that his Church would be eternal and unfailing, he was asserting at the same time that his kingdom was not of this world, that he had not come to found a civil empire, and that his promises were limited to the mystical body that was the work of his heavenly Father, not the political community created by civil governments, kings, and emperors.

10. Having established this distinction—without which no step in the right direction can be taken in a matter where civil and religious rights are so intertwined—it remains to us only to examine under which of these rights the clergy

possess the temporal wealth they enjoy, and, after having also determined the nature of such wealth, the origin and authority to which it is subject will be clear; for if it belongs to the clergy by civil right, it is and ought to remain subject to temporal authority; but if, on the contrary, its ownership comes to it by indisputable Divine right, it should be entirely independent of that temporal authority and subject exclusively to the authority of the pastors. That the ministers of the Church have an indisputable right to demand their food from the faithful to whom they give their spiritual service is a truth so evident that no one can dispute it. By natural law each person should live by the fruit of his labor, and it is a matter of strict justice that the toil and services of the ministers of the Church should be compensated by those who profit in some way from them. But this is not the question that occupies us right now; this right, which St. Paul affirms and to which he bears witness, is the personal right of each minister and not a right common to the whole body of the Church that we are discussing—so, therefore, the latter cannot be inferred from the former; the question we must resolve is whether the Church, considered as a mystical body, has a right to possess any wealth, and if so, by which right? From whom can it exact this wealth? And of what might this wealth consist?

11. If by the word *wealth* is understood the voluntary offerings of the faithful, designated not to form a fund to be administered but rather to be used precisely for the sustenance of the ministers of worship and for the expenses affiliated with worship, there is no doubt that the Church, even considered as a mystical body, has the right to possess it. The ministers are men like all others, requiring sustenance, and external worship involves material acts that entail this kind of expense. Until the conversion of Constantine the Church was only a mystical body and nevertheless possessed this type of wealth with neither controversy nor opposition; nor could it be otherwise, for it was not in the realm of possibility or justice that pastors not eat or drink, or that the faithful neglect the basic necessities of those who rendered such important service, providing them with spiritual food. Jesus Christ had designated Judas, one of his apostles, to collect alms from the disciples, who gave alms for his sustenance;[19] and the apostles, after they scattered throughout the world and devoted themselves to the exercise of their ministry, designated the deacons as the collectors and repositories of the offerings of the faithful, so that these offerings could be used for the sustenance of the ministers and aid for the needy, inasmuch as the expenses of worship then were few or none.

12. The history of the first three centuries of the Church preceding the conversion of Constantine does not supply a single example of ecclesiastics possessing other kinds of wealth. The most fervent among the faithful sold all their belongings and put the proceeds at the disposal of the apostles or of the succeeding bishops, not for them to administer those proceeds—because this word "administer" amounts to "transmutation," that is, some type of business deal—but rather so

---

19. Judas Iscariot is described in John 12:6 and 13:29 as keeping the moneybag or alms-purse. Mora does not pause to comment on the fact that Judas used this position to betray Jesus, but his readers undoubtedly understood the point.

that whoever received them would deposit them in their coffers, and afterwards take them out to distribute among the poor and the ministers. The less fervent kept all their wealth and assisted the ministers with partial offerings that had the same use and purpose. The first disciples of Jesus Christ never demanded anything from the faithful, nor can a single example be cited that would provide evidence that they did, for in the case of Ananais and Saphira, referred to in the Acts of the Apostles as having been punished by a violent and miraculous death for concealing part of their wealth,[20] it was not because they wanted to retain it or refused to lend it, but rather because, having offered it voluntarily, they subsequently tried to deceive St. Peter, hiding part of it from him; so what was punished was deceit, not resistance to divesting themselves of their fortune in deference to the Church. This and nothing more is what can be said and perceived from a simple reading of the sacred text.

• • • • •

14. And from whom could the Church, considered as a mystical body, demand the offerings that are its due? Could it be perhaps from its own faithful, or from civil governments? This question is rather important, no matter how trivial it seems at first glance, for the clergy claim that governments have an obligation to support their possession of their wealth and the collection of their revenues with external force, compelling citizens and subjects to comply with decisions rendered by the ecclesiastical authority for the maintenance and administration of their wealth, and asserting on the basis of such claims, that not only are the individuals who profess Catholicism subjects of the Church, but so also are governments. From this comes the clergy's constant demand that religious sins or failings be made civil offenses and be subject to temporal punishments, charging the Catholic princes who have refused to do so with transgression of this presumed obligation. Nevertheless, one must agree that this claim not only has no support in the Gospel but is, at the same time, unjust and unfounded. Jesus Christ, as he himself testifies in many passages of the New Testament, did not come to preach his doctrine to governments, but to men—nor to conquer kingdoms, but souls for his heavenly Father. Neither did he solicit the support of earthly powers, but rather turned directly to individuals and had them adopt his religion, using only persuasion and conviction or fear of eternal punishment, which he warned would be the consequence for those who, having heard the Gospel preached, refused to submit to it.

15. The Christians of the first centuries behaved in this regard exactly like their divine teacher. Sent out like lambs among wolves, they never turned to governments, to emperors, or to kings, to demand aid that would sustain their religion by force, nor did they ever think that denying them aid would be an indictment of the earthly powers; much to the contrary, they were always loyal

---

20. Acts 5:11.

and preached obedience to the emperors, who not only did not help them, but who actively persecuted them. Even when these emperors, after converting to Christianity, not only offered but also employed their temporal force to support the judgments of the Church, the most celebrated Fathers refused this cooperation as harmful to the Church itself. We could cite many passages from St. John Chrysostom, St. Augustine, and St. Jerome to support this truth, but it will be completely sufficient to cite those from St. Cyprian, the Sardican Council, St. John Chrysostom, and St. Hilary of Arles, which are conclusive on this topic.[21]

• • • • •

20.[22] Many other passages in the works of these and of other Fathers, as clear as the foregoing, confirm that it is not governments that must support the Church, and consequently that they are under no obligation to do so, for the Church recognizes as its sole subjects only individuals; and if governments are not subjects of the Church, how can anyone demand from them any type of contribution, revenue, or other wealth for the maintenance of its ministers? It must be shown that no prince or temporal authority, simply by having professed Catholicism, is under any obligation to compel his subjects to pay the expenses of the worship that he himself has adopted personally. The goal and objective of civil governments is to maintain social order, not to protect this or that religion; so then, just as it would be an absurdity to claim that the Church could not exist except in a nation that had a particular form of government, so it would be similarly absurd to assert that one cannot have a government without a particular given religion. Knowledge of the form of government of any nation to which the faithful belong is as irrelevant to the institution and objectives of the Church as is knowledge of the form of religion that its subjects profess to the institution and objectives of civil government. On the contrary, how many pious Catholic princes would have the reputation of behaving reprehensibly if it were a religious obligation to compel their subjects to profess a particular religion or to compel them to pay the levies that would sustain the worship of the true Church? Beginning with Constantine, the first protector of Christianity, and ending with Louis Philippe I, present king of the French, history supplies us with many examples of truly religious sovereigns who have not authorized, under civil law, the obligation to profess a particular religion nor the obligation the faithful have, under natural law, to sustain the ministers of the worship they profess. No one has dared to throw in the face of these princes their having failed in their religious duties, and the reason is very simple—because, considered as governments, they are not subject to the Church, nor do they have any obligations whatsoever relative to it, for this mystical and spiritual body

---

21. St. Augustine (354–430), Bishop of Hippo, one of the most important theologians of the Church; St. Jerome (c. 347–c.420), Church Father, greatest Biblical scholar of his age; St. Cyprian of Carthage (d. 258), Bishop of Carthage, a founder of Latin theology; Council of Sardica (343); St. Hilary of Arles (c. 315–c. 367), Bishop of Poitiers and Doctor of the Church.

22. Sections 16–19, omitted, provide specific citations to support Mora's argument.

founded by Jesus Christ, considered as such, recognizes as subjects only the individual faithful and not the governments to which they belong.

21. Having proven that the Church, even considered as a mystical body, can demand under natural law from the faithful, its subjects—and not from governments—some temporal assistance, improperly called wealth, it follows naturally to ask what type and amount of wealth the faithful must give to satisfy this obligation. This question would be unnecessary if the clergy had not maliciously confused the civil right to possess temporal wealth, a right which the Church has acquired as a type of political community, with the right that allows it, as a mystical body, to demand recompense for the services its ministers give. Under natural law, the faithful must support these ministers; but what cannot be required of the faithful is that any particular kind of wealth be designated for this support—whether the wealth be real estate or livestock, whether it consist of capital or rental income—because all these obligations, civil by nature, cannot exist except under the right that bears the name "civil." If the ministers of worship receive what they need to eat, dress, be lodged, and pay for the performance of rites and ceremonies that constitute worship, under natural law they cannot demand more nor insist that the wealth assigned to this use be of any particular nature nor have any specific value or valuation; in apostolic times and in the early centuries of the Church, pastors could not even formally demand this type of assistance. St. Paul, who recognizes this right for priests, professes that he never made use of it, and he tells us categorically that he lived by the work of his hands,[23] it being understood that he did so without ever neglecting the obligations of his ministry, to which, as everyone knows, this chosen vessel dedicated almost every moment of his existence.

22. His conduct in this respect was imitated in the early centuries by a very large portion of the first pastors, who subsisted on their physical labor; the rest of the pastors, the smaller portion, supported themselves with the voluntary offerings of the faithful, without ever pressuring or threatening them to force these offerings. To be sure, in those times it was not necessary to use threats to make the faithful fulfill such a strict and rigorous obligation; but this compliance depended in great part on the ministers' having made themselves loved by their gentle and soft manners, by their irreproachable conduct, and by their tireless labor and dedication to the exercise of their sacred ministry. If the faithful subsequently cooled off in this regard, they were certainly blameworthy; but such coolness was due in large part to the decadent conduct of their ministers. Today, in those countries where the Catholic religion is only tolerated, as it is in the greater part of Europe and Asia and in other no less considerable parts of Africa and America, the Church is as it was in the early centuries, and ministers maintain themselves by what their faithful subjects voluntarily offer; nonetheless, they have never wanted for necessities, nor have the faithful in general ever excused themselves from the obligation to pay. The reason is very obvious. The priest who knows that his sustenance cannot be secured by the coercive force of

---

23. 2 Thessalonians 3:7–10.

laws attempts to make himself acceptable to the faithful by his exemplary conduct and dedication to his ministry, and he thus secures—with greater profit—what others barely manage to get from the faithful when they appeal to civil authority to obtain wealth by temporal measures.

23. If from the foregoing we can legitimately infer that the Church can exist without lacking anything and without seeming less than perfect even though it might lack temporal wealth, this does not mean that the possession of such wealth is contrary to its principles, as some heretics have claimed; such an error must be rejected not only by the Catholic but also by the man of judgment as contrary to reason and to the evidence of centuries. If possession of temporal wealth is not foundational for the Church, neither is it loathsome; but as the Church cannot enjoy temporal wealth in its role as mystical body but only as a political community, the right to acquire and retain wealth is essentially civil, however much one might want to give it another name, and it must be entirely subject to temporal authority like that of all other political bodies. Indeed, the greatest right that the Church can assert regarding its wealth is that of property, and not only is property civil by its nature, but also one cannot conceive of its being anything else. Property consists of the owner's power to dispose of the wealth he has acquired in accord with the provisions of the laws, by using it, selling it, or exchanging it. And how could a body or community whose existence is not recognized or authorized by the laws acquire, sell, or exchange wealth? Such a claim would be as outlandish as the claim that a man I have conjured up here in my imagination could own capital or land. So if the Church comes to acquire either capital or land and calls itself the owner, this can only be in its capacity as a political community and by the right that pertains to all such communities, that is to say, by civil right. If this is so, as there can be no doubt, it is impossible to comprehend by what reason the Church should be the only community, among all those that society has created, that claims to be exempt from the norms that have been or will be written for entities of the same class, norms that arise from the temporal authority that has given being to those entities.

24. The most celebrated Fathers of the Church, who surely do not deserve to be reprimanded for abandoning the interests of the Church, did not think in this way nor make such claims; nonetheless, almost all of them recognized not only that the right of ecclesiastics to possess temporal wealth is purely civil, but also—as a necessary consequence of this recognition—that such possession is entirely subject to the laws that were prescribed by the temporal authority to acquire it, maintain it, or forfeit it. To support the truth of what we say we will cite some of the most notable passages from the works of the Fathers.

• • • • •

27.[24] To these and many other authorities that we might have cited are opposed, like an irrefutable argument, the resolutions of many conciliar canons

---

24. In the remainder of section 24, and all of 25 and 26, Mora provides citations to support his argument thus far.

and as many more papal bulls and decrees in which censures are fulminated against those who interfere with the Church in the possession of its wealth, many of them giving as a reason that Church wealth is entirely independent of civil jurisdiction. It would be useless and tiresome to enumerate all these documents, or even the principal ones, at length; naturally, we agree that they exist, and that they say everything those who cite them in their favor attribute to them. Our adversaries do not deceive the public in this, and all they lack is proof of one thing for their argument to be effective, and this is that such documents and their authors are competent judges of the matter. Naturally, we agree that these authors' authority is worthy of respect when they are judged as educated persons, but it is not infallible in this matter even when they are viewed as pastors of the Church. If the present question were about faith and practices, their decision would be free of error, and if it were about rites and ceremonies, it would have the character of law; but as it is neither about one nor the other, but rather precisely about temporal wealth, objects, and actions, their authority is and must be acknowledged as lacking jurisdiction in the present question. This is a truth for all that one may assert the opposite. Whenever the kings and the governments of all Catholic countries have found it appropriate, they have disregarded the resolutions that are quoted to us and the doctrines that we oppose and that are used against us, distancing themselves from these doctrines, conforming their conduct to the ones that contradict them, and disregarding the censures that were supposed to uphold them; all this they have done without leaving the pale of the Church or breaking the ties of Catholic unity, as we will see further on.

28. But one will ask us, is not ecclesiastical wealth in itself, in its administration and investment, covered by canon law? And is this law not distinct from the civil law, by which we claimed ecclesiastical wealth is regulated and to which we say it is and must be subject? To answer this objection, it is necessary to caution that canon law is part civil and part ecclesiastical; the civil part consists of the powers that temporal governments have expressly accorded to the Church or, by tacit consent, have permitted it to exercise; this part of canon law is entirely subject to civil jurisdiction; it exists only to the extent it has not been revoked by temporal authority, and it is subject to this authority that popes and councils organize the public conduct of the Church as a political community. Where the Catholic clergy have neither privileges nor immunities, where they possess no other wealth than the voluntary offerings of the faithful, where they are not permitted to exercise coercive authority nor to have anything to do with the civil contract of marriage, as is the case in countries where Catholicism is only tolerated, such as the United States, England, Prussia, a large part of the rest of Germany, Holland, France, and Russia—in those countries, we say, although there may be churches and Roman Catholics, the section of canon law that regulates public conduct has no standing, and this is the section that includes the subject of ecclesiastical wealth. The reason is that the sovereign authority of those countries has decided not to consider the Church a political community nor to confer on it the rights of such. Nonetheless, in those nations the churches should be governed, and are in fact governed, by the section of canon law that is ecclesiastical in nature and

through which are organized the duties of conscience, the rites, the ceremonies, and everything that pertains to the internal conduct of the Catholic community considered as a mystical body. So saying everything pertaining to the acquisition, administration, and investment of ecclesiastical wealth is by its nature temporal, and at the same time must be regulated by canon law, is not logically inconsistent nor contradictory, for canon law in this sense is actually civil law by another name, even though ecclesiastical authority exercises it by virtue of the powers it has received for this purpose from the temporal government, revocable in a case where that government finds doing so appropriate.

29. The most decisive proof of ecclesiastical authority's lack of jurisdiction in the subject we are considering is the low esteem in which the conciliar resolutions and papal bulls on public discipline and ecclesiastical wealth are held, even by the very Catholic governments that consider the Church a political body and concede to it the rights that belong to this kind of community. The Council of Trent[25] has never been accepted in France, and most of its resolutions on the subject of discipline are not nor have ever been in force in Spain nor in the other Catholic kingdoms; the bull *In Coena Domini* has been generally rejected in all of them;[26] their governments do not allow any mandates from Rome to become valid or enforceable in those kingdoms, except after examining them and granting the appropriate permit; and in exercising this right, they have many times refused to receive papal bulls, with the result that the popes themselves, in the widely known concordats with Catholic sovereigns, have recognized the sovereigns' right to suppress or accept the bulls. Well, then, what validity and what esteem can be given to bulls or resolutions whose doctrines are contrary to the universal practice of Catholic countries, a practice recognized by the pontifical sovereigns themselves, based in the Gospel, the doctrines of the Fathers, and the customs of the early centuries, and supported by very solid reasons? And could there still be any doubt that it is deceiving the public to lead it to believe that these bulls and resolutions are from an irrefutable and decisive authority on the subject?[27]

· · · · ·

52. In Mexico, the clergy and ecclesiastical wealth are neither limited nor insufficient for conducting worship and ecclesiastical service. All that is lacking is an appropriate distribution of both, for their current distribution could not

---

25. The Council of Trent (1545–1563), an ecumenical council responding to the Protestant Reformation, introduced tenets that confirmed Catholic doctrine and made reconciliation with Protestants impossible.

26. The bull *In Coena Domini* was originally promulgated in the fourteenth century and modified until 1627, opposed by the reigning civil powers, and therefore never published and made effective in any part of the Church. This bull promulgated a wide variety of prohibitions regarding various activities of individuals and governments.

27. Sections 30–51 discuss the historical background of tithes and other forms of ecclesiastical wealth and their administration.

be worse.[28] We must increase the number of bishops and decrease the income of each; equally important is building new parish churches, increasing the number of ministers in each, reducing parish territory, totally eliminating chaplains or simple benefices[29] as well as religious orders of both sexes. With the amount of capital now dedicated to chaplaincies or pious works and the wealth that the monastic orders enjoy, a fund can be created to provide adequately for the ministers of the parishes in each bishopric, increasing them by whatever number might be necessary, prohibiting anyone from being admitted to a religious order thereafter except in the capacity of serving in some specific parochial church or cathedral in the role of principal minister or assistant. In this way, the number of ecclesiastics will always be the same or even greater; but they will be reduced in numbers in the great population centers, where they are generally not needed and often harmful, and their numbers will not decrease in the small places and poor parishes where there is now so great a need. Another advantage can result from this arrangement, that of eliminating the unjust, hateful, and imprudent parish fees forever, for with a fund as substantial as the one that should result from the chaplaincies, pious works, and wealth of the religious orders, there will be enough for everyone. But if this arrangement does not occur, this hateful parish tax system should still be exchanged for another that would be less hateful and would be payable, not in the unfortunate way it is now payable, but in fixed and determined installments, as are all the others. The tithe must also be eliminated, or if it is believed necessary, it must be expanded to all the professions and made payable only with cash.[30]

• • • • •

87.[31] We have come to the end of this essay, in which we have tried to provide insight into the nature of wealth known as "ecclesiastical," and we have tried to prove that it is by its essence temporal, the same before as after having passed to the dominion of the Church; that the Church, considered as a mystical body, has

---

28. The number of priests and friars in Mexico plummeted from about 7,300 to 4,000 with the departure of foreign-born clergy after independence. The majority lived in Mexico City, both before and after independence; outside the capital, there were only about 1,000 parishes in the entire country, many of them serving 10,000 parishioners or more.

29. Chaplaincies and benefices were endowed clerical offices for clerics. In many cases, the family that created such an endowment would specify that the "benefited" priest should be one of their own descendents, in effect keeping the endowment in the family.

30. "Perhaps because of the views expressed in this essay, the Chamber of 1833 abolished the *civil* obligation of paying the *tithe,* leaving this business to the conscience of individuals. The measure has been so well received and universally approved that in the midst of the raging ecclesiastic-military reaction that has thrown everything over, including the constitution of the republic, this law and the one that abolished the compulsory monastic vows have remained in place and managed to survive. . . ." [This note is by Mora's unnamed editor.]

31. In the intervening sections Mora provides a detailed historical account of the political standing of religious communities.

no right to possess nor request this wealth, nor much less to demand it from civil governments; that as a political community the Church can acquire, hold, and preserve temporal wealth, but only by such right as corresponds to communities of its kind, that is to say, civil communities; that by virtue of this right, public authority can now and has always been able to determine for itself, and without assistance from ecclesiastical authority, the laws that it deems appropriate for the acquisition, administration, and investment of ecclesiastical wealth; that to the public authority belongs the exclusive right to set expenses of worship and provide the means of covering them; finally, that in a federal system, the civil power to which these rights belong is that of the states and not the federation.

88. The clergy probably will be offended by the resolution that has been given to the questions proposed, but it is in the interest of nations and of religion itself—and their interest is deep, in a matter as vital to the public well-being as ecclesiastical wealth—that they determine their rights and make known their obligations. Both their rights and their obligations are set out in the passage of the Gospel that serves as the epigraph for this essay: *Whose likeness is this?* Jesus Christ asked the Pharisees who consulted him on whether it would be permissible to pay tax to Caesar. *Caesar's,* they responded to him. *Then render unto Caesar,* continued the Savior, *what is Caesar's, and unto God what is God's.* Return it, says St. John Chrysostom, interpreting this passage, because you have received it from Caesar. Thus can we say to the clergy: Give back to Caesar—and, in his place, to the civil authority of which he is the trustee—what the coin designates, that is to say, the temporal wealth it represents; do it whenever it is asked of you, as Jesus Christ did when the tax collectors requested the head tax from him; and keep what is of God, that is to say, spiritual wealth and the keys to the kingdom of heaven. Do not claim to take possession of the kingdoms and wealth of the earth, nor aim to stir up malicious doubts to avoid handing these over; imitate the openhandedness of Jesus Christ and follow his example, clearly and straightforwardly fulfilling the command to let the wealth go. So you will be less rich but more like the Divine Savior, who protested repeatedly that his kingdom was not of this world, but purely spiritual.—Mexico, December 6, 1831.

Andrés Bello
(Venezuela/Chile)

Andrés Bello (1781–1865) is among the most respected and influential thinkers in Latin American intellectual history. He was prodigiously well-educated and contributed significantly to each field of learning to which he turned his attention. He was born in Caracas, Venezuela, to Bartolomé Bello and Ana Antonia López, parents of modest means and social standing. In 1814 Bello married Mary Ann Boyland, with whom he had three children. She died in 1821, and he remarried three years later; with his second wife, Elizabeth Antonia Dunn, he had twelve children.

Bello received a classical education under the direction of Fr. Cristóbal de Quesada of the Mercedarian Order. A superb student, Bello won a number of academic prizes while at university and graduated at the top of his class. During his university years he was a close friend of and teacher of geography and literature to Simón Bolívar and also befriended Alexander von Humboldt, through whom he came to know of Alexander's brother Wilhelm von Humboldt's work on language, an interest that would consume Bello throughout his life. Having secured his baccalaureate in 1800, Bello became secretary to the Central Vaccination Board, responsible for vaccinating Venezuela's urban and rural populations against smallpox. He was also becoming known as an important literary figure, a poet of exceptional grace and scope—though the manuscripts of many of his most famous poems were lost to fire and neglect—and a journalist who helped shape the editorial stance of Venezuela's most important journal of ideas, *Gazeta de Caracas,* to which he contributed original pieces and translations of works that had appeared in similar European outlets.

In 1810 Bello left for London, where he was to continue his studies and serve as an occasional diplomatic functionary for the next twenty years. There he encountered some of the most important British Utilitarian philosophers, including William Hamilton and James Mill. Having learned to speak and write French and English early in life, he was comfortable with the texts of the most important English and Scottish philosophers. Under their influence he wrote his *Filosofía de entendemiento* in 1881. During these years, Bello served several South American nations in a number of quasi-diplomatic roles. Through friends he received an offer from the Chilean government to serve in a high public position in Santiago.

On June 25, 1829, Bello arrived in Valparaíso and during the next thirty-five years he would become the most important intellectual figure in South America. At the same time, Bello began to address a number of issues he regarded as crucial to building his adopted nation. At the center of his concerns was education, without which a nation has neither a civil, economic, nor cultural future. First, upon the request of the Chilean government, he undertook reform of legal education, which he believed necessary to the life of a republic, and eventually wrote a textbook, *Princípios de derecho de gentes* (1832), which remains the foundation for legal education in Chile. He then moved to international law, in which his writings again became foundational, particularly with respect to the doctrine of territorial waters, so essential to a nation such as Chile, with its extraordinary coastline relative to its landmass. At the same time, he resumed his studies of language in general and Spanish in particular, arguing that a standardized form of Spanish with well-defined rules for orthography and pronunciation is necessary to develop the properly literate and educated citizenry so essential to a republic. Furthermore, standardizing Spanish is a necessary condition for creating a unified Latin American social and political culture.

Perhaps Bello's single greatest triumph was his appointment as first rector of the Universidad de Chile, a position he held until his death, after which it stood vacant for many years, so high was the regard in which his adopted nation held him. In one of the selections that follows, "Discurso pronunciado en la instalación de la Universidad de Chile el día 17 de septiembre de 1843" (translated as "Speech delivered at the installation of the University of Chile"), Bello argues that education at all levels, and particularly higher education, is a necessary condition for nation building and cultural preservation and advancement. In the second selection, he responds to José Victorino Lastarria's speech articulating the doctrine of the "Black Legend," the view that the Spanish colonial past left Latin America ravished and unprepared for self-governance. Bello holds that Europe is not only the source of values important to civilized society but also is an economic and political partner crucial to Latin America's future.

Further Reading

Bello, Andrés. *Obras completas de Andrés Bello*. 26 vols. Caracas: Fundación La Casa de Bello, 1981–1986.

———. *Selected Writings of Andrés Bello*. Translated by Frances M. López-Morillas. Edited by Iván Jaksič. New York: Oxford University Press, 1997.

Caldera, Rafael. *Andrés Bello: Philosopher, Poet, Philologist, Educator, Legislator, Statesman*. Translated by John Street. Caracas: La Casa de Bello, 1994.

Jaksič, Iván. *Academic Rebels in Chile*. Albany, N.Y.: State University of New York Press, 1989.

———. *Andrés Bello: Scholarship and Nation Building in Nineteenth Century Latin America*. Cambridge and New York: Cambridge University Press, 2001.

Lynch, John. *Andrés Bello: The London Years*. London: Richmond Publishing Co., 1982.

Murillo Rubiera, Fernando. *Andrés Bello: Historia de una vida y de una obra*. Caracas: La Casa de Bello, 1986.

Stoetzer, O. Carlos. "The Political Ideas of Andrés Bello," *International Philosophical Quarterly* 23, no. 4 (1983): 395–406.

Speech Delivered at the Installation of the University of Chile, September 17, 1843

. . . You know, ladies and gentlemen, all truths touch each other—from those that prescribe the course of the worlds in the open sea of space; from those that determine the marvelous agencies on which movement and life in the material universe depend; from those that constitute the structure of the animal, the plant, the inorganic mass on which we stand; from those that reveal the soul's intimate phenomena in the mysterious theater of consciousness, to those that express the actions and reactions of political forces; to those that sense the unshakable foundations of morality; to those that determine the precise conditions for the development of the seeds of industry; to those that guide and enrich the arts. Advances along all lines appeal to each other, are linked, encourage each other. And when I say *"advances along all lines,"* I certainly include the most important to the happiness of the human species, advances in the moral and political order. To what do we owe this progress of civilization, this yearning for social improvement, this thirst for liberty? If we desire to know this, let us compare Europe and our fortunate America with the gloomy empires of Asia, where despotism's iron scepter weighs down on necks already stooped from ignorance, or with the African hordes, where man, hardly superior to beasts, is, like them, an article for his own brothers' trade. Who in enslaved Europe set off the first sparks of civil liberty? Was it not letters? Was it not the intellectual heritage of Greece and Rome, reclaimed by the human spirit after a long era of darkness? There, there, this vast political movement, which has restored to so many enslaved races their freeborn rights, had its beginning; this movement, which is spreading in every direction, accelerated continually by the press and letters, whose undulations, here rapid, there slow, everywhere necessary, inevitable, will finally overcome whatever barriers are put up against them and will cover the surface of the globe. All truths touch each other, and I extend this assertion to religious dogma, to theological truth. Those who imagine there can be a secret antipathy between religion and letters slander one or the other—and here I am not sure which. I believe, on the contrary, that there exists—that there cannot help but exist—a close alliance between positive revelation and that other universal revelation in the book of nature that speaks to all men. If misguided understandings have misused their knowledge to impugn dogma, what does this show if not the state of things human? If human reason is weak, if it stumbles and falls, it is that much more necessary to provide it with substantial nourishment and solid support. Because one cannot extinguish this curiosity, this noble boldness that makes the mind confront nature's secrets, the future's riddles, without at the same time making that mind incapable of everything grand, indifferent to all that is beautiful, generous, sublime, holy; without poisoning the founts of morality; without deforming and debasing religion itself. I have said all truths touch each other, and I do not yet believe I have said enough. All human abilities form a system, in which there cannot be regularity and harmony without the cooperation of each one. Not a thread (if I may speak thus), not a single thread of the soul can be paralyzed, without all the others being weakened.

Sciences and letters—beyond this social value, beyond the gloss of pleasantness and elegance that they give to human societies and that we should also count among their benefits—have an intrinsic merit of their own to the extent that they increase the pleasures and delights of the individual who cultivates and loves them; exquisite pleasures to which the delirium of the senses does not carry us; pure delights, in which the soul does not say to herself:

> . . . *medio de fonte leporum*
> *surgit amari aliquid, quod in ipsis floribus angit.*
> (Lucretius)
> From amid the wellsprings of delight
> an unknown bitterness arises,
> that pierces the allure of the flowers.[1]

The sciences and literature carry in themselves the reward for the labors and night vigils dedicated to them. I am not speaking of the glory that enlightens the great scientific conquests; I am not speaking of the halo of immortality that crowns the works of genius. Few are permitted to expect them. I am speaking of the pleasures, more or less lofty, more or less intense, common to all classes in the republic of letters. For the understanding, as for the other human faculties, activity is in itself a pleasure—pleasure that, as a Scottish philosopher says,[2] shakes from us that inertia to which we would otherwise succumb, to our own detriment and that of society. Every path science opens to the cultivated mind reveals to it enchanting perspectives; each new facet discovered in beauty's ideal type makes the human heart, created as it is to admire and feel beauty, tremble with delight. The cultured mind hears in meditation's solitude the thousand voices of nature's chorus—a thousand wonderful visions flutter round the solitary lamp that enlightens its vigils. For the mind alone, the order of nature is unfurled on an immense scale; for the mind alone, creation is adorned in all its magnificence, in all its finery. But the letters and sciences, while giving a delightful training to the mind and imagination, also elevate moral character. They weaken the power of sensual seductions; they eliminate most of the terrors from fortune's vicissitudes. They are (after the humble and content resignation of the religious soul) the best preparation for the hour of sorrow. They bring comfort to the bed of the sick, to the refuge of the exiled, to the prison, to the scaffold. Socrates, on the eve of drinking hemlock, illuminates his cell with the most sublime speculations regarding the future of human destiny that pagan antiquity has bequeathed us. Dante composes his *Divine Comedy* in exile. Lavoisier asks his executioners for a bit of time to complete important research. Awaiting death

---

1. Lucretius, *De Rerum Natura*, Book VI. Editors' translation.

2. Thomas Browne [(1778–1820)]. [Bello's note; Browne's most influential work was *Lectures on the Philosophy of the Human Mind* (Edinburgh, 1820).]

at any moment, Chénier[3] writes his last verses, leaving them incomplete as he goes to the gallows:

Comme un dernier rayon, comme un dernier zéphyre
Anime la fin d'un beau jour,
Au pied de l'échafaud j'essaie [sic] *ancor ma lyre.*

As a last ray of sun, as a last gentle breeze
enlivens the end of a beautiful day,
at the foot of the gallows I again practice my lyre.

Such are the rewards of letters; such are their comforts. I myself, following so far behind their favored worshippers, I myself have been able to partake in their benefits and savor their delights. Letters adorned the morning of my life with happy cloudscapes and still preserve some tints in the soul, like the flower that beautifies ruins. Letters have done yet more for me; they nourished me on my great journey and put my steps on the right road to this land of liberty and peace, to this adoptive fatherland that has granted me such kind hospitality.

There is another point of view, from which perhaps we will struggle with specious worries. Are universities, are literary bodies suitable instruments for disseminating learning? But I hardly imagine how one can pose that question in an age that is supremely one of association and representation; in an age in which agricultural, commercial, industrial, and charitable societies everywhere teem; in the age of representative governments. Europe and the United States of America, our models in so many respects, will respond to the question.

If disseminating knowledge is one of the most important features of letters—because without dissemination, letters would do no more than offer a few points of light in the midst of dense shadows—the bodies to which we principally owe the speed of literary communications provide essential benefits to enlightenment and humanity. No sooner does a new truth arise in an individual's thought than the entire republic of letters takes possession of it. The learned men of Germany, of France, of the United States, appreciate its importance, its consequences, its applications. In this dissemination of knowledge, the academies, the universities, form so many other repositories where all scientific acquisitions tend continually to accumulate; and it is from these centers that the acquisitions spread most easily through society's different classes. The University of Chile has been established for this special purpose. If it meets the intent of the law that has given it its new form, if it meets the desires of our government, the University will be an eminently expansive and disseminating body.

---

3. Antoine Laurant Lavoisier (1743–1794), a French chemist and physicist, was a founder of modern chemistry. André Chenier (1762–1794), a French poet active in the French Revolution, was guillotined only three days before the end of the Terror. (Chenier, *Dernières poésies*, LXXVIII, lines 1–3.)

Others claim that the encouragement given to scientific instruction should preferably be given to primary instruction. Certainly, I am among those who see general instruction, the education of the people, as among the most important and privileged objectives to which the government can direct its attention—as a primary and urgent necessity, as the base of all solid progress, as the indispensable foundation of republican institutions. But for that reason, I believe necessary and urgent the encouragement of literary and scientific teaching. Nowhere has the elementary instruction demanded by the industrial classes—the great majority of the human race—been able to spread, except where sciences and letters already flourish. I am not saying that the cultivation of letters and sciences necessarily leads to the spread of elementary instruction; although it is undeniable that sciences and letters have a natural tendency to spread when artificial causes do not oppose them. What I am saying is that the sciences and letters are an indispensable condition for elementary instruction; that where sciences and letters do not exist, elementary instruction cannot be suitably carried out—no matter what may be the authority's efforts. The spread of knowledge supposes one or more hearths from whence light can emanate and spread, a light which, progressively extending over the intermediate spaces, will finally penetrate to the furthest regions. Making education universal requires a great number of competently instructed teachers; and the skills of these teachers, the ultimate distributors of education, are themselves more or less distant emanations of the great scientific and literary repositories. Good teachers, good books, good methods, the good management of education are necessarily the work of a very advanced intellectual culture. Literary and scientific instruction is the fountain where elementary instruction takes nourishment and comes alive—just as in a well organized society the wealth of the class most favored by fortune is the spring from whence flows the subsistence of the working classes, the well-being of the people. But in establishing the University anew, the law has not trusted solely enlightenment's natural tendency to spread itself, inasmuch as the press in our days provides a force and mobility never before known; it has joined intimately the two types of education; it has given to one section of the University body the special duty of watching over primary instruction, seeing to its progress, facilitating its spread, contributing to its improvement. The encouragement, above all, of the people's religious and moral instruction is a duty each member of the University takes on by virtue of being part of it.

• • • • •

Encouraging the ecclesiastical sciences—devoted to forming worthy ministers of the religion and, ultimately, providing the republic's people with competent religious and moral education—is the first and most important of these objectives. But there is another aspect under which we must view the dedication of the University to the cause of morality and religion. If cultivating the ecclesiastical sciences is important for fulfilling the priestly ministry, it is important also to extend to scholarly youth, to all youth who participate in literary and scientific education, adequate knowledge of the dogma and the annals of the Christian faith. It goes without saying that this goal should be an integral part of general education, indispensable to every profession and even for every man who wishes to occupy more than the least place in society.

The faculty of laws and political science opens into a vast field most capable of useful applications. You have heard it—practical usefulness, positive results, social improvements are what the government primarily expects of the University; they are what should primarily commend its work to the fatherland. Heirs to the legislation of Spain, we must cleanse our laws of the stains they contracted under the harmful influence of despotism; we must clear away the inconsistencies that tarnish a work to which so many centuries, so many alternatively dominant interests, so many contradictory inspirations have contributed. We must adjust it, return it to republican institutions. And what objective more important, or more magnificent, than the formation, the perfection of our organic laws, the upright and swift administration of justice, the protection of our rights, the integrity of commercial transactions, the peace of the domestic hearth? The University, I dare to say, will not welcome the prejudice that condemns the study of Roman law as useless or pernicious; I believe, on the contrary, that the University will give the study of Roman law a new stimulus and will set it on broader foundations. The University will probably see in that study the best training in juridical and forensic logic. On this point, let us listen to the testimony of a man who surely will not be accused of bias toward the old doctrines; to a man who in the enthusiasm for popular emancipation and democratic balancing has perhaps gone to the extreme. "Science stamps its seal on the law; its logic apprehends the principles, formulates the axioms, deduces the consequences, and from it derives innumerable consequences from the idea of the just by reflecting it. From this point of view Roman law admits no equal; some of its principles can be disputed; but its method, its logic, its scientific system, have made it and keep it superior to all other forms of legislation; its texts are masterpieces of juridical style; its method is that of geometry applied to moral thinking in all its rigor." So L'Herminier[4] expresses himself, and even earlier Leibniz[5] had said: *"In juris prudentia regnat (romani). Dixi saepius post scripta geometrarum nihil extare quod vi ac subtilitate cum romanorum jurisconsultorum scriptis comparari possit: tantum nervi inest; tantum profunditatis."*[6]

The University will also study the unique features of Chilean society from an economic perspective, which present problems no less immense, no less challenging to resolve. The University will examine the results of Chilean statistics,

---

4. Ferdinand Joseph L'Herminier (1802–1866), a French naturalist.

5. Gottfried Wilhelm Baron von Leibniz (1646–1716), German philosopher and mathematician.

6. "The Roman dominates in jurisprudence. I have said very often that there is nothing, after the writings of the geometricians, that can be compared for force and subtlety with the writings of the Roman jurisconsults; there is so much vigor, so much depth."

will contribute to creating the field, and will read in its figures the expression of our material interests. Because in this, as in its other branches, the University's program is entirely Chilean—if it borrows scientific deductions from Europe, it does so to apply them to Chile. All the paths along which the research of the University's faculty and the study of its students are directed converge on one focal point—the fatherland.

Following the same plan, medicine will research the particular modifications given to Chilean man by his climate, his customs, his food; it will deliver the rules for public and private hygiene; it will work tirelessly to extract the secret of the germination and devastating activity of epidemics, to the extent possible, see that knowledge of simple methods for maintaining and restoring health spread to the countryside. Shall I enumerate now the positive uses of mathematical and physical sciences, their application to a nascent industry, which barely uses even simple rude skills, without well-understood procedures, without machines, without even some of the most common tools; their applications for a land crossed in every direction by veins of ore, a soil fertile with vegetative riches, of substantial foods; a soil over which science has hardly cast a cursory look?

But, although I encourage practical applications, I am very far from believing that the University should adopt the unfortunate *"cui bono?"* as its motto, or that it should fail to appreciate sufficiently knowledge of nature in all its different departments. First, because to guide the practice correctly, the mind must rise to the highest points of science, to the appreciation of its general formulas. Surely the University will not confuse practical applications with the manipulations of a blind empiricism. And second, because, as I said before, the cultivation of contemplative intelligence that removes the veil from the mysteries of the physical and moral universe is in itself a positive result and of the greatest importance. On this point, so as not to repeat myself, I would cite the words of an English sage who has honored me with his friendship. "It has been," says Dr. Neil Arnott, "it has been a common prejudice, that persons thus instructed in general laws, had their attention too much divided, and could know nothing perfectly. But the very reverse is true; for general knowledge renders all particular knowledge more clear and precise. . . . The laws of Philosophy may be compared to keys which give admission to the most delightful gardens that fancy can picture; or to a magic power, which unveils the face of the universe, and discloses endless charms of which ignorance never dreams. The informed man, in the world, may be said to be always surrounded by what is known and friendly to him, while the ignorant man is as one in a land of strangers and enemies. . . . He who studies the methodized *Book of Nature,* converts the great universe into a simple and sublime history, which tells of God, and may worthily occupy his attention to the end of his days."[7]

---

7. Neil Arnott (1788–1874), Scottish physician and one of the founders of the University of London, *Elements of Physics; or, Natural Philosophy, General and Medical* (London, 1827), pp. xiii–xiv.

I pass, ladies and gentlemen, to that literary department that particularly and preeminently possesses the quality of polishing practices; that refines the language, making it a faithful, beautiful, transparent vehicle for ideas; that, through studying other tongues, both living and dead, allows us to communicate with antiquity and with today's most civilized, cultured, and free nations; that lets us hear the accents of foreign wisdom and eloquence, not through the imperfect medium of translations, always and necessarily unfaithful, but rather living, sonorous, vibrant; that, through contemplating ideal beauty and its reflections in the works of genius, purifies taste and reconciles the bold ecstasies of fantasy with the inalienable rights of reason; that at the same time it initiates the soul into rigorous studies—necessary aids to great literature and indispensable preparation for all the sciences, for all the careers of life—forms the primary discipline of the intellectual and moral being, expounds the eternal laws of intelligence with the goal of directing and affirming its steps, and penetrates the heart's deepest folds to preserve it from unfortunate deviations, to establish on solid foundations man's rights and duties. To enumerate these different objectives is to present you, ladies and gentlemen, as I conceive it, the program of the University in the philosophy and humanities section. Among those objectives, study of our language seems of the highest importance. I will never be an advocate of the exaggerated purism that condemns everything new in the matter of language; I believe, on the contrary, that the multitude of new ideas that pass daily from literary interaction into general circulation demand new voices to represent them. Will we find in the lexicon of Cervantes and Fr. Luis de Granada—no, I do not want to go back so far—will we find, in the dictionary of Iriarte and Moratín,[8] adequate means, clear symbols to express the common notions that today drift over reasonably cultivated intellects, to express social thought? New institutions, new laws, new practices; matter and form changed everywhere we look; and old words, old phraseology! That aspiration, besides being discordant—because it would conflict with language's primary purposes, the easy and clear transmission of thought—would be totally beyond reach. But language can be expanded, it can be enriched, it can be accommodated to all the demands of society and even to those of fashion—which exercises an undeniable rule over literature—without adulterating it, without corrupting its constructions, without doing violence to its genius. Is the language of Pascal and Racine[9] perhaps different from the language of Chateaubriand and Villemain?[10] And does not the language of these latter two writers reveal perfectly the social thought of France in our days, so different from the France of Louis XIV? But there is something more—if we give

---

8. Thomas de Iriarte (1750–1791), Spanish poet and dramatist; Leandro Fernandez de Moratín (1760–1828), Spanish dramatist and poet.

9. Blaise Pascal (1623–1662), French scientist and religious philosopher; Jean Racine (1639–1699), French dramatist.

10. François René Viscomte de Chateaubriand (1768–1848), French writer; Abel-François Villemain (1790–1870), French scholar and critic.

free rein to this type of pretentious literary style, if we give national identity papers to all the whims of extravagant neologisms, our America will reproduce within a short time the confusion of languages, dialects, and slang, the Babylonian chaos of the Middle Ages, and ten peoples will lose one of their most precious instruments for interaction and commerce.

The University will not only encourage the study of languages but also their literatures. But I do not know if I deceive myself. The opinion of those who believe that we should accept the synthetic outcomes of the European Enlightenment, excusing us from an examination of its merits, excusing us from analysis—the sole means of acquiring true knowledge—will not find support in the University. Respecting, as I do respect, different opinions, and reserving to myself only the right to debate them, I confess that relying on Herder's moral and political conclusions, for example, without studying ancient and modern history, would seem to me as inappropriate for nourishing the understanding, educating it, and accustoming it to thinking for itself, as adopting the theorems of Euclid without doing the underlying intellectual work of proof. I see Herder,[11] ladies and gentlemen, as one of the writers who has served humanity most usefully; he has given complete dignity to history, unraveling in it the designs of Providence and the destiny to which the human race is called on earth. But Herder himself did not propose to supplant knowledge of facts but rather to illuminate them, to explain them; nor can his doctrine be appreciated except through prior historical studies. To substitute deductions and formulas for those studies would be to present youth with a skeleton instead of a live copy of social man; it would be to give youth a collection of aphorisms instead of presenting it with the mobile, instructive, picturesque panorama of the institutions, the practices, the revolutions of the great peoples and the great men; it would be to take away from the moralist and politician the profound convictions that can only arise from knowledge of facts; it would be to take away from the experience of the human race the salutary power of their advice, at precisely the age most receptive to lasting impressions; it would be to take away from the poet an inexhaustible mine of images and colors. And what I say of history, it seems to me, we can apply to all the other branches of knowledge. In this way we impose on the mind the necessity for long, it is true, but agreeable studies. Because nothing makes instruction more disagreeable than abstractions, and nothing makes it easier and more pleasant than the process that, by furnishing the memory, simultaneously trains the mind and exalts the imagination. Reasoning must breed the theorem; examples deeply engrave the lessons.

And in this rapid outline, ladies and gentlemen, could I fail, even in passing, to refer to the most enchanting of the literary vocations, the perfume of literature, the Corinthian capital, as it were, of a cultured society? Could I, above all,

---

11. Johann Gottfried von Herder (1744–1803), German philosopher, critic, and clergyman. Among his important doctrines is that Divine Providence gives unity and purpose to human history, a doctrine with which such positivist thinkers as Auguste Comte and, after him, Lastarria took issue.

fail to refer to the instantaneous excitement that has made that constellation of young geniuses, who cultivate poetry with such ardor, appear on our horizon? I will speak frankly—their verses are sometimes incorrect; there are things in them that a polished and strict reason condemns. But correctness is the work of study and years; who could expect it of those who, in a moment of excitement, simultaneously poetic and patriotic, rushed into that new arena, determined to prove that also in Chilean souls burns that divine fire, of which, because of unfair prejudice, they had been thought deprived? Brilliant examples have already refuted it—and not limited to the sex that, until now, has almost exclusively cultivated letters among us. They have disproved that prejudice anew. I do not know if some small predisposition toward the efforts of young intellects misleads my judgment. I say what I feel: I find in those works undeniable sparks of true talent, and with regard to some of them I could even say, of true poetic genius. I find, in some of those works, an original and rich imagination, happily daring expressions, and (what it would seem only long practice could yield) a harmonious and fluid versification that deliberately seeks difficulties in order to struggle with them, and emerges successfully from this daring test. Encouraging our young poets, the University may say to them, "If you do not wish your name to remain imprisoned between the cordillera of the Andes and the Pacific Ocean, an enclosure too narrow for the abundant aspirations of talent; if you wish posterity to read you, study well, beginning with study of your native tongue. Do more—take up subjects worthy of your fatherland and posterity. Set aside the bland tones of lyric poetry, of Anacreon and Sappho;[12] the poetry of the nineteenth century has a higher mission. May humanity's great interests inspire you. May the moral sentiment pulse in your works. On taking up the pen, say to yourself, each of you, 'I, Priest of the Muses, sing for innocent and pure souls.'

> . . . *Musarum sacerdos,*
> *virginibus puerisque canto.*
> (Horace) [*Odes,* 3.1]

"And how many magnificent themes has the young republic already presented you? Celebrate its great days; weave garlands for its heroes; consecrate the shroud of the fatherland's martyrs." At the same time the University will remind youth of the counsel of a great teacher of our times. "It is necessary," said Goethe,[13] "that art be the measure of the imagination and transform it into poetry."

Art! Hearing this word—although taken from the very lips of Goethe—some people will place me among the supporters of the conventional rules that have for so long usurped the name of art. I solemnly protest such an accusation, and

---

12. Anacreon (c. 570–485 BC), Greek lyric poet; Sappho (c. early sixth century BC), greatest of the early Greek poets.

13. Johann Wolfgang von Goethe (1749–1832), German poet, dramatist, novelist, and scientist.

I do not believe my background justifies it. I do not find art in sterile academic precepts, in the inflexible units, in the rigid wall between different styles and genres, in the chains that have been used to imprison the poet in the name of Aristotle and Horace, sometimes attributing to them things they never thought. But I do believe in the existence of an art based on the intangible, ethereal relationships of ideal beauty; delicate relationships, but accessible to the sharp eyes of the competently prepared spirit; I believe in an art that guides the imagination in its most ardent transports; I believe that without such art, fantasy, instead of bringing the model of the beautiful to life in its works, spawns sphinxes, enigmatic and monstrous creations. This is my literary faith. Complete liberty—but in the orgies of the imagination I do not see liberty but rather wanton intoxication.

Liberty—as opposed, on the one hand, to the servile docility that accepts everything without scrutiny, and on the other hand, to the disorderly license that rebels against the authority of reason and against the noblest and purest instincts of the human heart—liberty will, without doubt, be the theme of the University in each of its different departments.

Response to Lastarria on the Influence of the Conquest (1844)[14]

I

What [Sr. Lastarria] says about the reasons he had for choosing the theme [for the first annual report on the activity of the faculty of the University of Chile] could provoke doubts about the appropriateness of the program indicated in the constitutional law of the University for the reports that must be delivered before this body in the solemn gathering of September. "I confess," Sr. Lastarria says,

> that I would have preferred to give you the description of one of those heroic events or brilliant episodes that our history relates to us, in order to move our hearts with the enthusiasm of glory or admiration, to speak to you of the good sense of Colocolo,[15] of the prudence and strength of Caupolicán,[16] of the skill

---

14. The Lastarria Speech to which Bello responds here appears, in part, on page 76 of this volume. This essay first appeared in *El Araucano* nos. 742 and 743, Nov. 8 and 15, 1844.

15. Colocolo (1515–1560), Araucanian leader opposed to the Spanish conquest; he and Caupolicán defeated Pedro de Valdivia in the Battle of Tucapel in 1553; the victory of the Araucanians has been attributed to Colocolo's plan of dividing into thirteen bodies and fighting in turn so as always to have fresh troops available.

16. Caupolicán (d. 1558) was an Araucanian leader who defeated the Spanish on numerous occasions but was ultimately killed.

and valor of Lautaro,[17] of the agility and daring of Painenancu;[18] but what real advantage would we derive from these alluring memories? What social utility would we obtain from directing our attention to one of the separate members of a great body, of which the analysis should be complete? I could have accomplished as much, and more suitably, certainly, of any of the important events of our glorious revolution; but I have been intimidated, I confess to you, by the fear of not being faithful and completely impartial in my research. I see that, with the heroes of those brilliant actions and the witnesses of their heroic deeds still living, even the simplest facts that remain to us regarding the influential events in the outcome of that sublime epic are contested and contradict each other. I do not dare to pronounce a judgment that condemns the testimony of some and sanctifies the testimony of others, stirring up passions that are in the last moments of their existence. My critique in such a case would be, if not offensive, at least tiresome and unsuccessful, for, as a young person, I feel I lack the genuine instruction and other conditions that might enable me to rise to a level necessary to judge events I have not seen and which I lack the means to study philosophically. Because our revolution is still unfolding, we are not in a position to produce its philosophical history but rather we are in a position to discuss and accumulate facts in order to transmit them with our opinion and the result of our critical studies to another generation that will possess the genuine historical viewpoint and the impartiality necessary to appreciate them.[19]

These reflections—expressed with a noble modesty that could serve as an example to writers younger than Sr. Lastarria—suggest, as we have said, some doubts regarding the possibility that the authors of these annual reports can limit themselves to the program of the constitutional law without stumbling into serious difficulties. It is no doubt difficult for the present generation to judge impartially the events and personages of the revolution; and we will say more, it is almost impossible that, even presented with impartiality and truth, these reports would not provoke protests, would not sound the alarm to slumbering passions that it would be desirable to let die out. But deprived of these themes, for which the very danger of stimulation provides a powerful incentive, and intimidated by the fear of traveling

---

17. Lautaro (1534–1557) was a Mapuche leader who, while serving as the personal servant of Pedro de Valdivia, Spanish conqueror of Chile, learned the maneuvers and skills of the Spanish army by observing Valdivia. When he escaped from Spanish captivity, he rejoined the Mapuches, introduced the use of the horse to them, and used his Spanish military tactics against the Spanish themselves.

18. Painenancu (also spelled Paynenancu) was an Araucanian leader who fought against the Spanish in the province of Arauco with only eight hundred men, who were able to put up stiff resistance. Even when twice defeated, he continued to harass Spanish settlements, but he was ultimately defeated and killed.

19. Lastarria, J. V., *Investigaciones sobre la influencia social de la conquista y del sistema colonial de las Españoles en Chile*. Santiago: Impr. del Siglo, 1844, pages 17–18.

. . . per ignes
Suppositos cineri doloso,[20]

on what historical discourses of Chilean interest could the authors of these reports practice their craft? Sr. Lastarria has anticipated them in a discourse entirely devoid of this risk: Unraveling the antecedents of the revolution, he has outlined a picture of dimensions so vast and has colored its different parts with such intensity that he seems to have left little or nothing to those who might wish to explore that field again. The subject, nonetheless, is fertile. Leaving out the diversity that can be given to such a theme by the different points of view from which it is contemplated, the diverse intellectual qualities, and the opposing opinions of writers, there are a thousand partial themes—small, if you will, compared with the impressive theme of the 1844 Report, but not for that reason unworthy of attention, rather for that very reason susceptible to those vivid hues and that individual formulation that bring the understanding of the past back to life at the same time that they supply the imagination with a delightful pleasure. What is lost in the breadth of perspective is gained in the clarity and intensity of the details. The domestic practices of a given era, the foundation of a town, the vicissitudes, the disasters of another, the history of our agriculture, of our commerce, of our mines, the just appreciation of this or that part of our colonial system, could offer a field for many and interesting investigations. There is no lack of materials to consult if one searches with wisdom or patience in private collections, in archives, in reliable oral traditions, which we must make haste to write down before they disappear completely or are forgotten. The war between the Spanish colony and the indigenous tribes would present many lively and interesting descriptions. Nor is history useful only because of the great and comprehensive lessons of its integrated results. The special circumstances, the eras, the places, the individuals, have particular attractions and also contain worthwhile lessons. If he who summarizes the entire life of a people is like the astronomer who depicts the age-old laws to which the great masses are subject in their movements, he who presents us with the life of a city, of a man, is like the physiologist or physicist, who, in a given body, makes us see the mechanisms of the material agencies that determine its forms and movements and stamp it with the appearance, the attitudes that distinguish it. An immense epic poem cannot be judged without seeing the position, the relationship of all its parts; but that is not the only, nor perhaps the most useful activity of history—the life of a Bolívar, of a Sucre,[21] is a drama in which play all the passions, all the strings of the human heart, and to which the focus and individuality provide a higher interest.

Limiting ourselves to the Chilean revolution, and at risk of personal biases, there is in the revolution a multitude of events in which we can avoid this pitfall; we do not see the danger of wounding some self-love, the danger of reducing

---

20. ". . . through fires / set beneath deceptive ash" (Horace, *Odes* II.1).

21. Antonio José de Sucre (1795–1830), Venezuelan hero of American independence who fought mainly in Peru and Ecuador.

some exaggerated pretension to its proper limits as worthy of consideration: such events as the occupation of Rancagua,[22] for example, with its scenes of extreme cruelty and atrocity that history must not forget; such as the battle of Chacabuco,[23] with so curious, so picturesque a history, and with its sudden change in the fate of the victors and the vanquished; such as the battle of Maipo[24] with its eager expectation, its uncertain outcome, and its joyful triumph; and such as so many others to which only the contemporary generation can give the vividness, the freshness, the dramatic movement without which historical works are nothing more than abstract generalizations or colorless notes. The most fascinating history is that of contemporaries, especially history written by the very actors in the events that it narrates; and, after all, that history is (with the toning down that a rigorous criticism prescribes, taking into account the partialities of the historian) the most authentic, the most worthy of belief. Can Plutarch be compared with Thucydides?[25] [Antonio de] Solís with Bernal Díaz del Castillo?[26] Does not Xenophon,[27] in his account of the *Retreat of the Ten Thousand,* combine the interest of the novel with the value of history? Nor are contemporary remembrances or handwritten memoirs so barren of useful instruction as Sr. Lastarria seems to think. Were the *Commentaries* of Caesar[28] not the favorite book of the great captains? If contemporary memoirs provoke complaints, so much the better. Posterity will be able to extract the truth from the opposing testimonies and reduce everything to its true value. If history is not written by contemporaries, future generations will have to write it from adulterated oral traditions (because nothing is distorted and falsified so quickly as the oral tradition), from newspaper articles, from impassioned effusions of political proclamations—the product

---

22. The Seige of Rancagua (October 1–2, 1814) spelled the defeat of the first independent Chilean republic with the rout of patriots under Bernardo O'Higgins by Royalist forces.

23. Battle of Chacabuco (February 12, 1817): victory over the Royalists by the Army of the Andes under Generals José de San Martín and Bernardo O'Higgins, setting the stage for eventual victory by independence forces.

24. Battle of Maipo (April 5, 1818), a victory of General José de San Martín's troops over the Spanish troops under Mariano Osario, which assured the independence of Chile.

25. Plutarch (AD 46–120), author of *Parallel Lives,* used much anecdotal material from archival sources; Thucydides (460–400 BC), one of the greatest ancient historians, had occasion to acquire firsthand information for his history as a general in the Peloponnesian War.

26. Antonio de Solís y Rivadeneyra (1610–1686), a Spanish historian and poet whose history of the conquest of Mexico is not considered a great history, for it ignores the Aztecs and glorifies Cortés. Bernal Díaz del Castillo (1492–1581), a participant in the conquest of Mexico, wrote his history based on events, scenes, and men he himself had known.

27. Xenophon (430–355 BC), a Greek historian who was part of the Greek force, "the ten thousand," a leader of the heroic retreat from the Persians, a story he tells in the greatest of his works, *The Anabasis.*

28. Julius Caesar (102–44 BC). His commentaries on the Gallic war and on the Civil War are considered masterpieces of clear, beautiful, concise Latin, and they are among the most reliable histories of antiquity as well as being classic military documents.

of first impressions—and from dry official documents of frequently suspicious veracity. *Vaticinari de ossibus istis,*[29] history then says to the writer who has in front of him only the skeletons of events; and if the writer wishes to give us a picture and not a disembodied narrative, he will have to compromise the truth, extracting from his imagination or from fallible conjectures what his fleshless materials no longer provide.

But let us return to Sr. Lastarria's Report and inquire with him into the influence of the Spanish arms and laws in Chile. Chapter I—where he deals with the conquest and the prolonged battle between the Chilean colonists and the indomitable sons of Arauco[30]—is written with the brisk energy the subject demands. It would have been difficult to provide, in broad outline, a more complete idea of those rancorous hostilities that, handed down from fathers to sons, from generation to generation, still today slumbers beneath the appearances of a peace that is in reality a truce. Excepting the occasional sentence that better belongs to oratorical emotion than to historical moderation, we do not see that there is much ground to classify as inopportune and impassioned the exposition of the cruelty of the conquistadors that this chapter gives us. One of history's duties is to relate the events as they were, and we must not mitigate them just because they might not seem to honor the memory of Chile's founders. Injustice, atrocity, treachery in war have not been committed by Spaniards alone but rather by all races in all times; and, if, even among related Christian nations and in times of civilization and culture, war has had and still has this character of savage and heartless cruelty that destroys and becomes blood-stained for the sole pleasure of destroying and spilling blood, what is strange about the murderous battles and harsh consequences of victory among peoples in which the practices, religion, language, physical makeup, color, were all different, all repugnant and hostile? The vassals of Isabel, of Carlos I, and of Felipe II were the first nation of Europe; their chivalric spirit, the splendor of their court, their magnificent and honorable nobility, the experience of their captains, the skill of their ambassadors and ministers, the valor of their soldiers, their bold undertakings, their enormous discoveries and conquests made them the target of disparagement because they were an object of envy. The reports of that century everywhere present us with horrible scenes. The Spaniards abused their power, oppressed, offended humanity—not brazenly, as Sr. Lastarria says, because it was not necessary to be brazen to do what everyone was doing with no limit but that of their own strength, but rather with the same courteous regard for humanity, with the same respect for the rights of people that the powerful states have always shown in their relations with the weak and of which even in our days of morality and civilization we have seen too many examples.

If we compare the practical ideas of international justice in modern times with those of the Middle Ages and those of ancient peoples, we will find much

---

29. "Prophesy upon these bones" (Ezekiel 37:4).

30. The Araucanian Indians, who occupied most of south central Chile at the time of the conquest.

similarity among them at their core under differences that are not very great in methods and forms. "[T]he attempt to bind nations by mere moral sanctions," says an English writer of our times,

> is to fetter giants with cobwebs. To the greatest of human restraints, the fear of a hereafter, they are insensible. . . . [B]ut experience does not justify the belief that national crimes, except those crimes of which one part of a nation is guilty towards another, are always, or even usually, punished. The principal states of continental Europe—France, Russia, Austria, and Prussia, have grown from small beginnings to powerful and flourishing monarchies, by centuries of ambition, injustice, violence, and fraud. The crimes which gave Wales to England, Alsace and Franche Compté to France, and Silesia to Prussia, were rewarded by an increase of wealth, power, and security. Again, nations are not restrained by fear of the loss of honour; for honour, in the sense in which that word is applied to individuals, does not apply to them. . . . Never has the foreign policy of France been more faithless, more rapacious, or more cruel, than during the reign of Louis XIV. For half a century she habitually maintained a conduct, a single instance of which would have excluded an individual from the society of his equals. At no time was France more admired, and even courted. At no time were Frenchmen more welcome in every court, and in every private circle. What are often called injuries to the honour of a nation, are injuries to its vanity. The qualities of which nations are most vain, are force and boldness. They know that, so far as they are supposed to possess these qualities, they are themselves unlikely to be injured, and may injure others with impunity.[31]

So among the great masses of men that we call nations the savage state of brutal force has not ended. It pays an apparent homage to justice, appealing to the clichés of security, dignity, protection of national interest, and others equally vague; premises from which with average skill can be derived every imaginable consequence. The horrors of war have been mitigated in part—not because humanity is more respected, but rather because material interests are better calculated and as a consequence of the very perfection to which the art of destruction has arrived. It would be insanity to enslave the vanquished if one gains more by making them payers of tribute and forced producers of the victor's industry. Highwaymen have been converted into merchants, but merchants who hold over the counter the scale of Brennus: *Voe victis*.[32] One does not colonize by killing indigenous populations—why kill them if it is sufficient to push them from forest to forest and from meadowland to meadowland? Destitution and hunger will do the work of destruction in the long run, without noise and without scandal. In the heart of each social family the practices are regularized and purified;

---

31. *Edinburgh Review,* no. 156, article 1, [pp. 308–9]. [Bello's note. The article is an anonymous review of Henry Wheaton, *Histoire du progrès du droit des gens en Europe* (Leipzig, 1841).]

32. Brennus (c. 389 BC), legendary Gallic leader. According to legend, when the tribute that the Romans had agreed to pay was being weighed, a Roman complained, whereupon Brennus threw his sword upon the balance scale crying, *Voe victis* (Woe to the vanquished).

liberty and justice, inseparable companions, extend their rule more and more; but in the relationships between races and between peoples, the savage state, with all its injustice and primitive rapaciousness, endures under a veneer of hypocrisy.

We are not accusing any nation but rather the nature of man. The weak appeal to justice; give them strength, and they will be as unjust as the oppressors.

<h1 style="text-align:center">II</h1>

The picture Sr. Lastarria paints for us of the vices and abuses of Spain's colonial regime is generally supported in documents of irrefutable authenticity and truth: laws, ordinances, histories, the *Noticias Secretas (Secret Reports)* of Don Jorge Juan and Don Antonio de Ulloa. But shadows have spread profusely across the painting. There is something in it that clashes with the impartiality that the law recommends and that is not incompatible with the emphatic tone of reproof with which the historian, advocate for the rights of humanity and interpreter of moral sentiments, must pronounce his judgment on corrupt institutions. To the dominant idea of perpetuating the colonies' wardship, Spain not only sacrificed the colonies' interests but her own as well; and to keep them dependent and submissive she made herself poor and weak. American treasures inundated the world, while the treasury of the metropolis was left exhausted and its industry embryonic. The colonies, which for other countries have been a means of stimulating population and the arts, were for Spain a cause of depopulation and backwardness. Neither industrial life nor wealth was detectable except in some trading centers that served as intermediaries for exchanges between the two hemispheres and in which the accumulated wealth of the monopoly highlighted the general poverty—scattered oases at great distances in a vast desert. But we must be just; that was not a *fierce* tyranny. It shackled the arts, clipped the wings of thought, stopped up even the springs of agricultural fertility; but its policy was of hobbles and deprivations, not of tortures or blood. Penal laws were administered loosely. In the punishment of sedition it was not extraordinarily rigorous; it was what despotism has always been and not more—at least with regard to the Spanish race and until the epoch of the general uprising that ended in the emancipation of the American dominions. The despotism of the Roman emperors was the model for Spanish government in America. The same inefficient benignity of the supreme authority, the same arbitrariness of magistrates, the same divinization of the throne's rights, the same indifference to industry, the same ignorance of the great principles that give life and richness to human associations, the same judicial organization, the same fiscal privileges; but on the other side of these odious similarities are others of a different character. The civilizing mission that moves like the sun from east to west, and of which Rome was the most powerful agent in the ancient world, Spain exercised on the western world, more distant and more vast. Without doubt the elements of this civilization were destined to blend with others that would improve it, just as Roman civilization was modified and improved in Europe by foreign influences. Maybe we are deceiving ourselves; but certainly it seems to us that none of the nations that arose from the ruins of the empire conserved a stamp more pronounced from the Roman spirit—the very language of Spain is the one that best retains the character of the language spoken by the rulers of the world. Spain's colonial administration shows something imperial and Roman even in material things. To the government of Spain America still owes everything she has of greatness and splendor in her public buildings. Let us confess it with shame; we have hardly been able to preserve those public buildings that were erected under the viceroys and captains general; and bear in mind that the crown's income contributed liberally to their construction, and there was no imposition of taxes and forced labor like those with which Rome burdened the provincials for its roads, aqueducts, amphitheaters, thermal baths, and bridges.

Neither do we find, to tell the truth, complete precision in the statement of the historical phenomena on which the attention of Sr. Lastarria was focused at the beginning of his Chapter III. We do not believe that the history of universal legislation "shows us clearly that the laws adopted by human societies have always been inspired by their respective practices, have been an expression, a genuine formula of the customs and sentiments of the peoples,"[33] and that among the colonized countries the sole and most obvious exception to this phenomenon is found among the Spanish colonies of America. We believe that between laws and practices there has been and always will be reciprocity; that practices influence laws and laws practices. How else could all the influences of some peoples on others be explained? Conquest, laws imposed by the victors on the vanquished—have these not often been a means of civilization at some times, a cause of regression and barbarism at others? Laws should be directed precisely at the satisfaction of local needs and impulses, assuming that the legislator has sensed them in himself from the cradle; even if he is capable of controlling those impulses he will have to accommodate to them the regulations that he promulgates in order to make them acceptable and effective. But outside forces frequently modify practices and after them the laws, or they alter the laws and as a consequence the practices. The ideas of one people are incorporated into the ideas of another; and as both lose their purity, what was in the beginning an aggregate of discordant parts comes little by little to be a homogeneous whole, which under different aspects will resemble its different origins and from certain points of view will also present new forms. From the clash of different ideas will be born a resulting idea that will approach more or less one of the driving forces according to the intensity with which these driving forces work and the circumstances that respectively favor them. It is true that, as laws modify practices and assimilate them, they are in the long run the expression and formula of those practices; but that formula then precedes the assimilation instead of being produced by it.

When two races mix, the idea of the immigrant race will prevail over that of the native race depending on what their relative numbers, their moral vigor, and

---

33. Lastarria, *Investigaciones*, pg. 53.

the greater or lesser advancement of its civilizations might be. The northern bar-barians gave a new mettle to the humiliated inhabitants of the Roman provinces and received in exchange a large portion of Rome's social forms; Rome's religion, language, and laws little by little replaced those of the proud and ferocious con-querors. But it can also happen that the discord among the elements that come together be such that an unconquerable repulsion does not permit them to per-meate each other fully and produce a true composite. Sometimes races will mix and they will reject each other's ideas. Thus the Arabs and Spaniards represented in western Europe two types of antipathetic civilization. Setting aside certain material and purely external peculiarities, nothing Arab was able to take root in Spain—the religion, the laws, the nature of the language, that of the arts, that of the literature, took little or nothing from the Mohammedan conquerors. Arab culture was always an exotic plant in the middle of the Iberian-Roman-Gothic composite that occupied the Iberian Peninsula. It was necessary that one of the two elements expel or suffocate the other; the struggle lasted eight centuries, and the Strait of Gibraltar was once more crossed by the vanquished and exiled civi-lization of Islam, destined everywhere to leave the field finally to the arms of the West and the Cross. In America, on the contrary, the judgment of destruction is pronounced on the native kind. The indigenous races are disappearing, and they will be lost in the long run among the colonies of transatlantic peoples, leaving no more traces than a few words adapted in the foreign languages and scattered monuments, about which curious travelers will ask in vain the name and description of the civilization that gave rise to them.

In the colonies that remain under the control of the mother country, among the populations of the founding immigrant race, the metropolitan spirit neces-sarily pervades the distant emanations and makes the populations receive its laws docilely, even when those laws clash with local interests. When the time arrives in which those local interests feel strong enough to dispute the supremacy, they are not strictly two ideas, two types of civilization that hurl themselves into the arena but rather two aspirations to power, two athletes who fight with the same arms and for the same victor's crown. Such has been the character of the Hispanic American revolution, considered in its spontaneous development—because it is necessary to distinguish between two things in it, political independence and civil liberty. In our revolution, liberty was a foreign ally that fought under the banner of independence and that, even after the victory, had to do not a little to consolidate itself and take root. The work of the warriors is finished, that of the legislators will not be finished as long as the imitated idea, the foreign idea, does not more intimately penetrate the hard and tenacious Iberian substance.

This is our way of conceiving the moral law on which Sr. Lastarria focuses. Our presentation will seem too obvious, too pedestrian; but it is the true sum-mary of the facts as we understand them. Spain's American colonies are not an exception, but rather a confirmation of the general rules to which such phenom-ena are subject.

We also feel great repugnance at agreeing that the people of Chile (and we say the same of the other Hispano-American peoples) are so *profoundly degraded,* reduced to so *complete a humiliation* so devoid *of all social virtue*, as Sr. Lastarria supposes [Bello's emphasis]. The Hispano-American revolution contradicts his assertions. Never has a profoundly degraded people, completely humiliated, stripped of all virtuous sentiment, been capable of carrying out the great events that inspired the campaigns of our patriots, the heroic acts of self-denial, the sacrifices of every type with which Chile and other American areas won their political emancipation. And anyone who observes the history of our struggle with the metropolis with philosophical eyes will recognize without difficulty that what has allowed us to prevail was precisely the Iberian element. Native Spanish perseverance has clashed with itself in the inborn perseverance of the sons of Spain. The fatherland instinct revealed its existence in American hearts and reproduced the marvels of Numantia and Zaragoza.[34] The veteran captains and legions of transatlantic Iberia were beaten and humiliated by the leaders and improvised armies of another young Iberia, which, renouncing the name, kept the indomitable spirit of the old Iberia in defense of their homes. It appears to us, then, inaccurate that the Spanish system *stifled in its germ the inspirations of honor and the fatherland, of emulation, and of all the generous sentiments from which civic virtues arise* [Bello's emphasis]. Republican elements did not exist; Spain had not been able to create them; its laws certainly gave souls an entirely opposite direction. But at the core of those souls there were seeds of magnanimity, of heroism, of lofty and generous independence; *and* if the practices were simple and modest in Chile, there was something more in those qualities than the foolish senselessness of slavery. This is so certain that even Sr. Lastarria himself has believed it necessary to limit his assessments, speaking of them, *at the least* in their exterior and *ostensible* appearances [Bello's emphasis]. But thus limited, they lose almost all their force. A system that has only degraded and debased in appearance has not degraded and debased in reality.

We are speaking of events as they are in themselves and are not looking into causes. That despotism debases and demoralizes is for us a dogma; and if it has not been enough either in Europe or in America to bastardize the race, to weaken in three centuries the resource of noble sentiments (because without them the moral phenomena of Spain and Spanish America in our day cannot be explained), causes that offset that pernicious influence must have coexisted. Might there be in races a peculiar makeup, an indestructible idiosyncrasy, so to speak? And inasmuch as the Spanish race has mixed with other races in America, would it not be possible to explain to a certain degree the diversities presented by the character of men and the revolution in the different American provinces by the diversity of the mixture? We have here a problem that would deserve being resolved analytically and on which it is not possible for us to linger

---

34. Numantia, an ancient Iberian city that fiercely resisted conquest by Rome even after a siege (134 BC) that killed almost all of its inhabitants, becoming a rallying cry for nineteenth-century Spanish nationalists; Zaragoza, a Spanish city that held out twice against months-long sieges by Napoleonic forces during the Peninsular War (1808–1809).

because we lack the necessary data and because we have already exceeded the limits that we had set at the beginning.

For the same reason we find ourselves having to pass over various interesting chapters of the *Report* where we encounter doubts and difficulties in fully accepting the ideas of its learned and philosophical author. But we cannot refrain from contemplating one moment with him, in his Chapter VIII, the spectacle of the Chilean revolution.

Sr. Lastarria observes well enough the double character—recently discussed—of the Hispano-American revolution, although he sometimes seems to forget it. The Americans were much better prepared for political emancipation than for the liberty of the domestic hearth. Two movements took place at once—the one spontaneous, the other imitative and exotic; they often hindered each other instead of helping one another. The foreign principle produced progress; the native element, dictatorships. No one loved liberty more sincerely than General Bolívar; but the nature of things subjugated him like everyone else; independence was necessary for liberty, and the champion of independence was and had to be a dictator. Hence, the apparent and necessary contradictions in his actions. Bolívar triumphed, the dictatorships from Spain triumphed; the governments and congresses still wage war on the practices of the sons of Spain, on the habits formed under the influence of Spanish laws—a war of vicissitudes, in which ground is won and lost; a covert war in which the enemy counts on powerful allies among us. The scepter was seized from the monarch but not from the Spanish spirit—our congresses obey ideas of Gothic inspiration without realizing it; Spain has entrenched itself in our courts; the administrative ordinances of the Carloses and the Felipes are the laws of our fatherland; even our warriors, adhering to a special code [the military *Fuero*] that conflicts with the principle of equality before the law, the cornerstone of free governments, show the rule of the ideas of that very Spain upon whose flags they trampled. "It fell," says Sr. Lastarria, "the despotism of the kings fell, and the despotism of the past remained standing in full force because it had to happen thus by virtue of history. The fathers of the fatherland and the warriors of independence operated in the sphere of their power . . . ; and when the rule of despotism dissipated with the smoke of the final victory, the cannons of Chiloé[35] announced to the world that the revolution of political independence had ended and the war against the powerful spirit that the colonial system inspired in our society was beginning."[36]

Sr. Lastarria triumphantly answers the critics of the American Revolution, who have condemned it as inopportune, reproaching it for its inevitable disorders and missteps. The misfortunes were the necessary consequence of the condition in which we found ourselves; in whatever era an insurrection might have broken out, the misfortunes would have been equal or greater, and success perhaps less

---

35. Chiloé is the largest of the Chilean islands; it was the last holdout of the Spanish Royalists, who were not defeated until 1826.

36. Lastarria, *Investigaciones*, p. 131.

certain. We were faced with the alternative of taking advantage of the first opportunity or of prolonging our servitude for centuries. If we had not received the education to predispose us for the enjoyment of liberty, we certainly could not hope to receive it from Spain; we had to educate ourselves no matter how costly the effort; we had to put an end to a tutelage of three centuries which in all that time had not been able to prepare the emancipation of a great people.

José Victorino Lastarria
(Chile)

José Victorino Lastarria Santander (1817–1888) is among the most influential of all Chilean *pensadores*. A man of enormous intellectual capacity, he was born in Rancaugua to a family of modest means, not among the leading ruling families of Chile. He was nonetheless able to rise to the highest social levels. He married Jesús Julia Villarreal on June 8, 1839; they had twelve children.

Lastarria was educated at two of Chile's most prestigious institutions, first at the Liceo de Chile, where he was a student of José Joaquin de Mora, and then with Andrés Bello at the Instituto Nacional. At the Liceo de Chile, he studied under the auspices of a federal scholarship until the government closed the school because of Mora's liberal philosophical and political leanings. He studied law at the Universidad de San Felipe, and upon completing his degree in 1839, he became a member of the Academy of Law. He had begun his teaching career in 1836 and by 1838 published two early works, *Manual de testamentos* and *Lecciones de geografía moderna,* primarily as aids for his students.

An indication of the status Lastarria had attained was his presence among the eighty-six professors who in 1842 made up the original faculty of the Universidad Nacional de Chile, of which Andrés Bello was the rector for the first twenty years of its existence. Lastarria served several times as dean of the Facultad de la Filosofía y Humanidades, for the first time in 1846.

Among the responsibilities the national government placed on the rector and faculty was to provide an annual account of the progress of research at the University, particularly as it pertained to Chile's own history and social condition. Rector Bello charged Lastarria with delivering the first of the *memorias* in 1844, and this was the occasion for one of Lastarria's most important works, *Investigaciones sobre la influencia social de la conquista i del sistema colonial de los Españoles en Chile* (translated as *Investigations Regarding the Social Influence of the Conquest and the Spanish Colonial System in Chile*).

Independently of his career as a university professor, Lastarria was a journalist, editor of literary and political magazines, advocate of education for the less privileged, deputy for numerous constituencies, minister of the treasury, minister plenipotentiary to Argentina, Brazil, and Peru, and, finally, toward the end of his life, supreme court justice.

Among the literary and political magazines he founded or for which he served as editor are *El Diablo Político, El Crepúsculo,* and *La Revista de Santiago.* He was also a founding member of the literary and political group known as the "Generation of 1842," which included, among others, Francisco Bilbao, and was the analog of Argentina's Generation of 1837. The Generation of 1842 was dedicated to both literary and liberal political ideals, particularly to the ideal of a Latin American literature that was free of European influence and would develop uniquely Chilean literary and aesthetic standards. In 1844 *El*

Crepúsculo published Bilbao's "Sociabilidad Chilena," (translated as "Chilean Sociability") for the content of which the government fined and sent him into exile. In direct response and as a protest to Bilbao's expulsion, Lastarria resigned his position in the ministry of the interior. Lastarria encountered his own political difficulties when he became a member of the Sociedad de la Igualdad, for which the government of Manuel Bulnes (1841–1851) accused him of being an agitator and sent him to Lima, Peru, in exile. He remained out of the country for about a year.

The first selection that follows contains two sections from Lastarria's famous *Investigaciones sobre la influencia social de la conquista,* one giving his philosophy of history and the other stating his version of the "Black Legend," the view that Spanish colonialism left the Americas unprepared for self-rule. The second selection is from *La América,* which contains a statement of what scholars call the "Western hemisphere idea," an advocacy of the unique place and destiny of the Americas in the history of the world and of the need for Americans, especially Latin Americans, to establish cultural independence from the European past.

Further Reading

Alamiro de Ávila Martel, ed. *Estudios sobre José Victorino Lastarria.* Santiago: Ediciones de la Universidad de Chile, 1988.

Cruz, Pedro Nolasco. *Bilbao y Lastarria.* Santiago: Editorial Difusión Chilena, 1944.

Fuenzalida Grandón, Alejandro. *Lastarria i su tiempo (1817–1888): Su vida, obras e influencia en el desarrollo político e intelectual de Chile.* Santiago: Imprenta Barcelona, 1911.

Fuenzalida Wendt, Hernán. *José Victorino Lastarria: Síntesis biográfica.* Santiago: La Nación, 1942.

Jaksič, Iván. *Academic Rebels in Chile: The Role of Philosophy in Higher Education and Politics.* Albany, N.Y.: State University of New York Press, 1989.

Jobet, Julio César. *Precursores del pensamiento social de Chile.* Santiago: Editorial Universitaria, 1955–1956.

Lastarria, José Victorino. *Literary memoirs.* Translated by R. Kelly Washbourne; edited by Frederick M. Nunn. New York: Oxford University Press, 2000.

———. *Obras completas.* 13 vols. Santiago: Imprenta Barcelona, 1906–1909.

Oyarzún, Luis. *El pensamiento de Lastarria.* Santiago: Editorial Jurídica de Chile, 1953.

Subercaseaux, Bernardo. *Cultura y sociedad liberal en el siglo XIX: Lastarria, ideología y literatura.* Santiago: Editorial Aconagua, 1981.

———. *Historia de las ideas y de la cultura en Chile.* Santiago: Editorial Universitaria, 1997.

Investigations Regarding the Social Influence of the Conquest and the Spanish Colonial System in Chile (1844)

[Lastarria's philosophy of history][1]

Introduction

Gentlemen:

History is for peoples what personal experience is for man. Just as man follows his path toward perfection, ever calling on his memories, on truths that have made him conceive his own sensibilities, on observations that the events surrounding him since his childhood suggest to him, society must likewise, in the various eras of its life, turn to history, that great mirror of the times, in which the experience of the entire human race is set down, to be enlightened by its reflections. What would be the fate of nations if they were delivered blind into the arms of destiny, making no effort to work at developing the moral laws that guide them irresistibly to their future! A nation's existence would then lack unity—it would be nothing but a succession of isolated events whose record would not begin to form an awareness of its true position nor have value for foretelling its future, because it would not conceive its natural and necessary connections; its activity along the path to perfection would develop slowly and painfully at the spontaneous prompting of events, and it would be as varied and capricious as are those events; its education would be entrusted to fortune, and it would necessarily contradict and conflict with itself, given that with each generation the experience and spirit of the eras would forever disappear—those lessons that humanity receives from the events that mark the course of the centuries, impressing their character on those centuries.

It is true that, on contemplating in the immense chaos of the times an ever-active higher power that regulates everything, an organic law of humanity ever constant and all powerful to which empires are subject in their prosperity, in their decadence, and in their ruin, which governs all societies, subjecting them to irresistible precepts, hastening the extermination of some and providing for the subsistence and future of the others; it is sure that, on seeing a harmony always notable and wise in the anarchic confusion that produces the clash and dislocation of the elements of the moral universe, the spirit is overcome by wonder and, as if exhausted, abandons all analysis, judging it not only excusable but also logically necessary to believe in destiny, to give in to that regulatory power of creation, "to entrust itself to the majestic order of the times and to doze off lulled by the hope that the power that has known how to weigh and balance the centuries and empires, that has counted the days of old Chaldea, of Egypt, of Phoenicia, of Thebes, that power of the Hundred Gates of heroic Sagunto,[2] of

---

1. In the opening section of the *Report,* Lastarria outlines his positivist theory of history.

2. Ancient city in Spain, which put up a stiff resistance to Carthage during the Second Punic War, 219 BC.

implacable Rome, will also know how to coordinate the few instants that have been reserved for man and those ephemeral movements that fill his time."[3] But we discover the error on which this reasoning, [this belief in predetermined destiny] so seemingly logical, is based when we lift our eyes to contemplate man's sublimity, when we focus on that liberty of action that man's creator has bestowed upon him. The succession of moral causes and effects, which constitute the great code to which the human race is subject by its very nature, is not strictly predetermined, that is, it does not operate without any participation on the part of man; but rather, the action of those causes is entirely null if man does not promote it through his acts. Man has a part so effective in his own destiny that, in the majority of cases, neither his good fortune nor his misfortune is anything other than a necessary result of his efforts, that is to say, of his liberty. Man thinks with independence, and his ideas are always the source and foundation of his will, so that his voluntary acts do nothing more than promote and hasten the unfolding of the natural causes that will produce either his happiness and perfection or his utter decline. The wisest and most profound philosophical historian of the last century teaches this truth when he establishes that:

> The deity has in nowise bound [men's] hands farther than what they were by time, place, and their intrinsic powers. When they were guilty of faults, he extricated them not by miracles, but suffered these faults to produce their effects, that man might the better learn to know them. This law of nature is not more simple than it is worthy of God, consistent and fertile in its consequences to mankind. Were man intended to be what he is, and to become what he was capable of becoming, he must preserve a spontaneity of nature and be encompassed by a sphere of free actions, disturbed by no preternatural miracle. All inanimate substances, every species of living creature that instinct guides, have remained what they were from the time of the creation: God made man a deity upon Earth; he implanted in him the principle of self-activity, and set this principle in motion from the beginning, by means of the internal and external wants of his nature. Man could not live and support himself without learning to make use of his reason; no sooner, indeed, did he begin to make use of this than the door was opened to a thousand errors and mistaken attempts; but at the same time, and even through these very mistakes and errors, the way was cleared to a better use of his reason. The more speedily he discerned his faults, the greater the promptitude and energy with which he applied to correct them: the farther he advanced, the more his humanity was formed; and this must be formed, or he must groan for ages beneath the burden of his mistakes.[4]

These observations, rigorously based on facts, prove to us too well that humanity is much more noble in its essence and is destined for much more

---

3. [Edgar] Quinet, "Introduction" to the work of [Johann Gottfried von] Herder entitled *Outlines of a Philosophy of the History of Man.* [Lastarria's note; translated by T. Churchill (London 1800).]

4. Herder, *Outlines of a Philosophy of the History of Man,* book XV, ch. 1. [Lastarria's note; translated by T. Churchill (London, 1800).]

magnificent ends than is imagined by those who consider humanity as dully subject to its laws as is matter.

To think that human societies should deliver themselves passively to a law that capriciously destroys them or makes them greater, without their being able to influence in any way their own well-being or misfortune, is as absurd and dangerous as to ordain that man must entrust himself to a power other than the one that nature has given him to cultivate his happiness, and in order to subject himself to the predetermined order of his destiny he must chain his active abilities to inertia.

Society possesses, then, that sovereignty of judgment and will that, in the individual, constitutes the capacity of working out his own well-being and greater glory so long as he does not offend justice. In the same way as the individual, society can be successful or lose its way, whether it be by hastening the course of those natural causes that must bring about its perfection as a necessary consequence, or whether it be by twisting nature itself, bringing upon itself, through its errors, decline or eternal ruin that leaves nothing more than the memory of its name and of its vices.

I cannot deny, nevertheless, that weakness, ignorance, or other accidents that are not foreign to the history of the world and that are difficult to avoid usually bring about the misfortunes of peoples, even when those peoples put all their strength into warding off the blow by which they perish; but this very consideration convinces us precisely of the urgent need that society has to take as its charge its own preservation and development, availing itself not only of its own elements but also the lessons that experience furnishes it, studying humanity in its virtues, in its aberrations, and in its vices, to extract from this very study the means to prevent evil or at least the way to neutralize evil's action. And where can it be found, that experience of societies? Where are its precepts deposited, if not in history, in that sacred repository of the centuries, in that tabernacle that holds all the splendor of the civilizations that time has cast down, all the wisdom that the great catastrophes of the human race contain!

History is the oracle that God uses to reveal his wisdom to the world, to counsel peoples and teach them to secure a happy future. If one considers history only a simple testimony of past events, the heart aches and skepticism begins to gnaw at the mind, because then nothing is perceived but a scene of miseries and disasters. Liberty and justice maintain a perpetual struggle with despotism and iniquity and almost always succumb to the repeated blows of these adversaries; the most prosperous and flourishing empires are shaken to their foundations, and, from one moment to another, immense ruins that astound the generations come to take the place those empires once occupied, testifying to the weakness and constant shifting of man's works; man wanders everywhere, presiding over destruction, spilling his tears and his blood in torrents; he seems to be chasing an altogether unknown good, which he cannot reach without devouring the entrails of his own brothers, without himself perishing under the executing axe that he ceaselessly swings against whatever surrounds him. However, history reveals itself to us in a different way if we consider it as a science of events; then philosophy shows us—in the midst of this intermi-nable series of vicissitudes in which humanity proceeds, trampling on humanity and hurling itself into the abysses that it digs with its own hands—a profound wisdom on which the experience of centuries has thrown light, a wisdom whose counsels are infallible because they rest upon the sacrosanct precepts of the law to which the Omnipotent adapted the organization of that moral universe. The peoples must penetrate into that august sanctuary with the torch of philosophy to learn there the experience that must guide them; let them flee—along with the men who direct their destinies—from that blind confidence in fatalism that would separate them from reason, destroying at their root the abilities that their own nature has bestowed on them to enable them to cultivate their happiness!

The human race has in its very essence the capacity for its perfection, pos-sesses the elements of its good fortune, and is the only being given the ability to direct and promote its own development, because the laws of its organization form a key that it alone can play to make it produce harmonious sounds. So as to know those laws and appreciate them in their natural consequences, man must open the great book of his life, in which the laws are written in indelible characters: In it man will see that the constant alternation of well-being and mis-fortune in which he has traversed the centuries is neither the fateful work of a blind power that precipitates him from event to event, nor the inevitable conse-quence of a caprice, but rather a natural effect of those laws, of that system of conditions to which by his nature he is subject. He will also see that if, in the physical universe the causes that serve him as laws to produce a necessary result develop spontaneously, the same does not happen in the moral universe, because man has the power to bring about the development of his own laws or to avoid their development through his liberty to act in whatever way best befits his hap-piness. Such is the supreme wisdom of the Divine Intelligence! Humanity nei-ther is nor has been strictly what it could be, given the circumstances of place and time, but rather what it should be, given the use that the men who have ruled and guided humanity have made of those circumstances. Humanity has an active part in directing its own destinies, because if this were not so, its freedom would be an insulting lie, its dignity would disappear, and the idea of justice could not exist in the world![5]

This is why I have said, Gentlemen, that society must resort to history, to that precious repository of experience, to derive from it the means to prevent misfor-tune and the light that should guide it through future shadows. Only in history can society learn the unchanging laws of its happiness or decline; in history alone can it see the dangers it must avoid, the influences of the past that can delay its progress, the errors that must lead it to its ruin; and finally, only in his-tory can it study the path that it has followed and the rank and position that it

---

5. Perhaps I could be called audacious because I depart here from the foundation of the bril-liant theories of more than one genius of modern times, but I beg pardon for this, if it is a fault, and I ask that I be permitted to use my freedom of thought. I do not believe in historical determinism, as some learned persons conceive it. [Lastarria's note.]

occupies on the scale of nations. Public men, those to whom has fallen the happiness of taking on the difficult task of guiding a state, must for this reason know in depth the history of the people whose fortune is entrusted to them. If, following the learned Sismondi,[6] the constitution of a society is, properly speaking, nothing other than its way of existing, its very life, the sum of all its laws and all its customs; if that constitution has as its base the record of the society itself, how would it be possible to know and follow it in its spirit if not by knowing philosophically the history of the people? If the legislator must guarantee the present to prepare for what should be and prudently encourage reforms and accelerate progress, what, if not history, can guide him on the thorny path he must pursue in such a lofty undertaking? How to discover, without this torch of divinity, what the terrible consequences of a past history are, what the antisocial practices that perpetuate themselves, what the inclinations, the vices rooted in the heart of the people, putting up insuperable opposition to its perfection?

I sincerely believe that if those who love their fatherland and truly desire its good fortune would regard the philosophy of history as an essential part of their knowledge in the social sciences, they would never commit those errors that impede the progress of societies and that often make them go backwards, because these errors are either very much the repetition of a cause that in earlier eras has developed in an unfortunate and lamentable way, or the actual echo of those prejudices that, had they been known in their origin and nature, should have already been eliminated and stigmatized with the disgrace of all prejudices considered shameful to humanity. I have rooted in my heart the hope that civilization's progress must come to a happy time when those degrading errors will no longer figure in the catalog of any cultured peoples' acts, and when the laws will have developed to such a degree of perfection that they punish as true criminals men of bad faith who might strive hard to perpetuate them. This hope could perhaps be regarded as genuinely utopian, but at least it will not have its foundation in one of those deceptive and bewildering chimeras that beguile the mind and lead it astray. This hope is innocent and not so impossible to realize as it appears!

Convinced of these truths, which philosophy has elevated to the category of dogmas, I consider full of wise foresight and rich in happy consequences that decree of the University statutes prescribing to this illustrious corporation the duty of periodically presenting a study on the history of our fatherland. This important work, entrusted for the first time to a man such as I—without doubt the least fit to carry it out in an honorable and satisfactory manner—will certainly not offer, even in broad perspective, the development that it would surely receive when performed by others of my colleagues, more worthy for their learning and talents and with more free time than I have to dedicate themselves to the difficult historical research and serious study of philosophy, which seeks wisdom among apparently remote and disconnected facts. Do not believe, Gentlemen,

---

6. Jean-Charles Léonard Simonde de Sismondi (1773–1842), Swiss economist and historian who warned against the perils of unchecked industrialism.

that in so expressing myself I am using one of those rhetorical clichés in which vanity often disguises itself in the trappings of modesty; no, this is the genuine expression of what is going on in my heart!

What is the history of our republic? What benefit can we derive from its study for directing its affairs in its current state? And here we have the questions that appear primordial as we focus our deliberation on this vitally important subject.

[Lastarria and the "Black Legend"][7]

The history of Chile remains that of a new people who count barely three centuries of a gloomy existence lacking movement; it is the history of a past era that the philosopher can subject to his research without great difficulty, and of a new era that we touch and that belongs to us, because it is the present. The origin and childhood of our society do not escape our gaze; they have not yet been lost in the shadows of time, and to study them we do not need criticism that compares and corrects to separate the false from the true, but rather criticism that classifies and orders known facts. Consequently, the culminating points of our history are two—the conquest and the revolution of independence. In these two great events can be recast and formulated all the rest that have contributed to completing them. The simple narration of the facts forming the history of the first of these events—as expressed by the writers who, making a skeletal chronicle of them, believe they have written the *History of Chile*—does not offer any genuine interest whatsoever, except the interest inspired by a barbarian people struggling to defend their independence from the authority of a foreigner; but the narration of the colony's revolution, even if written without any unity or philosophical discernment, is of greater interest, inasmuch as in those heroic events, which gratify our national love, we perceive the foundation of our political liberty and the origin of a happiness that feels much greater the fresher our memory is of the sufferings caused by the despotism from which we emancipated ourselves—this is a philosophical deduction that all of us instinctively make without the historian guiding us.

Nonetheless, the events that completed the conquest, producing as an immediate result the establishment of Spanish domination in Chile, deserve serious study, inasmuch as they are not so isolated from nor so independent of our era that we can regard them as having no influence on the republic's present state. Considered in their individuality, as the historians who have described the war of conquest have done, without paying attention to the necessary links among them, they not only appear to be events belonging to an era and a generation independent and distinct from ours, but it is also impossible to imagine that their study would have anything useful and advantageous for present society, and it is above all difficult to see them as experiential data that might contain

---

7. In what follows, Lastarria articulates his version of the "Black Legend."

some lesson for the future. So we must discover the relationships that link such events to see how they all conspire in bringing about a great occurrence in our history—the conquest and consequent establishment of Spanish power in Chile. Considering them in this way will lead us easily to study that great occurrence, that culminating episode in which are summarized and recast all the other particulars that produced it. Then we will be able to know philosophically the features of that era and how they function in society; we will be able to appreciate their influence on society's character and concerns; and finally, we will accurately calculate the power and intensity of the reaction begun in 1810. Only thus can studying the conquest's history be useful to us to see our current situation in its true nature and to guide our public affairs in a way favorable to developing our happiness and perfection.

II. Idea of the Spanish Colonial System

Not only did the conquest's character alter the existence of this nation; yet another element certainly exercised a more powerful influence over its spirit and social inclinations, namely, the colonial system adopted by Spain.

It is well-known that the Spaniards conquered America, soaking its soil in blood, not to settle it but rather to seize the precious metals that it so abundantly produced. Driven by the hope of gathering enormous riches at little cost, torrents of adventurers flooded the New World, and they directed their activity to this sole objective, using every possible expedient or outrage necessary to attain it. In the end reality made the illusion disappear, and the conquistadors, convinced by their own experience that the productivity of the American mines was not so great as they had imagined, began to abandon their reckless speculations and dedicate themselves little by little to agricultural and commercial enterprises. But this turn in their aspirations did not yield as much as it might have, given the advantages that American soil offered, because they had neither the taste nor the intelligence to exploit this new source of wealth, and, in addition, their government, with its absurd industrial system, brought to a standstill at the outset all the wealth that they could have expected.[8]

As it established its colonies in America, Spain transplanted to them all the vices of its absurd system of government, vices that multiplied infinitely for having their origin in the system itself. . . .[9]

Here we have an idea of the administrative power of the Chilean colonies; it was all reduced to a strict unity, it ruled in an absolute way, and it depended

---

8. The Spanish mercantile system of monopolies and trade prohibitions was aimed at protecting industrial production in Spain by eliminating potential sources of competition in the overseas Spanish possessions, for example, by prohibiting wine production in the Americas and establishing an absolute government monopoly on the manufacture and sale of tobacco products.

9. In intervening passages, Lastarria describes the actual organization of Chile by the Spaniards.

solely on the king, who not only regarded himself sovereign, but also lord and master of his American vassals and all the lands he had conquered in the New World, and whose rule had been sanctified by a papal bull.

The Spanish monarch governed the Americas through a supreme council, called the Council of the Indies, at which His August and Sacrosanct Majesty was considered present and from which emanated all the laws, all the regulations, all the measures—whether general or local—necessary to rule colonies that were at a distance of thousands of leagues and whose character and circumstances were not even remotely known. The noteworthy feature, with respect to the governance of America, is that any resolution issued by the agency of the ministers of the crown or by the Council of the Indies, so long as it was about some American situation, was given the full force of a genuine law even though it might not have had the characteristics of a law. The number of these resolutions had no end, because they were issued arbitrarily and without coordination, and their number increased so prodigiously that the time came when positive colonial legislation formed a veritable labyrinth. Properly speaking, it was an accumulation—with neither plan nor system—of letters patent, royal decrees, letters, writs, ordinances, legal proceedings, government edicts, and an infinity of other incoherent, heterogeneous, and absurd documents, not all of which had even come to the attention of the American vassals because of the distance and long traveling time between the provinces.[10] Various attempts were made to compile and arrange all these measures during the sixteenth century and into the seventeenth as well, until, during the reign of Carlos II in 1680, the famous *Compilation of the Indies* was created in four bulky volumes, taking into account the many attempts and projects of codification that had been undertaken earlier without the least result.[11]

Some partisans of the Spanish system have considered these laws the most just, correct, and adaptable for the prosperity of the American colonies, deducing from this outlandish opinion the strongest arguments against America's independence.[12] Even among us there are those persons who share this belief to a certain degree and

---

10. Law that declares the authority of the compendium of the Indies. [Lastarria's note. The reference is to the *Recopilación de leyes de los reynos de Indias,* commonly referred to as *Leyes de Indias,* an authoritative collection of laws governing the Spanish territories in the Americas, first published in 1681 and periodically thereafter through the nineteenth century.]

11. Ibid. [Lastarria's note.]

12. The London *Observer,* in its edition of January, 1820, said: "No nation has treated the peoples in their overseas establishments with more humanity and kindness than the Spanish nation. The most judicious writers recognize it, among them Baron [Alexander von] Humboldt himself. 'The mildness of Spanish legislation,' says he, 'compared with the Black Code of most other nations, [. . .] cannot be denied.'"

The *Observer* could also have cited the opinion of [Scottish historian William] Robertson who, deceived by the appearance of the laws of the Indies, tried in some passages of his *History of America* [(London, 1777)] to justify the monarchs of Spain and excuse their despotism. [Lastarria's note.]

who argue for the wisdom of this monstrous legislation, which—unfortunately and by I do not know what inexplicable absurdity—is still considered to be in force in a sovereign and independent republic that ceased needing colonial laws at the moment it proclaimed its independence. For that reason, Gentlemen, I believe it very appropriate at this point to make an examination, although brief, of the vices that raise this code to the highest degree of imperfection.

To this end it would be sufficient to cast a glance at the background of this code, at the elements used to compose this veritable mosaic, with its infinite variety and neither agreement nor harmony among its parts. Almost all those laws had been issued because of suggestions from the civil servants that Spain maintained in its colonies; in general, all referred to special circumstances, and those that did not have this character were aimed at regulating the government, without regard to the disturbances that could as easily result from the arbitrary rule of the leaders as from the various and unforeseen occurrences that influenced their management of affairs. The ills that arose from these causes—without even considering the tyranny and absurdity of such resolutions—were therefore not remedied by reducing all these contradictory measures to a single body with neither doctrine nor system, but on the contrary, they continued to exist and were multiplied infinitely, because the practice continued unabated of issuing letters patent and royal decrees for every case that arose without considering any precedents other than what the most base passions suggested to those who had an interest in their being issued. The number of these new resolutions very soon exceeded the number of those already compiled, and the contradictions also increased, to the point that it was not possible to distinguish the laws in effect from those that had been partially or completely revoked. For this reason, the science of Spanish colonial legislation came to be a veritable black magic in whose mysteries were initiated only those who had enough audacity to make their caprice or interest prevail, corroborating their claims by citing one or another of the Laws of the Indies or whatever other royal letter patent.

For this reason, an observer says that, "civil and criminal proceedings, matters of income, and matters of public policy endured such variation and conflict among royal decrees and orders that no foundation existed on which any claim, complaint, or petition could be based. Everything arose from, depended on, and ended in the arbitrary rule of the court's ministers and those of the leaders of America. They always lent each other a hand, and their decisions were mutually supported as suited their despotic ideas of governing. . . . At the same time, every forward step in American government faced the obstacle of some of the many exclusive charters and privileges of the corporations and professions that abounded in it."[13] All these vices had their origin and their greatest support in the laws themselves, and difficulties multiplied that made their application yet more obscure and absurd.

---

13. *La biblioteca Americana.* [Lastarria's note; referring to a literary journal published in London in 1823 by Rafael Caldera, Andrés Bello, and Juan García del Río.]

That was about the form of the legislation. Its foundation was another matter. One single overarching thought dominated all the resolutions of the court and the colonies' leaders, namely, always to keep America blindly dependent on Spain, to extract from its possession all possible profits. From this point of view, the metropolis did have a system, a spirit that gave unity to all its resolutions and sanctified all the judgments that came before it, no matter how wicked and unacceptable they might be. The New World was for Spain a very rich mine that it must exploit, taking advantage of its fruits even when it was exhausting that mine and making no effort to insure its future productivity. To this end Spain had subordinated the indigenous people to the most humiliating and gross servitude, declaring them slaves in certain cases and disguising the slavery in others, with a feigned and sarcastic respect for their liberty, while nonetheless subjecting them to the *mita,* to the *repartimiento*[14] and to other burdens with which it oppressed them. The tax laws were precisely calculated to benefit the royal coffers and extract all possible treasure from the colonies, even at the price of the very elements of production. Trade was monopolized to benefit the court itself, manufacturing and agriculture were caught in a thousand hobbles and burdened with so many taxes that it seemed obvious the intention was to contain them at their germ and block their development. Spain's financial system, with its genuinely exclusive character, was taken to America in this legislation, with no more difference than being overloaded with other vices and absurdities that made it easier for the court to obstruct and cut off the colonies' paths to progress. Communication and trade with foreign powers were prohibited in such a way that not only was it a crime to maintain these relations, but Spain also appealed to a deceitful sovereignty of the seas to order the governors, as was done in a royal letter patent of 1692, "that they treat as an enemy any foreign vessel that might sail the seas of America without license from the court, even though the nation to which it belonged be an ally."

The laws and resolutions issued to obstruct the intellectual development of Americans attest, on the other hand, to a perverse intention of keeping them in the most brutal and degrading ignorance, to make them submit perpetually to the yoke of their "natural sovereign" and of all the leaders who derived their authority from him. Selling and printing books of any type in America, even prayer books, was prohibited with severe punishments, and their importation required a license from the Council of the Indies or from another authority equally bent on not permitting the light of knowledge to penetrate the New World.[15] The few universities and colleges that the laws established and regulated

---

14. *Mita,* a draft labor system by which Andean Indians were forced to work for prescribed periods of time in Spanish enterprises, particularly the mines; a similar draft labor system was known in Mexico as *repartimiento.*

15. *Leyes de Indias,* Book 1, Title 24. [Lastarria's note. These laws did not actually prohibit the printing and sale of books in the Americas, but rather hindered the publishing industry by requiring prior approval from government and Church censors and levying heavy taxes; still, books were printed in colonial Spanish America.]

were absolutely intended to separate man from true knowledge; they were, let me use the happy expression of an American, "a monument to imbecility."[16] Because these establishments were subject entirely to a monastic set of rules, moral and intellectual education was abandoned with meticulous care; their only endeavor was to create ministers of worship and, at most, lawyers or doctors, but false doctrines were delivered to everyone, who grew accustomed to deceptive arguments and extravagant theories, and by means of its useless science and errors were made to adopt a vulgar and high-flown style. The court thus managed, through its laws and resolutions, to lead the Americans' intellect astray and distract them with some antisocial studies that had necessarily to lead them to the desired end of making them blind to reason so that they might not see "in the king of Spain anything but their absolute lord, who knew no superior nor any check on earth, whose power was derived from God Himself for the execution of his intentions, whose person was sacred, and before whose presence *everyone must tremble.*"[17]

In making this rapid examination of colonial legislation for the purpose of investigating its social influence, I must nonetheless provide testimony to the impartiality of my judgment, declaring that the tedium that this monstrous compilation creates takes a break at times with the reading of some measures that show their authors' pious sentiments. But nothing more than pious sentiments, because in them, just as in the rest, one does not find the common sense, the foresight that results from philosophical analysis of the facts, whose qualities are the most outstanding features of any legislator's wisdom. Indeed, various laws intended to regularize the natives' service in the *mitas, encomiendas,*[18] *and repartimientos,* to which they were subjected, as well as other laws that assessed their tributes so their exaction might not be excessively burdensome. Some laws were intended especially to protect the liberty of the Chilean Indians and concede to them more privileges and exemptions than to the Indians in the other colonies, without doubt with the object of winning them over and, by these mild and protective measures, cutting the war short.[19] And here we have the laws that doubtless have beguiled the minds of this legislation's defenders, if they speak in good faith, and from which they have derived their arguments to prove the wisdom of these laws and praise the protection Spain bestowed on its colonies; but remembering what I have argued above regarding the spirit of this code

---

16. The quotation is from a critique of colonial education by Colombian-born politician and journalist Juan García del Río (1794–1856), an associate of Andrés Bello who founded newspapers and literary journals in Chile, Peru, and London during the early independence period.

17. [Gregorio] Funes, *Ensayo de la historia civil del Paraguay, Buenos-Ayres y Tucumán* [*Essay on the Civil History of Paraguay, Buenos Aires and Tucuman,* Buenos Aires, 1816], quoted by the *Repertorio Americano* on this point. [Lastarria's note. *El Repertorio Americano* (1826–1827) was a London literary journal, successor to *La Biblioteca Americana.*]

18. The *encomienda* system obliged natives to tend the king's agricultural lands.

19. See *Leyes de Indias,* Book 6, Title 16, and some of the laws from Book 6, Title 2. [Lastarria's note. The Mapuches of southern Chile maintained hostilities against Spanish and Chilean intruders until the 1880s.]

and the system of the metropolis, what else were these laws but, at best, the expression of an isolated good desire or maybe a device to disguise the intentions and opinions that a corrupt and backward court had about the debased inhabitants of the New World? Whatever one might think, those protective laws were a silent exception without effect, a dead letter, from the moment that their execution, their interpretation, and even the right of modifying them were in the hands of the leaders of the colonies.

The metropolis untiringly insisted on naming individuals born in Spain to all offices and positions in the American colonies, this being the primary qualification it required, even when the candidate lacked the aptitudes and professional capacity the nature of the position demanded; so it was not unusual to see the judicial magistracy conferred on someone whose background lacked even the rudiments of jurisprudence, and Spain frequently invested with high military posts persons who had never brandished a sword and were ignorant of even basic tactics. Americans were strictly excluded from all public posts except for municipal council posts, which, because they came with no honors, income, or jurisdiction, were seen by peninsular Spaniards as burdens that only the colonists should bear. So blindly did Spain observe this insulting practice that any scruples the court might have had in establishing it as a legal principle were set aside, and the question of whether by law Americans would be excluded from public positions—thus declaring them incapable of carrying out offices of honor in the colonies—came to be argued before the full Council of the Indies, although it remained undecided. With thousands of facts, history further proves that Spain was completely in agreement with this resolve—of the one-hundred sixty viceroys in America, only four non-Spaniards were named, and among more than six hundred presidents and captains general, only forty fit that same category.[20]

History also makes obvious to us that all the civil servants Spain sent to America were turned into veritable despots who exercised the most arbitrary authority to secure for themselves their own profit—and this was a natural result of the position in which they were placed. The colonies' great distance from the metropolis and the consequent difficulties in communication between the continents made the impunity of their crimes easy; the doctrine that sanctioned as just and legitimate every atrocious act practiced against the settlers served them as sufficient excuse; the vagueness, latitude, and complexity of the legislation of the Indies made easy for them an immense, absolute authority, always a legal support whenever they had to cover up an abuse or legitimate a usurpation; finally, the need that the metropolis had to accept and defer to the agents' reports in all matters was a brilliant means to which they appealed to sanction with the will of the crown whatever might suit their tastes and interests. For this reason, every head civil servant was an absolute king, and his subordinates

---

20. Guzmán, *Historia de Chile,* lesson 69. [Lastarria's note; the reference is probably to José Javier Guzmán, *El Chileno instruido en la historia topográfica, civil y política de su país* (Santiago de Chile, 1834). Viceroys, Audiencia presidents, and captains general were the highest public officials in the Spanish territories.]

defended their own arbitrary rule and extravagances—if not with his master's approval, at least with his tolerance or example. From this, the frequent scandalous clashes, even among themselves, the sensational reprisals, and the use of all the mechanisms of influence and power to which one resorted to carry out a whim or leave some terrible crimes unpunished. From this also arose the impotence and the nullity of the laws themselves—the law of colonial America was merely the will of its immediate leaders. If one wishes to see a clear demonstration of this unquestionable fact, see what Don Jorge Juan and Don Antonio Ulloa state in their *Noticias Secretas* to the court of Spain about the miserable and humiliating state, the corruption, and the frightening social dislocation at which the colonies had arrived, because of the conduct of their governors, by the middle of the last century.[21] In the faithful and detailed account that these wise and impartial observers give, it becomes obvious that all the kind methods of the metropolis broke apart on the formidable reef of vulgar arbitrariness and insolent despotism that the governors and colonial civil servants put up against them, and this in all branches of the administration.

The navy and merchant marine services in the seas of South America were neither methodical nor reliable, but rather depended entirely on the whims and personal interests of those who carried them out, as many and as good as might have been the measures that the metropolis drew up to organize them. The fortresses were in complete disarray, and their heads were devoted to the profit that their posts could provide them. Their authority being, as it was, absolute, they took advantage of it to the same degree as any other functionary, even availing themselves of the money they were allotted for manning their garrisons and, by this and other means, tyrannizing those who had the misfortune of living in their employ, as was especially true of the governors of the fortress in Valdivia.[22]

Despite commerce being subjected to a complete monopoly whose restrictions and exclusions were calculated to reserve it exclusively to Spain, and in spite of its being burdened with heavy taxes in favor of the royal treasury, it was actually a source of earnings for those who were charged with maintaining this monopoly and guaranteeing its profits to the royal finance office, and at the same time commerce was a source of corruption for all who were involved in pursuing it, because they were accustomed to the fraud and illicit intrigues that civil servants sanctioned by their example. Those civil servants sponsored contraband and figured it as the principal advantage of their job, and if they sometimes resorted to laws to prevent fraud, they did so either because doing so helped them avoid an accusation or because they needed to avenge themselves on some

---

21. Jorge Juan and Antonio de Ulloa, *Noticias secretas de América, sobre el estado naval, militar, y político de los reynos del Perú* . . . (London, 1826; translated as *Secret Expedition to Peru,* Boston, 1851). Juan and Ulloa were Spanish scientists who conducted a survey of South America from 1735 to 1746. *Noticias Secretas* was a classified political report that accompanied their important and widely disseminated *Relación histórica del viage a la América Meridional* (Madrid, 1748; translated as *A Voyage to South-America,* London, 1758).

22. *Noticias Secretas,* vol. 1, ch 7. [Lastarria's note.]

enemy, availing themselves of their own authority. Exposing the serious faults of this branch of the administration, the authors cited say that it would be very normal to imagine that the place where the viceroys had their headquarters should be exempt from these disorders because of the viceroys' immediate presence, or that at least commercial fraud would be less there, in view of all the tribunals, all the ministers, all the judges, and the tremendous number of guards that were there to prevent it, but that this abuse actually reached its greatest height in these places. Contraband merchandise was introduced in the middle of the day without the least suspicion and was watched over by the guards themselves, who would even keep it in a safe place, free from the danger it might face while in its owners' possession. A similar thing happened with legal merchandise, so as to free it from paying the duties to which it was subject, and with this goal the most scandalous frauds were considered legitimate in both overland and maritime commerce. In this way, "neither conscience, nor fear, nor the awareness of these civil servants that they were being supported by the sovereign with very large salaries, served them as incentive to comply with their obligations."[23]

And if this was practiced by the functionaries who found themselves, by the nature of their employment, under more immediate inspection by the court and consequently more pressed to meet their obligations faithfully and accurately, what must have happened with those who exercised independent authority, with those whose actions were not so immediately interesting to the metropolis? It is not my intention to detail here the frightening arbitrariness, the countless abuses, the absurdities, the crimes that the governors, the military officers, the judicial magistrates, and even the very priests charged with the direction and spiritual care of the people executed and favored at each step;[24] I have only to submit myself to history to consider the facts in abstract and derive from examining them the logical conclusion that all iniquity ceased to be iniquity from the moment it was practiced on the Americans; that these latter, considered slaves and men different in nature and condition from the nature and condition of Europeans, were subject only to the laws that the Europeans' whims and interests imposed on them. The circumstance of being born American sealed the misfortune of the colonist, whatever might be his family's origin. With such a prejudice elevated into dogma, with the absolute power the leaders exercised, could any use, could any salutary effect come from the protective laws that the court used to issue as if to rest from the fierce despotism it exercised over the Americans?

In fact, despite those laws, the indigenous suffered all the weight of the prejudice that condemned them and all the harshness of the leaders who, instead of protecting them, believed themselves authorized to tyrannize them. "Such is the subject that we are about to treat," say the wise authors I have cited, in sketching the picture of the miserable state in which the natives found themselves when they [the authors] visited America, "that it is not possible to

---

23. *Noticias Secretas,* vol. 1, ch. 9. [Lastarria's note.]

24. See the work cited and this feature will not appear exaggerated. [Lastarria's note.]

enter into a discussion of it without the spirit being moved to compassion, nor is it possible to pause to think of it without unceasingly crying with pity for the miserable, wretched, and unfortunate fate of a nation that, without any other offense than simplicity nor more motive than natural ignorance, has come to be enslaved—and by a slavery so oppressive that, by comparison, the Africans whom the colonies' force and reason have condemned to servile oppression can be called happy; for good reason the fate of these [Africans] is envied by those who are called free and who the kings have so often requested be so regarded, for their state, subjection and miseries are much worse than those of the Africans."[25]

This expressive and sincere stroke of the pen saves me the distressing task of describing the frightful and miserable condition to which the indigenous were reduced by their conquerors and offers me unchallengeable testimony in favor of the truth I meant to prove.

A notable proposition follows from all these observations—that the practices of the Spaniards in America so neutralized the effect of the laws that were issued to govern them that they made the benefits of the good laws entirely useless, and the influence of the bad laws even more pernicious. When by chance, which is not rare in the history of the human race, there appears a wise or charitable law in the code of a corrupt people, the power of bad practices renders it useless, also corrupts it, and at the very least reduces it to a measure without force, which though perhaps venerated is never carried out, because it runs counter to the immoral interests and vices of those who should execute and obey it. Such has happened in Spanish America during the colonial period, but as the corruption had not risen to the same degree in all the colonies, the disorders and legal transgressions in the administration were not the same in all of them. Undoubtedly, greed was the corrupting element that had depraved the conquistadors to the point of making them lose all sense of humanity and religion: to the vices that, through their education, the backwardness of the era had inspired in them, to the false doctrines and antisocial prejudices that a foolish court encouraged in them as the best support of its stability, were thus added the immoral desires, criminal interests, and corruption that greed awoke in their hearts. Therefore, wherever this passion had no strong stimulus, neither the disorders nor the crimes were multiplied, nor was the despotism so ferocious. In Chile, for example, despite all the Spaniards having the same prejudices and the same corrupt practices as Spaniards in Peru, the abuses and transgressions of the laws were not so countless nor the tyranny so frightful as in the latter, because there did not exist in our land the incentives that awoke a more lively greed in Peru. Agricultural crops and precious metals were not exploited with the ease and exuberance as in the country of the Incas, and for that reason our history does not show the great crimes that tyranny, goaded on by thirst for gold, wrought among the descendents of those unfortunate monarchs. Our commerce, if what we had

---

25. *Noticias Secretas,* vol. 2, ch 1. [Lastarria's note.]

could be called that, did not offer broad opportunities for fraud and contraband as in Peru, because it was not abundant and rich, because it had no speculating capitalists, nor could it have had them because of the monopoly—and here we also have the reason why we do not find the excessive demoralization that is observed among the civil servants who in other colonies were specifically charged with carrying out the laws of the royal treasury. Thus, in every administrative branch, corruption did not exist among us with the same deformity, despite the fact that the same vices, the same prejudices, and, finally, the same destructive and antisocial elements existed in the administration of our colony as in the others.

The difference nonetheless is completely secondary and had no influence in Chile's favor during the era to which I refer, because, although the immediate effects show a difference, no such difference exists in its underlying causes. These causes, on the contrary, always work in the same way, influencing society and undermining its foundations.

America (1865)

Part One. America and Europe

I European Errors Regarding America

Although America and Europe are, in general, populated by different people from profoundly diverse social conditions, they nonetheless have traditions, sentiments, and practices deriving from the same origin and, above all, they have as their aim the same social end. Both continents are at the forefront of modern civilization and both are completely united in the enterprise of spreading that civilization and carrying it to its highest levels of achievement.

America knows Europe, studies it unceasingly, follows it step by step, and imitates it as its model; but Europe does not know America and, rather, disdains it and puts it out of sight like a misguided child for whom there is no hope. One European interest alone, the industrial interest, pays attention to America and takes the trouble to gather some statistical data on production and consumption in the New World, on those ports, commercial plazas, and population centers from which it can derive most profit.

But the agents of that interest—that is to say, the merchants of Birmingham, of Manchester and Glasgow, of Hamburg, of Le Havre and Bordeaux, of Cadiz and Genoa—come to America believing they are arriving in a savage country, and even though they are soon persuaded that civilized peoples live here, they never tolerate the belief that Americans are on the same level as Europeans, and they suppose Americans to be inferior in class. The industrial interest completely dominates the life of the European in America from this point on, and no matter how long his sojourn here might be, he never comes to understand the social and political interests of the people among whom he conducts his business, and he is disposed always to serve only his business, aligning himself with the one who guarantees his gains, albeit at the cost of the most sacred interests of the people from whom he buys and to whom he sells. Here we have the only tie that exists between Europe and Ibero-America. Here we have the only interest that European governments shelter and protect, the only one that its diplomacy and cannons have served to this point, the only one that inspires their relations with the American governments that they call barbarian and savage.

From time to time European presses issue an article or a book on one or another of the Ibero-American states; but generally, although those productions might be the result of a trip to America or a study financed by an American government, they are written with mean-spirited intent or with such superficiality that their data are deceptive, if not false and contradictory.

One need only open a travel book on America, above all if it is written in French, to find much to laugh at because of the wonders and grotesqueries it contains, and it is enough to read a report written by order of the government and under its protection, such as those frequently published about Brazil and the Argentine Republic, to see the truth disfigured for the sake of convincing Europe that what is not good is good, or that a great business operation can find something to do in these regions.

But these writings must be little read in Europe, inasmuch as the ignorance of its governments, its congresses, its statesmen, and its writers about America gushes and overflows on all occasions when they have to engage with our businesses and our circumstances. We do not even have to peruse history to gather facts to prove this—the ones before us are enough.

To what do we owe these facts if not the attempts that Spain today is beginning anew against Mexico, Santo Domingo, and Peru, ordering the war to continue on that island[26] and demanding from Peru much more than it obtained by the Agreement of Chinchas on January 20, 1865;[27] to what do we owe the unlawful, unprovoked, and unjustifiable war that Spain is waging against Chile on the pretext that Chile will not give Spain explanations for legal and inoffensive acts, which have, in fact, been given to Spain *ad nauseum;* to what France's invasion of Mexico, with the English government's acquiescence and applause—that war without precedent, because the history of humanity "has

---

26. The Spanish Caribbean colony of Santo Domingo was conquered and occupied by newly independent Haiti in 1821; it gained independence as the Dominican Republic after a revolt against Haitian rule in 1844. In 1861, Dominican dictator Pedro Santana arranged to have Spain re-annex the country. A guerrilla war (1863–1865) restored the country's independence.

27. The Chincha Islands are three islands off the coast of Peru, which became very valuable during the nineteenth century because of the extensive guano deposits they contained, which were marketed for fertilizer. Spain seized the islands in 1864, and after the failure of the 1865 treaty mentioned here by Lastarria, war erupted between Spain and a Peruvian-Chilean alliance.

never registered a single war more unjustifiable by its causes, more useless and pernicious in its objective, more illogical and self-contradictory, more condemned by its own allegations and by universal opinion, more dishonored in its alliances and in all its methods, and who knows if more suicidal;"[28] to what, finally, the attempts by Napoleon III to create a protectorate in Ecuador, and all the other political or industrial, public or private endeavors that Europe has set in motion in recent years against the independence of Ibero-America, against its liberal system, against its democratic ideas, against all its progress along the path of law?

Have we not seen newspapers founded and books written to spread the ridiculous theory that the "Latin" race has a nature different from, and conditions contrary to, those of the "Germanic" race, and that its interests and its fortune, therefore, force the Latin race to seek progress under the shelter of absolute governments, because the parliamentary system escapes it grasp? What a lie! We Americans well know that the fundamental principle of European monarchy, the social, political, religious, and moral base of Europe, is a "Latin" principle, that is to say, pagan, anti-Christian—the principle of the absolute unity of power, which kills the individual, annihilating his rights; but we also know that today neither the Latin nor the German race exists, nor can they exist, either in Europe or in America.

The Latin race disappeared or was profoundly modified and reshaped as soon as the peoples of the Germanic race conquered Roman dominions, and after fifteen centuries the French who descended from the Franks—the Germanic people who settled in Gaul, today called France—can scarcely be called "Latins"; nor can the Spaniards who were descended from the Goths and Visigoths, also Germanic peoples who conquered and settled the peninsula. What is Latin about the Germans who groan beneath the yoke of the "Latin" principle that consecrates absolute power, or the descendents of the Lombards, who are struggling in Italy to have a government that respects the law?

German, not Latin, are the European monarchies that follow the Latin, or pagan, principle of absolutism; so too are the peoples who are on their knees before the European monarchs, dragging their borrowed lives through the shadows of ignorance under which the dignity and rights of the individual have disappeared.

What this absurdity wishes to do is to make us "Latins" in politics, morals and religion—that is, to blot out our personality in favor of the unity of an absolute power that would dominate our consciences, our thoughts, our wills, and

---

28. *Cuestión de Méjico: Cartas de D. José Ramón Pacheco al Ministro de Negocios Estrangeros de Napoleón III, M. Drouyn de Lhuys*, New York, 1862 [*The Mexico Question: Letters of D. José Ramón Pacheco to Napoleon III's Minister of Foreign Affairs*]. [Lastarria's note. The reference is to the invasion of Mexico by France under the rule of Louis Napoleon (1861–1867). In the following paragraphs, Lastarria criticizes the intellectual justification of French intervention in the Americas, which was based on the then-novel idea that the former Spanish, Portuguese, and French dominions in the New World formed "Latin America."]

through this, all the individual rights that we won in our revolution; the theory of the races has been invented for that purpose. But such an aim proves one thing only, namely, that Europe is completely in the dark regarding our moral and intellectual progress; and just as it thus deceives itself through its ignorance when it seeks to return us to the rule of its kings, it also childishly deceives itself when it aspires to steep us in its errors, in those absurdities that constitute the faith of its peoples.

• • • • •

XIII Comparison of Europe's and America's Political Principles

What does the exhaustive review we have just completed of the theories and systems of the leading European experts in public law tell us about the present state of European political science regarding the state and individual rights, which together form what we call "Liberty"?[29] Does it not clearly demonstrate and finely reckon the enormous political distance separating the New World from the Old in political matters? Does the evidence not prove that the other nations on the European continent cannot understand American democracy any better than the unsatisfactory way the English do—given that the political dogma of those nations is the unity of the Latin monarchy, the universality of the absolute and controlling power over the conscience, over thought, over the will, annihilating the individual so as to enlarge the principle of authority supported by force?

In Europe this principle of authority dominates, and human activity in all its spheres is sacrificed to it—the individual and society exist for the state, individual rights are a favor that the latter bestows only when it wishes and then grants them only halfway.

In America "democracy tends to destroy the principle of authority supported by force and privilege but strengthens the principle of authority that rests on justice and the interests of society," as we have already noted some time ago.[30] The difference cannot be more profound and marked; and no human power will be able to make it disappear unless all Europe is moved in its innermost recesses to be converted from monarchy, as it is, into democracy, which it cannot be except after a general, painful, and prolonged revolution.

We have already seen it—the principles of Latin monarchy are the basis of Europe's civil and political existence, and they give to its life the action and form, the sentiment and prejudices that constitute all its social relationships, its

---

29. In the preceding several chapters, Lastarria has reviewed the accounts of the nature of the political mentality of Europe and America propounded by such European thinkers as Baron Wilhelm von Humboldt, John Stuart Mill, Jozsef Baron Eoetvoes, Jules Simon, Alexis de Tocqueville, Édouard René Lefèvre de Laboulaye, and Jean Gustav Courcelle-Seneuil.

30. *Historia constitucional del Medio Siglo* [Valparaíso, Chile, 1853]. [Lastarria's note].

entire mode of being—its judgment, its viewpoint for judging everything, its habits and practices, its acts and statements.

This is so certain that the very few noble intellects who rush from that chaos of sorrows and misery to the regions of philosophy in search of a remedy for the oppression of society, to find the fire of life—rights—now crushed and dead, cannot divest themselves of the dogma of European life nor of the prejudices to which they have been accustomed, and they end up inventing theories that in themselves are nothing more than a vicious circle, around which they race without finding a way out.

The most progressive—Humboldt and Eoetvoes in Germany, Mill and Macaulay in England, Tocqueville, Laboulaye, and Simon in France—sense the wrong, know the wound, touch it, but cannot cure it, because their methods are powerless. Courcelle-Seneuil and a few German philosophers have clearer views, even know the remedy, but, doubting its efficacy, aspire only to promote it as an ideal whose realization is distant because it requires conditions that are nearly impossible in Europe's present state.[31]

Among all these sages, those closest to the truth are the ones who perceive in America the light of the future, the ones who, like the voice that cries in the wilderness, announce to Europe, at the risk of wounding Europe in her pride, that she will not be saved if she does not imitate America, that she will not be redeemed from sin if she does not follow the new messiah of the new redemption, which is democracy. The light now returns from the west to the east; but Europe closes her eyes and refuses to see it.

Well now, if Europe is ignorant of America and refuses to study her because, in her old woman's pride, irritated by the bitter lessons of time, she scorns America without ever coming to understand that Christian civilization has found its strength and its form in American democracy; if, moreover, there is between the two continents a difference of ideas and political interests so profound that they cannot cease to be at two antagonistic extremes—who, then, other than a myopic person, could come to imagine that between the two continents there could exist the same community of interests and the same ties that respectively link together the peoples who form the social entity of each community?

Ideas give practices their essence and form. This is a proven truth. Because the dominant ideas in Europe and America are different and contrary—ideas on society and the state, on the power of the authority and the individual rights that

---

31. Alexander von Humboldt (1769–1859), German naturalist and explorer. Jozsef Baron Eoetvoes (1813–1871), Hungarian novelist, essayist, educator, and statesman. John Stuart Mill (1806–1873), English philosopher and political economist. Thomas Babbington Macaulay (1800–1859), English Whig politician, essayist, poet, and historian. Alexis-Charles-Henri Clerel de Tocqueville (1805–1859), French political thinker and historian. Edouard René Lefèvre de Laboulaye (1811–1883), French jurist. Jules François Simon (1814–1896), French statesman and philosopher. Jean Gustav Courcelle-Seneuil (1813–1892), French liberal economist; taught economics at the University of Chile, 1855–1858, under contract with the Chilean government, which made his writings part of the mandatory curriculum.

shape liberty—those practices that have their foundation in such ideas and the interests they form cannot help but also be different and opposing. And as those fundamental ideas have an intimate connection with the fundamental ideas of religion and morality, the difference goes farther than the practices we might call political, goes so far as to give civilization another moral and religious viewpoint that governs social interests.

Between the practices of Spanish America and those of Europe, that difference will still be embryonic, we admit, because the reform in political, moral, and religious ideas has not yet run its full course here; but we must also acknowledge that, when this reform is complete and reaches the level it has currently attained in English America, where the source of the practices has been purified because the old ideas have been reformed and the new have crystallized, then the difference will not be embryonic and will come to be as evident and striking as is the difference that today exists between European practices and those of North American democracy.

It is true that the work of Spanish American reform is slow because it is spontaneous, that is to say, because it operates solely by virtue of natural development, by virtue of the laws that govern humanity's progress. But when the men who are called to influence the fate of their generation come to realize that they are obliged to work for that reform, renouncing all European influences and prejudices, when they are persuaded that their mission is essentially American and that the model they should imitate is in the North and not in Europe, then the effect of the natural laws of humanity that govern our reform will not only be more effective but also more rapid, because nature will be helped by man's cooperation.

As the ideas that ruled the life of the Spanish American peoples during their infancy and under the sterile and destructive tutelage of Spain are studied and understood, the generations that have accepted the legacy of independence have the duty to reform those ideas in order to adapt them to the new circumstance, because each century is responsible for the way it *corrects and completes the experience* and education of its ancestors, because events and happenings are not the work of chance but rather the pure results of dominant ideas, and humanity is mistress of her fate and is under obligation to direct it, to develop her natural ends. We must rebuild social science,[32] as the Anglo-Americans have rebuilt it. If

---

32. "This science," says Courcelle-Seneuil, "has as its objective the voluntary activity of man considered in his totality and in his habits. To understand this activity well one must study in the individual the faculties that serve him to exercise it, the motives by which it is decided and the general conditions in which it develops." Many of the ideas of Spanish America about man and his voluntary activity are contrary to the new circumstance in which democracy has placed it, and they must be rectified so that the bits that emerge from these ideas might be more appropriate to our present mode of being. We have partly taken on this arduous task, writing for elementary schools our *Book of Gold,* which is intended to propagate exact ideas on the intelligent being, his activity, and his moral faculties, just as on his general relationships. [Lastarria's note.]

we accept European traditions blindly; if we continue the errors and prejudices bequeathed to us by the nation that has been the most backward of all Christian nations ever since it was converted into the *last bastion of uniformity,* of despotism and pagan ideas on the organization of society and the state; if we transplant to America precisely and without reflection the dominant historical, political, and moral views of European societies—views that could be called official, because they cannot be separated from the dominant principles of order, and that, when they rise above prejudices, are rejected or condemned, or, at the least, scorned as a utopia or a heresy; such blind acceptance is to thwart our reform, to hold it back, leading it astray from its natural course.

Let us teach history, philosophy, morality, law, the political sciences, not under the inspirations of the dogma of force, of the dogma of Latin monarchy, of the *imperium unum* that rules conscience and life in Europe, but rather under those of the new dogma of democracy, which is that of the future—which is our credo, which is the mode of being conferred on us by the sway of circumstances and conditions that produced and consummated that revolution of 1810, the greatest event of all centuries after Christianity.

This is not to deny the advances of European knowledge nor try to eliminate them in order to start out anew on that painful and long road that the intellect has traveled in the Old World to arrive at its present place. No, since 1842 we have said to the youth of our fatherland, and we have constantly repeated, that we must and can benefit from the experience of the centuries; that we must use European knowledge and make it our own; that Europe offers it to us completely finished; that we have only to learn it—but in order to adapt; to imitate, but not blindly, not forgetting that we are above all Americans, that is to say, democrats and, therefore, obligated to develop our life and prepare our future as such, and in no way destined to continue here the European life that has conditions diametrically opposed to ours.

In history, for example, Europe honors heroes of force, the scourges of justice and liberty, and presents as lofty examples of beneficial social transcendence events whose only outcome was to thwart and deform the development of humanity's aims.

Let us leave it to Europe to sanctify Caesar and be enraptured by admiration for Napoleon. "Tell me the names you honored in the past," exclaims Laboulaye; "I will tell you the vices or virtues you have in your heart."[33]

We must have other heroes; for us the events of lofty example and the lessons of history must have another character. In philosophy, in morality, in law, in the political sciences, Europe leaves all lofty conceptions of truth in the sphere of the ideal, in the category of the utopian, and it accepts as practical and necessary only those doctrines that adapt themselves to the official dogma and to the prejudices that serve as the basis for the domination of the false civilization by which the absolute state, dominator of social life, endures.

---

33. Édouard René Lefèvre de Laboulaye (1811–1883), French jurist.

In Spanish America those sciences must not be adulterated with the events and foolishness by which Europe lives; they must teach the truth that in Europe is scorned as unattainable; they must be emancipated from official conventions and dogmas; and, above all, they must strive to disseminate the new element of American life—to teach and realize in practice the great principle that is completely dominant in Anglo-American life and makes democracy there a reality, a natural mode of being, to wit: *"That Providence has given to every human being the degree of reason necessary to direct himself in the affairs which interest him exclusively—such is the grand maxim,"* says Tocqueville, *"upon which civil and political society rests in the United States. The father of a family applies it to his children, the master to his servants; the township to its officers; the province to its townships; the State to the provinces, the Union to the States."* [34]

This maxim, extended to the nation as a whole, comes to be the doctrine of the sovereignty of the people, and therefore this sovereignty ceases to be an isolated doctrine, unattached to the habits and the sum total of dominant ideas, and, on the contrary, one must see it as the final link in a chain of opinions that wraps around the entire Anglo-American world.

So, then, whenever we use European knowledge in our American sense, we will serve our reform well, and the triumph of our democratic civilization will make our antagonism with Europe as obvious as is that which exists today between Europe and Anglo-American democracy.

For this antagonism exists and compels us to establish our life and practices, our interests and rights, on different principles.

• • • • •

XVI Europe and America Are at Two Opposing Extremes in Politics. American Union

In politics Europe and America are at two opposing extremes no matter how much European knowledge, industry, and individuals might become acclimated in America and assist our progress. That antagonism, which has its foundation on the ideas dominating the existence and political interests of both continents, influences the international relations of the two directly and primordially, because Europe knows neither the power nor the conditions of American life. If Europe knew them, its antagonism would show up less and would be less harmful to us, because, finally, it is true that two entities whose principles are opposed can coexist to their mutual benefit when they know each other, understand each other, and respect each other.

Can this normal and necessary situation disappear with the speed required by the interests of humanity and the generous aspirations of many noble souls in

---

34. Alexis de Tocqueville, *Democracy in America*, translated by Henry Reeve, Ch. XVIII, Part IX.

Europe and America? Can it even be altered through commercial interests and the treaties that govern commerce or by the support of American governments for these interests and the European powers' claims to superiority?

Undoubtedly not, because a situation so deeply rooted is not changed by fleeting political agreements but by the slow action of time. How many years will it take for the studies that some eminent Europeans are beginning to make of conditions in American society to become generally known among European peoples and affect European governments? [. . .] How much must Americans themselves work to make themselves known among the peoples and governments of Europe, with which the Americans who—from ignorance or blindness, from egoism or treason, serve the purpose of making the spirit and domination of Europe prevail in America—have greater access, credit, and consideration because of their similarity of interests and sympathy of ideas?

And if those general efforts can only modify the situation at great cost and over the long term, can one expect the situation to change through the exchange of the ideas dominating the existence and political interests of the two worlds? For America's democratic revolution to regress would require twice the efforts—and more successful ones—than the efforts of the Roman Empire against Christianity and the efforts of Catholic powers against the Reformation. Revolutions that have their foundation in the rehabilitation and emancipation of man and society obey a natural law that no human power can block.

Such is the great providential law of humanity's progress, the fulfillment of which not even an alliance of all Europe could begin to hinder. But this fact is insufficient to prevent the attempts of monarchical interests against America, and it would be a childish illusion to depend on that fact and trust in the vain hope that European antagonism would be intimidated by the impossibility of holding back our democratic progress. Despotism is blind.

The ideas that will change, certainly, are those of European political life, because they do not conform to the law that governs the destiny of the human race. The changes and transformations in those ideas will happen slowly but visibly and clearly; and they will only become complete enough for the antagonism of the two worlds to disappear after profound revolutions and frightening social and political cataclysms, which will arise from the clash of the base and egotistic interests with the interests of the society that today is subjugated.

There are some facts that must be accepted as they are; there are unavoidable situations that cannot be modified by evasive expedients nor by incidental interests that advise a policy as ephemeral as they themselves are. American governments must accept their situation as it is and deal with it as the conditions of life and the progress of their societies, their sovereignty, and their independence require. To attempt the opposite, to abide by the demands of European policy in America, would be to serve the interests opposed to the Americans that such a policy represents.

This is the reason why American governments must establish, in a general congress or in partial treaties, the principles that should form the code of their mutual relationships, as an entity characterized by special circumstances that

distinguish it from every other political entity. With these principles established, a necessary consequence of their definition would also be to designate
the respective positions and duties each member of that American political
entity must respect should one of them become a victim of European antagonism—that is to say, of the opposing interests that the European entity can
assert against American interests, whether all the European powers act in con-
junction or only some of them.

Setting aside the profound difference that exists between American and European populations, [. . .] one cannot deny that the Spanish American nations, by
their familial characteristics, by their history, by their future, and by their institutions, form among themselves a true political entity, which, without doubt,
has a strong link with Anglo-American society in all those features, although the
familial characteristics might be different. This fact has been known and
accepted by all American republics and elevated to the category of a political
dogma since the time when, forty years ago, the United States proclaimed and
authorized it as a legal policy, the Monroe Doctrine.[35]

This fact has always been proclaimed in an official way and has served as the
basis for countless agreements and political negotiations. Chile's government,
which has asserted it constantly in continental politics, expressed it also in discussing with the Spanish representative the questions raised regarding "restoration" after Spain's occupation of the Chinchas. "The American republics of
Spanish origin form, in the great community of civilized nations, a group of
states united by close and special ties," it stated.[36] "A common language, a common race, identical forms of government, uniform religious beliefs and practices, multiple similar interests, special geographic conditions, common efforts
to win a national and independent existence—such are the principal features
that distinguish the Spanish American family. Each of the members that makes
it up sees its own successful progress, security, and independence as more or less
linked to the fate of the others. Such a community of destinies has formed a natural alliance among them, creating reciprocal rights and duties that stamp their
mutual relationships with a particular character. The external dangers that might
threaten some of them in their independence or security must not be a matter of
indifference to any of the others. In such complications, all of them must take an
interest arising from their own and the common concern. This interest will be
the more intense, the more legitimate and well founded their immediate proximity makes it. The ideas expressed here are so widely accepted in America that
they have become commonplaces. I would believe myself, then, excused from
reminding you of them, did I not feel obliged to do so by the surprise Your

---

35. The Monroe Doctrine proclaimed that European powers should neither colonize nor
interfere in the politics of the Americas. It was issued by President James Monroe in 1823 and
stated that any European invasion of the Americas would be viewed by the United States as an
action hostile to itself.

36. Note from Sr.[Álvaro] Covarrubias, minister of foreign relations of Chile, to the Spanish
minister, 28 May 1864. [Lastarria's note].

Excellency seems to show for the explanations requested in my earlier communications regarding the events of Chinchas. 'My government,' Your Excellency says, 'is unaware that Chile's government is exercising a protectorate over Peru, nor that it has any kind of public or private treaty of offensive and defensive alliance with Peru.' No protectorate exists, no offensive or defensive treaty of alliance exists between Chile and Peru; but a perfect and inalienable right does exist—namely, that of *self-defense,* which permits a state to intervene in the affairs of its neighbors, which binds nations together—as has happened more than once in Europe—to maintain their political balance, and which authorizes America, and Chile in particular, to stand guard over the territorial integrity and sovereignty of Peru."

What a splendid manifestation of the natural alliance that in fact exists among the American republics! All the peoples, all the governments sense and recognize it, and none of those dangers that have their origin and their motive in the antagonism of European interests against America has ever appeared, without at the same time there having also burst forth a feeling of community and intimacy among the members that constitute the American political entity.

This undeniable fact precisely describes the object and limits of that manifest community; it is therefore useless and futile not to acknowledge it or to object to it on the pretext that an alliance based on it might find a false and harmful application if some European nation, in defense of its offended rights and authorized by international law, were to start a war against an American republic that did otherwise satisfy the just demands made on it.

This situation stands outside the natural American alliance, and such a possibility cannot be the basis for a rational argument, either against the existence of the American political entity or in denial of the antagonism that, for obvious reasons and undeniable interests, Europe has against that entity.

Francisco Bilbao
(Chile)

Francisco Bilbao Barquín (1823–1865) is among the fieriest of all Latin American writers. In his brief life, much of it spent in exile, he participated in some of Chile's more liberal political movements.

Bilbao was born to Rafael Bilbao Beyner and Mercedes Barquín, whose circumstances were modest. His father advocated liberal republican views, based primarily in the thought of Rousseau, and held to a non-institutional form of Christianity, opposed to the hierarchy of the Catholic Church. His views came to the attention of the government, which exiled the family to Lima, Peru, in 1834, when Francisco was eleven. In Lima, the young Francisco studied astronomy, the physical sciences, and music. His father insisted he learn a trade, carpentry, and commit portions of the Gospel of John and Rousseau's *Social Contract* to memory; one sees features of both in his mature writing. When the family returned to Santiago in 1839, Francisco matriculated at the Instituto Nacional, where he came under the influence of Andrés Bello and José Victorino Lastarria. In 1844, Bilbao himself came to the attention of the Church and the government when he published "Sociabilidad Chilena" (translated as "Chilean Sociability") in Lastarria's literary journal *El Crepúsculo*. For his views on religion in this work, he was expelled from the Instituto Nacional, without possibility of completing his degree, and subsequently exiled. But the work, selections from which follow, became a benchmark document in Latin American intellectual life.

During a six-year exile in Europe, Bilbao studied at the Collège de France with Edgar Quinet and Jules Michelet, among others. He traveled throughout Europe and Africa, concentrating on understanding the plight of the dispossessed and those dominated by colonialism. With the political revolutions of 1848 in Europe, Bilbao returned to Chile.

There he found work in the Office of Statistics on the one hand and seems, on the other, immediately to have taken up his political activism. Within two months of his return, with other Chilean political dissidents, he founded La Sociedad de la Igualdad and the literary magazine, *El Amigo del Pueblo,* which opposed Manuel Montt's government and the Catholic clergy. The Sociedad had as its foundation the recognition of reason as the supreme authority and the sovereignty of the people as the only proper political foundation. Moral life was constituted by universal love and brotherhood. At its height, the Sociedad claimed three thousand members.

Conflict between Bilbao and the government and ecclesiastical establishment intensified from this point on. The government undertook a systematic campaign against members of the Sociedad, finally declaring it illegal. At the same time, the Chilean Catholic Church excommunicated Bilbao for his criticism of Catholic dogma in his *Boletines del Espíritu*. Finally, on April 20, 1851, partisans of the Sociedad, with Bilbao at their head, mounted a riot that controlled some of Santiago's principal streets, but government forces overcame them. Bilbao spent the next three months in hiding in Valparaíso, finally leaving for Peru in July. He was never to return to his homeland.

In Peru he became involved in politics and criticized the local clergy, which led to his persecution, from which he had to seek asylum in the French embassy. After three months and despite promising not to engage in political activity, he was at it again, participating in 1854 in a coup headed by General Ramón Castilla, who took control of the capital in 1855. Bilbao soon came into conflict with the new Peruvian authorities, accusing them in his pamphlet, *El Gobierno de la Libertad* (1855), of acting unconstitutionally. The government asked him to leave and he returned to Europe. There he wrote a number of essays addressing the political unity of Latin America based on the community of social interests of its countries. His *Movimiento social de los pueblos de la América: Idea de un congreso federal de las repúblicas* appeared in 1856. This work draws a firm distinction between "nuestra América," that is, South America, and the United States, which Bilbao already perceived as expansionist.

In 1857 Bilbao settled in Buenos Aires, undertaking at the behest of Justo José Urquiza, president of the Argentine Federation, the editorship of *El Nacional Argentino,* in which Bilbao supported the battle of the Argentine provinces against Buenos Aires for control of the government. Urquiza soon found Bilbao's positions too radical and relieved him of his charge.

The Spanish Crown's annexation in 1861 of the Dominican Republic and France's 1862 invasion of Mexico caught Bilbao off guard, but he quickly undertook denunciation of European despotism and political expansion in *América en peligro,* published in 1862.

Further Reading

Bilbao, Francisco. *Obras completas.* Edited by Pedro Pablo Figueroa. 4 vols. Santiago: Impr. de "El Correo," 1897–1898.

Cruz, Pedro Nolasco. *Bilbao y Lastarria.* Santiago: Editorial Difusión Chilena, 1944.

Jalif de Bertranou, Clara Alicia. *Francisco Bilbao y la experiencia libertaria de América: la propuesta de una filosofía Americana.* Mendoza, Argentina: EDIUNC, 2003.

Lipp, Solomon. *Three Chilean Thinkers.* Waterloo, Ont.: McGill University, 1975.

López Muñoz, Ricardo. *La salvación de la América: Francisco Bilbao y la intervención Francesa en México.* Mexico D.F.: Centro de Investigación Científica Ing. Jorge L. Tamayo, 1995.

Varona, Alberto J., *Francisco Bilbao, revolucionario de América: Vida y pensamiento. Estudio de sus ensayos y trabajos periodísticos.* Panama: Ediciones Excelsior, 1973.

Chilean Sociability (1844)

Our Past

> *A cry was heard at Ramah,*
> *Sobbing and loud lamentation*
> Matthew 2:18

Our past is Spain.

Spain is the Middle Ages. The Middle Ages were made up, in soul and body, of Catholicism and feudalism. Let us examine them separately. That society called feudal, made up of the remnants of Roman civilization, idealized by the Catholic religion, and renewed by the barbarian's distinctive practices, forms the nucleus, the knot that ties the ancient world to the modern world. Rome leaves her legislation, industry, and mythology; Catholicism—Scholasticism, the oriental myths with the coloring of revelation but with a notable perfection; the barbarians—the spontaneity of their beliefs and their glorification of individuality. Reflection, faith, spontaneity; Rome, Orient, the barbarians—there we have the elements. They clash, blood runs, but the barbarian-become-Catholic triumphed. Time unfolds, the system settles in, Catholicism rules, the barbarian does not completely abdicate his distinctiveness, and the Middle Ages rise from the ruins of the invasion, from the blood of so many years of combat.

There we have that society, that civilization secured in its castles, its cloisters, to resist the torrent of the world that collapses around it. True society, because it was one society, because it had a creed that nourished and gave it that distinctiveness so very distinctive; society of soul and body from this point of view. That is to say, Catholicism and feudalism, spirit and land, religion and politics—let us analyze the two phases separately.[1]

. . . We have examined the two elements that made up the Middle Ages. Spain, we said, is the Middle Ages, and we came from the Middle Ages of Spain. Let us look at the unique character that it had in Spain in order to see the character it had among us.

The Middle Ages fulfilled itself in Spain, that is to say, it developed most fully there. The isolation of Spain because of racial differences, tradition, climate, national pride heightened by traditions and differences from other peoples; the exclusivism that this produces as to the importance of all things foreign, the strengthening of its Catholic-feudal beliefs because of the opposition to African civilization; the union of all classes to support Spain's individuality, accosted in land and spirit; conquistadors and Mohammedans—here we have the causes of the complete development and embodiment of Spanish beliefs. Those beliefs were Catholic-feudal. They gained strength for reasons that we have stated, the importance, the strength, the absolutism, that characterized the Catholic domination of Spain.

---

1. In sections II and most of III Bilbao examines the land and spirit of Spain's Middle Ages.

America belonged to Spain and Spain imposed its seal on America; here we have our Spanish past on American soil. Here we come to Chile.

The Middle Ages was a true society because it had unity of beliefs. The idea dominates over form. The ideas of a people branch out because the idea is first in all forms that give rise to life. Thus we see the unity of faith, tradition, authority dominate and form the true character of our society.

Let us start with the family.

Indissoluble marriage.

Adultery was frightening. Marriage ties were established by family relations, requiring families of the same class. The state of lovers, that is to say, the state of spontaneity and liberty of the heart, was persecuted. Communication between the sexes arouses inclinations, uncovers qualities, and produces *new* distinctive relations or circumstances that cannot exist from the point of view of authority—so they must be prohibited. Authority and tradition weaken with innovations; hence, the aversion to the new, to *fashion,* and the hatred of whatever promotes it, and that is why one must live withdrawn and alone. Misanthropic isolation. The door to the street closes early and at the dinner hour. In the evening the rosary is prayed. Social visits, *communication,* must be declined except with persons one knows very well; sociability does not exist—neither new people nor strangers are admitted. The young woman's passion must be quieted. Heightened passion is the instrument of instinctive revolution. She is brought to the church, she is dressed in black, in the street her face is covered, she is prevented from greeting, from glancing to the side. She is made to kneel, she must mortify her flesh, and, what is more, the confessor examines her conscience and imposes his unappealable authority on her. The chorus of old women intones the litany of the danger of fashion, of contact, of the social call, of clothes, of looks, and of words. The monastic life, the stupid mysticism of physical suffering, is regarded as agreeable to the Divinity. This is the young woman. The man, although too proud to submit to such slavery, must nevertheless bear its weight. Woe to the young man if he goes home late, if amorous words are heard from him; poor him, if he is caught reading some book that they designate as prohibited, finally, if he strolls, dances, falls in love. The father's whip or *eternal* damnation are the curses! There is no reasoning between father and son. After his daily work, he will go to pray the rosary, to the *stations of the cross,* to the school of Christ, or to hear told the stories of witches, of spirits and purgatories. Imagine the young man of robust constitution, well-fed, impetuous imagination, with some impressions and under the weight of that mountain of worries! Imagine the drama of what he would feel stirring inside him; but we are cold chroniclers.

There we have the family. Education consists of six or eight years of Latin (Lord have mercy), some four of scholastic philosophy, and as many more of theology. If they go beyond the four fundamental principles of arithmetic, it is a lot; if they know what there is on the other side of the Andes, if they know that we move around the sun, it is a lot. The monks and clerics are teachers, and blows, crude insults, or the whip are the means of correction. Observe human dignity!

As men are in the political family called society, so they are in the family. Authority is power, and power is authority. The king is sent by God (*rex gratia Dei*), he is God's arm, and the pope the divine intelligence on earth. So—slaves of the governor; the governor, of the king; and the king, of the pope. Man includes nothing beyond this circle. God willed it, "His will be done!" is the final word on questions of liberty. So there are neither citizens nor people. There are slaves and a flock of sheep.

This is the political-monarchical viewpoint. Let us examine the organization at the base of civil society, that is to say, property, and we will discover Chilean feudalism.

The lack of communication and of new needs, the lack of capital shareholdings, the lack of teaching and of the need for artistry, the lack of trade because of the oppressive and exclusionary system, the coercive system, and the exaction of *tithes* from the work of the poor—these things prevent the rise of a middle class that would pave the way for liberty, as did the bourgeoisie in Europe.

The rich man owns property as did the barbarian of the conquest—by force. The land owner, the hacienda owner, owns land either under protection of the monarch by his monarchical power—that is to say, to the most enslaved and to the one who rules most despotically, the greatest the reward—or by original occupation through the conquest. The rest of the people are the rabble, the unwashed, the vile, who must serve, for there were *two* Adams (exaltation of pride). Eternal separation—master and servant, rich and poor, proud and humble, nobles and peasants. With neither intellectual nor physical industry, no one will be able to rise except the rich, and as the rich are the land owners and the land owners are the aristocrats, it follows that the ruling class has an interest in monarchical-feudal organization. The rich man or the property owner, so that there might be logic in privilege and caste, must be noble; if he is not, the monarch will ennoble him, selling the titles of count or marquess for cash, or bestowing them as gifts on his favorite subjects. The poor man needs to eat and looks for work. Work can come only from those who have industry or capital. Industry or capital are the land—so the hacienda owners determine who works, whether wages rise or fall. Wealth or privilege can go on for some time without the work of the poor. But hunger does not allow for waiting—so the rich man determines the conditions of salary—and here we have feudal despotism. Intellectual bread—the sermon—makes the unfortunate resign themselves and justifies the established order. *Theft* is defined as taking away from another what that person *possesses,* without considering the despotism of the rich. Immediately the tax necessary for maintaining worship falls on the poor.

> The priest knows not how to plow
> Nor how to yoke an ox,
> But by his very own law
> Without having to sow he reaps.

When he goes out for a stroll,
He exerts himself little or not;
His income guaranteed,
He sits back and takes his ease.
Going through life with no cares,
No one earns more than the priest.

Here we have the expressive language of the common person, primal literature, the expressive language of despotism. The slavery we have analyzed was logical. Its origins were divine institutions. Absolute monarchy, absolute property, absolute authority of the clergy. The clergy fended off *theft* and sanctioned disproportionate *possession,* acquired and preserved without *work.* In all these things, we see Catholic unity, the society of the Middle Ages. Examine any relationship. See the humiliation of the common person, his servility, his lack of personality. Domestic service—it is not a contract. The servant or serf cannot defend his rights; if he defends them by force or by insult, he commits a crime, a *rebellion.* How could he prosecute his master before the law? The judge has no jurisdiction over such a claim. The *testimony* of the poor man has no value; he is not a person. If he avenges himself personally, the whip, prison, confound him. If the master insults him, he bears the insult; the poor man has no honor. Civility, that human treatment without differentiating among persons, does not exist for the common man. He is made to get out of the way on the road, he is made to take off his hat in the street to speak, and "your grace," "my master" are the only words of his that are heard. Slavery, degradation, here we have the common man! Here we have the past.

God grant that our lines (written with focused indignation) transform themselves into the eternal epitaph of that past and lock away forever the eternal curse that dashes human dignity, so long degraded. Let us leave that past, that underworld of crimes, that inferno of sorrows; let us go out into the daylight, let us bathe our faces in the light of the breaking dawn, and let us praise the Divinity, for we are going to speak of revolution.

Revolution

Who goes there?—The fatherland
Who are you?—A citizen

Glory to God!

Who, before sketching revolution, does not first attempt to sing a hymn to Divinity?—Because it is true, God exists. And it is in these moments of exaltation for the glories of humanity; in these volcanic moments that entrance us when we recognize human dignity; in these moments when we sense the inadequacy of our expressive language, of our substance, of our *self,* to express and sustain the poetic torrent that engulfs us; in these moments when we would be attempting suicide because we know that we would be diving headlong into the infinite that we had foretold—it is then that we acknowledge as living that Creator of so great a humanity, of a being so sublime as the man of liberty. It is then that, in prostrating ourselves before the greatest of His creations, we genuinely prostrate ourselves before His true altar by prostrating ourselves before His greatest creation—and it is then that we would like to kick the earth with contempt, and so raise ourselves up to the mansion of time and of space.

But let us contain our heart's impulses, let us repress the rumor of victory, and let us examine the field.

Our past, as we have said, has come out of the *Middle Ages,* out of Spain. Our revolution, with past or future, has come out of the *new* age, out of Europe. The new age broke out in France; let us then link our revolutionary thinking to French thinking of the revolution.

That society, organized under the Catholic creed, dominated. Its life was uniform; its course was systematized. It knew from whence it came, where it was, where it was going. Paradise was its cradle, sin the origin of all its ills, hope or the heavens the certain end, the final aspiration, the crown of life. All doubts, all problems, were answered. Turn to the text with faith in your eyes, and you will see the truth. If you have sorrows, the priest consoles you. All the family's despotism, all political and religious despotism is nothing. This world is one of misery; the will of God be done on earth as in heaven. The consequence was great, for all the power of the individual, his passions, were glorified in his sufferings. What does it matter that there be some secret indignation in the back of one's mind? The world is tranquil, what more do you want? Do you not see how sweetly he bears the cross of his sorrows? Do you not see the flock that walk silently to the corral that we have for it? Oh magnificent harmony of servile obedience! Let us praise this state of silence and tranquility—what more do you want, you evil spirits?

There we have, then, in that faith, the circle of fire that the cherub guards with its terrifying sword, there we have the Herculean pillars of thought—there we have the Rubicon of Catholicism, of the Middle Ages.[2]

But will there be no genius, no Columbus, no Caesar of thought to cross it?

In the middle of solitary tribulations, some spirits harbor in their breast all the power of individual conscience. They rise to the contemplation of the laws of nature, perceive divine harmony, and then the human contrast revolutionized them. They conceived, through the grandeur of the love that animated them, the love of the God that created them, and they wondered—Does God, or what is the same, infinite love, reign over this spectacle of tears? Is God—who has given us the unsubduable countenance of liberty, placing on it the seal of his

---

2. The Pillars of Hercules were the promontories flanking the entrance to the Strait of Gibraltar, considered the farthest end of the navigable world. The Rubicon was a small river in northern Italy that marked the northern boundary of the ancient Roman heartland. Julius Caesar led his army across the Rubicon in 49 BC, flouting long-established law and making armed conflict inevitable.

noble pride—is God gratified by seeing the priest of his worship or the leader of men tread on that liberty?

Does God, who has given us a brain where infinity can fit, authorize, then, those in possession of his law to fit in only so much as they want? Impossible! Great God, you have not authorized such things. You have not given man the wings of genius only to place into his hands the sword to cut them off! You have not wanted the adoration of slaves—this would be unworthy—but rather the fierce adoration of him who recognizes and praises you on his own account. You have not urged him on with your breath so that in your name man might stop him.

You have not placed in his breast the magnet of your love so that man might bind him with chains. You do not reveal yourself to him radiant and clear in nature, for him to be transported to adore you in another mansion as limited as is man. Finally, you do not place over his majestic head any roof but the heavens...............There we have the doubt that reveals itself, the germ of revolution; there we have the dawning of liberty—thought in search of its object, that is to say, of nature and God.

Thought evolves—Abelard, Luther, Descartes, and most lately Voltaire, Rousseau, etc.,[3] betake themselves to the sacred ark,[4] offer it the worship of their life in the temple of their intellects, until the prophets of the new law assume the mantel of the tribune,[5] put their lips to the bugle of the printing press, and the worship became popular.........Doubt becomes incarnate, the system of beliefs falls to the floor, human dignity raises itself. The individual must question in order to believe.

To question is to deny faith, to submit oneself to the rule of individual reason. To submit oneself to reason is to have faith in oneself, to have confidence in one's strength; it is the exaltation of the *human self,* voluntary and intelligent, subjective and objective, that is to say, individual and social, particular and general, human and divine, possessing in its psychological makeup the foundation of universal harmony. The individual system released, the individual frees himself from the old system, from the old foundation of belief and synthesis, but he did not isolate himself in misanthropic egoism, but rather he tries to rest the social bond on another foundation and in another system of relationships that would let in facts that the Catholic synthesis set aside. The new spirit emerged

---

3. Peter Abelard (1079–1142), medieval logician who focused on moral issues. Martin Luther (1483–1546), German theologian, Augustinian monk, and ecclesiastical reformer whose teaching inspired the Reformation. René Descartes (1596–1650), progenitor of modern subjectivism. Voltaire, pen name for François-Marie Arouet (1694–1778), French Enlightenment writer, essayist, deist, and philosopher. Jean-Jacques Rousseau (1712–1778), formulator of the French social contract theory who made liberty an object of almost universal aspiration.

4. Ark of the Covenant, the sacred wooden chest of the Hebrews, representative of the Divine and that in which scripture was kept.

5. One of the officers of ancient Rome, whose office is closely associated with the struggle of the lower class against the upper class to achieve a more equitable position in the state.

from the old era to raise a new one—greater, more majestic, worthy of God's being, and of man's being, who appreciated recognizing absolute liberty of thought as the only means of communicating legitimately with God. The foundations of the structure are still being debated, all the thinkers run to place their stone. As with the old synthesis—that is to say, the unified mass of beliefs about man, his origin, his essence, his purpose, his relationships and duties—the assault was on its principles of faith and tradition, it is clear that all the branches of the system would feel the quaking that shook its foundations. We thus see that in their philosophical elaboration, the works diverge. Some attack a relation, an obligation, a principle; others, the foundation of faith; others, the agreement between the Hebraic tradition and the teachings of geological science. By this we see that the elaboration is huge, that the works are encyclopedic, and that they all have in common the desire to give human beliefs a scientific foundation. Majestic sight! Gigantic work! Babel of genius! Eighteenth century!—humanitarian battle that joins the noise of the battering ram that destroys with the horrible groans of those being buried. You have placed on liberty the Gothic weight of so many centuries, but you do not see the unhappy woman who, with a black veil over her face, is paying close attention to the unknown voice that says to her, *The hour of mystery has struck! The hour of the deceitful symbol has sounded. Man has followed the course of the river and has seen his origin; he has gone up to the summit of the mountain and has left the cloud beneath his feet.*

Bolt of lightning, divine flash of fire, liberty shakes its head. It strikes the earth, the universe trembles, the eighteenth century arises. . . . Mortals! Fall to your knees, receive the baptism of the new law! . . . But the work is not finished. The poor are raised up; the political, religious power, the feudal power—the positive power, in a word—all unite to stifle innovation and nail the new word once again to a cross. The prisons fill, the aristocracy despairs and governs despotically, the Inquisition terrifies, the denunciations are filed, the Jesuitical malevolence corrodes. And the enemy, where is he? Which is the weapon so terrible that one wants to blunt it? . . . Look at that man of the people who walks sullenly; observe the storms that his countenance reveals; look at the ferocity that his gaze casts. That is the enemy, that person carries the destructive weapon called, "The beginning of wisdom is knowing how to doubt." There we have his battering ram; move to one side, let him go by, you men of the black robe, you nobles burdened with pomp. Ah! You insult him, you spit in his face; you call him philosopher, heretic, common tradesman. Fine, he accepts the affront, but he shows you a tomb. At the time, you did not see it, but at the appointed hour you felt it.

The earthquake shook civilization to its roots and all its branches also shook. We, entwined, as we have said, with Europe's past, also felt that explosion. Some Americans went to study and travel in Europe, some communication had begun through the upheaval of Spain, invaded by the revolution; a few hidden books filtered in; the splendor of the French renewal was too radiant to keep out every last bit of its light. The revolution germinated among us and exploded at the prudent time. The rest we know; let us proceed to the consequences.

Chile

Spread your mantle, flag of my country! Blaze in our mountains; wave in the ocean's breeze, reflecting the rays of the sun when you are displayed in the purity of Chile's blue! Spread your mantle, which is the book of our fatherland. Let your children read you and make known the great mysteries that you encompass.

Glory to you, Tricolor!

Our revolution is the violent change of the former organization and synthesis to replace them with the indefinite but true synthesis that modern philosophy promulgates. Our revolution was not insularly political, insularly industrial, insulated from the progress of humanity, but rather, it was a *sedibus imis*,[6] from the root—from the unity that existed—with all its ramifications. Our revolution, finally, is the destruction of the past synthesis and the enthroning of the modern synthesis. It was not a partial event, not solely analytical, but rather complete and synthetic, even vaguely perceiving the actualization of future problems. But the work of establishing the new system of beliefs—the spiritual bread that needed to be given to the people after the destruction of the old system of beliefs—has not yet been able to work itself out in a satisfactory way. The reason is this.

The solutions necessary for a society to know what it is, from whence it came, where it is going, were provided by the faith. With the faith destroyed, we must answer those questions scientifically, that is to say, rationally. The pertinent science, which had occupied itself so exclusively with the critique of the past, could not, did not have the opportunity to occupy itself in such a way. To put in doubt a past system of belief is simply a huge task. So let us then leave scientific activity—the compilation of all human knowledge—to prepare for the coming of the future Messiah, that is to say, of the future system, of the future synthesis, of the future genesis, of the future testament, and, finally, the future apocalypse. For now, our revolutionaries, armed solely with critical philosophy, have found themselves with a burden on their hands that they did not know where to set down. In such cases, human impotence turns to look at the past and settles the sacred burden on the ruins of the very pillar that has been destroyed. Terrible mistake. This is what is known as reaction, that is to say, counterrevolution. This is what has happened among us. Let us pause for a minute.

Our revolution was reflective in its instigators and spontaneous in the people. The reflective revolution was skepticism in new beliefs, but as it involved a limited number of individuals—*educated* ones—it could do without the new beliefs. The only certitude they had was in the liberty they had won and their knowledge of the falsehood of past beliefs. They had, one might say, unity of skepticism, because of which all beliefs branching off from the destroyed unity were similarly overturned. But the people, who had embraced the new cause with all the purity of inspiration, with all the warmth of genuine enthusiasm; the people, who had felt only the political excitement, the conquest of civic rights; the people saw in

---

6. Virgil, *Aeneid*, Book 1, line 84, "from the deepest seat."

political liberty only an isolated fact, separated from all the other matters that the reflective revolution had overturned, and the people remained with the old.

The men who led the reflective revolution, finding themselves impotent to organize the beliefs logically related to political liberty, turned to reaction in religion and politics on the people's behalf. Thus, among many peoples we find constitutional despotism and the encouragement of sermons. Thus, at the outset, were almost all American governments. Thus, those military capabilities fell through an inability to organize society logically. Thus fell Bolívar in Colombia and O'Higgins in Chile.[7] They became reactionaries in organization when the heat of the republican war was still making itself felt. On the other hand, those governments also fell, which, after the spirits of the revolutionary people had cooled, tried to pass reforms in separate acts rather than in the logical unity of the revolution. What was the high point of the revolution of the eighteenth century and of the American revolution? The liberty of man; the equality of the citizen. The individual who had reclaimed all his rights and every implementation of these rights. The equality of man's origins, of his rights, and of his purposes was recognized. As a result, the conditions necessary to fulfill these equalities were logically due to men. The individual, as man in general, demands liberty of thought, from which is born liberty of worship. The individual, as *free spirit*, exposed to good and evil, needs *education* to know what is good. The individual, the *human self*, body and soul, needs *property* to fulfill his purpose on earth. He needs property to develop his intellectual life, his physical life, and the lives of his children. As a result, the conditions necessary to acquire it and to acquire it fully are due him. From this arises the destruction of privilege, of feudal property, and the raising of wages as human dignity soars.

These are, then, the high points of the revolution. If the governments had understood that the development of equality was the sacred testament of the revolution, that equality is historical destiny in its development, they would not have perished. By standing firmly on the *land* and by raising the glorious countenances of heroes, the people would have upheld the governments because they would have upheld themselves. And then, with legitimate authority, from the glory with which they entrance, from the justice with which they legislate, the governments would have been able to establish, through general education, the complete renewal of the people, who had remained old in their beliefs. If they did not have a complete system to give the people, they should have given them the glorification of the indomitable will and knowledge of the rest of the individuals as so many other indomitable wills—that is to say, they should have introduced them to the equality of liberty.

And here we have the unmistakable point of departure, the touchstone for all human systems, the *idea* of social existence, as certain as the idea that bodies occupy space.

---

7. Bernardo O'Higgins (1778–1842), liberator of Chile, became supreme director of the country for six years. He resigned under pressure in January, 1823.

The equality of liberty.

Here we have the Paradise from which we have been banished; here we have the infinity of human grandeur; here we have the kingdom of God on earth.

The equality of liberty is the universal religion; it is the government of humanity; it is the future unity.

Liberty is infinite,[8] it is the fulfillment and apex of human creation; so equality, which has no limit other than liberty itself, is the connection, the development of understanding, the happiness of the absolute good.

From this we will derive the theory that societies and governments should hold.

Who are those men in the governments that we have had and still have, the ones who boast of being wise in guiding society? Who boast of possessing the secret of happiness, while preserving the old traditions, respecting the organization of property? Who shun the noble development of men, while fueling beliefs destroyed by the revolution and governing the country by laws inferior to the enlightenment, the circumstances of the people who are governed?

Shall we say that our governors are leaders organized for society when they accept both traditions and reforms, both good and evil?

Let us take a rapid look at the logic of our men in the spirit and body of Chile, in the *Chilean self.*

We speak from the height of our revolutionary *point of view.*

Either we proceed from the revolution or not.

If we proceed from it, our duty is to finish it; if not, our duty is to define what we are and what our tradition as a nation is. The governments have proceeded either from the heart of revolution, in which case their existence is legitimate, or not, in which case, they are not recognizable as authorities for revolutionary people. This is the basis on which we can assess governments in evaluating Chile's new life. We have had two civil revolutions.

We have had, consequently, two classes of government. Government in the republican tradition, that is to say, revolutionary, and government in the tradition of the old order.[9]

• • • • •

---

8. *La libertad es infinita.* This proposition is not true except as a conception of the *idea* "liberty," which is identified as the law. Liberty as law—the law as the embodiment of the power of freedom: the autonomy, autocracy, and nomocracy [self-governance] of a free being. [Note to the third edition; Pedro Pablo Figueroa, 3rd edition, Santiago, 1897.]

9. What follows is a discussion of the presidencies of Bernardo O'Higgins (1778–1842) and Francisco Antonio Pinto Díaz (1785–1858), which Bilbao sees as governments in the revolutionary tradition. O'Higgins failed because he tried to reform only one aspect of the old order and because in the face of the peoples' protests he became despotic. Bilbao describes Pinto's government as having "all the elements that modern republicanism had produced."

But let us take off the wreath of flowers, let us veil our faces, let us uproot happiness from our hearts because we are about to step inside the mansion of shadowy silence.

There was peace, there was prosperity, there was liberty, but all those men favored by the now shattered privilege, all those men of the old education, all those men who fell into insignificance after the fall of the order that had made them great, all the ignorant people—the Spanish indigenous element that cannot in its pride put up with innovation in beliefs, in forms of government, in liberal customs in the public and private sphere—chafed at the bit in the silence of their rage. Education invaded Spanish beliefs. The authorities supported that invasion. So, let us destroy those authorities.

The government was destroying privileges and industry. So, we privileged ones, let us destroy that government.

The political power examined and touched the *land holdings* of the supporters of the old order. So, let us, the monks and priests and privileged ones, destroy that political power.

The government is heretical, it wants to update the old beliefs of the common people; it wants to enlighten. So let us incite the old Catholic common person against enlightenment and heresy.

Let us identify the elements of the reaction that is being prepared.

The new education is the elevation of individual consciousness; it is liberty.

The destruction of privilege is equality and promotes the liberty of all to own property; it is liberty. To take away the *land-based* foundation from the upholders of the old order is to destroy their authority. To destroy the authority of the upholders of the faith is to elevate liberty.

To update the beliefs of the common people, to give them a philosophical education instead, is to give them their individual consciousness, is to make the revolution secure. To make the revolution secure is to promote liberty.

There we have the new elements. Now, the old order! Absolutist creeds, a despotism from the Middle Ages! Spain of the conquest, aristocracy of man, rejoice!

That tombstone that was thrown over you is going to fall. Grab its rubble and use it to inflict wounds. You are going to rise up, as gloomy and infernal as the mansions into which truth had cast you!

Resurrection of the Past

The horse's influence on the character of the life of any people is striking. The influence of the occupation for which the horse is necessary also has the greatest influence on the character of the inhabitants. The care of livestock, separated and scattered over mountains and plains, requires an active rider to tend it. Hunting in the Andes, even agriculture, require a rider to roam or to thresh the grains that have been sown. Riders who herd, riders who hunt, and riders searching for adventure are the principal classes of men who, among us, spend their lives on a horse.

The *guaso*,[10] who has the qualities we have noted, certainly has his most singular, most original, and most untamed character in places that are favorable to livestock breeding because of their pastures and natural shelter. In Chile, the south is more extensive, has more water, has better land for pasture, and has a better climate for man and animal; it is cold and stimulates activity; mountainous, it accustoms one to perseverance, to *separation*, and finally, to the physical development of the chest.

These influences of locale produce moral consequences. The *guaso*, racing along the crest of the mountains, breathes in independence as he rides.

The *guaso* hidden among the mountains is separated from moral communication; he is solitary, rustic. Isolation gives him pride. He always sees and has seen the same. He only knows what his parents taught him, and this is for him the end point of his intellectual work. The rest he rejects. But, know less than that? His pride does not permit it.

One sees emerge from here the traditional spirit of the horsemen who spend their lives drifting or traveling in circles. The beliefs of our *guasos* are Catholic and Spanish. These beliefs—traditional and tenacious in themselves, embodied in men whose spirit it is to conserve and who cannot, because of the life they lead, witness a variety of different sights—should lead to a complete development of isolation, of barbarism, and of conservatism. The south of Chile, the region of the indigenous element, is the one with the most obvious locales for preserving the old traditions and beliefs among the people of the horse. So the antirevolutionary, anti-liberal reaction, should emerge from there, or have among that people its most resolute supporters.

This is the theory; let us look at the facts.

Do you remember those days when all the doors to the houses of Santiago were closed and fear covered the faces of its residents?

Those days when the cannon was heard inside the gates of the capital?

Yes; the events are recent, the images are still too vividly palpable for us to have forgotten them.

Well, then, did you not see in those days of dreadful silence a multitude of men who rushed out through the streets?

Who wore the *guaso's* headband, field boots, and poncho?

Who waved the hatchet in one hand and the dagger and reins in the other?

Who had vandalism in their eyes and rabid foam at their mouths?

Who hauled away carpets, smashed furniture and clothes of the city's residents?

Who passed in groups, yelling and creating a demonic din?

Those men are the ones who have come down from the mountains and plains of the south at the call of those who glorified their fanaticism and promised

---

10. *Guaso,* the Chilean rural worker or peasant, a figure who was comparable in many parts of the country to the Argentine gaucho or the cowboy of the U.S. West.

them plunder. There we have them! See the rustic spirit in action, the ignorant savage's spiteful spirit against whatever is new and civilized.[11]

• • • • •

Let us examine the institution of the victorious order. We shall give only the most important consequences and institutions.

The reaction is supported by the old unity of beliefs. That unity was Catholicism. So all similar institutions are to be encouraged; all inherent prejudices are to be satisfied. From this emerges the return of all *properties* to the communities.[12] The establishment of the religion at an elevated and magnificent level. There is a ministry of worship, processions and feasts are carried out; a larger amount of the public treasury is dedicated to such purposes.

Free education is revolutionary. Free education is the current of thought that inevitably rushes headlong in the direction determined by gravity; in education gravity is the logic of liberty. So let us confront that logic and redirect the torrent. From this emerges the institution of the seminary, the censorship of books, limitations on studies, and their circumscribed sphere.

From this emerges the promulgation of monkish missions, the promulgation of fanatical books. The sales of novenas and mystical books are up.

The epithets "enlightened" and "heretical" are hurled at the fallen order.

Industry and trade must be coercive, that is to say, they must glorify nationalism against European perfection.

Spreading and easing the means of acquisition stimulate individual activity. The elevation of the individual is contrary to despotism's centralized organization. The establishment of a class favored by monopoly is the most active means for conserving a system of organization. So let monopolies and a restrictive system of trade be established.

Centralized power is the means of imposing the seal of the old order on provincial individualities. Provincial liberty seems to break despotic strings and to elevate individuals through public spirit. So the provincial administration must be made entirely dependent on the central one. The intendant [provincial governor] must be appointed and removed by the central government.

Spanish legislation is developing. Its barbarism can be inferred from its legal bulletins. The people are content and satisfied with the restoration of prejudices. So let us keep the people mired in prejudices and let us work on the people as we

---

11. Here Bilbao goes on to provide more detail of the 1829–1830 civil war between Liberals and Conservatives, which triggered the conservative reaction.

12. The forced sale of community land in order to spread private ownership of land was a major Liberal project in many Latin American countries in the mid-1800s. The idea was to take land away from "feudal" collective institutions and put it in the hands of individuals, but in some countries where these sales were carried out, the land went to a small number of landowners while the proceeds went to the national government, leaving peasant communities impoverished and increasing peasant support for Conservative causes.

wish. Judicial terror is excellent for submission. Punishments are not textbook lessons, corrective; that would require moral and philosophical organization.

So let us apply the whip, individual degradation, stiff fines for slander, and let us call down the condemnation of God on the *carros*.[13]

The despotic organization that has been built on top of the defeated republicanism must extinguish any resistance that might arise. From this emerges the need for extraordinary powers and the despicable budgeting of secret expenses.

The consequence was great. Enlightenment was scorned. Anyone who did not submit scrupulously to the old forms of past creeds was looked down on in public and in the salons. The monasteries become crowded, the seminary fills, the public spirit is alarmed. Individual liberties are violated, despotism foments denunciations, and manners become debased. Mutual confidence disappears, social gatherings are frowned upon, fear spreads, the isolation of egoism is disseminated. One fears giving one's opinion in public, the spirit contracts, and conspiracies erupt one after the other. Despotism raises dangers, surprises individuals, imprisons them, exiles them, and even murders them.[14] The extraordinary powers wave their omnipotent hand over the head of the citizen, and the citizen is terrified, hides, denounces and deceives, or feels its tremendous weight.

But the common people see the president taking communion and confessing. This is enough, this is a guarantee against heresy. As for the rest, what does it matter? Let the supreme will be done, let us be docile in the yoke. We have fireworks on the 18th and outings to La Pampilla.[15] We have processions, prayers and missions; what more do we want? Blessed be the government we have!

Here we have a weak, cursory, and incomplete picture of that vaunted decade that we call the resurrection of the past.

Let us swoop down on the present and on the present administration.

Is the present government a continuation of the past and consequently reactionary, or is it a continuation of the revolution?

There we have the question.[16]

• • • • •

---

13. The *carros* were prisons for those arrested by the justice [system], who were condemned to public work [note to the 3rd edition].

14. I am referring to the jury trial of *El Diablo Político*. The jury found the writer innocent, and consequently implied that the government was guilty of murder. [Note to the 3rd edition. In early 1840, Juan Nicolás Álvarez was charged with sedition and slander for his writing in *El Diablo Político* (*The Political Devil*), the liberal journal that he had founded a few months earlier. A large and supportive crowd surrounded the court, influencing the jury to find Álvarez innocent of slander, though he was fined 200 pesos for sedition and threatened with exile.]

15. 18 September 1810: the anniversary of the Chilean Revolution. Holiday celebrated by all classes and by the government. [Note to the third edition. La Pampilla de Coquimbo, a coastal town about 200 miles north of Santiago, is famous for its 18 September celebrations.]

16. What follows is a passage in which Bilbao discusses the events and elections that brought President Manuel Bulnes to power.

The forms of the past administration have been respected. No law marks the transition from a reactionary to a progressive government. The present administration has been constructed on reactionary beliefs, and we do not see the progressive character that it boasts of having taken. The immortality of a government in the history of its people consists of comprehending the highest idea that the century presents to it for actualization and actualizes it. For us the highest idea as heirs of the revolution is to complete the revolution. To complete the revolution is to support democracy in the spirit and the land, in education and in property. This work is the destruction of the authoritarian synthesis of the past and the substitution of the principles that philosophy recognizes with the seal of immortality. This work signifies the revolution. Its success would be probable but its outcome in the history of human activity is inevitable. This work of social renewal must always emerge from the philosophical legislative *representation* of the nation, that is to say, the legislator.

We lack representation capable of reorganizing a propaganda squad. So the executive power, which exercises such an important power among the new peoples, must be the leader of the revolution. Now, if the head of the executive power combines the popularity of traditions and glories, no one would be more capable than he of successfully leading the synthetic revolution among the masses. And here we have the brilliant position of the present administration, the opportunity that history sets out for it, together with the threat of losing the opportunity and jumbling it up among the multitude of those who are ignorant and incapable of immortality. You will keep the peace, you will maintain order, you will fashion a way, you will pass through the countryside, you will be saluted on the 18th, but the oblivion or anathema of history is preparing an epitaph of impotence for you. There we have the unique position of President Bulnes. If he does not understand it, pity the man who holds in his hand the torch of truth and extinguishes it because he cannot bear its brilliance.

But let us finish developing the traditional character that the administration presents.

The constitutional code that organized the republic in such a despotic, unitary fashion is the one that governs us. This prevents provincial individualities from arising and prevents life from returning to Chilean territory.

The code that legally organizes despotism still exists, destroying all the guarantees that republicanism acquired, which are the necessary forms for the security of individual rights.

The same respect for the forms of the past synthesis exists in the government. Monks are brought from Europe, and this fact alone is enough to characterize the ignorance of an administration in our time. Ecclesiastical organization exercises an influential power independent of political influence. The Catholic system reigns everywhere. The priest still collects tithes, the priest traffics in matrimonies and baptisms. The public treasury spends copiously on worship, creates bishops, archbishops. Ecclesiastical power holds an important position and the government tolerates it; the government is hypocritical. In the sphere of commerce and industry the remains of the prohibitive and privilege-based synthesis still exist. The Monopoly exists; money is taken out of circulation to form a bank. To take money out of circulation is to bog down the way. To keep it for purposes of amassing it is to lose the use of capital; it is to lose.

The interior regime of the intendants [provincial governors] is so well known that we will not pause to examine it.

Education is divided into two classes. The first very little advanced, the other quite backward. Consider what unity of civilization is being prepared. The Institute[17] fans the fire of the intellect a little bit.

The seminary and the convents keep it indoors. The somewhat less backward education is heterogeneous. There one finds the new with the old, philosophy with Catholicism, philosophical legislation with the canonical texts. But as for the unity of collegiate studies, it is a matter for another article, and we have dealt with it previously. Education there is linked to the old synthesis burdened with rituals and lacking in knowledge relative to social and humanitarian life. The old synthesis, which should be reformed, is being propagated. The books that are given to the schools are old and relate to past times. Let us say, then, whether the conservative and reactionary character of the present administration is not encapsulated in the cursory observations we have put forward. In education, in worship, in finance, and in interior governance. This means it is no more than a small program of opposition.

But the highest point, where every administration either comes to grief or receives a crown from history, remains unapproached. We are speaking of the elevation of the masses to national sovereignty, to the actualization of democracy.

There we have the great spectacle; the people, the image of the infinite, if there can be an image of it. See them there, as they come and go tranquilly, unaware of their internal power. See them there, as they fill the prisons, as they supply the gallows with fodder, as they moan in the *carros,* as they enrich the landowner, as they endure the insult; see them there, working for the priest, for the State, and for the rich; see them there, accepting the passing of days with stony stares and without the divinity of Light reflecting in their eyes. The mysterious night receives them, exhausted, and in their animal slumber, shelters them. The day breaks and the luminous sun of Chile serves only to dry the sweat of their anguished brows. . . .

The people thus, unaware of their individuality and their social position, brutalized by the work of the day and for the day, are the throng and torrent that threatens destruction of our progress on hearing the voice of sedition. The danger is visible, the abyss is palpable, and nothing rushes to fill it in. Do you want it to be filled with bodies? Or do you believe you have strength sufficient to leap over it? *Error.* The raised hand of the common man is the mountain sliding down. That hand will only stop when it picks up the ashes of what it

---

17. Instituto Nacional de Chile in Santiago, founded 1813.

has destroyed. Keep him from raising that hand; put an instrument in his hand, bore into his brain with the word, point out the happy future to him, and then you will see the people-as-association, not the people-as-flock, not the people acting like a boa constrictor with its threatening mouth. Here we have, then, the work, here we have the politics, here we have the character of an historic administration. This can only be neglected, this can only be forgotten, this can only be ignored, if it is viewed with the palliative and miserable gaze of conformity.

Some beneficial works are being instituted, but works, institutions that are veneer on a building that is collapsing. Examine the foundations, examine the ground, examine the fellow with a pickax who is undermining it, and then you will have examined the question. Meanwhile you are doing nothing but patching up the same old thing.

Here we are. The question of the century is this; the humanitarian question is this, the question that signifies our historical destiny is this. Are you not taking it into account? Then go away to mix in with the mob, descend from the heights that you unworthily occupy. But if you stay as you are, resign yourself to having as your only memorial the compassion that ignorance inspires or the hatred that evil causes.

Conclusion and End

The development of the revolution has been the law that has guided us in assessing our political life.

To develop the revolution is to continue the destructive work on things that live in the past and organize beliefs that can be extracted from the humanitarian chaos.

The organization of society is the consequence of the organization of beliefs.

The unity that organized past beliefs has been destroyed, and the *Que suis-je, où vais-je et d'où suis-je tiré*—What am I, where am I going, and from whence have I come—[18] is obvious and demands a scientific solution.

Consequently, what we need is scientific religion.

Here we are.

Now we ask if the work of the socialist, of the legislator, or of him who governs is to despair, or to remain indifferent, or to stick with the old solutions to human problems.

No. To despair is for the weak. To remain indifferent is for beasts unworthy of the name of human beings. To stick with the old solution is for the impotently ignorant. What to do? Here we have the question.

The present spectacle is lamentable. We observe the intellectual anarchy, but anarchy is transitory. The triumph of the old is on full display in the forms of

---

18. Voltaire. [Bilbao's note. The line is from "Poème sur le désastre de Lisbonne" ("Poem on the Lisbon Disaster"), 1756].

the old civilization. There are still monarchies, there is still aristocracy, there is still papal and ecclesiastical authority. This is to pay attention to the human and miserable husk of things. Social metaphysics sometimes takes giant steps, but we always witness the struggle between the soul and the brain. The first to enthrone hope and the second to tear down the heavens. Nonetheless our duty, the question with which we ought to push, is to inquire into the *law* and its obligatory character *as law*. Given this stoic step into science, we will be able to wait for everything else, resting one hand on individual conscience and with the other invoking immortality.

As a consequence, our task in the political and religious sphere is to accept every fact that we recognize as indisputable and make it known.

Just as doubt recedes before the consciousness of the existence of the *self*, so also political and religious doubt stops to contemplate the magnificent and inescapable spectacle of liberty that we have won philosophically.

The liberty of the individual as a body and as a thinking thing. There we have a fact.

The equality of my fellow being insofar as he is another temple where God has also placed liberty. There we have another fact.

Liberty and social equality, meaning equality for everyone—*sovereignty of a people*. There we have another fact.

The liberty to conceive of the divine, that is to say, religious democracy. There we have another fact.

Liberty and political equality, that is to say, democracy properly stated. There we have another fact.

The consciousness of free rights, which gives one the right to defend rights and to spread rights to convert into free individuals those who are not, that is to say, the right to civilize and increase the children of divinity. There we have another fact.

From these facts emerges the foundation of the future system of beliefs. They are few but they are irrefragable. They are indisputable. So they must serve as the foundation in a future religion.

Meanwhile, we poor well-intentioned devils, we will do the best we can and we will pull out for ourselves the following conclusions:

Order, religion, and politics.

As for number one, we simply must abide by the moral universe that we recognize.

Thou shalt not kill
Thou shalt not steal
Thou shalt not commit adultery
Thou shalt not bear false witness nor lie.

As for stealing, it remains indeterminate until property has been defined in relation to the right of everyone to develop morally and physically.

As for adultery, it remains indeterminate until it has been defined according to the freedom the woman has achieved, the sphere of her duty in relation to the husband.

The exaltation of individual dignity produces the feeling of honor, but honor necessitates fixed principles to which it can appeal in the situations that arise in life. It remains, then, to define honor in its relationships. Question of insult and question of duels.

Thou shalt love the Creator. It remains, of course, to define the Creator's essence popularly and scientifically, and to decide whether it is thought and extension or a *personal being.* The sublime inspirations that strike us tell us that it is a personal being. The creation of liberty is for me the proof of divine liberty. Divine liberty is the individualization of the Creator.

Thou shalt love your neighbor. Fraternity is a principle and a sentiment. Splendid refuge against the hardships of life and against ghastly indifference. How could you not love your *neighbor,* your brother, if you recognize in yourself the omnipotence of liberty. My neighbor is another "I" He is the repository of the same spirituality as am I; so the bond, the love between the community and identity of so great an essence is necessary. Here we have the unassailable fundament of democracy.

Governments must then generalize what science presents, clearly, without abstractions; enough of lies. This is the logic of the time and of the revolution. To encourage past beliefs and forms is to regress.

In *politics* let us likewise accept the principles expressed and let us accept the new forms that liberty of worship brings with it; it is a necessary step to prepare better the new synthesis and the new worship.

The elevation to sovereignty of all individuals, that is to say, to the fraternity of liberty, is our defining goal. So let the rights of the laborer and of the lowest common man be represented. Right is indivisible. So there can only be one representation of their rights, that is to say, a single legislative chamber.

His rights represented, the proletarian will have representation for his right to knowledge; *education,* or his right to own *property.* Education is established at the expense of the rich land holdings, which will have to raise the wages of the poor man so that he will be able to educate himself.

The senate chamber represents the conservative interests or the propertied aristocracy. In the first case, it tries to preserve the present organization, and in the second case, the same. So in both cases it tries to preserve inequality. This is its sentence of abolition.

Responsibility is relative. Punishment is corrective.

So punishment by death, which does not assess responsibility and does not correct, is unjust. The penalty of death is incapable of correcting.

The hand of hell can still be plainly seen grasping onto the *carros.*

To demand their abolition is to insult the government that has not expunged that barbarism in all this time and allows their groaning to be heard. Etc. etc. etc. These are facts regarding which doubt is not possible. Until we have scientific solutions to human problems, let us realize the eternal principles of development that appear clearly and logically before the revolutionary point of view. If the old symbol has fallen, let us replace it with the yet unformed spirit of philosophy. The truth has advanced very far on its journey, compared with the state in which we find ourselves. Let us try not to distance ourselves from the truth, giving the old word for lack of a new word.

Let us have doubts, let us suffer, let us carry the weight of transitory eras, but let us not regress to rest beneath the collapsing monument. Let us continue, let us cry if you wish, but let us live with whatever small amount of truth we have grasped. Let us not separate the people from us any farther than they are already separated.

Let us educate the people in the theory of individuality, of the right of equality, and of honor. Thus they will find themselves fit to receive the baptism of the new word without it costing us the blood of the greater number of them nor the centuries other beliefs have taken to organize society. Let us keep an attentive ear to the inspirations of a moral nature; let us grasp them in their mysterious flight; and let us bring them to the people who anxiously await us so that we might present them rationally. Let us exalt sentiments, let us push the imagination to formulate them and let us bring these intimate revelations to the receptacle of reason so it may imprint them with its truth. Let us always bear in mind, in our moments of moral tribulation, in those moments when indifference begins to show its satanic smile, the immense power that we feel, that power terrible in its grief, and our awareness of that power will tell us that we are something. This something is life, it is the revelation that tells us that we carry a charge and that the being that has given it to us glorifies us in commending to us a gigantic work.

Then let us return to life and in elevating ourselves to titanic heights with the knowledge of the stormy liberty that we contain, we will raise to God the hymn of the martyr's faith, and we will pass through this life with our heads held high to repel the thunderbolt and with our gaze defying the cloud that hurls it.

Domingo Faustino Sarmiento
(Argentina)

Domingo Faustino Sarmiento (1811–1888) was one of the most prolific and varied contributors to his native Argentina—educator, writer, sociologist, soldier, diplomat, governor, and, ultimately, president of the country. His path to developing his talents was not easy. Born in one of the poorest neighborhoods of the capital city of the province of San Juan, he was the fifth child and only son of José Clemente Sarmiento, who had been a soldier with San Martín, and Paula Albarracín. His education was often interrupted by political upheavals, and much of it came from self-directed reading, which focused on literature, the contract theory of political life, and, most particularly, Benjamin Franklin, who became his major influence, inasmuch as Sarmiento identified with Franklin's life and circumstances. Because of Sarmiento's own experience, he developed an abiding interest in the education of the young, and he was known as the school teacher president. He was particularly taken with the educational system that the United States was implementing at the urging of Horace Mann, who became a close friend.[1]

Sarmiento's introduction to political life at age sixteen was not auspicious; forced to join the provincial militia, he was jailed for insubordination. When he later fought as a defender of political unitarianism under General José María Paz against the *caudillo* Juan Facundo Quiroga, he was captured and sentenced to house arrest in San Juan. In 1831 he went into the first of several exiles in Chile, returning to San Juan briefly to fight against Quiroga, but leaving again for Chile when the latter reestablished his political supremacy. Over the next five years he successively took jobs as teacher at a remote school in the Andes, clerk in Valparaíso, and foreman in a mine, from where he began his literary career. In 1836, after Quiroga's murder, Sarmiento returned to San Juan, founded the Colegio de Santa Rosa de América for young women in 1839, and a newspaper, *El Zonda,* espousing democratic politics. The federalist governor of San Juan took offense, closed the newspaper, and imprisoned Sarmiento in 1840, whereupon Sarmiento yet again left for Chile to begin his literary career in earnest.

Arriving in Chile with neither money nor prospects, he immediately wrote an article for *El Mercurio,* published in Valparaíso, which brought him to the attention of Chile's main literary lights and secured him a position as an editor of that newspaper, thereby allowing him to assume a leadership role in Chilean intellectual life. That same year he used his newspaper forum to advance the fortunes of conservatives in the political campaign of 1841 and was rewarded

---

1. Horace Mann (1796–1859) advocated schools and education that would be available and equal for all persons. He believed that such education was the birthright of every American child.

with a position as director of South America's first normal school. Also in 1841 he founded *El Nacional* and in the next year he founded *El Progreso,* Santiago's first daily newspaper. From the forum of these newspapers, and especially *La Crónica,* which he founded in 1849, he mounted an unrelenting attack on Argentina's new dictator, Juan Manuel de Rosas. He became a member of the Faculdad de Filosofía y Humanidades at the Universidad de Chile and published important works on education.

Upon his return to Argentina a few years after the defeat in 1852 of Rosas, Sarmiento began a dramatic climb to the very pinnacle of educational influence and political power. He became editor of *El Nacional* of Buenos Aires, joined the city government, and was elected to the national Senate from San Juan. He became head of schools in Buenos Aires and founded the periodical *Anales de la Educación Comúm.* He served as minister of the interior and of foreign affairs under President Bartolomé Mitre and was governor of San Juan from 1862 to 1864. From 1865 to 1868 he was minister plenipotentiary and envoy extraordinary to the United States. Leaving the United States in 1868, he knew he was among the leading candidates for his country's presidency, but only when his ship entered the port of Pernambuco, Brazil, and was greeted by a twenty-one gun salute from a U.S. warship did he know that he had won the election. He served in the position for six years, a period marked by the same kinds and levels of success he had achieved in other posts. Although many of his reforms were significant, the most lasting were in education, which he understood to be the very foundation of democratic civil institutions. The selection that follows is from his most acclaimed work, *Facundo o civilización y barbarie* (translated as *Facundo, or Civilization and Barbarism* [1845]).

Further Reading

Bellotta, Araceli. *Sarmiento: Maestro del éxito.* Buenos Aires: Grupo Editorial Norma, 2000.

Botana, Natalia R. *Domingo Faustino Sarmiento.* Buenos Aires: Fondo de Cultura Económica, 1996.

Bunkley, Allison Williams. *The Life of Sarmiento.* Princeton, N.J.: Princeton University Press, 1952.

Criscenti, Joseph T., ed. *Sarmiento and His Argentina.* Boulder, Colo.: L. Rienner Publishers, 1993.

Donghi, Tulio Halperín. *Sarmiento, Author of a Nation.* Berkeley and Los Angeles, Calif.: University of California Press, 1994.

Foster, David William. *The Argentine Generation of 1880: Ideology and Cult Texts.* Columbia: University of Missouri Press, 1990.

Martínez Estrada, Ezequiel. *Sarmiento: Meditaciones sarmientinas; Los invariantes históricos en el Facundo.* Rosario, Argentina: Beatriz Viterbo Editora, 2001.

Sorensen Goodrich, Diana. *Facundo and the Construction of Argentine Culture.* Austin, Tex.: University of Texas Press, 1996.

Facundo, or Civilization and Barbarism (1845)

Chapter I

The Physical Features of the Argentine Republic and the Characters, Habits, and Ideas it Engenders

The expanse of the pampas is so great that on the north they are bordered by palm forests and in the southern part by eternal snows. Head[2]

The American continent ends in a point at the south where, at its outermost part, the Strait of Magellan forms. To the west and at a short distance from the Pacific, the Chilean Andes extend parallel to the coast. The land that remains to the east of that chain of mountains and to the west of the Atlantic, following the *Río Plata*[3] to the interior going up the Uruguay, is the territory that was called the United Provinces of the *Río Plata,* and where blood is still being spilt to determine whether it be called the Argentine Republic or the Argentine Province. To the north lie Paraguay, El Gran Chaco,[4] and Bolivia, its presumptive boundaries.

The country's immense expanse in these extremes is completely unpopulated, and it has navigable rivers that not even a small fragile boat has penetrated. The misfortune troubling the Argentine Republic is its expanse—desert surrounds it on all sides and insinuates itself into its innermost recesses; the solitude, the wilderness lacking all human habitation, are in general the unquestionable limits between its provinces. Here, immensity everywhere—immense plain, immense forests, immense rivers, the horizon always indefinite, always blending with the earth between clouds and haze that do not allow one to distinguish from a distance the point where land stops and sky begins. To the south and to the north savages watch, waiting for moonlit nights to fall like packs of hyenas on livestock grazing in the fields and on defenseless settlements. In the solitary caravan of wagons that lumbers across the pampas and stops for a few moments' rest, the crew, gathered round the scant fire, turns their gaze mechanically toward the south at the faintest whisper of wind moving the dry grass to sink their gaze into the profound darkness of the night in search of the sinister shapes of the savage horde that, unnoticed, can surprise them at any moment. If the ear hears no sound, if the eyes fail to penetrate the dark veil that covers the silent solitude, they turn their looks, to calm themselves about everything, to the ears of some

---

2. Francis Bond Head, an Englishman, took an administrative post with the Río de la Plata Mining Association, but left when the government in Buenos Aires took over the mines.

3. The *Río Plata* is the River Plate (River of Silver), which forms the boundary between Argentina and Uruguay and drains nearly one-fifth of the South American continent. The term also refers to the land mass constituted as the Viceroyalty of la Plata, which included Bolivia, Paraguay, Uruguay, and Argentina.

4. El Gran Chaco is the largest dry forest left on earth, centrally located in South America.

horse close to the fire, to observe whether those ears are motionless and carelessly slanting back. Then they continue their interrupted conversation or raise to their mouths the half-scorched jerky with which they feed themselves. If it is not the proximity of the savage that troubles the man of the country, it is fear of a tiger lying in wait for him, of a viper on which he might step. The insecurity of life, habitual and permanent in the countryside, impresses on the Argentine character, it seems to me, a certain stoic resignation toward violent death, which makes of it one of life's inherent misfortunes, a way of dying like every other, and can perhaps explain, in part, the indifference with which they impart and receive death, not leaving on survivors any deep, lasting impressions.

The inhabited part of this country, graced with gifts and containing every climate, can be divided into three distinct regions that imprint diverse characters on the population, depending on the way it adapts to the natural world around it. To the north, mixing with the Chaco, a dense forest covers, with its impenetrable branches, expanses that we would call extraordinary if, in gigantic shapes, there were nothing extraordinary in the entire expanse of America. In the center, and in a parallel zone, the pampas and the jungle have contended a long time for the territory; the forest dominates in parts, reducing itself to unhealthy and thorny scrublands, the jungle appears anew thanks to some river that favors it, until finally, in the south, the pampas triumphs and displays its smooth and downy brow, infinite, without known limit, without notable irregularity; it is the image of the sea on the earth; the earth as on the map; the earth waiting still to be commanded to produce plants and all types of seeds.

As a notable feature of this country's face, one could designate the agglomeration of navigable rivers that rendezvous in the east, from all directions on the horizon, to come together in the *Río Plata* and worthily present their tremendous tribute to the ocean, which receives it in its flank, not without visible indications of turbulence and respect. But these immense waterways, excavated by the obliging hand of nature, introduce no change in national habits. The son of the Spanish adventurers who colonized the country detests navigation and considers himself imprisoned in the narrow limits of the boat or launch. When a great river blocks his way, he calmly undresses, prepares his horse and guides it, swimming, to some islet he makes out in the distance. Reaching it, horse and rider relax, and moving from islet to islet, they finally complete the crossing.

In this way, the greatest favor that Providence provides a people the Argentine gaucho disdains, seeing in it more an obstacle blocking his movements than the most powerful means for facilitating them; in this way, the source of national growth, which brought fame to distant Egypt, which brought growth to Holland and is the reason for North America's rapid development—navigation of the rivers or the building of canals—is a dead element, unexploited by the inhabitants of the banks of the Bermejo, Pilcomayo, Paraná, Grande, and Uruguay. From the *Río Plata*, a few small boats manned by Italians and Genoese go upriver, but the movement proceeds a few leagues and almost completely stops. The Spanish were not given the instinct for navigation that the Saxons to the north have to so high a degree. A different spirit is needed to stir those arteries where today the life-giving fluids of a nation stagnate. Of all those rivers that should be carrying civilization, power, and wealth to the most hidden depths of the continent and making Santa Fe, Entre Ríos, Corrientes, Córdoba, Salta, Tucumán, and Jujuy so many other towns swimming in richness and overflowing population and culture, there is only one that is rich in benefits for those dwelling on its banks—the *Río Plata,* which brings them all together.

At its mouth are situated two cities, Montevideo and Buenos Aires, today alternately reaping the benefits of their favorable position. Buenos Aires is destined one day to be the most gigantic city in all the Americas. Beneath a mild climate, mistress of the navigation of a hundred rivers that flow at her feet, reclining luxuriously on an immense territory, and with thirteen interior provinces that know no other outlets for their products, it would already be the American Babylonia if the spirit of the pampas had not blown over it and stifled at its source the tribute of wealth that the rivers and the provinces must always carry to it. It alone, in the vast Argentine expanse, is in contact with European nations; it alone exploits the advantages of foreign trade; it alone has power and income. In vain, the provinces have asked it to allow a little European civilization, industry, and population to pass through to them; a stupid and colonial policy made it deaf to these clamors. But the provinces took revenge, sending Rosas,[5] and with him, much—and too much—of the barbarism they had in excess.

Dearly have those paid who said, "The Argentine Republic ends at the Arroyo del Medio."[6] Now it goes from the Andes to the sea; barbarism and violence have brought Buenos Aires to a level lower than that of the provinces. We must not complain about Buenos Aires, which is great and will be even more so because that is its lot. We should rather complain first to Providence and request that it more favorably reconfigure the land. This not being possible, let us accept as well-made what the hand of the Master has made. Let us complain of the ignorance of this brutal power that sterilizes, for itself and for the provinces, the gifts that nature lavished on a people gone astray. Now, instead of sending learning, wealth, and prosperity to the interior, Buenos Aires sends it only chains, exterminating hordes, and petty little tyrants. It also takes revenge for the evil that the provinces did in sending it Rosas!

I have pointed out this circumstance of the monopolizing position of Buenos Aires to show that there is an organization of the land so central and unified in that country, that even had Rosas screamed in good faith *federation or death!* it would have ended in the unified system that he has established today. We, however, wanted unity in civilization and liberty, and we have been given unity in barbarism and slavery. But another time will come when things will enter upon their regular channel. What concerns us now is to know that the progress of civilization is accumulating in Buenos Aires alone; the pampas is a very poor

---

5. Juan Manuel de Rosas (1793–1877), Argentine landowner, military leader, governor of Buenos Aires, dictator of Buenos Aires from 1835–1852.

6. The natural limit of the province of Buenos Aires with the province of Santa Fe.

conductor for carrying and distributing it to the provinces. And we will certainly see what results from this. But over all these accidents peculiar to certain parts of that territory predominates a general, uniform, and constant feature: whether the land is covered with lush and colossal tropical vegetation, whether unhealthy, thorny, and unpleasant shrubs reveal the meager portion of humidity that gives them life; whether, finally, the pampas displays its unobstructed and monotonous face, the surface of the land is generally flat and smooth, with the mountain ranges of San Luis and Córdoba in the center and some advanced ramifications of the Andes in the north not sufficient to interrupt this limitless continuity. This is a new unifying element for the nation that may one day populate these great solitudes, because one knows well that mountains interposed between some countries and other natural obstacles maintain the isolation of peoples and preserve their original characteristics. North America is destined to be a federation, less for the original independence of the settlements than for its wide exposure to the Atlantic and the diverse approaches that lead to the interior—the St. Lawrence in the north, the Mississippi in the south, and the immense waterways in the center. The Argentine Republic is one and indivisible.

Many philosophers have also believed that the plains prepare the way for despotism just as the mountains provided a handhold for those who fight for liberty. This unbounded plain, which from Salta to Buenos Aires, from there to Mendoza, for a distance of more than seven hundred leagues, permits enormous and heavy wagons to roll over roads where the hand of man has scarcely needed to fell any trees or cut any underbrush without encountering any obstacle—this plain constitutes one of the most notable features of the interior face of the republic. To prepare routes for communication, individual effort and the results of brute nature alone suffice; if skill might want to give nature assistance, if the forces of society attempted to make up for individual weakness, the colossal dimensions of the work would frighten away the most enterprising, and the inadequacy of the effort would make it inopportune. Thus, with respect to roads, wild nature will rule for a long time, and civilization's action will remain weak and ineffective.

Moreover, this expanse of the plains imprints on the life of the interior a certain Asiatic hue, which remains quite pronounced. Many times, on seeing the moon rise tranquil and resplendent between the grasses of the earth, I have greeted it mechanically with these words by Volney in his description of the ruins: *La pleine lune à l'Orient s'élevait sur un fond bleuâtre aux plaines rives de l'Euphrate.*[7] And in effect, there is something in the Argentine solitude that brings to mind the Asiatic solitude; the spirit finds a certain analogy between the pampas and the plains that lie between the Tigris and the Euphrates; some kinship in the solitary group of wagons that crosses our solitude to arrive at the end of a trek of months at Buenos Aires and the camel caravan traveling toward

---

7. Constantin-François de Volney (1757–1820), French scholar; *Les Ruines: Ou, méditation sur les révolutions des empires*, 1791. "The full moon in the east rose over the bluish bed of the flat banks of the Euphrates."

Baghdad or Smyrna. Our wagons are a sort of squadron of small vessels, whose people have peculiar customs, language, and dress that distinguish them from other inhabitants, as the sailor is distinguished from men of the land.

The leader is a *caudillo,* as in Asia the chief of the caravan; for this post is needed an iron will, a character bold to the point of recklessness, to control the audacity and turbulence of the freebooters of the land who he alone has to govern and dominate in the forsaken wilderness. At the least sign of insubordination, the leader raises his iron *whip* and unloads on the insolent person blows that cause contusions and wounds; if the resistance is prolonged, before calling on pistols, whose assistance he disdains in general, he jumps from his horse with a formidable knife in hand and very quickly recovers his authority by the superior dexterity with which he knows how to handle it. He who dies in these executions by the leader has no right to protest, the authority that has killed him being regarded as legitimate.

This is the way—through these peculiarities—the predominance of brute force, the preponderance of the strongest, unlimited authority without accountability in those who command, justice administered without formulas and without debate, all begin to establish themselves in Argentine life. Moreover, the group of wagons carries weapons—a rifle or two per wagon, and at times a small revolving cannon in the lead wagon. If the barbarians attack, the wagons, tied to each other, form a circle and they almost always victoriously resist the covetousness of the savages, greedy for blood and plunder.

Mule trains, on the other hand, frequently fall, defenseless, into the hands of these American Bedouins, and rarely do the cowboys escape having their throats cut. On these long journeys, the Argentine proletariat acquires the habit of living far from society and of struggling individually with nature, hardened by deprivations and counting on no resources other than their capability and personal knack for guarding against all the risks that continually surround them.

The people inhabiting these expansive regions are of two different races, which, when mixed, create imperceptible hues, Spanish and indigenous. The pure Spanish race predominates in the countryside around Córdoba and San Luis, and it is common to find in the fields, herding sheep, young women as white, as rosy and beautiful as the elegant women of the capital would like to be. In Santiago del Estero, the bulk of the rural population still speaks *quichua,* which reveals its Indian origin. In Corrientes, the peasants use a very amusing Spanish dialect: "Give me, general, a *chiripa,*" Lavalle's soldiers used to say to him.[8]

In the countryside around Buenos Aires, the Andalusian[9] soldier is still recognized, and foreign surnames predominate in the city. The Negro race, now

---

8. *Chiripa,* gaucho dress trousers. Juan Lavalle (1797–1841), one of the most important leaders of the unitarian party.

9. Andalusia is a province in the south of Spain from which many of the Spanish settlers came.

almost extinct—except in Buenos Aires—has left its *zambos* and *mulattos*,[10] inhabitants of the cities, as a link that binds the civilized with the rustic man; a race inclined toward civilization, endowed with talent and with the loveliest instincts for progress.

Apart from this, a homogeneous whole has resulted from the fusion of these three families, distinguished by its love of laziness and lack of capacity for industry, unless education and the demands of a social position come to goad it on and extract it from its habitual pace. The incorporation of indigenous people that colonization brought about must have contributed greatly to producing this unfortunate result. The American races live in laziness and show themselves incapable, even under compulsion, to dedicate themselves to hard and steady work. This laziness suggested the idea of introducing Negroes into America, which has produced such fatal results. But the Spanish race has not shown itself more prone to act when abandoned to its own instincts in the American wildernesses.

Comparing the German or Scottish colony south of Buenos Aires with the town that has grown up in the interior makes one feel pity and shame in the Argentine Republic; in the first, the little houses are painted, the front of the house always clean, adorned with flowers and charming small shrubs; the furnishings simple but complete, the tableware of copper or tin always gleaming, the bed with charming, small curtains, and the inhabitants constantly moving and acting. Milking cows, making butter and cheeses, some families have managed to make colossal fortunes and retire to the city to enjoy the conveniences. The native town is the unworthy reverse of this medallion—children, dirty and covered with rags, live with a pack of dogs; men stretched out on the floor in the most complete inactivity; filth and poverty everywhere; a little table and leather trunk the only furnishings; miserable huts for dwellings and a distinct general appearance of barbarism and negligence.

This misery, which is now disappearing, and which is a characteristic of the pastoral countryside, doubtless motivated the words that the indignation and humiliation of English arms elicited from Walter Scott. "The vast plains of Buenos Aires," he says, "are populated only by Christian savages known by the name of *guachos* (that is to say, *gauchos*), whose main furniture consists of horse skulls, whose food is raw meat and water, and whose favorite pastime is riding horses to exhaustion in hard races. Unfortunately," adds the good gringo, "they preferred their national independence to our cottons and muslins."[11] It would be good to propose this to England simply to see how many yards of linen and how many pieces of muslin it would give to own these plains of Buenos Aires!

• • • • •

---

10. A *zambo* is a person of mixed African and Indian blood; a *mulatto* is a person of mixed African and Caucasian blood.

11. *Life of Napoleon Buonaparte*, v. 2, ch. 1. [Sarmiento's note in the first edition.]

The man of the city wears the European suit, lives the civilized life as we know it everywhere—here are laws, ideas of progress, means of instruction, some municipal organization, regular government, etc. Moving outside the city, everything changes aspect—the man of the country wears a suit I will call American, because it is common to all the peoples; his habits of life are different, his needs specific and limited; they seem to be two distinct societies, two peoples estranged from one another. There is even more—the man of the countryside, far from aspiring to be like the man of the city, disdainfully rejects his luxury and refined manners; and the city person's dress, the swallowtail coat, the cape, the saddle, no such European symbol can appear with impunity in the countryside. Everything civilized in the city is blocked here, proscribed outside; and, for example, he who dares show himself in a frock coat, mounted on an English saddle, would attract to himself the mockeries and brutal aggressions of the peasants.

Let us now study the external face of the vast countryside surrounding the cities, and let us penetrate the internal life of its inhabitants. . . . Pastoral life unintentionally brings to mind the memory of Asia, whose plains we imagine always covered here and there with the tents of the Kalmuck, the Cossack, or the Arab. The primitive life of peoples, the eminently barbarous and static life, the life of Abraham, which is that of today's Bedouin, appears in the Argentine countryside, although strangely modified by civilization.

The Arab tribe wandering through the Asiatic solitudes lives united under the command of a tribal or a warrior chief; society exists, although it is not established at a specific place in the land; religious beliefs, immemorial traditions, invariability of customs, respect for the elders, collectively form a code of laws, uses, and governmental practices that maintain morality, as they understand it, order, and tribal organization. But progress is stifled because there cannot be progress without permanent possession of the land, without the city, which develops man's industrial capacity and permits him to extend his possessions.

On the Argentine plains the nomadic tribe does not exist—the shepherd has property rights to the land, he remains in one place that belongs to him; but for him to occupy it, it has been necessary to dissolve the association and scatter families over an immense area. Imagine an expanse of two thousand square leagues, completely populated but with homes situated at four leagues' distance from each other, sometimes eight, at the closest, two. Acquiring movable property is not impossible, the enjoyment of luxury is not totally incompatible with this isolation—wealth can raise a superb building in the desert; but the stimulus is absent, the example disappears, the need felt in the cities to show a certain dignity is not felt here in the isolation and solitude. Unavoidable deprivations justify natural laziness, and frugality of pleasures brings with it all the outward appearances of barbarism. Society has disappeared completely; there remains only the feudal family, isolated, withdrawn within itself; and, without united society, all forms of government become impossible—the municipality does not exist, the police cannot function, and civil justice has no way of reaching offenders.

I do not know if the modern world presents a form of association as monstrous as this. It is the complete opposite of the Roman *municipium,* whose entire population was concentrated in one space and from there went out to work the surrounding fields. There existed, then, a strong social organization, and its resulting benefits are still felt today and have prepared modern civilization. It is similar to the old Slavonic *sloboda*[12] with the difference that the *sloboda* was agricultural and therefore more readily governable—the population's dispersion was not so extensive as is ours. It is different from the nomadic tribe because the nomadic tribe is hardly a society inasmuch it does not own the land. It is, finally, somewhat similar to the feudalism of the Middle Ages, when the barons resided in the countryside and from there harassed the cities and devastated the countryside; but here the baron and the feudal castle are missing. If power rises in the countryside, it is temporary, it is democratic—it is neither inherited nor can it be preserved for lack of mountains and strongholds. For this reason, even the savage tribe of the pampas is better organized for moral development than is our countryside.

But what this society offers of note with regard to its social aspect is its affinity with ancient life, with Spartan or Roman life, if it did not differ in one radical way. The Spartan or Roman free citizen placed on his slaves the burden of material life, the concern for providing the means of support, while he lived free of care in the Forum, in the public square, occupying himself solely with matters of state, of peace, war, partisan struggles. Herding provides similar advantages, and the inhuman role of the ancient Helot is played by cattle. Spontaneous procreation creates and extends fortune indefinitely; man's hand is unnecessary; his work, his intelligence, his time, are not necessary for the preservation and augmentation of the means of living. But if none of this is needed for life's material aspects, he cannot use the energy he conserves as did the Roman—he lacks the city, the municipality, the intimate association, and therefore he lacks the base of all social development; because hacienda owners do not gather, they have no public needs to satisfy—in a word, there is no *res publica.*

Moral progress, the culture of intelligence, neglected in the Arab or Tatar tribe, is not only neglected here but also impossible. Where to place the school so that children spread out at ten leagues' distance in all directions can go to receive lessons? Thus, then, civilization cannot be actualized, barbarism is normal,[13] and we can give thanks if domestic practices preserve even the slightest trace of morality. Religion suffers the consequences of society's dissolution; the parish is nominal, the pulpit has no audience, the priest flees from his solitary chapel or becomes demoralized by the inactivity and the solitude; vices, simony, and normal barbarism penetrate into his cell and convert his moral superiority into sources of fortune and ambition, because at last he ends up a partisan *caudillo.*

---

12. *Sloboda* is an early political organization, either tribal or pastoral, in the Slavic regions.

13. In the year 1826 during a year of residence in the sierra of San Luis, I taught six young people of an affluent family to read, the youngest of whom was 22. [Sarmiento's note to the first edition.]

I have witnessed a rural scene worthy of the world's earliest days, before the establishment of the priesthood. I found myself in 1838 in the San Luis mountain range in the house of a hacienda owner whose two favorite occupations were praying and gambling. He had built a chapel, in which on Sunday evenings he himself prayed the rosary in place of the priest and the Mass, which for years had been absent. That was a Homeric picture—the sun set in the west, the flocks of sheep returning to the sheepfold split the air with their confused bleating; the owner of the house—a man of sixty years with a noble face, in which the pure European race was obvious in the whiteness of the skin, the blue eyes, the ample and wide forehead—chanted, answered by a dozen women and some strapping lads whose horses, not yet well broken, were tied up near the chapel door. The rosary concluded, he made a fervent offering. Never have I heard a voice more full of devotion, a fervor more pure, a faith more firm, nor a prayer more beautiful, more appropriate to the circumstances than the one he recited. In it he asked of God rains for the fields, fecundity for the cattle, peace for the republic, security for the travelers . . . I am very given to crying, and that time I cried until sobbing because the religious sentiment had been awakened in my soul with exaltation and like an unknown feeling, because I had never witnessed a more religious scene; I believed I was in the time of Abraham, in his presence, in God's, and in the presence of the nature that reveals him; the voice of that man, simple and innocent, made the fibers of my being quiver and penetrated my bones to the marrow.

Here is what religion is reduced to in the pastoral countryside—to natural religion; Christianity exists, like the Spanish language, in a kind of tradition perpetuated but corrupted, embodied in vulgar superstitions, without instruction, without worship, and without convictions. In almost all the countryside remote from the cities, it happens that, when traders from San Juan or Mendoza arrive, people present them with babies a few months or a year old to baptize, satisfied that because of the traders' good education they can do it properly; and it is not rare that, when a priest arrives, strapping lads present themselves, taming their colts, on which the priest places oil and administers the baptism *sub conditione*.[14]

Lacking all means of civilization and progress, which cannot be developed except on condition that men come together in societies of a certain size, observe the education of the man of the country. Women keep house, prepare the food, sheer the sheep, milk the cows, make the cheeses, and weave the coarse fabrics in which everyone dresses. The woman performs all domestic occupations, all the household industries. Almost all the work falls to her. And she is fortunate if some men decide to cultivate a little corn to feed the family, for bread is not an ordinary part of the diet. The children exercise their strength and for pleasure teach themselves to handle the lariat and *bolas*,[15] with which they unceasingly

14. *Sub conditione* is conditionally baptized, used for baptisms of foundlings and converts.

15. Lariat, a rope of greased leather with an iron ring at one end through which the other end passes and is used to hunt vicunas and horses, etc. *Bola,* instrument used for hunting by indigenous people and adopted by gauchos.

harass and chase calves and goats; when they become riders, and this happens immediately after learning to walk, they do some chores on horseback; later, as they grow stronger, they roam the fields, falling off and getting back up, intentionally wandering among the vizcacha burrows,[16] jumping precipices, and training themselves to handle horses well; when puberty arrives, they dedicate themselves to breaking wild colts, and death is the least punishment that awaits them if at any moment their strength or courage fails them. With first youth come complete independence and idleness.

Here begins the gaucho's public life, I will call it, because his education has now ended. We must see these men as Spaniards, if only in language and the confused religious notions they maintain, to appreciate the indomitable and proud characters that emerge from this struggle of the isolated man with untamed nature, of the rational with the brute; we must see these faces thick with beards, these grave and serious countenances, like those of the Asiatic Arabs, to judge the pitying disdain inspired in them by the sight of the sedentary city man, who may have read many books, but who does not know how to bring down and kill a wild bull; who, on foot and with no one's help, cannot provide himself with a horse in an open field; who never has stopped a tiger, receiving it with a knife in one hand and a poncho wound around the other to thrust in its mouth while piercing its heart and leaving it spread out at his feet. This habit of triumphing over opposition, of showing himself always superior to nature, of challenging and conquering it, develops to an extraordinary degree the feeling of individual importance and superiority. The Argentines, of whatever class they may be, civilized or ignorant, have a great awareness of their value as a nation; all other American peoples throw this vanity in their face and appear offended by their presumption and arrogance. I believe the charge is not completely unfounded, and I do not regret it. Woe to the people that does not have faith in itself! Because of it, great things have not been done; how much will the arrogance of these Argentine gauchos—who never have seen under the sun better than themselves, neither the wise nor the powerful man—have contributed to the independence of America? The European is for them the lowest of all, because he does not last even two bucks of the horse.[17] If the origin of this national vanity among the inferior classes is mean, the consequences are not for that reason less noble, just as the water of a river is not less pure for being born of muddy and contaminated springs. The hatred that the cultured man inspires in them is inexorable; their irritation with his clothes, customs, and manners is insuperable. From this dough are kneaded Argentine soldiers; and it is easy to imagine what habits of this kind can yield in valor and suffering in war. Add to this that from childhood

---

16. Deep, large holes made by vizcachas, a rodent abundant in the pampas, dangerous for horses because if their legs get caught in them they can break and cripple the animal.

17. General Mancilla said in the House during the French blockade, "What can they do to us, those Europeans, who can't even gallop all night?" And the immense plebeian crowd drowned out the voice of the orator with the deafening noise of their applause. [Sarmiento's note to the first edition.]

they are habituated to kill cattle and that this necessary act of cruelty familiarizes them with spilling blood and hardens the heart against the victims' wails.

The life of the country, then, has developed the gaucho's physical abilities but none of his intellectual ones. His moral character is affected by his habit of triumphing over obstacles and the power of nature—he is strong, proud, energetic. Without any instruction, without needing it either, without means of livelihood as without needs, he is happy in the midst of his poverty and his deprivations, which are not really poverty and deprivations for him—he has never known greater enjoyment nor desired more. So if this disintegration of society takes root deeply, barbarism, because of the impossibility and uselessness of moral and intellectual education, will always have its own attractions. The gaucho does not work; he finds food and clothing prepared in his house; his cattle supply him with both if he is the owner; or the house of his patron or relative if he has nothing. The attention required by cattle is reduced to riding and games of pleasure. Branding, which is like the farmers' harvest, is a fiesta whose arrival is received with transports of joy—here is the gathering place of all the men from twenty leagues around; here showing off incredible skill with the lasso. The gaucho arrives at the branding at the slow and measured pace of his best *parejero*,[18] which stops some distance away; and to enjoy the spectacle better, the gaucho crosses his legs on the horse's neck. If the spirit moves him, he gets down from the horse slowly, unwinds his lasso, and throws it over a bull passing with the speed of lightning from forty paces away—he catches it by one hoof, which was what he intended, and goes back calmly to roll up his rope.

Chapter IV

The Revolution of 1810

> *When the battle begins, the Tatar gives a terrible scream, comes*
> *close, wounds, disappears, and returns like a lightning bolt.*
> Victor Hugo

I have had to go the whole way we have just traveled to arrive at the point where our drama begins. It is useless to take time on the character, aim, and end of the revolution of independence. In all of America they were the same, born of the same source, which is the movement of European ideas. America acted in this way, because all peoples acted in this way. Books, events, everything brought America to associate itself with the drive that North America and France's own writers gave France, and that France and its books gave Spain. But what I need to note for my purpose is that the revolution, except in its exterior symbol, independence from the king, was interesting and intelligible only for the Argentine cities, alien and uninteresting for the countryside. In the cities there were books, ideas, municipal spirit, courts, rights, laws, education—all the points of contact

---

18. *Parejero,* a horse trained for racing.

and community that we have with the Europeans; there was a base of organization, incomplete, backward, if you will; but precisely because it was incomplete, because it was not yet at the level it knew it could be, the revolution was adopted with enthusiasm. For the countryside, the revolution was a problem; to get out from under the authority of the king was agreeable, inasmuch as it was to get out from under authority. The pastoral countryside could not view the question in any other way. Liberty, the obligations of power, all the questions the revolution was trying to resolve, were alien to its way of life, to its needs. But the revolution was useful to it in this sense—that it was going to give purpose and outlet to that excess of life we have indicated, and it was going to add a new center for gathering, better than the very circumscribed one to which throughout the entire countryside the men went daily.

Those Spartan constitutions, that physical strength so very developed, those warlike dispositions squandered in stabbing and cutting each other, that Roman idleness lacking only a Field of Mars[19] to be put into active maneuvers, that antipathy for authority with which they lived in constant struggle, everything finally found a pathway to go out into the light, to display and develop itself.

The revolutionary movements began, then, in Buenos Aires, and all the interior cities responded decisively to the call. The pastoral countryside was stirred up and joined the momentum.[20]

• • • • •

The mounted rebel horde, as it appeared in the first days of the republic under the command of Artigas, already presented that character of brutal ferocity and terrorist spirit, which was reserved for the immortal bandit, for the rancher of Buenos Aires to convert into a system of legislation applied to cultured society and to present it in the name of shamed America for the contemplation of Europe. Rosas has not invented anything; his talent has consisted only in plagiarizing from his predecessors and making the brutal instincts of the ignorant masses a coldly thought out and coordinated system. The strip of skin taken from Colonel Maciel, out of which Rosas had made a horse hobble that foreign agents have seen, has its antecedents in Artigas and the rest of the barbarous, Tatarlike *caudillos*. Artigas's mounted rebel horde *enchalecaba* its enemies—that is, sewed them inside a sack of untanned leather and left them like that abandoned in the fields. The reader will supply all the horrors of that slow death. In the year [18]36 this horrible punishment was repeated with a colonel of the army. Executing with a knife, *cutting the throat*, rather than shooting, is the instinct for butchery that Rosas knew how to make use of to give gaucho forms even to death and horrible

---

19. Field of Mars was an area outside Rome used for military training.

20. In the next passages, Sarmiento describes the role of the "countryside," in the revolution, specifically how Uruguayan general José Gervasio Artigas (1764–1850), having joined the patriot side with a thousand gauchos, ended up leading an independent force, "a mounted rebel horde," that "became the enemy of the royalists and the patriots at the same time."

pleasures to the killer; above all, to change the *legal* and accepted forms in cultured societies for others he calls American and in the name of which he invites America to come to his defense, when the sufferings of Brazil, of Paraguay, of Uruguay call on the alliance of the European powers so this alliance could help them free themselves from this cannibal, who has already invaded them with his bloody hordes. It is impossible to maintain the tranquility of spirit necessary to research the historical truth when at each step one stumbles over the idea that he has been able to deceive America and Europe for so long with a system of murders and cruelties tolerable only in Ashanti or Dahomey in the interior of Africa!

Such is the character that the rebel horde has presented since its appearance—a singular type of war and justice that has antecedents only among the Asiatic peoples that inhabit the plains and should never have been confused with the habits, ideas, and practices of the Argentine cities, which were, like all American cities, a continuation of Europe and Spain. The rebel horde can be explained only by examining the intimate organization of the society from which it proceeds. Artigas,[21] smuggler, who is making war on civil society, on the city, a campaign commander by agreement, *caudillo* of the masses on horseback, the same type that with slight variations continues reproducing itself in each campaign commander who has come to make himself *caudillo.* Like all civil wars in which profound dissimilarities of education, beliefs, and objectives divide the factions, the interior war of the Argentine Republic has been long and stubborn until one of the elements has won. The war of the Argentine revolution has been double—first, war of the cities, initiated in European culture against the Spaniards, with the goal of giving greater expansion to that culture; second, war of the *caudillos* against the cities, with the goal of liberating themselves from all civil domination and developing their character and hatred of civilization. The cities triumph over the Spaniards and the countryside over the cities. Here we have explained the enigma of the Argentine revolution, whose first shot was fired in 1810, and the last has not yet sounded.

I will not go into all the details this subject requires—the struggle is more or less long; some cities succumb rather sooner, others later. The life of Facundo Quiroga[22] will give us the opportunity to show the details in all their nakedness. What I must note now is that, with the triumph of these *caudillos,* every *civil* form, even as the Spaniards used it, has disappeared, totally in some parts, in a partial way in others, but visibly moving toward its destruction. The masses are not capable of differentiating between some eras and others; for them the present moment is the only one on which they cast their gaze—this is why no one has observed until now the destruction of the cities and their decline; in the same way the peoples of the interior do not foresee the total barbarism toward which

---

21. Artigas had been a smuggler until 1804, when the civil authorities of Buenos Aires forced him to serve as a military commander.

22. Juan Facundo Quiroga (d. c. 1835), military and political leader noted for his authoritarian methods, provincial conservatism, and his alliance with Argentine dictator Juan Manuel de Rosas.

they are clearly marching. Buenos Aires is so powerful in elements of European civilization that it will ultimately educate Rosas and contain his bloody and barbarous instincts. The high post he occupies, his relations with European governments, the need he has seen to respect foreigners, his need to lie to the press and deny the atrocities he has committed to save himself from the universal disapproval that pursues him, all, in the end, will contribute to containing his excesses, as is already occurring; but this is not keeping Buenos Aires from becoming, like Havana, the richest city of America, but also the most subjugated and degraded.

Four are the cities already annihilated by the rule of the *caudillos* who today support Rosas, namely, Santa Fe, Santiago del Estero, San Luis, and La Rioja. Santa Fe, situated at the confluence of the Paraná and another navigable river that flows nearby, is one of America's most favored places, and nonetheless it does not have today two thousand souls; San Luis, capital of a province of fifty thousand inhabitants, and where there is no other city than the capital, does not have fifteen hundred.

To make sense of the ruin and decline of civilization and the rapid progress that barbarism makes in the interior, I need to take two cities, one already wiped out, the other moving toward barbarism without knowing it—La Rioja and San Juan. La Rioja has never been a city of first rank; but, compared with its current state, its own sons would not recognize it. When the revolution of 1810 began, it had a growing number of capitalists and notable persons who have distinguished themselves in arms, at the bar, in the tribunal, in the pulpit. From La Rioja has come Dr. Castro Barros, deputy to the Tucumán Congress and renowned expert in canon law; General Dávila, who liberated Copiapó from the Spanish power in 1817; General Ocampo, President of Charcas; Dr. don Gabriel Ocampo, one of the most famous lawyers of the Argentine bar; and numerous lawyers with the surnames of Ocampo, Dávila, and García, who today live scattered throughout Chilean territory, as do various learned priests, among them Dr. Gordillo, a resident of Huasco.

For a province to have produced in a given era so many eminent or illustrious men, learning must have been spread among a great number of individuals and been respected and eagerly sought. If in the first days of the revolution this was occurring, what growth in learning, wealth, and population should we be able to note today, had not a terrible regression to barbarism prevented that poor people from continuing its development? Which Chilean city, no matter how insignificant, cannot enumerate the progress it has made in ten years in learning, increase of wealth and adornment, without even excluding from this number those cities destroyed by earthquakes?

Well then, let's look at the state of La Rioja, according to the answers given to one of the many inquiries I have made to ascertain the facts on which I base my theories. Here a respectable person speaks, unaware of my objective in questioning his recent memories because he left La Rioja only four months earlier.[23]

---

23. Dr. don Manuel Ignacio Castro Ramos, canon of the cathedral of Córdoba. [Sarmiento's note to the second edition].

1. What is the approximate number of La Rioja's current population?
   R.—*Scarcely fifteen hundred souls. It is said that there are only fifteen adult males resident in the city.*

2. How many notable citizens reside in it?
   R.—*In the city there will be six or eight.*

3. How many lawyers have an office open?
   R.—*None.*

4. How many doctors tend the sick?
   R.—*None.*

5. How many learned judges are there?
   R.—*None.*

6. How many men wear swallowtail coats?
   R.—*None.*

7. How many young Riojans are studying in Córdoba or Buenos Aires?
   R.—*I know of only one.*

8. How many schools are there and how many children attend?
   R.—*None.*

9. Is there some public charitable establishment?
   R.—*None, nor primary school. The one Franciscan brother in that convent takes some children.*

10. How many ruined churches are there?
    R.—*Five; only the main church is used for anything.*

11. Are new houses being built?
    R.—*None, nor are collapsed ones being repaired.*

12. Are the existing ones being ruined?
    R.—*Almost all, because there are so many floods in the streets.*

13. How many priests have been ordained?
    R.—*In the city only two adolescents—one is parish clergy, the other is a religious of Catamarca. In the province, four more.*

14. Are there great fortunes of fifty thousand pesos? How many of twenty thousand?
    R.—*None; all very poor.*

15. Has the population increased or diminished?
    R.—*It has diminished by more than half.*

16. Does any feeling of terror predominate among the people?
    R.—*The greatest. One fears speaking of even innocent matters.*

17. Is the coined money of full value?
    R.—*The provincial money is debased.*

Here the facts speak with all their sad and horrifying harshness. Only the history of the Mohammedan conquest over Greece presents examples of such a rapid *barbarization* and destruction. And this is happening in America in the nineteenth century! Nonetheless it is the work of only twenty years! What is occurring at La Rioja is exactly applicable to Santa Fe, to San Luis, to Santiago del Estero, skeletons of cities, decrepit and devastated little villages. In San Luis for ten years there has been only one priest and there is no school, nor a person who wears a swallowtail coat. . . .[24]

This is the history of the Argentine *cities*. All of them must restore past glories, civilization, and noteworthiness. Now the level of *barbarization* weighs them all down. The barbarism of the interior has even come to penetrate the streets of Buenos Aires. From 1810 to 1840 the provinces, which contained so much civilization in their cities, were nonetheless barbarous enough to destroy with their momentum the colossal work of the revolution of independence. Now that nothing remains for them of what they had in men, learning, and institutions, what is going to become of them? Ignorance and poverty, which are the consequences, are like birds of carrion waiting for the cities of the interior to give their dying gasp in order to devour their prey, to turn them into field, ranch. Buenos Aires can return to what it was because European civilization is so strong here that, despite the brutalities of the government, it must be sustained. But in the provinces, how will civilization be supported? Two centuries will not be sufficient to return them to the road they have abandoned, because the present generation educates its children in the barbarism that has come to it. Let us now ask ourselves, why are we fighting? We are fighting to return to the cities their very life.

Chaper XV

Present and Future

With everything I have presented, should there remain doubt that the present struggle of the Argentine Republic is only between barbarism and civilization, it would be proof enough that there is at Rosas's side not a single writer, a single poet, of the many that this young nation has. For three consecutive years Montevideo has witnessed the literary competitions of the 25th of May, a day when scores of poets, inspired by passion for the fatherland, have competed for a laurel.[25] Why has poetry abandoned Rosas? Why does the soil of Buenos Aires not produce any rhapsodies today when in another time it was so rich in songs and rhymes? In foreign countries, four or five writers' associations have undertaken to collect facts to write the history of the republic, so full of events, and the great quantity of materials they have gathered from all parts of America is truly astonishing—manuscripts, printed matter, documents, old chronicles, journals, travel diaries, etc. Europe will one day be amazed when such rich materials come to

---

24. In the rest of this section, Sarmiento examines in detail the conditions prevailing in San Juan and shows that at an earlier time a cultured city did, in fact, exist in the interior and can, perhaps, exist with good government.

25. A laurel was the traditional prize awarded to Greek poets and playwrights, particularly during the Olympiads.

light and swell the voluminous collection of which Angelis has not published even a small part.[26]

How great a benefit will these Argentine peoples reap from the day, now not far off, when spilled blood drowns the tyrant! How many lessons! How much experience gained! Our political education is complete. All the social questions aired—federation, unity, freedom of worship, immigration, navigation of the rivers, political powers, freedom of religion, tyranny, all has been discussed among us, all have cost us torrents of blood. A feeling of authority is in all hearts, at the same time that, through his atrocities, Rosas has implanted the need to curb the arbitrariness of power. Now there remains for us only to do what he has not done and repair what he has destroyed.

Because for fifteen years *he* has not taken one administrative measure to support domestic trade and our provinces' nascent industry, the people will devote themselves zealously to developing their resources for wealth, their communication routes, and the *new government* will dedicate itself to reestablishing postal service and securing the roads nature opens throughout the republic's entire expanse.

Because for fifteen years *he* has not secured the southern and northern frontiers with a line of forts, because this work and this good done for the republic would not give him any advantage over his enemies, the *new government* will locate the permanent army in the south and secure territories to establish military colonies, which in fifty years will become flourishing cities and provinces.

Because *he* has vilified the European name, opposed the immigration of foreigners, the *new government* will establish large associations to introduce population and distribute it in fertile territories on the banks of immense rivers, and in twenty years what happened in North America in the same time will happen here—cities, provinces, and states have arisen like magic in the wildernesses where a short time ago herds of wild bison grazed; because the Argentine Republic finds itself today in the situation of the Roman Senate, which, by decree, ordered five hundred cities to rise at one time, and the cities arose at its voice.

Because *he* has placed an insuperable barrier on our interior rivers, the *new government,* so the rivers can be freely navigated, will encourage preference for fluvial navigation; thousands of boats will go up the rivers as far as Bolivia and Paraguay to extract the riches that today have neither outlet nor value, enriching in their course Jujuy, Tucumán and Salta, Corrientes, Entre Ríos and Santa Fe, which will become rich and beautiful cities like Montevideo, like Buenos Aires. Because *he* has squandered the abundant revenues of the port of Buenos Aires and in fifteen years wasted the forty million silver pesos that it has produced in carrying out his lunacies, crimes, and horrible revenges, the port will be declared national property so its revenues can be dedicated to furthering the welfare of the entire republic, which has a right to that port of which it is a tributary.

---

26. Pedro de Angelis (1784–1859), liberal intellectual who collected important documents of Argentina's past.

Because *he* has destroyed the colleges and taken revenues from the schools, the *new government* will organize public education throughout the republic, with adequate revenues and a special ministry as in Europe, as in Chile, Bolivia, and all civilized countries—because knowledge is wealth and because a people that vegetates in ignorance is poor and barbarous, as are those of the African coast or the savages of our pampas.

Because *he* has put the press in chains, not permitting dailies other than those he has appointed to vomit blood, threats, and death, the *new government* will extend the benefit of the press throughout the entire republic, and we will see abound instructional books and publications dedicated to industry, literature, the arts, and all the works of the intellect.

Because *he* has persecuted to death all learned men, allowing only his whim, his lunacy, and his thirst for blood to govern, the *new government* will surround itself with all the republic's men, who today wander scattered all over the earth, and the gathering of all their learning will benefit everyone in general. Intellect, talent, and knowledge will be summoned anew, as in all civilized countries, to guide public destinies.

Because *he* has destroyed the guarantees that secure the citizens' life and property among Christian peoples, the *new government* will reestablish representation and forever secure the rights of every man not to be disturbed in the free exercise of his intellectual abilities and his activity.

Because *he* has made crime, murder, castration, and throat-cutting a system of government; because *he* has brought out all the evil instincts of human nature to create accomplices and partisans, the *new government* will make of justice, of accepted forms among civilized peoples, the means of punishing public crimes and will work to stimulate the noble and virtuous passions that God has placed in man's heart, his happiness on earth, making of those passions the stepping stone whereby men raise themselves and influence public affairs.

Because *he* has profaned the altars, putting on them his vile portrait; because *he* has cut the throats of priests, abused them or made them leave the country, the *new government* will give worship the dignity due it, and will elevate religion and its ministers to the stature necessary to make the people moral.

Because for fifteen years *he* has screamed, "Let the unitarian savages die," giving to believe that a government has a right to kill those who do not think as it does, branding an entire nation with a label and a ribbon, so that he who wears the *brand* is believed to think as they order him—with lashes—to think, the *new government* will respect diverse opinions, because opinions are not deeds or crimes and because God has given us reason, which distinguishes us from beasts, free to judge by our own free will.

Because *he* has been continually provoking quarrels with neighboring governments and the Europeans; because *he* has deprived us of trade with Chile, has stained Uruguay with blood, incurred the hatred of Brazil, drawn a blockade from France, insults from the North American navy, hostilities from the English navy, and entered into a labyrinth of interminable wars and protests that will come to an end only with the depopulation of the republic and the death of all his partisans, the *new government*, friend to the European powers, kind to all American peoples, will undo at one stroke that tangle of foreign relations, and will establish both interior and exterior tranquility, giving to each his right and progressing by the same routes of conciliation and order by which all cultured peoples progress.

Such is the task that remains for us to realize in the Argentine Republic. It may be that such good will not be secured immediately and that, after a subversion so radical as the one Rosas worked, it may still take a year or more of oscillations for society to enter into its proper groove. But with the fall of that monster, we will enter, at the very least, onto a path that leads to such a beautiful future, instead of a path which, under his unfortunate influence, each day moved us further away and made us recede by giant steps into barbarism, demoralization, and poverty. Peru suffers, no doubt, from the effects of internal convulsions; but in the end, its sons have not left by the thousands, and for dozens of years, to wander through neighboring countries; a monster has not arisen who surrounds himself with cadavers, suffocates all spontaneity and all feeling of virtue. What the Argentine government needs more than anything, what Rosas will never give it because it is no longer his to give, is a situation in which life and men's property do not hang on a word indiscreetly uttered, on a whim of one who rules; given those two foundations, security of life and property, the form of government, the political organization of the state, time, events, circumstances will give it. Hardly a people in America has less faith than the Argentine in a written agreement, a constitution. Illusions are now gone; the constitution of the republic will be made imperceptibly, of itself, without anyone having planned it. Unitarian, federal, mixed, it must come from completed deeds.

Nor do I believe it impossible that when Rosas falls order will follow immediately. However much it seems from a distance, the demoralization that Rosas has caused is not so great—the crimes to which the republic has been witness have been *official*, mandated by the government; no one has been castrated, had his throat cut, nor been persecuted without an express *order* to do it. On the other hand, peoples work always by reactions; the state of uneasiness and alarm in which Rosas has kept them during fifteen years has necessarily to be followed by calm; for the same reason that so many and such horrible crimes have been committed, the people and the government will flee from committing even one, so that the ominous words *Mazorca!*[27] Rosas! will not come to ring in their ears like so many avenging furies; for the very reason that the exaggerated claims of liberty harbored by the unitarians have caused such calamitous consequences, in the future politicians will be prudent in their resolutions, the parties measured in their demands. On the other hand, believing that peoples become criminals and that unruly men who kill when a tyrant drives them to it are basically evil, is to be ignorant of human nature. Everything depends on the prejudices that dominate at certain moments, and the man who today rages in blood for fanaticism was

---

27. *Mazorca* was the name of Rosas's secret police, often accused of being death squads.

yesterday an innocent devotee, and will be tomorrow a good citizen, as soon as the stimulus that led him to crime disappears. When in 1793 the French nation fell into the hands of those implacable terrorists, more than a million and a half Frenchmen were immersed in blood and crime, and after the fall of Robespierre and the Terror, scarcely sixty famous evil doers had to be sacrificed with him to return France to its habits of peacefulness and morality; and those same men who had perpetrated so many horrors were afterwards useful and moral citizens. I would say that in the factions of Rosas, even among members of the *mazorca,* there are, beneath the criminal exteriors, virtues that one day will deserve to be rewarded. Thousands of lives have been saved by the warnings that members of the *mazorca* gave secretly to the victims they had been *ordered* to sacrifice.

Independent of these general motives of morality that pertain to the human race in all times and in all countries, the Argentine Republic has elements of order that many of the world's countries lack. One obstacle that stands in the way of calming spirits in convulsed countries is difficulty in calling public attention to new objectives that might well extract it from the vicious circle of ideas in which it lives. The Argentine Republic has, luckily, so much wealth to exploit, such newness with which to attract souls after a government like that of Rosas, it would be impossible to upset the peace necessary to move on to new goals. When a cultured government is occupied with the nation's interests, what enterprises, what industrial movement! Pastoral peoples occupied with propagating the *merino* sheep that produce millions and keep thousands of men busy every hour of the day; the provinces of San Juan and Mendoza dedicated to raising silk worms, which in four years, with the government's support and protection, would require workers for the agricultural and industrial labors it needs; the northern provinces dedicated to cultivating sugar cane and indigo, which is produced spontaneously; the river banks, with free navigation that would give movement and life to interior industries. In the midst of such movement, who makes war? To what end? Only if there is a government as stupid as the present one which tramples on all these interests and, instead of giving men work, carries them off to armies to make war on Uruguay, Paraguay, Brazil, everywhere, finally.

But the principal element of order and morality on which the Argentine Republic counts today is European immigration, which by itself and despite the lack of security offered it, gathers from day to day in the *Río Plata,* and were there a government capable of directing its movement, that immigration alone would be enough to heal, in not more than ten years, all the wounds that the bandits from Facundo to Rosas have inflicted on the country they have dominated. Every year, at least half a million men who possess an industry or trade leave Europe to seek their fortune and settle where they find land to own. Until the year 1840 this immigration made its way principally to North America, which has been covered with magnificent cities and filled with an immense population thanks to immigration. At times the craze to emigrate has been so great that entire German towns have transported themselves to North America with their mayors, priests, school teachers, etc. But what finally has happened is that, in the coastal cities, the increase in population has made life as difficult as in

Europe, and the émigrés have found here the malaise and the misery from which they were fleeing. Since 1840 one reads notices in the North American dailies warning of the difficulties émigrés encounter, and the consuls in America have published similar notices in the dailies of Germany, Switzerland, and Italy so that more do not emigrate. In 1843 two ships loaded with men had to return to Europe with their cargo; and in 1844 the French government sent to Algeria twenty-one thousand Swiss who, in vain, had been going to North America.

That stream of émigrés that no longer finds advantage in the north has begun to sail the coast of America. Some made their way to Texas, others to Mexico, whose unhealthy coasts repel them; the immense littoral of Brazil does not offer them great advantages because of the work of the Negro slaves, who take away the value of production. They have, then, to reach the *Río Plata,* whose gentle climate, fertility of land, and abundance of the means of subsistence attracts and keeps them. Since 1836 thousands of émigrés began to arrive in Montevideo, and while Rosas put the native population of the republic to flight with his atrocities, Montevideo grew in a year into a flourishing and rich city, more beautiful than Buenos Aires and more filled with movement and trade. Now that Rosas has carried destruction to Montevideo, because this cursed spirit was born only to destroy, the émigrés are crowding together in Buenos Aires, taking the place of the population that the monster butchers daily in the armies, and already this year he proposed to the Assembly that Basques be enlisted to replace his decimated cadres.

The day, then, that the millions now wasted in waging disastrous and futile wars and in paying criminals are directed by a new government to the objective of national usefulness, the day all Europe knows that the horrible monster now destroying the republic and screaming daily, "Death to foreigners," has disappeared, that day the industrious immigration of Europe will find its way in mass to the *Río Plata;* the *new government* will be charged with distributing it throughout the provinces—the engineers of the republic will proceed to design plans for cities and towns that must be constructed for their residence in all suitable places, and fertile lands will be granted them, and in ten years there will be cities along all the rivers, and the republic will double its population with active, moral, and industrious residents. These are not chimeras, for it is enough to want it and to have a government less brutal than the present one to achieve it.

In 1835 five hundred thousand six hundred fifty souls emigrated [from Europe] to North America. Why would one hundred thousand per year not emigrate to the Argentine Republic if the horrible fame of Rosas did not frighten them? Well, then, one hundred thousand per year would make in ten a million industrious Europeans spread throughout the republic, teaching us to work, exploiting new riches, and enriching the country with their properties; and with a million civilized men, civil war is impossible, because there would be fewer of those who would desire it. The Scottish colony that Rivadavia[28] founded to the

---

28. Bernardino Rivadavia (1780–1845) was an Argentine statesman who served as president of the United Provinces from 1826 to 1827.

south of Buenos Aires proves it to the point of certainty; it has suffered war, but it has never taken part—and no German gaucho has abandoned his work, his dairy, or his cheese factory to go chasing around the pampas.

I believe I have demonstrated that the revolution of the Argentine Republic is now finished and that only the existence of an execrable tyrant that it created prevents it, even today, from entering onto a path of uninterrupted progress that some American peoples could envy very quickly. The struggle of the countryside with the cities has ended; the hatred of Rosas has united all elements; the old federalists and the old unitarians, like the new generation, have been persecuted by him and have become united. Recently his very brutalities and unruliness have led him to compromise the republic with a foreign war in which Paraguay, Uruguay, and Brazil would inevitably make him succumb if Europe itself had not felt compelled to come and break down that scaffolding of cadavers and blood that props him up. Those who still harbor prejudices against foreigners can answer this question: When an outlaw, a raving or crazy wild person manages to take hold of the government of a people, should all the other governments tolerate and allow him to destroy without running any risk, to kill without mercy, and for ten years to cause uprisings in all the neighboring nations?

But the remedy will not come to us only from outside. Providence—at the unfolding of our revolution's bloody drama—has wanted the parties so many times defeated, people so trampled, to find themselves with weapons in their hand and the capability to make the victims' complaints heard. The heroic province of Corrientes has today six thousand veterans who at this moment will have entered into a campaign under the command of the victor of Tablada, Oncativo, and Caaguazú, the *boleador*, the one-armed Paz,[29] as Rosas calls him. How many times will this enraged person [Rosas], who has futilely sacrificed so many victims, have bitten and bloodied his lips in rage, remembering that he held in prison for ten years and did not kill that same one-armed *boleador*[30] who today is preparing to punish his crimes! Providence will have wanted to grant him this torture of the damned, making him jailer and guardian of the one who was destined from on High to avenge the republic, humanity, and justice.

May God protect your weapons, honorable General Paz! If you save the republic, there will never have been glory like yours! If you succumb, no curse will follow you to the tomb; the peoples will associate themselves with your cause or later deplore their blindness or their degradation!

---

29. José María Paz (1791–1854), a military and political leader opposed to Rosas, was held prisoner by Rosas (1831–1839), then organized an army against him (1841–1842).

30. A *boleador* is a person who uses bolas (a weapon consisting of two or more balls attached to the ends of a cord) to catch animals.

Esteban Echeverría
(Argentina)

Esteban Echeverría (1805–1851) was one of ten children of José Domingo Echeverría, a Basque merchant, and Martina Espinosa. He was born in Buenos Aires. Somewhat after completing his early education, he fell into a dissolute existence, which came to an end only after the death of his mother. In 1822, he enrolled in the department of preparatory studies at the university, and in 1825 he left for Paris. While there, he finished his education, though not formally, coming under the influence of the romantic movement in literature. He read such authors as Montesquieu, Lammenais, Goethe, Schiller, Byron, and Lamartine. He also came to know the doctrines of Saint Simonean socialism and the romantic nationalism of Giuseppe Mazzini's Young Italy organization. He became fully involved in the cultural and intellectual life of the country, writing a series of articles entitled "Ilusiones," designed to show the dreams and idealistic aspirations of youth. In July, 1830, just at the point at which romanticism was reaching its peak in Europe, he had, for economic reasons, to return to Buenos Aires. As soon as he arrived, he published two poems in *La Gaceta Mercantil,* called "Regreso" and "En celebridad de Mayo," which would later become part of *Los consuelos,* a collection of his poems. With these and several other poems he published in the next few years, he brought the romantic spirit to Argentine literature.

In 1832, Echeverría published anonymously "Elvira o la novia del Plata," a love story in poetic form that did not have the reception he desired or anticipated, leaving him much deflated. Because of the dictator Juan Manuel de Rosas's repression, which even caused many university faculty to leave, Echeverría went to Mercedes, Uruguay, where he remained for six months, a time that was very productive for writing his poetry. On his return to Argentina, he published "La Diamela" and "Adiós al Río Negro." In 1834, Echeverría published *Los consuelos,* consisting of thirty-six poems, the first book of poems by an Argentine published in Buenos Aires. This work received great acclaim.

In 1837, Marcos Sastre, an organizer and supporter of young writers and other intellectuals, opened the Salon Literario in his bookstore. That same year, Echeverría published his best known, most admired poem, "La Cautiva," which represented an adaptation of romantic ideas to Argentine reality. He immediately became a recognized leader in the Salon. Because the Salon was such an open forum and some of its members were beginning to form a political opposition to Juan Manuel de Rosas, the bookstore was forced to close in 1838, and meetings of the Salon ended. In their place, some thirty-five young men came together on June 23, 1838, to form a new, clandestine society called Young Argentina, modeled after the romantic political organizations of Young Italy and Young Europe. Echeverría turned his romanticism to politics, becoming one of the primary founders and the intellectual leader of what ultimately came to be known as the Association of May. The Association became a center for opposition to Rosas's political sensibilities, methods, and goals. Echeverría's *Dogma socialista,* (translated as *The Socialist Doctrine*) which captures the idealism and enthusiasm of the early meetings of this group, became the intellectual platform for its programs. The selection that follows is from this work, first published in its final form in 1846, although an earlier version appeared in *El Iniciador* in 1839.

One of Echeverría's most important contributions to intellectual life in South America was his concern for the education of youth, a topic to which he devoted a great deal of attention from both Argentina and Uruguay in subsequent years. His *Manual de enseñanza moral,* published in 1846, gave him a position as one of the leading advocates of public education. He also helped found the Instituto Histórico y Geográfico del Uruguay. In September of 1847, he was named a member of the Instituto de Instrucción Pública de Uruguay, the sole official position he held in his life. Almost immediately after receiving the appointment, his health began to decline. Echeverría died in 1851, a year before Rosas was overthrown.

Further Reading

Anastasía, Luis V. *El espíritu nuevo y Esteban Echeverría.* Montevideo, Uruguay: Fundación Prudencio Vázquez y Vega, 1989.

Barcia, Pedro Luis. *Homenaje a Esteban Echeverría, 1805–1851.* Buenos Aires: Academia Argentina de Letras, Academia Nacional de la Historia, 2004.

Echeverría, Esteban. *Obras completas.* Buenos Aires: A. Zamora, 1972.

González, Liliana C. *Repensando el dogma socialista de Esteban Echeverría.* Buenos Aires: Instituto Torcuato Di Tella, 1994.

Katra, William H. *The Argentine Generation of 1837: Echeverría, Alberdi, Sarmiento, Mitre.* Madison, N.J.: Fairleigh Dickinson University Press, 1996.

Knowlton, Edgar C. *Esteban Echeverría.* Bryn Mawr, Pa.: Dorrance, 1986.

Kohan, Martín. *Los cautivos: El exilio de Echeverría.* Buenos Aires: Editorial Sudamericana, 2000.

Mercado, Juan Carlos. *Building a nation: The Case of Echeverría.* Lanham: University Press of America, 1996.

Palermo, Pablo Emilio. *Esteban Echeverría: Historia de un romántico argentino.* Editorial Dunken, 2001.

Segovia, Gonzalo. *Esteban Echeverría: El credo romántico y la heterodoxia política, romanticismo y liberalismo ortodoxo.* Mendoza, Argentina: Editorial de la Facultad de Filosofía y Letras de la Universidad Nacional de Cuyo, 1997.

The Socialist Doctrine of the Association of May (1846)

To the Argentine Youth and All Worthy Sons of the Fatherland:

1.—Tyrants have sown discord and erected their throne of iniquity on the rubble of anarchy.

2.—For us there is neither law, nor rights, nor fatherland, nor liberty.

3.—Wandering and exiled, we pass like the children of Israel in search of the promised land.

4.—Here we have the inheritance that has fallen to us by chance: Gloom, humiliation, servitude. Such is the patrimony that the revolution and the fruit of our heroic fathers' blood and sacrifices have bequeathed us.

5.—Cursed race, we seem destined by an unjust law to suffer punishment for the crimes and errors of the generation that gave us being.

6.—Our torment is the torment of Tantalus:[1] We desire and we cannot satisfy, we yearn and we cannot fulfill. Our love of liberty is a chimera, our wishes for the fatherland ineffectual.

7.—We are of age and we feel ourselves possessed of sufficient vigor to don the manly toga, but triumphant foolishness prevents us from doing so—we want to voice our complaint, and it puts a gag on us.

8.—As infants, at the roar of the cannon we saw a fatherland in a dream, and as awakening adults we find instead a wilderness strewn with cadavers and ruins, a blood-stained and fratricidal banner waving over them.

9.—There, in its shadow, is seated despotism, mute and in perpetual adoration of itself, and surrounding it the blind multitude shrieks and clamors like the misguided Israelites around the idol of Baal.[2]

10.—"We have here my fatherland," it exclaims. "We have here the protective god of the Argentines; come and adore him; prostrate yourselves, humble, at the feet of his sublime throne, and he will lavish blessings on you; adore him or you will be cursed; shame and ignominy will fall on you."

11.—Thus they speak to their brothers, "Believe or you will be wiped out." Egoism incarnate is their God, and they have made for him an altar of their unclean hearts.

12.—Pitiful are you who, more foolish than the beasts, prostrate yourselves before the monstrous idol.

13.—Pitiful those who hesitate when tyranny rages in the depths of the fatherland.

---

1. Tantalus, son of Zeus and king of Sipylos, uniquely favored among mortals in being invited to share the food of the gods. When he abused the guest-host relationship, his punishment was being "tantalized" with hunger and thirst. He was immersed up to his neck in water but when he bent to drink, the water all drained away. Fruit hung on trees above him, but when he reached for it, winds blew the fruit beyond reach.

2. Baal, Canaanite fertility deity, often associated with the sun; his religion was frequently accepted among ancient Jews, the object of priestly and popular worship.

14.—Pitiful are those who, laughing at their own clamorings, are going to offer themselves in sacrifice to the tyrant's wicked ambition.

15.—For them is ignominy, for them slavery, for them the shame and inexorable anathema of the generations.

16.—And what will we say? Will they go, the sons and the heroes of May and July? Will the generation of the giants go to be united with the chorus of the perjured idolaters who have no other god but egoism, no other fatherland than their mean ambitions, no more idea of the dignity of man than the dignity of brutes?

17.—What would they say there in their forgotten tombs, those famous martyrs of American independence!

18.—Hear, hear their cry. Hear the clamor of their immaculate blood.

19.—"Our mission was to give you independence and leave you a fatherland as inheritance."

20.—"What have you made of it? You have put it on public auction; you have sold it and prostituted it, like a whore, to the tyrants; you have mocked it in the eyes of the world; you have placed it as something vile in the mouth of slanderers; and now that you see its decorum shrunken, its cool freshness and exuberance wilted, you cast it aside and repudiate it as you would a prostitute."

21.—"Arise, arise Argentine patriots, young sons of the fathers of the fatherland, respond; may our hopes not be thwarted."

22.—"Are you also going to leave shame and servitude as an inheritance for your own sons?"

23.—"Break those chains that oppress you; unite with an indissoluble bond and open the sanctuary of your hearts to the fatherland that shelters you."

24.—"Be brothers and work together; do not fall into your fathers' error. We were lost because we cried *liberty, liberty,* but we were not brothers; lack of unity rendered all our sacrifices useless."

25.—"The greedy egoists incited this lack of unity so as to collect the fruit of our sweat, and the fatherland is dying in their impure hands."

26.—"Slaves, or men subject to absolute power, have no fatherland, because the fatherland is not tied to the land of birth but to the free exercise and full enjoyment of the rights of citizens."

27.—"You do not have a fatherland; only the citizen has a fatherland. The law bestows it and tyranny takes it away. A mob of slaves sold your fatherland, but it has not been able to sell your noble hearts."

28.—"Arise, worthy sons of the fathers of the fatherland, and march united toward securing liberty and the proud destinies of the Argentine nation."

29.—"'In union is strength; the kingdom divided will perish,' said the savior of the world."[3]

30.—"Become partners, unite your intelligence and your arms to resist oppression; it is the only means of one day coming to create the fatherland."

---

3. Luke 11:17–18.

31.—"Unite and progress—your mission is great and, indeed, as great as ours."

32.—"Fear must not frighten you, nor dangers daunt you; remember that your brothers are also oppressed. You will not recover your liberty and theirs except with blood. From courage comes triumph; from patriotism, the reward; from prudence, success."

33.—"Remember, virtue lies in action, and all thought not actualized is a chimera unworthy of man."

34.—"Always be prepared, because the time of the crusade for emancipation is approaching. The reign of truth will not come without war."

35.—"What awaits you will be harsh, but you will triumph with the help of God and your perseverance and fortitude."

36.—"Fall a thousand times, but raise yourself as many. Liberty, like the giant of legend, recovers new spirit and strength with each fall; storms make liberty larger and martyrdom makes it divine."

37.—"What you secure will be the liberty of half the world; working for the emancipation of your fatherland, you are working for the emancipation of the American spirit."

38.—"Initiative belongs to you, as the initiative of American independence fell to your fathers."

39.—"No, when all the world's peoples are moving and walking from east to west, from north to south, as if driven by a hidden force toward securing glory and well-being, you remain stationary."

40.—"Do not lie down to sleep in the tent your fathers raised, because it harbors sadness, and tyranny is lying in wait for you to let down your guard."

41.—"The world is moving forward; move forward with it if you want to elevate yourselves to the status of free men."

42.—"But remember that to triumph you must unite, and that only with harmonious coordination of all your strengths will you manage to fulfill your mission and guide your fatherland to the status of a free, independent, and powerful nation."

Here we have God's mandate, here we have the fatherland's outcry, here we have the young generation's sacred oath.

To whomever adulterates with corruption, anathema.

To whomever offers incense to tyranny, or sells himself to its gold, anathema.

To whomever betrays liberty's principles, honor and patriotism, anathema.

To the coward, the egoist, the perjurer, anathema.

To whomever hesitates on the great day of the sons of the fatherland, anathema.

To whomever looks backward and smiles when the trumpet of the fatherland's regeneration sounds, anathema.

Here we have the wish of the new generation and of generations to come.

Glory to those who do not get discouraged in conflicts and who have confidence in their strength—from them will come victory.

Glory to those who do not despair, who have faith in the future and in humanity's progress—from them will come the reward.

Glory to those who work tenaciously to make themselves worthy sons of the fatherland—from them will come the blessings of posterity.

Glory to those who do not tolerate any type of tyranny and feel a pure, free, and gallant heart beating in their chest.

Glory to the Argentine youth who yearn to emulate the virtues and actualize the great thought of the heroic fathers of the fatherland—Glory forever and prosperity.

• • • • •

§ III

3. Brotherhood. — 4. Equality. — 5. Liberty

"Human brotherhood is mutual love, that noble disposition that inclines man to do unto others what he would wish them to do unto him."[4]

With his blood, Christ made brotherhood divine, and the prophets sanctified it with their martyrdom.

But at that time man was weak because he lived for himself and only within himself. Humanity, or the *harmony of the human family,* agreeing on an identical goal, *did not exist.*

Tyrants and egoists easily clouded the divine light of the redeemer's word with their deadly breath, and, in order to rule, incited fathers to fight with sons, brothers with brothers, families with families.

Man, blind and walled up in his *I,* believed it right to sacrifice the well-being of others to his passions, and peoples and men made war among themselves and tore each other to pieces like wild animals.

"By the law of God and humanity, all men are brothers. Every act of egoism is an offense against human brotherhood."[5]

Egoism is the death of the soul. The egoist feels neither love, nor charity, nor affection for his brothers. All his acts are directed toward the satisfaction of his *I;* all his thoughts and actions revolve around his *I;* and duty, honor, and justice are hollow words without meaning for his depraved spirit.

Egoism deifies itself and makes its heart the center of the universe. All tyrants are egoism incarnate.

It is the duty of every man who knows his mission to wage hand-to-hand combat with egoism until he annihilates it.

Brotherhood is the golden chain that must link all pure and truly patriotic hearts; without this chain, there is neither strength, nor union, nor fatherland.

Every act, every word that tends to weaken this chain is an offense against the fatherland and humanity.

---

4. Young Europe. [Echeverría's note, referring to Giuseppe Mazzini's revolutionary organization of the same name.]

5. Young Europe. [Echeverría's note.]

Let us cast a veil of forgetfulness over our ancestors' errors; man is fallible. Let us judge their works fairly and let us consider what we would have done in the same circumstances. What we are and what we will be in the future we owe to them. Let us open the sanctuary of our hearts to those who were very much worthy of the fatherland and sacrificed themselves for it.

The egoist and evil doers will receive their just deserts; posterity's judgment awaits them. The motto of the new generation is brotherhood.

"By the law of God and humanity, all men are equal."[6]

To make equality real, men must understand their rights and mutual obligations.

Equality consists in everyone supporting and equally accepting those rights and duties, in no one being exempt from the effect of the law that expresses those rights and duties that each man, proportional to his intelligence and work, share equally in enjoyment of rights. *All privilege is an affront to equality.*

Equality does not exist where the rich class superimposes itself and has more privileges than other classes.

Where a certain class monopolizes public posts.

Where influence and power paralyze the law's effect for some and strengthen it for others.

Where only factions, not the nation, are sovereign.

Where levied taxes are not divided equally and in proportion to the wealth and accomplishments of each one.

Where the poor class alone bears the most difficult social burdens, like military service, etc.

Where the least of the government's henchmen can violate with impunity the citizen's security and liberty.

Where compensations and jobs are not awarded to the deserving, as evidenced by the facts.

Where every employee is a mandarin,[7] before whom the citizen must bow his head.

Where employees are servile agents of the government, not salaried employees dependent on the nation.

Where factions grant rights and rewards at their whim.

Where talent and probity have no claim to merit, only despicable foolishness and flattery do.

All privilege granted to civil, military, or religious, academic, or university corporations also offends equality, as does every exceptional and particular law.

---

6. Young Europe. [Echeverría's note.]

7. Mandarin, a pedantic official in the Chinese empire.

Society and the government that represents it owe equal protection, security, liberty to all their members; if these are granted to some and not to others, there is inequality and tyranny.

Social power is not moral, nor is it in keeping with its goals, if it does not protect the weak, the poor, and the needy, that is to say, if it does not use the means society has given it to make equality real.

Equality has a connection to citizens' learning and well-being.

To enlighten the masses regarding their genuine rights and obligations, to educate them with the goal of making them capable of exercising citizenship, and to infuse them with the dignity of free men, protect them and encourage them so that they work and are industrious, provide them the means of acquiring well-being and independence—here we have the way to raise them to equality.

The only *hierarchy* that should exist in a democratic society is one that originates in nature and is invariably and necessarily like nature.

Money can never be a reason for entitlement if it is not in pure, charitable, and virtuous hands. A foolish and villainous soul, a depraved and egoistic heart, may be favored by luck, but neither its gold nor the flattery of lowly common people will ever instill in them what nature *denied them—republican talent and virtues.*

God—supreme intelligence—wished man to excel in reason and intelligence so that he might have dominion over creation and be master of the rest of the creatures.

Intelligence, virtue, talent, proven merit—here we have the only hierarchies of natural and divine origin.

Society recognizes only merit attested to by works. It asks of the general replete with ranks and medals, "What useful victory have you won for the fatherland?" To the government agent and the rich person, "How have you alleviated the miseries and needs of the people?" To the individual, "For what works have you merited respect and consideration from your fellow citizens and humanity?" And to everyone in general, "In what circumstances have you shown yourself talented, virtuous, and patriotic?"

He who has nothing to reply to these questions and who nonetheless shows pretentiousness and aspires to supremacy is a fool who merits only pity or scorn.

The challenge of social equality is contained within this principle: "To each man according to his ability, to each man according to his works."[8]

"By the law of God and humanity all men are free."

---

8. Saint Simon. [Echeverría's note, referring to Claude Henri de Rouvroi, compte de Saint-Simon, 1760–1825, French social philosopher who foreshadowed classical positivism.]

"Liberty is the right each man has to use his abilities in pursuit of his well-being with no hindrance whatsoever and to choose the means that will be useful to him for this objective."[9]

The free exercise of individual strengths should not cause injury or violence to the rights of others; do not do to another what you would not want him to do to you. Human liberty has no other limits.

Liberty does not exist where man cannot alter his situation as he pleases.

Where he is not permitted to make use of the fruits of his industry and his work.

Where he has to sacrifice his time and his wealth to the government.

Where he can be maltreated and insulted by the hired assassins of an arbitrary government.

Where, without having violated the law, without previous judgment nor any due process, he can be imprisoned or be deprived of the use of his physical or intellectual faculties.

Where his right of proclaiming his opinions in speech or writing is limited.

Where a religion and worship different from what his conscience judges true is imposed on him.

Where he can be arbitrarily disturbed in his home, snatched from the bosom of his family, and banished from his fatherland.

Where his security, his life, and his wealth are at the mercy of a government agent's caprice.

Where he is obliged to take up arms without absolute necessity and without the general interest requiring it.

Where obstacles and conditions are put on him in the exercise of whatever industry, like printing, etc.

§ IV

God, Center and Periphery of our Religious Belief. Christianity His Law.

Natural religion is that imperative instinct that leads man to offer homage to the Creator.[10]

The relationship of man with God is of a moral nature, like that of son to father. Because God is the pure source of our life and abilities, of our hopes and joys, we, in exchange for these riches, present Him the only offering for which He could yearn, the tribute of our heart.

---

9. Young Europe. [Echeverría's note.]

10. In various paragraphs, and in this one especially, there are some critical opinions, suggested by the exceptional situation in which our country found itself, whose drift was not hidden from the readers of the Río Plata. Nonetheless, we are making the precaution because considered in "the abstract" those opinions can seem erroneous or contradictory to readers unfamiliar with our situation. (E.A.) [Note to the 1944 edition of *Dogma socialista*.]

But natural religion has not been enough for man because, lacking of certainty, of life, and of sanction, it did not satisfy the needs of his conscience, and it has been necessary for the positive religions that support his authority over historic deeds to proclaim the laws that should govern those intimate relations between man and his creator.

Christianity is the best of the positive religions because it is nothing other than the revelation of humanity's moral instincts.

The Gospel is the law of God because it is the moral law of conscience and reason.

Christianity brought to the world brotherhood, equality, and liberty, and, restoring the human race to its rights, redeemed it. Christianity is essentially civilizing and progressive.

The world was submerged in the shadows, and the word of Christ illuminated it, and from the chaos sprang a world. Humanity was a cadaver and received life and resurrection with His breath.

The Gospel is the law of love, and as the Apostle James says, the perfect law, that is, the law of liberty. Christianity must be the religion of democracies.

Examine everything and choose the good, says the Gospel; and thus it has proclaimed the independence of reason and liberty of conscience—because liberty consists, principally, of the right to examine and choose.

All religion presupposes a worship. Worship is the visible part, the exterior manifestation, of religion, just as speech is a necessary element of thought.

Religion is a tacit pact between God and human conscience; it forms the spiritual link that unites creature and maker. Man, as a consequence, will have to guide his thought to God in the way that he judges most suitable. God is the only judge of the acts of man's conscience, and no earthly authority must usurp that divine prerogative, nor will it be able to do this even if it wanted, because conscience is free.

If liberty of conscience is repressed, the voice and hands will exercise the practices of worship automatically, if required, but the heart, deep within itself, will renounce this and will keep liberty in its inviolable sanctuary.

If liberty of conscience is a right of the individual, liberty of worship is a right of religious communities.

With liberty of conscience acknowledged, it would be contradictory not to recognize liberty of worship as well, which is nothing more than the direct application of the former.

The profession of beliefs and worship will be free only when no obstacle is placed in the way of preaching the doctrine of the former or the practice of the latter, and when individuals of every religious community are equal in civil and political rights with all other citizens.

Religious society is independent of civil society; the former directs its hopes to another world, the latter concentrates its hopes on earth; the mission of the first is spiritual, that of the second is temporal. Tyrants have forged from religion chains for man, and from this emerged the impure league between the government and the altar.

It is not incumbent on the government to regulate beliefs, putting itself between God and human conscience, but rather to protect those principles of society that sustain it and keep social morality under its protection.

If any religion or worship had a tendency, publicly or directly, by actions or by writings, to injure social morality and alter the system, it will be government's duty to work actively to repress that religion's excesses.

The jurisdiction of the government with respect to forms of worship will be to constrain itself to keeping watch so they neither harm each other nor sow social discord.

The state, as a political body, cannot have a religion because, not being an individual person, it lacks a conscience of its own.

The dogma of the dominant religion is moreover unjust and offensive to equality because it pronounces social excommunication on those who do not profess its belief and deprives them of their natural rights without exempting them from social obligations.

The principle of liberty of conscience will never be reconcilable with the dogma of state religion.

If liberty of conscience is acknowledged, the state must not declare any religion dominant nor support it. All religions must be respected and protected equally as long as their morality is pure and their worship does not offend the social order.

The word *tolerance,* in the matter of religion and of worship, not only declares the absence of liberty but carries an insult to the rights of humanity. The inhibited or the bad is tolerated; a right is recognized and proclaimed. The human spirit is a free essence; liberty is an indestructible element of its nature and a gift from God.

The priest is a minister of worship; the priesthood is a public post. The mission of the priest is *to moralize;* to preach brotherhood, charity, that is to say, the law of peace and love—the law of God.

The priest who from the pulpit inflames passions and provokes revenge is impious and sacrilegious.

"Love your neighbor as yourself; love your enemies," says Christ—here we have the priest's spoken word.

The priest must preach tolerance, not persecution against indifference or impiety. Force makes hypocrites, not believers, and ignites fanaticism and war.

"How will they have faith in the word of the priest if he himself does not observe the law? He who says that he knows God and does not keep His commandments is a liar and there is no truth in him."[11]

"We do not demand blind obedience," says St. Paul. "We teach, prove, persuade." *"Fides suadenda non imperanda,"*[12] repeats St. Bernard.

---

11. The Epistle of John, 9:2. [Echeverría's note, referring to the passage that can be found in the King James version of the Bible at 1 John 2:4–5.]

12. One version of St. Bernard of Clairvaux's (1090–1153) motto, which appears in some places as *"Fides suadenda, non imponenda"* (By persuasion, not by violence are men won to the

The mission of the priest is exclusively spiritual, because mixing himself in worldly passions and interests compromises and stains the sanctity of his ministry, and brings upon him contempt and hatred instead of love and veneration.

The vicars and ministers of Christ must not exercise employment nor assume any temporal authority. *"Regnum meum non est de hoc mundo,"*[13] their divine teacher has said to them, and thus has signaled to them the limits of his church's government.

Ecclesiastics, as members of the state, are under its jurisdiction and cannot form a privileged and separate social body. Like all other citizens, they will be subject to the same duties and obligations, to the same civil laws and punishments, and to the same authorities. All men are equal; only merit and virtue beget supremacy.[14]

§ V.

1. Honor and Sacrifice, Motive and Norm of our Social Conduct

Morality governs the private man's acts, honor the public man's.

Morality belongs to the jurisdiction of individual conscience and is the norm of man's conduct regarding himself and his peers. Honor enters into the jurisdiction of the conscience of social man and is the norm of his actions with respect to society.

There exists a certain disagreement between some evangelical precepts and the actual organization of societies.[15]

There are certain actions that morality approves in the private man and censures in the public man. It is for that very reason necessary to adopt the word "honor," which is commonly applied to the public man who conducts himself with honor and probity, since it immediately designates morality.

Honor and morality are two identical endpoints that have an identical result.

Morality will be the dogma of the Christian and of the private man, honor, the dogma of the citizen and the public man.

---

faith), and *"Fides suadenda, non impodenda"* (By persuasion, not by imposition, are men won to the faith). St. Bernard adopted this motto as a reaction to the Inquisition in France.

13. John 18:36. "My kingdom is not of this world."

14. We have not been able nor wanted to touch on all the points that are contained in the religious question; we have contented ourselves with signaling those more essential for now and those that the state of our society tolerates. (E.A.) [Note to the 1944 edition of *Dogma socialista.*]

15. Christianity teaches abnegation of worldly things, detachment from earthly interests, absorption of man into God or into the exclusive idea of the salvation of his soul, doctrines entirely the opposite of the duties of social man and of the citizen. Christianity preaches humility and says, "If they strike you on one cheek, present the other to the hand of your adversary,"—humility that the honor of the social man does not tolerate. Christianity says: "regnum meum non est de hoc mundo," etc. [Echeverría's note.]

The man of honor does not betray principles.

The man of honor is truthful, he does not fail to keep his word, he does not violate religion with blasphemy; he loves the genuine and just, is charitable and kind.

The man of honor does not fail in his public duty, has rectitude and probity, does not sell his favors when he finds himself in high position.

The man of honor is a good friend, he does not betray the enemy who puts himself under his protection; the man of honor is virtuous, a good patriot, a good citizen.

The man of honor detests tyranny because he has faith in principles, and he is not an egoist; tyranny is egoism incarnate.

The man of honor sacrifices himself, if necessary, for justice and liberty.

There is neither honor nor virtue without sacrifice; nor will there be room for sacrifice in inactivity.

He who does not act when honor calls him is not worthy of being called a man.

He who does not act when the fatherland is in danger is worthy of being neither man nor citizen.

The virtue of virtues is action leading to sacrifice.

Sacrifice is that noble character of the spirit that leads man to consecrate his life and abilities, often drowning out temptations from personal interest and egoism, to defend a cause that he considers just; to attain a good common to his fatherland and peers; to fulfill his duties as man and as citizen always and despite everything; and to shed his blood, if necessary, to carry out so high and noble a mission.

All men, then, have a mission. Every mission is obligatory.

Only he is worthy of praise, who, knowing his mission, is always ready to sacrifice himself for the fatherland and for the sacred cause of liberty, equality, and brotherhood.

Only he is deserving of glory who works for the progress and well-being of humanity.

Only he earns for himself respect and deference who counts his worth by his ability and virtues.

"You know that those who are recognized as rulers over the Gentiles exercise lordship over them and their great ones exercise authority on them.

"But it shall not be so among you; rather whoever wishes to be great among you will be your servant.

"And whoever wishes to be first among you will be the servant of all.

"For the Son of man did not come to be served but to serve and give his life as a ransom for many."[16]

The doctrine of Christ is ours, because it is the doctrine of salvation and redemption.

---

16. Matthew 10:42–45. [Echeverría's note. But in actuality he refers to Mark 10: 42–45.]

He who wishes to raise himself up will sacrifice himself for others.

He who wishes to see his name exalted will look for a foundation in the heart of his fellow citizens.

He who yearns for glory will build it with the forceful action of his intelligence and strength.

Liberty is acquired only at the price of blood.

"Liberty is the bread people must earn with the sweat of their brow."[17]

Egoism labors for itself, sacrifice for others.

Sacrifice is the decree of death for egoistic passions. These passions have brought war, disaster, and tyranny to the soil of the fatherland. Only in sacrificing ourselves will we manage to redeem the fatherland, emulate the virtues of those who gave it being, and win noble laurels.

§ VIII

10. Independence from Reactionary Traditions That Subordinate Us to the Old Regime.

Two ideas always appear in the theater of revolutions—[18] the static idea that requires the *status quo* and depends on the traditions of the past, and the reforming and progressive idea—the old regime and the modern spirit. Each of these ideas has its representatives and sectarians, and from their antipathy and struggle are born the war and disasters of a revolution.

The triumph of the revolution is for us the triumph of the new and progressive idea; it is the triumph of the sacred cause of the liberty of man and peoples. But that triumph has not been complete, because the two ideas still silently harass each other and because the new spirit has not completely annihilated the spirit of darkness.

The American generation's blood is contaminated with the habits and tendencies of another generation. On its brow are noted, if not the slave's dejection, the recent scars of past servitude.

Its body has been emancipated but not its mind.

It could be said that revolutionary America, now free of the Spanish lion's claws, is still subject to the fascination of its looks and the prestige of its omnipotence.

As a sign of its vassalage, independent America retains the accessories from the imperial robe of its former mistress, and independent America is also graced with her moth-eaten livery.

What a monstrosity! A virgin full of life and strength covered with tattered rags; democracy adorned with the monarchy's coat of arms and the aristocracy's

---

17. La-Mennais (E.A.). [Note to the 1944 edition, referring to Félicité Robert de Lamennais (1782–1854), French Roman Catholic apologist and liberal.]

18. We do not understand by revolution the riots or turbulences of civil war, but rather the complete overthrow of an old social order, or the absolute change, as much in the interior system as in the exterior of a society (E.A.). [Note to the 1944 edition.]

powdered wig; a new century crammed into an old one; youth walking at the pace of old age; a cadaver and a living person covered with the same shroud; revolutionary America still wrapped in the swaddling clothes of its former stepmother!

Two terrible legacies from Spain are what principally shackled the progressive movement of the American Revolution—its customs and its legislation.

A new political order demands new elements to constitute it.

The customs of a society founded on the inequality of classes will never be able to fraternize with the principles of democratic equality.

Spain left us as an inheritance the *routine,* and routine is nothing in the moral order other than abnegation of the right to examine and choose, which means suicide of the race; and in the physical order, to follow the well-worn path, not to innovate, always to do things in the same mold, adapting them to the same method. Democracy demands action, innovation, constant exercise of all man's abilities, because movement is the essence of democracy's life.

Spain inculcated in us the dogma of blind respect for tradition and the infallible authority of certain doctrines; but modern philosophy proclaims the dogma of reason's independence and recognizes no authority other than what reason sanctions, nor other *criteria* to decide on principles and doctrines than the uniform *consent* of humanity.

Spain recommended that we respect and defer to the opinions of grey-haired people, but grey hair can be evidence of old age, not intelligence and reason.

Spain taught us to be obedient and superstitious, but democracy wants us to be submissive to religious and civic law.

Spain educated us as vassals and colonists, but in accord with the dignity of free men the fatherland demands that we be enlightened.

Spain divided society into bodies, hierarchies, professions, and guilds, and brought clergy, nobility, commoners, or the anonymous crowd to the laws. Democracy, leveling all conditions, says to us that there are no hierarchies other than those the law establishes for the governance of society; that the magistrate, outside the place where he exercises his functions, is no different from other citizens; that the priest, the military man, the lawyer, the merchant, the artisan, the rich, and the poor, are all one; that the least of the common people is a man equal in rights to the rest and carries imprinted on his brow the dignity of his nature; that only probity, talent, and character beget supremacy; that he who exercises the humblest industry, if he has ability and virtues, is not less than the priest, the lawyer, or any other who employs his abilities in whatever other profession; that there are not some professions more noble than others, because nobility does not consist in a full-length habit or in bearing some title but rather in actions; and that, in sum, in a democratic society, only those inclined to use their natural strengths for the good and prosperity of the fatherland are worthy, wise, virtuous, and deserving of respect.

To destroy these noxious seeds and emancipate us completely from those stale traditions, we need radical reform in our practices; such will be the work of education and laws.

A semi-barbarous legislation—dictated in dark times by the caprice or will of a man to protect the interests and secure the superiority of certain classes; a legislation made, not to satisfy the needs of our society but rather to strengthen the tyranny of the metropolis; a legislation intended for colonists and vassals, not for citizens; a legislation that indefinitely prolongs disputes and differences, causing the ruin of individuals and the state; that opens the field wide to bad faith and abuses; that leaves room for the deliberations of a gloomy and vacillating jurisprudence, bristling with scholastic sophistries; a legislation, in sum, that has no root whatsoever in the mind of the nation, and that destroys at their foundation the principles of equality and democratic liberty—that semi-barbarous legislation will never be suitable for an independent America.

Our legislation must be born of the mind and practices of the nation.

Educating the people, tempering them for it, will be the means of preparing the elements of a legislation suitable to our social state and needs.

The work of legislation is slow because customs are not modified at a single stroke.

The laws have influence beyond measure in improving practices. When laws are bad, practices become depraved; when good, they improve.

The vices of a people are almost always buried deep in the core of its legislation. America attests to it. American practices are the children of Spanish laws.

Our positive laws must be in harmony with principles of natural law. *Jus privatum latet sub tutela juris publici.*[19] Because, in this way, as reason is the foundation of all rights, natural law is the original principle and the source of all other laws.

Our laws will be personal, or equally obligatory for everyone. The strength of law consists only in that it applies to everyone.

Our laws will, for each citizen, fix the limits of his rights and obligations and will teach him what is useful or noxious to his particular interests or society's collective interests.

If the law should be one for everyone, no civil, military, or religious class will have special laws, but will rather be subject to common laws.[20]

Actualization of these principles must guide our legislators' views.

A complete body of American laws, prepared in light of the gradual progress of democracy, would be the solid foundation for the magnificent edifice of the American spirit's emancipation.

---

19. Bacon. [Note to the 1944 edition, probably referring to Francis Bacon, 1561–1626, English philosopher, essayist, and statesman. "Private right is under the protection of public right." Source unknown.]

20. The association of the young Argentine generation pledges itself to make a complete classification of all those Spanish laws in force among us that are in open opposition to the principles of equality and democratic liberty, passing them through the crucible of a true philosophical critique. The nature of this work does not permit going into detail now. (E.A.) [Note to the edition of 1944.]

§ IX

11. Emancipation of the American Spirit

The great thought of the revolution has not been made real. We are independent but not free. Spain's arms do not oppress us, but its traditions crush us. The counter-revolution was born in the innermost recesses of anarchy.

The static idea, the Spanish idea, emerging from its dark den triumphantly raises anew its slow-witted head and hurls anathemas against the reforming and progressive spirit.

But its triumph will be ephemeral. God has wanted and the history of humanity shows that the ideas and events that have existed disappear from the world stage and are engulfed forever in the abyss of the past as the generations disappear one after the other. God has wished that today's day not resemble yesterday's day; that the present century not be a monotonous repetition of the previous one; that what once was, not be reborn; and that in the moral world, as in the physical, in the life of man as in the life of peoples, everything moves and progresses, everything is in incessant activity and continuous movement.

The counter-revolution is nothing other than the slow death knell of a worn-out century, of the reactionary tradition of the old regime, of some ideas in history that were already completely empty. Who, violating the law of God, will be able to reanimate that specter which rises in its delusions already wrapped in the shroud of the tomb? The impotent force of some blinded spirit? Chimera!

The revolution rumbles voicelessly in the innermost recesses of our society. To raise its head it awaits the reappearance of the generative star of the fatherland; in the darkness it sharpens its arms and whets its tongues of fire in the prisons where they oppress and muzzle it; it ignites all patriotic hearts; it matures its plans for reform in silence and, inactive, it gains greater intelligence and power.

The revolution proceeds, but shackled. It falls to the young generation to break the shackles into pieces and secure the glory of the initiative in the great work of the emancipation of the American spirit, which is summed up in these two problems: *political emancipation and social emancipation.*

The first is resolved; the second lacks resolution.

The fatherland's liberty is tied to its social emancipation.

We can obtain American social emancipation only by repudiating the legacy Spain left us and by concentrating all our efforts on the goal of constituting American sociability.

A people's sociability is made up of all the civilization's elements—the political, philosophical, religious, scientific, artistic, industrial.

American politics will tend to organize democracy, or, in other words, equality and liberty, assuring to all and each of the association's members, by means of adequate laws, the broadest and freest exercise of their natural faculties. It will recognize the principle of the independence and sovereignty of each people, drawing with letters of gold on the high summit of the Andes, in the shadow of all the American standards, this divine symbol—*citizenship in a nation is sacred.*

It will establish the rules that must govern their mutual relationships and their relations with the rest of the world's peoples.

Philosophy recognizes individual reason as the sole judge of everything that touches the individual and it recognizes collective reason, or the general *consensus*, as the sovereign arbiter of everything that concerns society.

Philosophy in the association will attempt to establish the covenant of alliance between individual reason and collective reason of citizen and fatherland.

Philosophy enlightens faith, explains religion, and also subordinates it to the law of progress.[21]

Philosophy in inert nature searches for the law of its generation; in animality, the law of the development of the life of all beings; in history, the thread of the progressive tradition of each people and of humanity, and, as a consequence, the manifestation of the intentions of Providence; in art, it searches for individual and social thought, which it confronts and explains; or, in metaphysical terms, the harmonious expression of finite and contingent life and of absolute, infinite, humanitarian life.

Philosophy brings the industry and the material work of man under the control of rational laws.

Philosophy, in sum, is the science of life in all its possible manifestations, from the mineral to the plant, from the plant to the infusorial insect, from the insect to man, from man to God.

Philosophy is the eye of the intellect, examining and interpreting the laws necessary to rule the physical and moral world or universe.

Religion is the moral foundation on which society rests, the divine balm of the heart, the pure fount of our future hopes, and the mystical ladder by which earthly thought ascends to heaven.

Science teaches man to have knowledge of himself, to penetrate the mysteries of nature, to raise his thought to the creator, and to find the means of individual and social improvement and perfection.

Art embraces in its divine inspirations all the moral and emotional elements of humanity—the good, the just, the genuine, the beautiful, the sublime, the divine; individuality and society, the finite and the infinite; love, misgivings, the visions of the soul, the vaguest and most mysterious intuitions of consciousness; it penetrates and embraces everything with its prophetic spirit; it looks at everything through the brilliant prism of its imagination, animates it with the fiery

---

21. Philosophy already presents and announces the birth of a rational religion of the future, broader than Christianity, that serves as the base of the development of the human spirit and reorganization of European societies and that fully satisfies humanity's present needs. Who will reveal that religion?—humanity itself. This idea, which constitutes the fundamental principle of the doctrine of Leroux and his school, has not yet emerged from the sphere of speculation and reduces us to announcing it, because it is not yet time to air the questions it involves among ourselves. Our faith in Christianity is complete. We adopt it moreover as the religion of the people, even though we would like to see it reign with all its purity and majesty (E.A.). [Note to the edition of 1944.]

breath of its generative word, embellishes it with the bright colors of its palette and translates it into ineffable or sublime harmonies. It sings of heroism and liberty and solemnizes all great acts, internal as well as external, of the life of nations.

Industry places in man's hands the instruments to master the forces of nature, cause its well-being, and win dominion over creation.

Politics, philosophy, science, religion, art, industry—all of them will have to guide democracy, offer it their support, and cooperate actively in strengthening it and laying its foundations.

In the natural, harmonious, and complete development of these elements, the problem of the emancipation of the American spirit is enumerated.

§ X.

12. Organization of the Fatherland on a Democratic Foundation

Equality and liberty are the two central axes, or better, the two poles of the democratic world.

Democracy starts from a necessary fact, that is to say, the equality of classes, and proceeds with firm step toward securing the reign of a broader liberty—*of individual, civil, and political liberty.*

Democracy is not a form of government, but rather the very essence of all republican governments or governments instituted by everyone for the good of the community or the association.

Democracy is the rule of liberty based on the equality of classes.

All modern political associations tend to establish equality of classes, and can be assured, observing the progressive movement of the European and American nations, "that the gradual development of the equality of classes is a law of providence, because it shares in its principal characteristics; it is universal, lasting, withdraws itself daily from human power, and all events and all men unknowingly conspire to extend and strengthen it."[22]

Democracy is government of the majority, or the uniform *consent* of the reason of everyone, working for the creation of law and working to decide authoritatively everything of interest to the association.

This general and uniform consent constitutes the *sovereignty of the people.*

Sovereignty of the people is unlimited in everything pertaining to society—politics, philosophy, religion; but the people are not sovereign over what touches the individual—his conscience, his property, his life, and his liberty.

The association has been established for the good of all; it is the common fund of all individual interests or the symbol animated by the strength and intelligence of each one.

---

22. Tocqueville (E.A.). [Note to the 1944 edition of *Dogma socialista*, referring to Alexis de Tocqueville, 1805–1859, French liberal political writer.]

The purpose of the association is to organize democracy and assure all and each of the associated members, *the most extensive and freest enjoyment of their natural rights, the most extensive and freest exercise of their abilities.*

The sovereign people or the majority, then, cannot violate those individual rights, restrict the exercise of those abilities that are at the same time the origin, the bond, the condition, and the purpose of the association.

From the moment it violates them, the covenant is broken, the association is dissolved, and each one will be absolute master of his own will and actions and can base his right on his own strength.

Therefore, the limit of collective reason is *right,* and the limit of individual reason, the *sovereignty of the people's reason.*

The right of the individual man is antecedent to the right of the association. The individual, by the law of God and humanity, is exclusive master of his life, his property, his conscience, and his liberty. His life is a gift from God; his property, the sweat of his brow; his conscience, the eye of his soul and the intimate judge of his acts; his liberty, the necessary condition for developing the abilities that God gave him to live happily, the very essence of his life, inasmuch as life without liberty is death.

Consequently, the right of the association is circumscribed by the orbit of individual rights.

The sovereign, the people, the majority, dictate social and positive law for the purpose of strengthening and sanctioning the original law, the natural law of the individual. So, far from man's giving up a part of his liberty and his rights upon entering society, he has, on the contrary, united with the rest and formed the association with the goal of guaranteeing and extending his liberty and rights.

If the positive law of the sovereign conforms to natural law, its right is legitimate and everyone must obey it on pain of being punished as an offender; if positive law violates natural law, it is not legitimate and is tyrannical, and no one is obligated to obey it.

The individual's right of resistance against tyrannical decisions by the sovereign people, or the majority, is, consequently, legitimate, as is the right of repelling force with force and of killing the thief or the murderer who threatens our property or life, since this right arises from the very conditions of the social covenant.

The sovereignty of the people is unlimited to the extent that it respects the right of man—first principle.

The sovereignty of the people is absolute to the extent that it has reason as its norm—second principle.

Collective reason alone is sovereign, not collective will. The will is blind, capricious, irrational; the will wants; reason examines, weighs, and decides.

Therefore, the sovereignty of the people can reside only in the *reason of the people,* and it is called only to exercise the judicious and rational part of the social community.

The ignorant part remains under the guidance and safeguard of the law prescribed by the uniform consent of the rational people.

Democracy, then, is not the absolute despotism of the masses nor of the majority; it is the rule of reason.

Sovereignty is the greatest and most solemn act of a free people's reason. How will they be able to agree to this act—those who do not know its importance? Those who for lack of learning are incapable of discerning good from evil in the matter of public affairs? Those who, ignorant as they are of what might be appropriate, have no opinion of their own and are consequently prone to accede to the suggestions of people with bad intentions? Those who by their imprudent ballot might compromise the liberty of the fatherland and the existence of society? How will it be possible, I say, that the blind see, the lame walk, the mute speak, that is to say, that he who has neither capacity nor independence agree to sovereign acts?

Industriousness is another condition of the exercise of sovereignty. The idler, the vagabond, he who has no position also may not participate in sovereignty, because not being tied to society by any interest he will easily give away his ballot for gold or threats.

He whose well-being depends on the will of another and does not enjoy personal independence will be less able to enter into the enjoyment of sovereignty, because it will be difficult for him to sacrifice his interest to the independence of his reason.

The tutelage of the ignorant, of the vagabond, of the one who does not enjoy personal independence, is, consequently, necessary. The law does not forbid them to exercise sovereign rights for themselves, but only while they remain in a state of tutelage. It does not deprive them of their rights, but rather imposes on them a condition for possessing them—the condition of emancipating themselves.

But the people, the masses, do not always have in their hands the means of achieving emancipation. The society or *government* that represents society and that is the agent of emancipation must put the means to emancipation within their reach.

It will encourage industry, destroy the fiscal laws that hobble its development, will not overload it with taxes, and will allow it to pursue its activity freely and rigorously.

It will spread learning everywhere in society and will extend its beneficent hand to the poor and helpless. It will endeavor to raise the proletarian class to the level of the other classes, first emancipating its body, with the aim of subsequently emancipating its reason.

To emancipate the ignorant masses and open to them the road to sovereignty, it is necessary to educate them. The masses have nothing but instincts; they are more emotional than rational; they desire the good and do not know where it is; they wish to be free and do not know the path of liberty.

Education of the masses must be systematized.

Religion, making them more moral, will nourish in their hearts the seeds of good practices.

Elementary instruction will put them in a position to acquire greater learning and to arrive one day at developing an understanding of the rights and obligations that citizenship imposes.[23]

The ignorant masses, nevertheless, although temporarily deprived of the exercise of the rights of sovereignty or of political liberty, fully enjoy their individual liberty. Like those of all the members of the association, their natural rights are inviolable. Civil liberty also protects them, as it does everyone. The same civil, penal, and constitutional law, dictated by the sovereign, protects their life, their property, their conscience, and their liberty; it calls them to judgment when they commit an offense and condemns or absolves them.

They may not be present at the making of the law that formulates the rights and obligations of the associated members while they remain in tutelage and in their minority; but that same law gives them means to emancipate themselves, and in the meantime they stand under its protection and safeguard.

Democracy leads to the leveling of conditions, to the equality of the classes.

The equality of classes includes individual liberty, civil liberty, and political liberty. When all the members of the association are in full and absolute possession of these liberties and together exercise sovereignty, democracy will have been constituted definitively on the unshakable foundation of the equality of classes—third principle.

We have worked out the spirit of democracy and traced the limits of the peoples' sovereignty. Let us now move on to investigate how sovereignty operates, or in other words, which apparent, visible form transmits its decisions; how it organizes democratic government.

By making the law, sovereignty delegates its powers, reserving for itself the sanction of the law.

The delegate represents the sovereign's interests and reason.

The legislator exercises a limited and temporary sovereignty; his criterion is reason.

The legislator dictates the organic law and formulates in it the rights and obligations of the citizen and the conditions of the covenant of association.

He divides the social domain into three great powers, for which he outlines the limits and jurisdictions, which constitute the symbolic unity of democratic sovereignty.

The legislative represents the people's reason, the judiciary its justice, the executive its action or will. The first crafts the law, the second applies it, the third carries it out; the first votes on expenditures and taxes and is the immediate organ of the desires and needs of the people; the second is the organ of social justice expressed in the laws; the third is administrator and unerring manager of social interests.

These three powers are, in truth, independent; but, far from being isolated and condemned to immobility, offering mutual resistance to maintain a certain

---

23. The association will present at an opportune time a complete plan for popular instruction and propose adequate means for putting it in place. [Echeverría's note.]

illusory equilibrium, they will set out harmoniously by different routes to a single end—social progress. The strength of social progress will be the result of the three united strengths; their wills will be united into one will; and just as reason, feeling, and the will constitute the moral unity of the individual, the three powers will form the generative unity of democracy, or the legitimate organ of sovereignty, destined to pass judgment without appeal on all questions of interest to the association.

The conditions of the covenant are written; the cornerstone of the social building, placed; the government organized and animated by the spirit of the fundamental law. The legislator presents the law to the people; the people approve it if that law is the living symbol of its reason.

The work of the constituent legislator is concluded.

If the organic law is not the expression of public reason proclaimed through its legitimate representatives; if the latter have not spoken in that law of the interests and opinions of their constituents; if they have not endeavored to interpret their thought; or in other words, if the legislators—ignoring their mission and the vital needs of the people they represent—have begun like despicable plagiarists to copy from here and there articles of constitutions from other countries instead of making one that has living roots in popular consciousness, their work will be an aborted monster, a body without life, an ephemeral law without action that the public criterion will never be able to sanction.

The legislator will have betrayed the confidence of his constituent; the legislator will be an imbecile.

If, on the contrary, the work of the legislator fully satisfies public reason, his work is great, his creation sublime and similar to God's.

So neither the people, nor the legislator, nor any social authority will be able to raise its sacrilegious hand to that sanctuary, where is traced with divine letters the supreme and inviolable law—the law of laws, which all and each one has recognized, proclaimed, and sworn to respect before God and men.

Sovereignty has been embodied in that law, so to speak—in that law is the people's reason and consent; in that law is order, justice, and liberty; in that law is democracy's safeguard.

This law can be revised, improved with time, and adjusted to the progress of public reason by an assembly chosen *ad hoc* by the sovereign; but if, in the meantime, that era which the law itself determined has not arrived, the power of the law is omnipotent; its will dominates all wills; its reason is superimposed on all reasons.

No majority, no faction, no assembly will be able to infringe on it at the risk of being usurpatory and tyrannical.

That law serves as the touchstone of all other laws; its light illuminates them, and all the thoughts and actions of the social body and of constituted powers arise from it and converge at its center. It is the driving force that provides impetus and around which gravitate, like stars around the sun, all the partial forces that make up the world of democracy.

Constituted thus, democracy, the sovereignty of the people, starts from that point, and begins to exercise its unceasing and unlimited action; but always rotating in the orbit that the organic law traces for it—its right goes no further.

It, through its representatives, makes and unmakes laws, innovates every day, carries its activity everywhere, and imprints an unceasing movement, a progressive transformation, on the social machine.

Each act of its will is a new creation; each decision of its reason a step forward.

Politics, religion, philosophy, art, industry; it examines it all, elaborates it, subjects it to its supreme desire and sanctions it—the voice of the people is the voice of God.

From this statement we will deduce that if the people have neither learning nor morality, that if the seeds of a constitution are not, so to speak, disseminated in the people's practices, feelings, memories, traditions, the work of organizing the constitution is unachievable; we can further deduce that the legislator is not called to create an organic law or acclimate in his country the law of other countries, but rather he is called to know instincts, needs, interests, everything that forms the intellectual, moral, and physical life of the people that he represents and to proclaim and formulate them into a law; and we will deduce, finally, that only those who unite the highest ability and honest virtue, the most complete knowledge of the spirit and needs of the nation, can and should be legislators.

From this we can also deduce that, if the legislator is conscious of his duty before investigating what form of government would be preferable, he should ascertain whether the people are ready to be governed by a constitution; and if so, he should offer them not the best and most perfect in theory, but one that adapts itself to their condition.

I have given to the Athenians, said Solon,[24] not the best laws, but rather those that they find themselves in a state to receive.

From this we can infer that when public reason has not matured, the constituent legislator has no mission whatsoever and, not being able to raise awareness of his position nor of the importance of his role, figures in a farce that he himself does not understand and issues or copies laws with the same lack of restraint with which he would make petitions in his office or adjust the accounts of his business.

From this, in sum, we will deduce the necessity of preparing the legislator before entrusting the work of a constitution to him.

The legislator will not be able to be prepared if the people are not. How will the legislator be able to create the good if the people are ignorant of it? If they do not appreciate the advantages of liberty? If they prefer inertia to activity? Their habits to innovations? What they know and touch to what they do not know and see only from afar?

It is indispensable, for that very reason, to prepare the people and the legislator, *first to elaborate the substance of the law,* that is to say, make known the ideas

---

24. Solon (c. 638–558 BC), Athenian lawmaker.

that will have to be embodied in the legislators and actualized in the laws, circulate them, popularize them, incorporate them into the public spirit.

It is necessary, in a word, to enlighten the reason of the *people* and of the *legislator* on political questions before beginning to *constitute the nation.*

Only on this condition will we achieve what we all earnestly desire—that the *future legislator* appear, or a national representation capable of understanding and remediating the ills that society suffers, of satisfying its wishes, and of laying the unshakable and permanent foundation of a social order.

If the public spirit has not acquired the necessary maturity, *constitutions* will only fuel anarchy and incite in peoples' minds disdain for all law, for all justice, and for the most sacred principles.

Democracy, being the *government* of the *people* for *itself,* demands the constant action of all man's abilities and will not be able to establish itself except with the aid of learning and morality.

Democracy, beginning with the principle of the equality of classes, endeavors to establish itself in the people's ideas, practices, and feelings, and elaborates its laws and institutions in a way that tends to extend and secure its predominance.

All the forces of our governments and our legislators must be directed to fulfilling the intentions of democracy.

The Association of the young Argentine generation believes that in our society democracy exists in germ; the Association's mission is to preach democracy, spread its spirit, and consecrate the action of its powers to the end that one day democracy will be constituted in the republic.

The Association is aware of how many obstacles will be put up by certain aristocratic bad habits, certain reactionary traditions, the laws, the lack of learning and morality.

It knows that the work of organizing democracy cannot be done in a day; that constitutions are not improvised; that liberty is not established except on the foundation of learning and practices; that a society is not enlightened and made moral at a single stroke; that the reason of a people that aspires to be free is matured only with time; but, having faith in the future and believing that the lofty intentions of the revolution were not only to destroy the old social order, but also to build a new one, will work with all the fullness of its abilities so that the coming generations, gathering the fruit of its labor, might have in their hands better elements than we to organize and constitute the Argentine society on the unshakable base of equality and democratic liberty.

Lucas Alamán
(Mexico)

Lucas Alamán (1792–1853) is one of the foremost conservative thinkers and spokesmen of nineteenth-century Mexico. He was a political and intellectual figure, authoring many well-known works on Mexican history and serving both the Spanish crown and independent Mexico in a number of political posts. His writings, while reflecting his traditional outlook on history and political culture, also demonstrate well the difference between European and American conservative thought. Although he admired such European conservative thinkers as Edmund Burke and Joseph de Maistre, his thought did not fully belong to the European era defined by conservative Austrian Prince Klemens Metternich, with its deep devotion to the old order. Alamán accepted independence as a fact of Mexican life, but he believed that independence did not carry great benefits, largely because of the liberal republicans and their methods for ruling. He regarded Spanish rule as having been generally good for the American colonies, the Catholic Church as a stabilizing influence and the logical institution for educating Mexico's youth, and he believed that, in the interests of stability, the new liberal ideas should be rejected in favor of returning to some time-honored Spanish colonial practices. He respected Spain as the wellspring of Mexican culture—its language, its form of government, its religion. Mexican history began, for him, with the Spanish conquest.

Alamán, a well-educated creole aristocrat, was born in the mining city of Guanajuato. He was the son of Juan Vicente Alamán of Spain and María Ignacia Escalada; in 1823, he married Narcissa Castrillo García. His family was involved in the mining industry, a factor that almost surely influenced Alamán's economic thought, which was one element of his thought shaped far more by liberal British economic thinkers than French and Spanish political conservatives. In 1810 he began studying at the Colegio de Minería de México in Mexico City. On one of his trips to Europe, he became interested in the technology of the Freyburg mines of Germany, which he hoped to put to use in Mexican mining. Much later, he helped found the United Company of Mines in Europe, whose director he became in 1825, and attracted English and French investment.

Alamán had many talents and interests, among them writing and political life. His first publication was in 1812 in *El Diario de México,* and it was with his connection to this newspaper that he first developed his interest in politics. It is probable that his opposition to democratic forces was born in 1810, when he witnessed the results of the Hidalgo uprising with which the revolution against Spain began. The horror of seeing the slaughter of Spanish men by Hidalgo's indigenous forces may well be what turned Alamán into a lifelong conservative. Later he wrote for, and probably edited, the conservative paper *El Universal.* His most important works are his historical writings, including the *Disertaciones sobre la historia de la República Mexicana desde la conquista hasta la independencia*

(1844) and *Historia de México desde los primeros movimientos que prepararon su independencia en el año 1808* (1849–1852).

Alamán's public life spanned thirty-nine years. He visited Europe several times on scientific and diplomatic trips; the first was in 1813 when he received an honor from the Royal Seminary. In 1820, he was named Guanajuato's Secretario de la Junta de Sanidad by the Viceroy Count of Venadito, the first of his many public posts. He was immediately elected representative of New Spain to the courts of Spain and argued successfully before them to obtain the right of sales in Spain for Mexico's mines. The new Mexican imperial government of Agustín de Iturbide named him diplomat to the French king. He held the post of minister of the interior and foreign affairs and remained minister of foreign relations throughout several presidencies. In this post he worked out a treaty of border limits with the United States before the Mexican-American War and tried to protect the eastern provinces of Mexico from U.S. expansionism. Under President Anastasio Bustamante, as part of the Junta de Fomento de la Industria, he worked to industrialize Mexico, including organizing the Banco de Avío, Mexico's first national bank, through which he created new textile industries, improved cattle raising, and favorably renegotiated Mexico's European debts. In 1849, Alamán organized the Conservative Party for elections. He was elected as representative for Jalisco in 1851 and as senator in 1852.

Finally, Alamán was active in educational and other intellectual pursuits. He created the Archivo General de la Nación and Museo de Antigüedades e Historia Natural. He worked with José María Luis Mora on projects that included the reform of scientific education under President Valentín Gómez Farías in 1833. He was responsible for creating the Dirección General de Instrucción Pública.

The Alamán selection that follows is from the last volume of his highly regarded five-volume *Historia de México* (History of Mexico).

Further Reading

Lira, Andrés. *Espejo de discordias: La sociedad Mexicana vista por Lorenzo de Zavala, José María Luis Mora y Lucas Alamán.* Mexico D.F.: Secretaría de Educación Pública, 1984.

Méndez Reyes, Salvador. *El hispanoamericanismo de Lucas Alamán, 1823–1853.* Toluca, Mexico: Universidad Autónoma del Estado de México, 1996.

Quintanilla Obregón, Lourdes. *El nacionalismo de Lucas Alamán.* Guanajuato, Mexico: Gobierno del Estado de Guanajuato, 1991.

Valadés, José C. *Alamán, estadista e historiador.* Mexico D.F.: Universidad Nacional Autónoma de México, 1977.

The History of Mexico (1849–1852)

Seeing, in so few years, this immense loss of territory;[1] this collapse of the treasury, leaving behind an onerous debt; this annihilation of a select and courageous
army, leaving no means of defense; and, above all, this complete extinction of the
public spirit, which has made the whole idea of a national character disappear;
then finding no Mexicans in Mexico, and contemplating a nation that has gone
from infancy to decrepitude without having enjoyed more than a glimpse of the
exuberant growth of youth or shown signs of life other than violent convulsions—it seems correct to acknowledge with the great Bolívar that independence
has been purchased at the cost of all the wealth that Spanish America enjoyed,[2]
and to give its history the same title that the venerable Bishop Casas gave to his
general history of the Indies, "The History of the Destruction of the Indies,"[3] for
what has happened in Mexico has been repeated with very few and temporary
exceptions in all of what were the Spanish possessions, Mexico feeling the effects
of the disorder more painfully because it has a powerful neighbor that has contributed to causing those effects and has known how to profit from them. These
disastrous consequences have given us reason to discuss whether independence
has been a good or an evil and whether or not it should have been encouraged.[4]
The question is pointless after the fact, all the more so because these great
national events are never the result of careful calculations but rather the effect of
coincidences or variables beyond human foresight, and the course of things has
been such that if Mexico had not gained her independence in 1821, she would
have done so a little later, being pushed to it by the very measures the Spanish
government might have taken to prevent it, and even more by the war of succession that has made it uncertain who will occupy the throne in the metropolis
until the test of arms has decided it.[5] On the other hand, the prosperity that New

---

1. The original territory of Mexico at independence included the mainland possessions of
Spain from Costa Rica to California. The Central American republics seceded peacefully in
1823, followed by Texas after a war in 1836–1839. The U.S. annexation of Texas provoked
the Mexican-American War of 1845–1848, ending with the Treaty of Guadalupe-Hidalgo,
which reduced Mexico's territory by more than half. Northern Mexico became the present-day
U.S. states, in whole or in part, of Texas, New Mexico, Arizona, California, Nevada, Colorado, and Utah.

2. Thus said Bolívar in a public document. [Alamán's note.]

3. Bartolomé de las Casas (1474–1566), Spanish ecclesiastic famous for denouncing Spanish
maltreatment of Indians.

4. Sr. Don Luis Cuevas, in his work cited. [Alamán's note. Like Alamán, Luis G. Cuevas
(1799–1867) was a conservative who believed that Mexico could only achieve unity through
centralist rule and an emphasis on its Spanish heritage.]

5. The Carlist wars in Spain, 1833–1876. After Fernando VII of Spain died without a male
heir, conflict arose between his designated heir, the infant Isabel II, and the late king's brother
Carlos. The second Carlist war, 1847–1849, had not yet concluded when Alamán wrote these
lines.

Spain enjoyed had begun to disintegrate even before the French invasion under the old regime,[6] as a result of the seizure of ecclesiastical wealth applied to the consolidation fund for royal promissory notes, which, causing their owners' ruin, had already awakened in them the desire for emancipation, and that same prosperity shows that it was possible to form an independent nation.[7] But in order not to alter the nation's natural course, it would have been necessary to use all the elements that had originally produced the nation, and since, as we have said elsewhere, everything was organized in America's various viceroyalties and captaincies general in such a way that nothing was missing but the monarch for them to be independent monarchies, it would have been very easy to complete the political system by adding this one missing element.

Independence, then, was not only possible but would not even have seemed premature had the number of innovations introduced along with it not been so excessive, given that such innovations would never be possible at any point in the existence of those nations not originally created with the kind of innovative institution that one has tried to establish here. All damage to the nation derives from this state of affairs, and the lack of men for governing the State, which can be seen in everything that has happened since the formation of the provisional governing junta that assumed sovereign power [in 1821], would not have seemed so noteworthy if those same men who have proved so incapable in the new system had done nothing more than follow the order of things to which they had been accustomed, and, much more importantly, had Archbishop [Pedro de] Fonte, the regent of the Audiencia [Miguel] Bataller, and others experienced in these matters been able then to remain in the country, men whose wisdom would have been very useful in founding the government.

In the midst of such a complete upheaval of all elements of society, the only one that has remained unchangeable is the Church, and this is because neither the Congress nor the government has been able to lay a hand on either its administration or the election of its ministers, the bishops having opposed with admirable energy the government's exercise of the right of patronage.[8] The government had been demanding this power since the regency, acting on the assumption that all Catholic governments have this right without requiring a concordat or pontifical declaration.

---

6. This passage refers to the Napoleonic invasion of the Iberian Peninsula, 1808–1814.

7. In 1798 the Spanish crown ordered the sale of property of public and religious institutions in Spain to ease a financial crisis, and in 1804 it extended this decree to the colonies for the consolidation of its *vales reales,* bonded debt. In the New World, however, most funds of religious institutions were invested in loans to hacienda owners, merchants, miners, and others. This consolidation, then, threatened a powerful debtor class with the loss of property or bankruptcy. Negative reaction to these measures, particularly in New Spain, was widespread.

8. The Spanish kings since Fernando and Isabel held the "royal patronage" (*patronato real*), the right to appoint bishops and priests within their realms. Bishops throughout the Americas resisted the independent Spanish republics' claims to have inherited this power from the Crown.

• • • • •

This right of patronage was useful when truly Christian princes granted the Church the protection it needed, and they exercised the power of patronage because of the institutions they had established and the wealth with which they had endowed those institutions; but, as a result of extending the boundaries of this protection, patronage became true oppression. At the very least, by subordinating the clergy to the civil government, it turned the clergy into flatterers, attracting to such capital cities as Madrid crowds of claimants to canonships and prebendaries, who were not always the most meritorious and virtuous, which tended to put these favored appointees in the position of disseminating courtly vices and decadence throughout the provinces—do not forget that a Duke of Orléans,[9] regent of France, so unfortunately famous for his dissolute habits, elevated to the episcopate Father Dubois,[10] a minister worthy of such a ruler. The same can be said of the right to withhold papal bulls and rescripts, which, if used moderately and with intentions that are both religious and politic, is necessary for the preservation of kingdoms and republics; this right can become destructive for the religion when governments, guided by other principles, use it as a device to block what is genuinely in religion's interest. These dangers are greater in governments that owe their origin to chance or to the intrigues of periodic elections, which can elevate to the nation's or states' supreme authority—and, unfortunately, this probably happens all the time—absolutely impious men, who consider religion a superstition that must be tolerated until it can be destroyed or who are so indifferent to the religion that when filling bishoprics and benefices they pay attention only to their own biases and party interests, making appointments to them as they might appoint officials to maritime customs posts. Thus, when the Yorkists[11] took over the government, if the government had exercised the right of patronage, the bishoprics would have been given to ecclesiastics who were the Venerables of lodges[12] and the parishes to the worst clergymen in each diocese. But just as it is advantageous that the chapters

---

9. Duke of Orléans (1674–1723), regent of France 1715–1723, known for an excessive taste for pleasure. His regency is regarded as one of the most corrupt periods of French history.

10. Guillaume Dubois (1656–1723) was the childhood tutor of the Duke of Orléans and was equally dissolute. The Duke named him Archbishop of Cambrai in 1720.

11. In early republican Mexico, before political parties were formed, the York Rite Masons identified with a liberal and federalist program, while the Scottish Rite Masons furthered the interests of elites and members of the former ruling groups that had remained in Mexico. The Yorkinos took power from the Scottish Masons in 1825. Alamán himself was a Scottish Mason.

12. This is what Governor Salgado of Michoacán proposed to President Guerrero in a confidential report that I discovered in the Ministry of the Interior when I returned to that post in 1830, opposing the proposal by the Michoacán diocesan chapter and requesting a new proposal be made in which the nominees would be genuine patriots—and one knows what that phrase meant at the time. [Alamán's note. Venerables of lodges were the presiding officers.]

participate in filling the bishoprics, it is also necessary to regulate their participation so that elections do not always go to the chapter heads of these bodies, but instead that attention is paid to the rest of the individuals among the clergy, as was done in filling six vacant bishoprics in 1830, for which General Bustamante[13] nominated two ecclesiastics from among the canons, two from among parish priests, and two from the regular orders. It would be highly advisable to renew the wise regulations prescribed by the Laws of the Indies so that the merit, knowledge, and virtue of those who were to be favored would be kept in mind, and to reestablish the scale that the Spanish government used both in the Church and in the judicial system, according to which men ascended from the churches and tribunals of least importance to the highest positions of the court and altar—the consequence of which was that these highest positions went to men filled with knowledge and experience and accustomed to running enterprises, whose knowledge can only be acquired through practice.

The disadvantages that result from the exercise of patronage and the unlimited right of withholding bulls will become greater and greater because of the principles by which the youth, who in time will fill all the positions of the State, are being educated. We have already noted that, in the plan of studies that was drawn up and that is currently in use, special care had been taken to exclude all influence of the clergy from public education. One could say that in Spain and its possessions, since the expulsion of the Jesuits, no plan of studies has had any great moral aim as its foundation, its parts interrelated in such a way that they formed a complete and uniform system.[14] Six highly capable Jesuits had shaped the study plan through many years of work and reflection, giving it the finishing touch in the fifth general congregation celebrated in 1590, improving and expanding it yet more in the seventh; it was published and ordered to be followed in all Jesuit schools in 1616.[15] With the expulsion of the members of that order, the instruction that they gave in the various territories where they had established schools ceased in New Spain, or was continued in a very imperfect way, with instruction limited to certain professions but without following the

---

13. Anastasio Bustamante (1780–1853), creole general who brought six thousand troops to Iturbide's army, supporting Iguala, went on to become vice president and, following exile and coup, president/dictator, 1837–1841.

14. The Jesuit order, which had run virtually the entire educational system of colonial Spanish America, was forcibly expelled from the empire in 1767 by order of Carlos III. The order was subsequently suppressed in all Catholic countries from 1773 to 1814. It was not reestablished in Mexico until 1854.

15. The *Ratio atque institutio studiorum Societatis Iesu* (the official plan for Jesuit education) is the document that formally established the worldwide system of Jesuit education in 1599. Most of the work was done by an international team of academics at the Jesuit *Collegio Romano* in Rome. A committee of six was formed in 1584: John Azor of Spain, Gaspar González of Portugal, James Tyrie of Scotland, Peter Busée of Holland, Anthony Ghuse of Flanders, and Stephen Tucci of Sicily. The document this committee produced underwent several trials before being officially adopted in 1599.

general system in its entirety. The foundation of this system consisted of religion and the morality that acknowledges this religion as its source; once this principle was established, instruction in the sciences and literature rested on it.[16]

The French Convention created a plan that has given rise to all the other plans that various nations have established by imitation—the Cortes of Spain made its version extraordinarily and impractically long[17]—and that is also the origin of the Mexican Republic's plan. And just as the essential aim of the Jesuits' educational plan was, above all, to form religious men who were also literate and knowledgeable, the French Convention's plan intended only to educate lawyers, doctors, and naturalists, without basing the instruction essential to these professions on religion, and instead, excluding it completely, from which, consequently, came the exclusion of clergy from all participation in the instruction of youth—and, as the character of the century is superficiality, the subjects of education multiplied without any of them being sufficiently deepened. Reestablished in many countries of Europe and America, the Jesuits tried to adapt their plan of studies to the advances in all the sciences, and, when the necessary reforms had been made to the plan by men of great knowledge from all nations who had gathered in Rome for this purpose, it was circulated by the current vicar general, Father John Roothaan,[18] to the provincials of all the order's provinces on July 25, 1832, with a letter in which, explaining the reasons why all the innovations introduced into instruction since the expulsion had not been accepted, he says, "This great variety of many subjects and bodies of knowledge—from which children, instead of drinking, do nothing but moisten their lips—produces no other result than making them believe they know a lot, increasing the crowd of half-educated people who know nothing well and solidly, harming both knowledge and, most especially, the republic." *Ex omnibus aliquid; in toto nihil.* "A little of everything, but nothing of substance."

Besides this fundamental defect in the Mexican plan of studies, which it has in common with the plans formed in various parts of Europe, it suffers in practice from other defects inherent in the prevailing ideas and political system. Schools have been created in various states with no consideration at all to distributing them appropriately and without there being men capable of teaching,

---

16. In Article 1 of the "Ratio studiorum" or System of Studies of the Company, the aim of this plan is defined in the following terms: "So that the young are excited to know and love our Creator and Redeemer." If all plans of study that have been created since showed the same good faith as the Jesuits' plan, the aim that they had would be found, which in many of them has been the opposite. [Alamán's note.]

17. When this plan was being discussed, the Count of Toreno used to say that the Cortes was composing a romance or legislative novel. [Alamán's note. During the French Revolution the National Convention or the Convention sat as the constituent and legislative body of France from 1792–1795. The Cortes to which Alamán here refers was the short-lived liberal Spanish parliament that met in Cadiz in 1812–1814 and in Madrid in 1820–1822. Count Toreno was a deputy to both Cortes; Alamán was a deputy from Mexico to the Cortes of 1821.]

18. The twenty-first General of the Society of Jesus (1785–1853) served 1829–1853.

which leads to a situation in which something that should be so useful and beneficial becomes of little value, and maybe even harmful, because it lacks a plan and its teachers are insufficiently trained. As if the republic's primary need were to increase the number of lawyers—a career that, by its very nature, attracts enough students already, because lawyers are the group who have gained the most from the revolution and who most readily find posts in the congresses, tribunals, and courts of justice in those same states—law is the field that is taught by preference in these new schools, when, on the contrary, one must orient Mexican youth towards the craft trades and agriculture, for which no establishment has been created. Although the minister of the interior tried in 1831 to found a school of craft trades in Mexico, for which government funds were appropriated, and he himself, as director of industry, made great progress in 1845 toward the creation of a theoretical and practical school of agriculture, for which he had purchased the building where it was to be put and adjacent land where all the field work would be performed,[19] everything fell with its author, and these ideas have not been fostered since. It is noteworthy that, although a school has been established in Guanajuato, a mining and agricultural area, and another in Toluca, where wealth depends on farming, mines and the cultivation of the fields are not the special focus of these schools; agriculture is barely beginning to feel the effect of the great advances in Europe, only because some French agriculturists in the valley of San Martín Texmelucan have introduced the new tools and the use of fertilizer.

This lack of appropriate administration is to blame for the imperceptible fruits of the great methods used in public instruction, for there is no country, not even among the most enlightened ones of Europe, where free education in all areas is offered as widely as in Mexico—but nonetheless one sees that, even after fifty years of having an overabundantly funded school of mining, it is very difficult to find a person capable of directing labor in a mine or the processing of ore, and we must resort to hiring some foreigner who is taken at his word that he knows what he is doing, or some merchant who has no grasp at all of the business, even though there is no lack of talent or industry among our youth, and in the school of medicine we see hardworking students being educated every day. Primary instruction, which should be the foundation for what follows, is the object of individual preferences—some families send their children to Jesuit schools in England and the United States, a situation that introduces the odd phenomenon that, to be educated in entirely religious principles, Mexican youth go to Protestant countries to learn to be Catholics.

Education, although superficial and not including the fields most important to public happiness, has nonetheless produced the benefit of better writing that has a propriety unknown in the first years of independence. All those filthy works with unseemly titles that came off the Mexican presses in that era have

---

19. See the Reports on Industry for 1844, 1845, and 1846. [Alamán's note. The minister in question was Alamán himself.]

disappeared, and the periodicals that are published in their place have, even in their physical format, a different appearance, scientific works being published that would have been impossible to fund at that time, and in the serial stories of these journals some useful things appear—although other harmful ones as well, depending on the propensities of the editors. With these changes, the printing houses have increased greatly—employing a substantial number of people, and the publications have become comparable to the most beautiful ones from Europe. Advances in lithography have also followed, and in place of the small and very poor illustrations that were previously engraved by chisel and gave mean employment to some few artists, a multitude of portraits, landscapes, and well-executed designs are now published. In the fine arts, there has been great progress in painting and sculpture because of the backing that has been given to the Academy of San Carlos,[20] and the many buildings that have been erected have given employment to foreign architects, many of them with exquisite taste, who have established themselves in the country, although similar praise cannot be given generally for the decoration of the churches, in which it would be better not to have changed any of the old part, because the modern style that is being substituted for it is quite inferior.

In the midst of so many reasons for backwardness, the country has nonetheless made notable strides, not so much because of government stimulus but, more likely, because the country has overcome the obstacles that its institutions and political difficulties put in its way. Although foreign mining companies might not themselves have been profitable, mining has progressed extraordinarily, and the treasures extracted from Veta Grande, El Fresnillo, Rayas, and now from the mine of Nuestra Señora de la Luz in Guanajuato have raised mining to a level of prosperity equal to or greater than what it had been before, the sums minted annually being slightly less than what was being minted before the insurrection. We may expect still greater increases because of the abundance of quicksilver—owing to the great quantities of this ingredient, indispensable for amalgamation, coming from California—reducing the price to less than half of what it was when the mines of Mexico were restricted to getting quicksilver only from the Almadén mines in Spain, which were leased to individuals; miners now acquire quicksilver at almost the same price that the Spanish government gave them before independence.[21] Agriculture has returned to the very prosperous state of that era, and its products are selling at higher prices than they have in many years. Great industrial establishments have been created, where goods are made that are far superior to those that had been made until now, and the progress would have been greater if the entry of raw cotton had not been prohibited. Well-being is seen among all who do not depend on salaries from the general government for their livelihood:

---

20. The Royal and Pontifical Art Academy of San Carlos was founded in 1783 and introduced the neo-classical style to Mexico.

21. Almadén is the oldest and largest quicksilver (mercury) mining region in the world. Quicksilver's value derives from its use in the amalgamation process of separating gold and silver from other elements in mined ore.

artisans and craftsmen have found work to do, and in the fields there are not enough people for all agricultural operations; the low price of the essential clothing goods allows the popular classes not only to cover themselves but even to adorn themselves in luxury; in the capital and other principal cities there are crowds for all kinds of entertainment, enough to support several theatres and two bull rings in the capital when there was only one before. None of this is exactly the result of independence, for it could have occurred without it, and just as the loss of territory and other hardships cannot be blamed on independence, neither should independence be given credit for the wealth that has derived from general progress in the civilized world, in which Mexico would have shared to a greater degree with tranquility and good government or from coincidences unrelated to political matters like the bonanzas of the mines and the abundance of the harvests.[22]

Whereas foreign debt occasions the great misfortune of a continuous outflow of money with no compensation whatsoever, the loans that businesses make against customs duties or by receiving as compensation salt mines and other national and Church lands, in spite of having been so ruinous for the public treasury, have produced the good of creating a number of large- and medium-sized fortunes that, together with those that have come from the mines and those that have been created by people who have benefited from the abuses or weaknesses of government, have remained rooted in the country and have made the price of rural properties rise considerably, contributing to beautifying some cities, especially Mexico and Guanajuato, with sumptuous edifices; some public buildings having also been constructed at great cost, like the theatre of Santa Ana in Mexico City and the customs house and warehouses in Veracruz. This accumulation of wealth, the perfection that various arts have attained, and the opportunities offered by dressmakers, tailors, and French cooks have introduced on the other hand a luxury so excessive that, along with gaming and dissolute behavior, it has ruined a number of fortunes—especially the fortunes of people enriched by the mines—before those fortunes were fully formed, and this is the reason for frequent commercial failures. There is no city in Europe or the United States in which, proportionate to the population, there are so many private coaches as in Mexico City, and there are three times as many available for hire at public posts or stands as there were before independence.

• • • • •

The effect of the ideas that have prevailed since the past century has been to destroy all hereditary or administrative inequality. When the distinctions among nobility or those coming from public employment were greatly esteemed, an

---

22. The governor of the state of Michoacán, in a public speech celebrating the 16th of September [Independence Day] this year, attributes everything to independence, but he sees nothing other than prosperity, without taking into account the woes it has caused. [Alamán's note.]

illustrious name, a cross on the chest, an academic gown, a religious sinecure, an insignia of colonel or even captain, along with a moderate fortune or middling salary, created for those who possessed them a place among the most distinguished classes of the State; so men strove to acquire those distinctions through great services, risking their lives on military campaigns or by the easier method of palatial pretensions and the sacrifice of money, for in Mexico, when all else had disappeared, only the army retaining a certain splendor, some of its ranks could still be bought while the government still had extraordinary powers to bestow them, even if those ranks would later be rescinded by a congressional decree. Society was also, at least in Spanish America, much less wasteful. The wealthiest men—especially the Spanish—scarcely differentiated themselves in their domestic comportment from those with moderate fortunes, and because of this, by living frugally, they accumulated great fortunes, which they used on celebratory occasions to serve the sovereign, making them worthy to receive those medals they so valued, or as a last resort, they invested it in pious establishments, many of which are still preserved and, with them, the memory of those who knew how to make so noble a use of their wealth.

All of this fell before the forces of the irreligious and antisocial philosophy of the eighteenth century, and no other distinction remained than wealth. Coming up with money is the sole aim of everyone's efforts; making money by whatever means is considered legitimate. And—because money is not invested in the distinctions that were previously purchased when not merited by other qualifications; because no one feels obligated to serve the country with his fortune, so that when a government without prestige needs financial help in the nation's greatest afflictions, it finds nothing but hardened hearts and closed purses that open only with harder terms the more urgent the need; when men like Basoco and Yermo, like Meave and Aldaco, would be considered foolish,[23] because no investment other than material pleasures remains possible for the great fortunes, obtaining material pleasures is ambition's sole aim. Because of this employees are disloyal, because of this abuses are committed in administering public affairs, and because of this governments have no stability whatsoever. The basis on which they have attempted to found these governments, under the name of the representative system, has been individual interest, under the assumption that

---

23. In the course of this history, we have referred to the great services that the first two men lent the Spanish government, to whose names could be added the Count of La Cortina and many other Spaniards of that time. Meave and Aldaco were the creators of the magnificent Colegio de las Vizcaínas. [Alamán's note. Antonio de Basoco y Castañiza (1738–1814); Don Gabriel Joaquín de Yermo (1757–1813); Ambrosio de Meave (1710–1781); Manuel de Aldaco (1696–1770); all four were of Basque origin, and, in Mexico, became wealthy merchants, mine owners, and general supporters of the royal government. Basoco forgave more than two million pesos in loans to the crown and was named Count of Basoco in 1811. Yermo turned one of his estates into the headquarters for royalist forces during the independence war. Meave and Aldaco founded Vizcaínas, a school for "orphaned girls and unprotected widows," built between 1732 and 1767 and still in operation.]

people will make an effort to establish and maintain the greatest order possible, based on their own personal benefit; from this principle they try to derive the consequence that, when all these armed men have formed the national guard, which the Marquis de Lafayette[24] called the armed opinion of the nation, they will necessarily uphold certain institutions to protect their own well-being. But what has not been considered is the following: That because the fundamental principle of modern society is egotism, it cannot be the foundation of any political institution; that men who aspire solely to enjoy themselves in accord with the doctrines of Epicurean philosophy can neither submit their opinion to the deliberations of an assembly, which might constrain their pleasures, nor risk their lives in the dangers of military service; that both things assume work, strength of spirit, abandonment of comforts, and these comforts are the only things they desire; that, consequently, such a society must fall, and fall the more quickly to the extent others who strive to enjoy the pleasures—and cannot or do not aspire to obtain them through honest work—seek them by means of revolutions, which are the easier to make the more governments are deprived of all status and respect, and all the institutions that should sustain and strengthen them have been destroyed, while the comfortable class—indifferent to everything that does not cohere with its personal interests—wakes up only with the clamor of a revolution that threatens it with immediate ruin, and then to save itself from disaster, throws itself—as happened in France—into the arms of the first one who says, "Come here so I can protect you."

What I have said is sufficient to explain easily the origin of the present era's social woes, and because it is a subject with which the most famous writers of Europe have been and are occupied, it must not delay us any longer, as we lack only an examination of the most important point of our own situation, which can be considered the most essential aim of this entire work. *Iter hujus sermonis quod sit, vides: ad respublicas firmandas et ad stabiliendas vires, sanandos populos omnis nostra pergit oratio.* "Notice," said Cicero[25] in his admirable treatise on the laws, "what the aim of this discourse is. All our efforts go to strengthening the republic, establishing its forces, and remedying the people's misfortunes." If I cannot flatter myself by suggesting the means by which our misfortunes might be cured, I will at least have shown with clarity and truth what they consist of so that others may have the glory of discovering how to reform them. And of course this question arises: We have shown that, in the midst of so many contrasts, well-being in the Mexican republic is general; that wealth has increased; that mines and agriculture are prospering; that the arts of luxury have risen to a level not previously known; that all that supposed abundance, like carriages, entertainments, comforts of all types, is greater, relative to the population, in the republic's

---

24. Marie Joseph Paul Roch Yves Gilbert du Motier, Marquis de Lafayette (1757–1834), French aristocrat famous for his participation in the American revolutionary war and early French Revolution.

25. Cicero, book I of the *Laws,* ch. 13. [Alamán's note. Marcus Tullius Cicero (106–43 BC), orator and statesman of ancient Rome.]

capital city than in other cities of Europe and America. How is it, then, that with all these elements of prosperity, the government lacks resources to cover the costs of administration—even though greatly reduced—and to pay the interest on the foreign debt? How can there not be means of defense necessary for the security of this very country? Why is the existence of this nation so uncertain?

These and many other questions of like nature that we might ask can be answered clearly and demonstrably by an example taken from what all the residents of the capital of the republic see, that all feel and experience for themselves, although perhaps few understand everything it signifies. We have said that Mexico City has been enlarged and beautified with magnificent business establishments, in whose stores are displayed the most costly jewels and all the most refined articles of luxury. Well, the streets in which these sumptuous palaces are built, in which so many diamonds and silks sparkle, have stone pavement on which superb carriages with beautiful horses that pass through them can hardly roll, and many are depositories of filth that create the saddest and most shocking contrast to the beauty of the business establishments in them!!! These establishments and streets encapsulate the state of the republic. Everything that could be done by the work of nature and the efforts of individuals has progressed; everything that should have known the hand of public authority has regressed. The elements of the nation's prosperity exist, but the nation as a social body lives in poverty. The conclusion we can deduce from these incontestable premises, which has all the rigor of a mathematical proof, is this: The political institutions of this nation are not the ones it needs for its prosperity, and so it is essential to reform them, and this reform is urgent and must be the most important concern of every good citizen.

One might reply that if the country is making progress in its present state it is not obvious why reform is so necessary, and that if Mexico is so anomalous a nation that it does not need government, everything can be left as it is without any harm at all, just as in the capital one moves among magnificent buildings over impassable stone pavements with no problems other than great inconvenience. If things are as this argument presents them, everything could in fact remain the same, which is the false and ill-fated plan that the government has followed since the Treaty of Guadalupe, to which we owe the fact that we have reached so critical a state; that plan was feasible only while the funds of the American indemnity lasted,[26] but it fell and had necessarily to fall when those funds ran out, for following the principles that were adopted at that time—convenient and advantageous for those who exercised power, but ruinous for the nation—it was impossible to create secure and sufficient resources for when those funds ran out. Moreover, the path we should best follow must be varied, as we are dealing with things that in reality are very different, for we are not talking about small and tolerable misfortunes but rather the issues most essential to a

---

26. In exchange for its territorial gains in the Mexican-American War, the United States agreed to pay $15 million to the Mexican treasury and assume $3.25 million in Mexican debt.

nation's existence. In fact this nation cannot exist without resources to pay its expenses; the interest on foreign debt cannot be ignored, much less so after entering into a highly advantageous agreement with the nation's creditors; an attempt must be made to pay off this debt, which is a cancer that is slowly consuming the republic's resources, and it is indispensable that the republic have a military to defend it and make it respected.

These are the necessary conditions for every nation that claims to deserve the name of nation, but in the case of Mexico there are other circumstances even more imperative, which are unique to it. Its territory has been considerably reduced and runs the risk of being invaded again. "This," to make use here of the very words of the official document,[27] "is a question of life or death for the nation, because it does not deal solely with the usurpation of its territory, but also with establishing another race in its territory, be it by eradicating the Hispanic-American race, be it by reducing it to the humiliating state of foreigner in its own territory, as the Anglo-Saxons have done with the creoles who lived in Florida and other Southern states." To avoid this, we must be prepared with all necessary means, "under pain of becoming the object of the curses of future generations, other nations, and history, which will unanimously accuse the present generation of the Mexican race of unworthiness to be a nation and of having aspired to such a lofty title with neither the elements nor public spirit necessary to merit that title." As grave as is this danger, it is neither less a danger nor more immediate than that of the invasion by the barbarians[28] who—with the advances they have made and our failure to take appropriate measures to contain them at the border—will arrive within sight of the capital to destroy the country homes of the Mexican potentates. Whatever the type of invader, be they entrepreneurs who, as in the sixteenth century, came on their own account to speculate on the field of conquests, or be they barbarians who want only to plunder and withdraw, they will put into motion the very dangerous elements that exist in the country, and the present owners will see their properties snatched from their hands after these properties have been ravaged and destroyed, while the states, as a result of these very risks and perhaps also believing that they are able to protect themselves against those risks, will split apart to attend to their own defense or, because of their individual quarrels, create, as in Guatemala, as many other nations as there were provinces of the Captaincy General, all weak, all unacknowledged by the others, all exposed to seizure by whoever wants to invade them. All this is urgent and cannot be left to the vicissitudes of events; one must guard against it and remedy it with wisdom; Mexicans leaving their fatherland must be able to hold their heads high and speak the name of their country without fear that this name might be one of humiliation and insult.

---

27. Decree of October 2, 1846, of Don José Mariano de Salas, who came into the executive power as a result of the revolution of August 4th of that year. [Alamán's note.]

28. Referring to the Apaches of the former northern Mexican territories, who by this time had acquired horses and rifles, and, pushed out by the invading Anglo-Americans, were making raids as far as 500 miles south of the new border.

Do not think that the consequences of the future fate of Mexico are limited only to this republic; they include territorial and commercial interests of the highest importance for the European powers and for the maintenance of a principle that England has been so determined to establish, that all other nations have adopted with ardor, and to the observance of which they have been tied by the most solemn treaties: the abolition of slavery. The existence of Mexico as an independent nation on a respectable footing is the one thing that can guarantee that Spain will hold onto the islands of Cuba and Puerto Rico, or that England will keep Jamaica and the other Antilles and, what is more, that secures for England its possessions, its influence and power in India, which will all become the object of the designs of those who, should they become of masters of the entire expanse of the Pacific coast from California to Tehuantepec and of as much farther as they wish to occupy up to Panama, shall have a large navy that would completely dominate the expanse of seas that separates the American continent from Asia after cutting a connection through the Isthmus of Tehuantepec to the Gulf of Mexico. Inasmuch as a great part of these coasts and all those of the Gulf lie in a climate that is inhospitable to the white and copper-colored races, one should not believe that the inhabitants of the southern regions of the United States—who, with this addition of territory, will either separate from the Union or secure a decided predominance in it, and who are interested in continuing the slave trade, knowing that without the African race all these lands can never be populated nor made productive—are concerned with the interests of humanity rather than finances to the point of renouncing the enormous output they can extract from certain regions that are useless without slavery. They will, then, bring in slaves despite all prohibitions, and moreover will subject to a more or less harsh servitude the Indians and *castas*[29] of the region they occupy, who cannot hope to receive from their future dominators a code of privileges like the one the Spanish monarchs made on their behalf, nor the legal equality that Mexican laws grant to them. The immense expenditures that England has made to liberate the slaves in her colonies will have been lost, then, and all the treaties with which it has believed forever to prevent traffic in blacks will be thwarted.

But even agreeing with all this, many despair that a reform can ever be made that satisfies the desires of those who see it as necessary and that remedies the nation's misfortunes. They say all the ways have been tried, and none has been able to improve conditions. Extraordinary powers have been conceded numerous times to those who have held power, and only new abuses have resulted. Congresses have come, one after the other, of one, of two chambers, or the two meeting jointly, and nothing has improved. The Spanish Constitution [of 1812] gave way to the Federal Constitution in 1824; the latter became the Central Constitution in 1836 and was modified in 1844, and the results were the same; finally, the second edition of the Constitution of 1824 has arrived, and everything has been worse. It has been said for some time, moreover, that this nation,

---

29. *Castas* are people of mixed race.

which once appeared to us as the wealthiest and richest in the universe, is very poor and cannot cover its expenses. But the only thing all this proves is that what has previously been found insufficient should not be repeated, that it will be necessary to find new ways, and, as for the alleged national poverty, we must respond that if the ideas of extraordinary wealth were exaggerated, the opposing ideas that are now given credence are no less so, and that as experience has demonstrated, in times when the administration has been well regarded and honest, revenues have surpassed all that the country's condition could demand.

Very far, then, from being persuaded by these arguments that there is no remedy, that the position is desperate, I dare to think exactly the opposite and to believe that the desired remedy is easy, provided that it is applied appropriately and with regard to the nature of the misfortune. Fortunately, this challenge is not as great as it should be, given the way it was created—the Spanish race, bent on self-destruction, has not managed to arouse against itself those whom it has been inciting with unjust and imprudent harangues; depravity in religious matters has not yet gone beyond some individuals in the trade crafts of the capital and some other large cities. The people, peaceful and moderate, ask nothing, and, content to the extent they are left their festivals and celebrations, to the extent they are not burdened with excessive taxes, do not have the aspirations that seductive writings have inspired among some of Europe's peoples, who have been aroused to rebellion, from which they derive only dismal disillusion and fall under a more absolute power than the one they shook off.[30] All those components of modern society's great misfortunes have not taken root among us; the bad newspapers and journals are abhorred and cause only scandal and horror among the general population. This population still strongly adheres to the religious doctrines that they received from their ancestors, and this deep religious sentiment—which not only has not been weakened but on the contrary has been strengthened through enlightenment—is the bond of union remaining to Mexicans when all other bonds have been broken and is the only protection that has kept them from all the disasters into which those desiring to break that bond have wanted to fling them. All the means exist, then, to make a nation happy. Why should it be impossible to find an effective remedy for the misfortunes from which our nation suffers? We have agricultural, mineral, and manufacturing wealth; we have a docile and well-disposed people; these people produce excellent soldiers, courageous when necessary, better than others at suffering all the hardships and deprivations of battle—those soldiers are the ones who distinguished themselves so very much in the courageous corps that, with the names of Column of Grenadiers, Corona, Mexico, Faithful of Potosí, and so many others, made up the army that fought with glory under the banners of Spain and that have fought with courage, when well led, under the banners of independence. Let us see then what reasons prevent us from taking advantage of all these

---

30. Referring to the publication of the *Communist Manifesto* and the wave of liberal revolutions that swept Europe in 1848 and were defeated by a reactionary backlash in 1849.

means to prosperity; let us examine in the history of our errors the causes that have led us to commit them; let past experience be useful to us, and let us seek with this light the path to guide us more successfully in the future, reforming present institutions, keeping in mind what may be good and suitable in them, and changing all those things that a period of thirty years and so many repeated revolutions have made us recognize as impractical, defective, weak, or harmful.

Those who have carefully followed the series of events related in this second part of our history, may have noted that some of the ills the Mexican nation suffers are the result of the general course of things and the spirit of the century; these are not easy to remedy quickly because, as the harm has been done slowly, it must also be corrected little by little, making use of all the benefits that those same misfortunes have brought with them. Fortunately, as we have already said, those ills are not yet of great importance, and we have created them ourselves by imitating what happens in Europe rather than because our country has produced them. They can, then, be remedied with appropriate methods, and, with the guidance of the necessary wisdom, it is still possible to avoid all the difficulties and get all the advantages that events in other parts of the world can produce. Other ills are the results of institutions; these consist principally of the following: In the executive branch, the weakness of its action and the lack of effective protection on behalf of citizens against the abuse of its own power, which, on the one hand is weak in conforming to the law, but on the other hand absolute in breaking it; in the legislative branch, the excessive authority that it exercises and the defective composition of legislative bodies, the result of these two factors being that Congress, as now constituted, is not only useless but an obstacle to the regular formation of a government that might meet the nation's needs; and in the states, their excessive power and their disproportionate inequality. We must remedy these ills without colliding with those trends that have manifested themselves over time, but rather, to the contrary, by complementing and favoring those trends, for otherwise the reform would be neither popular nor lasting; nor by attempting to alter everything by means of absolute change—which, like all strong jolts, cannot but meet resistance—but rather by conserving everything advantageous in the present system and eliminating only what is harmful and noxious.

Of these trends that have formed roots deep in the public spirit, one of the most important—which has contributed much to the origin, reestablishment, and conservation of the federal system—is small town loyalty, that is, provincialism, which, contained within just and wise limits, should produce the beneficial result that the individual interests of each population center and each state will be more carefully managed; this trend is the reason why instruction has been encouraged in the states, and some useful works of comfort and finery and even sheer ostentation have been produced. This fondness for the place where each person was born, lives, or owns land can be seen in some attempted revolutions, which also characterize respect for and loyalty to the nation's ancient capital. Thus we see Colima separate from Guadalajara in 1823 to become subject to the government of Mexico as a territory of the federation. Orizaba, Mazatlán, Aguascalientes, and other population centers have petitioned to do the same, and many others incline toward doing so, with the result that, if the present states were now divided into their constitutive departments or districts, all those departments would readily accept this change, which, with its broad consequences, would by itself be enough to bring the nation out from under all the difficulties in which it finds itself, establishing a simple, symmetrical, uniform, and not very costly system throughout the nation. Before explaining these points, I must say that this is not an innovation, but rather the reestablishment of the old system of government of New Spain before the intendancies were created that afterwards became states,[31] and also that the principle is not so general that there should be no exceptions with respect to states with small land areas and populations, like Chiapas, Nuevo Leon, Querétaro, and Tabasco, which ought not be further divided; instead by carrying this plan in those states with greater land area and population—taking parts from some states to combine with others, when the occasion calls for it—the result would be that each would have the necessary equality, as occurred in France when the old estates and provinces were divided into departments—a division that has been so beneficial to that country that all the governments that have followed since the National Assembly have kept it, and that today is linked to that nation's entire administrative system. . . .[32]

The religious and judicial divisions of the republic should match its civil divisions. It is essential to establish more bishoprics, and these and the original ones should encompass a certain number of entire states, not the fragments of states that now needlessly impede the actions of both authorities. But before forming new dioceses, the clergy's subsistence must be guaranteed by fixed resources that will be equal for all workers and independent of the government; the process for making appointments to bishoprics, prebendaries, and parishes must be set up; the administration and use of ecclesiastical wealth and the appointment of priests to chaplaincies whose sponsorship has reverted to the revenue of the bishoprics, must be regulated, which should lead to endowments for churches, making the administration of the sacraments as cost-free as possible—with the approval of the Holy See, which will doubtless be very well-disposed to accede to all this insofar as it redounds to the benefit of religion.

For the administration of justice, the necessary tribunals must be established, suitably distributed, and situated for the convenience of those who must come before them, creating the legal codes for administering justice that will inform all citizens what their duties are and what the penalty will be if they fail in them—an effort that has been tried so many times, on which considerable sums

31. The provinces of New Spain were grouped into intendancies (*intendencias*), the predecessors of the states of modern Mexico, in 1786, as part of the Bourbon Reforms, a series of measures taken by the Bourbon family monarchy of Spain, designed to enhance political and economic control over Spain and its American colonies.

32. In the next several pages, Alamán provides details of the plan he is proposing, specifically exploring the distribution of states, the makeup of the army, and the nature of the legislative body.

have been spent, and in which no progress has been made. To complete all this requires time, and the economies that should result from the decrease in the number of tribunals will not be immediately noticeable, because it is unjust to ignore the employment tenure rights that have been acquired by the present magistrates and by other employees who find themselves in similar situations.

In this way we will establish a system suitable to the state of the nation, symmetrical and uniform everywhere, economical in its expenses, consistent with established opinions and tendencies, and not only will the principles of the federation be preserved by "*sublato jure nocendi*,"[33] "abolishing its right to cause harm," but all the means of doing good will multiply as everything that is useful in this system spreads generally. The government's action, barely perceptible, will be more effective not facing opposition, and the action of the states' congresses and governments, when limited to providing for the states' own well-being and progress, will be seen as the effect of a paternal authority without becoming oppressive—as it has at present become in some states, where government action has consequently become loathsome, arousing discontent and revolution. The landed class will take greater part in public affairs because such affairs touch their interests closely; and inasmuch as an essential condition for the complete enjoyment of a good is the security of enjoying it forever, they will commit to securing the good when they see that doing so depends on themselves. This will give rise to public spiritedness, now completely dead, and will reestablish the national character that has disappeared. Mexicans will again have a name to preserve, a country to defend, and a government to respect, not out of a servile fear of punishment, but rather because of the benefits it dispenses, the decorum it acquires, and the consideration it deserves. To obtain these distinctions, it is not necessary that power fall to men of great talent—decorum and integrity are all that is necessary. To these qualities was owed the skill in governing of those viceroys—paragons of virtue—who in the past century pulled New Spain up from the state of disorder and decadence into which it had fallen during the last reigns of the monarchs of the Austrian dynasty,[34] and not only did these viceroys leave all branches of administration in good order, but they also foresaw possible future improvements. The Duke of Linares, the Marquess of Casafuerte, Bucareli, and Revilla Gigedo had no other secret.[35] Apodaca, with no other means than these, reestablished the treasury in circumstances much more difficult than the present ones. Their principles were those of Christian morals, and when they served their

---

33. Horace [*Ars Poetica,* l.284] says that Augustus improved on ancient comedy in this way. [Alamán's note.]

34. The Hapsburgs. The branch of the Hapsburg family that ruled Spain and its overseas empire died out in 1700 and was replaced by a branch of the French Bourbons.

35. Among the most active viceroys of Bourbon-era New Spain were the Duke of Linares (1710–1716), the Marquess of Casafuerte (1722–1734), Antonio de Bucareli (1771–1779), and the first and second Counts of Revilla Gigedo (1746–1755 and 1789–1794). Juan Ruiz de Apodaca, whom Alamán goes on to mention, was effectively the last viceroy in Mexico (1816–1821).

king faithfully, their loyalty was based on the firm conviction that in this way they also served God. The same principles informed that respectable class of employees who aspired to nothing more than to rise in their career by fulfilling their obligations, and to whose zeal and intelligence the good order of their offices was owed. They transgressed, it is true; they sometimes abused their offices because they were men; but when these men were fully aware—as the Duke of Linares was, of the fact that, "the most exacting of final accounts is the one that the viceroy will undergo when he is personally judged by the Divine Majesty"—it was not possible for them to fall into those excesses to which men who do not hold this conviction rush headlong.

Without this or some other reform that would give rise to new interests, that would energize spirits, it is futile to expect any great result. The change from the federal to the central system and the return of the former to primacy, left the same things in place with different names; the sole difference this change has produced has been to make both systems hateful. In the federal system, public wealth is in the hands of the governments of the states, which use it to pay state employees, leaving the employees of the national government in poverty. The change of system puts the funds at the disposition of the national government, which means that when the employees of national offices are paid, those of the departments languish, but when an attempt was made to pay some attention to everyone by raising the consumption tax on foreign goods to create a special fund for that purpose—set at fifteen percent—this became the motive or pretext for a revolution. Such change inspires no interest whatsoever, just as there is no interest in the repetition of a drama whose ending is already known. The institutions in their present state have fallen into the greatest disrepute, as one sees with the national holiday of October 4, designated as a memorial to the day the present constitution was promulgated and sworn, which is celebrated with complete indifference, seeming more like a funeral procession than a festival consecrated to a laudable end, providing an opportunity for nothing more than fresh criticism of the same institutions or for some sarcasm regarding the authorities established by those institutions. The same thing would happen with the national holiday of September 16 if the people were motivated only to show enthusiasm rather than to attend entertainments provided to them by spending money.[36]

"All of this," the response will be, "supposes that the order of things that will produce so much wealth has already been established, or at least that there are means to establish it. But what can these be, when amending the constitution requires so many formalities and is so slow, and every change depends on the approval of the state legislatures? Even were there not this difficulty, it would be impossible for a congress to make such a substantial reform, even over many

---

36. September 16, 1810, was the date when Miguel Hidalgo y Costilla declared independence from Spain; it remains the most important national holiday in Mexico. October 4, 1824, was the date of the adoption of the first federal constitution of Mexico, superseded after this writing by the Constitution of 1857.

years, along with the legal codes and laws necessary for putting it into practice." To this I answer that without a doubt, subject to the letter of the constitution, it would be impossible to reform that document, because ordering such reform depends on the very people at whom the reform would be aimed; but can one doubt that the existence and well-being of a nation must not be sacrificed to the forms that those who gave it that constitution wanted to tie it, assuming that they had made such a good one that it was necessary to prevent any changes to it—and, moreover, it would be absurd to follow the example of the Cortes of Spain, which allowed the loss of the entire American continent because it observed the letter of the constitution, and, afterwards, preferred to repeal the entire constitution rather than make any beneficial change to it. When nations are put in the predicament of perishing because they adhere to observing institutions that do not suit them, or getting rid of these institutions to save themselves by the violent method of revolution, Congress and the government have the responsibility to avoid the misfortunes that revolution would necessarily cause and to save the nation by some means conducive to the essential goal of preservation, as they have done many times through the concession of extraordinary powers that are obviously contrary to the constitution. As the reform of the constitution cannot be the work of a congress, to this very body falls the responsibility of specifying the means to bring about the reform.

It is worth noting that whenever the need to create a code of laws or make some change in the constitution arose, ancient nations—even when they had established congresses—authorized special commissions for the purpose. So to draw up the Laws of the Twelve Tables, the Roman Senate appointed the decemvirate;[37] to reform the constitution, it made Sulla dictator, and Sulla made the reform in such a way that the republic could have sustained itself had Pompey's ambition not destroyed everything Sulla had established; later, the reason for appointing the triumvirate was so that they could constitute the republic.[38] Such works cannot be carried out in any other way, for a large body can neither follow a set plan nor proceed with the necessary promptness, because of the time that deliberations require, and for this reason congresses are by their nature more suitable for preserving what exists than for creating new things. So, if a nation where everything must be created because everything that existed has been destroyed must depend on an ordinary congress to have a treasury system, a legal code, and all those organizational laws without which the general principles contained in a constitution cannot be developed and applied, it will never make

---

37. The Law of the Twelve Tables was the basis of the constitution of the Roman Republic. A decemvirate (board of ten men) was appointed to draw up a code defining the principles of Roman administration. During the decemviri's term in office, all other magistracies were suspended.

38. Lucius Cornelius Sulla Felix (c. 138–78 BC), who as dictator enacted a series of reforms. Gnaeus Pompeius Magnus (106–48 BC), Roman military and political leader, known as Pompey, who, with Julius Caesar and Marcus Crassus, formed the first triumvirate. In attempting to dominate Rome personally, Pompey ended up in civil war with Julius Caesar.

them. It is not the least of the misfortunes of this kind of system that, not only does it lack the means to provide everything necessary for the happiness of a people, but also it is an obstacle to the people ever obtaining it. To work with the terrible energy it had, the French Convention stopped being a congress and transformed itself into as many dictatorships as it had committees, each of which proceeded independently of the others; while the organization that Napoleon finally gave to France and the legal code that carries his name resulted from the deliberations of his Council of State.

In light of these antecedents, it would be appropriate that a commission of not more than three or five individuals be named and charged with constituting the nation, which would be understood to have empowered the commission for this purpose. No one will oppose the small number of these individuals, because in the fiction of the representative system, the nation can as readily be considered represented by five as by one hundred. This commission would have the authority to name as many more commissions as it believes necessary to organize each of the branches, according to the general plan that it proposes, and all the authorities and offices of the republic would be obligated to support its work and to supply it with all the facts and information it might need, so that at the end of one year, at most, everything would be complete, without precluding putting each individual part into effect when it is ready. This is the only possible way of putting into complete and simultaneous order all the branches of the administration, but since, in a matter so delicate, one does not expect to be successful in everything from the outset, and experience quickly reveals difficulties that could not be foreseen before putting a political system in practice, at the end of two years all of it should be reexamined—keeping in mind the observations that will have been made about each of the parts—in order to adjust for and amend whatever seems to require it, afterwards leaving it to Congress to make any changes that the course of time might demand.

Joining the authority to amend with the power to govern, as has been done in the republic, has the serious drawback that the absolute power given to the former extends to the latter, and it is very difficult to make whoever holds in his hand the ability to do anything he wants, do only what he must. In difficult circumstances, in countries where the representative system has been well established, Congress is convened in order to make appropriate resolutions; among us, on the contrary, Congress has not found itself capable of doing anything more appropriate than dissolving itself and leaving absolute authority in the hands of the president. He, passing suddenly from a very restricted power to the opposite extreme, loses sight of the objective for which he was granted such broad authority; when this kind of authority was given to defend the republic from a Spanish invasion, as in 1829, it was used to declare null a will that had been written many years earlier, or to establish a house for invalids and to declare the freedom of the slaves. The latter two things were very good, but they had no relation whatsoever to the objective for which authority was granted to the government, which—as almost always happens when one attempts to legislate for show and not for necessity—permitted the continuation of slavery in the Texas colonies for prudential reasons, and so it ended up declaring free those who did not need this declaration to be free, because they were free in fact, and it made slaves of those who had not been slaves, because, having set foot on the territory of the republic, they had, under earlier laws, acquired freedom by this act alone.[39] The use of this authority was of short duration on this occasion, but when in a subsequent epoch it was prolonged for more time and was applied to a multitude of objectives, especially in the branch of finance, the only result was an excessive increase in foreign and domestic debt, a multitude of transactions costly to the national treasury, the destruction of some useful establishments, and the creation of a crowd of superfluous employees; and, although some magnificent public buildings were built, they were constructed at enormous cost, and instead of ennobling the character of the citizens, flattery and baseness were promoted, subjecting the highest authorities to humiliating indignities. The idea of dictatorship, which tends to have some advocates, must then be absolutely excluded from the methods one can consider for reforming the constitution.

All citizens who can be considered fit should be called to labor in this great work. That work must secure its destiny, establishing a system of government that will be more advantageous than the existing one, at least by being well defined. At present, the confusion that has been introduced is such that, although the present order of things is called a federation, in reality nothing whatsoever exists to which a familiar name can be given. There are popular elections, but these elections lead to nothing, because in the end the governors of the states and the national government in its turn appoint whomever they feel like appointing to congresses and councils, riding roughshod over even the appearance of liberty. A congress exists, but it does none of the things it ought to do. In vain the state of the nation is presented to it each year in the ministers' reports, which have become very costly and completely useless academic exercises, for they never seem to be taken into consideration and may not even be read by those who should be seeking in them the standards of their operations. Responsibility has become a party weapon, not a legal method for restraining arbitrariness. The decisions of the tribunals are not respected, their jurisdiction being so doubtful that it is not yet known which tribunal has jurisdiction over a sensational lawsuit that for years has been pursued at great cost.[40] And the administration of the treasury goes along at the whim of the government, without budgets or accounting. To give the name "constitutional system" to such disorder distorts the meaning of the words, and to govern *ad hoc*—issuing isolated rulings according to the circumstances—cannot make a nation happy, because doing so is both uncertain and not very secure for the government itself, which can neither count on firm support nor rely on a party in which it can place its trust.

---

39. President Vicente R. Guerrero on September 15, 1829, issued the Guerrero Decree, which abolished slavery in the then-Mexican state of Texas. The decree never went into effect.

40. The dispute over ownership of fifteen bars of silver from the rich mine of La Luz in Guanajuato. [Alamán's note.]

I do not presume to believe that the reform I have proposed is the best, but my having expressed ideas on which I have reflected for a long time will perhaps be a reason for others to expound theirs with greater clarity, leaving the worn path of centralism or federalism. To work with determination for the father-land's salvation, it is enough not to lose hope. The misfortunes that the father-land has experienced, the mistakes that have been made and that it has been my duty as a historian to present undisguised throughout this work, must not dis-hearten the spirit nor discourage the hopes of those who love their country. All nations have had periods of disheartenment; all present in their history lamenta-ble events—battles, bloodshed, excesses of all kinds; but their perseverance in the face of adversity, the prudence of their governments, and the enlightened cooperation of their citizenry have rescued them from situations that seemed hopeless and have elevated them afterwards to the height of power and glory. In the Mexican Republic we have passed, as we have already noted, from excessive ideas of wealth and power to an equally unfounded discouragement, and because we previously expected too much, it seems that nothing is left now for which to hope; and so, with the vitality of party spirit exhausted, not only has public spirit failed to take its place but even the stimulus from the factions has disappeared. Certainly, a great deal has been lost, and some of these losses are irreparable, like the loss of territory; but all the rest can be repaired, and frugality and prudence are what must repair it, while a bright future for Mexicans still remains possible. Let it get off to a start by encouraging it with the necessary institutional reform; the outcome will be an abundance of resources to meet both the needs of the nation and the organization of the armed forces, which is indispensable for the nation's defense. Internal security and the esteem that the republic will win abroad will follow from this, and the day that signals the beginning of this new era should be the great national holiday, which, by not commemorating any ill-fated origin, shall connect the happy citizenry with the benefits they may enjoy and with their hopes for more benefits to come.

But if, instead of making the efforts necessary to achieve this goal, we continue along the ruinous path on which we have embarked, the results will be most lamentable. In the comparative table at the end of this chapter[41] one can see at a glance everything that Mexico as a nation has lost since becoming independent: more than half its territory; a foreign debt of 52 million; the national debt con-tinuing the same as it was in the earlier era, if not increased, although it should have been greatly reduced by the many negotiations in which credits have been given like money; revenues reduced by half, and the army to nothing. This is the dismal conviction to be drawn from reviewing this document, in which every-thing is indisputable because only numbers are presented, and these numbers are taken from the annual ministerial reports, regarding which there can be no doubt whatsoever. This work of destruction, begun with independence itself, gathered great momentum in 1827, 1828, and 1829; it was held in check from 1830 to

---

41. Table is not included in this selection.

1831, but it returned to increase rapidly after 1832. Since that time, the foreign debt has almost doubled; more than thirty million pesos in new domestic debt has been incurred; revenues, which had finally been reestablished on a pre-independence footing, have begun to decline again; the army has disappeared; and since then—and for reasons that, if they did not originate at that time, were increased then—the loss of territory took place. Let the multiple elements of happiness that Divine Providence has bestowed on this privileged nation continue to be squandered; let the great good of independence continue to be abused instead of being considered a foundation and beginning for all the rest; let armed adventurers be called to the most distant and difficult-to-defend states, so that they can become masters of those states; let the rich states waste the resources in which they abound, investing them in unnecessary enterprises; let the national government waste on unnecessary things the few resources on which it counts, while it lacks the resources necessary for the nation's defense; let writers continue lulling the nation to sleep with flattering fictions, leaving it ignorant of its origins and presenting it not with its history but with novels, in which, by excusing or concealing bad acts and even extolling them as good, they influence the nation to continue committing them, and by depriving the author of independence of the glory that belongs to him and to those who cooperated with him in creating it, they attribute this glory to those who, for whatever reason, were not the ones who secured independence; let this unjust plunder, this act of ingratitude, continue to be commemorated with a national holiday; let him who speaks the truth be considered a bad citizen, and let speaking the truth be taken as a crime the nation will never pardon, as a writer in these days has said; let the most important affairs of state be conducted with indifference, as they have been until now; let its management be given over to inept or disloyal hands—the result is sure, and the picture, receiving its final brush strokes, will soon be complete.

Mexico will be a prosperous country, without a doubt, because its natural elements provide prosperity, but it will not be prosperous for the races that reside here now, and, as appears inevitable, the peoples who established themselves in it in various and distant eras will disappear from its territory, leaving scarcely a memory of their existence—just as the nation that constructed the buildings of Palenque and the others that are admired on the Yucatan Peninsula was destroyed without anyone knowing what it was nor how it disappeared; just as the Toltecs perished at the hands of the barbarian tribes coming from the north, leaving no memory of themselves except the pyramids in Cholula and Teotihuacan;[42] and

---

42. Palenque, a Mayan archeological site in the state of Chiapas that had recently been discovered in Alamán's time. Mexican intellectuals, particularly conservatives, were reluctant to believe that the Mayas could have built this and other Mayan sites, such as Chichen Itza, Coba, Kalakmul, Tikal, and Uxmal. The Toltecs were a pre-Columbian native people who dominated much of central Mexico between the tenth and twelfth centuries AD. The Great Pyramid of Cholula is the largest pre-Columbian pyramid by volume, built between the second century BC and the early-sixteenth century AD. Teotihuacan is a city built around 300 BC and reaching its height of power between 150 and 450 AD.

just as, finally, the ancient Mexicans fell under the power of the Spaniards, the country winning enormously in this change of rule but the old masters being laid low—so also the present inhabitants will be destroyed, and, without even receiving the compassion that their predecessors were shown, what a celebrated Latin poet said of one of the most famous persons in Roman history will be applied to the Mexican nation of our days: *Stat magni nominis umbra.* "Only the shadow remains of the name celebrated in other times."[43]

May the Almighty—in whose hand the fate of nations lies, who by ways hidden to our eyes brings them down or raises them up according to the design of His Providence—grant to our nation the protection with which He so many times has deigned to preserve it from the dangers to which it has been exposed!

---

43. Lucan, *Pharsalia*, [Book I, line 135] speaking of Pompey. [Alamán's note.]

Juan Bautista Alberdi
(Argentina)

Juan Bautista Alberdi (1810–1884), is widely regarded as Argentina's most important philosopher of law; he is considered the father of the Argentine Constitution. Alberdi was born in San Miguel del Tucumán to Salvador de Alberdi, a wealthy merchant, and Josefa de Aráozs, who was from a traditional aristocratic northeastern Argentine family. Alberdi studied at the Colegio de Ciencias Morales, where he read French Enlightenment philosophers. At university he studied law, though he was also much attracted to music. He wrote several works on the aesthetics of music and its performance, and he was a pianist and composer.

In his early days as a student, Alberdi was attracted to literary salons, but as he matured he became increasingly involved in student clubs whose primary focus was the discussion of political philosophy, history, and the future of the American peoples. He was deeply influenced by the British liberal tradition, particularly Locke and Bentham, as well as the Scottish moral sense tradition. He shared his fellow Latin American intellectuals' admiration of Auguste Comte's positivism, which he believed to be key to understanding how Spanish America might rapidly improve its political and economic standing. He admired the ability of the United States to, as he saw it, civilize itself and accommodate emerging political realities. Finally, along with Esteban Echeverría and Domingo Faustino Sarmiento, Alberdi was a member of the "Generation of 1837" and, more particularly, the Association of May, a group dedicated to republicanism in government, free trade, individual freedoms, and material progress, all policies opposed to Argentine dictator Juan Manuel de Rosas's political inclinations.

By 1837, Alberdi had begun to establish his literary presence and position, publishing *El fragmento preliminar al estudio del derecho* and founding and editing *La Moda,* a periodical devoted to customs, music, and art. He left Argentina in 1838, unhappy with Rosas's government, to practice law and journalism in Montevideo, Uruguay. While there, he wrote for several literary and political journals, including *El Nacional, El Grito Argentino,* and *El Iniciador;* he also was cofounder of *La Revista del Plata.* After a brief visit in 1843 to Europe, he went to Chile, where he remained until 1855 working as a lawyer, journalist, and writer of essays and literature.

With the fall of Rosas in 1852, Alberdi saw a unique opportunity for Argentina to reflect on the challenges it faced and move forward on the basis of a rational analysis of the strategies through which reform might be effected. He thus undertook the writing, in 1853, of his most influential book, *Bases y puntos de partida para la organización política de la República Argentina* (translated as Foundations and Points of Departure for the Political Organization of the Republic of Argentina), which provides the model for what he saw—and what was finally adopted—as Argentina's future organization. The selection that follows is from this work. The following year he published *Elementos del derecho público provincial Argentino,* a statement of his ideas about public law for provincial institutions, and applied them to the constitution of Mendoza province. In 1854 he published the *Sistema económico y rentístico de la Confederación Argentina, según la constitución de 1853,* which articulates the relationship between law and economy and explains what a nation must do to achieve economic liberty. These three works, along with *El fragmento preliminar* (1837) are generally regarded as the basis for Argentine law and civil life.

When General Justo José Luis Urquiza became president of Argentina he named Alberdi, still living in Chile, a traveling diplomat to represent Argentina to the governments of various European nations and the United States, a role in which he served from 1855 to 1862. When Bartolomé Mitre became president of the republic, he relieved Alberdi of his diplomatic mission. Alberdi responded in 1869 with a series of pamphlets denouncing Mitre's war in league with Brazil against Paraguay, collected under the title *El Imperio del Brazil.* Much later, when Mitre was no longer president, Alberdi tried his hand at politics. He was elected deputy to the national Congress for Tucumán, returning to Argentina after a forty-year absence in 1879 to take up that post. He left Argentina again, this time for France, in 1881, and died there three years later. His remains were repatriated in 1889.

Further Reading

Academia Nacional de Derecho y Ciencias Sociales. *Homenaje a Juan Bautista Alberdi: Sesquicentenario de las bases (1852–2002).* Córdoba: Academia Nacional de Derecho y Ciencias Sociales de Córdoba, 2002.

Aguirre, Gisela, *Juan Bautista Alberdi.* Buenos Aires: Planeta, 1999.

Alberdi, Juan Bautista. *Obras completas.* 8 vols. Buenos Aires: La Tribuna Nacional, 1886.

———. *Escritos póstumos de Juan Bautista Alberdi.* 16 vols. Buenos Aires: Universidad Nacional de Quilmes, 2002. (Originally published Buenos Aires: Imprenta Europea, 1895–1901.)

Ghirardi, Olsen A. *La filosofía en Alberdi.* Córdoba: Academia Nacional de Derecho y Ciencias Sociales de Córdoba, 2000.

Halperín Donghi, Tulio. *Alberdi, Sarmiento y Mitre: Tres proyectos de futuro para la era constitucional.* Santa Fe, Argentina: Universidad Nacional del Litoral, 2004.

Katra, William H. *The Argentine Generation of 1837: Echeverría, Alberdi, Sarmiento, Mitre.* Madison, N.J.: Fairleigh Dickinson University Press, 1996.

Lannes, Federico A. M. *El pensamiento económico de Alberdi.* San Miguel de Tucumán: Universidad Nacional de Tucumán, Ediciones del Rectorado, 2003.

Lucas Verdú, Pablo. *Alberdi, su vigencia y modernidad constitucional.* Buenos Aires: Ciudad Argentina, 1998.

Thonis, Luis. *Estado y ficción en Juan Bautista Alberdi.* Buenos Aires: Paradiso, 2001.

Foundations and Points of Departure for the Political Organization of the Republic of Argentina (1853)

Only those great means of an economic nature—namely, the nourishing and strength-giving action of material interests—will be able to extract South America from the utterly untenable situation in which it finds itself.

That situation comes from the fact that America has become a republic through governmental law, but the republic is not a reality in its territory.

The republic is not a reality in South America because the people are not prepared to rule themselves under this system, a system that exceeds their ability.

Would returning to the monarchy of another time be the way to give this America a government suitable to its capability? If the republic is not practicable, given the present condition of our people, does it then follow that monarchy would be more practicable?

Decidedly not.

The truth is that we are not sufficiently mature to implement any representative government, be it monarchical or republican. The partisans of monarchy in America are not mistaken when they say we are incapable of being republicans; but they are more mistaken than we republicans if they think we have greater means for being monarchists. The idea of a representative monarchy in Spanish America is most inadequate and foolish; it even lacks common sense, it seems to me, if we concentrate on the present moment and the state to which things have come. The monarchists of our first era could be pardoned for their dynastic plans—the monarchical tradition was only at one step's remove, and there still existed an illusion about the possibility of reorganizing it. But doing so today would not occur to anyone with a sense of what is practical. After an endless war to convert into monarchies what we have changed into republics by a twenty-year war, we would be very happily returning to a monarchy more unsettled than the republic.

Brazil's noble example should not delude us; let us congratulate that country for the good fortune that has come its way, let us respect its form, which knows how to protect civilization, let us learn to co-exist with it and proceed in harmony to the common goal of all forms of government—civilization. But let us refrain from imitating it in its monarchical way. That country has not experienced being a republic for even a single day; its monarchical life has not been interrupted for an hour. It passed from colonial monarchy to independent monarchy without interregnum. But those of us who have practiced republicanism for forty years, although terribly, would be worse monarchists than republicans because today we understand monarchy less than we do the republic.

Would the new elected monarchy take root? It would be something never before seen. By its essence monarchy has tradition as its origin. Would we elect our friends, who are our equals, as counts and marquesses? Would we consent freely to be inferior to our equals? I would like to see the face of the one who considers himself competent to be elected king in republican America. Would we accept kings and nobles of European extraction? Only after a war of re-conquest. And who would imagine, much less consent to that madness?

The problem of what government is possible in the former Spanish America has only one sensible resolution—it consists in elevating our peoples to the level of that governmental form necessity has imposed on us; in giving them the ability they lack for being republicans; in making them worthy of the republic we have proclaimed, which today we can neither make workable nor abandon; in improving the *government* by improving the *governed;* in improving *society* to secure the improvement of the *government,* which is its expression and direct outcome.

But the road is long, and there is a great deal to anticipate before we come to its end. Would there not be in such a case a suitable and adequate government to move us through this period of preparation and transition? Fortunately, we have one and do not need to leave the republic.

Happily the republic, so rich in forms, permits many stages and lends itself to all the needs of the age and the space. To know how to adapt it to our age is the entire art of constituting it among us.

That solution has a fortunate precedent in the South American republic, and we owe it to the good sense of the Chilean people who have found in the energy of presidential power the public guarantees for order and peace that monarchy offers without giving up the nature of republican government. To Bolívar is attributed this profound and spiritual saying: "The new states of the former Spanish America need kings with the name of presidents." Chile has resolved the problem without dynasties and without military dictatorship through a constitution, monarchical at base and republican in form, law that entwines the tradition of the past with the life of the present. The republic can have no other form when it immediately follows upon monarchy; the new regime must contain something of the old; the last ages of a people do not leap ahead. The French Republic, offspring of monarchy, might have saved itself in that way, but the excesses of radicalism will return it to monarchical rule.[1]

How to make, then, democracies in fact of our democracies in name? How to convert our written and nominal liberties into facts? By what means will we manage to elevate the current capacity of our peoples to the level of their written constitutions and proclaimed principles?

By the means I have indicated and everyone knows—by educating the people, working through the civilizing action of Europe, that is to say, by immigration; by a civil, commercial, and maritime legislation with adequate foundations; by constitutions in harmony with our time and our needs; by a system of government that favors those means.

• • • • •

---

1. The Revolution of 1848 in France resulted in republics, but by the time Alberdi's book was published in 1853, President Louis-Napoleon Bonaparte had assumed dictatorial powers after a coup; at the end of that year, following a plebiscite, he was crowned Emperor of France.

XIV

The South American republics are products of and living testimony to Europe's activity in America. What we call independent America is nothing other than Europe established in America; and our revolution is nothing other than the dismemberment of a European power into two halves, each of which today manages itself by itself.

On our soil, everything civilized is European; America itself is a European discovery. A Genoese sailor discovered it, and the discovery excited a Spanish sovereign. Cortés, Pizarro, Mendoza, Valdivia,[2] none of whom were born in America, populated it with the people who today possess it and who certainly are not indigenous.

We do not have a single important city not founded by Europeans. Santiago was founded by a foreigner named Pedro Valdivia and Buenos Aires by another foreigner named Pedro de Mendoza.

All our important cities received European names from their foreign founders. The very name *America* was taken from one of those foreign discoverers—Amerigo Vespucci of Florence.

Even today, with independence, the indigenous person does not figure in or make up the world of our political and civil society.

We who call ourselves Americans are nothing other than Europeans born in America. The shape of our skulls, our blood, color, everything comes from outside.

The indigenous person does us justice; even today he calls us *Spaniards*. I do not know one distinguished person in our societies with a *Pehuenche*[3] or *Araucano*[4] surname. The language we speak is European. To the humiliation of those who abhor its influence, they must curse it in a foreign language. The language of the Spanish is "Spanish."

Our Christian religion has been brought to America by foreigners. If it were not for Europe, America would today be worshipping the sun, the trees, the beasts, burning men in sacrifice, and would not know marriage. The hand of Europe planted the cross of Jesus Christ before the heathen in America. For this alone, blessed be the hand of Europe!

Our former and present laws were handed down by foreign kings, and today, with their aid, we have civil, commercial, and criminal codes. The laws of our fatherland are copies of foreign laws.

---

2. Hernan Cortés (1485–1547), Spanish conquistador who defeated the Aztecs in 1521; Francisco Pizarro (c. 1475–1541), Spanish conquistador who defeated the Incan empire; Antonio de Mendoza (1490–1552), first viceroy of New Spain and viceroy of Peru; Pedro de Valdivia (1497–1553), Spanish conquistador who led an expedition into Chile, of which he became governor.

3. The *Pehuenche* were an indigenous people of the southern Andes, whose name derives from their dependence on the piñon nut.

4. The *Araucano* were an indigenous people of the southern Chilean Andes, also known as the Mapuche.

Our administrative system in finance, tax, income, etc., is the work of Europe almost to this very day. And what are our political constitutions if not the adoption of European systems of government? What is our great revolution with respect to ideas if not a phase of the French Revolution?

Enter our universities and show me learning that is not European, into our libraries and show me a useful book that is not foreign.

Observe from head to foot the suit you are wearing, and it will be unusual if even the soles of your shoes are American. What do we call "elegant," if not what is European? Who governs our fashions, our elegant and comfortable manners? When we say *confortable,* convenient, *bien, comme il faut,* are we alluding to Araucanian things?

Who knows a gentleman among us who boasts of being a pure Indian? Who would not a thousand times rather see his sister or daughter married to an English shoemaker than to an Araucanian nobleman?

In America everything not European is barbarian. There is no other division than the following: 1. the indigenous, that is to say, the savage; 2. the European, that is to say, we who were born in America and speak Spanish, who believe in Jesus Christ and not in Pillán (god of the indigenous).

There is no other division of American man. The division into man of the city and man of the country is false; it does not exist. It is reminiscent of Niebuhr's studies on the original history of Rome.[5] Rosas has not ruled with gauchos, but with the city.[6] The main *advocates of centralization* were men of the country, such as Martín Rodríguez, the Rámos, the Miguens, the Díaz Valez; on the other hand, the men of Rosas, the Anchorénas, the Medrános, the Dorrégos, the Arana, were educated in the cities. The *mazorca*[7] is not composed of gauchos.

The only subdivision Spanish American man recognizes is *man of the littoral* and man *of the interior* or *mediterranean.*[8] This division is real and profound. The first is the fruit of Europe's civilizing activity in this century, which derives from commerce and from immigration into the peoples of the coast. The other is the work of sixteenth-century Europe, of Europe at the time of the conquest, which is preserved intact, as though in a container, among the interior peoples of our continent, where Spain settled it with the intention of keeping it that way.

From Chuquisaca to Valparaíso[9] there is a distance of three centuries; and it is not Santiago's National Institute[10] that has created this difference in favor of this

---

5. Barthold Georg Niebuhr (1776–1831), German statesman and historian whose work, *Roman History,* 1812–1828, broke new ground in its subject matter and historiography.

6. Juan Manuel de Rosas (1793–1877), conservative Argentine *caudillo.*

7. Rosas's secret police, often accused of being death squads.

8. In Spanish, literally, "in the midst of the land."

9. Chuquisaca is the ancient name of Sucre, Bolivia, a city of the interior. Valparaíso was Chile's most important port city, located about fifty kilometers from Santiago.

10. Instituto Nacional de Chile, founded in 1813 for the purpose of educating citizens for the Chilean Republic, served as one of Chile's major sources of higher education throughout the nineteenth century and continues to do so up to the present.

city. It is not our poor colleges that have put the South American littoral three hundred years ahead of interior cities. In fact, the littoral lacks universities. The immense progress of its cities relative to the interior cities is a result of the intense activity of present-day Europe in the form of free trade, immigration, and industry in the South American coastal towns.

From the sixteenth century until today, Europe has been the wellspring and origin of this continent's civilization. Under the old regime, Europe played that role through Spain. That nation brought us the highest expression of the Middle Ages and the beginning of the rebirth of civilization in Europe.

With the American Revolution[11] the activity of Spanish Europe on this continent ended, but the activity of Anglo-Saxon and French Europe took its place. Today's Americans are Europeans who have changed masters; the Spanish initiative has been followed by the English and French. But it is always Europe that is the producer of our civilization. The means of action has changed, but the product is the same. Official or governmental activity has been followed by social activity—of people, of race. In America present-day Europe does nothing but complete the European task of the Middle Ages, which here remains embryonic, half-formed. Its present means of influence will not be the sword, it will not be conquest. America is already conquered; it is European and for that very reason is unconquerable. The war of conquest supposes rival civilizations, opposing states—e.g., the savage and the European. This antagonism does not exist; the savage is conquered; in America it has neither dominion nor lordship. We, Europeans by race and civilization, are masters of America.

It is time to recognize this law of our American progress and again appeal to Europe for help with our incomplete culture, to that Europe that we have fought and defeated by arms on the battlefield, but that we are far from defeating in the fields of thought and industry.

Feeding circumstantial resentments, there remain those who are alarmed at even the name "Europe"; there remain those who harbor fears of perdition and slavery.

Such sentiments constitute a state of illness in our South American spirit, extremely ominous for our prosperity and, for that very reason, worthy of study.

The kings of Spain taught us to hate, under the name *foreigner,* all who were not *Spanish.* The liberators of 1810, in turn, taught us to detest, under the name *European,* anyone who had not been born in America. Even Spain was included in this hatred. The question of war was set up by these terms—*Europe* and *America*—the old world and the world of Columbus. Hatred of the European was called *loyalty* and the latter in turn *patriotism.* In their time, these hatreds were useful and convenient resources; today they are prejudices tragic for the prosperity of these countries.

The press, instruction, history—prepared for the people—must work to destroy the prejudices against what is foreign, seeing these prejudices as obstacles

---

11. Alberdi here refers to Spanish-speaking Latin America's revolution against Spain.

to this continent's progress. Aversion to the foreigner is barbarous in other nations; in South American nations it is something more—it is the cause of the ruin and dissolution of a society Spanish in character. We must fight that ruinous tendency with the weapons of the very credulity and vulgar truth that lie within reach of our masses. The press, by way of introducing and promoting the true spirit of progress, must ask the men among our people these questions: Whether they consider themselves indigenous in race; whether they take themselves to be Indians of *pampas* or *pehuenches* origin; whether they believe themselves descendents of savages and heathens rather than descendents of the foreign races that brought the religion of Jesus Christ and the civilization of Europe to this continent, which in an earlier time was the fatherland of heathens.

Our apostolate of civilization must put clearly and in all their material simplicity the following facts of historical evidence before our good people, who are poisoned by prejudice against what makes up their life and progress: Our holy pope, Pius IX, present head of the Catholic Church, is a foreigner, an Italian, just as all those popes who have preceded him have been foreigners and just as all those who follow in the Holy See will be. The saints who are on our altars are foreigners, and everyday our believing people kneel down before those meritorious foreign saints who never set foot on the soil of America, nor spoke, most of them, Castilian.

St. Edward, St. Thomas, St. Gall, St. Ursula, St. Margaret,[12] and many other Catholic saints were English, foreigners to our nation and tongue. If our people heard them speak in English, which was their language, our people would not understand them and would, perhaps, call them *gringos*.

Saint Ramon Nonato was Catalonian, Saint Lawrence, Saint Philip Benecio, Saint Anselm, Saint Sylvester,[13] were Italians, the same in origin as those foreigners that our people scornfully called *low-class foreigner*, forgetting that we have an infinite number of *low-class foreigners* on our altars—Saint Nicholas was a Swiss, and Saint Casimir was Hungarian.[14]

Finally, the Man-God, our lord Jesus Christ, was not born in America but in Asia, in Bethlehem, a small city of Judea, a country twice as distant and foreign to us as Europe. Our people, hearing his divine word, would not have understood it because he did not speak Castilian; they would have called him "foreigner" because, in fact, he was; but does not that divine foreigner—who

---

12. St. Edward the Martyr, King of England (962–979), died a young, violent death; St. Thomas More (1477–1535), Lord Chancellor of England, writer, author; St. Gall, seventh-century Irish saint; St. Ursula, fourth-century virgin and martyr; St. Margaret, Margaret of Scotland (1050–1093), known for her charitable and pious life.

13. St. Ramon Nonato (the Unborn) (1204–1240), delivered by caesarian section after the death of his mother, is the patron saint of midwives and persons falsely accused of gossip; Saint Lawrence (d. 258), martyred for having distributed the Church's wealth to the poor; St. Philip Benicio (d. 1285); St. Anselm of Canterbury (1033–1109), born in Lombardy, known for his doctrine of "faith seeking understanding"; St. Sylvester (1177–1267), founder of the Sylvestrine Order.

14. Blessed Nicholas of Flü (1417–1487); St. Casimir (1458–1484), patron saint of Poland.

has eliminated borders and made a family of brothers of all the earth's peoples—consecrate and ennoble, so to speak, the condition of the foreigner by the fact that he is one himself?

Let us remind our people that the fatherland is not the soil. We have had the soil for three centuries, and we have had the fatherland only since 1810. The fatherland is liberty; it is order, wealth, civilization organized on native soil, under its flag and in its name. Well then, this has been brought to us by Europe, that is to say, Europe has brought us the notion of order, knowledge of liberty, the art of wealth, the principles of Christian civilization. Europe, then, has brought us the fatherland, if we add that it even brought us the population that makes up the people and body of the fatherland.

The patriots of our first era are not the ones with accurate ideas for how to make this America prosper, as much as they are the ones who, with such accuracy, knew how to remove the Spanish power. Notions of patriotism—the contrivance of a purely American cause which they used as a means to a war appropriate for that time—dominate and possess them still. Thus, up to 1826 we saw Bolívar agitating for alliances to contain a Europe that sought nothing, and in 1844 we saw General San Martín applauding the resistance of Rosas to the casual claims of some European states. Having been agents for a real and great need of the America of that time, they are today somewhat ignorant of this continent's new requirements. The military glory that absorbed their life still preoccupies them more than does progress.

Nonetheless, the need for profit and amenities has succeeded the need for glory, and warrior heroism is no longer the tool appropriate for the prosaic needs of commerce and industry that constitute the present life of these countries.

Enamored of their work, the patriots of the first era are frightened of everything they believe compromises it.

But we—more focused on the work of civilization than on the work of a certain era's patriotism—we are not fearful in the face of all that America can produce in great deeds. Having understood that America's current situation is in transition, that its future destiny is as great as it is unknown, nothing frightens us, and in everything we have lofty hopes of improvement. America is not well; it is uninhabited, solitary, poor. It begs population, prosperity.

From where will this come in the future? From where it came in the past—Europe.

XV

In the future, how, in what form, will the life-giving spirit of European civilization come to our land? As it came in every other era—Europe will bring us its new spirit, its habits of industry, its practices of civilization in the immigrations it sends us.

With his habits, every European who comes to our shores brings us more civilization—which he then communicates to our inhabitants—than do many books of philosophy. Perfection not seen, touched, or felt is poorly understood. The most instructive catechism is an industrious man.

Do we wish to plant and acclimate in America English liberty, French culture, the industriousness of the man from Europe and the United States? Let us bring living pieces of them in their inhabitants' practices, and let those practices take root here.

Do we want the habits of order, discipline, and industriousness to thrive in our America? Let us fill our America with people who possess those habits inherently. Those habits are contagious; by the side of the European industrialist the American industrialist is immediately formed. The plant of civilization does not spread by seeds. It is like the grape vine; it requires grafting.

This is the only method by which America, today uninhabited, might in a short time come to be a world of abundance. By itself reproduction is the very slowest method.

If we wish to see our states grow larger in a short time, let us bring their elements from outside, already formed and ready.

Lacking large populations there is no development of culture, there is no considerable progress, everything is petty and small. Nations of one-half million inhabitants can have these latter characteristics throughout their territory; throughout their district will be provinces, villages; and all their affairs will always carry the petty stamp of "provincial."

Important warning to the men of the South American State—primary schools, high schools, universities, are, by themselves, very poor means for progress without great productive enterprises, which are the offspring of large numbers of men.

Population—the South American need that symbolizes all the others—is the accurate measure of our governments' capability. The minister of state who does not double the census of these peoples every ten years has wasted his time in bagatelles and excessive detail.

Make the *roto,* the *gaucho,* the *cholo*[15]—fundamental unit of our popular masses—go through all the transformations of the best system of instruction; in a hundred years you will not have in him an English worker, who works, consumes, lives well and comfortably. Place the one million inhabitants, which form the average population of these republics, on the best educational foundation possible, as well-instructed as the Canton of Geneva in Switzerland, as the most cultured province of France—will that give you a large and flourishing state? Certainly not—a million men in a territory that can easily accommodate fifty million, is it anything other than a paltry population?

The argument that is made is this: by educating our masses, we will have order; having order, population will come from outside.

I will reply to you that you are reversing the true means to progress. You will have neither order nor popular education except with the influx of masses who have those deeply rooted habits of order and good education.

---

15. *Roto* is a term for a "lower-class person"; *gaucho* is a South American cowboy; and *cholo* is a derogatory name for a person of mixed race.

Increase conscientious populations and you will see those foolish agitators with their plans for frivolous revolts become unsuccessful and isolated in the middle of a world that is absorbed by serious occupations.

How to achieve all this? More easily than by wasting millions in endless petty attempts at improvements.

Foreign Treaties.—Sign treaties with the foreigner giving him guarantees that his natural rights of property, civil liberty, security, acquisition, and transit will be respected. Those treaties will be the most precious part of the constitution— the external part, which is key to progress for those countries called to receive their growth from outside. To make this branch of public law inviolable and last- ing, sign treaties for an indefinite or very extended term. Do not be afraid to chain yourselves to order and culture.

To fear perpetual treaties is to fear that individual guarantees will endure in our land. The Argentine treaty with Great Britain has prevented Rosas from turning Buenos Aires into another Paraguay.[16]

Do not fear giving away our industry's distant future to civilization if there is a risk that internal barbarism or tyranny will seize it. Fear of treaties is left over from the first warlike era of our revolution. It is an old and out-of-date principle, or an unwise and poorly-carried-over imitation of the foreign policy [George] Washington counseled to the United States under circumstances and for reasons totally different from those facing us.

Treaties of friendship and trade are honorable means of placing South Ameri- can civilization under the protection of the world's civilization. Would you not want our constitutions and all the guarantees of industry, of property and civil liberty confirmed by them, to exist inviolable under the armed protection of all peoples without diminishing our own nationality? Then consign the rights and civil guarantees that those constitutions bestow on your inhabitants to treaties of friendship, of trade, of navigation with the foreigner. Maintaining—having the foreigner maintain the treaties—will only serve to maintain our constitution. The more guarantees you give the foreigner, the more secured rights you will have in your own country.

Treat with all nations, not with a few; concede to all the same guarantees so that none can subjugate you and so that some serve as obstacles to the aspira- tions of the others. If in the *Río Plata*[17] France had had a treaty like England's, there would not have existed this secret desire for equality under the cloak of an

---

16. "In 1824 . . . Britain conferred diplomatic recognition on the United Provinces. Under the Treaty of Friendship, Navigation, and Commerce, the two countries gave each other the status of most-favored nation in trade, along with security of property for each others' resi- dents, freedom of religion and exemption from military service" (David Rock, *Argentina: 1516–1987* [Berkeley and Los Angeles, Calif.: University of California Press, 1985], p. 100).

17. The *Río Plata* is the River Plate (River of Silver), which forms the boundary between Argentina and Uruguay and drains nearly one-fifth of the South American continent. The term also refers to the land mass constituted as the Viceroyalty of la Plata, which included Bolivia, Paraguay, Uruguay, and Argentina.

alliance that for ten years has kept affairs uneasy along the *Río Plata,* half working and always with an eye to conserving exclusive and partial advantages.

Immigration Plan.—Voluntary immigration is the true and great immigration. Our governments must bring it about, not making themselves impresarios, not for petty concessions of plots of land habitable by bears, in deceptive and usurious contracts more harmful to the citizenry than to the settler, not by a small handful of men, through typical side agreements to provide business for some influential speculator—that is the lie, the farce of fruitful immigration—but by the great, generous, and disinterested system that in four years has given birth to California, by lavish liberty, by grants that make the foreigner forget his condition, persuading him that he is living in his fatherland, facilitating, without method or rule, all legitimate aims, all useful tendencies.

The United States is so advanced as a people because it is composed and has been continually composed of European elements. In all eras it has received an extraordinarily abundant European immigration. Those who believe that immigration dates only from the era of independence are mistaken. Lawmakers in the individual states were very wisely inclined toward immigration; and one reason for perpetual disagreement with the metropolis was the barrier or hindrance that England wished to put on this immigration, which was imperceptibly converting its colonies into a colossus. That reason for disagreement is invoked in the act of the Declaration of Independence of the United States itself.[18] In light of this, consider whether the gathering of foreigners prevented the United States from winning its independence and creating a great and powerful nation.

Religious Tolerance.—If you want moral and religious settlers, do not encourage atheism. If you want families that form private mores, respect every creed at your altar. Spanish America, reduced to Catholicism and excluding every other religion, is like a solitary and silent convent of monks. The dilemma is unfortunate—either exclusively Catholic and unpopulated, or populated and prosperous and tolerant in the matter of religion. Appealing to the Anglo-Saxon race and the populations of Germany, Sweden, and Switzerland, and denying them the practice of their religion, is the same as appealing to them only as a formality, as a hypocrisy of liberalism.

This is literally true—to exclude dissenting religions from South America is to exclude the English, the Germans, the Swiss, the North Americans who are not Catholic, that is to say, the populations of which this continent is most in need. To bring them without their religion is to bring them without the agent that makes them who they are; whoever lives without religion becomes atheist.

Some desires lack common sense, and one such is to want population, families, habits and at the same time surround the matrimony of the dissenting settler with barriers—it is to try to ally morality and prostitution. If you cannot

---

18. In the Declaration of Independence, one charge listed against the King of England is that "He has endeavoured to prevent the population of these States; for that purpose obstructing the Laws for Naturalization of Foreigners; refusing to pass others to encourage their migrations hither, and raising the conditions of new Appropriations of Lands."

destroy the unconquerable affinity of the sexes, what are you doing robbing natural unions of their legitimacy? You are increasing the number of concubines rather than wives; condemning our American women to the mockery of foreigners; making Americans begin their lives tarnished; filling all of our America with gauchos, prostitutes, sick people—in a word, ungodliness. That cannot be undertaken in the name of Catholicism without insulting the magnificence of this noble church, so capable of being associated with all human progress.

Does it make sense to wish to promote morality in the customs of life and yet to persecute churches that teach the doctrine of Jesus Christ?

In support of this doctrine, I provide nothing more than praise for one of my country's laws that has received the approval of experience. Since October, 1825, freedom of religion has existed in Buenos Aires, but it is necessary that this provincial grant be extended to the entire Argentine Republic by its constitution as a means of extending European immigration to the interior. It is already so under the treaty with England, and no local interior constitution should be an exception or derogation of the national compromise contained in that treaty of February 2, 1825.

Spain was wise to employ Catholic exclusivity as a tactic for monopolizing the power of these countries and for civilizing the indigenous races. For that reason the *Code of the Indies*[19] began guaranteeing the colonies' Catholic faith. But our modern constitutions should not copy the legislation of the Indies in that respect, because to do so is to reestablish the old regime of monopoly that benefited our first Catholic settlers and to damage the broad and noble aims of the new American system.

XVIII

This entire book has been dedicated to expounding goals that the new South American constitutional law should promote; nonetheless, in this chapter we are going to enumerate those goals with greater precision with respect to the constitution of the Argentine Republic.

In the presence of the desert, in the middle of the seas, at the beginning of life's unknown paths and uncertain and great endeavors, man needs to find his support in God and to deliver to His protection half the outcome of his plans.

As in the sixteenth century, religion today must be the first purpose of our fundamental laws. It is to the character of the people what purity of blood is to the health of individuals. In this political writing, we will view it only as a source of social order, as a method of political organization, for, as Montesquieu[20] has said, it is admirable that the Christian religion, which distributes the happiness of the other world, also distributes the happiness of this world.

---

19. Spanish colonial law, compiled as the "Law of the Indies," specified that all Indians were to be treated as minors.

20. Charles-Louis de Secondat, Baron de La Brèd et de Montesquieu (1689–1755), French Enlightenment political thinker.

But on this point, as on many others, we must separate our modern constitutional law from Indian or colonial law and from the constitutional law of the first era of the revolution.

On the matter of religion, colonial law was exclusionary, as it was on the matter of commerce, population, industry, etc. Exclusivity was its essence in everything it enacted, for it is sufficient to remember that it was a colonial law, one of exclusion and monopoly. Exclusive religion was employed in the sense of that policy as a state resource. On the other hand, Spain excluded dissident religions from its dominions in exchange for concessions that, in their interest at the time, the popes made to their majesties. But our modern American politics—which, rather than excluding, must lean toward attracting, conceding—cannot ratify and reestablish the colonial system on exclusion of religions without damaging the ends and purposes of the new American system. It must maintain and protect the religion of our fathers as the first need of our social and political order; but it must protect religion through liberty, through toleration, and through all the means that are peculiar and appropriate to the democratic and liberal system and not, like the old Indian law, by exclusions and prohibitions of other Christian religions. In their practices, the United States and England are the most religious nations on earth, and they have arrived at this outcome by the very means we wish to see South America adopt.

In the first days of the American Revolution, our constitutional policy did well to offer Catholicism the respect of its old privileges and exclusions on this continent, because it proceeded with equal discretion, declaring to the Spanish throne that the revolution was advantageous to it. They were tactical concessions required for the success of the enterprise, but America would not be able to continue today with the same constitutional policy without leaving illusory and ineffectual the revolution's goals of progress and liberty. We must confirm Catholicism as the state religion, then, but without excluding the public practice of other Christian religions. Religious liberty is as necessary to the country as the Catholic religion itself. Far from being irreconcilable, they mutually need and complement each other. Religious liberty is the means of populating these countries. The Catholic religion is the means of educating those populations. Fortunately, at this point, the Argentine Republic will have to do nothing other than ratify and extend to all its territory what for twenty-five years has existed in Buenos Aires. For the last twenty years, all the bishops received into the republic have sworn obedience to those laws of freedom of religion. It would now be late for Rome to raise objections on this point regarding the modern constitution of the nation.

As has been shown in this book, the other great goals of the Argentine constitution will not be today what they were in the first period of the revolution.

In that era it was a question of securing independence by arms; today we must try to assure it by our peoples' material and moral growth.

The great goals of that time were political; today, economic goals must especially concern us.

The great constitutional goal of the first era was to move away from Europe, which had held us as slaves; the constitutional goal of our time must be to attract

Europe so that with her populations that continent might civilize us as free people, just as through its governments Europe civilized us as enslaved people.

With scarcely one million inhabitants as the total population in a territory of two hundred thousand leagues, the Argentine Republic has nothing of the nation about it except the name and territory. Its distance from Europe merits its being recognized as an independent nation. The lack of population that prevents it from being a nation also prevents it from acquiring a complete central government.

Accordingly, populating the Argentine Republic, today deserted and solitary, must for many years be its constitution's great and fundamental goal. It must guarantee implementation of all means to attain that vital outcome. I will call these means *public guarantees of progress and growth*. On this point the constitution must not be limited to promises—it must give guarantees of performance and actualization.

Thus, to populate the country, it must guarantee religious liberty and facilitate mixed marriages, without which it will have population, but scarce, impure, and sterile.

It must *lavish* citizenship and domicile on the foreigner without imposing them on him. Lavish, I say, because it is the word that expresses the means required. Some South American constitutions have adopted the conditions under which England and France concede naturalization to foreigners, of whom they have no need, given their already excessive population. It is imitation carried to folly and absurdity.

The constitution must reconcile the civil rights of the foreigner—for whom we have vital need—with the civil rights of the national, without conditions of an impossible, illusory, and absurd reciprocity.

It must give them access to second-level public employment, more in the country's interests than for their own advantage; in that way the country will make use of their aptitude for managing our public affairs and will, through the activity of practical example, facilitate the official education of our citizens, as in the transactions of private industry. This system will be extremely advantageous to the municipal government. A former English or North American councilman, set down in our countries and taken into our municipal or local councils, would be the most enlightening or instructive teacher in this area, where we Spanish Americans ordinarily discharge our duty in a petty and narrow way, as with our policy in our private homes.

Because developing and exploiting the elements of the Argentine Republic's wealth is the principal feature of its growth and the strongest incentive for its necessary foreign immigration, its constitution must recognize as among its great goals the inviolability of property rights and complete freedom of work and industry.

· · · · ·

Freedom of work and industry as set down in the constitution will be nothing more than a promise unless at the same time the constitution guarantees the abolition of all the old colonial laws that enslave industry and the sanction of new laws intended to give performance and reality to that industrial freedom set down in the constitution and to do so without undermining those new laws with exceptions.

Of all the known industries, maritime and terrestrial trade is the one that forms the Argentine Republic's particular calling. Argentina derives that calling from the type, productions, and extent of its territory, from its marvelous rivers that make that country the agent of exchange for all South America, and from its situation relative to Europe. Accordingly, freedom and development of domestic and foreign trade, maritime and terrestrial, must figure among the Argentine constitution's first-order goals. But this great goal will remain illusory if the constitution does not at the same time guarantee that it will implement the means for its realization. Freedom of domestic trade will be only a name as long as there are forty internal customs houses that represent forty denials placed on freedom. The customs house should be one and national with respect to producing income; and with respect to its regulatory system, the colonial or fiscal customs, the inquisitorial customs—illiberal and petty of another time—the intolerant customs of monopoly and exclusions must not be the customs of a system of freedom and national growth. We must set out guarantees of reform in this dual regard and solemn promises that fiscal regulations will not undermine freedom of trade and industry.

Freedom of commerce without freedom to navigate the rivers is a contradiction because, all Argentine ports being fluvial, closing the rivers to foreign flags blocks the provinces and cedes all commerce to Buenos Aires.

· · · · ·

The following guarantees, which in that treaty[21] were established only in favor of the English, should be applied to everyone. Everyone should enjoy *constitutionally,* not necessarily by treaties:

> Freedom of trade;
> The privilege of coming securely and freely, with their boats and cargoes, to the ports and rivers accessible by law to all foreigners;
> The right to lease and occupy properties for purposes of commerce;
> Protection from paying differential duties;
> The right to negotiate and perform all trade activities in their own name without being required to employ persons of this country for the purpose;
> The right to exercise in the republic all the civil rights inherent in citizenship;
> Protection from the obligation to perform military service;
> Freedom from forced loans, exactions, or military requisitions;
> The maintenance in force of all these guarantees despite any possible dispute with the nation of the foreigner residing in the *Plata;*

---

21. The treaty with England of February 2, 1825.

> Enjoyment of complete freedom of conscience and of religion, freedom to build churches and chapels any place in the Argentine Republic.

. . . . Today more than ever the adoption of this system would be useful, calculated as it is to receive those populations which, thrown out of Europe by civil war and industrial crises, now pass through the rich regions of the *Río Plata* to seek in California the fortune they could find more easily here, with fewer risks, and without putting themselves at such a distance from Europe.

Peace and internal order are among the other major goals that the sanction of the Argentine constitution must keep in view, because peace is essential for developing institutions, and without it all efforts made on behalf of the country's prosperity will be vain and sterile. Peace, in and of itself, is so essential to the progress of these countries in formation and development that the constitution that provides only that one benefit would be admirable and fruitful in consequences. Farther on, I will touch on this point of decisive interest for the fate of those republics that march to their disappearance down the road of civil war, by which *Mexico* has already lost the most beautiful half of its territory.

Finally, through its nature and spirit, the new Argentine constitution must be an absorbing, attractive constitution, endowed with such power to assimilate that whatever foreign individual comes to the country makes it his own, a constitution calculated especially and directly to provide in a very few years four or six million inhabitants for the Argentine Republic; a constitution designed to transfer the city of Buenos Aires to a street of San Juan, La Rioja, and de Salta, and to carry these peoples to the fruitful borders of the *Río Plata* by railroad and electric telegraph, which abolish distances; a constitution that in few years makes of Santa Fe, Rosaria, Gualeguaychú, Paraná, and Corrientes so many other Buenos Aireses in population and culture by the same means that has made Buenos Aires great, namely, by immediate contact with civilized and civilizing Europe; a constitution that, attracting European inhabitants and assimilating them to our population, makes our country so populous in a short time that we will never have to fear official Europe.

A constitution that has the power of the fairies who constructed palaces in a single night.

· · · · ·

XXXI

What name will you give a country—what name does a country deserve—that is composed of two hundred thousand leagues of territory and a population of eight hundred thousand inhabitants? A wilderness. What name will you give the constitution of that country? The constitution of a wilderness. Well then, that country is the Argentine Republic, and whatever its constitution might be, for many years it will be nothing other than the constitution of a wilderness.

But what is the most suitable constitution for a wilderness? The one that helps make it disappear—the one that helps make the wilderness cease being a wilderness in the shortest possible time, converting it into a populated country. So this must be the political goal—and it cannot be any other—of the Argentine constitution and, in general, of all South American constitutions. For now and for many years, the constitutions of unpopulated countries can have no more serious and rational goal than to give the solitary and abandoned territory the population it needs as a fundamental tool for its development and progress.

Independent America is summoned to continue the work begun in its territory and left half done by the Spain of 1450. The colonization, the population of this world, new even today despite the three hundred years that have passed since its discovery, must be achieved by the American states themselves, constituted as independent and sovereign bodies. The work is the same, although the authors are different. In another time Spain populated us; today we populate ourselves. To this primary end we must direct all our constitutions. We need constitutions, we need a policy of creation, of population, of conquest over solitude and wilderness.

American governments as an institution and as persons, have no mission more serious for now than to fashion and develop the population of the territories under their governance, called states before their time.

Population everywhere, and principally in America, forms the substance around which all the phenomena of social economy are realized and developed. By it and for it everything in the world of economic events is stimulated and actualized. The principal tool of production, it yields to its benefit distribution of national wealth. Population is simultaneously the *end* and the *means*. In this sense, economic science, according to the word of one of its great organs, could be taken up again completely in the science of population; at least the science of population constitutes its beginning and end. This has been taught everywhere by an economist admiring of Malthus,[22] the enemy of population in countries that have it in surplus and in moments of crisis that result from that excess. With how much more reason will it not be applicable to our poor America, enslaved in the name of liberty and unconstituted for no reason other than absence of population?

The goal of constitutional policy and government in America is, then, essentially economic. Thus, in America, to govern is to populate. To define government in any other way is to be ignorant of its South American mission. The government receives this mission from the need that symbolizes and rules all the rest of our America. In economic matters, as in all the rest, we must accommodate our law to the special needs of South America. If these needs are not the same that have inspired a certain system or economic policy in Europe, our law must follow the voice of our need and not the command that expresses different or contrary needs. . . . For example, in the presence of the social crisis that occurred in Europe at the end of the last century from the imbalance between

---

22. The Rev. Thomas Robert Malthus (1766–1834), author of *An Essay on the Principle of Population,* predicted that population would outstrip food supply, the former growing geometrically while the latter grew arithmetically.

food and population, economic policy, expressed by the pen of Malthus, protested against population increase, because in such increase he saw the certain or apparent origin of the crisis; but to apply it to our America—for which population constitutes precisely the best remedy for the European ill feared by Malthus—would be like putting an infant weakened by lack of food under the rigor of a Pythagorean diet[23] because of that treatment's having been advised for a body sick from superabundance. The United States, with its practical example in the matter of population, takes precedence over Malthus; with its very rapid increase, it has worked miracles of progress that have made it the surprise and envy of the universe.

XXXII

Without population, and without better population than we have for the practice of representative government, all resolutions will remain illusory and without effect. You will have brilliant constitutions that completely satisfy the country's illusions, but disillusionment will not be long in demanding from you an account of the value of the promises; and then it will be obvious that you play the role of charlatans if not of children, victims of your own illusions.

In effect, constitute the Argentine provinces as you wish; if you do not constitute anything other than what they contain today, you constitute a thing of little value for practical liberty. Combine in every way your current population, you will do nothing other than combine old Spanish colonists. Spaniards to the right or Spaniards to the left, you will always have Spaniards weakened by colonial servitude, not incapable of heroism in victories when the occasion calls for it, but certainly incapable of the virile forbearance, of the immutable vigilance of the man of liberty.

Take, for example, the thirty thousand inhabitants of the province of Jujuy;[24] put on top those who are below, or vice versa; raise the good and knock down the bad. What will you accomplish by that? Double the customs income from six to twelve thousand pesos, open twenty schools instead of ten, and some other improvements of that sort. That is what will be accomplished. Well then, that will not prevent Jujuy from remaining for centuries with its thirty thousand inhabitants, its twelve thousand pesos of customs income, and its twenty schools, the most progress it has been able to achieve in its two hundred years of existence.

Something has just occurred in America that puts the truth of what I maintain beyond doubt, namely, that without better population for industry and for independent government, the best political constitution will be ineffective. What has produced California's instantaneous and marvelous regeneration is not necessarily the promulgation of the North American constitutional system. That

---

23. Pythagoras, Greek philosopher of the sixth century BC, was the first prominent vegetarian in the West. "Pythagorean diet" came to mean avoidance of the flesh of slaughtered animals.

24. Jujuy, the extreme northeast province of Argentina.

system has been proclaimed in all of Mexico since 1824 and is still being proclaimed; and in California, former province of Mexico, it is not as new as is thought. What is new in California—the real origin of the favorable change—is the presence of a people made up of inhabitants capable of industry and a political system that the old Spanish-Mexican inhabitants did not know how to effect. Liberty is a machine that, like the steam engine, requires for its management machinists who are English in origin. Without the cooperation of that race, it is not possible to adapt liberty and material progress anywhere.

Let us cross our people, eastern and poetic in origin, with that English race, and we will give our people the aptitude for progress and practical liberty without losing its character, its language, or its nationality. Doing so will save it from disappearing as a people of Spanish character, with which Mexico is threatened by its intractable, petty, and exclusive policy.

I am not trying to humiliate my own people. Devoid of ambition, with the same disinterest with which I have always written the truth, I am speaking now the practical and complete truth, which bursts illusion. I know the flattery that obtains ready sympathy for ambition; but I will never be the courtier for prejudices that cause attitudes I do not feel, nor of a popularity as ephemeral as the misconception on which it rests.

Let us suppose that the Argentine Republic is made up of men such as I, that is to say, of eight hundred thousand lawyers who know how to write books. That would be the worst population it could have. Lawyers do not build railroads, make navigable and navigate the rivers, work the mines, cultivate the fields, colonize the wilderness; that is to say, we do not give South America what it needs. Well then, the current population of our country serves those ends, more or less, as if it were composed of lawyers. It is an unhappy misconception to believe that primary or university instruction is what can make our people suitable for material progress and the exercise of liberty.

In Chiloé[25] and in Paraguay all the men of the town know how to read; and nonetheless they are uncultured and wild next to an English or French worker who many times does not know the letter "*o.*"

It is not the alphabet, it is the hammer, it is the crowbar, it is the plow that the man of the wilderness must possess, that is to say, the man of the South American people. Do you believe that an Araucanian would be incapable of learning to read and write Castilian? And do you think with that alone he could cease being a savage?

I am not so modest as an Argentine citizen to claim that only in my country does the truth I have just written apply. In speaking of it, I describe the situation in South America, for all of which this is the case, as is evident to all who want to see the truth. It is a half-populated and half-civilized wilderness.

• • • • •

---

25. Chiloé is the second largest island in South America after Tierra del Fuego.

To populate the wilderness, two primary things are necessary—open its gates to let everyone enter, and assure the well-being of those who come; liberty at the gate and liberty within.

If you open the gates and harass within, you will lay a trap rather than organize a state. You will have prisoners, not settlers; you will catch some unwary people, but the rest will flee. The wilderness will remain victorious rather than conquered.

Today the world is completely filled with favorable places so no one needs to be imprisoned by necessity, much less by desire.

If, on the contrary, you create guarantees within, but at the same time close the gates to the country, you will only guarantee solitude and wilderness; you will not constitute a people but a territory without people, or at the most a municipality, a wretchedly founded town, that is to say, a town of eight hundred thousand souls, cut off from each other by hundreds of leagues. Such a country is not a state—it is a political limbo, and its inhabitants are errant souls in the solitude, that is to say, South Americans.

The colors of which I avail myself will be strong; they may be exaggerated but not deceptive. Take several degrees away from the color yellow, and the remaining color will always be pallid. Fewer carats will not alter the strength of the truth, just as they will not alter the nature of gold. One must give exaggerated forms to truths that escape the sight of ordinary eyes.

Eugenio María de Hostos
(Puerto Rico)

Eugenio María de Hostos y Bonilla (1839–1903), commonly known as the Citizen of the Americas and revered as an educator and tireless worker for independence, was born in Río Cañas, Mayagüez, Puerto Rico, to a well-to-do family. His father was Eugenio de Hostos y Rodríguez; his mother was Hilaria de Bonilla y Cintrón. In 1876, he married the Cuban Belinda Otilia de Ayala Quintana.

Hostos studied at the Instituto de Segunda Enseñanza in Bilbao, Spain, and then attended the Universidad Central de Madrid, where he studied law, philosophy, and letters. In 1863, Hostos wrote his first and possibly his greatest work, *La peregrinación de Bayoán*. He left Spain, disillusioned, when the new Spanish Constitution of 1869 did not grant Puerto Rico its independence.

He arrived in New York City that year and soon began a campaign for the emancipation of Cuba and Puerto Rico. Although part of his dream was to unify Latin America, he was above all a citizen of the Spanish Antilles—Cuba, the Dominican Republic, and Puerto Rico. He believed that his Pan-American ideals could best be carried out through effective education, and to this project he dedicated his life.

Although Hostos's greatest legacy was his educational activity, he was also an effective journalist and a committed worker for independence. From 1871 to 1873, he lived in Chile, where he edited the newspaper *La Patria* and wrote several works, including *La reseña histórica de Puerto Rico* (1873), *Plácido* (1873) (biography of a great Cuban poet), and his much acclaimed 1873 discourse advocating women's education, "Por la enseñanza científica de la mujer" (translated as "The Scientific Education of Women"). A selection from this discourse follows. He also, that same year, wrote his important essay, "Hamlet." In 1873–1874 in Argentina he published a series of articles arguing for a trans-Andean railroad to unite Argentina and Chile; when this railway was built, the first Argentine locomotive was named for Hostos. He left for New York in 1874 intending to join an armed invasion that would fight for the liberation of Cuba; however, it was called off.

His work as an educator was more fruitful. In Venezuela in 1876, he took a position as a director of the Colegio de la Paz, followed by appointment to the position of rector of the Colegio Nacional de Asunción and, finally, as professor in the Instituto Comercial. In 1878, in Santo Domingo, he opened the Escuela Normal, which he directed until 1888. His address to its first graduating class is the second selection that follows. In the Instituto Profesional de la Universidad he held a chair in constitutional, international, and penal law, and political economy and social morality. In 1891 he founded another Escuela Normal in the Dominican city of Santiago de los Caballeros. In 1888, the president of Chile asked Hostos to assist in the reform of Chilean instruction. As he carried out this charge, he also served as rector of two secondary schools and as professor in the Universidad de Santiago.

When Hostos foresaw that there was to be a war between Spain and North America, he returned to New York, hoping to argue on behalf of the rights of the Antilles. Alarmed at U.S. preparations to invade Puerto Rico, he and a group of Puerto Rican patriots traveled to the U.S. capital to speak with the secretary of state and the president; meanwhile, U.S. General Nelson R. Miles occupied Puerto Rico. Hostos then convoked a meeting in New York of persons formerly active in the movement to free Cuba and Puerto Rico to organize them as the Liga de Patriotas Puertorriqueños. Shortly thereafter, Hostos returned to Puerto Rico after an absence of thirty-five years, hoping to inflame Puerto Ricans with the desire for liberty, but the U.S. government had decided to retain the territory and Hostos left the country, never again to return.

He went to the Dominican Republic where he died in 1903. He is buried in the National Pantheon in Santo Domingo, where, following his final wishes, his remains will stay until Puerto Rico is finally independent. In 1938, in the Octava Conferencia Internacional Americana, held in Peru, Hostos was consecrated as "Citizen of the Americas and Teacher of the Youth."

Further Reading

Adriana Arpini, ed. *Razón práctica y discurso social latinoamericano: El "pensamiento fuerte" de Alberdi, Betances, Hostos, Martí y Ugarte.* Buenos Aires: Biblos, 2000.

———. *Eugenio María de Hostos, un hacedor de libertad.* Mendoza, Argentina: Editorial de la Universidad Nacional de Cuyo, 2002.

Borda de Sainz, Joann. *Eugenio María de Hostos: Philosophical System and Methodology: Cultural Fusion.* New York: Senda Nueva de Ediciones, 1989.

Ferrer Canales, José. *Martí y Hostos.* Río Piedras: Instituto de Estudios Hostosianos, Universidad de Puerto Rico; San Juan: Centro de Estudios Avanzados de Puerto Rico y el Caribe, 1990.

Hostos, Eugenio María de. *Obras completas.* 20 vols. Havana: Cultural, s.a., 1939.

Maldonado-Denis, Manuel. *Eugenio María de Hostos y el pensamiento social iberoamericano.* México, D.F.: Fondo de Cultura Económica, 1992.

Méndez, José Luis. *Hostos y las ciencias sociales.* San Juan: Editorial de la Universidad de Puerto Rico, 2003.

Reyes Dávila, Marcos F. *Hostos: Las luces peregrinas.* Humacao, P.R.: Revista Exégesis, Universidad de Puerto Rico en Humacao, 2004.

Zea, Leopoldo. "Hostos como conciencia latinoamericana." *Handbook of Latin American Studies* 3, no. 16 (1989): 49–57.

"The Scientific Education of Women" (1873)[1]

Gentlemen:

. . . This Academy[2] desires a literary art based on truth, and beyond science there is no truth; it desires to serve the truth by means of the word, and beyond what wins converts for science, there is no word; it desires, must desire, the diffusion of demonstrated truths, and beyond continuous promotion, there is no diffusion; it desires, must desire, effectiveness for its promotion, and beyond transmission by emotion, there is no effectiveness of scientific truth among childlike peoples who have not yet come to the free use of reason. As heat revives the most decrepit organisms, because it makes itself felt in the most hidden channels of life, so emotion awakens the love of truth in peoples not habituated to thinking about the truth, because there is a moral electricity, and emotion is the best conductor of that electricity. Emotion is an unstable, transitory, and inconstant faculty in our sex; it is a stable, permanent, constant faculty in woman. If our end is to serve the truth by means of literary art, and in the present state of Chilean life the most adequate means to that end is emotion, and emotion is most active and therefore most persuasive and effective in woman, by a logical chain of ideas, by a rigorous deduction, you will arrive, as I have arrived, at one of the ends contained in our first principle—the scientific education of woman. She is emotion. Educate her and your promotion of truth will be effective. Make your redemptive promotion effective by means of woman, and you will disseminate everywhere the eternal principles of science. Disseminate those principles, and on every tongue you will have words of truth. Give me a generation that speaks the truth, and I will give you a generation that does what is good. Give yourselves mothers who scientifically teach their children what is good, and these mothers will give you a fatherland that obeys reason in a manly way, that actualizes liberty conscientiously, that resolves little by little the major problem of the New World, by basing civilization on science, on morality, and on work, rather than on corrupting force, or on indifferent morality, or on the exclusive predominance of individual well-being.

But to educate woman for science is an undertaking so arduous in the eyes of almost all men, that even those men in whom the light of reason is most alive and the will's energy healthiest prefer the darkness of error, prefer the inactivity of their energy, to the struggle that this task imposes. And you will not be the only ones, gentlemen, who, in bringing to the peace of the home the harsh afflictions that the spectacle of the moral and intellectual anarchy of our century instills in every man's essence, you will not be the only ones who are alarmed at imagining that there, in the loving heart, in the idle brain, in the uncultivated spirit of woman, there probably lies the fundamental principle of the new social

---

1. A lecture read before the Academia de Bellas Letras de Santiago de Chile.

2. The Academia de Bellas Letras de Santiago was founded and presided over by José Victorino Lastarria from 1873 to 1881.

life, of the new moral world that you, in vain, demand from governments, from customs, from laws. You will not be the only ones who are alarmed at imagining this. Educated exclusively as she is by and for the heart, systematically isolated as she lives in the sphere of unhealthy idealism, the woman is a plant that vegetates, not a consciousness that is aware of its existence; she is a sensitive mimosa that contact with facts bruises, that brutalities of reality wither; not a being of reason and consciousness who, supported in her life by reason and consciousness, struggles to develop them, can develop them in order to live them, can live them freely and actualize them. Vegetation, not life; determined development, not free development; instinct, not reason; a bundle of irritable nerves, not a bundle of educable faculties; determined systole-diastole that expands or contracts her existence, not voluntary development of her life; this is what the errors that weigh her down—the social, intellectual, and moral traditions that crush her—have made of woman, and it is not extraordinary that, when we imagine in the total rehabilitation of woman the hope for a new social order, the hope for moral and intellectual harmony, we are alarmed. To deliver the direction of the future to a being to whom we have not yet been able to deliver the direction of her own life is a terrible risk.

And nonetheless, it is necessary to confront the risk, because it is necessary to overcome it. That risk is our work, it is our creation; it is the work of our errors, it is the creation of our weaknesses; and we men, we who monopolize force, which we are almost never able to exercise justly; we who monopolize social power, which we almost always conduct with a feminine hand; we who make laws for ourselves, for the masculine sex, for the strong sex, at our pleasure, fool-heartedly leaving out half of the human race, we are responsible for the woes that cause our continuous infraction of the eternal laws of nature. One eternal law of nature is the moral equality of men and women, because woman, like man, is a producer of life; because, to redeem this precious ministry, she, like he, is endowed with the creative faculties that complete the physical formation of the man-beast through the moral formation of the man-god. We violate that law when, reducing the ministry of woman to mere cooperation in the physical formation of the animal, we take away from her the right to cooperate in the psychic formation of the angel. To respect the laws of nature, it is not enough that our laws recognize the personhood of woman; these laws must establish that personhood, and there is personhood only where there is responsibility and where the responsibility is actual. More logical in our customs than we are used to being in the speculations of our reason, we have still not dared to declare woman responsible for moral and intellectual disorder, because, even knowing that she shares in the guilt for that disorder, we are ashamed to make her responsible for it. From magnanimity? From fortitude? No. From strict fairness, because if woman is accessory to our failings and accomplice to our woes, she is so from ignorance, from moral impotence; because we men have, in a cowardly way, abandoned her in the intellectual discussions that in error we keep to ourselves, because we have abandoned her cruelly to the anguishes of the moral cataclysm that darkens the moral consciousness of this century. Let us reconstitute the personhood of woman, let us establish her responsibility with respect to herself, with respect to the home, with respect to society; and to do this, let us reestablish the law of nature, let us respect the moral equality of the two sexes, let us give back to woman the right to live rationally; let us have her know this right, let us instruct her in all her duties, let us educate her consciousness so that she will be able to educate her heart. Educated in her consciousness she will be a responsible person; educated in her heart, she will answer for her life with the kindly virtues that allow us to live with a moral and corporal satisfaction as well as an intellectual resignation.

How?

You already know—by obeying nature. More just with man than he is with himself, nature foresaw that the being whom it endowed with consciousness of his destiny could not have resigned himself to having a mere mammal for a companion; and in giving to man a life's collaborator in woman, it endowed her with the same faculties of reason and made her collaborator in their destiny. For a man to be a man, that is to say, worthy of realizing the ends of his life, nature gave him consciousness of it, the ability to know his origin, his favorable and contrary elements, his significance and relationships, his duty and his right, his liberty and his responsibility; the ability to sense and to love what he senses, the ability to desire and to actualize what he desires; the ability to perfect himself and to improve by himself the conditions of his being, and by himself to elevate the ideal of his existence. Idealists or sensationists, materialists or positivists might describe the faculties of the spirit according to the order of innate or pre-established ideas or in accord with the development of the soul through the development of the senses, sometimes as mere material modifications, sometimes as categories; but all philosophers and all psychologists have found themselves forced to recognize three orders of faculties that jointly constitute human consciousness, which, functioning in isolation, constitute the faculty of knowing, the faculty of sensing, and the faculty of desiring. If these faculties are distributed with different intensity in man and in woman, it is a problem; but that they completely and partially determine the moral life of both sexes is an axiom; that positivists assign to instinct the greater part of the means that idealists attribute to the faculty of sensing; that Spinoza and the Scottish school distinguish the senses as the greater of the aptitudes, a distinction that the rationalists declare exclusive to reason; that Krause would make consciousness into a kind of faculty of faculties; that Kant would reduce all the faculties of knowledge to pure reason and all the determinations of judgment to practical reason; all these views are of little importance, inasmuch as none of them have demonstrated that knowing, sensing, and desiring are exercised in an absolutely different way in each sex. It will never be demonstrated, and the foundation for the scientific education of woman will always be the moral equality of human beings. Woman must be educated so as to be human, so as to cultivate and develop her faculties, so as to exercise her reason, so as to live her consciousness, not to function socially with functions exclusive to woman. The more the human being knows and senses herself, the more woman will want to be and know how to be.

If you would permit me to divide into two groups the faculties and activities of our being, I would call the first *consciousness,* the second *heart,* to express the two great phases of woman's education and to make it understood that if reason, emotion, and will both can and should be educated to the degree that they are faculties, they can be guided only to the degree that they are activities. Education is a form of guidance, but it is external, indirect, mediated, extra-personal; guidance is in its essence direct, immediate, internal, personal. As a conscious human being, woman is educable; as a heart, she alone can guide herself. That she will better guide her heart when her consciousness is better educated, that her activities will be more wholesome the more developed her faculties are, is so evident and so obvious that it is therefore necessary, indispensable, obligatory, to educate woman scientifically.

Science is the entirety of demonstrated truths or demonstrable hypotheses, whether they refer to the exterior or interior world, to the self or the not-self, as ancient metaphysics would say; it comprises therefore all the objects of positive and hypothetical knowledge, from matter in its various elements, forms, transformations, ends, necessities, and relationships to the spirit in its multiple aptitudes, rights, duties, laws, finality, and progressions; from the worm to the idea; from being to not-being; from knowledge of the evolutions of stars to knowledge of revolutions of the planet; from the laws that rule the physical universe to those that rule the moral world; from the axiomatic truths on which the science of beauty is based to the fundamental principles of morality; from the entirety of the hypotheses that refer to the origin, transmigration, civilization, and decline of the races to the entirety of facts that constitute sociology.

This overwhelming diversity of areas of knowledge, each one of which can absorb entire lives, and in each one of which successive differences, divisions, and separations are established by the method, the logical rigor, and the specialization of facts, of observations, and of experiments that had not previously been proven, this diversity of areas of knowledge is virtually reduced to the unity of truth and can be, by a straightforward generalization, contained in a simple series. All that is knowable must refer necessarily and absolutely to one of our means of knowing. We know by means of our faculties, and our faculties are so intimately linked to each other, that what knowing is for some faculties is the same as feeling is for others, and the same as desiring is for the remainder; and sometimes the will is emotion and knowledge, and frequently emotion supplements or completes the illumination of the faculty that knows and the faculty that realizes. Dividing, then, all known science into as many categories as we have faculties to know the truth, to love it, and to act on it, let us synthesize it in its transcendental unity; and without needing to know it in its abundant variety, we will acquire all its foundational elements, in which all of us, man or woman, can know the general laws of the universe, the inherent characteristics of matter and spirit, the fundamental elements of sociability, the necessary principles of right, the motives, determinations, and elements of the beautiful, the essence and necessity of the good and of the just.

All of these things woman can know, because she has faculties for all these areas of knowledge. All of these things she must know, because by knowing it all she will emancipate herself from the tutelage of the error and the bondage in which the very idleness of her intellectual and moral faculties keeps her. One loves what one knows to be beautiful, good, true; the universe, the world, man, society, science, art, morality, all of it is beautiful, good, and true in itself; knowing it all in its essence, would it not all be more loved? And as the scientific education of woman will necessarily entail a correlative development of her faculty of loving, would she not love more, knowing all the things that today she loves without knowing? Loving more and with greater love, would her mission in society not be more effective? Educated by her, now knower and creator of the immutable laws of the universe, of the planet, of the spirit, of the societies, now free of superstitions, of errors, of the terrors upon which her emotion, reason, and will continually founder, would she not come to be the first and last educator of her children, the first to guide their faculties, the last to moderate their activities, presenting to them always the beautiful, the good, the true as goal? Woman is always mother; of her children, because she has revealed existence to them; of her beloved, because she has revealed happiness to him; of her husband, because she has revealed harmony to him. Mother, lover, wife, every woman is an influence. Arm that influence with scientific knowledge, and dream of the ineffable existence, happiness, and harmony that men on the planet would enjoy, if the giver, if the beautifier, if the companion of life were, as mother, our scientific guide; as beloved, the reflective lover of our ideas and of our virtuous plans; as wife, the companion of our body, of our reason, of our emotion, of our will and our consciousness. He would be a complete man. Today, he is not.

The man who educates a woman will live in the fullness of his being, and there are in the world some men who know how to live their whole life; but they are not the world, and the infinite number of crimes, of atrocities, of infractions of every law that in every hour are committed in all areas of the world are crying out against the bestial passions that woman's ignorance nourishes everywhere, against the infernal interests that an educated woman would moderate in the heart of each child, of each husband, of each father.

This American woman, who possesses so many spontaneous virtues, who nurtures so many noble dreams, who displays such high reason in counseling the family, and who sets such a firm will against misfortune, who manifests such a surprising perspicacity and with such powerful intuition absorbs the knowledges that the increase of civilization dilutes in the intellectual atmosphere of our century; this American woman, who is so rebellious because she is so worthy, just as she is docile and educable because she is so good, is worthy of the scientific initiation that is destined to give her back the integrity of her being, the liberty of her consciousness, the responsibility for her existence. In her, more than in anyone, one perceives the importance of the change that is occurring in the spirit of humanity in Latin America, and if she does not know where the anxious vagueness of her desires is coming from, where the mortal sorrows that depress her are heading, where the ideal resides in which she would like to bring back to life her heart, more withered than fully formed, she does know that she is ready to consecrate the new moral world where, truth converted to reality, the idea of the beautiful converted into truth, virtue converted into kindly beauty, the three graces of the symbolic myth will descend to earth and, their hands joined tightly—just as the faculty of knowing the truth, the faculty of desiring the just, and the faculty of loving the beautiful are tightly joined—science, consciousness, and charity may greet each other.

"The Purpose of the Normal School" (1884)[3]

Mr. President of the Republic:
Secretaries of the State:
Honorable Magistrates:
Mr. Rector of the Professional Institute:
Commissioners:

. . . You know very well, Gentlemen, that every kind of revolution had been tried in [this] republic[4] except the only one that could restore it to health. It was dying for lack of reason in its goals, for lack of moral awareness in its conduct, and nothing was happening to restore its moral awareness and its reason. The great patriots among us, who had wanted, through the restoration of studies, to complete the restoration of the rights of the fatherland, had in vain prescribed rules, established classrooms, supported the intellectual development of youth, and even educated young people who today represent the actualized hopes of the fatherland; but their meritorious efforts were annulled in the confusion of anarchic passions, or else the lack of an order and system prevented their sacred work from coming to full fruition.

Anarchy, which is a social condition rather than a political fact, was everywhere, even in the legal relationships of the nation, and that anarchy was in teaching as well as in the impersonal and personal instruments of teaching.

For the republic to recover, it was absolutely essential to institute—in the very design of public education—a rational order for studies, a reasoned method for teaching, the influence of a harmonizing principle for teaching positions, and the ideal of a system superior to all others.

It was essential to create an army of teachers who would fight, throughout the republic, against ignorance, against superstition, against stupidity, against barbarism. It was essential, so that those soldiers of truth might triumph in their

---

3. Speech Delivered by the Director of the Normal School of Santo Domingo at the Investiture of Its Students, the First Normal School Teachers of the Republic, 1884.

4. From 1845 through 1882, the Dominican Republic was wracked by a string of chaotic changes in government. In 1882, dictator Ulises Heureaux had taken power.

battles, that they carry in their minds so clear an idea, and in their will so firm a resolution, that the more they fought, the more the idea would enlighten them and the more they would be driven by steadfast resolve.

Neither love of truth, nor even love of justice, is sufficient for a system of education to take a man from where he is to where he must be if the notions of right and of duty do not develop on an equal footing with those two sacred loves—the notion of right, to help him know and practice liberty; that of duty, to spread the natural principles of morality in a practical way from the citizen to the fatherland, from the fatherland as it is to the fatherland conceived, from brothers in the fatherland to brothers in humanity.

Together, therefore, with love of truth and justice, it was necessary to instill in the spirit of student generations a powerful sense of liberty, a deep and fundamental knowledge of the positive power of virtue, and such a profound, positive, and firm knowledge of the duty to love the fatherland—in the good of all, by the good of all, and for the good of all—that never again would it be possible for the fatherland to cease being the mother-soul to sons born on the fatherland's sacred soil or to adoptive sons who are brought to that soil by work, exile, or the tenacious pursuit of an ideal.

Each and every one of these partial aims was subordinate to an overarching aim; or, in other words, it was impossible partially to realize one or a few of these aims as long as the principal aim—that of educating men in all the lofty fullness of human nature—remained unknown or undiscovered.

And how was this aim to be actualized? In one way only, the sole way that nature has set out as the universal means for the moral formation of human beings—by developing reason. I will express this idea much better if I use the word "rationality," that is to say, the capacity for reasoning and making connections, for conceiving and thinking, for judging and knowing that only man, among all the beings that populate the planet, has received as a distinctive, notable, exceptional, and transcendent characteristic.

And to develop the greatest possible amount of reason in each rational being, what principle had to be the norm, what conduct had to be the means, what end had to be the goal of education?

Should we have left things as they were? We would have continued getting from the yearned-for system of education what the system as practiced is giving the republic—a few men of very powerful natural intellect, who, by virtue of their own efforts and in the face of their deficient intellectual education, could elevate themselves to a pure and more real contemplation of the true and the good than the generation of harmful or harmless bipeds that surrounded them.

Should we have gone on to reestablish the artificial culture that scholasticism is still determined to resuscitate? We would have continued having that monstrous education of human reason to thank for the vacuous sophists who, in Europe's Middle Ages and Latin America's colonial centuries, siphoned off reason, leaving as an impure residue the hundred generations of voluntary slaves who live bound by the chains of human power or by the chains of divine power, and who, when they found themselves in modern society, finding themselves in a world depopulated of their old gods and their old heroes, were unable, in Europe, to position themselves with good men to create liberty, and were unable, in Latin America, to position themselves with the best of men to forge independence.

Should we have sought the model we ought to follow along the path that the Renaissance gave to moral and intellectual culture? We are not here to do that. We are here to be our own men, masters of ourselves, and not borrowed men; useful men in all the activities of our being, and not men who always depend on the form that necessities, emotions, passions, desires, judgments, and the conception of nature took in Greco-Roman literature and science. We are here to think, not to express; to be awake, not to dream; to know, not to chant; to observe, not to imagine; to experience, not to infer the objective reality of the world from subjective conditions.

Should we, finally, have adopted an educational organization that might have given us the outline but not the content of science?

What would we have made of the organization of North American, German, Swiss, French studies if we lacked the generative element of organization? Could any Condorcet ever imbue a facsimile of man with the vital principle?[5] Could any Cuvier ever set in motion his restored anatomical organizations?[6] Could any Pygmalion ever give the divine spark of life to the beautiful ideal that modeled his statuary?[7]

Like the glorified dreamer of Greece, like the paleontologist who was France's gift to science, like the philosopher whom the French Revolution destroyed, we needed not the statue, not the bones, not the image—we needed life.

But even more than life. For educated reason to give us the vital principle that we were going to require of it, we needed to return it to health.

A healthy reason is not one that functions the way reason commonly does in the segment of human society to which we belong. A healthy reason is one that reproduces objective realities with scrupulous fidelity and gives us, or gives itself, a fit interpretation of the physical world; one that reproduces subjective realities with stoic impartiality and gives itself, or gives us, a clear explanation of the moral activities of the being that lies in the depths of the animal structure that we all are.

A healthy reason is not one that flashes unequal rays of light, first shining with the brilliance of fantasy, then dazzling with the mirages of memory, illuminating an uncertainty or a doubt with solar clarity, then taking pleasure in the

---

5. Marie Jean Antoine Nicola Caritat, Marquis de Condorcet (1743–1794), traced human development through nine epochs and predicted perfection of man in the tenth epoch.

6. Georges Léopold Chrétien Frédéric Dagobert, Baron Cuvier (1769–1832), whose reconstruction of the soft parts of fossils deduced from their skeletal remains greatly advanced the science of paleontology.

7. Pygmalion, king of Cyprus in Greek mythology, is said to have fallen in love with a beautiful statue of a woman that he himself had sculpted and to have prayed to Aphrodite to breathe life into it.

shadows or in the incomplete, walking through life as the traveler without fore-sight goes down the world's pathways—stumbling and falling and getting up, to stumble and fall and get up again. A healthy reason is one that functions strictly subject to the natural conditions of its organism.

And that is when a healthy reason—director of all the physical and moral forces of the individual, establisher of the norms of all the relationships of its associated body, creator of the ideal of each individual existence, of each national existence, and of the supreme ideal of humanity—finds its own way to truth, directs the emotions toward the beautiful, directs the will toward the good, regulates the relationships of family, community, fatherland by means of right and of duty, forges the ideal of the whole man in each man; the ideal of fatherland blessed by history in each patriot; the ideal of universal harmony in all truly rational beings, and using this ideal to light the bitter path that nature, turning a deaf ear, unwaveringly indicates for each human being, carries him from century to century, from continent to continent, from civilization to civilization, to the always dark and always radiant Golgotha,[8] from where one discovers with astonishment the eternity of effort that it has cost to accomplish the simple goal of making rational the earth's only inhabitant endowed with reason.

To bring reason to that degree of full development and to teach how to allow oneself to be brought by reason to that complete control of life in all forms of life, is not an end that education can actualize with any of the principles and pedagogical methods that either empirical or classical instruction employs. The former omits reason. How can one then direct reason? The latter amputates it. How can it make reason whole? The first would make us fossils, and life is not a natural history room. The second would make us men of letters, and life cannot be reduced to, nor are the creative forces of man summed up in the imitation or admiration of the harmoniousness of the beautiful. Life is a battle for bread, for principle, for position, and one must present oneself in life with the armor and slogan of the stoic: *Conscientia propugnans pro virtute,* "As a consciousness fighting for good."[9]

Life is dissonance. It demands that we learn—moaning, crying, working, perfecting ourselves—to bring into a harmony superior to the passively contemplated or imitated classical one, the continually discordant notes that, in man's individual, national, and universal evolutions through space and time, are emitted at each moment by the lyre of a thousand strings,[10] the lyre that with the name of History sobs or sings, praises or rebukes, exalts or censures, blesses or curses, deifies or demonizes the acts of humanity in all spheres of action—

---

8. Jesus' place of crucifixion; metaphorically, a place of suffering and transcendence.

9. The Spanish *conciencia* means both "conscious awareness" and "conscience."

10. According to legend, Apollo received his lyre from Hermes and it was distinguished by its well-ordered, i.e., rational, music. He passed this lyre to Orpheus, a celebrated Thracian musician, whose music was said to soothe wild beasts, make trees and rocks dance and rivers stand still.

organic, moral, and intellectual—that make of humanity a second creator and a continuous creation.

If scholasticism is monstrous and classicism impotent, what kind of instruction was necessary to realize the health-giving revolution in this society so tired of murderous revolutions?

True instruction—instruction that has nothing to do with historic purposes, partial methods, artificial procedures—paying attention exclusively to the subject of knowledge, which is human reason, and to the object of knowledge, which is nature, favors the union of both and rests in the confidence that this happy union will produce truth as its fruit.

Give me the truth and I will give you the world. You, without the truth will destroy the world, and I, with the truth, with only the truth, will rebuild the world as many times as you might destroy it. And I will not give you only the world of material organizations; I will give you the organic world, together with the world of ideas, together with the world of the emotions, together with the world of work, together with the world of liberty, together with the world of progress, together—to lay out the entire thought—with the world that reason constructs enduringly over and above the natural world.

And what might I be, a pitiful worker of nothingness, for me to have this great virtue? What all of you could be, what all men can be, what I have wanted the upcoming generations to be, what, with all the devotion, with all the anointing of a moral consciousness that bears a foresight of a new moral and intellectual world, I would want all beings who possess reason to be—a subject whose understanding is nurtured by nature, the eternal object of understanding.

The truth that would arise from this nurturing is such a force that you can see it, it is in your sight; the face we see on present-day humanity, so different from that of past humanity, is the work of no other worker, and the effect of no other cause, than the great amount of truth that the man of today possesses in his mind. We owe this great amount of truth to no other operation of alchemy or miracle working than the simple operation of observing the world's reality as it is.

And why, if not for this, do we have senses? And why, if not for this, do they transmit their sensations to the brain? And why, if not for this, does reason function in the brain?

And nonetheless, to do this—which is what nature has wanted man to do on the planet it has given him—has seemed, to unreflecting persons everywhere, a crime against nature, and to unreflecting persons here, a crime against God. But Lord, Providence, first cause, fundamental truth, efficient reason, universal moral consciousness, whatever you are, how long must innocence remain a crime? How long must aspiring to good be an evil? How long must he who most strives to be nature's faithful creature be estranged from nature? How long must he who wants only to be a defender of reason be an offender?

Of reason? Of the particle of reason that you, certainly you, centripetal reason, have imparted to the spirit of man, so that, evolving independently from his source, he might hurtle into truth's endless space, and, keeping your bosom as his fixed center, might imitate the vortex of worlds that rush into the infinite, tracing in it their invisible orbits, possessed of a vertigo that distances them from their center, they are, like human reason, greater proof that the center they obey exists, the deeper they plunge into the depths of the infinite.

What body in space, what reason in the world of men, what virtue in the soul of children, can be more orderly than when they respond naturally to their centers of attraction?

Just as the center of the planetary world is the sun, and the center of reason is the world it contemplates, so the center of all virtue is reason. To develop reason in children, nourishing it with reality and truth, is to develop in them the very principle of morality and virtue.

Morality is based on nothing other than reason's recognition of duty; and virtue is neither more nor less than fulfillment of a duty in each of the conflicts that continuously occur between reason and instinct. What we have of the rational is, then, victorious over what we have of the animal, and that is virtue, because that is to fulfill the duty we have always to be rational, because that is strength (*virtus*), the constituting essence, the nature of rational beings.

To achieve this end—higher and better than any other, inasmuch as it is, to use an expressively redundant phrase of German metaphysics, the *final end* of man on the planet—to achieve this end, the great masters, from Confucius to Aristotle, from Mencius to Socrates, from Comenius to Pestalozzi, from Fénelon to Froebel, from Tyndal to Locke, from Mann to Hill,[11] have aimed to support reason in its constant evolution toward truth. To achieve this end, the aim here, too, was to apply the system and rational procedure of education.[12]

• • • • •

In wanting to educate whole men, I did not want only to form them, I did not want only to provide new agents for truth, new workers for the good, new soldiers for justice, new patriots for the Dominican fatherland—I wanted also to provide new assistants for my vision, new hearts for my dream, new hopes for my plan of forming an entire fatherland from the fragments of fatherland that we, the sons of these lands, have.

May he throw the first stone at me who, among you, feels incapable of such egotism.

---

11. Confucius (c. 551–479 BC), Chinese philosopher; Aristotle (384–322 BC), Greek philosopher; Mencius (c. 371–288 BC), Chinese philosopher, follower of Confucius; Socrates (c. 469–399 BC), Greek philosopher; Jon Amos Comenius (1592–1670), Moravian churchman and educator; Johan Heinrich Pestalozzi (1746–1827), Swiss educational reformer; François de Salignac de la Mothe Fénelon (1651–1715), French theologian and writer; Friedrich Wilhelm August Froebel (1782–1852), German educator and founder of the kindergarten system; Wiliam Tyndale (1494–1536), English biblical translator and martyr; John Locke (1632–1704), English philosopher and founder of British Empiricism; Horace Mann (1796–1859), U.S. educator; Sir Roland Hill (1795–1879), British educator.

12. In the omitted passages, Hostos discusses the problems he encountered in actualizing his vision.

I will not rely on that man for this lofty enterprise. And, when the legions of those whose moral consciousness and reason have been reformed, seeking logical ways to apply truth to a goal in life necessary for the liberty and civilization of man in these lands and for the greatness of these peoples in history, begin putting their patriotic virtue to work to create the Confederation of the Antilles, which moral consciousness and reason, duty and truth, set forth as the ultimate objective of our life in the Antilles, the Confederation will pass over his dead body. And when, in reflecting on the efficacy of the intellectual process that will have been employed to achieve the Confederation, someone says that the Confederation of the Antilles is more a confederation of minds than of peoples, he who now accuses me will be left out of the host of minds that will have led to that lofty end.

But if the dreamer should not arrive at the realization of the dream, if the worker should not see the work completed, if the apostasies should destroy the apostolate, neither troubled life nor early death will be able to take away from the teacher the hope that in the future the seed he has sown in the present might sprout, because from the soul of his students he has tried to make a temple for reason and truth, for liberty and the good, for the Dominican and the Antillean fatherland.

And when, most desperate, he closes his eyes in order not to see the misfortune that might follow, from the back of his retina springs up again the scene that most movingly has proved to him the excellence of this work.

We were in the midst of it. We were working to deliver these men at last to the republic. One of them was about to be examined, and the signal had been given. The organ, with its majestic voice, resounded in that sublime interlude, which, with four notes, penetrates into the depths of moral sensibility and awakens it in the corners of physical sensibility, and sets the nerves in the flesh on edge.

The school was in that moment what it is in essence; and the silence and spiritual absorption testified that it was officiating at the altar of the eternal redemption that is the truth.

Suddenly, passing by the door, a woman from the countryside stops, sets the tools of her work and of her life on the pavement, tries to cross the threshold, becomes intimidated, wavers between the emotion that attracts her and the fear that repels her, raises her feeble arms, makes the sign of the cross, kneels down, bows low, prays, rises silently, timidly retraces her steps, and thus consecrates the temple.

The thoughtless students laughed, the organ continued groaning its sublime melody, and, so as not to interrupt the music nor interrupt the religious emotion that moved me, I did not express to the students the fervent desire that I express before you and before the fatherland of today and tomorrow.

May the day soon arrive in which the school will be the temple of truth before which the passerby might kneel down, as yesterday the country woman did! And then may you not reject her with your laughter, may you not intimidate her with your mockery; open the doors wide to her, open your arms wide to her, because that poor feeble woman is the personification of the society of the Antilles, which wishes but does not dare to enter into the worship of truth.

Juan Montalvo
(Ecuador)

Juan Montalvo (1832–1889) is an Ecuadorian writer whose intellect tended toward attack and criticism rather than theory building, and many see him as a writer in the tradition of Cervantes, Montaigne, and Voltaire. He was born in Ambato, Tungurahua Province, Ecuador, the ninth of sixteen children born to José Marcos Montalvo, a textile merchant, and Josefa Fiallos. He studied in Quito at the Colegio de San Fernando (1846–1848), finishing his studies in philosophy at the Seminario de San Luis in 1851. He studied law for a time at the Universidad Central but did not finish. He returned to Ambato in 1854, dedicating himself to reading Greek and Latin classics and modern European authors.

Montalvo had the opportunity to experience an intense intellectual life in Europe when, in 1857, former president José Maria Urbina appointed him to diplomatic posts in Italy and France. In Paris he met many French intellectuals, including the poet Alphonse de Lamartine. He returned to Ecuador in 1859 and married María Adelaida Guzmán in 1865. A number of his travel narratives and poems were published in *La Democracia*. Some of his essays also appeared in *La Cosmopolita*.

Montalvo used his literary talent to serve liberal political causes in Ecuador and, by extension, all of Spanish-speaking America. He reserved his particular vitriol for such dictators as Dr. Gabriel García Moreno and General Ignacio de Veintimilla, both of whom he attacked relentlessly for their autocratic and theocratic governing styles. His opposition to Moreno led to seven years' exile, which he spent in Colombia. When his pamphlet, *La dictatura perpetua,* against Moreno, inspired some young people in Quito to assassinate the dictator, Montalvo is said to have exclaimed, "It is my pen that killed him!" With the advent of the new government, Montalvo returned from Colombia and took up the liberal cause in a new periodical, *El Regenerador,* and several other writings. When General Veintimilla led a revolution in 1876 and began showing dictatorial tendencies, Montalvo mounted a campaign to bring down that regime as well. He wrote twelve polemical pamphlets, *Las Catilinarias;* for this effort he received two more exiles, both in Paris, one for four months during 1876–1877, and the other from 1879 until his death in 1889.

Besides attacking dictators, Montalvo focused his pen on Juan León Mera, a contemporary novelist, poet, and essayist who was also born in Ambato and who espoused conservative ideas. Montalvo's attack on certain views held by the Catholic Church hierarchy—expressed with great erudition, biting wit, and not a little anger—in his most highly regarded book, *Siete tratados* (*Seven Treatises*), caused the Archbishop of Quito, Monseñor Ordóñez, a long-time enemy of Montalvo, to have the book placed on the Index of Prohibited Books. Almost immediately Montalvo wrote and published a diatribe against the archbishop entitled *Mercurial eclesiástica, libro de las verdades.* A selection from the third of the seven treatises follows. While in exile in Colombia, Montalvo also wrote dramas, many essays, and *Los capítulos que se le olvidaron a Cervantes* (first published in 1895). Montalvo's most intense political output came in 1875, when he produced a large number of political tracts, among them "El último de los tyranos," "Constitución nueva," and "Misiva patriótica."

During the years before his death, he published three volumes of *El Especta-dor,* a work that received wide international acclaim, although the third volume was also placed on the Index of Prohibited Books. Throughout his career, Montalvo was revered as a writer and reviled as a political polemicist: his conservative opponents blocked his appointment to the prestigious Real Academia de la Lengua Española, yet the many memorials to Montalvo in France, Spain, and Ecuador bear witness to the respect his work inspired.

Further Reading

Albornoz Peralta, Osvaldo. *Montalvo: Ideología, pensamiento político.* Quito: CIPAD Publicaciones Tercer Mundo, 1982.

Agromante, Roberto. *La filosofía de Montalvo.* 3 vols. Quito: Banco Central del Ecuador, 1992.

Barriga López, Franklin. *Vida y pensamiento de Montalvo.* Loja, Ecuador: Universidad Nacional de Loja, Instituto Ecuatoriano de Crédito Educativo y Becas, 1985.

Grijalva, Juan Carlos. *Montalvo: Civilizador de los bárbaros ecuatorianos: Una relectura de las Catilinarias.* Quito: Universidad Andina Simón Bolívar, Abya Yala, Corporación Editora Nacional, 2004.

Mead, Robert G., Jr. "Montalvo, Hostos y el ensayo hispanoamericano." *Hispania* 39, no. 1 (1956): 56–62.

Miño, Reinaldo. *Juan Montalvo: Polémica y ensayo.* Guayaquil, Ecuador: Tall. Gráf. de Editorial "Claridad," s.n., 1990.

Paladines Escudero, Carlos. *Aporte de Juan Montalvo al pensamiento liberal.* Quito: Fundación Friedrich-Naumann, 1988.

Pérez, Galo René. *Un escritor entre la gloria y las borrascas: Vida de Juan Montalvo.* Quito: Banco Central del Ecuador, 1990.

Sacoto, Antonio. *Juan Montalvo, el escritor y el estilista.* Cuenca, Ecuador: Casa de la Cultura Ecuatoriana "Benjamín Carrión," Núcleo del Azuay, 1987.

Salvador Lara, Jorge. *Ensayos sobre Montalvo y Mera.* Quito: Comisión Nacional Permanente de Conmemoraciones Cívicas, 1991.

Spindler, Frank MacDonald. "Lamennais and Montalvo: A European Influence upon Latin American Political Thought." *Journal of the History of Ideas* 37, no. 1 (1976): 137–46.

———. *Nineteenth Century Ecuador: A Historical Introduction.* Fairfax, Va.: George Mason University Press, 1987.

Spindler, Frank MacDonald, and Nancy Cook Brooks, trans. and eds. *Selections from Juan Montalvo Translated from the Spanish*. Special Studies no. 23. Tempe, Ariz.: Arizona State University Center for Latin American Studies, 1984.

Seven Treatises (1882)

Third Treatise: Reply to a Pseudo-Catholic Sophist

If you were of one heart with me in the essential issues, we would have little to say about the secondary ones—eliminate the contrast you have drawn between pagan and Christian virtues, between Mary, Mother of God, and Arria, wife of Caecina Paetus,[1] and those "dark abysses"[2] with which you like to make us shudder are sealed off. Our insistence that women should acquire some notion of ancient history does not indicate less regard for modern history; on the contrary, we previously assumed a necessary and complete religious education, so that we might propose ancient history as something new, as knowledge that would be desirable. "Mary" is the first name a little girl pronounces; with it her speech begins to form; with it, her tongue becomes free. Do you not see how she makes little altars, where she hears the Mass that one of the family's boys says for her? I can easily grasp that pure and clean virtue, heaven's virtue, lies in Christian law, the law of God; but if for the most part the ancient Greeks and Romans practiced that law, shall we say they had no virtue because the savior had not yet come into the world? Virtue belonged to Socrates, wisdom to Plato. How can this be! Socrates, practicing and teaching suffering; Socrates, suffering and advocating poverty; Socrates, putting modesty into action and prescribing it; Socrates, always speaking the truth; Socrates, humble, temperate, prudent; Socrates, kind, neat, gentle—and not genuinely virtuous? Everything Jesus Christ preached later, Socrates practiced before; almost everything Socrates practiced before, Jesus Christ taught later. Had Socrates lived in Jesus' time, he would have been the first of his disciples; he would have baptized Jesus in the Jordan. Socrates is like a prophet, a precursor of the Messiah in a way, whom the centuries have venerated, honored almost as a divinity of the human race. A philosopher without equal, a man inferior only to Jesus, a sublime soul—

---

1. When in AD 42, Claudius ordered Caecina Paetus to put an end to his own life for conspiracy and Paetus hesitated, Arria, an image of courage and self-control, took the dagger and stabbed herself, after which she handed the dagger to her husband, supposedly saying, "It doesn't hurt, Paetus." Simon Hornblower and Anthony Spawforth, eds., *The Oxford Classical Dictionary*, 3rd ed. (Oxford and New York: Oxford University Press, 2003), p. 175. Hereafter cited *OCD*.

2. "Dark abysses" (*abismos tenebrosos*), a reference to hell, from the Spanish translation of 2 Peter 2:4 and Jude 1:6.

Socrates, are you not he who with a firm hand tears away the thick mantle that enveloped the world and with a clear gaze discerns there one eternal God? Are you not the one who establishes a school of greatness of soul and goodness of heart? Is it not you who dies for wisdom? The Savior was still far from beginning his great work, and already on Earth there was a man proclaiming him with his own works—this was Socrates. And because he did not have the name of "Christian," nor could he have had it, do we have to look askance at proposing him as an example of morality and wisdom? We have not said that we must sacrifice a cock to Mercury[3] at the moment of death. Except for this vain indulgence, Socrates was a genuine and good Christian, and the father of the universe has baptized him in the city of God. *Sancte Socrate, ora pro nobis!* exclaims Erasmus,[4] in an outburst of admiration for the virtue of this extraordinary man—Saint Socrates, pray for us! And Erasmus was not a pagan, but a Christian, and very Christian—more charitable, without a doubt, than the saints who arbitrarily and cruelly sent to hell the brightest and most virtuous men produced by the human species. "Woe to you, Aristotle!" says St. Jerome,[5] "You are praised where you are not," that is, in the world, "and you are tormented where you are," that is, in hell. And how does St. Jerome know Aristotle is in hell? St. Thomas[6] saw this philosopher as being in heaven when he presented him to the world as the model to be held up to us when considering the ideas of metaphysics, natural sciences, and sentiments of the mind. And Bacon,[7] striking the first blow against Aristotelianism, should be an arch-heretic in the eyes of the Church, which for so many years held Aristotle's doctrine as its own. Certainly the Church paid little attention to St. Jerome when it burned Etienne Dolet[8] for having translated Plato rather than Aristotle; and it exiled Ramus,[9] persuaded that he thought differently from the philosopher. If St. Jerome's sentence affects the final judgment, the Church has fallen into mortal guilt, publicly proclaiming one of the damned as its doctor and guiding light; if the Church is right, the verdict of St. Jerome carries within itself neither justice nor

---

3. At *Phaedo* 118a, Plato records Socrates' last words as: "we ought to offer a cock to Asclepius. See to it, and don't forget." *The Collected Dialogues of Plato,* ed. Edith Hamilton and Huntington Cairns. New York: Random House, 1964, Tredennick translation.

4. Desiderius Erasmus (1469–1536), Dutch Humanist.

5. St. Jerome (c. 347–420), Christian scholar, Father of the Church, Doctor of the Church.

6. St. Thomas Aquinas (1225–1274), Italian philosopher and theologian, Doctor of the Church.

7. Sir Francis Bacon (1561–1626), English philosopher, essayist, and statesman.

8. Etienne Dolet (1509–1546), French scholar and printer who lived in Lyons. Printed by his own press, his translations of the Bible and other classical works brought him into conflict with civil and religious authorities, who arrested, tried, convicted, and executed him for heresy.

9. Petrus Ramus (1515–1572), French humanist, logician, and philosopher, noted for formulating a system of logic emphasizing precision and clear, fine distinctions that was influential among Protestants, most notably Bacon and Milton.

truth. Count Joseph de Maistre,[10] flag bearer for the modern ultramontanists,[11] uses Plato's principles to prove the immortality of Christian maxims, and, presenting the ideas of the Academy with respect to original sin, he says, "This is precisely the Christian doctrine."[12] We do not understand, then, how those who, by force of divine inspiration, have anticipated the fundamentals of Christian doctrine should be condemned by the Church to eternal fire. In Justinian's reign, Plato was condemned in this very way by a well-attended synod, according to Gibbon. What a wonder when, for the same reason as the founder of the Academy, Origen,[13] Doctor and Father of the Church, was also so condemned![14] Now, then, if the sentence of the synod was carried out, it is foolish and contradictory to use the authority of the damned to give weight and lofty lineage to Christian doctrine; if Plato, immortal spirit, vanished and became one with the eternal flame, the synod's resolution is futile and even impious.

Observe the similarity between Socrates and Jesus. Both are of humble birth; both live poor, diligent, beneficent lives; both have disciples; both are denounced, accused, persecuted; both consume the bitter cup; both die at the hands of those they wish to save—Jesus died for the redemption of humankind; it was not from vanity that Socrates died. There is merely one difference between these two teachers; but great, infinite, is the difference between heaven and earth. If we wish to imitate Socrates we are not casting Jesus into oblivion. The difference will lie in the nature of the works we contemplate and produce. If they have philosophical education as a basis, and the authors focus on the learning of human societies and on the common course of life, then, given as well-established and admitted what already belongs to religion, no one will take away

---

10. Joseph de Maistre (1753–1821), French author and diplomat whose finely honed prose aimed to undermine eighteenth-century rationalism. His attacks on rationalism and his support of the pope's absolute right to rule the world independently of all secular authority are the basis for Montalvo's assertion that he is an ultramontanist.

11. Advocates of the absolute supremacy of the papacy in all matters of religion and politics.

12. *Veladas de San Petersburgo.* [Montalvo's note. The *St. Petersburg Dialogues,* Second Dialogue, states, "Plato tells us *that in contemplating himself he does not know if he sees a monster more arrant, more evil than Typhon, or rather a moral, gentle, and beneficent being who partakes of the nature of divinity.* He adds that man, so torn between these opposite natures, cannot act well and live happily *without mastering that power of the soul in which evil resides, and without setting free that which is the abode and the agent of virtue.* This is precisely the Christian doctrine, and original sin could not be more clearly admitted." (Count Joseph de Maistre, *The Saint Petersburg Dialogues,* Second Dialogue, translated by Jack Lively, http://maistre.ath.cx:8000/st_petersburg.html).]

13. Origines Adamantius (c. 185–254), born in Egypt, probably Alexandria. One of the most important early Christian philosophers and scholars, whose strict asceticism—he castrated himself—made him a disputed figure from early in his career, giving his own bishop, Demetrius, reason to order him banished and deposed after the bishops of Jerusalem and Caeserea had ordained him.

14. The apparent reference is to Edward Gibbon.

from the philosophers and great men of antiquity what they themselves valued. If someone is speaking of Athens and Rome; do you have to bring up St. Thomas and St. Toribio?[15] Be aware, Pharisees, and be careful, too—if you start by now throwing stones at Socrates, you risk running the fate of Anytus and Meletus,[16] who earned universal hatred, with the horror of both good and evil persons, for having accused the Teacher. Centuries and generations have anointed Socrates; he is like a great pontiff. Whoever touches him is cursed. Now, to condemn and discredit him, you remind us of the arrogance of this pagan before the thirty tyrants; yet you will not hesitate to present him as a model of humility to throw our own pride in our faces. But not even in this regard does the comparison between the two teachers break down. Jesus' modesty had no limits with regard to personal humiliation and physical suffering, yet, proceeding from his divine authority, he always showed in his demeanor and his words, and even in his works, an exaltation and power that made officials and lords tremble. Wounded by the high priest's servant, with a serene face he turns and asks, "If I have erred in what I have said, show me the error. If I have spoken the truth, why do you mistreat me?"[17] No differently, in the street Socrates receives a slap in the face and continues on his way without giving any indication of having noticed the insult. Now put Jesus before Annas,[18] who throws in his face the arrogance and presumption of calling himself the "Son of God," and you will see how that divine man maintains what he has said, the eternal fire of the Divine gleaming in his gaze. And perchance is he humble when he enters the Temple and with lashes throws from it the merchants who have profaned his father's dwelling? Seeing the crowd that had left him almost alone reassemble behind him, he turns toward them and bitterly addresses them: "You seek me out not for the miracle but for the bread that fills you."[19] Peace and serenity were the moral characteristics of Jesus Christ: cry—he often cried; laugh—he never laughed, because the joy of the world was not his. Anger, holy anger, a sudden emotion, and often a necessary one, did indeed move him from time to time. The Holy Scripture mentions God's wrath at every step; this is not arrogance. It was not arrogance in Jesus Christ, because such a passion does not pertain to the Divine; it was not arrogance in Socrates, because that vice has no part in true philosophy, which is nothing other than the love of God through the knowledge

---

15. St. Toribio Alfonso Mogrovejo (1538–1606), Archbishop of Peru, the Grand Inquisitor of Spain, famous for having predicted the day and hour of his death, among other notable accomplishments.

16. Plato represents Socrates as saying to the Athenian tribunal: "There you have the causes which led to the attack upon me by Meletus and Anytus and Lycon. Meletus being aggrieved on behalf of the poets, Anytus on behalf of the professional men and politicians, and Lycon on behalf of the orators" (23e–24a, Tredennick translation).

17. John 18:23.

18. High Priest at Jerusalem, a Roman sympathizer. John 18:13–24.

19. John 6. [John 6:26, Montalvo's note.]

of things and the practice of virtues. Socrates in the presence of the thirty tyrants, reminding them boldly of the sentence of Apollo, is a sublime person. "The Oracle at Delphi, questioned by Caerephon about me, responded: There is no man more just, free, nor wise than Socrates."[20] Boastfulness, no; vanity no— the gods speaking to the world are the ones who say such grand things. In the same way, Jesus, a most respectable oracle, declares that he is the Son of God, the messiah announced to the world by the prophets in the ancient law. I know very well that Jesus Christ is the model of virtue—his Imitation,[21] one of the greatest books that has come forth from the heart of man. But when we are not concerned with him, who prohibits us from turning to the ancient sages? You certainly imply, and all but set down as a principle, that virtue cannot exist outside the Church. Sticking with the same philosopher, since those pagan names disagree with you so much, tell us: Charity in itself is a Christian virtue—in St. Bruno[22] it is, in St. Theresa[23] it is—and would it not be so in Socrates? If in the latter it was not virtue, what was it? Vice, or something indifferent? "Truth on this side of the Pyrenees, error on the other side"[24]—that is the principle of false Christians, those who pay the tithe of their millet and rye but neglect the essence of the Lord's precepts. But do they not know he has cursed those who pay the tithe yet do not abide by the precepts, much as he has cursed those who fast from delicacies but not from hatred, egotism, and defamation? "Cursed are you!" he is crying on the peak of Ebal. Then he passes to the peak of Gerezim[25] and cries anew, "Come to me, oh you who profess my law and fulfill it. My law is truth, my law is faith. Blessed are you in the name of my Father."[26]

> "If with pure heart you extend your arms to heaven and you deny iniquity and do not live in sin, you will raise your unblemished brow, you will forget your misery and not remember your woes except as waters that have passed. And your glory will gleam like the noonday sun, and when you judge yourself complete, you will be reborn like the morning star."[27]

20. *Apology,* 21e ff. in *The Collected Dialogues of Plato,* op. cit.

21. *The Imitation of Christ,* the devotional manual of the Brothers of the Common Life (Dutch, 14th century, Roman Catholic community) and by tradition attributed to St. Thomas à Kempis (1380–1471), German Catholic monk.

22. St. Bruno (1030–1101), founder of the Carthusian Order, dedicated to the contemplative life to the extent that each member of the order lives individually, coming together with the others only for worship.

23. Theresa of Avila (1515–1582), Spanish Carmelite nun, Doctor of the Church, one of the principal saints of the Roman Catholic Church and one of the greatest of mystics.

24. Blaise Pascal (1623–1662), *Pensées.*

25. The reference is to Deut. 27–28, where the Israelites are commanded to pronounce curses and blessings from these two mountains upon entering Canaan.

26. Deut. 11:26–29. Montalvo's quotation seems to be a paraphrase or from memory.

27. Job 11:13–17.

"Lord, who will inhabit your tabernacle and who will rest on your holy mountain? He who travels the road of innocence and practices virtue; he who speaks truth in his heart and does not conceal artifice in his words; he who does no harm to his brother, nor provokes him with insults—that one whose presence confounds the perverse and honors the man fearful of God—who swears an irrevocable oath against evil, who gives no money to usurers nor receives gifts to judge with injustice; that one, that one, will not go hesitatingly through eternity."[28]

Thus spoke the prophets who took it upon themselves to enlighten you four thousand years before the miserable little bubble from which you have emerged arose from nothingness, you hypocrites, younger brothers of Satan. You have faith not in the doctrine of Jesus, which is love, compassion, and brotherhood, but rather in your doctrine, which is hatred, pride, and persecution. Don't you know that God does not want the death, but rather the life of the sinner, and that he is awaiting him over there with eternal health? Justice, mercy, and faith, this is the law, says the Lord. Doctors of the law, you are ignoring it. I say more—you are obscuring it. And more yet—you are knowingly violating it. Your sacrilege will be posted against your account in divine wisdom, and so you are approaching and holding out your hand for the reward promised to those who are good; but here is one who meets you on the path saying, "Go back, impure ones; go far, far away. Your road is the pit obscured in shadows that you see over there, black and deep."

"Tribulation and anguish for the soul of every man who does evil—for the Jew, of course, and then for the gentile—but honor, glory, and eternal peace to all who do good—to the Jew and to the gentile—because God does not make a distinction between persons."[29]

Did you hear that? If God does not exclude those who are good, be they Jews or be they gentiles, we cannot flee from them as though they were the damned. Virtue is virtue in every time and place; there are rich springs of virtue in those lands that you cloak with darkness and condemnation. The Lord is magnanimous, the Lord is merciful. There are many dwellings in the house of my Father, He Himself says, and you work to make this house narrow and mean, where there is room for no one but your chosen ones and not for the chosen ones of the Lord—inhospitable house, palace of egotism, similar to that of the impious, where the only ones who may enter are the rich, arrogant, vain, shameless, gluttonous, and those dressed from head to toe in purple and fine jewelry—house of the profane, of tyrants, on whose facade is engraved this inscription in bloody characters: "Here those beggars called virtues may not enter." The owners of that house order that the Temple at Epidaurus[30] be cast to the ground, taking as an

---

28. Psalm 15 or 14, depending on edition.

29. Letter of St. Paul to the Romans. [2:9–11, Montalvo's note.]

30. Epidaurus, a small state on the peninsula of the Saronic Gulf dating from the late Bronze Age, is dedicated to the healing cult of Apollo's son, Asclepius (*OCD,* p. 534).

insult the warning on the facade: "Here may enter only pure souls." True it is that certain sectarians take humble vows, but with a back door through which they proceed to pride and condemnation. They take a vow of poverty so they may become rich, a vow of obedience in order to command popes and monarchs, a vow of chastity to make their way through the world of sin silently and with ease. The Benedictine monk who made this noble declaration did not know that a great historian would transmit it to future generations.[31] We, who, if we do not find the doors of the Temple of Epidaurus wide open to us, are not guests at the other palace either; we do not take the vows of the Jesuit or the Benedictine, and, like the sage, we ask only two things of the Lord. We ask him to keep us far from vanity and lying, and to overwhelm us neither with extreme poverty nor with excessive wealth. Give us, Lord, we say, what is necessary, that we may not fall into despair or arrogance. St. Paul affirms that the love of riches has made many Christians lose their faith. The Benedictine whose vow of poverty had produced for him two and a half million reals per year had lost faith in Jesus Christ. Treasures do not produce glory; poverty accepted, relished, used well, that is wealth. And to use poverty well is precisely to find one of fortune's riches in the study of morality and the exercise of virtue. Riches got by the sweat of the brow, without the help of avarice—why not? Possessed with indifference, used with discernment, far from being dangerous for its master, wealth can be the road to salvation. No one more than the rich person has the ability to be useful to his fellow creatures, giving food to the hungry, drink to the thirsty, clothing to the naked, and instruction to the ignorant. If heaven is not filled with the rich and powerful, it is because the demon opens its mouth over them, spews its putrid breath upon them, and enraptures them with its magic, and attracts them as the serpent does certain birds, swallows them, and rushes to vomit them into the darkness of hell.

In your writing, I read with surprise, "Will we go to ancient Greece or to ancient Rome in search of morality or virtue? They are the daughters of our religion." And I also read this passage from Bossuet,[32] which comforts me: "Around the same time, Thales, the Milesian, founded the Ionian sect from which emerged those great philosophers Heraclitus, Democritus, Empedocles, Parmenides; Anaxagoras, who showed that the world was the work of an eternal spirit;[33] Socrates, who somewhat later persuaded the human race to observe good habits and was the father of moral philosophy." Carneades, Plutarch, and other disciples of Plato, disciple of Socrates, carried this moral philosophy to Rome and taught it. Arulenus Rusticus,[34] favorite of and minister to the

---

31. [Edward Gibbon,] *Decline and Fall of the Roman Empire* [ch. 37, pt. 2, note 57]. [Montalvo's note.]

32. Jacques-Bénigne Bossuet (1627–1704), the bishop of Meaux, one of the greatest of all French orators. Montalvo frequently cites his *Discourse on Universal History* (1681).

33. The foregoing list of names is a catalog of the most influential pre-Socratic philosophers.

34. Junius Arulenus Rusticus (d. AD 93), a friend of Pliny and Tacitus, was later executed by the emperor Domitian. Plutarch relates this (probably apocryphal) story in his discourse on Inquisitiveness.

emperor, stands among thousands of bystanders listening to a philosophical dis-
quisition by Plutarch.[35] An official enters and presents to Arulenus Rusticus a
folded paper from the monarch, informing him that it was a matter of the greatest urgency. The teacher stops talking. Everyone remains silent, awaiting the
courtier's departure. But the courtier asks the orator to continue, and he does
not open the imperial note until the discourse has been concluded. Observe how
philosophers and moralists commanded respect in ancient Rome, and see moral
philosophy there—morality and virtue, with the good habits toward which
Socrates inclined the human race. My God! These days I cannot cling to the
authority of a pagan. Bossuet, Bossuet is my support; Bossuet, Bossuet is my
guide; Bossuet, Bossuet is my guiding light.[36] He makes me see that those
pagans whom you despise are great philosophers. He makes clear to me that
those men, incapable of morality or virtue, are the fathers of morality. He per-
suades me that those idolaters, reprobates through and through, see the world as
made by an eternal spirit and proclaim one single God.

If there could not have been virtue before the birth of the Christian religion,
as you contend, you come by your own path, eyes blindfolded, to the edge of a
gloomier abyss than the one I have wanted to dig for you. Moses, Aaron, Joshua,
and you, great Melchizedek, did not know morality. David, Jonathan, and you,
venerable Razis,[37] had no idea of virtue. Ezekiel, Jeremiah, and you, sublime Isaiah, did not develop wisdom. Nonetheless, not only were you leading up to Jesus
Christ, but you were also his image and represented his mysteries. Elisha, imprisoned and shackled; Ezekiel, drowning in a sea of anxieties and sorrows; Elijah,
up to his neck in trouble; Zachariah, stoned to death; Isaiah, mocked and
taunted by the people; Daniel,[38] thrown to the lions—all foreshadowed Jesus
Christ, sent by the Father to announce the Son two thousand years in advance.
Knowers of the truth, they reveal it to men; masters of the doctrine, they preach
it; devotees of justice, they suffer for it; inspired prophets, wisdom is their
nature; saints from birth, their lives are a collection of virtues. And nonetheless,
inasmuch as before the Christian religion there could be no morality or virtue,
those precursors of the Savior neither practiced nor knew them. Here are the
inventions of ignorance, sharpened by egotism and informed by malice. To listen to those priests of Teutates,[39] one imagines seeing Nestorius[40] as he extends
his hands to the emperor so that the emperor might kill the heretics, who for
him were the Catholics, and as Nestorius offers the emperor the heavenly kingdom in exchange for the sea of blood for which he is asking. When Jesus asks the

---

35. Mestrius Plutarchus (c. 50–120 AD), Roman philosopher and biographer.

36. Jacques-Bénigne Bossuet (1627–1704), the bishop of Meaux.

37. 2 Maccabees 14:37.

38. This list is a catalog of important and symbolic figures found in the Hebrew Bible.

39. Ancient Celtic god.

40. Nestorius (d. c. 421), Bishop of the Church, formulated the doctrine that Jesus was two
persons in one.

learned man, who is preaching impiety and extermination, for his name, the learned man has to respond, "My name is Legion, because we are many. Many, yes many. . . . Many are called, but few are chosen."[41] I am no Jacobite, but I would gladly cast a stone at the tombs of those mutilators of the Divinity, who pare it down and defame it to such a degree that it might well fit into an Asian pagoda. Their obsession is to make those who are not heretics pass for heretics, as if that would not be lacking in charity, breaking the law, being impious themselves. But how different are the judgments of God from those of men! While you condemn us, he absolves us.[42] And the Holy Father, who is absolved by the supreme judge despite his enemies, does not want his fellow men to participate in that absolution. On the contrary, with a wave of the arm he casts half the human race into the fires of hell and laughs to hear the sizzling of their flesh on the satanic grates and the crunch of their bones breaking in the teeth of Lucifer's dogs. "What peals of laughter will be mine, what raptures of pleasure, when I see so many kings, so many great ones, who the common person believes are in heaven—when I see them, I say, howling in the profound darkness of hell!"[43] The reader, terrified, imagines himself in the presence of Galerius,[44] who claps his hands and dies of laughter on seeing how the lions devour the live men he throws them for pure pleasure. The greatest difficulty of wisdom is to possess it with measure, said a great pagan author,[45] agreeing with the Apostle, who had said: Be wise temperately; do not be so more than is necessary.[46]

"You are generous with the generous, you shall be ferocious with the wicked.

"You are the one, oh Lord, who feeds the torch that gives me light; enlighten my darkness.

"With your help, oh my God, I will cross the field of my enemies; with you I will have the strength and agility to leap their ramparts."[47]

"God is higher than the heavens; you, miserable creature, you cannot reach him, deeper than hell, impenetrable to your eyes. God is greater than the earth, vaster than the sea.

"God knows the vanity of mortals, He sees transgression in the midst of the shadows."[48]

---

41. Mark 5:9.

42. [Tertullian,] *The Apology* [ch. 50]. [Montalvo's note.]

43. Attributed to Pius IX directed at Victor Emmanuel, who had curtailed the Vatican's secular powers.

44. Galerius (d. 310), Roman Emperor 305–310, prompted the persecution of the Christians.

45. Probably Aristotle.

46. The "Apostle" here is probably Socrates, and the citation is a paraphrase of arguments in Plato, *Charmides,* 164.

47. A paraphrase of Psalms 18:25–29.

48. Psalms of David. Judges. Job, Old Testament. [Montalvo's note. A paraphrase of Job 11:8–9, 11.]

Yes, God is and does all of that. God sees the transgressor in the midst of the shadows. You, miserable creatures, what do you see? Do you want perchance to be equal to God, becoming what we cannot see in the midst of the obscurity that surrounds us? How quickly they come to condemn their fellow men, those good people, those pious ones who wish to see in religion nothing but a narrow prison cell where man can neither move nor look about! God is higher than the heavens, deeper than hell, greater than the earth, vaster than the sea; and what God is, his religion is, high, deep, broad, and vast in all directions. And you reduce it to miserable ends? And you reduce his infinite stature? And you take away his depth and make it superficial and transitory? "Little earthen man, what makes you so proud and haughty? Dust and ashes, why do you exalt and magnify yourself?"[49] You are not able to grasp God and measure him and form him in accord with your passions and your mean nature. Leave him high, deep, broad, vast, that is to say, unknown by us. Do you not know that Plato, notwithstanding who he was, regarded as impious someone wishing to discover the nature of the gods? The holiest, the wisest is to accept not knowing that nature—a lesson from a great Doctor of the Church, from which you could benefit, if bad faith and ignorance did not keep you far from virtue and wisdom. You not only covet knowledge of God's nature, but you claim to know it; and knowing it, what sad disillusionment you must have endured, for you see him foolish, egotistical, spiteful, exactly like you, in whose image your lunacy forms him. My God is a mystery, a great mystery; *and mysteries are death's hopes.* Now then, as death's hopes are what give force to life, I judge that we live by the force of a mystery that will be revealed to us when these hopes are fulfilled.

You do not want to go to Greece or to Rome because you are of the opinion that you will not find virtues there. Let's look for them. If we find them, what do you lose? I am not the Sybil of Cumae who guides pious Aeneas through the Averno,[50] nor the shade of Virgil who conducts Dante Alighieri through the Elysian Fields.[51] But I am not blind; I can see because of my sincerity; you cannot see. Follow me through the ruins of Greece and Rome. What is the first of the virtues? The first is a natural law engraved deeply in the heart of man—religious feeling, love and fear of the Divine, sometimes we call it the gods, sometimes God. Let us see if the Greeks loved and feared it. Alcibiades,[52] idol of the people for his bravery and beauty, leaves an orgy one night, and, drifting

---

49. Fray Luis de Granada, *Libro de la oración y de la meditación.* In *Obras completas,* vol. 2 (Madrid: 1906), p. 137.

50. Priestess of Apollo mentioned by Virgil as a guide to Aeneas in the *Aeniad.* The ancient Romans regarded the Averno, a volcanic crater lake, because of its sulphuric haze, as the entrance to hell.

51. In Dante's *Divine Comedy,* Virgil leads Dante toward salvation through hell, purgatory, and the Elysian Fields, the happy netherworld reserved for heroes favored by the gods.

52. Alcibiades (450–404 BC), Athenian statesman and general; guest in Plato's *Symposium;* friend to Socrates.

between reason and delirium, staggering along through the streets of Athens, he mutilates the sacrosanct Hermes or statues of the guardian gods. The reprobate flees the next day. The Athenians, worked up, infuriated, unanimously condemned him. The handsome libertine can be as insolent as he wishes with men, they said; he must pay for his insults against the divinity with his life. This is in Greece. Let's see what happens in Rome.

The Gauls have entered the city by force of arms. Camillus Furius,[53] in exile; the Senate, massacred in the precinct of the laws. The rest of the citizenry had hidden on the Capitoline Hill, where they are saved by the ruggedness of the place and the providence of the household gods. The enemy surrounds the citadel; no one leaves without paying for his audacity with mandatory death. Caius Fabius Dorso gets up one day, dresses in priestly garb, takes the standards of Rome, and with firm step begins to walk toward the Quirinal Hill, where his family had established a place of sacrifice. The Gauls, in dumbfounded silence, open ranks and let him pass freely. Having completed the sacrifice, the young priest, peaceful, serious, still carrying his standards, returns, crosses the enemy camp, and enters the Capitoline unharmed. Here we see the love of life subordinated to religious passion. The Christian martyrs could not have shown greater strength of character. As for the audacity—that is the heroic virtue.[54]

For love of country, observe young Curtius,[55] as he comes over there, a horseman decked out in his richest clothes, making the prancing and swerving steps of a conqueror. He measures the distance, turns the horse, spurs him on, and, weapons glistening in the sun, throws himself headlong into the open chasm at the foot of the Temple of Peace. The oracle had said that if what was most precious in Rome was not thrown into the abyss, the misfortunes of the country would be great. Curtius thought that a great heart such as his was the most precious thing Rome had, went, and for Rome cast himself into the abyss.

Greece does not lag behind Rome in the matter of love of country. On Themistocles'[56] advice, the Athenians had resolved to abandon the city to the conquering Persians and take refuge with their liberty and gods in the sacred Salamis. A man named Cyrsilus, a good orator, stands up and says in a loud voice, "Athenians, do you want to know what is best for you and has the best outcome? Throw out this chatterbox who is leading you to ruin and remain in Athens. The conqueror will be magnanimous with a submissive people." The

---

53. Marcus Furius Camilus (d. 365 BC), Roman hero, elected dictator after the sack of Rome by the Gauls in 387 BC.

54. This story, first written by Livy, was retold in many popular nineteenth-century European histories of ancient Rome.

55. M. Curtius, young Roman knight, part of a myth explaining the name of *Iacus Curtius* in the Roman forum.

56. Themistocles (524–460 BC), Athenian political leader and military commander, defeated the Persians at Salamis.

Athenians, furious, stone him and go with their leader, fleeing from servitude. Athens is, they said, where there are free Athenians.

The three hundred members of the Fabian clan,[57] beheaded on the banks of the Cremera, the three Decii,[58] sacrificed for the country; all this is patriotism— patriotism boiled in the crucible, so refined and pure that it passes over us like an invisible flame without cutting away our soul nor inflaming our brain. You patriots who have accused Rome of lacking love of country, let us see you throw yourselves into that oracular lake like so many Curtiuses; or attack with the Samnites, a holy family of three hundred persons, and die without a single survivor; or expose your unprotected chest to the enemy army like the Decii. Do you know what you have said, you cowards? Patriotism is Rome's virtue—love of country was what made her mistress of the world. The great actions of our times do nothing to obliterate from memory the treasure trove of feats that remain in antiquity. Palafox's answer to the French ("War, unto the knife!");[59] the act of one of the latter in swallowing the papers that might have given away their plans to the enemy; Antonio Ricaurte, setting fire to the powder box:[60] These are truly heroic deeds. But if we keep rowing up the same stream, we come to Mucius,[61] to Horatius Cocles,[62] and to other brilliant characters from Roman history. If studying Roman and Greek history were mandatory for the youth of today, if by law they had to know these histories by memory, how many heroes, how many martyrs would make our centuries greater! Plutarch's *Parallel Lives* of the illustrious heroes has been the school of great men.

The Athenians, despite their frivolous character, did not place the useful before the honest. The report that Aristides[63] gave regarding Themistocles' plan

---

57. From the fifth century BC on, among the most distinguished of Roman families.

58. Mus Publius Decius, the father of the Fabian clan, during the Samnite war rode, as an act of devotion, into the enemy lines, disrupting them and sacrificing himself; the son of the same name is reported to have acted similarly on a later occasion, though without specification of the occasion. (*OCD.*)

59. José de Palafox y Melzi (1776–1846), Spanish general who sent this message in reply to the French commander's demand that the city of Zaragoza surrender.

60. Antonio Ricaurte (1786–1814), a Colombian military man who fought for Venezuelan independence, died after setting fire to a store of gun powder in order to prevent the capture of weapons.

61. Gaius Mucius Scaevola, part of a Roman legend, according to which he stole into the opposing king's camp but killed the king's secretary by mistake. With his arrest he showed indifference to torture by thrusting his own right hand into a fire. His name, Scaevola, means "the left-handed."

62. Horatius Cocles, according to Roman legend, he and two companions held a bridge across the Tiber against an invading army.

63. Aristides, fifth-century BC Athenian politician, archon 489–488 BC, often represented as an upright foil to devious Themistocles (524–459 BC), Athenian politician and archon 493–492 BC.

to set fire to the Lacedemonian fleet anchored in Pireus is well known: "Athenians," said the just Aristides, "no idea can be more useful to us than that of Themistocles, but neither is any more wicked. I advise you to reject it." The Athenians, without asking what the archon's plan might be, rejected it. Copenhagen's destruction by the English, the burning of Peking's fortress by the French, the shelling of Valparaíso by the Spanish would not have been counseled by Aristides. As for the Romans, good faith was the divinity that encompassed all the gods. Numa[64] established a solemn sacrifice in its honor; the priest who celebrated the sacrifice went in a covered wagon, his right hand concealed in a silk cloth. Good faith is blind; it sees nothing but the just. It has no eyes for what is advantageous if the advantageous falls outside the just. It is possible that today an honorable and self-respecting soldier might reject the order they give him to poison the enemy general; but it is also probable that he would not send the culprit in chains to the general, denouncing the despicable proposal. Gaius Fabricius,[65] pale with anger, had Pyrrhus's doctor tied up and sent him to the conquering prince. If on occasion the Romans broke their word, the ire of the gods was warded off with a sacrificial victim. The treaty made by the consul who passed through the Caudine Forks was not ratified by the Senate; and the very consul who had made it was the one who argued most forcefully against it, taking on himself the punishment for this disgraceful agreement.[66] The same thing happened with the one who made an improper treaty with Numantia; the Senate censured it, and the consul at his own request was placed naked, tied hand and foot, below the walls of the offended city. When Rome had promised something, it would have died before failing to keep its word; and when, despite this, she had committed an injustice, she set it right at the first opportunity with a solemn act of reparation, and the dignity of the republic rested on this point. Ardea and Aricia[67] have a dispute over boundaries, and for the sake of peace they agree to abide by the decision of the Roman people. The Roman people, on the advice of a wicked old man, decide to rid itself of the outcries of the disputants by adjudicating the contested territory to itself, and, in fact, it is so adjudicated. The Senate, boiling with anger, waited its turn in silence; as soon as it was possible to lay down the law for the mob in the Forum, it returned the contested territory to its owners without receiving compensation. This is a great people.

Even today we see acts of faithfulness. Turenne[68] had meetings in his camp

---

64. Numa Pompilius (d. 673 BC) was the second of the kings of Rome, succeeding Romulus.

65. Gaius Fabricius Luscinus, elected Roman consul in 282 and 278 BC. When at war with Pyrrhus, Fabricius angrily refused Pyrrhus's physician's offer to poison Pyrrhus.

66. In the Battle of Caudine Forks (321 BC), the consuls leading a Roman army acknowledge their defeat at the hands of the Samnites by passing under a yoke of spears. The Senate later rejected the peace terms agreed to and turned over the consuls to the Samnites for punishment.

67. Roman cities near Rome, both ancient; the dispute over borders occurred in 446 BC.

68. Henri de la Tour d'Auvergne, Vicomte de Turenne (1611–75), Marshall of France, one of the greatest of French commanders.

with his enemy, the Great Condé.[69] Learning of it later, the queen, Anne of Austria, reproached her captain, saying, "Why did you not take the prince when he came to your camp?" "Because I feared that he might take me, Madam," he responded valiantly. But I suggest that, if a general today were to free a certain number of prisoners on condition that, if the enemy did not accept such and such a proposition, the released men would have to return to their prison, not all of them would in fact return. The two hundred Roman prisoners whom Pyrrhus conditionally set free did return and gave themselves up as prisoners; the Senate had not accepted the peace. The ten prisoners sent by Hannibal were untrue to their word; the Senate declared them despicable and not fit for public duty. Here we see the good faith and loyalty of a wise people. Among us it is very common to put in danger a generous official who trusts in the word of a prisoner and gives him permission to go secretly to get some air and to revive with a breath of freedom. The dishonorable prisoner does not return; this would not have happened in Rome. These great virtues shone in public only because they had examples in the home. A base people, corrupt in life's private relations, will not be serious and sublime in matters of state. When the small household gods go into the street, they grow and turn into Apollo and Minerva, higher divinities. The Romans were politically great because they were wise in life's everyday actions. For a man to be of good faith with other peoples, he must be of good faith with individuals. Thus, Quintus Scaevola,[70] believing that the price of the piece of property he was trying to acquire was unfairly low, suddenly added one hundred thousand sesterces. "The farm that they have sold me is worth that," he said. If the noble Roman had given for the property what they had asked, he would not have been in breach of the law, but he would have been in breach of his conscience. Knowing for sure that it would have been a great wrong, those hundred thousand sesterces were for him a secret robbery; and even given that the contract had been finalized and could never be protested, it was not quite right in his own eyes, and he felt it better to raise the price scandalously than to possess unfairly something good and cheap. These are indeed not actions of our time; rather, fraud, stinginess, and abuse set the law in our buying and selling. It is absolutely certain that we would consider it stupid to give ten thousand pesos more for a thing than the seller is asking; and at the least it would be a complete idiot who had qualms paying twenty for a horse worth two hundred, if someone were willing to sell it for so little. Quintus Scaevola was undoubtedly not an authority on sharp practices; but if we have never yet taken the occasion to honor the memory of that good man by imitating him, we the poor second sons of the nineteenth century can flatter ourselves for having given twenty florins to the fundraiser who requested four for a hospice for the blind in a city on the

---

69. Louis II de Bourbon, Prince de Condé (1621–86), French general, called the Great Condé.

70. Quintus Publius Scaevola Pontifex (d. 82 BC), an early authority on Roman law. This story is told by Cicero (*De Oficiis*, III:xv).

Rhine;[71] or for paying a *duro* to a blind girl who sold us a flower while singing laments to the Virgin. One of those old men who thought it unbecoming to beg for alms when he could earn a living by the sweat of his brow was selling hand-made combs on a street corner. "What's that?" "Your change, sir." "Don't you have children, good man?" "I have a daughter and three little grandchildren, whom I support with my work." "Keep the change, and here's a little bit more, to buy bread for those children." The old man looked at us with seeming surprise and said, as we were walking away, "Go with God, noble foreigner."

Likewise, we are reminded of having responded with a harsh refusal to an overly pious person of very bad appearance who approached us once in Seville to request a *duro* for Our Lord of the Defenseless, and we never gave even a cuadrante[72] to a disgusting beggar who, in the city of Nice, came begging "for tobacco," eyes shut, pipe in his mouth, spitting yellow while he was begging. Had the above mentioned asked on behalf of "the Defenseless," we would have given her a hundred thousand sesterces; but she asked for Our Lord, who neither eats nor drinks, and smashing her with a vulgarity against the wall was a question of conscience. "Our Lord of the Defenseless" was probably a no-account cleric rolling in money, one of those who chase away with dogs the poor who appear on their door steps, or one of those priests who threaten to deny burial to a corpse if they do not give him a hundred pesos for his concubine's trinkets. May God save us all our lives from contributing to the vices or encouraging the avarice of certain enemies of God and of men; but hunger will be a divine sensation for us if we should have an occasion to take bread from our own mouths to give to the disinherited person who arrives and falls all but dead at our door. For Our Lord of the Defenseless, for the holy candle wax, for the blessed souls of purgatory, all is for the priest, that heartless man who eats a whole chicken and refuses to give even the chicken bones to the beggar, the priest who drinks the expensive stuff and does not keep a jar in his corridor for the thirsty to wet their lips. We have had the misfortune of knowing a Pharisee who once went with a whip all the way out to the street after some unfortunate women who, with tears in their eyes, had come to beg him to reduce the burial fee just a little. "Don't they know that the priest eats chicken?" cried the impious man. "Don't they know that the priest drinks wine?" On the doorstep of these bad Christians is printed in fat characters the inscription from the mysterious house of Pompeii: *Cave canem.* Beware the dog!

The Vicar of Wakefield; Padre Cristoforo of *The Betrothed;* good and holy priests are not included in this account.[73] Who would be so audacious as to

---

71. In Wiesbaden. The government contributes two-thirds; foreigners complete the budget of that benevolent institution. [Montalvo's note.]

72. Roman coin.

73. Oliver Goldsmith, *The Vicar of Wakefield* (London, 1766), in which the vicar, the novel's main character, is known for strength of character in difficult circumstances; Alessandro Mazoni, *I Promessi Sposi* (*The Betrothed,* Florence, 1828), which features a kindly priest, Padre Cristoforo.

censure the works of the true apostles of Christian doctrine and charity? A religion that has created such men as St. Bruno,[74] St. Charles Borromeo,[75] celestial spirits in human form, is, without doubt, the mother of the virtues. We hurl ourselves only against prevaricators, those phantoms who in silence and secret are scourges that open the flesh on the unhappiest part of the human race. These men, if they buy things, do not pay for them like Quintus Scaevola. They say that they split the fruit of their manipulations with the Church, in God and in good conscience; in the same way, all along the Sea of Azov, if the fisherman does not loyally leave half his catch for the wolves, the wolves destroy the nets. Give us the evangelical man—the man who fasts and does not hate the man who eats; the man who believes and does not curse the man who thinks; the man who preaches and condemns neither the wise nor the ignorant. Piety, charity, and benevolence are the marks of the perfect priest; and the latter is a saintly person, made angelic by the love of God and by the love professed to him by his fellow men, who are amazed to find so many and such great virtues radiating from his august person.

If any of the Roman virtues has been lost almost completely, it is altruism. There are examples, and great ones, but they are so rare in our time that they are altogether a marvel to those who contemplate them. Altruism stood out sublimely among the Romans. Even the salary—the despicable salary that today corrupts and dishonors so many people—was unknown in the great epoch of Rome. Her leading men never served the fatherland for wages, nor did they set their sights on riches. Tiberius Gracchus,[76] entrusted by the Senate with a serious embassy, had only five denarii per day for strict essentials; and what was essential for those men was so little that they could live on nothing. Today, the ambassadors of the great powers have 50,000 *duros* of annual income; plus office expenses; plus a palace in which to be housed like princes. And I wonder whether these illustrious men would give a fifth of their income to their country if it were at risk of falling for lack of that amount! Well, do we poor little republicans of the new world not understand that giving less than 12,000 silver coins to a minister plenipotentiary in Europe would diminish the stature of the nation and expose that public official to hunger and shame? Other times, other customs. Today, necessity and respect demand these fortunes, and we do not have to usurp the glories of antiquity, taking from them virtues that are not for us. It remains established, nonetheless, that the ancient Romans practiced them in a grand way, like the good faith of Fabricius and the altruism of Curtius. The senators, when they were considering imposing a tax as part of a law, imposed it first upon themselves and always for an amount greater than for the rest. Many times the people were excluded from these general taxes, where the rich gave much, the poor little. The people, said an orator,

---

74. St. Bruno (c. 1030–1101), German monk, founder of the Carthusians.

75. St. Charles Borromeo (1538–84), Italian churchman, exemplary pastor.

76. Tiberius Sempronius Gracchus (d. 133 BC), Roman statesman and social reformer.

contribute enough by feeding their children. But not now, when the parliamen-
tarians have exempted themselves in some areas, or have tried to exempt themselves even from paying their debts, thanks to immunity, like the Lords of Great
Britain. And we in our democratic republics are seeing each day even the parish
deputies and gendarmes defrauding the public treasury, assuming privilege *ex
officio* over postal revenues. Do precisely those who have a salary not have to
contribute one damned thing to the common expenses? A no-account tyrant
using ignorance as an excuse, not content with doubling his year's pay, actually
had his eunuchs set an additional salary aside for his cook, his servants, his
horses—and this is not an exaggeration, nor a manner of speaking, but rather
the genuine truth. Let us compare this illustrious man with those of antiquity,
and let us decide whether our times offer us more examples of pride and greatness than those that you call abysmal. "There has not been a people on earth
among whom frugality, economy, poverty have been more, nor for more time,
honored than in Rome." Have you, with no doubts at all, you the enemies of
Rome, found a way to give the lie to the great Bossuet, when you say that the
love of ancient history means eternal damnation of the Christians? May you be
forgiven your guilt thanks to your dimwittedness; but if malice has its part in
such extraordinary nonsense, come here, gossip-mongers of the devil, and
know that "cadaverous obedience"[77] has no room in hearts where the love of
God and the human race are boiling, ignited by the intelligence that descends
over and increases them and turns them into giants. Fabricius, Curtius, Aemilius Papus,[78] conquerors of the richest peoples of Italy, spurned their gifts and
had nothing in their homes but clay dishes. Rufinus,[79] respected counselor, was
ignominiously expelled from the Senate by the censor because he had silver and
gold tableware. Let us then replace admiration with slander and, lacking
knowledge of this great people, let us marvel at our own, because we are Catholics, you say, even though our morality is contemptible and our corruption per-
verts our judgment, resulting in our inability to distinguish good from bad,
large from small. A people among whom great events and humble virtues had
crowns—and the crown of least intrinsic value was the most esteemed—is certainly a hazardous example for the young, whose studies are chains that bind
their soul to the destructive will of those gloomy teachers who teach the crushing of the spirit and direct their influence to the center of the world's governance through bondage and ignorance. The Council of Carthage[80] already
prohibited bishops from reading authors prior to Christianity. These ministers

---

77. Referring to *Kadavergehorsmankeit,* the "corpse-like" obedience demanded of Prussian
troops, which became a byword for blind obedience in politics and religion.

78. Aemilius Papus, Roman consul in 282 and 278 BC.

79. Flavius Rufinus, Roman consul in AD 390.

80. Council convened and conducted by St. Augustine, Church Father and author of *The
Confessions,* in AD 411 to resolve the question of the supposed donation by Constantine of his
lands to the Church.

invested by the Church were to have no knowledge of Plato's *Phaedo,* nor of Sophocles' *Oedipus the King,* nor of Cicero's *Book of Duties.* The Council wanted to take revenge, no doubt, for St. Augustine's owing his conversion to this sublime author, as he himself declared in his *Confessions.* In the *Phaedo,* Plato teaches before anyone else the doctrine of the immortality of the soul. In the tragedy cited, Oedipus, cleansed and pure with tears of grief, ascends to heaven without dying, like another Elijah. Cicero makes Christians holy with his works; and we, in the name of Christ and of the Church, prohibit these works. We, no; you, Catholics of few obligations, you have prohibited them, and you have done well. Gregory I,[81] going through the city of Rome, hatchet on his shoulder, without anybody standing ground against this raging destroyer, has left you a great example—statues, porches, libraries, everything falls to dust before this holy founder of Christian civilization. If Titus Livy[82] appears, he is reduced to ashes; and the world, in fervent gratitude, will sanctify the memory of this great pontiff. His tiara is gold, studded with diamonds. The Roman's most honored crown was the *corona graminea,* or grass crown; this crown could be won only by the person who had completed the greatest exploits.[83] I doubt that the *servum servorum* of the Christians holds the grass crown in greater esteem than the gold. Among the pagans, the latter was the least.

Justice, love of country, selflessness, good faith, altruism, we have already seen them. Now let us see something else among the ruins of ancient Rome. "What would we go to find in ancient Rome?" you have asked. "Could it be liberty?" Yes, in ancient Rome we will go look for liberty that, unfortunately, we do not know in the majority of modern nations. We speak of political liberty, that liberty that the remote peoples of the Tiber sow and harvest on Mt. Aventino. Do not forget that I refer only to ancient Rome; when the emperors arrive, my admiration for Rome stops. I do agree that the Mariuses and the Sullas, the Pompeys and the Caesars[84] were not emperors, but these do not belong to ancient Rome either. The Rome of the Curtiuses, the Rome of the Decii, the Rome of the Scipios, the Rome of the Lucretias, the Rome of the Cornelias, the Rome of the Veturias and Bolumnias—that is ancient Rome.[85] We will go to it to find selflessness, throwing ourselves with the Decii into the middle of the enemy to save the fatherland. In it we will go to look for unfathomable integrity, refusing with Scipio[86] to give reports to men before thanks to the gods. In it we

---

81. St. Gregory I, The Great (540–604).

82. Titus Livius (59 BC–AD 17), Roman historian.

83. *Corona quidem nulla fuit graminea noblior* [there was no crown more noble than the crown of grass]. Pliny, *Natural History* [22:4]. [Montalvo's note.]

84. Roman political leaders between the classic years of the Roman Republic and the beginning of the Roman Empire.

85. Important political figures during the classic Roman Republic.

86. Cornelius Scipio Aemilianus Africanus (b. 185 or 184), known for probity in all matters.

will go to look for evangelical poverty, scorning riches with Fabricius. In it we will go to look for good faith, returning with Regulus[87] to Carthage.

The Porcian law[88] was a guarantee of the inviolability of the citizen; the Valerian law[89] prohibited the punishment of anyone who appealed to the people. One could patiently endure the fact that the civilized and cultured nations of Europe—where what they call "individual guarantees" actually do serve as safeguards of the citizens—might ridicule ancient Rome as a slave; but in our pretend republics—where the laws are down there, and the dictators up above; where individual guarantees are not suspended legally, and the best patriots suffer in prison, loaded down with chains that the constitution prohibits; where the law is one thing and the blind will of whoever has weapons in his hand is another; where property does not exist with a secure or perpetual character, for there is no triumphant revolutionary who does not violate it with a thousand heinous confiscations or with penalties that spell the ruin of families; where the soldier is master of the horse, the burro that he finds in the road, and the Indian or peasant farmer may pay for his imprudent protest with his life; where each day the sanctuary of the domestic hearth suffers brutal desecrations; where colleges and schools are quarters for public enemies who wander to and fro, calling themselves "troops;" where eminent patriots fall to the dagger that the "supreme leader" puts into the assassin's hands—among peoples and governments like these, I say, who is so ignorant or evil as to praise them, while endeavoring to arouse distrust of or aversion to truly free and great institutions and nations? Never in Rome did the government or its officials use force against citizens. When consuls or tribunes wanted to eject disruptive persons from elections, they used this moderate formula: *Si vobis videtur, discedite, Quirites*—"Romans, withdraw if you please." This is not the same thing as having *cholo* soldiers[90] go out with their guns to bash in the heads of voters at the electoral tables with blows of their rifle butts, or having black lancers knock down and disperse people when they attempt to exercise their rights. And I would ask a voter with a broken head whether, when they clubbed him on his bald spot, he heard them say: *Si vobis videtur, discedite, Quirites?* What he heard was something else, as was what he felt—blood streaming over his ear.

A people for whom liberty is the effect of the laws, and the laws are sacred, is of necessity a free people. "The people most jealous of its liberty that the universe has ever seen was at the same time the most respectful of legitimate power and the

---

87. Marcus Atilius Regulus (d. 250 BC), Roman general and consul in the First Punic War, taken prisoner by Carthage in 255 BC. According to a story told by Horace (*Odes,* iii.5), Regulus was sent by the Carthaginians to negotiate peace with Rome; instead, he urged continued war, then fulfilled his promise by returning to Carthage where he was tortured to death.

88. The Porcian Law, enacted 454 BC. The second *lex Porcia,* enacted in 195 BC, provided that no one should bind, scourge, or kill a Roman citizen without appeal.

89. Among several laws so named, probably refers to the *lex Valeria Publicola* (449 BC), which granted the right to appeal any judicial decision to the Roman people.

90. *Cholo,* an Andean term for an urbanized Indian, or an "Indianized" mestizo.

most obedient to magistrates." When the Bishop of Meaux[91] made this declaration in his *Discourse on Universal History*, he did not think that a half-barbarian Catholic would later give him the lie. Catholicism would be a sad thing if, in order for it to prevail, it were necessary to destroy everything good and holy that the world has had, declaring the use of intelligence impious and the investigation of truth sinful in the domains of the history and philosophy of the most brilliant epochs of the human race. The liberty of Rome was the result of its laws. Liberty is great justice, natural justice, and the Roman laws were the work of divine inspiration. Thus, as God has spoken supernaturally through the prophets, so he has spoken naturally through Roman legislators, says a great Doctor of the Church. I deliberately seize on this class of authorities to confound you with them and make you see that if there is someone impious and deviant, it is not I, but you who are going against the current of indisputable truths for theologians and saints. In you one sees what the Bishop of Salisbury in his travels describes regarding that woman whose epitaph reads, "Going too far in piety, she became impious." Thus you: Trying too hard to appear wise, you let your ignorance show; to acquire a reputation as "pure Catholics," you display an abominable love for servitude; trying to show off your piety, you fall into impiety like the woman of the epitaph and become impious. Hutchinson grew furious with Newton[92] and called him an evil-intentioned imposter for wanting to spoil the Pentateuch's system of the universe and proclaimed the Pentateuch the sole requirement for the happiness of the human race. The law of universal gravity, the ordering of the stars and their rhythmical rotations in their orbits, the perpetual turning of the earth around the sun were frauds and iniquities for this Jewish visionary. Our Catholic rabbis live precisely thus, committed to circumscribing human wisdom to the circle of the Index and Encyclicals, finding useless and even harmful the knowledge of things that, well established, are true science.

You want "the freedom to think, speak, work, learn, and teach," you enemies of the liberty of thought, speech, work, learning, and teaching. How does it happen that you come to want what you in no way want? If we are in perpetual contradiction, and in our combative style we show that we follow diametrically opposed directions, it is precisely because of the impious war that you are pursuing against all the liberties that are the human race's privilege. Liberty of thought is the liberty to form concepts and opinions, and this sacred right is fatal for faith. Your great principle is faith, the annihilation of reason—hence, you do not work for the rule of this liberty, but rather for its ruin and neglect. Liberty of reason leads directly to liberty of conscience. This is prohibited by your sovereign, and thus you cannot want it without falling into rebellion and apostasy, or else you are the miserable playthings of an ignorance that does not meet the test

---

91. Bossuet (see footnote 32).

92. Sir Isaac Newton (1642–1727), British natural philosopher and physicist. John Hutchinson (1674–1737), English theologian whose book *Moses's Principia* (1724) attacked Newton's theory of gravity on theological grounds.

of difficulties. Nothing is less suitable for your ends than liberty of thought. If that liberty were among your principles, you would not have thrown into the infamous fire of the Inquisition those who have committed the crime of thinking freely. You would not have violently pushed into the inferno those who took the liberty of thinking. You would not have threatened excommunication nor thrown curses on those who thought like philosophers and worked like sensible persons. You mean-spirited and tyrannical sect, who have prohibited the history, philosophy, and even the arts that are expounded in the best books of our times, do you dare claim that what you want is liberty of thought? Liberty of thought is liberty to read. He who does not read does not think. Now then, must we grant that someone can think as a learned man and argue as a free man, when his reading is a crime that carries infernal punishments? Slavery of the body is nothing—bonds, chains are enough to disable it. Slavery of the spirit—where reason finds itself imprisoned, natural discourse in shackles, and the soul in fetters—that is sad, despicable. Physical servitude—the most illustrious men have suffered. Plato was a slave of the tyrant Dionysius. Diogenes[93] was a slave, but this philosopher said, how mad are those who feel sorry for me! Do they not see that those who hold me captive are the slaves? Catholics of learning and conscience view with horror the corpse that symbolizes the dead soul—by dead soul I mean the soul that has been abandoned by all liberties, extinguished, reduced to ashes. Montalembert,[94] a supreme authority for these sectarians when he is not using his freedom of thought, has just given them a knocking down: on the eve of his death, he turns to the famous anti-infallibilist Doellinger,[95] boiling with holy ire against the drafts that were about to be made into dogmas by the ecumenical council.[96] "The Gallican Church has been turned into a chicken coop,"[97] he says in his noble polemic, and he cries out for the great wise men of France to rise up against the destroyers of thought and conscience. Ay! Dupanloup,[98] in

---

93. Diogenes the Cynic (c. 412–321 BC) was captured by pirates and sold as a slave; asked his trade, he said he knew only how to govern men and should be "sold to a man who needs a master."

94. Charles Forbes Comte de Montalembert (1810–1870), French political leader and writer, hoped to forge French Catholicism into a united political force; he associated Catholicism with liberalism and worked for civil liberty; he also opposed the doctrine of papal infallibility.

95. Johann Ignaz von Doellinger (1799–1890), German priest and historian, excommunicated for having opposed the pope's dogma of infallibility, 1871, became the leader of the "Old Catholics."

96. Vatican Council I, 1869–1870, convened to decide the issue of papal infallibility.

97. The Gallican Church originally referred to the Catholic Church in France when it was under direct control of the king (1682–1790). Nineteenth-century Gallicanism was the movement, opposed to ultramontanism, which advocated the national autonomy for Catholic churches under the leadership of the monarch rather than the Pope. It was effectively crushed by Vatican I. "Chicken coop" (*gallinero*) is a pun on "Gallican."

98. Félix Antoine Philibert Dupanloup (1802–1870), bishop and educator who implemented important innovations in religious higher education. At the First Vatican Council he absented

whom the great Montalembert, sincere and knowledgeable Christian, put his faith; Dupanloup upheld his principles with valor. Once these principles were declared erroneous by the majority of the enemies of reason, he yielded to that terrible authority in whose innermost recesses lurks the Tribunal of Vehme.[99] . . . Dupanloup, the new Augustine, said for himself, "I would not believe in this if the authority of the Church did not oblige me to believe." Bellarmine and Baronius,[100] sinister officials of this Vehmic court, finally persuaded the skeptics. Since the retraction by Galileo[101] at torture's gate, there is nothing that the authority of the Church cannot achieve.

Freedom of speech without freedom of thought does not exist—unless it means we have the freedom to publish foolish nonsense, to muddle the rights of man, and to utter curses against those who take up the defense of those rights as their own. This is the only liberty that Catholics who disagree with Montalembert and Dupanloup enjoy, together with that of having work shackled with tithes, the human body with mortuary fees, and the spirit with the keys of hell. Freedom of speech—something the unworthy priest has when he defiles his lofty charge of sacred eloquence by stuffing us with insults and stupidities. Something a writer of bad faith has when he calls on religion to incite peoples against each other. Something the bloodthirsty devotee has when, like Nestorius, he requests that the tyrant exterminate men of knowledge and understanding, whom he calls "heretics" because they do not salute his avarice nor welcome his lechery. This is the freedom of speech touted and enjoyed by the owners of the keys of hell, at whose signal hell's gates open up to let in the legion that thinks and speaks with freedom restrained by courtesy and lit by the light of intelligence. Among peoples where papist prophets walk with stones in hand, ready to throw them at anyone who speaks, are there any papists so foolish and dishonest as to dare throw in our face our love of ancient Rome on the pretext that they want freedom of speech? They also claim to want "the freedom to work." False—what they want is the freedom to live off others' work, to get rich from the sweat of the people's brow; to eat, drink, and sleep basking in laziness, soundly as a log, dreaming of the wedding of Camacho,[102] and snoring to raise the rafters. This is the liberty that they defend like life itself.

---

himself at the time of the vote on the principle of papal infallibility rather than either betray his own views or come into direct conflict with the Church.

99. An extralegal criminal tribunal in Medieval Germany that used methods of torture in secret proceedings.

100. Bellarmine (1542–1641), Italian cardinal. Caesare Baronius (1538–1607), ecclesiastical historian and cardinal.

101. Galileo Galilei (1564–1642), Italian astronomer, mathematician, and physicist, was warned not to hold or teach the heliocentric system of the universe but continued to do so, which led to his trial and incarceration by the Inquisition.

102. An episode in Cervantes' *Don Quixote,* Part II, chs. XX–XXI. An extraordinary feast accompanied Camacho's wedding.

José Martí
(Cuba)

José Julián Martí y Pérez (1853–1895), one of the most famous, prolific, versatile, and talented of all Latin American writers, had humble beginnings. He was born in Havana, Cuba, to Mariano Martí y Navarro, a rope-maker's son who had come to Cuba as a sergeant in the Spanish army, and Leonor Pérez y Cabrera of Spain. He was brother to seven sisters and husband to Carmen Zayas Bazán, with whom he had a son. The marriage ultimately fell apart in 1890, the casualty of Martí's revolutionary activities and their unhappy consequences. Martí devoted his life and his talents in poetry, journalism, and essay writing to freeing Cuba of Spanish colonial rule and keeping her free from the control of any other country, particularly the United States.

Martí studied at the Colegio de San Pablo, whose director, Rafael María de Mendive, was a revolutionary poet and journalist. Mendive, who was ultimately arrested for political activities, was one of the important early influences on Martí. When the Ten Years War broke out against Spain in 1868, the fifteen-year-old Martí wrote a patriotic drama in verse form, "Abdala," glorifying the revolution and the revolutionaries, which was published in Mendive's journal, *La Patria Libre*. He also wrote a sonnet, "10 de Octubre," during that year, which was published clandestinely. Mendive was soon exiled, and Martí was arrested and condemned to six years of hard labor for treason, having written an anti-Spanish letter with one of his friends. Although he only served six months of the treason sentence in hard labor, he was sent on to another prison for a while and, finally, in 1871, exiled to Spain. Even so, the hard labor had ruined him physically. In Spain, between 1871 and 1874, he studied at the universities of Madrid and Zaragoza and continued his political activities, publishing a pamphlet denouncing political imprisonment in Cuba.

Once he had earned his bachelor of arts degree and obtained his license in civil law, Martí left Spain for Mexico City, spending two years there as a journalist and obtaining some recognition as a literary figure. But that move was just the first in a virtual odyssey. His journeys included two visits to Mexico, a professorial position in Guatemala, two short stays in Cuba, exile in Spain, a professorial position in Venezuela, and two sojourns in the United States, the last from 1881 to 1895. During this latter period in the United States he often visited cities with large Cuban populations, trying to inspire another war for Cuban independence. He was a correspondent for numerous newspapers, both in Latin America and the United States. His articles showed that he admired some sides of life in America but disliked others. He especially began to fear U.S. expansionist tendencies, which he followed closely from his position as consul in the United States for Uruguay, Argentina, and Paraguay. When U.S. secretary of state James G. Blaine called a Pan-American conference in Washington, D.C., in 1889–1890, ostensibly to build a community of interest among all American countries, Martí exposed it, in a damning two-part article in Argentina's prestigious *La Nación,* as a veiled attempt to expand U.S. interests into Latin America.

In 1891, Martí began to devote himself exclusively to preparations for revolution in Cuba. In May, he published his last correspondence piece in *La Nación.* In October, he resigned his consular posts and his presidency of the Sociedad Literaria Hispanoamericana. In visits to Tampa and Cayo Hueso, Florida, and other cities with Cuban exile communities, he gave speeches outlining his revolutionary and republican ideals for Cuba. In 1894 he went to Mexico looking for assistance and funds. By the beginning of 1895, it was clear the revolution was just a matter of days away. On February 24, the war broke out in certain parts of Cuba, and on the 25th Martí and Máximo Gómez issued the *Manifiesto de Montecristi* (translated as *Manifesto of Montecristi*) announcing the new revolution. On May 19, on the island of Cuba, José Martí was killed instantly as he rushed on horseback to the front lines to do battle with the Spaniards. He had just turned 42.

"Nuestra América" (translated as "Our America"), the work that follows, is one of Martí's most famous pieces of writing. It first appeared in the journal *La Revista Ilustrada de Nueva York* in 1891 and shortly thereafter in the journal *El Partido Liberal* of Mexico.

Further Reading

Alemany, Carmen, Ramiro Muñoz, José Carlos Rouira, eds. *José Martí: Historia y literatura ante el fin del siglo XIX.* Alicante, Spain: Universidad de Alicante, 1997.

Canales, José Ferrer. *Martí y Hostos.* San Juan: Centro de Estudios Avanzados de Puerto Rico y el Caribe, 1990.

Guerra, Lillian. *The Myth of José Martí: Conflicting Nationalisms in Early Twentieth-Century Cuba.* Chapel Hill, N.C.: University of North Carolina Press, 2005.

Kirk, John M. *José Martí: Mentor of the Cuban Nation.* Tampa, Fla.: University of South Florida Press, 1983.

Martí, José. *Obras completas.* 28 vols. Havana: Editorial de Cuba, 1963–1973.

Montero, Oscar. *José Martí: An Introduction.* New York: Palgrave Macmillan, 2004.

Ripoll, Carlos. *José Martí, the United States, and the Marxist Interpretation of Cuban History.* New Brunswick, N.J.: Transaction Books, 1984.

Rodríguez, Luis. *Re-reading José Martí: One Hundred Years Later.* Albany, N.Y.: State University of New York, 1999.

Sacoto, Antonio. *José Martí (1853): Estudios y antología en el sesquicentenario de su nacimiento.* Quito: Casa de la Cultura Ecuatoriana, 2003.

"Our America" (1891)

The vain villager believes the whole world is his village, and so long as he can stay on as mayor, or annoy the rival who stole his girlfriend, or see that his savings are growing in his piggy bank, he will continue to consider the universal order good, unaware of the giants in seven-league boots who can grind him underfoot, or of the battle of comets in the heavens, comets that travel unconsciously through the air gulping down worlds. What remains of the village in America must wake up. These are not times for sleeping with the covers over our heads, but rather with weapons for pillows, like the self-confident men of Juan de Castellanos[1]—the weapons of the mind, which triumph over other weapons. Trenches of ideas are worth more than trenches of stone.

No prow can cut through a cloud of ideas. A radical idea, billowing at just the right time, may, like the mystic flag of the last judgment, stop a squadron of battleships. Peoples who do not yet know one another must hurry to become acquainted, like peoples who are about to fight together. Those who shake their fists at each other, like jealous brothers who both want the same parcel of land, or the brother with a small house who envies the brother with a better house, have to join hands so that they become one. Those who, under the protection of a criminal tradition, have cut away the land of their conquered brother, of the brother punished far beyond his guilt, using a sword stained with the same blood from both their veins, should return the land to their brother if they do not want people to call them thieves. The honorable person does not charge money to repay debts of honor, at so much per slap. We can no longer be a people of leaves, living in the air, in the treetops loaded with flowers, crackling or humming, depending on how the caprice of light caresses it or storms beat and devastate it; the trees must form ranks so that the giant in seven-league boots cannot pass! It is the hour of reckoning and for advancing together united, and we must move forward phalanx-like, as compact as the silver deep in the Andes.

Only babies born in the seventh month[2] will lack courage. Those who have no faith in their land are men of seven months. Because they lack courage, they deny its existence in others. They cannot climb the high tree with their feeble arms—their arms of painted fingernails and bracelets, their arms from Madrid or Paris—and they say that the tree cannot be climbed. We must load the boats with those harmful insects that gnaw away the bone of the fatherland that nourishes them. If they are Parisians or Madrileños, let them go to the Prado[3] by lamplight or to Tortoni[4] in a top hat. These sons of a carpenter, who are ashamed that their father is a carpenter! These people born in America, who are ashamed of

---

1. Juan de Castellanos (1522–1607), Spanish chronicler, author of *Elegías de varones ilustres de Indias,* an epic poem of the conquest of the New World.

2. *Sietemesino,* born seven months after conception, i.e., prematurely.

3. Paseo del Prado, a fashionable street in Madrid, Spain.

4. A well-known Parisian café of the times.

the mother who reared them because they wear an Indian apron[5] and—those rogues!—renounce their ailing mother and leave her alone in her sick bed! Well, which one is the real man? He who stays with the mother to cure her illness, or he who puts her to work out of sight and lives from her support in putrid lands, wearing his wormy tie, cursing the womb that bore him, displaying the label of traitor on the back of his paper dress coat? These sons of our America, which must save herself with her Indians and is going from less to more; these deserters who take up guns in the armies of North America, which is drowning its Indians in blood and is going from more to less! These delicate ones who are men but do not wish to do the work of men! Did Washington, who made this land for them, go away to live with the English, to live with the English during those years when he saw them coming against his own land? These "incredibles" of honor, who roll their honor through foreign soil, just as the "incredibles" of the French Revolution,[6] dancing and gloating, used to roll their *R*s!

And in what country can a man feel more pride than in our suffering American republics, raised up among the mute masses of Indians, on the bloody arms of a hundred apostles to the sound of struggle between the book and processional candlestick? Never, in less historic time, have nations so advanced and so solid been created from such disparate elements. The arrogant man believes that this land was made to serve as his pedestal because he has a facile pen or colorful speech, and he accuses his native republic of incompetence and hopelessness because its virgin jungles do not provide him with endless means to travel the world as a famous political boss, driving Persian ponies and spilling champagne. The fault is not in the emerging country, which seeks forms that suit it and a useful kind of greatness, but rather in those who want to rule original peoples, which have come together in unique and sudden ways, with laws inherited from four centuries of free practice in the United States, of nineteen centuries of monarchy in France. The *llanero's* colt does not come to a halt with a command from Hamilton.[7] The stagnant blood of the Indian race does not quicken with a phrase from Sièyes.[8] To govern well, one must pay attention to the way things are in the place to be governed; and the person who governs well in America is not he who knows how the German or the Frenchman is governed, but rather he who knows the elements that make up his country and how he can gather them together to arrive—by methods and institutions born of the country itself—at

---

5. The term is *delantal,* which is elusive because it refers not only to women's aprons but also to aprons worn by workmen and servants. It may also refer to the apron worn by members of Masonic orders.

6. The "incredibles" (*incroyables*), dandies of Revolutionary France, who were devoted to radical politics and high fashion in equal measure.

7. Alexander Hamilton (1755–1804), one of the founding fathers of the United States who served as secretary of the treasury under George Washington. *Llanero,* a plainsman of the wild plains in the south of Venezuela, one of the legendarily free lands of South America.

8. Emmanuel-Joseph Sièyes (1748–1836), French revolutionary and statesman, author in 1789 of the famous pamphlet, "What Is the Third Estate?"

that desirable state where each man knows himself and is active and everyone enjoys the abundance that nature provided for all those among the people who make the land fertile with their work and defend it with their lives. Government must be born of the country. The government's spirit must be that of the country. The government's form must conform to the country's natural constitution. Government is nothing other than the balance of the country's natural elements.

In America, for that reason, natural man has triumphed over the imported book. Natural men have triumphed over artificially learned men. The native mestizo has triumphed over the exotic creole.[9] There is no battle between civilization and barbarism, but rather between false erudition and nature. Natural man is good, and he respects and prizes superior intelligence, unless that superior intelligence uses his obedience to harm or offend him by disregarding him, which is something natural man does not pardon, disposed as he is to recover by force the respect of anyone who insults his sensibilities or harms his interest. By working with these disdained natural elements, the tyrants of America have risen to power, and these tyrants have fallen as soon as they have betrayed the natural elements. The republics have paid in tyrannies for their inability to know the country's true elements, to derive the form of government from them and to govern with them. Among a new people, governing means creating.

In peoples made up of cultured and uncultured individuals, where the cultured ones do not learn the art of governing, the uncultured will govern because they are used to attacking and resolving doubts with their fists. The uncultured mass is lazy and timid in matters of intellect and wants to be governed well; but if the government hurts it, it will shake the government off and govern itself. How is it possible for those who govern to come out of universities if no university in America teaches the basics of the art of government, which is the analysis of the elements characteristic of America's peoples? Our youths go into the world wearing Yankee or French glasses and aspire to rule by guesswork a people they do not know. Entrance to a career in politics should be denied to those who are ignorant of the rudiments of politics. The prize in literary competitions should not go to the best ode, but rather to the best study of the political factors in the country where one lives. In the newspaper, in the school, in the academy, the study of the actual factors of the country must be carried forward. Knowing them is enough, without blindfolds, without beating around the bush; because he who deliberately or unknowingly sets aside a part of the truth ultimately fails because of the truth he lacked, which grows when neglected and destroys whatever is built in its absence. Solving a problem after coming to know its elements is easier than solving the problem without knowing them. The natural man comes, outraged and strong, and destroys the accumulated justice of books, because it is not administered compatibly with the country's obvious needs. To know is to solve. To know the country and to govern it coherently with that

---

9. "Mestizo," a person of mixed racial background (typically part indigenous, part European); "creole," a person of Spanish descent born in the Americas.

knowledge is the only way to liberate it from tyrannies. The European university must yield to the American university. The history of America from the Incas to the present must be taught thoroughly, even if the history of the archons[10] of Greece goes untaught. Our Greece is preferable to the Greece that is not ours. We need ours more. National politicians must replace foreign ones. Let the world be grafted onto our republics; but our republics must be the trunk. And let the vanquished pedant be silent, for there is no fatherland in which man can have more pride than our suffering American republics.

With our roots in the rosary, with the white heads and dark bodies of Indian and creole, we came boldly into the world of nations. With the standard of the Virgin we set out to win liberty. In Mexico, a priest, a few lieutenants, and a woman raised the republic on the shoulders of the Indians.[11] A Spanish cleric under cover of his cape teaches French liberty to a few magnificent baccalaureate students, who place the Spanish general at the head of Central America against Spain.[12] With monarchical vestments and the sign of the sun on their chest, the Venezuelans in the north and the Argentines in the south applied themselves to building peoples into nations. When the two heroes collided and the continent began to tremble, one, and not the lesser, relinquished the reins.[13] And because heroism in peace, being less glorious, is scarcer than in war; because for a man it is easier to die with honor than think with order; because it is easier to govern when feelings are excited and unanimous than it is to set scattered, arrogant, alien, or ambitious thoughts straight after the fighting is done; because the powers that had been crushed by the epic attack were undermining, with the feline cunning of the species and the weight of reality, the structure that had raised—in the harsh and singular regions of our mestizo America, among people with bare feet and long Parisian jackets—the flag of the peoples nourished by wise government in the continuing practice of reason and liberty; because the hierarchical makeup of the colonies resisted the democratic organization of the republic, or the bow-tie cities left the riding-boot countryside out in the cold, or the book-driven redeemers did not understand that the revolution, having triumphed with the soul of the land unleashed by the savior's voice, would have to govern with the soul of the land, not against it nor without it; for all these reasons America

---

10. Officers of state in Athens and other Greek cities.

11. The priest is Miguel Hidalgo y Costilla (1753–1811), who launched Mexico's revolution of independence in the town of Dolores. Josefa Ortiz de Domínguez (1768–1829) wife of the mayor of Querétaro, warned the revolutionaries that Spanish forces were gathering to subdue them. Most of the footsoldiers for independence were Indian or of Indian descent.

12. The general in charge of Spanish royalist forces in Mexico, Agustín Iturbide, was persuaded to switch sides in 1821 and quickly led Mexico (which at that time encompassed Central America) to independence.

13. Símon Bolívar (1783–1830) and José de San Martín (1778–1850) led revolutions of independence from opposite ends of South America. They met in July in 1822 in Guayaquil, Ecuador, at which meeting San Martín gave up his title, Protector of Peru, and left South America.

began to suffer, and she suffers still from the fatigue of reconciling the discordant and hostile elements that she inherited from a despotic and perverse colonizer and the imported ideas and forms that have delayed logical government for lack of local reality. Kept disjointed for three centuries by an authority that denied the right of man to exercise his reason, the continent—neglecting or ignoring the ignorant peoples who helped it to redeem itself—entered into a government that had reason as its base, the reason common to all in matters concerning all, and not the university reason of some over the rural reason of others. The problem of independence was not the change of forms but, rather, the change of spirit.

Common cause had to be made with the oppressed to secure a system opposed to the interests and ruling habits of the oppressors. Frightened by the powder flash, the tiger returns at night to the place of his prey. He dies with flames shooting from his eyes and grasping the air with his claws. He cannot be heard coming because he comes on velvet paws. When the prey awakens, the tiger is upon him. The colony continued living in the republic, and our America is saving itself from its great errors—the arrogance of the capital cities, the blind triumph of the scorned country people, the excessive importation of foreign methods and ideas, the unjust and discourteous scorn for the aboriginal race— through the superior virtue, nourished by the necessary blood, of the republic that struggles against the colony. The tiger waits behind each tree, curled up in every corner. He will die with his claws in the air, flames shooting from his eyes.

But "these countries will be saved," as Rivadavia the Argentine[14] announced, he who was so urbane in rude times; a silk sheaf does not suit a machete, nor in a country that was won with a spear can the spear be thrown aside, because it becomes angry and takes its place in the door of Iturbide's Congress "to have them make the blond man emperor."[15] These countries will be saved because, with the spirit of moderation that seems to rule in the continent of light, through the serene harmony of nature and through the influence of critical reading that, in Europe, has replaced the superficial and propagandistic reading on which the previous generation gorged itself, there is being born to America in these real times, the real man.

We were a vision, with an athlete's chest, a dandy's hands, and a child's face. We were a masquerade, with English trousers, a Parisian vest, a North American overcoat, and a Spanish bullfighter's hat. The Indian, mute, walked all around us, and went away to the mountain, to the mountain's crest, to baptize his children. Alone and unknown, the Black, always being watched, sang the music of his heart in the night between the waves and the wild beasts. The countryman, the creator, blind with indignation, turned against the scornful city, against his

---

14. Bernardino Rivadavia (1780–1845), Argentine politician who fought in the revolution of independence, elected president of the republic in 1826.

15. Agustín de Iturbide (1783–1824), Mexican soldier and statesman, leader in the Mexican independence movement. He had himself proclaimed president of the governing junta and, in 1822, after being proclaimed emperor by his soldiers, abolished the representative body and governed as a dictator.

creation. We were epaulets and academic gowns in countries that came into the world with sandals on their feet and headbands on their brows. The stroke of genius would have been to use the heart's charity and the founders' boldness to unite the headband and the academic gown, to release the Indian, to make more space for the able Black, to tailor liberty to the bodies of those who rebelled and triumphed in liberty's name. We were left with the judge, and the general, and the man of letters, and the prebendary. The angelic youth, as if from the arms of an octopus, threw its head crowned with clouds heavenward to fall with glory, sterile. Natural people, driven by instinct, blind with triumph, carried off the golden staffs of office. Neither the European book nor the Yankee book provided the key to the Spanish American enigma. They tried hatred, and each year the countries came to less. Tired of useless hatred, of the opposition of the book to the spear, of reason to the processional candlestick, of the city to the country, of the impossible rule of the divided urban castes over the tempestuous or inert natural nation, we begin almost unknowingly to try love. The people stand up and greet each other. "How are we?" they ask each other; and they start telling each other how they are. When a problem appears in Cojímar, they do not seek its solution in Danzig. The frock coats are still from France, but the thought is beginning to be from America. The youth of America roll up their shirtsleeves, sink their hands into the dough, and make it rise with the leavening of their sweat. They understand that there is too much imitation and that salvation lies in creating. "Create" is this generation's password. Wine of plantains; and if it comes out sour, it's our wine! It is understood that the forms of a country's government must accommodate themselves to its natural elements; that absolute ideas, so as not to collapse because of an error in form, must be put into relative forms; that liberty, to be viable, must be sincere and full; that if the republic does not open its arms to everyone and move forward with everyone, the republic will die. The tiger from within enters through a fissure, and so will the tiger from without. The general holds the march of the cavalry to the infantry's gait. If he leaves the infantry behind, the enemy will surround the cavalry. Politics is strategy. Peoples should live in continual self-criticism, because criticism is health—but with a single heart and single mind. Bend down to the unfortunate ones and lift them up in your arms! Melt clotted America with the heart's fire! Drive the natural blood of the country boiling and bubbling through the veins! Standing, with workers' joyful eyes, the new American men salute one another, one people to another. From the direct study of nature natural statesmen arise. They read to apply, not to copy. Economists study the difficulty at its source. Orators begin to temper their words. Playwrights bring native characters to the stage. The academies discuss practical subjects. Poetry shears its Zorrilla-like locks[16] and hangs its red vest from the glorious tree. Prose, sparkling and refined, is idea-laden. Governors in the republics of Indians learn Indian.

---

16. José Zorrilla (1817–1893), Spanish writer and poet of extensive influence and known for wearing his hair long.

America is saving herself from all her dangers. Over some republics the octopus still sleeps. Others, by the law of equilibrium, are plunging in to recover the lost centuries with mad, sublime speed. Others, forgetting that Juárez[17] rode in a mule-drawn carriage, use the wind as their coach and soap bubbles for coachmen; poisonous luxury, enemy of liberty, corrupts the fickle man and opens the door to the foreigner. Others with the epic spirit of threatened independence refine their virile character. Others beget in predatory war against their neighbor the undisciplined troops that can devour them. But our America may face another danger that does not come from within, but rather from the difference in origins, methods, and interests between the continent's two elements, and the hour is near when an enterprising and powerful people draws close to our America demanding intimate relations, a people that does not know our America and scorns her. And as all virile peoples, self-made with rifle and law, love other virile peoples and love them only; as the hour of unrestraint and ambition—which North America might yet avoid by the ascendancy of the purest of her blood, or into which her vengeful and sordid masses, the tradition of conquest, and the self-interest of a skillful leader might thrust her—is not yet so close, even in the eyes of the most easily alarmed, that there is not time for the continuous and discreet demonstration of pride with which our America might be able to confront and turn North America away; as, in the eyes of the attentive peoples of the universe, North America's honor as a republic places a restraint on it, which childish provocation or ostentatious arrogance or the parricidal discord of our America must not remove, the urgent duty of our America is to show herself as she is, one in soul and intent, rapid victor over a suffocating past, stained only by the fertilizing blood that the struggle with ruins extracts from fighting hands and from the veins that our masters left punctured. The scorn of the formidable neighbor that does not know our America is the worst danger she faces; and it is urgent—because the foreseen day is near—that the neighbor know our America, that it know our America soon, so that it not scorn her. From ignorance, perhaps, North America would come, coveting our America. From respect, as soon as it knows our America, it would take its hands off her. We must have faith in the best in man and distrust the worst in him. We must give opportunity to the best so that it might reveal itself and prevail over the worst. If not, the worst prevails. The peoples have to have one pillory for those who stir up pointless hatreds, and another for those who do not tell them the truth in time.

There is no racial hatred, because there are no races. Feeble thinkers, thinkers of dim lights, string together and reheat bookshelf races that the just traveler and the friendly observer vainly seek in nature's justice, where man's universal identity appears in victorious love and turbulent appetite. The soul, equal and eternal, emanates from bodies diverse in form and color. He who foments and spreads conflict and hatred among the races sins against humanity. But in the

---

17. Benito Juárez (1806–1872), Zapotecan Indian, Mexican politician, served as governor of Oaxaca and president of the republic and issued the wide-ranging laws of the Reform.

proximity of other diverse peoples, in the kneading of the peoples, innate and active characteristics are condensed—characteristics of ideas and habits, of expansion and acquisition, of vanity and avarice—which, from a dormant state of national prejudices could, in a period of internal disorder or from rash growth of the cumulative characteristics of the country, turn into a serious threat to the isolated and weak neighboring lands that the strong country declares transitory and inferior. To think is to serve. Nor should we allow a village-like antipathy to impute an innate and deadly wickedness to the continent's blond nation because they do not speak our language, nor see their homes as we see ours, nor resemble us in political defects that are different from ours, nor think very highly of the quick-tempered and dark-skinned men, nor look charitably from their still poorly secured eminence on those who, less favored by history, ascend by heroic stretches the road that republics travel. Nor should we conceal the obvious facts of the problem that can be resolved through timely study and tacit and urgent union of the continental soul, bringing centuries of peace. Because the unanimous hymn already sounds, the present generation carries industrious America on its shoulders down the road sanctioned by its sublime fathers; from the Bravo to the Magellans, the Great Cemí,[18] seated on the back of the condor has sown, throughout the romantic nations of the continent and the suffering isles of the sea, the seeds of the new America!

---

18. The Rio Bravo/The Rio Grande, the U.S.-Mexican border; the Strait of Magellan, separating South America from Tierra del Fuego and other islands south of the continent; the Great Cemí, the traditional totemic symbol of the Taino peoples of Puerto Rico.

Soledad Acosta de Samper
(Colombia)

Soledad Acosta de Samper (1833–1913) is considered the most important woman Colombian writer of the nineteenth century and among the most talented writers of her generation, male or female. The only child of historian, geographer, and patriot of independence, Joaquín Acosta y Pérez de Guzmán, and Carolina Kemble Rou, Acosta de Samper received an education uncommon for girls of that time. She first studied in Bogotá in the Colegio de la Merced, but at age twelve, she went to Halifax, Nova Scotia, Canada, where she continued her education for a year while living with her maternal grandmother. She next moved to Paris with her parents, where, from 1846 to 1850, she received her formal education in several schools and where, with her father, she attended literary and scientific gatherings, giving her access to some of the most important writers in Europe.

Returning to Colombia, she married the writer and politician José María Samper Agudelo in 1855. They moved to Paris in 1858, and Acosta de Samper began to publish diverse works under the pseudonyms of Aldebarán, Renato, Bertilda, and Andina. She began her public career in 1858 as a correspondent in Paris, later in Lima, Peru, for the two most important Latin American literary journals of the time: *El Mosaico* and *La Biblioteca de Señoritas*. While in Paris, she also helped her husband with the journals he edited and sent some of their collaborations to Peruvian dailies. In 1862, she and her family, now with four daughters, moved to Lima, where her husband had been named editor-in-chief of the daily *El Comercio*. While there, Acosta de Samper and her husband established *La Revista Americana*. When they returned to Bogotá, Acosta de Samper's husband was named a member of Congress and rose to become one of the most important people in Colombian politics. Acosta de Samper began to publish short stories in literary periodicals and novels in installments. The first of these was "Dolores, cuadros de la vida de una mujer," which appeared in *El Mensajero* in 1867. Her first book, *Novelas y cuadros de la vida Suramericana*, appeared in 1869; it was a collection of narratives she had published in various periodicals, mostly under pseudonyms. With the publication of *José Antonio Galán: Episodios de la vida de los comuneros en 1870* (1870), she moved into the genre of the historical novel. Plays like *Las víctimas de la guerra* (1884) followed, and, finally, she began to write histories, the first of which was the *Biografía del General Joaquín París*, which won an award in a contest in Bogotá (1883).

Her works for women and the family are noteworthy. Acosta de Samper founded and edited the biweekly publication *La Mujer*, published exclusively for women. During 1878 and 1881, she published five volumes of *La Mujer*. In 1884, she founded a monthly review, *La Familia*, and in 1888, she began to edit *El Domingo de la Familia Cristiana*. The French publishing house, Garnier, published three of her books on sociological topics pertaining to women: *La mujer en la sociedad moderna* (1895), *Consejos a las mujeres* (1896), and *Conversaciones y lecturas familiares sobre historia, biografía, crítica, literatura, ciencias y conocimientos útiles* (1896) all of them adapting the ideas of the Scottish Samuel Smiles in his book *Self Help* to the education of women.

Acosta de Samper moved again to Paris with her mother and her daughters in 1888 after the death of her husband. In 1892 she was named Colombia's official representative at the ninth international congress of students of American studies in Spain and represented Colombia in the commemorative congresses of the fourth centennial of the discovery of America. There she presented various *Memorias,* which won a prize. She also published a novel in French and translated two works into Spanish from English.

Acosta de Samper was a prolific writer. She has 194 works attributed to her, including more than 20 novels, almost 50 other brief narrations, and hundreds of articles on various themes. The essay that follows, "The Mission of the Woman Writer in Spanish America," appeared in *La mujer en la sociedad moderna* (1895).

Further Reading

Acosta de Samper, Soledad. *Diario íntimo y otros escritos.* Bogotá: Alcaldía Mayor of Bogotá: Instituto Destrital Cultura y Turismo, 2004.

———. *Una nueva lectura.* Bogotá: Fondo Cultural Cafetero, 1988.

Gómez Ocampo, Gilberto. *Entre María y la vorágine: La literatura colombiana finisecular (1886–1903).* Bogotá: Fondo Cultural Cafetero, 1998.

Gonzales Ascorra, Martha Irene. *La evolución de la conciencia feminina a través de las novelas de Gertrudis Gómez de Avellaneda, Soledad Acosta de Samper y Mercedes Cabello de Carbonera.* New York: Peter Lang, 1997.

Jaramillo, María Mercedes. *Y las mujeres?: Ensayos sobre literatura colombiana.* Medellín, Colombia: Editorial Universidad de Antioquia, 1991.

Miller, Yvette E., and Charles M. Tatum, eds. *Latin American Women Writers: Yesterday and Today.* Pittsburgh: Latin American Literary Review, 1977.

"The Mission of the Woman Writer in Spanish America" (1895)

Translated by Mary Louise Pratt[1]

The question that I propose—I will not say to elucidate, for I lack the strength to do so—but to touch in passing, is first of all this: What is the mission of

---

1. Soledad Acosta de Samper, "The Mission of the Woman Writer in Spanish America," translated by Mary Louise Pratt, in *Rereading the Spanish American Essay: Translations of 19th*

woman in the world? Undoubtedly, to moderate customs, to promote morality and Christianity in societies—that is, to give them a civilization adequate to the needs of the time and, in the process, to prepare humanity for the future. But now let us ask another question: What is the mission of the woman writer in the New World?

Let us first examine what Mr. Varigny says in his volume on *Women in the United States.* "Every race," he writes,

> has formed its own ideal of what woman should be. Ideas, like languages, vary; let me explain my own thinking. For the *French,* woman personifies and incarnates all the delicate and exquisite perfections of civilization; for the *Spaniard,* she is a virgin in a church; for the *Italian,* a flower in a garden; for the *Turk,* a device for pleasure [*mueble de dicha*]. Let us not forget the artless complaint of the young Arab woman: "Before he was my husband he kissed the ground I walked on, and now he hitches me up with his ass to his plow and makes me work." The *Englishman,* precursor of the American, sees in woman above all the mother of his children and the mistress of his house. On leaving England, the women who went to live in North America did not leave their customs and traditions in Europe. All emigrants, rich or poor, carry a world with them, an invisible world of ideas, the result of their early upbringing, the legacy of previous generations, things they never leave behind even when they are leaving behind everything, things they reverently conserve.

Thus for North Americans the ideal is the same as for the English, though in North America the woman is even more the mistress of her house than in England.

The Spanish American, more advanced in these matters than his Spanish ancestors, sees in woman something more than "a virgin in a church." It has been observed that in all the republics formed after independence, efforts have been made from the outset to give women a better education and a broader role in social life. Governments have made great efforts to redeem us from the lower status—let us say the lowest rather than lower—to which colonial customs condemned us daughters of the Spaniards.

In Colombia, for example, young women receive a fairly progressive education at the normal school and afterward become primary school teachers for both sexes. It has been observed that in primary education they are greatly superior to male teachers in their level of learning, orderliness, conduct, and so on. In Bogotá there is a Music Academy for girls that has produced first-class teachers; in the past there was an Academy of Drawing and Painting in which the female students achieved equally with the young men. The School of Telegraphy, directed by a lady dedicated to teaching this subject, has produced very talented employees who serve the government in many national offices. The School of Medicine in Bogotá has admitted young women who attend classes and are

and 20th Century Women's Essays, edited by Doris Meyer (Austin, Tex.: University of Texas Press), pp. 71–76. Reprinted by permission of the University of Texas Press.

highly respected by the male students. A broader horizon is thus opening up for women's aspirations in Colombia and in other Spanish American nations, as we have seen elsewhere in this book. Soon it will come to pass in these republics as in North America that women's influence will be considered essential to the successful functioning of society.

Once woman has conquered the important position she now occupies in Spanish American society, she must reflect on that position and recognize what is expected of the influence she will exercise in these new countries, which now seem to be leaving behind the period of political turbulence and conspiracy that obscured the social horizon of the new republics for more than eighty years. She must dedicate herself to work, to a judicious unfolding of progress. We must reflect with maturity on the role women will play in the new order of things that is emerging.

These governments have concluded the period of ferment that, according to the laws of nature, is essential to produce *a nation* out of heterogeneous, distinct, and arbitrary elements. "I would compare," said Carnot (the father of the man who became president of France), "a revolutionary country to our great wine harvest barrels: In the vat of the passions everything stirs around from top to bottom, from the most generous of wines to the most disgusting sediments; but the fermentation purifies and ennobles the liquor."

From this time forward we will doubtless witness public upheavals, changes of government and perhaps of entire political systems, but our nations will be safe in the arms of civilization, whose laws will prevent them from falling behind on the paths of progress they now so knowingly traverse, and the governments will quickly reconstruct themselves on solid and respectable footing.

The United States, whose prosperity so astounds, should provide Spanish America with wholesome examples in this regard. And in that country, which finds itself ahead of all others in material advances, woman enjoys an immense and acknowledged influence. Why is this? Because she is respected by all. And why is she respected? Because her actions, her character, her moral courage make her respectable; because, besides fulfilling her duties as wife and mother, she is genuinely and positively the companion of man. She is not a flower, a dream, a toy, a decoration, a servant. She is the equal of her husband and her brother, through the soundness of her education, her noble strength of character, her spiritual gifts. Hence all careers are open to her, except one, the least desirable—that of politics. In North America, not only do women work as public employees, lawyers, doctors, farmers, bankers, and so on, but they also compete with men in these positions as equals. They are given nothing as a favor, they are praised only when they deserve it; they are given awards and positions of honor only because they are more entitled to hold them than any man. This is true justice, and we should aspire to it as well if we wish to exercise a genuinely positive influence on our fellow citizens. But to deserve this justice we must work seriously, renounce special treatment, demand strict justice and nothing more.

Among the nations of the Spanish race, women are still regarded as inferior beings, as children, and whenever they raise themselves slightly above mediocrity they are praised with embarrassing exaggeration. Nevertheless, we should reject certain kinds of adulation almost as an offense, for they confirm that so little was expected of us that anything we do involving learning or talent is alien to our sex and must be applauded as an uncommon rarity. Let us not pride ourselves, then, with passing praise that is soon gone with the wind, for it has no weight. Let us attend to the mission that we ourselves must undertake.

The moral redemption [*moralización*] of Spanish American societies, soured by a long series of revolutions, disorders, and bad governments, is undoubtedly in the hands of women whose influence, as mothers of the future generations, as teachers of the young in their early years, and as writers disseminating good ideas, will save society and set it forth on the right path.

But, it will be said, though there are women writers in Spanish America, in fact they are so few; and they rely so little on their intellectual faculties that they could not possibly have even the smallest influence on the workings of society. So it seems in fact, and yet there would be more women writers if they were less timid, if they convinced themselves that they have a beneficent mission to carry out—women of character always want to be useful, and they forget obstacles if they are convinced they have a chance to do good.

In Colombia at least, women are highly respected, and I trust that other South American republics will not, please God!, repeat the situation in Spain where, in the words of the renowned writer and diplomat Don Juan Valera, "any woman who tries to be a writer must be more courageous than the nun Alferez or even Pentesilea herself. . . . Every dandy she happens to meet," he adds, "will be an Achilles against her, more to kill her than to weep for her beauty after death. Leaving mythologies aside, I mean that in literature, women writers are looked upon like those odd older bachelors, somehow abnormal, disorderly, and improper, posing problems for the prospects of a good marriage, etc., etc."

No, among us in Spanish America, it is not like this, and a woman who writes for the press is not looked down upon in society. On the contrary, she is listened to and respected (unless she is being undermined out of envy). This respect must arise from the fact that our women poets have all been mistresses of their households as well. They have not neglected this role merely because in their idle hours they scribble on paper. Thus they have readily been permitted, and even encouraged, to write verse and prose, and they are praised highly by the press—too highly, as we said earlier, because such praise deludes the novices.

Once the career of writer is open and women can embrace it freely, all who feel called to it should focus on one thing: The good they can do with their pens. If God has given them intellectual capacities, let them use those abilities to push the cart of civilization in their own particular way. Let us not imitate the fashion today in foreign literatures, especially the French; let us depict not the vices of others but rather the virtues of our own homeland. Providence did not endow America with the riches of the most beautiful nature in the world in order for us to recoil from describing it; God has not put us in these new countries struggling to form themselves so that we will neglect their history and customs and the teachings to be distilled from them.

While the masculine side of society deals with politics, remakes laws, attends to material progress, and orders social life, would it not be truly great for the feminine side to undertake the creation of a new literature? A *sui generis* American literature, American in its descriptions, in its inclinations, doctrinaire, civilizing, artistic, beneficial to the soul; a literature so beautiful and so pure that its works could appear in all the salons of the countries where the language of Cervantes is spoken; a literature that could be placed in the hands of our daughters, that would elevate the ideas of whoever read it, that would instruct and at the same time display the newness and originality of the countries in which it was born. In this literature of our dreams would be found no descriptions of crimes or scenes depicting the wicked ways imported to our societies from the corrupt civilization of Europe. For whatever the modern writers might say, the novel should not simply be the exact description of what happens in real life among degenerate people; the novel can be interesting *despite* being moral. It should graphically depict human existence and at the same time the ideal, what should be, what men and women could be if they conducted themselves well.

What greater mission for a woman than conveying gratifying and heartwarming lessons to society? Take note that all the works that still hang from the branch of great literature not only possess moral grounding but also use an elegant, polished language that awakens only pure and beautiful images. The exceptions to this rule are few, and they confirm it.

Our countries are beginning to take shape. Like the sapling that can grow straight or crooked, we must see to it that our ways of life develop straight and well formed, and that we the women writers of the new South American world can present ourselves with the same distinction, the same healthy and altruistic vitality as our counterparts in North America.

In societies that have not only reached maturity but have begun to slide down the slope of decay, writers can stop along the way to pick the poisonous flowers, point out the swamps, describe the cesspools of vice they encounter. There, one finds readers of all classes, and many whose intelligence, perverted by the excesses of civilization, requires a dish spiced with descriptions ever more violently exaggerated and pictures that move their sensibilities dulled by a refinement bordering on corruption. The ripest fruit has already begun to rot. But our societies have not reached this point. They are growing up, and they require an intellectual sustenance that is healthy and hygienic. What a glory it would be for American women if they could offer our incipient societies the literature they need to live with their souls, after using their faculties to work for the material side of our social and political institutions!

We do not believe that one morally educates readers by putting in front of their eyes pictures of vice and corruption, even when afterwards one intends to point out the drawbacks of those vices. Readers devour the descriptions, their attentions so absorbed they often forget the moral of the story—but not the scenes of disorder and the bad examples—and care little about the punishment of vice.

274   *Soledad Acosta de Samper (Colombia)*

There exists a concern that the virtue and sacrifice of noble souls, the adventures and happenstance of good people cannot make an interesting plot, that only the arrows of love attract attention, provided they are sinful, that readers will enjoy only farfetched intrigues that offend modesty and should not be read by girls. But this is a concern and nothing more. The unified *truth* of an agreeable style will always be popular and last longer than any narrative that addresses those false, inconstant, frivolous passions that pass without a trace like fashions and are forgotten like the cut of last year's dress. No. The women writers of America must dedicate themselves seriously to making a lasting name for themselves, doing good with literary works written to fulfill the mission that I believe they have in the new Spanish American literature that is dawning.

Justo Sierra
(Mexico)

Justo Sierra Méndez (1848–1912), considered the greatest liberal thinker of the post-Reform era in Mexico, began his literary career as a romantic poet. While still quite young, he published poems in the periodical *El Globo*. From poetry, he moved into the literary essay, publishing his first in 1868. From there, he moved on to works on education and the improvement of Mexican intellectual life and edited various journals. He wrote for a number of periodicals, including *El Monitor Republicano, El Renacimiento, La Tribuna* and *El Federalista*. He came to public attention as a writer when he published his poems "Playera" and "Conversaciones del domingo" in *El Monitor Republicano* in 1868. But his greatest works were histories. The primary influence on his philosophical thought was positivism and, perhaps, the social evolutionary thought of Herbert Spencer, both of which inspired him to see Mexican history as movement in a linear and positive direction through distinct stages toward a time of perfection. Sierra's opposition to the Church, unlike the more focused views of earlier liberals, takes the form of regarding the superstitious elements of religion as vestiges of a stage of history through which Mexican culture and civilization has passed. His ideas on race fall into place in the same way. He views the future optimistically, in keeping with the concept that the future eventually improves on the past as it progresses toward perfection.

Sierra was born in the port city of Campeche to Justo Sierra O'Reilly, well-known attorney and intellectual, and Concepción Méndez Echazarreta. He attended the clerical Colegio de San Miguel Estrada and, when his family moved to Mérida, the Liceo Científico y Comercial in that city. He also attended the Liceo Franco Mexicano in Mexico City and later studied at the Jesuit Colegio de San Ildefonso. He received his law degree in 1871. Although he did practice law, he soon discovered that he preferred letters. He served as a deputy to the Congress several times and became a magistrate of the Supreme Court of Justice.

Sierra's public life focused on education. He taught history in the Escuela Nacional Preparatoria and there prepared the well-known *Compendio de historia* (1878), a widely known and respected textbook. He was one of the directors of the *Revista Nacional de Letras y Ciencias* in 1889–1890. President Porfirio Díaz named him undersecretary of education in the Secretaría de Justicia e Instrucción Pública y Bellas Artes (1901–1905) and, afterwards, he became its director/secretary (1905–1910). During this time Sierra reestablished the Universidad Nacional de México by bringing together the separate liberal arts colleges and integrating the curriculum. He saw the university as the center of what he referred to as the "mental revolution." He believed the only way to spread education, learning, and enlightened thought throughout society is to begin with an enlightened minority who takes that diffusion as its charge. He also supported intellectuals and artists, creating a higher council for public education, composed of well-known intellectuals and artists, whose duty was to revise plans and programs of study, methods, and books of instruction. He sent promising students like the artist Diego Rivera to Europe on scholarship. He reformed the Escuela Normal to prepare superior elementary teachers and founded a standard system of kindergartens. One of his great accomplishments was establishing primary schools all over Mexico, building on the legacy left by his predecessor, Gabino Barrera.

President Francisco Madero named Sierra minister plenipotentiary to Spain in 1912. When Sierra died in Spain that same year, his body was brought to Mexico and buried with great public honors. At the first centennial celebration of his birth, the national university named him "Maestro de América," and his remains were moved to the Rotonda de los Hombres Ilustres.

Sierra's best known work is *La evolución política del pueblo Mexicano* (1900–1902) (translated as *The Political Evolution of the Mexican People*), which traces the history of Mexico since the arrival of the Spaniards. This is one of the few examples of a positivist-influenced historical work. It traces Mexican history from the earliest times to Sierra's day, just before the 1910 Mexican Revolution. The selection that follows analyzes the presidency and character of Porfirio Díaz.

Further Reading

Dumas, Claude. *Justo Sierra y el México de su tiempo, 1848–1912.* 2 vols. Mexico, D.F.: Universidad Nacional Autónoma de México, 1986.

Hale, Charles. *Justo Sierra: Un liberal del porfiriato.* Mexico, D.F.: Fondo de Cultura Económica, 1997.

———. *The Transformation of Liberalism in Late Nineteenth-Century Mexico.* Princeton, N.J.: Princeton University Press, 1989.

Landa, Josu. *La idea de la universidad de Justo Sierra: Ensayo crítico.* Campeche, Mexico: Universidad Autónoma de Campeche, 1998.

Rivero Alvisa, Daisy. *Justo Sierra y la filosofía positivista en México.* Havana: Editorial de Ciencias Sociales, 1987.

Saez Pueyo, Carmen. *Justo Sierra: antecedentes del partido único en México.* Mexico, D.F.: Facultad de Ciencias Políticas y Sociales, Editorial Porrúa, 2001.

Sierra, Justo. *Obras completas.* 15 vols. Edited by Agustín Yáñez. Mexico, D.F.: Universidad Nacional Autónoma de México, 1948–1949.

Yáñez, Agustín. *Don Justo Sierra: Su vida, sus ideas y su obra.* Mexico, D.F.: Universidad Nacional Autónoma de México, Centro de Estudios Filosoficos, 1950.

"The Present Era" from *The Political Evolution of the Mexican People* (1900–1902)

We have come to the end of our great task; in embarking on it, we feared it might be greater than our abilities, and only because of the fascination that the magnitude and almost insuperable difficulty that an intellectual enterprise exercises on educated men did we have the boldness to undertake it; in the end we confess ourselves defeated. The task was, indeed, greater than our vigor. It could not be less in a country where statistical works have hardly begun to take shape; where devotion to collected and classified data has not existed except in a very individual and deficient way; where our archives, still without organization, catalogs, work facilities, are immense accumulations of old papers that time and neglect are reducing to dust; where our writers, basing their evaluations only on very obvious and very readily explained facts, have made of their works weapons of partisanship, as was inevitable, and linked the theories with which they have interpreted our history and the prejudices with which they have falsified it. And we have deliberately disregarded the possibility of official documents, also very incomplete, because these never have had proven worth except when meticulously compared with various other sources, given that official documents exist for very specific purposes.

To sum up, the fact—the phenomenon—determines ostensible history, whether political or administrative or economic or juridical or moral, sometimes minor and in any case hidden or veiled by events in the foreground and determined by environmental and hereditary conditions. The social fact—in its constitutive elements—almost always escapes us because either it did not leave traces or its traces have been lost. And without the social fact, all study ends up frustrating, ephemeral, and provisional at the very least.

And this we have done—a provisional work; with a larger quantity of data, more scientifically refined, others will rework what we have tried to do and with greater success. But our effort will nonetheless not have been futile. In the first place, if we have attempted to study the dynamic conditions of our society without prejudgment, we have not studied it without a system. We are not concerned to explain it here in an academic way; but the title of our book alone indicated that, even when we could have disagreed with the formula for social laws, and some people—following the Spencerian school—might assimilate social laws to biological laws, and others might consider social laws essentially psychological—agreeing with Giddings—and most might believe them fundamentally historical—agreeing with Auguste Comte and Littré—all of us have shared this one concept: Society is a living being, therefore growing, developing, and transforming itself; the intensity of this perpetual transformation depends on the level of internal energy with which the social organism reacts on external elements to assimilate them and use them to further its progress.[1]

---

1. The title of the three-volume book in which this essay was first published is *Mexico: Its Social Evolution;* the volume for which this was the conclusion is entitled *The Political Evolution of the Mexican People.* Herbert Spencer (1820–1903), English philosopher, saw societies as evolving systems; Franklin Henry Giddings (1855–1931), one of the founders of sociology as a discipline in the United States, who saw social phenomena as occurring and evolving through "consciousness of kind," the sense among individuals of their belonging to social groups; Auguste Comte (1798–1857), French philosopher credited with founding the philosophy of positivism and coining the term "sociology"; Émile Maximilien Paul Littré (1801–1881), French lexicographer and philosopher, remembered for his monumental dictionary of the French language but known to Sierra as a popularizer of Comte.

Science, converted into a prodigiously complex and effective instrument for work, has accelerated the evolution of certain human groups by many hundreds of times; other groups either subordinate themselves unconditionally to the major groups and lose awareness of themselves and their personality, or grounding themselves on ideals that are moral forces—as perfect a reality as physical forces—tend to take advantage of every external element to consolidate their personal equation and manage as a result to put a stamp of progress on their evolution, which, if not equal to the progress of those who are in the vanguard of human movement because of their own specific conditions, is nonetheless what they need for their self-preservation and well-being.

Using this criterion, we have written about those Mexican social phenomena that books and documents and our own observations have brought to our attention; and we have inferred logically that, if all the facts of which we were certain pointed, even to very different degrees, to a recent movement that resulted from the confluence of internal and external progress, that movement is Mexican social evolution. We have abided by this final conclusion, even when the intimate and profoundly genuine conditions and reasons for that evolution may be, for lack of data and studies, more conjectural than actually known.

III [2]

The country was a wreck; the civil war had heaped debris and misery together everywhere amidst great pools of blood; everything had collapsed; below, among the rural people, conscription, one of the endemic maladies of Mexican labor, had intensified (the others are alcohol and ignorance)—conscription redistributed people from the fields into the army as cannon fodder; into the guerrillas, as units regressing into the life of the savage mob; and into gangs, the nomadic school of all antisocial vices. In the cities the urban people, whether in factories, idle from fear of war or from the futility of producing for overstocked markets, or in workshops lacking work, either fell into idleness or ran off to join the riot[3]

---

2. In Part I of this concluding chapter Sierra traces the rise to power of Benito Juárez after the decade-long War of the Reform (1857–1867) and his success in leading the Mexican people into a period of political discipline, order, and peace. Mexico's economic recovery and its reform of education made it seem as though "a new republic of concord and love was about to rise in the dawn of the new era." In Part II of this concluding chapter, Sierra discusses the period of unrest during which there were disturbances all over the country. President Juárez died; Sebastián Lerdo de Tejada became president and began to carry out Juárez's program to begin economic transformation and incorporation of the Reform laws into the Constitution. José María Iglesias became chief justice (a position that doubled as vice president under the 1857 constitution) and nullified Lerdo's reelection decision, naming himself as the constitutional president. The Tuxtepec Revolution, which had as its platform the abolition of reelection and effective suffrage, started in Oaxaca, spread throughout the country, and was finally victorious under General Porfirio Díaz.

3. "The riot," *la bola,* Mexican slang for a riotous mob, extended ironically to refer to the wars and rebellions of the nineteenth century, and here referring specifically to Porfirio Díaz's "Tuxtepec Revolution."

or allowed themselves to be roped in and carried off to the barracks. People in the middle class, squeezed dry without pity by local petty tyrants or governments in conflict, hid their money and withdrew their sympathies; they had regarded the fall of the central government with pleasure (except in two or three states where Lerdism signified emancipation from hated local tyrannies); but they had been indifferent to Sr. Iglesias's attempted takeover, which looked to them like fine constitutional hairsplitting with all the appearances of a coup by lawyers and poets, and they were assailed by profound misgivings and fears in the face of that heterogeneous mass of insatiable appetites, implacable resentments, and shameful interests, which, with the name of the Tuxtepec Revolution,[4] had taken control of the republic, and it was a summary of all the elements of disorder eliminated by civil war. They believed in the good faith of the revolution's leader, believed in his honesty, but believed him, then as before, hopelessly subordinate to the very energetic but very narrow ambitions of a group of his advisors; and if they conceded him his administrative gifts, they persisted in denying him his political gifts; this man, it was repeated among urban groups, in our familiar way of condensing opinions, this man "won't pull the ox out of the ditch."

That was society. The official factors were appalling—the federal army—disoriented, confused, discontent with itself—had been divided between two flags that called themselves constitutional but had in its immense majority remained faithful to duty and now entered en masse into the army of the victorious revolution and felt humiliated, repressed, impatient, quick to shake what it considered a chain and a yoke; their principal leaders either had abandoned it or viewed contemptuously the crowd that surrounded them with a secret desire for revenge. The revolutionary crowd was resolved to strip the legitimate army of all its ranks and prerogatives and cast it down into the street, disarmed and naked, and punish it, and demanded this spoil of war from the revolution's leader.

As for the bureaucratic phalanx, minimally paid when it was paid, it barely fulfilled its duty; it mercilessly censured the customs and ignorance of the victors, it organized the great nether conspiracy of unfaithful servants, or it deserted; the makeshift leaders of the ephemeral government that had arisen from the revolt publicly solicited employees for administrative posts and usually received contemptuous rebuffs.

Abroad, the vicissitudes and the end of the civil war had created an embarrassing impression. It was proven—Mexico was an ungovernable country; the United States should put a stop to such disorder now that Europe was powerless to renew its attempted takeover. Sociologists took us as an example of the organic inability of the national groups that had been formed in America from the remains of Spain's colonial domination, and the United States ambassador assumed an attitude of haughty and dissatisfied tutor relative to the revolutionary executive.

---

4. The Tuxtepec Revolution is the 1876 coup that brought down the Lerdo and Iglesias governments and swept Díaz into the presidency.

The constitution had been buried beneath the rubble of legality. The reforms that the revolution had proclaimed were clearly Jacobin—neither Senate nor reelection, that is to say, the omnipotence of the popular chamber, weakening of the executive branch by the constant forcible change of its leader. There remained the court to protect individual right. But when has a tribunal ever served as a positive barrier to the despotism of political power if that tribunal is also subject to popular election, perennially manipulated in Mexico by our official prestidigitators?

And to make it all worse, the press either cruelly opposed the government or, when the press was loyal to the government, scolded and incessantly lectured it, both factions agreeing on the demand for strict fulfillment of the revolutionary promises, among which two stood out as the country's paramount aspirations—respect for free suffrage, that is to say, the abandonment of local and general elections to the governors and their agents, and the abolition of the "revenue stamp" tax, a most popular promise, whose fulfillment would amount to financial suicide for the administration.

The true desire of the country—the low hum that escaped from all the cracks in that enormous accumulation of legal, political, and social ruins, the infinite yearning of the Mexican people that manifested itself through all the organs of expression, public and private, from one end of the republic to the other, in the workshop, in the factory, on the ranch, in the school, in the church—was for peace. That feeling was in reality what undermined the resistance of the vice president of the republic, despite his constitutional authority.[5] No one wanted the continuation of war with the exception of those who could live only in confusion, those who are most reprehensible in any normal situation. Everything was sacrificed for peace—the constitution, political ambitions, everything, peace above all. Few times in the history of a people has there been an aspiration more pressing, more unanimous, more resolute.

On that feeling—well-perceived and well-analyzed by the leader of the victorious revolution—he founded his authority; that feeling coincided with a resolve as profound and firm as the national aspiration—to make another general revolt impossible. With the securing of this resolve, which he considered, as we already noted, a service and a supreme duty at the same time, he wanted to redeem for history the terrible responsibility incurred in two horrific fratricidal struggles[6]—the blood of his brothers would be pardoned him if in it and from it he made the tree of permanent peace bloom.

The way to achieve what seemed to be that unrealizable dream was to involve all higher and lower interests in the work; the *caudillo* believed that faith in him and fear of him were necessary to achieve that. Faith and fear—two feelings that,

---

5. José María Iglesias, as the head of the Supreme Court, was constitutionally the next in line to succeed Lerdo after the president's resignation.

6. The War of the Reform and the War of French Intervention, both of which were primarily civil wars.

because profoundly human, have been the foundation of all religions—had to be the sources of the new politics. Without losing a day or neglecting an opportunity, President Díaz has marched in that direction for twenty-five years; he has founded the political religion of peace.

As a result of the legal state's disappearance, return to a normal regime seemed impossible; everyone, we repeat, trusted in the energy, the ascendancy, the rectitude of the triumphant *caudillo;* nobody supposed him to have true political and administrative gifts; however, the progress of three of his advisors was followed with interest—the three oracles of the new government (Srs. Vallarta, Benítez, and Tagle);[7] to them was conceded much talent but much passion. The first political step was the return to constitutional order; for this it was urgently necessary to reconstitute the legal agencies of government. Only one branch had been half-way respected, the Supreme Court of Justice; for the rest, renovation was necessary.

An election held under the auspices of the revolutionary authorities and with the actual abstention of most qualified voters, gave, if not legitimacy, at least legality to the *caudillo;* he was president of the republic—his action was less restricted and firmer. But at the same time, the danger was clearly indicated; partisans of the overthrown president, exploiting the prestige of venerable names in the army, encouraged conspiracies inside and outside the country, conspiracies that everywhere threw off sparks in an attempt to ignite a fire for which there was everywhere an immense accumulation of combustible material. The external threats on the American border were neutralized because of good luck. All the threats were focused inside, and just when the plots were at the point of exploding in a terrible conflagration, they were extinguished with blood—the disaster was avoided. The emotion was extraordinary—there were protests and sorrow; many innocents seemed to be sacrificed, but the attitude of the president was surprising; fear, government's great resource—not to be confounded with terror, instrument of pure despotism—became general in the country. Peace was a fact; would it last?

In this country, as we have already said, there are really no fixed classes, because those so-called fixed classes are separated from one another by the changeable boundaries of money and manners; here no class is more open and mobile than the middle class; it absorbs all the active individuals of the lower groups. Among these we include those who could be called intellectual plebeians. These intellectual plebeians, after the final triumph of the Reform, were created from, first, a good number of the descendents of the old creole families who have not mentally disentailed themselves,[8] but rather live in the past and

---

7. Ignacio Vallarta (secretary of foreign relations), Justo Benítez (secretary of the treasury), and Protasio Tagle (secretary of the interior) were three key members in the first cabinet of Porfirio Díaz, who became known for governing through technically accomplished advisors.

8. Disentailment (*desamortización*), in the historical sense of selling off the entailed estates of the Church, was a key aim of Enlightenment economic thought and was enthusiastically embraced by the Reform in Mexico. The twin aims of disentailment were to create a capitalist

come into the present world with astonishing slowness; and second, the illiterate. Both groups are subject to the rule of superstition, and, moreover, the second to alcohol; but among both, the middle class makes converts every day, assimilating some by means of the budget and others by means of the school. The division of races, which would seem to complicate this classification is, in reality, losing its influence as a barrier to social evolution, because between the conquering race and the indigenous, a mixed race has formed, each day growing larger, that we have solidly affirmed is the true national family; in this mixed race the dominant middle class has its center and its roots. We must state, nonetheless, that all these considerations about the distribution of the social mass would be totally artificial and constitute genuine sociological lies if they were regarded as absolutes; no, there is a constant infiltration between the social classes, an osmosis, a physicist would say; thus, for example, the middle class has not managed to emancipate itself from alcohol or superstition. These are socio-pathogenic microbes that swarm in colonies wherever the medium of culture is favorable to them.

This middle class, which has absorbed the old oligarchies, both reformist and reactionary, whose genesis we have studied elsewhere—this middle class became conscious of its being, understood where it should go and by what route to become master of itself on the very day it felt itself governed by a man of character who would balance everything to achieve one result—peace. Army, clergy, reactionary relics; liberals, reformists, sociologists, Jacobins, and, from the social perspective, capitalists and workers—as many in the intellectual domain as in the economic—formed the nucleus of a party that, as was natural, as will always happen, took as its common denominator a name, a personality—Porfirio Díaz. The Mexican middle class, as it is constituted at present, is a work of this statesman, because he determined the condition essential to its organization; a government that would not allow itself to be discussed is, in turn, the creator of General Díaz; the immense authority of this ruler—that authority of an arbiter, not only political but also social, which has permitted him to develop and will permit him to secure his work, not against the crisis, but indeed maybe against disasters—is the product of the Mexican middle class.

Never has peace worn with greater clarity the character of a primordial national necessity than it did the day after the triumph of the Tuxtepec revolt. This is why, to avoid paralysis, the industrial development of the United States, already huge twenty-five years ago, demanded as a necessary condition the concomitant development of the railroad industry. American *go ahead* would not tolerate paralysis, and because of complex economic phenomena that we need not analyze here, what entered necessarily into the calculus of managers of the great systems of communication that had approached our frontiers was to complete

---

economy by freeing property from the "dead hands" (mortmain, *manos muertas*) of feudal institutions, putting it instead in the active and productive hands of individuals, and to benefit the public treasury with the profits of the sales. Here and elsewhere, Sierra uses "disentailment" as a metaphor for other forms of liberating individuals from the dead weight of the past.

those systems in Mexico, which, from the point of view of communications, was considered one single region with the southwestern United States. The financial outcome of incorporating our country in the immense American rail network rested on the hope of dominating our markets industrially.

This enormous North American need could be satisfied either by declaring Mexico ungovernable and unpacifiable and intervening in the guise of protecting the interests of the railroad people, or peacefully and normally if it came to believe that a Mexican government existed with which it could negotiate and contract, a government whose action could make itself felt in the form of a guarantee to the labor and business of the entire country, and whose viability was sufficient to pledge the good faith of succeeding generations. The civil war was, then, from that moment, not only a serious, the most serious of national woes, but also a danger, the greatest and most immediate of international dangers. Sr. Lerdo tried to stir it up by resorting to the assistance of European capital; it was futile, completely futile. European capital would come to Mexico only after many years, underwriting American business. The political virtue of President Díaz consisted in understanding this situation and—convinced that our history and our social conditions put us in the situation of being coupled to the formidable *Yankee* locomotive and being pulled into the future—in preferring to do this under the auspices, vigilance, policy, and action of the Mexican government, because in that way we would become free partners, committed to order and peace, and thereby command respect and affirm true national integrity and achieve progress.

Many of those who have tried to perform a psychological analysis of President Díaz—who, without being either the apocalyptic archangel toned down by Tolstoy or the tyrant of melodramatic grandeur of Bunge's fantastic tale,[9] is an extraordinary man in the true sense of the term—find in his spirit a grave deficiency; in the process of his volitions, as they say in school, of his determinations, there is a noticeable inversion of logic—the decision is rapid, the deliberation follows this first act of will, and this interior deliberation is slow and laborious and usually attenuates, modifies, sometimes nullifies the initial decision. The consequences of this mental disposition—perhaps typical of all individuals of the mixed family to which the majority of Mexicans belong—gives rise to the imputations of Machiavellianism or political perfidy (deceive to persuade, divide to rule) that they have directed at him. And there would be much to say, but we will not say it here, about these imputations, which, because they are contradicted by the qualities everyone recognizes in the private man, do not indicate, insofar as they are true, anything but reflexive, defensive, and corrective reactions to multiple demands and solicitations. In effect, by means of these solicitations and demands, certain individuals put themselves in contact with

9. Russian novelist Leo Tolstoy (1828–1910) reportedly called Porfirio Díaz "a prodigy of nature." Argentine philosopher Carlos Octavio Bunge (1875–1918), who introduced positivist sociology to Argentina, wrote about Díaz in his scathing analysis of Latin American society and politics, *Nuestra América: Ensayo de psicología social* (Buenos Aires, 1903).

power, certain individuals of this Mexican society, which—from the idiosyncrasy of the indigenous race and from colonial education, and from the perennial anarchy of the eras of revolt—has inherited the suspicion, the dissimulation, the infinite distrust with which it views governments and receives the government's decisions; what we criticize is, probably, our own reflection in the one criticized.

Be that as it may, it will always be true that the revolutionary *caudillo's* original resolution in the matter of international railroads was immediate, definite, did not change afterwards; it was the first day what it is now; and it was certainly necessary to overcome the anxiety regarding the future with an immensely bold and calm spirit and have unshakable faith in the destiny of the fatherland and demand with singular moral energy a source of strength and grandeur for what appeared to be the required path of our economic servitude, in order to have opened our borders to the American railway and industry. And in what times! One of Sr. Lerdo's unconquerable fears—both justified and truly rational—was the seedbed for very dangerous conflicts with the United States that would perhaps arise from the agreement to pay subventions, which the state of our national treasury could never fulfill. Sr. Díaz—trusting in the certainty of avoiding those conflicts and the necessity of the economic and, therefore, financial transformation that the country would undergo with the completion of the projected railroads—dared to contract national obligations amounting to many millions of pesos at a moment when our national treasury was exhausted and there was no money in the coffers to pay the wages of the army.

Indeed, the financial question threatened to paralyze the president's entire effort toward material improvements of national import; because the northern border was completely disorganized by the complacency or weakness of the local authorities relative to the kings of contraband, this business took on huge proportions; the republic's interior marketplaces were inundated by illegally imported merchandise, and the drop in customs duties had produced a state of terrifying unease, because it was thought irremediable. The entire political struggle came to complicate this situation, not the political struggle that sought the favor of voters—neither literate nor intelligent, who vote at the secondary level—but rather the one that struggled to obtain a majority in the president's spirit, for he now had sufficient moral authority that even a suggestion of his would be acceded to by the electoral colleges. But the end of the presidential term was drawing near; General Díaz then tossed aside the crutches of Sixtus V,[10] broke resolutely with his advisors who wanted to impose a candidate on him, chose his own, actually put him at the head of the army, and in the middle of a situation pregnant with threats but not devoid of hopes, left power to one of the most audacious, the most courageous, the most loyal of his revolutionary

---

10. According to an old story, Sixtus V (1520–1590) entered the conclave that elected him pope in 1585 pretending to be an old man supported on crutches, but upon his election he threw away the crutches and began to govern with vigor.

collaborators. The nation was perplexed by the new president. General Gonzáles was all soldier. Was he a man of government? [. . .]¹¹

Something like angry unanimity had returned the old *caudillo* of the revolution to power; events in the capital seemed a sure indication of the precarious state of the peace and the ease with which it could fall back into the old ruts of civil war; administrative anarchy and financial penury made the situation appear like the last period of legal government in 1876, and to everyone it seemed that eight years had been lost and that everything would have to begin anew; opinion imposed power on President Díaz as if demanding the fulfillment of a duty, like a responsibility that had come due.

In the enormous political bankruptcy of 1884, the liability was overwhelming; we had to rebuild our credit abroad—without which we would not have been able to find the sums necessary to achieve the great works of the future—by making the principal obligation fall on the future that it benefited, and that work seemed impossible, given the blind unpopularity of acknowledging the English debt, key to that credit; we had to rebuild the disorganized treasury, and it was necessary to begin with a partial suspension of payments; we had to lend authority to justice, impose respect for the law, undo certain loose coalitions of local governments, a sure sign of morbid weakness in the central authority; we had to give solemn, tangible, lasting guarantees for labor in its industrial, agricultural, mercantile forms . . . such was the liability. Among its assets, the new administration counted the great completed railroads and the name of General Díaz. But for the president to carry out the great task imposed on him, he needed maximum authority in his hands, not only legal authority but also political authority that would permit him to assume the effective direction of the political branches, including legislative chambers and state governments; the social authority, being constituted by general consent, supreme arbiter of peace in Mexican society, an authority which is not ordained but rather can flow only from everyone's faith in the honest judgment of the citizen to whom was entrusted the power of resolving conflicts; and moral authority—that indefinable power, intimately tied to the equivalent of what astronomers call the "personal equation"¹²—the way of life characteristic of an individual who reveals his feelings through absolute transparency of his home life (and that of General Díaz's character has always been illuminated by deep and gentle virtues capable of serving as an inspiration and an

---

11. Here Sierra gives an account of the presidency of Manuel González, who served from 1880 to 1884 under Díaz's close supervision. González's presidency was marked by, first, a boom created by U.S. money invested in construction, followed by a disastrous scarcity in the public treasury when spending for railway construction slowed down. The result was furious protest in the press and in the streets, exacerbated by the government's acknowledgment of the unpopular English debt and monetary devaluation after an attempt to issue cheap, alloyed coins. Díaz returned to office in the midst of this unrest.

12. "Personal equation," in early twentieth-century astronomy, was a corrective factor used to account for biases in measurement that were taken to be typical of each individual observer.

example) and through absolutely extraordinary freedom from vanity and pride, in spite of power, flattery, and good fortune; such were the inestimable elements of that moral authority.

With all these factors taken into account, the work progressed, not without serious snags; the general demand, here and abroad, among everyone who had entered into contact with our affairs—among holders of Mexican bonds, among the lenders of the enormous amounts of capital already invested in the railroad—was clear, compelling, imposing; it demanded full assurance that General Díaz would continue his work until it was safeguarded from disastrous accidents. This assurance was satisfied, to the degree that was humanly foreseeable, by reestablishing—first partially and then totally and absolutely—the original text of the constitution, which permitted the unlimited reelection of the president of the republic.

With this measure the program of the Tuxtepec Revolution had been wiped out. Giving the appearance of democratic principles, the dogmas of the Tuxtepec Revolution wrapped together, like all Jacobin creeds, the satisfaction of a momentary passion—a satisfaction designed to fan the fire of struggle and hasten the triumph—and absolute ignorance of the nation's normal needs; and those dogmas had died one by one; it was a negative program, fundamentally composed of three abolitions—the Senate, the revenue stamp tax, reelection—not one had been carried out. It had not even brought about a dominant group of new men, except halfheartedly. Losers and winners shared the budget in peace. The only result of this profound and bloody upheaval was a new situation; but this new situation was a transformation—it was the regular arrival of foreign capital to exploit the entailed wealth of the land; and this was, it is worth saying here, the last of our history's three great disentailments—that of Independence, which gave birth to our national personality; that of the Reform, which gave birth to our social personality; and that of the Peace, which gave birth to our international personality—they are the three stages of our total evolution. To achieve the last stage, which gave full value to the ones that went before, we needed—we will keep repeating it—like all peoples in their hours of supreme crisis—like the people of Cromwell and Napoleon, certainly, but also like the people of Washington and Lincoln and Bismarck, of Cavour and Juárez—we needed a man, a conscience, a will to unify the moral forces and transmute them into normal progress; this man was President Díaz.

An ambition to be sure; but capable of subordinating everything to the preservation of power? Posterity will judge. But that power which in all times has been and will be the irresistible magnet, not for supermen of thought, perhaps, but certainly for supermen of action, that power was a *desideratum* of the nation; there is not in Mexico a single citizen who would deny it or even doubt it. And that nation, which en masse applauds the man, has built up this man's power with a series of delegations, of abdications if you will, extralegal abdications, for they belong to the social order, without his soliciting that power, but without his sidestepping this formidable responsibility for even a moment—and is that dangerous? Terribly dangerous for the future, because it forms habits, themselves incongruous with self-government, without which there can be great men but not great peoples. But Mexico has confidence in that future, as in its star, the president; and Mexico believes that—now that the supreme condition of peace has been achieved without any possible fear that it might be altered and disintegrate—everything will come later, will come in its own time. Let us hope we are not wrong! . . .

Thus, without breaking a single legal formality, President Díaz has been invested, by the will of his fellow citizens and by the applause of foreigners, with a de facto life-long magistracy; until now—because of a combination of circumstances that it is not reasonable for us to analyze here—it has not been possible for him to put into place his program of transition between one state of things and another, which would be its logical consequence in a given sequence of events. This investiture—the submission of the people in all its governing agencies, of society in all its active elements, to the president's will, can be christened with the name of social dictatorship, of spontaneous Caesarism, of whatever it may be; the truth is that it has distinguishing characteristics that do not permit its logical classification among the classic forms of despotism. It is a personal government that enlarges, defends, and strengthens legal government; it is not about a power that sees itself elevated because of the country's growing depression, as the daydreamers of Spanish American sociology seem to assert, but rather a power that has risen in a country that has also risen proportionally, and risen not only in the material order but also in the moral, because that phenomenon is child to the national will to emerge finally from anarchy. For that reason, if our government is eminently authoritarian, it cannot, at the risk of perishing, stop being constitutional, and it has been conferred on one man, not only to achieve peace and to direct economic transformation, but also to put the government in a condition to neutralize the despotisms of other powers, to wipe out *cacicazgos*,[13] and to disarm local tyrannies. To justify the all-embracing authority of the republic's present leader, the measure that will have to be applied to him will be the difference between what has been demanded of that authority and what has been achieved.

In sum, the political evolution of Mexico has been sacrificed to the other phases of its social evolution; one very obvious, unchallengeable fact suffices to demonstrate this truth—there does not exist a single political party, organized active group, gathered around a program rather than a man. Every step ever taken in this direction has been stopped by the government's suspicion and by general apathy; they were, then, artificial attempts. The day a party manages to maintain its organization, political evolution would once more be underway, and the man, more necessary in democracies than in aristocracies, would follow; the function would create an agency.

But if we compare Mexico's situation at the instant when the suspension of its political evolution began with the present moment, we will have to agree that

---

13. *Cazicazgo,* the rule of a *cacique* or local political boss, was common across rural Latin America at the time.

the transformation has been amazing—and in this we anticipate with absolute certainty the verdict of our posterity. Only we who have been present at the events and have witnessed the change can fully appreciate its value. The pages of the great book we are finishing today show this abundantly. It was a dream to have a peace of ten to twenty years—the most optimistic allotted a century for this to come about; ours has lasted a good quarter of a century. It was a dream to cover the country with a railroad system that would unite the ports and the center with the interior and link it to the world, that would serve as an endless iron furrow along which foreign capital cast like seeds would produce abundant harvests of our own wealth; it was a dream, the appearance of a rapidly growing national industry, and it has all been realized, and everything is moving, and all this is in progress, and *Mexico: Its Social Evolution,*[14] has been written to show it so, and it stands proven.

The great work of the current administration—no matter how severely the administration may be judged—does not consist in having made the change that perhaps a set of external phenomena would have destined and made inevitable, but rather in having taken admirable advantage of that change and having facilitated it conscientiously. In this work nothing has been more fruitful for the country—and history will etch it in bronze—than the intimate collaboration between the president's unswerving aims and the extraordinary convictions and skills of the man who, in the management of Mexican finances, symbolized the desire to apply scientific processes to financial administration.[15] To that collaboration is owed the organization of our credit, the balancing of our budgets, the freedom of our domestic trade, and the concomitant growth of our public income. To that collaboration will be owed—is perhaps already owed—the fact that certain consequences are neutralized and may, by chance, become favorable to us, that is, the consequences of the alarming depreciation of silver, which was the richest of our consumer and export products,[16] a depreciation which if, on the one hand, with the ease of communications and the exploitation of natural forces, has been an extremely energizing factor of our industrial life, on the other it threatened, through price fluctuations, to isolate, circumscribe, and smother

---

14. This essay originally appeared in a three-volume work edited by Justo Sierra and Santiago Ballescá, with the endless title *México, su evolución social: Síntesis de la historia política, de la organización administrativa y militar y del estado económico de la federación mexicana; de sus adelantamientos en el orden intelectual; de su estructura territorial y del desarrollo de su población y de los medios de comunicación nacionales y internacionales; de sus conquistas en el campo industrial, agrícola, minero, mercantil, etc., etc.* (Mexico City: J. Ballescá y cía., 1900–1902).

15. José Y. Limantour (1854–1935), served as secretary of the treasury under Díaz from 1893 until the fall of the regime in 1911. He was considered the political leader (while Sierra was the intellectual spokesman) of the *científicos,* the technocratic advisors surrounding Díaz who based their approach to social questions on "scientific" positivism.

16. The repeal in 1893 of a U.S. law mandating large federal purchases of silver, in combination with greatly increased supplies of the metal since the beginning of the Colorado silver boom in 1879, led to an immediate collapse and the long-term devaluation of silver prices.

our mercantile evolution. The net effect, then, is impossible to calculate when we try to weigh the losses against the gains at the end of the present era.

There exists, we repeat, a Mexican social evolution; our progress, composed of foreign elements, reveals on analysis a reaction of the social element on those foreign elements to assimilate them to it, to take advantage of them in developing and intensifying our life. Thus our national personality, put in direct relationship with the world, has been strengthened, has grown. Without doubt, that evolution is just beginning; in comparison to our state before the last third of the past century, the road we have traveled is immense, and it is so even by comparison with the road traveled during the same period by our neighbors—and that comparison must always be our firm observation and reference, without illusions, which would be deadly, but without fears, which would be cowardly—our progress is no longer insignificant.

It remains for us to return life to the earth, the mother of the strong races who have known how to fertilize it by irrigation; it remains to us—this method more sure than any other—to attract the immigrant of European blood, which is the only one with whom we must attempt the crossbreeding of our indigenous groups if we do not want to pass from the level of civilization to which our nationality has risen to some inferior level, which would not be an evolution but a regression. There remains for us to produce a complete change in the indigenous mentality by means of education in the school. This, from the Mexican point of view, is the supreme task presented in both urgent and enormous characters. A great and pressing task, because either this or death.

To convert the native into a social asset (and only because of our apathy is he not), convert him into the principal settler on an intensively cultivated land; blend his spirit and ours through unity of language, of aspirations, of loves and hates, of mental and moral judgments; let shine before him the divine ideal of a fatherland for everyone, of a great and happy fatherland; create in sum the national soul—this is the goal assigned to the effort of the future, that is the program of national education. Whatever leads to its actualization, and only that, is patriotic; any obstacle that holds, or retards, or detracts from it is almost treason, it is an evil deed, it is the enemy.

The enemy is close; it is the possibility of passing from the indigenous language to a foreign language within our borders, obstructing the way to our national language; it is superstition, which only the secular school, with its human and scientific spirit, can successfully combat; it is the civic irreligiosity of the impious who, abusing the Mexican's ineradicable religious sentiment, persist in setting the principles that are the basis of our modern life against those that have been the religious basis of our moral being; it is the skepticism of those who, doubting that we will ever become fit for liberty, condemn us to death.

And thus the duty is defined; educate, that is to say, strengthen; liberty, essence of lions, has only been, individually and collectively, the patrimony of the strong; the weak have never been free. All of Mexican social evolution will have been totally abortive and futile if it does not arrive at that final goal—liberty.

Euclides da Cunha
(Brazil)

Euclides Rodrigues Pimenta da Cunha (1866–1909), Brazilian engineer, journalist, and essayist, was born in Cantagalo (state of Rio de Janeiro) to Manuel Rodrigues Pimenta da Cunha and Eudóxia Moreira da Cunha. Because his mother died of tuberculosis when he was three, he was raised by relatives. The time during which he grew up was a politically turbulent one in his country's history, and he chose to be a full participant in that turmoil. As time went on, he became dedicated to making Brazil a republic.

In 1883–1884, while a student in the Colegio Aquino, da Cunha came under the considerable influence of the great republican advocate and writer, Benjamin Constant. Constant's influence is apparent in da Cunha's subsequent political activity and writing. Da Cunha began writing at this time, but as he was gifted in mathematics and the exact sciences, he decided, in 1885, at age nineteen, to study engineering. He enrolled at the Escola Militar da Praia Vermelha in Rio de Janeiro and studied military engineering. There he once again had Constant as a teacher and began participating in the republican movement. In 1888 da Cunha directed his leadership against the minister of war, Tomás Coelho, in a political protest that became known as the "episode of the sword," in which da Cunha threw a weapon at Coelho's feet. The incident led to his expulsion from the school and his subsequent imprisonment. He was readmitted to the Escola in 1889, at the behest of Constant, when the republic was proclaimed. In 1890 he married Anna Emília Ribeiro, daughter of Major Frederico Solon Sampaio Ribeiro, one of the leaders of the republic. The couple had five sons.

In 1891 da Cunha was admitted to the Escola da Guerra. Because the curriculum of the military school was influenced by the writings of the great French positivist, Auguste Comte, Comte's writings came to influence da Cunha. He received his bachelor's degree in mathematics and physical and natural sciences in 1892. Although he worked for the Brazilian government as a military engineer from 1892 until his death in 1909, and undertook a number of civil engineering projects, his literary career took precedence. In 1897, when he went with the army as a correspondent for the newspaper *O Estado de São Paulo* to the Canudos campaign against a rebellious group of peasants, his life took its most dramatic literary turn. He accompanied the 21st Brigade of the Divisão Auxiliar on this campaign at the request of the editor of *O Estado de São Paulo,* who greatly admired da Cunha's earlier writings on republicanism. The ultimate result of this assignment was his masterpiece, *Os Sertões* (translated as *Rebellion in the Backlands*), which describes the campaign of Canudos in all its geological, zoological, botanical, geographical, social, and military complexity. First published in 1902, the work had many subsequent editions and has been translated into dozens of languages; the next year he was elected to the Academia Brasileira de Letras and the Instituto Histórico e Geográfico Brasileiro.

In 1904 da Cunha led a Brazilian-Peruvian commission charged with determining the border between Brazil and Peru. One result of this commission's work was the publication of his essay "Peru versus Bolivia." In 1909 he became chairman and teacher of logic at the Colegio Pedro II, a public secondary school, a position he was never able fully to pursue because of his untimely death. He was killed in a duel by Dilermando de Assis, a seventeen-year-old cadet at the Escola Militar and lover to da Cunha's wife. Dilermando was ultimately absolved of criminal murder and subsequently married Anna, only to abandon her later.

The selection that follows is from *Rebellion in the Backlands*. Other works by da Cunha include *Á margem da história* (1909) and articles collected in *Contrastes e confrontos* (1907).

Further Reading

Abreu, Regina. *Coisas boas p'ra pensar.* São José do Rio Pardo, Brazil: Casa Euclideana, 1998.

Bastos, Abguar. *A visão historico-sociologica de Euclides da Cunha.* São Paulo: Companhia Editorial Nacional, 1986.

Cunha, Euclides da. *Obra completa.* Edited by Afranio Coutinho. 2 vols. Rio de Janeiro: Aguilar, 1966; revised, 1995.

Fernandes, Rinaldo de, ed. *O Clarim e a oração: Cem anos de Os sertões.* São Paulo: Geração Editorial, 2002.

Levine, Robert M. *Vale of Tears: Revisiting the Canudos Massacre in Northeastern Brazil, 1893–1897.* Berkeley: University of California Press, 1992.

Moura, Clóvis. *Introdução ao pensamento de Euclides da Cunha.* Rio de Janeiro: Editôra Civilização Brasileira, 1964

Oliveira, Franklin de. *Euclydes, a espada e a letra: Florianistas e castilhistas no massacre de Canudos, Comte e outras influências reacionárias, as antecipações do autor de Os sertões.* Rio de Janeiro: Paz e Terra, 1983.

Ventura, Roberto. *Retrato interrompido da vida de Euclides da Cunha.* São Paulo: Companhia das Letras, 2003.

Rebellion in the Backlands (1902)[1]

Translated by Samuel Putnam

THE SERTANEJO

The *sertanejo,* or man of the backlands, is above all else a strong individual [. . .][2]

His appearance, it is true, at first glance, would lead one to think that this was not the case. He does not have the flawless features, the graceful bearing, the correct build of the athlete. He is ugly, awkward, stooped. Hercules-Quasimodo

---

1. Euclides da Cunha, *Rebellion in the Backlands,* translated by Samuel Putnam (Chicago: University of Chicago Press, 1944), pp. 89–91, 104–6, 110, 117–19, 160–62, 190–95, 405–9, 411–15, 481. Reprinted by permission of the University of Chicago Press.

2. I did encounter in the backlands (*sertanejo*) type an ethnic subcategory already formed and one which, as a result of historical conditions, had been freed of the exigencies of a borrowed civilization such as would have hindered its definitive evolution. This is equivalent to saying that in that indefinable compound—the Brazilian—I came upon something that was stable, a point of resistance reminiscent of the integrating molecule in the initial stage of crystallizations. And it was natural enough that, once having admitted the bold and inspiring conjecture that we are destined to national unity, I should have seen in those sturdy *caboclos* [Brazilian Indian] the hearty nucleus of our future, the bedrock of our race.

The bedrock . . . . . This locution suggests an elegant simile. The truth of the matter is, our formation, like that of a block of granite is due to three principal elements. Whoever climbs a granite hillock will encounter the most diverse constituents: Here, pure clay, of decomposed feldspar, variously colored; a little farther along, bits of gleaming mica scattered over the ground; and, beyond that, the sand dust of pulverized quartz. But from a distance, the hill has the erratic appearance of a *roche montannée* [glaciated rock], while all around is to be seen a mixture of these same elements, with the addition of other, adventitious ones, the whole going to form an arable terrain that is non-characteristic and extremely complex. Down beneath, however, when the surface layer has been removed, will be found a nucleus of hard, solid rock. The elements which on the surface are scattered and mixed in a highly diversified manner—for the reason that the exposed soil retains even the foreign matter brought in by the winds—are here, down below, rendered firm and resistant, with their proportions stabilized. And so it is, the deeper he goes, the closer the observer will come to the definite matrix of the locality in question.

Precisely the same thing happens with respect to race, as we leave the cities of the seaboard for the villages of the backlands. At first, there is an astonishing dispersion of attributes, from all shades of color to all types of character. There is no distinguishing the Brazilian in this intricate mingling of whites, blacks, and mulattos, with the blood of all races in their veins, in every conceivable blending. We are as yet on the surface of our *gens;* or, better, if we are to follow out to the letter the comparison which we have begun, we are here treading the nondescript humus of our race. But, as we make our way deeper into the land, we come upon the first fixed groupings—in the *caipira* of the South and the *tabareo* of the North. [General terms for backwoodsman, countryman, rustic.] The pure white, the pure Negro, and the pure Indian are now a rarity. The generalized miscegenation, meanwhile, has given rise to every variety of racial crossing; but, as we continue on our way, these shadings tend to disappear, and there is to be seen a greater uniformity of physical and moral characteristics. In brief, we have struck bedrock—in the man of the backlands. [Da Cunha's Note V to the third edition.]

reflects in his bearing the typical unprepossessing attributes of the weak. His unsteady, slightly swaying, sinuous gait conveys the impression of loose-jointedness. His normally downtrodden mien is aggravated by a dour look which gives him an air of depressing humility. On foot, when not walking, he is invariably to be found leaning against the first doorpost or wall that he encounters; while on horseback, if he reins in his mount to exchange a couple of words with an acquaintance, he braces himself on one stirrup and rests his weight against the saddle. When walking, even at a rapid pace, he does not go forward steadily in a straight line but reels swiftly, as if he were following the geometric outlines of the meandering backland trails. And if in the course of his walk he pauses for the most commonplace of reasons, to roll a *cigarro,* strike a light, or chat with a friend, he falls—"falls" is the word—into a squatting position and will remain for a long time in this unstable state of equilibrium, with the entire weight of his body suspended on his great-toes, as he sits there on his heels with a simplicity that is at once ridiculous and delightful.

He is the man who is always tired. He displays this invincible sluggishness, this muscular atony, in everything that he does: In his slowness of speech, his forced gestures, his unsteady gait, the languorous cadence of his ditties—in brief, in his constant tendency to immobility and rest.

Yet all this apparent weariness is an illusion. Nothing is more surprising than to see the *sertanejo's* listlessness disappear all of a sudden. In this weakened organism complete transformations are effected in a few seconds. All that is needed is some incident that demands the release of slumbering energies. The fellow is transfigured. He straightens up, becomes a new man, with new lines in his posture and bearing; his head held high now, above his massive shoulders; his gaze straightforward and unflinching. Through an instantaneous discharge of nervous energy, he at once corrects all the faults that come from the habitual relaxation of his organs; and the awkward rustic unexpectedly assumes the dominating aspect of a powerful, copper-hued Titan, an amazingly different being, capable of extraordinary feats of strength and agility.

This contrast becomes evident upon the most superficial examination. It is one that is revealed at every moment, in all the smallest details of back-country life—marked always by an impressive alternation between the extremes of impulse and prolonged periods of apathy.

It is impossible to imagine a more inelegant, ungainly horseman: No carriage, legs glued to the belly of his mount, hunched forward and swaying to the gait of the unshod, mistreated backland ponies, which are sturdy animals and remarkably swift. In this gloomy, indolent posture the lazy cowboy will ride along, over the plains, behind his slow-paced herd, almost transforming his "nag" into the lulling hammock in which he spends two-thirds of his existence, but let some giddy steer up ahead stray into the tangled scrub of the *caatinga,*[3] or let one of

---

3. Earlier, da Cunha has described the backlands *caatinga* as a "turbulent maze of vegetation standing rigid in space . . . representing, as it would seem, the agonized struggles of a tortured, writhing flora" (p. 30).

the herd at a distance become entrammeled in foliage, and he is at once a different being and, digging his broad-roweled spurs into the flanks of his mount, he is off like a dart and plunges at top speed into the labyrinth of *jurema* thickets.

Let us watch him at this barbarous *steeple chase*.

Nothing can stop him in his onward rush. Gullies, stone heaps, brush piles, thorny thickets, or riverbanks—nothing can halt his pursuit of the straying steer, for *wherever the cow goes, there the cowboy and his horse go too*. Glued to his horse's back, with his knees dug into its flanks until horse and rider appear to be one, he gives the bizarre impression of a crude sort of centaur: Emerging unexpectedly into a clearing, plunging into the tall weeds, leaping ditches and swamps, taking the small hills in his stride, crashing swiftly through the prickly briar patches, and galloping at full speed over the expanse of tablelands.

His robust constitution shows itself at such a moment to best advantage. It is as if the sturdy rider were lending vigor to the frail pony, sustaining it by his improvised reins of *caroá* fiber, suspending it by his spurs, hurling it onward—springing quickly into the stirrups, legs drawn up, knees well forward and close to the horse's side—"hot on the trail" of the wayward steer; now bending agilely to avoid a bough that threatens to brush him from the saddle; now leaping off quickly like an acrobat, clinging to his horse's mane, to avert collision with a stump sighted at the last moment; then back in the saddle again at a bound—and all the time galloping, galloping, through all obstacles, balancing in his right hand, without ever losing it once, never once dropping it in the *liana* thickets, the long, iron-pointed, leather-headed goad that in itself, in any other hands, would constitute a serious obstacle to progress.

But once the fracas is over and the unruly steer restored to the herd, the cowboy once more lolls back in the saddle, once more an inert and unprepossessing individual, swaying to his pony's slow gait, with all the disheartening appearance of a languishing invalid.

$$\bullet\ \bullet\ \bullet\ \bullet\ \bullet$$

The Drought

And then, of a sudden, there comes a tragic break in the monotony of their days. The drought is approaching.

Thanks to the singular rhythm with which the scourge comes on, the *sertanejo* is able to foresee and foretell it. He does not, however, take refuge in flight, by abandoning the region which is being little by little invaded by the glowing inferno that radiates from Ceará.[4] Buckle[5] has a striking passage in which he draws attention to the strange fact that man never learns to accustom himself to the natural calamities that surround him. There is no people more

---

4. Ceará is one of the states of Brazil.

5. Henry Thomas Buckle (1821–1862), English historian and author of a history of civilization.

afraid of earthquakes than is your Peruvian; yet, in Peru, children in the cradle are rocked by the earth's tremors. The *sertanejo,* on the other hand, is an exception to the rule. The droughts do not frighten him; they serve merely to round out his tormented existence, framing it with tremendously dramatic episodes. And he confronts them stoically. Although this grievous ordeal has occurred times without number, as is borne out by traditions that he knows well, he is nonetheless sustained by the impossible hope of being able to hold out against it.

With the scant help afforded him by his own observations and those of his ancestors, in which common-sense directions are mingled with extravagant superstitions, he has studied this affliction as best he could, in order that he might understand it and be able to bear or avert it. He equips himself for the struggle with an extraordinary calmness. Two or three months before the summer solstice, he props and strengthens the walls of the dams or cleans out the water pits, he looks after his fields and plows up in furrows the narrow strips of arable land on the river's edge, by way of preparing these diminutive plantations for the coming of the first rains.

Then he endeavors to make out what the future holds in store. Turning his eyes upward, he gazes for a long time in all directions, in an effort to discover the faintest hints that the landscape may have to offer him.

The symptoms of the drought are not long in appearing; they come in a series, one after another, inexorably, like those of some cyclic disease, some terrifying intermittent fever on the part of the earth. The brief period of October rains, the *chuvas do cajú,* goes by, with numerous showers that are quickly evaporated in the parched air, leaving no trace behind them. The *caatingas* are "mottled," here, there, and everywhere, speckled with grayish-brown clusters of withered trees, and the number of these splotches, which look like the ash heaps left by some smothered conflagration, without flames, all the time increases; the ground cracks; and the water level in the pits slowly sinks. At the same time it is to be noted that, while the days are scorching hot, even at dawn, the nights are constantly becoming colder. The atmosphere, with the avidity of a sponge, absorbs the sweat on the *sertanejo's* brow, while his leathern armor, no longer possessing the flexibility it once had, is stiff and hot on his shoulders, like a breastplate of bronze. And, as the afternoons, growing shorter every day, fade into evenings without twilights, he sorrowfully contemplates the first flocks of birds leaving the region and flying away to other climes.

• • • • •

The drought is inevitable.

• • • • •

MESTIZO RELIGION

Isolated in this manner in a country that knows nothing of him, and engaged in an open warfare with an environment that would appear to have stamped upon his physical organism and his temperament its own extraordinary ruggedness, the *sertanejo,* either a nomad or with few roots in the soil, does not, to tell the truth, possess the organic capacity for attaining a loftier place in life. The restricted circle of his activities retards his psychic development. His religion is a monotheism that he does not understand, marred by an extravagant mysticism, with an incongruous admixture of the fetishism of the Indian and the African. He is the primitive individual, bold and strong, but at the same time credulous, readily permitting himself to be led astray by the most absurd superstitions. An analysis of these will reveal a fusion of distinct emotional states.

His religion is, like himself, mestizo in character. A résumé of the physical and physiological characteristics of the races from which he springs would likewise serve to summarize their moral qualities. It is an index to the life of the three peoples. And the *sertanejo's* religious beliefs reflect this violent juxtaposition of distinct tendencies. It is not necessary to describe them. The hair-raising legends of the waggish and wanton *caapora,* mounted on a peevish *caitetú* and crossing the plains on mysterious moonlit nights; the diabolic *sacy,* a vermilion-colored bonnet on its head, assaulting the belated traveler on unlucky Good Friday eves; along with the werewolves and the night-wandering headless she-mules; all the temptations of the evil one, or Devil, that tragic bearer of celestial grievances, commissioned to the earth; the prayers addressed to São Campeiro, canonized *in partibus,* to whom candles are lighted on the plains[6] to obtain his help in recovering lost objects; the cabalistic conjurings for the curing of animals, for "bruising" and "selling" fevers; all the visions, all the fantastic apparitions, all the fanciful prophecies of the insane messiahs; and the pious pilgrimages and the missions and the penances—all these complex manifestations of an ill-defined religiosity are wholly explicable.

•••••

It would not be too far amiss to describe them as miscegenation of beliefs. Here they are, plain to be seen: The anthropomorphism of the savage, the animism of the African, and, what is more worthy of note, the emotional attitude of the superior race itself in the period of discovery and colonization. This last is a notable instance of historical atavism.

•••••

---

6. The name of this local saint, Campeiro, is derived from *campo,* a field or plain. [Translator's note.]

ANTONIO CONSELHEIRO, STRIKING
EXAMPLE OF ATAVISM

It was natural that the deep-lying layers of our ethnic stratification should have cast up so extraordinary an anticlinal as Antonio Conselheiro.[7]

The metaphor is quite correct. Just as the geologist, by estimating the inclination and orientation of the truncated strata of very old formations, is enabled to reconstruct the outlines of a vanished mountain, so the historian, in taking the stature of this man, who in himself is of no worth, will find it of value solely in considering the psychology of the society which produced him. As an isolated case, this is one lost amid a multitude of commonplace neurotics; it could be included under the general category of progressive psychoses. Taken in connection with the social background, on the other hand, it is sufficiently alarming. It is at once a diathesis and synthesis. The various phases of this man's career do not, it may be, represent the successive stages of a serious ailment, but they most certainly afford us a condensed summary of a very grave social malady. As the upshot of it all, this unfortunate individual, a fit subject for medical attention, was impelled by a power stronger than himself to enter into conflict with a civilization and to go down in history when he should have gone to a hospital. For to the historian he is not an unbalanced character but rather appears as the integration of various social traits—vague, indecisive, not readily perceived when lost in the multitude, but well defined and forceful when thus summed up in a human personality.

All the naive beliefs from a barbarous fetishism to the aberrations of Catholicism, all the impulsive tendencies of lower races given free outlet in the undisciplined life of the backlands, were condensed in his fierce and extravagant mysticism. He was at once an active and a passive element of that agitation that sprang up about him. A highly impressionable temperament led him merely to absorb the beliefs and superstitions of his environment, in which process his mind, tormented by adversity was at first little more than the morbidly passive recipient; and, reflected by a consciousness that was in a state of delirium, these influences, greatly strengthened, in turn reacted upon the surroundings that had produced him.

In this particular case, it is difficult to draw a dividing line between individual and collective tendencies. The life of this man at once becomes a synoptic chapter in the life of a society. In tracing the individual tendencies, we at the same time draw a rapid parallel for the social forces, and, in following out these two lines, we have a perfect example of the reciprocality of influences.

In surveying the scene about him, this false apostle, whose excessive subjectivism predisposed him to a revolt against the natural order of things, was in a manner observing the formula of his own madness. He was not a misunderstood being. The multitude acclaimed him as the natural representative of their highest

---

7. Literally, "Anthony the Counselor." Conselheiro (pronounced "cohn-sel-yeh-ee´-roo") is a sobriquet. [Translator's note.]

aspirations. That was as far as it went with them; they were not concerned with his madness. As he continued to traverse a curve that would have led to the complete obscuration of reason, the milieu in its turn reacted upon him; it afforded him protection and corrected his aberrations to a degree, compelling him to establish some sort of unassailable logic even in his wildest imaginings, a certain show of order in his hallucinations, and a perduring consistency in everything he did. He manifested always a rare spirit of discipline in the control of his passions; and, as a consequence, the impressionable backlands for long years could behold in his every word and deed the tranquility, the moral elevation, and the sovereign resignation of an ancient apostle of the faith.

He was in reality a very sick man to whom one could only apply Tanzi e Riva's concept of paranoia. In his ideational hallucinations the ethnic note was always prominent; one might say that it was the only one to be detected. He was a rare case of atavism. His morbid constitution led him to give a whimsical interpretation to objective conditions, thereby altering his relation to the external world, and this appeared as basically a retrogression to the mental state of the ancestral types of the species.

$$\bullet\ \bullet\ \bullet\ \bullet\ \bullet$$

Why Not Preach Against The Republic?[8]

He preached against the Republic, there is no denying that. This antagonism was an inevitable derivative of his mystic exacerbation, a variant of his religious delirium that was forced upon him. Yet he did not display the faintest trace of a political intuition; for your *jagunço*[9] is quite as inapt at understanding the republican form of government as he is the constitutional monarchy. Both to him are abstractions, beyond the reach of his intelligence. He is instinctively opposed to both of them, since he is in that phase of evolution in which the only rule he can conceive is that of a priestly or a warrior chieftain.

We must insist upon this point: The war of Canudos marked an ebb, a backward flow, in our history. What we had to face here was the unlooked-for resurrection, under arms, of an old society, a dead society, galvanized into life by a madman. We were not acquainted with this society; it was not possible for us to have been acquainted with it. The adventurers of the seventeenth century, it is true, would encounter in it conditions with which they were familiar, just as the visionaries of the Middle Ages would be at home among the *demonopaths* of Varzenis or the Stundists[10] of Russia; for these epidemic psychoses make their appearance in all ages and in all places as obvious anach-

---

8. In the intervening pages, da Cunha goes further into the personal history and mentality of Conselheiro as well as his rise to power. Da Cunha also describes the Canudos region and its populations, especially the religious mentality and practices there.

9. Da Cunha uses this word as a near synonym for *sertanejo*.

10. In Verzegnis, Italy, in 1878, there was an epidemic of hysterical demonopathy. [Editors' note.] [The Stundists were] an evangelical sect of southwest (Czarist) Russia, widespread among

ronisms, inevitable contrasts in the uneven evolution of the peoples—contrasts that become especially evident at a time when a broad movement is vigorously impelling the backward peoples toward a higher and civilized way of life. We then behold the exaggerated Perfectionists breaking through the triumphant industrialism of North America, or the somber *sturmisch* sect inexplicably inspired by the genius of Klopstock, sharing the cradle of the German renascence.

With us, the phenomenon is perhaps still more readily to be explained. After having lived for four hundred years on a vast stretch of seaboard, where we enjoyed the reflections of civilized life, we suddenly came into an unlooked-for inheritance in the form of the Republic. Caught up in the sweep of modern ideas, we abruptly mounted the ladder, leaving behind us in their centuries-old semidarkness a third of our people in the heart of our country. Deluded by a civilization that came to us second hand; rejecting, blind copyists that we were, all that was best in the organic codes of other nations, and shunning, in our revolutionary zeal, the slightest compromise with the exigencies of our own national interests, we merely succeeded in deepening the contrasts between our mode of life and that of our rude native sons, who were more alien to us in this land of ours than were the immigrants who came from Europe. For it was not an ocean that separated us from them but three whole centuries.

And when, through our own undeniable lack of foresight, we permitted a nucleus of maniacs to form among them, we failed to see the deeper meaning of the event. Instead, we looked at it from the narrow-minded point of view of partisan politics. In the presence of these monstrous aberrations, we had a revealing fit of consternation; and, with an intrepidity that was worthy of a better cause, we proceeded to put them down with bayonets, thereby causing history to repeat itself, as we made yet another inglorious incursion into these unfortunate regions, opening up once more the grass-grown trails of the *bandeiras*.[11]

In the backlands agitator, whose revolt was a phase of rebellion against the natural order of things, we beheld a serious adversary, a foeman representing a regime that we had done away with, one who was capable of overthrowing our nascent institutions.

And Canudos was our Vendée.[12]

• • • • •

the peasantry. Apparently founded by German evangelical pastors, chiefly Lutheran, among the German settlements of that district (*Encyclopedia of Religion and Ethics,* ed. James Hastings [New York: Scribner's, 1925], XI, 342–43). [Translator's note.]

11. Colonial armed bands made up primarily of adventurers from the São Paolo regions who went into the backlands in search of precious metals and stones.

12. The Vendée in the French Revolution refers to the bloody 1793–1796 uprising of peasants in that area of France against the government. Reprisals were horrific. [Editors' note.]

THE WAR OF THE CAATINGAS[13]

Those doctors of the art of killing who today in Europe are scandalously invading the domain of science, disturbing its calm with an insolent jingling of spurs as they formulate the laws of war and the equations of battle, have well defined the role of forests as a tactical factor, both in offensive and in defensive action. And those wise old field marshals—warriors from whose hands the heroic *francisca*[14] has fallen, to be replaced by the pencil of the strategist—would certainly have laughed had anyone tried to tell them that our impoverished *caatingas* have a more clearly defined and important function in a military campaign than do the great virgin forests. For the former [the forests], notwithstanding their importance in the defense of a territory—bordering the frontiers as they do and serving to break the shock of invasion while hindering rapid mobilization and rendering impossible the transport of artillery—nevertheless become, in a manner of speaking, neutral in the course of the campaign. They may favor, indifferently, either of the belligerents, offering to each the same foliage for ambuscades and making equally difficult for both all those deploying and other maneuvers that strategy imposes upon the contending armies. They are variables in the formula of the dark problem of war, capable of representing the most opposite values.

With all this, the *caatingas* are an incorruptible ally of the *sertanejo* in revolt, and they do in a certain way enter into the conflict. They arm themselves for the combat, take the offensive. For the invader they are an impenetrable wilderness; but they have numerous paths by which they are accessible to the backwoodsman, who was born and grew up there. And so, the *jagunço* turns warrior-thug,[15] hard to lay hands on.

The *caatingas* do not so much hide him as extend him their protection. Upon catching sight of them in the summertime, a column of soldiers is not alarmed but continues to make its way, painfully, along the winding paths. Being able to see over the top of the leafless undergrowth, the men do not think of an enemy's being near. Reacting to the heat and with that relaxed air that is natural on long marches, they go along with a confused babble of conversation all down the line, punctuated by the clinking of their weapons and their jovial, half-repressed

---

13. In the intervening passages, da Cunha describes a mission in which Friar João Evangelista de Monte-Marciano and two other priests went to Monte Santo in the Canudos region to try to convince Antonio Conselheiro that he should give up preaching against the republic and become more religiously orthodox. This mission failed, and he left. Reacting to a small incident, largely based on rumor, one hundred soldiers were sent to a town where it was thought the followers of Antonio Conselheiro might attack. Warned of the soldiers' approach, the followers of Conselheiro attacked first and, although more in number, were repelled by the superior arms of the soldiers. But so alarmed was the government of the state of Baía that it decided to send another military expedition to put down what it perceived as a revolt of the backlanders.

14. "A battle-ax used by the ancient Franks with a slightly curved, long, narrow head, and an outwardly curved edge, the head forming a slightly obtuse angle with the pole" (*Funk & Wagnalls' Standard Dictionary*). [Translator's note.]

15. The word in the original is *guerrilheiro-thug*. [Translator's note.]

laughter. There is nothing, so it seems, that should alarm them. Certainly, should the enemy be so imprudent as to confront them here, they would make short work of him. These shoots of foliage could be slashed to bits by a few strokes of the sword, and it is not credible that this fine underbrush could impede the execution of prompt maneuvers. And so they go marching along, heroically unconcerned.

Suddenly, from the side, close at hand, a shot rings out.

The bullet whizzes past them, or perhaps one of their number lies stretched on the ground, dead. This is followed, after a while, by another, and another, whining over the heads of the troop. A hundred, two hundred, a thousand anxious eyes scan the foliage round about them, but can see nothing. This is the first surprise, and a shudder of fear runs from one end of the ranks to the other. The shots continue, not many of them, but there is no letup; they keep on coming at measured intervals, from the left, from the right, from in front of them, with the entire band now under a constant and deadly fire.

It is then that a strange anxiety lays hold of even the bravest ones whose courage has many times been put to the test, in the presence of this antagonist who sees them, but whom they cannot see. A company of sharpshooters is quickly formed, being with difficulty separated from the main mass of the battalions caught in the narrow path. These men now spread out around the edge of the *caatinga,* whereupon a voice can be heard giving a command, and there is a resounding hail of bullets though the branches of the stunted undergrowth.

But constantly, always at long intervals, the missiles from those other sharpshooters, the invisible ones, keep humming, all up and down the line. The situation rapidly grows worse, calling for energetic action. Other combat units are now detached and are detailed along the entire stretch of road, ready to act at the first word of command. The commanding officer resolves to launch an assault on the hidden enemy but soon finds that he is assaulting a phantom foe. With their bayonets, his men impetuously beat down the undergrowth, amid a widening range of bullets. They go forward rapidly, and the enemy appears to fall back somewhat. And then it is, at this moment, that the *caatinga* shows what a formidable antagonist it can be. The details rush on to the points from where the gunfire had been heard and are brought up short by the yielding but impenetrable barrier of *jurema* thicket. They become entangled in a *liana* bed, which trips them up, snatches their weapons from their hands, and will not let them pass; and so they are compelled to turn aside and make their way around it. There may now be seen what looks like a running flame, a row of bayonets along the dried brushwood. It glitters for a few moments in the rays of the sun, filtered down through the leafless boughs, and then is gone, to be seen, gleaming, here and there farther on, beating against the dense rows of *chique-chiques,*[16] bunched together in the close squares of an immovable phalanx, bristling with thorns.

---

16. "A relatively low-growing plant with thorn-laden, curved, creeping boughs" (da Cunha's description, p.34).

In great bewilderment the soldiers make a wide detour, spreading out, on the run, they plunge headlong into the labyrinth of boughs and branches. Tripped by the slipknot lassos of the creeping *quipá* vines, they fall, or else are brought to a standstill, their legs held motionless by the powerful tentacles. They struggle desperately, until their uniforms are in tatters, in the feline claws of the *macambiras* with their crooked thorns.

They stand there cursing impotently, in rage and disappointment, as they struggle furiously but without avail to free themselves. Finally, the tumult dies away as the men spread out more and more, firing at random, without aim, with an utter lack of discipline, their bullets likely as not hitting their own comrades. Reinforcements come up, and the anguished struggle with the underbrush is repeated all over again, on a yet larger scale, as the confusion and the disorder increase—and meanwhile, round about them, steadily, rhythmically, fall the deadly well-aimed missiles of the terrible enemy, safe in his hiding-place.

Of a sudden, the firing ceases. The enemy is gone, and no one has had so much as a glimpse of him. The detachments with their numbers depleted now return to the column after all this futile beating of the brush. It is as if they were coming back from a hand-to-hand encounter with savages; their weapons are lost or hopelessly battered; there are deep gashes on their hands and faces; they are limping, crippled, and it is all they can do to keep from crying out with the infernal pain inflicted upon them by the prickly leaves of the *caatinga,* the thorn wounds that they bear.

The troop is then reorganized and the march is resumed. Two abreast, it goes on down the paths, the blue uniforms of the soldiers with their vermilion stripes and the brightly gleaming, swaying bayonets giving a strong dash of color to the ashen-gray of the landscape. And so they march on until they are lost to sight in the distance.

Some minutes pass, and then, at the scene of the struggle, from the scattered thickets, five, ten, twenty men at the most rise up, and swiftly, silently, slip away among the parched shrubbery.

They meet on the highway and stand there for a moment or so gazing after the troop that is now barely visible on the horizon. And brandishing their muskets, still hot from firing, they hastily make for the trails that lead to their unknown dwellings.

As for the members of the expeditionary force, they will be more cautious after this. As they march along in silence, the soldiers cannot help thinking anxiously of this intangible enemy and are haunted by visions of sudden assaults. The commanding officer surrounds them with every possible precaution; detached companies skirt their flanks, and up ahead, a couple of hundred yards in advance of the column, is a squadron of picked men. Upon descending a rugged slope, however, they come to a ravine that has to be crossed. Fortunately, its sides have been swept clean by floods, leaving only a little grass stubble, a few slender cacti standing out here and there among the stone heaps and the dead and white-peeling boughs of the *umbú* trees, victims of the drought.

The advance guard goes down the side of the ravine, followed by the first of the battalions, slowly straggling after. One can see them now, down below, the entire vanguard of the column, following the twists and turns of the narrow valley, their weapons gleaming in the sun like some dark torrent shot with rays of light.

Then they suddenly haul up short with a convulsive shudder that they cannot control. A bullet has just whistled past them. This time the shots, fired at intervals as usual, appear to come from above and from a solitary marksman. Only discipline preserves order in the ranks now and restrains a panic that is on the verge of breaking out. As before, a detachment is told off and goes up the slope in the direction of the shots; but, owing to the bedlam of echoes, it is hard for the men to keep their bearings; and in this overheated atmosphere the sharpshooter's hiding-place is not revealed by the smoke from his weapon, owing to the absence of condensation; and so he continues firing, leisurely but with terrifying effect, assured meanwhile of his own safety.

At last the firing ceases, and it is in vain that the soldiers, roaming over the slopes, seek for their vanished assailants. They return exhausted, the bugles sound, and the band is on its way once more, with a few men less. And when the last of them are out of sight, beyond the roll of the hill, there rises up from among the stone heaps—like a sinister caryatid amid these cyclopic ruins—a hard and sunburned face, followed by the rude and leather-clad torso of an athlete. Running swiftly up the steep sides of the ravine, this dreadful hunter of armed men is gone in a few moments' time.

The troops continue on their way, completely demoralized. From now on, these hardened veterans are as timid as a child. A shiver runs up and down their spines at each bend of the road, at every dead leaf that crackles in the brush. The army has come to feel that its very strength is its weakness. Without any maneuverability, in a state of continual exhaustion, it must make its way through these desert regions under the constant threat of ambuscades and be slowly sacrificed to a dreaded enemy who does not stand and fight but flees. The conflict is an unequal one, and a military force is compelled to descend to a lower plane of combat; it has to contend not merely with man but with the earth itself; and, when the backlands are boiling in the dry summer heat, it is not difficult to foresee which side will have the victory. While the mighty Minotaur, helpless in spite of his steel armor and bayonet claws, feels his throat drying up with thirst and, at the first symptoms of hunger, turns back to the rear, fleeing the inhospitable and menacing desert, the aggressive flora of this region, on the other hand, takes the *sertanejo* to its friendly, caressing bosom.

Then it is—in these indeterminate seasons between the "green" and the "lean,"[17] when the last trickles of water are to be found in the mud of the marshlands and the last yellowed leaves on the boughs of the *baraúnas,* as the frightened stranger flees the imminent scourge of the drought—then it is the

---

17. "*Verde e magrem,* names that backwoodsmen give, respectively, to the rainy season and the season of drought" [da Cunha's note, p. 38.]

backwoodsman is blessed by knowing the ins and outs of every long and winding trail; for know them he does, knows by heart every nook and cranny of this enormous roofless home of his. It does not matter to him if the journey is long and the houses are few and far between, if the water in the wells is dried up, while the lowland coverts, where the weary cowboy is wont to take his noonday ease, are slowly thinning out. He is sustained by a sense of the long familiar. These trees are for him old companions. He knows them all. He and they were born and grew up together, like brothers; they have both had the same difficulties to face, have had to struggle with the same hardships, and have shared the same days of tranquility. . . .

Yes, Nature protects the *sertanejo,* renders him an indomitable Antaeus. And this is the bronzed Titan who causes armies to waver in their march.[18]

BEYOND THE BOUNDS OF THE FATHERLAND

The new expeditionaries, upon reaching Queimadas, were aware of [a] violent [geographic] transition. Here was an absolute and radical break between the coastal cities and the clay huts of the interior, one that so disturbed the rhythm of our evolutionary development and that was so deplorable a stumbling-block to national unity. They were in a strange country now, with other customs, other scenes, a different kind of people. Another language even, spoken with an original and picturesque drawl. They had, precisely, the feeling of going to war in another land. They felt that they were outside Brazil. A complete social separation expanded the geographic distance, giving rise to the nostalgic sensation of being very far from home. The mission that had brought them there merely served to deepen the antagonism. There was the enemy out there to the east and to the north, hidden away in those endless highland plains; and far, far away, beyond the plains, a terrible drama was being unfolded.

It was, surely, a paradoxical kind of fatherland whose own sons had to invade it, armed to the teeth, with martial tread, ripping out its very entrails with their Krupps cannon.[19] And, all the while, they knew nothing whatever about it; they

---

18. At this point, the national government realized the necessity of putting down this revolt and sent troops, although still under the state flag of Baía. A third expedition went into the backlands, but it was repelled by the *sertanejos,* and the church bells of Canudos rang out the victory. With the failure of the third expedition, a fourth expedition of troops from all regions of Brazil went to Canudos, but it too had to retreat, defeated by the backlanders. The government sent reinforcements, and the entire operation came under the command of Marshal Carlos Machado de Bittencourt, who organized the logistics of the campaign in such a way as to sustain an attack. He did so by the simple but effective expedient of purchasing one thousand domesticated burros to serve as a supply train. As da Cunha notes, "Marshall Bittencourt . . . unmoved by the impatience of the general public, organized supply trains and purchased mules. For the truth is, this bloody and truly dramatic campaign was to be brought to a successful conclusion in one way, and one way only, and the solution was a singularly humorous one. A thousand domesticated burros in this emergency were worth 10,000 heroes" (p. 398).

19. Krupps was the premier German manufacturer of heavy arms in the nineteenth century.

had never seen it before but viewed with amazement the arid earth, rugged and brutal, bristling with thorns, tumultuously littered with stone heaps and pulverized mountains, torn asunder with caverns and ravines, while all about were the parched and barren tablelands, great, rolling, steppe-like plains.

What they were being called upon to do now was what other troops had done—to stage an invasion of foreign territory. For it was all a geographic fiction. This other was the reality, plain for all to see from what had gone before. The soldiers felt this and were obsessed by the thought. Here were those unknown woodsmen sending back to them, day by day, mutilated and defeated, their comrades who, a few months previously, had gone down that same road, strong of body and proud in spirit. As a result, there was no heart left in them; they had not the courage to strike out, unconcerned with what might happen, into the depths of those mysterious and formidable backlands.

IN CANUDOS

Happily, upon their arrival at Queimadas, the effect of all this was counteracted to a degree by the receipt of encouraging news from the front. There had been no further disasters, and, in spite of the enemy's daily fusillades, our forces were still holding the positions they had won. The Girard Brigade and the São Paulo Battalion had reached Canudos in time to fill the gaps in the thinning ranks; and, meanwhile, the rebels were beginning to show the first signs of discouragement. They no longer rang the bell of the old church, by way of showing, vaingloriously, how unconcerned they were; for there was no bell to ring;[20] and, in the intervals of firing, their melancholy litanies were no longer to be heard. They had ceased their attacks on our lines; and at night there was not a flicker of light, not a sound, as the settlement lay submerged in darkness.

The rumor then began going the rounds that the Counselor was being held prisoner by his own followers, who had revolted when he announced his intention of surrendering and giving himself up to martyrdom. Other details were cited, all of them pointing to a rapid dying-down of the conflagration.

PRISONERS

Indeed, the new combatants fancied that it had been extinguished even before they reached Canudos. Everything appeared to indicate as much. The first prisoners were at last being brought back, after all these months of fighting; and our men could not help noticing, without attempting to explain the fact, that there was not a full-grown man to be found among them. These captives, escorted under heavy guard, were pitiful ones indeed: Half-a-dozen women with infants wizened as fetuses at their bosoms, followed by older children, from six to ten years of age. The soldiers crowded around to stare at them curiously as they made their way through the town—a town swarming with uniforms of every branch of the service and of every rank.

---

20. The bell had been knocked out earlier by fire from a Witworth 32, which the *sertanejos* had named "the Killer."

It was a sorry spectacle as these ragged creatures, under the gaze of all those eyes—insatiable eyes that seemed to look straight through their tatters—came into the square, dragging their young ones by the hand. They were like animals at the fair, an amusing sight. Round about them could be heard comments of every sort, in every tone of voice, whispered comments, with lively interjections and expressions of astonishment. This wretched band was for the time being something to take one's mind off things; a pleasing diversion to lighten the long and tedious hours spent in camp. It excited the curiosity of all without touching their hearts.

THE CHILD IN THE KEPI

One of the children—a thin little mite, barely able to stand—wore on its head an old kepi that it had picked up along the road and which came down over its shoulders, covering a third or more of its emaciated bosom. This big, broad hat kept swaying grotesquely at every step the child took, and some of the spectators were so unfeeling as to laugh at the sight. Then the child raised its face and looked them in the eye. Their laughter died on their lips; for the little one's mouth was a gaping bullet wound, from side to side!

• • • • •

ANOTHER CHILD

. . . A lad of less than nine years but with the shoulders of an embryonic athlete amazed them all with his precocious swaggering and his craftiness. His answers were given between stout puffs on a *cigarro,* as he drew on it with the self-assured nonchalance of an old roué. He volunteered a stream of information, almost all of it false, revealing the astuteness of the consummate rogue. His interlocutors took it all in, religiously, for this was a child speaking; but, when a soldier entered with a Comblain rifle in his hand, the boy stopped his babbling and, to the astonishment of all, remarked in a tone of conviction that a "*comblé*" was no good. It was a "sissy" gun; it made a "damned big noise," but there was no force behind it. For himself he preferred a "*manulixe*"; that was a rifle that was a rifle. And so they handed him a Mannlicher, and he proceeded to work its lock as easily as if this had been some favorite childish plaything. They asked him if he had ever fired one of them at Canudos.

"What do you think?" he said. "Those soldiers down there are a bunch of old fogies! . . . but when the young bucks get after 'em, they give 'em what for, and they have to take it like a bull in a corner; the jig's up then; we take 'em down a peg or two."[21]

This lad was, of course, tremendously depraved; but he was a lesson to those who heard him, all the same. Here was a finished bandit, cast up by this backlands

---

21. "*A cabrada fechava o samba desautorisando as praças,*" etc.; the lad speaks a backlands patois. [Translator's note.]

conflict, with a formidable legacy of errors resting upon his boyish shoulders, nine years of life into which had been packed three centuries of barbarism. It was plain that the Canudos Campaign must have a higher objective than the stupid and inglorious one of merely wiping out a backlands settlement. There was a more serious enemy to be combated, in a warfare of a slower and more worthy kind. This entire campaign would be a crime, a futile and barbarous one, if we were not to take advantage of the paths opened by the artillery, by following up our cannon with a constant, stubborn, and persistent campaign of education,[22] with the object of drawing these rude and backward fellow-countrymen of ours into the current of our times and our own national life.

But, under the pressure of difficulties demanding an immediate and assured solution, there was no place for these distant visions of the future. The minister of war, after stopping four days in Queimadas, where he removed the last obstacles to the mobilization of our forces, departed for Monte Santo.

• • • • •

IN MONTE SANTO

By the time they reached Monte Santo, the new troops felt little martial ardor. They were dejected. Their spirits were revived, however, as they entered the village that constituted the base of operations.

Within a few days' time Monte Santo had shed the shrunken, stagnant appearance that is common to backlands settlements where for a hundred years and more not a house has gone up. It was now a vastly larger place. The surrounding plains were white with tents, two thousand of them, forming a new quarter and one larger than the town itself in normal times, with long avenues that were plainly to be seen, the level-lying ground presenting no obstruction to the view. There were six groups of these tents, and, over them all, banners were floating in the breeze, and from them all, at almost every moment, came the vibrant, metallic notes of bugles and the beat of drums.

The town was now crowded with a multitude of new inhabitants from foreign parts, filling the square and overflowing down the narrow lanes, a heterogeneous assortment of men from all walks of life. There were officers of every rank and from all branches of the service; wagon-drivers, dust-begrimed from long journeys; soldiers bending under the weight of their equipment; the wounded and convalescent, limping along; women in tattered garments; busy tradesmen;

---

22. This sentence expresses one of da Cunha's core beliefs, namely, that Brazil would never develop a proper national life until such time as it had biologically and educationally unified its people: "We do not possess unity of race, and it is possible we shall never possess it. We are destined to form a historic race in the future, providing the autonomy of our national life endures long enough to permit it. In this respect, we are inverting the natural order of events. Our biological evolution demands the guaranty of social evolution. We are condemned to civilization. Either we shall progress or we shall perish. So much is certain, and our choice is clear" (p. 54).

groups of merry students; journalists eager for news, who went about asking questions incessantly—all this gave to the scene the appearance of a city *praça* on the day of a parade. Marshal Bittencourt at once put the town under strict martial law and lost no time in adopting such measures as accorded with the complex needs of the situation. The military hospital now became a reality, thoroughly well equipped and under the charge of skilled surgeons, aided by a number of students from the faculty of Baía who had volunteered their services. A proper discipline was everywhere established; and, at last, the question that had originally brought the minister there—that of the transport service—was definitely settled. Almost daily, partial supply trains were leaving for and returning from Canudos.

The results of these efforts were immediately visible. They were apparent in the news coming from the battlefront, where everything pointed to a new spirit on the part of the besiegers, who were now engaging in decisive tactical maneuvers.

If this was so, it was owing to one individual, an individual seemingly so incapable of any enthusiasm, who even at the base of operations declined to lay aside his bourgeois alpaca coat, clad in which he reviewed the brigades.[23] It was due to the fact that this man, thanks to the high degree of devotion that he displayed—and this is said without any desire to offend the sensibilities of those who were engaging the enemy at close range—had made himself, in reality, the supreme commander in this conflict. At a distance of forty miles from the front, he was in fact directing that conflict, without any boasting, without any weighing and balancing of strategic plans, but by spending his days in the rude company of pack-drivers at Monte Santo; he could frequently be seen, amid a throng of them, rising to his feet impatiently, watch in hand, as he gave the signal for departure.

For each supply train that was sent was worth battalions, it was a battle won. It gave the fighting men fresh hope of victory and little by little was doing away with that stagnation that had paralyzed our siege lines. This was what one gathered from the latest reports.

IN CANUDOS

The month of September, the truth is, began auspiciously enough. Early in the month—on the fourth, to be exact—one of the *jagunços'* leading chieftains had been killed by a rifle bullet. He fell near the churches, and the haste with which the inhabitants of the settlement threw themselves on his corpse, to take it away, showed that he was a person of importance. On the sixth there was an event of greater significance, when, one after the other, the towers of the new church crashed to the ground. This happened after six consecutive hours of bombardment, and was entirely unexpected, being attributable to an unpleasant circumstance that had arisen. In dispatching munitions to the front, someone had made a mistake and, in place of grenades, had sent plain cannon balls for the

---

23. Marshall Bittencourt.

Krupps, which were little suited for the purpose in hand, and it was accordingly decided to use them up by firing on the churches.

The surprising result was commemorated in a couple of enthusiastic orders of the day. The army at last had been freed of those high battlements from which the besieged had fired upon it with so deadly an effect; for the two towers had commanded our entire lines, reducing the effectiveness of our trenches. Ever since the eighteenth of July they had been manned by expert marksmen whose sharp eyes let nothing escape them, so that no one dared so much as show his face from behind the shelter of the huts. When the supply trains arrived, they had been greeted with a violent fusillade from the church towers, just as they reached the last lap of their journey and were crossing the river, before entering the gully that formed a covered passageway. It was from there that the newcomers, the auxiliary brigade, the São Paulo Battalion, and the Thirty-seventh Infantry, as we have seen, received the enemy's first savage salute.

ENTHUSIASTIC JEERS

And now, at last, those towers had fallen. It was an impressive sight to see them tumble, one after the other, carrying away with them large sections of the wall in the form of huge blocks and burying the bold sharpshooters in the ruins; the stones fell with a great crash into the village square, amid a cloud of pulverized mortar, as our entire army ceased firing and rent the air with triumphant cries. The commander of the First Column well described it in his order of the day: ". . .our advance line and the supporting troops in the camp behind, on this occasion, breaking out with enthusiastic jeers directed at the *jagunço* rabble."[24]

That is a good description of the campaign itself. From beginning to end, one saddening hue and cry, "Enthusiastic jeers . . . "

However that may be, the enemy's spell was broken now, the enormous settlement had of a sudden shrunken in size. It seemed smaller and more squat than ever, appeared to be huddled more deeply than ever in the depression in which it was built, being deprived of those two tall and slender white towers that had been a landmark for herdsmen for miles around, and which, reaching up to the blue and mysteriously dissolving in it, or gleaming brightly on starlit nights, served to objectify the rude and credulous *sertanejo's* ingenuous mysticism, bringing nearer to the heavens his propitiatory prayers.

---

24. Headquarters of the Commander, First Column, Canudos, sixth of September, 1897, Order of the Day No. 13. [Translator's note.]

Clorinda Matto de Turner
(Peru)

Clorinda Matto de Turner (1852–1909) is a Peruvian writer, whose nascent nineteenth-century feminism and passion for social justice with respect to the indigenous served to bring some of Peru's political and social realities into nineteenth-century intellectual discourse.

Matto de Turner was born in Cuzco to Ramón Matto y Torres and Grimanesa Usandivares and also lived at her family's hacienda in Calca Province. She had two younger brothers. Having grown up speaking both Spanish and Quechua, the indigenous language of the Andes, she always felt close to Andean indigenous culture. She studied in the Colegio Nuestra Señora de las Mercedes del Cuzco, and at fourteen began writing dramatic essays that were performed in a private theater. After marrying the English physician and merchant Joseph Turner in 1871, she moved with him to the town of Tinta where she continued her literary career, writing poetry and articles published under pseudonyms in *El Heraldo, El Ferrocarril, El Rodadero, El Eco de los Andes,* and *El Mercurio.* In 1876, she founded the weekly newsmagazine *El Recreo.* She had the opportunity to interact with other intellectuals when she moved to Lima and attended literary gatherings organized by the Argentine writer Juana Manuela Gorriti. Eventually, Matto de Turner began to hold such gatherings herself.

Two years after the death of her husband in 1881, Matto de Turner moved to Arequipa, where she became editor-in-chief of the important daily newspaper, *La Bolsa.* In 1886, she moved back to Lima where she took up the life of an intellectual, joining, by invitation, the prestigious literary societies, Círculo Literario and Ateneo de Lima. In 1888, the Ibero-American Union of Madrid extended honorary associate membership to her. In 1889, she became director of one of South America's most notable literary weeklies, *El Perú Ilustrado.*

Her charmed literary life now turned sour. Shortly after she took over leadership of *El Perú Ilustrado,* the Archbishop of Lima pronounced a prohibition, under pain of mortal sin, against reading, selling, or otherwise disseminating that publication, giving as his reason a "sacrilegious" work the magazine had published. Although Matto de Turner claimed the article had been published without her knowledge or consent, there appeared to be an underlying motive for the censure, the publication the year before of her novel, *Aves sin nido* (1889) (translated as *Birds without a Nest*), in which she had denounced the corruption of the clergy. In the end, Matto de Turner, now excommunicated by the archbishop and having been burned in effigy by crowds in Arequipa, felt forced to resign her post in order to open the way for the archbishop to lift the ecclesiastical censure against the weekly. Her novel was placed on the Index of Prohibited Books.

With her siblings, Matto de Turner then established an independent press staffed by women, La Equitativa, which published the bi-weekly periodical, *Los*

Andes. However, because of her open support, in print, of General Andrés A. Cáceres and his Constitutional Party, rebel troops entering Lima plundered her house and seized her, but she was able to flee and hide in the home of some friends. The troops then sacked Matto de Turner's publishing house, destroying its presses and manuscripts. Matto de Turner left for Chile and, finally, for Argentina, where she took up residence in Buenos Aires for the rest of her life.

Never a woman to admit defeat, in 1896 in Buenos Aires, she founded the magazine *Búcaro Americano,* which became the official organ of the Sociedad Proteccionista Intelectual, and which she edited until shortly before her death. In 1896, she began teaching in three schools: the Escuela Normal de Profesoras de la Capital Federal, the Escuela Normal Norteamericana, and the Escuela Comercial de Mujeres. She collaborated in numerous publications in Buenos Aires, Montevideo, and Caracas. She was elected to membership in the Consejo Nacional de Mujeres de Argentina, which in 1908 financed her six-month trip to Europe to study women's education there. Clorinda Matto de Turner died in 1909. Years later, a Congressional resolution in Peru paved the way for her remains to be repatriated.

The selection that follows, "The Woman Worker and the Woman," is from *Cuatro conferencias sobre América del Sur,* which was published in Buenos Aires in 1909.

Further Reading

Arellano, Ignacio, and José Antonio Mazzotti, eds. *Edición e interpretación de textos andinos: Actas del congreso internacional.* Pamplona: Universidad de Navarra; Madrid: Iberoamericana; and Frankfurt am Main: Vervuert, 2000.

Carrillo E., Francisco Eduardo. *Clorinda Matto de Turner y su indigenismo literario.* Lima: Ediciones de la Biblioteca Universitaria, 1967.

Cornejo Polar, Antonio. *Clorinda Matto de Turner, novelista: Estudios sobre* Aves sin nido, Indole y Herencia. Lima: Lluvia Editores, 1992.

Manrique, Nelson. *La piel y la pluma: Escritos sobre literatura, etnicidad y racismo.* Lima: CiDiAG: Sur Casa de Estudios del Socialismo, 1999.

Meyer, Doris, ed. *Reinterpreting the Spanish American Essay: Women Writers of the Nineteenth and Twentieth Centuries.* Austin, Tex.: University of Texas Press, 1995.

Tauro, Alberto. *Clorinda Matto de Turner y la novela indigenista.* Lima: Universidad Nacional Mayor de San Marcos, Dirección Universitaria de Biblioteca y Publicaciones, 1976.

Parra, Teresita J., and María Luisa Bombal. "Feminist Ideas in the Works of Clorinda Matto de Turner." In *Multicultural Literatures through Feminist/Poststructuralist Lenses,* edited by Barbara Frey Waxman, pp. 153–72. Knoxville, Tenn.: University of Tennessee, 1993.

"The Woman Worker and the Woman" (1904)

Translated by Mary G. Berg and Elena C. Berg[1]

LADIES:

Since I have no wish to bore this intelligent audience, I will not embark here upon an extensive analysis of the many definitions of that ominous word "strike," and of what this term has come to signify with modern society. I would like instead to remark briefly upon a series of issues and to discuss some examples that will be familiar and vivid to every woman who works for the cause of women under the slogan "Not for Herself Alone but for Humanity," which the National Council for Women of the Argentine Republic has engraved on the hearts of its members just as it prints it on its propaganda flyers.

Many are the authoritative voices that have shared the wealth of their wise thoughts through newspapers, magazines, lectures, and books intended to inform working women. They have investigated various topics, sought ways to improve conditions, and proposed plans of action designed to accelerate the improvement of present conditions through increases in salaries and better hygiene in factories where women work. The women who have spoken out include those who are about to give birth, those who are breastfeeding the workers of tomorrow, those who are virgins and in danger of premature moral deflowering, and those who are destitute widows: almost all of these are women who have been bestialized by ignorance and deprived of their ideals and hopes!

It is only honest to admit that these examples suggest a much darker picture than truth would demand, because the situation of the working woman in America, especially in Buenos Aires, is less grievous than in Europe. In fact, if our society were more intent on following its own common sense, and if the news that reaches us by telegraph were not so provocative, it is quite possible that we would not yet have witnessed the phenomenon of strikes here. Those who have actually visited the European centers in order to study the social structure of towns and workers' conditions can testify to us that salaries, housing, food, and general living conditions of European workers are inferior, far inferior, to those in America.

There, the worker receives a very low salary, can afford to eat meat on only two or three special days of the year, and lives in cramped quarters. If he is a farmer, he tills the land in order to give the landowner the best of the harvest, able to keep for himself only what is left over, and he dresses in the roughest of cloth. Hence those who come to hear something about this New World get so enthusiastic that they hurry to emigrate to this Promised Land where their hopes

1. Clorinda Matto de Turner, "The Woman Worker and the Woman," translated by Mary G. Berg and Elena C. Berg, in *Rereading the Spanish American Essay: Translations of Nineteenth and Twentieth Century Women's Essays,* edited by Doris Meyer, 90–8 (Austin, Tex.: University of Texas Press, 1995). Reprinted by permission of the University of Texas Press.

are fulfilled: From the moment they disembark at their port of entry here, they are welcomed as ladies and gentlemen, and they find that everything is set up for the beneficial transformation of their lives. If they want to work, work is available that is appropriate to their skills and abilities, and government assistance is readily available to them through the Department of Immigration. Farmers rejoice at the prospect of vast expanses of Argentine soil with all of its varied crops, where everything the farmers harvest or earn belongs to them, to them alone, and does not have to be shared with anyone else. Our fraternal republic offers them equality before the law, and the sublime energies of philanthropy, the soul of which is woman, open the doors of asylums to those who meet with misfortune.

Evidence of the well-being of honest workers who love order and hard work may be seen on every public sidewalk and in the public schools attended by their children; all the children are well cared for and if in some of the poorer neighborhoods we do see occasional ragged children, it is because there are problems there that are real exceptions to the general rule we are discussing: matters of dubious parentage, lazy people who are dissatisfied but do not choose to work, or that ridiculous type of men who live off women.

Very well then. If, as Spencer sustains, a society is an organism whose development and growth depend upon the components that constitute it, then our workers' society is very well established and so can generate other organisms or perfect those that are undeveloped or weak, like pale sapless plants that have sprouted in the dark and cannot be expected to contribute much to national progress. Only yesterday, ladies, it was said that all greatness distances itself from the common crowds: The eagle seeks heights and the thinker isolates himself in his garret; but today, in this age of new technology, when it is man himself who controls light through his understanding of electricity, the eagle flies from the peaks into the hands of men, and the thinker mingles with the populace, hearts draw nearer, and physical force and intellectual power, in intimate fusion, turn the great wheel of human progress. Strikes are perturbations that only momentarily interrupt the forward motion of that great wheel, without providing any positive benefit for anyone.

This disagreeable subject has been studied at length by men of such moral probity as Dr. Eduardo Dato, a former Spanish government minister and author of laws protecting workers; José Canalejas y Méndez, president of the Academy of Jurisprudence and Legislation; José Gascón y Marín; and others who are no less eminent. They describe grievous situations that have resulted from conflict of interest between owners and workers. However, these clashes, which embitter and intensify the struggle between capital and labor, are rare in this country, as rare as many of the social vices that are unknown in the homes of our pure young workers. The aforementioned Mr. Canalejas tells us of the many different factors that contribute to the gravity of these struggles. It will suffice to recall that once the worker has stopped being a *slave and servant* and has become a *free individual,* which represents undeniable progress, he continues to be a salaried proletarian. That is to say, he lives in conditions that are more conspicuously inferior than ever when he is aware of the contrast between his situation and that of the few men or groups of men who have been privileged by fortune and who have accumulated enormous wealth. This extreme inequality does not exist among us, for in Argentina we are all free in the most ample definition of the word "liberty." Our republican government consecrates equality as state law, and the precepts of Jesus Christ, teacher of true and pure socialism, are established as fundamental. Our basic law is that *All good that stems from evil is reprehensible.*

It is true as Mr. Dato affirms, with respect to Bilbao society, that the most popular movement, both here and in Spain, is a socialism that has been adulterated by subsequent theories, such as those of the evolutionists. Although utopian concepts such as total equality of social classes, work-sharing by everyone, and collective property would undoubtedly lead to general chaos if they were ever put into practice, these are still the dreams that seduce many workers. Without stopping to realize that differences between classes will always exist, without taking into account that social inequalities are as immutable as the laws of physics, imposed by God upon Humanity, and without noticing that we all have different abilities, that some of us are more virtuous or more beautiful than others, that we do not all share the same feelings, and that some of us are blonds while others are brunettes, these misguided workers give themselves up to unfulfillable promises and put themselves right into the hands of agitators who seek a political end or personal notoriety, often without any sense of civic responsibility.

In our view, the worker is the most respectable element of our society because it is he who carries the banner of progress and he who is the priest of the sublime religion of work in whose temple the joy of life is born.

A sharing of all labor! Who would direct it? Who would have to do the unhealthy and dangerous jobs? What difference would there be between intellectual and mechanical labor? Who would decide the salaries? How would we take into account the needs of each man, whether single or married, with or without a family? What would we do about the vagrant, the criminal, the dull-witted? The mind must ponder these profound and complex matters!

No! The honest worker, conscious of his acts, does not wish for collectivism. He will accept Christian socialism when it is likely to improve his condition and bring him happiness, but he knows perfectly well that a glowing utopian future is an illusion. When he recognizes liberty stemming from legal right, he must say to himself, "I have the freedom to decide whether to work or not, but I do not have the right to deprive others of their freedom to work." And following from this is the whole code of the perfectibility of relationships between all the men of the world. *Do unto others as you would have others do unto you.*

At the level of civilization we have reached, there is no reason to impose a sacrifice on anyone; it is more a question of insisting upon equality in decision-making procedures on the part of both owners and workers.

Does the owner wish that the worker not squander time or money? Well then, he should not cheat the worker. . . . Does he demand equality and justice for himself? Well then, he should want that same equality and justice for the laborers, without changing its terms. Those who became enemies in a time of egotism and inhumanity will become friends today and live together in the fraternal city of light, where there are no blizzards that paralyze the generous impulses of the spirit beneath the ice of positivism.

Until now, we have focused on the statements of others regarding strikes in general. Having established that the merit of man should be measured by the good he does to his fellow men, it is now time for us to move on to discuss the main topic of this speech, the woman worker. We could certainly say that she regards matters of social equality from a rather different point of view than do men, for her natural talents and observations have focused upon her sewing machine, and she dedicates her energies to the perfection of her assigned tasks, to the precise completion of the garments she sews. When they have been observed in large factories, women have proved extraordinarily capable of making the fine adjustments of bobbins and shuttles that produce perfect results.

Women, then, with their ability to make quick assessments and their perceptive feminine intuition stemming from their close attunement to domestic matters, understand the delicacy and importance of labor negotiations, and thus the woman worker, honest and thoughtful, does not go on strike.

For the same reasons, she will dissuade her husband and her children from participating, because she knows what a week without work means for her family, and she knows from experience not to place her trust in collective promises. She knows that strikes that influence the industrial world endanger the worker more than anyone else: The lost wages are never recovered, the vices her husband acquires during his days of being laid off stay with him, and when the strikers have triumphed, it usually means that the factories will close, thus reducing them to poverty. There will be less employment, fewer places to work, and . . . children who cry for bread!

Our sisters, the women who work, are mistrustful of the women who urge them along the path of disorder. Our working sisters are guided by their instinct for maintaining domestic harmony, a harmony that is the immediate result of uninterrupted labor. It is urgent that we who work with these women should draw closer to them in order to be able to convince them that to be both skilled and employed is to be happy. Our propaganda should have as its object, then, that the woman worker should love her work, orderliness, and domestic economy, without being ignorant that all living beings drag the same chains of suffering and march on toward the same unknown finality of death.

The doctrine of evolution, which is the synthesis of the Spencerian system I have just mentioned, must surely bring incalculable advantages to the cause of the *individual woman* [*la mujer persona*] without violating the boundaries of reason by suggesting a ridiculous absolute equality between men and women, for there are biological differences impossible to ignore.

To reduce this to its simplest terms: How can a man be a mother?

But we should remember, too, that both men and women are made up of spirit and physical matter, are one with infinite creation, and are nurtured by woman's milk.

This is the propitious moment, when those of us who have upheld the cause of protectionism for women must act. We must move on to further achievements and not allow ourselves to be intimidated by our egotistic detractors' derision of our cause, we must remember the initial struggles of all the great movements and all the great causes that have contributed to human progress, and this solidarity will uplift our spirits.

When Stephenson utilized Fulton's discovery of the uses of steam in order to make railroad engines run, what did the skeptics say? That it was surely the work of the devil, one of those heretical inventions that threatens the faith of simple folk. But those instigators of universal progress did not give up so easily, and within a half century, we saw that progress was taking hold, like Galileo's view of the earth, gradually establishing itself as irrefutable. The locomotive triumphant, the iron monster taking over the surface of the earth: the plains, the peaks, and all the spaces in between. We have come to accept this pandemonium on wheels, this metallic microcosm, this harbinger of civilization in every country. To this serpent without coloring or scales, the miles are its steps, and the different countries its flights and stages; its brow is horned like the unicorn and all the forms of terrestrial animality are fused in it; as Jaime Puig y Verdaguer said: It roars like a lion, bellows like a bull, twists around curves like a snake and forges ahead like a dragon.

Lion, bull, snake, and dragon, it charges along, racing, rushing, roaring, and obliterating inertia and all the immovable forces of the earth, in order to wake them to the life of work.

Many tons of coal are its daily nourishment, its boiler is its belly and the flames its heart; the steam is its blood, the wheels its muscles; it harbors safety in its breast, where men of all latitudes take refuge, to be transported across the miles, crossing mountains and cities congealed in the soot of time, amidst great stone boulders that will soon be transformed into arches, columns, and pillars that will support temples or art, science, and peace built by the efforts of the laborer and by the daring of the capitalist.

Yes, they must ever be coupled, in harmonious unity, and just as the steel giant has forged ahead, so, too, will the cause of the working woman gain more adherents with the passage of time. The growing strength of the movement for the betterment of working conditions for women is grounded in recognition of the virtue of freely chosen work, for the only free individual is the one who is self-sufficient. The sun of hope is rising in the east smiling at the woman worker as she takes over the world. Everywhere, she works with faith: in schools, workshops, academies, factories, offices, businesses, writing, teaching, and journalism. This purposeful effort results in the immediate reduction of delinquency and criminal activity.

In our research about women and crime, we have gathered the following statistics: of a hundred criminal cases, seventy-eight were motivated by love, twenty by greed, twenty by pathological or hereditary causes, and two by other factors. Studies of women criminals indicate that there are very few working women in their numbers. In many of the studied cases, poverty and abandonment by a man figure as causes of women's crime, especially when neglect or abuse of children is involved. Even when she is not at fault, it is the woman who is labeled as dishonored by separation from her spouse, one of those "conventional lies" discussed by Max Nordau.[2]

Let me repeat that we are now at an opportune moment, and that we should spare no effort to put the growing current of positive progress on the right track, serving the woman worker ever more effectively as we become better acquainted with her. We do not wish to exalt her fantasy with utopias that will disappoint her, nor to turn her head with unwholesome prospects, but rather to make her love her work, showing her that she need envy no one, not even the high-born nor the so-called wealthy, many of whom yearn for a restorative night's sleep, a good appetite, simple pleasures, and sound health.

Once we have examined the differences that exist between the American woman worker and the European, it is clear that the former has all the advantages over the latter. Let us awaken in her heart a fraternal love without continental boundaries, demonstrating with deeds that a strong chain, its links forged together by honor, interconnects good women from every part of the globe. In any case, the woman worker already knows that she should not participate in disastrous strikes nor have anything to do with boycotts or blacklists, for she has already learned from her own experience that "when the wheels are kept turning, busy hands are kept earning." She knows something more, ladies, that when she is putting bread on the table at home, her family is happy, and the goddess of harmony presides over spouses who are united by the bonds of love, bonds that are less likely to sunder in modest homes than in sumptuous mansions where the golden glitter dazzles us but where unknown problems underlie the shining surface.

Let us take care to provide education and guidance for women workers, for they are the precious antidote we are able to offer mankind to counteract the poison of social perturbations. Thus may truly civilized behavior prevail in the workplace.

We must admire the astronaut who adventures through space in his dirigible. We must applaud the engineer who constructs railroads on the surface and deep under the earth. And we must encourage the founder of factories, asking him for both equity and justice for workers, and appealing to him to turn over the future well-being of the young American nations to the well-established efforts of women.

Let us remind the woman worker that she has no reason to covet diamond diadems when her perspiring brow is encircled by the halo of holy work and of the sublime and universal law. It is our job to provide effective support for the working woman, our sister. Let us "comfort vacillating spirits and troubled hearts." Let us extend the field of action; let us ascertain that her work is properly remunerated since factory owners do exist who pay women less simply

2. Max Nordau (1849–1923), *The Conventional Lies of Our Civilization,* an 1884 best-seller in Germany, translated very soon thereafter into English (1885), Spanish, and other languages. [Translator's note.]

because they are women, even though their work is identical to that of men. Ah! These are the ones who forget that the buzz of the bee is more useful than the roar of the lion.

Let us found centers for education and recreation, and societies that protect the rights of women workers without the disruption of strikes, strikes that accord so poorly with woman's true nature, which is gentle, consonant with peace and conciliation.

As women struggle to make the best of their lives, let us inspire them with evidence of the beauty of orderly labor. And may they be even more stimulated by the radiantly beautiful example of the woman worker herself, her enlightened spirit manifest as a halo of true virtue. She is an ideal energy source for the creation of well-being and happiness both in her own home and in our entire nation.

In conclusion, let us turn to those who are most concerned about and most influential in social causes, in order to encourage them to support not only workers but all the needy classes. We should ameliorate their condition by implementing our brotherly and sisterly love. We end with Victor Hugo's message: *Responsibility,* get to work, for your hour has come: improve the human soul!

Francisco Alonso de Bulnes
(Mexico)

Francisco Alonso de Bulnes (1847–1924) is a Mexican public philosopher who seemed to enjoy courting controversy. His eclectic background and ability to stir up the anger of his critics make him an especially interesting person and writer. He was both a politician and a historian during the presidency of Porfirio Díaz, although his education and training was in mining and civil engineering and his writing preference seemed to be for sociological analysis of Mexico's problems. In his histories, especially his well-known *El porvenir de las naciones hispanoamericanas ante las conquistas recientes de Europa y los Estados Unidos* (translated as The Future of the Latin American Nations), Bulnes manifested the influence of positivism. Even as a politician, he believed with the positivists in a science of government. The selection that follows is from this work.

Bulnes was born and lived most of his life in Mexico City. He was the son of Manuel Alonso de Bulnes y de Ayerdi and María Muñoz Cano, descendents of northern Spanish families. His wife was María Teresa Irigoyen y de la Vega. Bulnes attended the Colegio de Minería where he became a civil and mining engineer, and he went to Japan in 1874 as part of a scientific commission charged with observing the passage of Venus in front of the sun. He wrote about this trip in his work, *Sobre el hemisferio norte: Once mil leguas* (1875). Despite this background in mining and engineering, he always had inclinations toward sociology and history, and he was also a teacher. He taught at the Colegio de Minería, in the Escuela Nacional Preparatoria, and at the Nacional de Ingenieros. He was a journalist at various times, editor and editor-in-chief of *La Libertad,* editor of *Siglo XX, México Financiero,* and *La Prensa* and contributing journalist to *El Universal.* He also served as a congressional deputy and senator for more than thirty years and was a consultant to various ministries. He served on a number of commissions, including one that wrote Mexico's first banking law and one that introduced the Mining Code of 1884 and reforms to that code in 1892. He also served on a commission concerned with the public credit and wrote laws for regularizing the public debt in 1886. He wrote about and advocated settlement of the English debt, a very unpopular opinion in Mexico at that time. He was especially effective in his role on the commission that sought to find the best ways to counteract the effects of the depreciation of silver. In his political role, he authored treatises on constitutional law, metallurgy, and agriculture.

Bulnes regarded the Mexican Revolution with skepticism. Further, when the revolution led by Venustiano Carranza broke out against Francisco I. Madero, Bulnes, in one of his articles, used a sentence of French historian Hyppolite Taine to describe Carranza's revolution: "The butcher of today will be the cattle of tomorrow." Carranza, taking offense, ordered Bulnes to be shot at his house. The order was never carried out because, fearing Carranza's anger, Bulnes had left for voluntary exile in the United States and Cuba. Very shortly after his departure, constitutionalist forces broke into his house, plundered it, and seized his library. While in exile in the United States, Bulnes wrote and had published in English *The Whole Truth about Mexico: President Wilson's Responsibility* (1916). He did not return to Mexico until 1921, three years before his death. During those few years he wrote a history of the Porfirian era and the revolution, *El verdadero Díaz y la revolución.*

In his writings, Bulnes often searched for the origins of the problems faced by Mexican society, writing about them in such works as *Las grandes mentiras de nuestra historia* and *Los grandes problemas de México.* He was especially critical of President Benito Juárez, writing several books about the man and his presidency, such as *El verdadero Juárez y la verdad sobre la intervención y el imperio* and *Júarez y las revoluciones de Ayutla y de Reforma,* which brought the ire of Juárez's supporters down upon him. But his titles show also a man of eclectic interests. He wrote, for instance, *El pulque: Estudio científico,* a detailed study of the popular Mexican drink, which posited that *pulque* has a lower alcohol level than other drinks and that the microorganisms it contains are not harmful to humans. On the other hand, he published books that showed his great grasp of finances, such as *La deuda Inglesa.*

Further Reading

Bulnes, Francisco. *The Whole Truth about Mexico: The Mexican Revolution and President Wilson's Part Therein, as Seen by a Científico.* Translated by Dora Scott. Detroit: Blaine Ethridge, 1972. (Original edition, New York: M. Bulnes, 1916.)

Bulnes, Francisco, and Norma de los Ríos. *Francisco Bulnes / Norma de los Ríos, compilación e introducción.* Mexico City: Senado de la República, 1987.

Didapp, Juan Pedro. *Explotadores políticos de México: Bulnes y el partido científico ante el derecho ajeno.* Mexico, D.F.: Tip. de los sucs. de F. Diáz de Leon, 1904.

González Roa, Fernando. *The Mexican People and Their Detractors.* New York: Latin American News Association, 1916.

Lemus, George. *Francisco Bulnes: Su vida y sus obras.* Mexico, D.F.: Ediciones De Andrea, 1965.

The Future of the Latin American Nations (1906)

Superorganic Elements of Latin America

Patriotism should be regarded as social energy of the first order for a country's preservation and progress. Unfortunately, the majority of Latins understand well what patriotism demands in times of foreign war but are almost completely ignorant of what it requires in periods of peace and cloudless noonday suns. In general, peacetime patriotism has served to drum up wars through **Punic**

hatreds, perverted ambitions, and impure interests. Glory, the tragic diva in the disheveled garb of devastation that occupies almost the entire stage of human history, has considered peace an unworthy social state, leading to the epic of the **hucksters**, to the agitation of the legal sharks, to the dictatorship of the courts, to the imposing prestige of the law codes. Justice has had three invincible enemies in the world up to now: Religion, Glory, and the Sovereignty of the people.

If one studies patriotic peoples, one sadly finds that in the name of patriotism they have reduced their country to living comfortably within the model of economic and mental indigence. In Spanish America we have a distinctly Latin patriotism, which consists in using peace to admire war, even if our wars have gone badly for us, and to prepare new catastrophes. Our patriotism cannot live without windmills, without battlefields, without the balm of Fierabras.[1] We never hear the alarm bells of patriotism ringing when it is a matter of obeying a law that goes against our own interests or against our pipe dreams; while, on the other hand, our patriotism catches fire when the drums roll, reverberating like a peal of exterminating laughter against the people we have been taught, justly or unjustly, to hate.

The first deficiency I have noted in Latin American patriotism is the lack of national unity. Not only sociology, but even the Jewish Gospel has said: *Omne regnum divisum contra se desolabitur* (every kingdom divided against itself is brought to desolation).[2] Union indisputably is strength. But what kind of union is the one we need? Union in the Catholic faith, in absolute obedience to the prince anointed by God, in the firm belief that everything our fathers did is our only command for the future, in the unyielding ambition of the Jesuit, in gloomy admiration for the Inquisition? Is the union we so badly need that of the regiments, that of the cloister, that of the railroad tracks, that of the shark's teeth, that of sheep following their shepherd's dog, that of convicts bound by clanking, groaning chains? That union was Spain's in the seventeenth century, in the century when Spain was defeated, humiliated, annihilated; the century when the Moors were expelled, when the glories of Spain were eclipsed, when its legends were forgotten, when its armor was melted down—not in a pure crucible, like that of the **incandescent Buddhist** faith, but rather in the dirty and opaque oil lamp of a refectory's fanaticism, of a sacrilegiously impregnated concubine, of concentrated fires of libidinous prostitution, and of horror for scientific truth. That union of all through a lie has produced the sort of crumbling nation that will die without ever having succeeded in seeing a genuine sun.

That union, altogether opposed to individual sovereignty, is a morbid legacy of classic Latinism. The Romans treated everything organic with a political algebra identical to its military algebra; they did not take into account individual rights because they had no sense of **the political individual**. For them, political

---

1. Referring to episodes in Cervantes' *Don Quixote,* First Part, chs. X, XVII. The balm of Fierabras was a medicinal elixer whose curative powers were decidedly unpredictable.

2. Matthew 12:25.

facts could only be about groups; in public law nothing existed but moral persons[3]—the State, the Army, the City, the Province, the foreign Barbarians, the Law, the Senate, the People, the Empire—never the individual, never men, only intangible things and groups of men as intangibles.

Where should national unity be sought in a civilized society? In every false tree of science there is a serpent that hypnotizes with its breath and an imbecile who loses paradise to eat a bitter apple. Mirabeau,[4] in an outburst of exaggeration, repeated a legendarily foolish remark: **"The truth is one and indivisible."** This sentence is theocratic and has the direct implication that all men must live united within the truth and subject to the manager of that sole, indivisible truth. The truth is that the number of truths is indefinite, and no man, no matter how wise, can hold in his consciousness all the truths of an advanced era of civilization. Savages anywhere, being physically, morally, and economically identical, can live unified under the authority of two or three truths; but in a nation, the more civilized it is the more it divides its mental tasks among its members—to the degree that a first-rate physician, a lawyer, an engineer, a pharmacist, a historian, can scarcely master, respectively, knowledge of even a part of medicine, of law, of mechanics, of physics, of chemistry, of the events that have taken place during the vast life of the human species.

To discover the truth, to recognize it well, to be able to test and to check it, is the most difficult of the sciences; nevertheless, as Spencer[5] has said, all men believe themselves capable of assessing truth and falsehood in sociological matters. Every era travels with its baggage of received truths, of **dubious truths** that will be errors in the next era. Truths and lies are equally good at standardizing consciousness, and even if it were possible one day to eliminate all errors from public thought, the fusion of men within truths acknowledged to be irreproachable would never take place, because in fully developed civilization supposed truths arise each day, challenging the skills of thinkers in order to become accepted.

But what is most difficult for the doctrine of the union of men in truth is that there is not, nor can there be for civilization, any truth that has the **authority of an established thing**. Individual thought can never lose or give up the right to **test** whether what is true for a nation is false for science. The most horrible attack against the individual has been the institution of moral persons such as the Church, the State, the Army, vested with the power to **declare** what is false and what is true, that is to say, what should be believed, not by means of logical proofs, but rather by means of policemen, executions, confiscations, torture, and

---

3. *Personas morales,* the evocative Spanish term for corporations recognized as legal entities.

4. Honoré-Gabriel Riqueti, Comte de Mirabeau (1749–1791), French revolutionary orator.

5. Herbert Spencer (1820–1903), English social and political philosopher who coined the phrase "survival of the fittest" in his writings on evolution, as well as the term "superorganic" in reference to the division of labor in civilized societies.

the gallows—complete chapters in the logic of terror, producer of brutalization and hypocrisy.

It is the right of each individual to be the sole judge in matters of his conscience; therefore, **union** within truth must be voluntary; but, as I have said that the number of truths is indefinite and the individual consciousness is incapable of holding them all even without judging them, it is impossible to actualize the union of all men within one sole truth, inasmuch as these truths are innumerable and necessarily hidden from the majority of individuals.

National unity in a civilized society must deal with a very limited number of truths, equally undeniable for all social classes, accepted freely by each individual, subject to solemn and energetic purification by the best telescopes, microscopes, and reagents of critical analysis. These truths, accepted without reservation by every social class, must correspond to interests of moral and economic well-being common to all social classes. In sum, patriotic union can develop only by the Anglo-Saxon formula, as opposed to the Latin formula. The Anglo-Saxon precept says, **The fatherland is for the individual;** the Latin formula maintains, **The individual is for the fatherland.**

In the Anglo-Saxon formula, **"The fatherland is for the individual,"** each individual has a right to form the fatherland in accordance with the ideal of his individual well-being, limited by the rights of others, which is the expression of social rights. A fatherland, as the word itself affirms, is a protection like that of a father, or even more nobly, like that of a mother, equally tender toward all her children; for a mother, there are not slave children and prince children. In the philosophical existence of a fatherland, the common mother is a moral person whose only consciousness and strength are the duties, rights, and wealth that **all her children by common agreement** want to give her. The fatherland, therefore, cannot demand any sacrifice; the duties of the individual toward the fatherland are those that he has imposed on himself in agreement with everyone else, in order to achieve present or future well-being or both; the fatherland does not demand anything, and individuals sacrifice themselves heroically to achieve the preservation of their families, their wealth, their customs, their territory, their way of life, in which they find happiness. The individual defends this whole set of historic, moral, intellectual, and material riches because it is his in part, because he has the right to reform it, to increase it, and, in a word, because he needs and enjoys the equitable protection of the whole community, which develops it in happiness, and whose rules cannot be modified without taking his will into account. For an Anglo-Saxon, the fatherland is duty, justice, liberty!

For a Latin, the fatherland has been the State, the Church, the Army, the Aristocracy—never the people nor he! Each one of those moral persons has represented the particular interests of a certain number of privileged people. Prove to a bishop that he is an adulterer, and he will reply that you are insulting the Church, and that, as the Church is the fatherland, you are a traitor who deserves the scaffold. Tell a king that a monarchy is contrary to the rights of man, and they will always behead you as a traitor, because the king is the fatherland! Shout "Long live Dreyfus!" in the Paris of 1899, and they will drive a dagger into you, because the inquisitorial verdicts of the Council of War must be venerated in every case of injustice, and the Army is the fatherland and every French patriot must prove it by yelling **hurrahs** at the Army at least seven times a day. But if the Army is conquered by the people, as in 1789, then any demagogue can be king, and you should believe that the guillotine is the fatherland. To sum up: The fatherland of the Latins until now has been the will of those who oppress them; **the individual for the fatherland** has been, according to history, **the individual against the fatherland** and in favor of those who are destroying it.

National unity in patriotic matters ought to signify the mutual respect of all social classes; the unconditional recognition of the rights and duties of each individual; altruism extended to the well-being of all, understood as the well-being of each one; and the community of general beliefs about the nation's past, present, and future, including philosophical and legal watchfulness over the interests of each class and individual.

Do the Spanish American nations possess these conditions of national unity in matters of patriotism? They must either possess them, or have them wrong, because all of them have proclaimed democracy as their social and political system.

The Apologists for the Colony

In Latin America, social classes are profoundly divided by cordilleras of prejudices and by chasms of which the most notable are hatred and scorn. Can the Indian be a patriot in our America? When four hundred years go by in a territory and the conquering and conquered races do not completely disappear through crossbreeding, giving way to a whole, mixed race in which the qualities · of the components dominate, that means that a great wall exists between the two races, which no one has wanted or been able to demolish.

Baron Humboldt, giving his opinion about New Spain, says: "That defect of sociability that is common throughout the Spanish possessions, and the hatreds that divide the castes closest to each other and, as a result of which, the life of the colonists appears full of bitterness, **derive solely from the political principles** by which those regions have been governed since the sixteenth century. A government enlightened in the true interests of humanity will be able to spread enlightenment and instruction and succeed in increasing the physical well-being of the settlers, gradually eliminating **that monstrous inequality of right and wealth, but it will have to overcome immense difficulties when it wishes to make the inhabitants sociable and teach them to treat each other mutually as citizens.**"[6]

---

6. Alexander von Humboldt (1769–1859), German naturalist and political thinker whose expeditions through the Spanish empire shortly before independence revolutionized the fields of geography and statistics in the Americas. The passage cited is from his *Political Essay on the Kingdom of New Spain* (Paris, 1811; London, 1811), book 2, chapter 7.

When a grown man is subject to protective legislation for minors, it is because he is considered demented or an idiot.[7] The supposedly wise Laws of the Indies were educational laws complementary to the rule of Aztec castes. Those laws were unjust, not because they burnt people at the stake and raised racks of torture; they were unjust for the human souls they dishonored; they forbade the Indians the right of owning land or possessions, the right to ride a horse, that of dressing like the Spaniards, that of leaving their villages, that of living on equal footing with the whites, that of marrying white individuals, that of working freely, that of being educated by their parents in the national religion, that of refusing *encomienda* service.[8] I do not understand how, but people who have never spent time in prison have warm feelings for the abominable precepts of a law code deemed "wise" by its authors and by those who benefited from such repugnant wisdom.

The conquest uprooted the Indian from his religion, his territory, his honor, his home, his children, his liberty, his wealth, his tradition, his history, his intelligence, his will, his memory, and, while in Latin America the upper classes have not wanted or been able to restore the Indian to his status as a human being, we make pastoral poems to praise the Indian's patriotism, such as we have understood it relative to our interests, always the interests of the dominant races. Lamennais has eloquently said: "The stable where the service animals eat and sleep is not a fatherland."[9]

Has the independence of the Spanish colonies in America radically modified, as it should, the state of the aboriginal races? No! In every Spanish American nation there is a Spanish clerical party, rabid with admiration for the conquest, scheming to resurrect the system of rule by greengrocers and theocrats developed after the conquest, passionate for continuing the *encomiendas* with or without the law, worshipping the treatment meted out to the Indians, and enthusiastically partisan of the wisdom of the Laws of the Indies.[10]

$$\bullet \ \bullet \ \bullet \ \bullet \ \bullet$$

The Evolution of Societies

In Latin America, as throughout the world, the liberal party has arisen from the professional middle class, whose function is to promote and sustain intellectual progress. The territorial propertied class, again as everywhere, has seized the

---

7. Spanish colonial law, compiled as the "Law of the Indies," specified that all Indians were to be treated as minors.

8. *Encomienda,* a grant of Indian labor given to the conquerors and their immediate descendents by royal authority.

9. Hugues Félicité Robert de Lamennais (1782–1854), French priest and philosophical writer who eventually fell out of favor with the Church because of his liberal politics.

10. In the following passages, Bulnes quotes several persons to substantiate the foregoing characterization of the attitude he finds so distasteful and retrograde.

natural and legal privileges dictated by its wealth and represents the conservative party. For the ignorant man, extensive agriculture is the perpetual rotation of a selfsame event, and this seemingly unchanging nature of the physical environment creates the fixed conscience as a crystallization of the conservative party.

In England, the struggle of the propertied class against the industrial and professional classes has almost completely ceased. In Catholic countries, especially among the Latins, the struggle continues—brutal, cruel, and without any possible outcome other than the extinction of Catholicism. The Catholic Church openly struggles wherever it has not been subjugated by force, but where it is kept in check like a dangerous evil-doer, it conspires treacherously, attempting to sustain a dangerous anarchic state that will force peaceful people to beg for its intervention for the sake of public tranquility.

Reconciliation is not possible in the struggle between clericalism and liberalism. The principle of scientific liberalism is to recognize and contribute to something that no one can deny—the evolution of human societies. While the societies of bees and ants are viewed as unchanging, and therefore deserving of religious institutions, human societies are evolutionary; the European society from the Paleolithic period is not the thinking, industrial, and artistic European society of 1899. Clericalism represents the **unchanging,** and as a result theocratic governments are impossible, regardless of the numerous and energetic attempts made to rule societies by means of religious political institutions. The words **religious politics** express an oxymoron—politics is the clearest evolutionary manifestation of a society, while religion is the most precise manifestation of purported immobilities. To say "religious politics" is the same thing as saying: **proceed without moving**.

An eminently evolutionary society cannot be governed by a moral person named "religion," which is eminently immobile, stationary, having tradition—that is, the past—as its ideal, if science does not say, because it cannot say, what the true ideal of humanity is, for it is not yet completely discovered. Theocracy is the effort that an artilleryman would make to have his weapon always fire out the back, which is the same as expecting that society should throw itself toward tradition.

Humanity lived for more than two hundred thousand years without religion; religion is a relatively modern, accidental fact in the world, given that it does not date back more than six thousand years before 1899; if it was a matter of social evolution that religion should have existed during society's agricultural period, it was also a matter of evolution that, after the markedly evolutionary industrial period arrived, evolution itself, in fulfillment of its powerful laws, has brought about the reality of breaking the ties that were attempting to turn man into an intellectual corpse, preserved in his rustic juices.

From the moment that two truths are recognized—first, that humanity, like all organic species, both plant and animal, is evolving; and second, that humanity possesses within itself the means to keep evolving indefinitely—one can be sure that there is no risk whatsoever that religions can rule again as in the past. An individual or a nation can go backwards, passing through all the periods of regression until it returns to the shape of the ancestral primate; but other nations, to the contrary, will move forward, and humanity in its enormous entirety will continue developing intellectually, economically, and morally. Civilization cannot lose; the liberal party's thesis of justice and science is winning on our planet as it is throughout the Cosmos.

But for patriotism, the important thing is to know which nations are condemned to perish because their inability to evolve renders them incapable of becoming civilized. Up until now, the nations marked as victims of their own morbid nature are, with total certainty, Spain and Portugal; those with a chance of being saved are France, Italy, Belgium, and Austria. In Latin America, only Chile, Argentina, Brazil, Mexico, and Uruguay have any chance of salvation.

In this matter, theology is of absolutely no use; the logical syllogism is like a **hundred thousand ton battleship** against a glass rowboat. Does anyone doubt that the **world moves**, as Galileo said, in the astronomical sense; **that the world progresses**, as Pelletan asserted; or that the **world evolves**, as Spencer has shown?[11] No one can deny evolution. Can anyone deny the unchanging nature of the dogmas that are the principles of action for religion? No one can deny that unchangeability either, because dogma is the divine word of revelation, and evolving revelations cannot exist. On the other hand, **what is unchanging cannot be the principle that governs what is evolving**; therefore, every government that is religious or mixed in with religion is antisocial, and the society that proceeds against its own laws commits suicide, like the individual who moves against his life.

So much does Catholicism recognize the unlimited supremacy of the argument that I have just expounded, that the Church itself has recognized it ever since Pius IX,[12] who openly condemned progress, in order that the Church itself might not perish. Indeed, Catholicism does not have a dogma condemning the use of *caoutchouc* for making rubber shoes, and it finds combating malaria with quinine orthodox. But when the most noble of the sciences—criticism—together with its general staff—paleontology, geography, archeology, philology, geology, history—asks the Church for its titles of divine authority to deliver its laws to men, then Catholicism excommunicates, slanders, demands punishment to suppress in man the first of his rights—to be the master of his beliefs, the sole, absolute king of his conscience.

The first moral duty of a civilized government is to recognize the rights of man; there cannot be progress without justice, and there cannot be justice without recognizing in man rights superior to those of all religions. No one can be

---

11. Galileo Galilei (1564–1642), Italian astronomer; forced by the Inquisition to recant the theory that the earth was not the fixed center of the universe, he allegedly said, "but it still moves." Charles Camille Pelletan (1846–1915), French politician and journalist. Spencer, see note 5.

12. Pius IX (1792–1878; pope, 1846–1878) denounced the limitations on Church power enacted by liberal politicians in Latin America and called himself "the prisoner of the Vatican" after the unification of Italy in 1870 reduced the Papal States to Vatican City.

obliged to accept the yoke of a religion, nor to remain silent before its dogmas, nor to give up the right of combating its errors and of speaking to the rest of men in the name of truth or of lies.

From the moment Catholicism does not recognize in man the rights that the liberals have discovered in him, there can be neither justice nor moral progress. From the moment Catholicism attempts to dictate to a country what it can read and what its instructional materials must be, intellectual progress no longer exists. What intellectual progress has Spain or the nations of Europe made by means of the Catholics? A great deal of intellectual progress is due to the friars who ceased to be orthodox, such as Luther, Wycliffe, Huss, Bruno, and others.

Religion and Economy

Regarding material progress, it is true that Catholicism does not oppose making rubber shoes, but it does oppose men's earning a sufficient day's wage to buy them. Catholicism has dogmas contrary to the most fundamental and rigorous principles of political economy, for example its dogma of accumulating all social riches in the hands of the clergy in order to distribute it to the poor. Even if that were to be carried out, which it never has, political economy declares that when a society does not use its wealth to contribute to the development of labor, that wealth will necessarily come to an end. Society cannot be a refuge for beggars.

Another of Catholicism's very serious economic errors is that it not only recognizes the professional liberty of the priesthood, but it imposes on society the obligation to support anyone who devotes himself to an ecclesiastical career. What would we say of a government that said, "The State is in charge of providing the necessities for all doctors, lawyers, dentists, engineers, and chiropodists, both foreign and domestic"? Catholicism is even worse, because one need not study to belong to some monastic order. How would a legislator be judged who commanded, even if he did so with noble aims: "The army in peace time will have an unlimited number of soldiers who will be treated decently and even opulently"? This is not theology, it is social economy, which does not acknowledge sophisms. Though sophistry can bind the human stomach, the brain quickly clears. Before he is a religious, moral, and political animal, man is an economic animal like all the rest, and, like all animals, with rare exceptions he will sacrifice everything for food, beginning with religion when he realizes that religion is snapping up his food. The Catholic is not inferior to the dog; when he senses that they are laying hands on the bone he is gnawing—he growls and bites.

To make liberalism triumph, political philosophy has not wasted its time on unintelligible metaphysical dissertations or on correct positivist syllogisms against Catholicism. It has made Catholics sense openly that their church has taken away the bread of their labor or the profits of their capital, and the Catholic animal, as economic as the dog, has revolted against the Church. Philosophers have been few and poor, but they have had the intelligence to tell the German princes and the English barons of the sixteenth century: "Wars have ruined you, you don't know how to work, but the Church is very rich; we will make you a gift of its money." "By what authority do you make this present?"

responded the princes and barons. "By our syllogisms." And the ruined but ambitious nobles understood the syllogisms without ever having heard them.

To the peasants, the Reformation of the sixteenth century said: "Philosophy authorizes you to deny the Church the tithe and all the contributions with which it plundered you," and the peasants understood philosophy instantly. In Mexico, the liberals were a handful of honorable men, of incomparable valor, of immense patriotism, and they told the hacienda owners and the landed gentry: "The clergy is the true owner of your wealth, your sons will beg for alms, we are selling you that wealth in the name of progress for a plate of lentils that you will eat." And the men of ardent faith understood progress and kept the greater part of the clergy's wealth. The Church has worshiped the **golden calf** more than anyone else, and the Catholic who has plundered the Church still follows this dogma by worshiping, in the Church, a golden calf.

The Church has skillfully managed to make the most of its defeat. Today it says, through its eloquent thinkers: "Why speak of the voraciousness of the monastic orders and their terrifying number when they scarcely exist anymore? Why speak of executioners and persecutions and confiscations when we have gone almost a century without a single case? Why impugn the Church's riches if we are poor? Why make a display of laicism if we do not participate in politics? Why designate us as theocrats if all forms of government are the same to us? Why rail against the crimes of our clergy if justice is yours, if we do not have prisoners anymore, and if your police can take us before your harsh tribunals to apply to us the law, to which we submit? The Church," they add, "has nothing left but meekness and charity; it is pacified."

This speech is as if the leader of a gang of bandits, condemned to the galleys for life, were to say: "Why speak of my crimes if for many years I have not committed a single one? Why oppose my freedom if I am sober, chaste, almost ascetic inside my cell? Why not give me back my horse and my weapons if I provide evidence that I do not love anything but tranquility, the sun in the morning, and sweet dreams? Why not return me to the mountains where I made raids, when everyone knows that my errors are forever behind me, and I have nothing but thoughts of love for my neighbor? No one has a right to attack me, as my life is as exemplary as it is virtuous."

When dealing with a physical person, cures are possible; but a moral person that believes it is authorized to decide what is good or evil, licit or illicit, virtuous or criminal—like a prisoner who believes that the judges, the jurors, the policemen, and the prosecutors are the criminals, and that only brute force has been able to deprive him of his liberties—is nothing more than a hypocrite when it exclaims: "Look at my life, clean as the inner core of an ideal of virtue."

If Catholicism does not oppress certain peoples as it once did, it is because they do not allow it, but if the resources with which the Church dominated were returned to it, the Church would dominate again, and the European world would once more pass through the Middle Ages. What resources are those? Two very simple ones—putting the Church in charge of public instruction and giving it the right to gag its enemies. To deliver the child to the Church is to deliver civilization to it; it is to decapitate the future. That is everything for which the Church contends; it no longer wants gold or palaces, nor Inquisition, nor armies, nor tithes, nor the Bank of Indulgences, nor convents; it wants only that by which it can recover everything—the education and instruction of children. It wants the soul of youth so that it can fabricate new wings with which to descend again to the cold chaos of tradition. The Church no longer wants anathemas or excommunications; it will open the gates of heaven to every liberal atheist who dies; what it wants is the article of the **Concordat** that decrees: "The Church will direct instruction." It wants an article as ignominious for national honor as that of the Concordat of Colombia.[13]

The nation that entrusts public instruction to the Church must perish. France, Austria, Italy, and Belgium have refused to deliver their youth to brutishness, the same as Chile, Argentina, Brazil, Guatemala, and Mexico—all these nations, if they do not turn to reaction, have great chances for salvation.

The Work of Theocracies

Faithful Catholics have a very defective intelligence from the moment when the facts they face no longer make an impression on them. When Christianity was ascetic, it was perfectly logical: The filthier towns were, the more clearly the quality of the world was seen as a **valley of bitter tears**; groups of beggars, bandits, and serfs, the three forces of the Middle Ages, fit in well with the dogma that **the kingdom of God is not of this world;** but when Catholicism, terrified by the submission of the human conscience to the demands of indefinite progress, finds no better way to avoid being renounced as incompatible with the present and future of the species than to maintain that theocracy is the only possible path to progress, you would have to have the nervous system of a crustacean to practice Catholic politics.

In the first place, no people has ever managed to practice theocracy, because even approaching this ultimate degradation has caused its death. The Jewish people were the ones who most endeavored to be theocratic and the ones who have suffered the greatest misfortunes. Catholicism has committed the despicable crime of persecuting the Jews, not as a nation, but rather as men, and the worst is that our so-called morality is so depraved that we find the fact natural. Egypt, that great empire, when it was deathly rotten, laid itself down in its pyramids as if on cushions and delivered its body and spirit to the shameless priests who had submerged it in grief and dishonor. Theocratic India lost all its strength and fell, disintegrating into separate parts, turning its fragments toward savagery without innocence. To Rome. Constantine made it a theocracy, and the barbarians conquered it, violated it, destroyed it. The theocratic Spain of Recaredo was conquered in hours by a squad of daring Arabs; the Spain of Felipe III, stooping

---

13. A *concordat* is a diplomatic agreement between a pope and a sovereign ruler or government on Church matters. The 1887 concordat with Colombia reversed liberal measures enacted in the 1850s and reestablished the Catholic Church as "that of the Nation."

to theocracy, was lashed for a century by defeats, famines, humiliations, and it owes its sad life to the **European balance of power** imposed on Louis XIV by arms. Paraguay, converted into a flock with Jesuit shepherds, served to demonstrate under Dr. Francia and his successors the boundlessness of human shame.[14] What theocracy has succeeded? When has a nation directed by ecclesiastics ever progressed? We wish to see the progress that Catholicism causes—not as a rule, not as a logical conclusion; we simply wish to see one case, one exception that goes along with the assertion that a system of government burdened with ecclesiastical types is the origin of great popular progress.

Something that has never been seen when it should have been, cannot exist. Every other system of government, even the worst, has had its artistic moment and has executed its masterpiece. Piracy made Greece commercial, opulent, philosophical, artistic. The Ionic archipelago could never be a nation, but it was a sumptuous **guesthouse** occupied by fractious divinities. Greece did not wish to die in the arms of theocracy, and for that reason its soul remained in the world to ennoble it. The Muslim empire has been theocratic, but it has not died because it is a theocracy without a body of priests, with one sole cleric—the Sultan. The feudal spirit has given us the political greatness of England and the philosophical loftiness of Germany. Pure aristocracy made the Russia of Peter the Great first among military powers. The consular dictatorship and Caesarism of Rome destroyed the heroic anarchy of the three continents and disciplined the European hordes, the foundation of present civilization. Italian anarchy brought with it the Renaissance, a fresh injection of the pagan world that put an end to scholasticism, founded humanism, and concluded by creating religious liberty with Protestantism. Feudal monarchy created the brilliant reign of Fernando and Isabel in Spain, and democracy has created the masterpiece among masterpieces—the United States. What is the masterpiece of Catholicism? Rome should have been the social Eden of all peoples and all generations, but the facts—the only authority for all wise men—show us the Rome of temporal power as a sewer of all corruptions and the **conciliar seminary** of all vices. Rome, until 1870, had the look of a garbage dump functioning as a sepulcher of pagan opulence.

Protestantism is an **evolved** and evolving Catholicism. In accordance with Protestant doctrine, the spirit of the believer is the sole interpretation of the law of God given in the Bible; if this view advances the interpretation of the Bible, it will reach the point where it becomes clear that the Bible is a book as supernatural as the **Thousand and One Nights** or the children's stories of the simple Perrault.[15]

· · · · ·

---

14. Paraguay was originally founded as a province of Jesuit missions in the seventeenth century. Dr. José Gaspar Rodríguez de Francia (1766–1840), a doctor of theology who became the first president of Paraguay following independence from Spain in 1811, took on dictatorial powers and even declared himself the head of the Catholic Church in that country, for which he was excommunicated.

15. Charles Perrault (1628–1703), French writer of fairy tales.

Global Possessions of Europe and the United States[16]

Nations	Territory in Square Kilometers		
	Metropolitan	Non-tropical	Tropical
Great Britain	314,951	15,177,000	9,301,000
France	528,572	1,076,000	8,635,000
Germany	540,518	374,000	2,668,000
Italy	288,540	—	560,000
Portugal	89,625	—	2,076,000
Holland	33,000	—	1,000,000
Belgium	29,455	—	2,330,000
Austria-Hungary	625,168	61,060	—
Denmark	38,302	228,000	360
Spain	500,443	630,000	—
Russia	22,429,998	200,000	—
Turkey	2,090,340	—	—
Sweden/Norway	775,997	—	—
Romania	129,447	—	—
Greece	64,688	—	—
Bulgaria	63,976	—	—
Serbia	48,582	—	—
Switzerland	31,213	—	—
United States	9,331,360	—	—
	39,934,700	17,836,600	27,883,653[17]

Imperial China is in the process of being divided up, its emperor bereft of sovereignty, because it is directed by a syndicate of mercantile powers. Afghanistan and Baluchistan are pledged to England and Russia. Japan, which declared war on China to liberate Korea from the sovereignty of that empire, almost has responsibility for China, for it has been converted into its tutor and protector, making laws for it and giving or lending it money.

We find that the European powers; the United States, military power of America; and Japan, military power of Asia, possess, or are en route to possessing, the following territory:

	Square Kilometers
Metropolitan Territory	40,317,147
Non-tropical Territory	30,628,000
Tropical Territory	27,884,000
	98,829,147

16. Based on fundamental economic data, Bulnes here begins an assessment of the imperialistic dangers South America faces from established world powers.

17. The three columns, reprinted here as in the original, actually add up, respectively, to 37,954,175; 17,746,060; and 26,570,360.

	Square Kilometers
In Latin America	19,932,057
Independent Arabia	2,507,390
Persia	1,648,195
Transvaal	285,363
Orange Free State	107,439
Abyssinia	333,279
African Deserts	6,180,426
Mountainous African Territories & Nomad Tribes	3,490,000
Uninhabited Regions & Islands	2,725,576
	136,038,872

Which is the total land area of our planet.

Independent Arabia, Persia, Abyssinia are almost unusable territories because of their aridity; the African deserts and uninhabited territories and uninhabited islands are completely useless. Only the small territories of the Orange Free State and the Transvaal and Latin America have great value. It can be said that the Transvaal already is, although slightly, under England's sovereignty. The Orange Free State is an African country conquered by private European individuals.

Separating the useless from what is still left unconquered by the great powers or individual Europeans on the globe, only Latin America remains—a continent-sized region with a value much higher than all of the African continent that has now been conquered by the hunger of Europe and by the great hopes of assuring a grand future for the European races and sovereign nations.

How can one explain why the European powers, with no more rationale than their immense military power, having before them the magnificent, the good, the acceptable, and the bad, are rushing after the good, the bad, and the acceptable, leaving the magnificent to one side? The European powers have education enough to know the great economic value of Latin America. Why not reach out and take it?

As for reaching out to take it, France did so with Mexico in 1862 and wanted to do so with Brazil in 1897; England has reached out to dismember or absorb Venezuela and Nicaragua; and Germany, which only flexes its muscles to reach out and take what it can, would gladly already have taken Tarapaca's fields of nitrate—of which it consumes so much—along with the Chilean Republic, not forgetting to annex non-tropical Brazil and Uruguay so as to have a view of both oceans in its **new house**.

Why has Europe not proceeded logically in its determined program of conquest and expansion against weak nations that occupy huge territories they have not been able to populate, which Europe would populate immediately with its great surplus of population?

Is it for fear of resistance by the Spanish American nations? No; with the exception of the Latin American nations with great tropical territories, fevers, malaria, swamps, and impenetrable mountain ranges crossing populated territory, which can offer serious resistance for more or less time—nations such as Argentina, Chile, non-tropical Brazil, Uruguay, upper Peru, and upper Bolivia—they are in no condition to resist a European coalition for two months, once the weak South American fleets are annihilated in a couple of minutes; and frankly, there could not be more valuable territories in the world—outside of Canada—than Argentina, Chile, non-tropical Brazil, and non-tropical Mexico.

Why, then, so much respect for the weak in America? It is not for the sake of justice, because justice applies just as well to the Chinese and the African Negroes as it does to the Latin Americans. Nor is it because of the principles of international law, because in practice they have nothing more than a certain musical value. Their influence is purely artistic and serves only to model friendly arrangements when two or more weak or strong nations do not want to go to war. But when war suits a strong one, like a powerful industrial machine that produces colonial government, then international law, the **eternal principles of justice, the immutable precepts of morality,** are verses in a call and response with cannon fire.

If Latin America is still independent and can be so indefinitely in the face of Europe's exasperating expansion, it is because of the Monroe Doctrine.[18] Much better said, it is because of the battleships on which the Monroe Doctrine depends, for if the hundreds of doctrines that make up international law are worth nothing in themselves in the face of force, a doctrine that the entire world is permitted to debate is worth even less.

It is evident that the United States at the present time does not have a navy capable of facing up to the navies of all the great European powers. But England is and will be with the United States, because Canada is united to the United States by land, and all of Europe can do nothing in the face of the territorial military power of the United States. In America there are many English possessions, and there is nothing else in the world comparable to the immense development of commerce between England and the United States. The Anglo-American alliance is not a pact of blood and steel signed by two Caesars on a battlefield, but rather an urgent necessity of the world's two most powerful and civilized nations. The Anglo-American alliance today is a scientific fact—necessary, unassailable, inviolable—that is imposed on the two allies themselves, and one that imposes on the entire world.

England has adopted, as an unwavering principle, that it will keep the size of its fleet equal to the size of the world's next two most powerful fleets combined. This is the theory, but in practice England exceeds its goal and can say that its fleet is always equal or superior to the three most powerful foreign fleets combined. If to this is added the increase in tactical naval units that the American nation constantly acquires and the elevated reputation that it has justly acquired in its war with Spain, it will be clear that none of the great European powers except England can think of taking even a square centimeter of land from Latin America.

---

18. See footnote 35 on page 100.

On the other hand, so long as England is more than halfway involved in America, it will not abandon the North American alliance. In the conflict between the United States and Spain, we have seen that England has been invited several times by such powers as France, Germany, and Austria-Hungary, acutely interested in helping Spain, and we have also seen that England's negative response to the **imposed intervention** has been enough for Spain to be left with neither protection nor hope. It is, then, to the Anglo-American alliance, upholder of the Monroe Doctrine, that Latin America owes and will continue owing its inviolability in the face of Europe's territorial lust.

$$\bullet \ \bullet \ \bullet \ \bullet \ \bullet$$

The Potential Danger

The sole and formidable danger for Latin America is the United States; this danger is not imminent, however, but rather purely probable and far off, for reasons I am going to state.

The United States does not need non-tropical land, because by placing the land it already has under intensive cultivation, it can sustain a population of **two billion inhabitants;** that is to say, it can hold and feed all of present humanity. The ideal of the United States has always been self-sufficiency, and it lacked tropical land. It needs, by its own account, to stop buying annually more than two hundred million dollars worth of sugar, coffee, rubber, fruits, and tropical woods. The production of Puerto Rican, Cuban, and Philippine coffee is enough to supply a part of its population with coffee.

In the United States there are no religious interests to spread, nor crusades to Jerusalem, nor military interests of a spear-and-armor aristocracy; the political interests of the United States are purely economic interests in action, making its struggle to prevail evident.

In the United States, the great political powers are capital and labor. Capital has industrial, commercial, agricultural interests. Labor has one interest only— high and steady daily wages.

The commercial interest of the United States demands communication between the Atlantic and the Pacific, breaking the continent at Panama or Nicaragua. This work has to be achieved, through war or through peace, and the North Americans will possess more or less territory ceded, bought, leased, or conquered in Central America or in the Republic of Colombia. No human force can oppose this need of the great North American republic.

With respect to the interests of American industry, Asia, where more than half of humanity lives, is as attractive for the North American market as the foreign consumption of fifty million inhabitants of Latin America.

The political problem, legitimately resulting from the social problem in the United States, is the peaceful and intelligent—not anarchic—struggle between capital and labor. The large workers' associations in the United States have decided to impose protective laws against free importation of foreign workers, in the same way that industrial capitalists have obtained laws against free importation—or with regulated rights over foreign industry.

American industrial production has greatly exceeded domestic consumption despite population growth, and it requires having no foreign competition in the domestic market and selling abroad indefinitely. Workers in the United States, to avoid a reduction in their daily wage caused by an unlimited supply of foreign labor, have dictated laws restricting immigration considerably, giving up producers of labor and, at the same time, domestic consumers, for every immigrant is also a consumer.

To sell industrial and agricultural products abroad and preserve high daily wages, North American capitalists stimulate the invention of machinery. The ideal for the bosses in the United States is to work only with workers made of steel, fed by a little coal. The ideal for North American workers is to live organized for general strikes, which they call sympathy strikes, with the goal of earning daily wages that consume all of capital's profits.

The European capitalist is still a master; in the United States, he is an abject slave of his workers. American bosses, like Tantalus,[19] see delicious indigent workers abroad who would be content with a low daily wage, but the law prevents them from importing them. Moreover, the American capitalist could previously take as a worker whomever he wished within the territory of the United States; today, he cannot freely choose among unsalaried North Americans. Under threat of sympathetic strikes, labor unions prohibit him from taking into the service of his industry workers who are not members of certain associations.

This nation of enslaved capitalists and sovereign workers can only live in this way because of its magnificent natural resources, among them the cheapest agricultural foodstuff production, and because of the American genius for invention, stimulated to such a degree that, during the same time when all of Europe issued nine hundred thousand patents on inventions, the United States issued more than a half-million, and in the last year of Mr. Cleveland's presidency, twenty-one thousand patents were granted on inventions and industrial improvements.

So long as the United States, with its low-cost agricultural production and its constant invention of machines, devices, and industrial methods, can preserve the balance between its population growth and the sales of its products in the domestic and foreign markets, everything will go smoothly; but from the moment the supply of North American workers exceeds the consumption of North American goods in domestic and foreign markets, either American industry or its high daily wages will have to disappear.

Since the United States market is overflowing with domestic merchandise, the sale of this merchandise abroad is an urgent necessity. Europe, with the

---

19. Tantalus, son of Zeus and king of Sipylos, uniquely favored among mortals in being invited to share the food of the gods. When he abused the guest-host relationship, his punishment was being "tantalized" with hunger and thirst. He was immersed up to his neck in water but when he bent to drink, the water all drained away. Fruit hung on trees above him, but when he reached for it, winds blew the fruit beyond reach.

exception of England, fends off the invasion of North American products by locking its doors with tariff bolts, but Africa, Asia, Latin America, and Australia remain competitive territories.

If the inhabitants of Asia, Africa, Latin America, and Oceania were all free, the competition would be equally free, and the nation that produced goods most cheaply with equal quality would triumph. It can be said that the North American worker deserves his high daily wage because, of the world's workers, he is the one who, by his physical strength, intelligence, and sobriety, produces the most profitable labor. Europe, with the exception of England, by locking the tariff bolts against the importation of American merchandise, has proved that it cannot compete with the United States in the great day-to-day production that is the largest type of consumption, and to save itself it has gone about locking its old foreign consumers in the cage of colonialism, in order to gain the right to create tariffs for all of Africa, all of Asia, and all of Oceania. Through these means, Europe believes it will win against the growing competition that the United States gives it, barring North American products from all the continents and islands it has converted into colonies.

Latin America is an excellent commercial client, for it buys in foreign markets, in relation to its population, more than the United States, which, in 1898, imported only 616 million in gold pesos.

Imports to Latin America (1897)	$430,000,000 gold
Imports to the United States (1897–1898)	$616,005,000 gold
Imports to China, India, and Japan (1897)	$560,000,000 gold

One sees, then, that the **fifty million** inhabitants of Latin America consume more foreign goods than the seventy-four million North Americans, and more than the **seven-hundred and forty million** Asians who occupy China, English India, and Japan.

As Latin America is such a valuable customer, it would be worth imposing foreign sovereignty on it in order to obligate it, by force of arms and humiliations, to obtain everything it needs from the shop counters of its masters. It would be in the United States' interests to impose its commerce on all Latin America, because, at present, it has:

Total annual imports to Latin America	$430,000,000 gold
Net American merchandise among these imports	$53,000,000 gold

The United States has only **twelve percent** of Latin America's import trade. Mr. Blaine[20] emphasized this fact, and to remedy it he came up with the idea of

---

20. James G. Blaine (1830–1893), congressman from Maine, Republican presidential candidate in 1884, and U.S. secretary of state in 1881 and 1889–1892.

treaties of reciprocity, which would hurt Brazil especially, because this republic consumes **six times fewer** American goods relative to Brazilian goods consumed by the United States. But a very high, almost prohibitive duty, imposed by the United States on Brazilian coffee, would have hurt a popular foodstuff in the United States, for all the other coffee-producing nations together would not be able to satisfy the North American market.

With respect to Argentina, North Americans buy wool from it for their own industry, and to tax the raw material of an industry with high duties is to destroy the industry to which this material gives rise.

Inasmuch as the celebrated treaties of reciprocity have not produced the desired effect, can the United States, in accord with its economic interests, proceed immediately or in the short term to the armed conquest of all or part of Latin America?

• • • • •

The Lie of Race

The distinguished South American writer who published "**The Sick Continent**"[21] proposes, as a practical solution favorable to the Spanish American nationalities in the face of the danger that threatens them, the immediate execution of Bolívar's idea: "A confederation or defensive alliance of all the Latin American republics to maintain their complete independence."

Bolívar was a great warrior who deserves the world's admiration for his patriotism; but as a statesman he was a **great simpleton** who deserves the sympathy of experts in domestic and diplomatic political science. Let us picture the United States as the aggressor nation versus the Spanish American nations. Is it possible to imagine that, in such an instance, the North Americans would act like Don Quixote or Orlando Furioso,[22] hoisting a lance with a challenging banner on its tip that reads: "**The American people, from the trustworthy mouth of its heralds,** challenges to single naval and continental battle the fifty million inhabitants of Latin America"? And even were that the case, it would be disastrous for Latin America, because it is no more than **an archipelago in a cold ocean of rocks** called the Andes and because it lacks strategic mobilization, without which all campaigns are lost.

If there were a North American aggression aimed at devouring Latin America, it would be partial, for the United States would not have great advantages in a general attack; the preservation of its conquests would be impossible, because it would have to maintain an army of much more than a million men, paid at great expense, with a per-soldier salary equal to that of a Mexican captain, an

---

21. *El continente enfermo* (New York, 1899), by Venezuelan writer and politician César Zumeta (1860–1955).

22. Orlando Furioso is the main figure in the epic poem of the same name written by Ludovico Aristo.

encumbrance that would rise with all the other costs of war to one and a half billion pesos per year.

The United States, or any great European power that might decide to conquer Latin America, would do so partially, that is to say, eating in order, **mouthful by mouthful**—in other words, nation by nation; and what would the other Spanish American nations do? Exactly the same as they did in the dispute between Venezuela and England, the same as they did in the wars of Mexico with the United States and France, the same as they did in Cuba's war of independence: they would keep quiet, maintaining the greatest composure on the official level, and, at most, in the desolate regions of private conversation they would post their sympathies as guardsmen. In sum, the nation under attack would have what Spain had in its war with the United States—sympathy, primarily from her numerous creditors, who would not want to see her ruined; but not a soldier, not a peso, not a word of bellicose diplomatic intervention.

And this conduct is natural—nations are moral persons devoted solely to their own interests; they have passions, sympathies, and kindnesses among themselves when their economic interests demand it; but when a pound sterling comes between two peoples, profound hatred arises between them both, and if war does not always take place, it is because the usual doctrine of the strong is to respect each other highly, something that we do not find in history when difficulties arise between strong and weak.

Bolívar's idea of keeping the Latin race united is a lovely, almost symphonic bit of foolishness; but the first difficulty it faces is that there is no Latin race. There is and has been in the world a Latin way of being; never has there been an imperial Latin race. The Roman Empire, like every empire before and since, represented an **emulsion of races** very difficult and very pointless to analyze. Precisely because there have never been imperial races, only imperial politics sustained by arms, as soon as the latter have suffered reverses, the empires have broken into separate nations, and as those nations have progressed, they have adopted a federal form of government that permits individualization within the nation.

The peoples that have been called Latin in race have in common their language, the firstborn child of Latin; a religion named Roman for having copied the organization of the Roman Empire, claiming a universal political empire; and legislation, customs, sentiments, and ideas of the public and private order similar or equal to those of the Roman Empire.

In their private way of life, the countries of Latin race have accepted pagan military Latinism and Catholic spiritual Latinism; these authorities, which come from history with formidable suggestive power, determine the abominable vices of Latins in public life. Latinism, both pagan and Catholic, condemns the **rights of man** and represents two cells for imprisoning men with the political consciousness of domestic animals. The Latin nations have become sufficiently civilized to cast far from their existence the customs, sentiments, and ideas of the Latin public order. At present, all Latin nations recognize that the aim of every civilized government must be to recognize and guarantee the rights of man, which leaves Latinism condemned, buried, and even forgotten as an impossible foundation for public virtues in a period of full civilization.

With respect to the private virtues of the Latin family, noble as they are in their goals, such as the protection and love of children, they have reached such a level of exaggeration that they have caused two evils—estranging the young people of the rich class from labor and plunging them into prostitution, and crushing society with the weight of the flood of professional classes. The other very serious evil in the Latin family is the ecclesiastical enslavement of woman, a misfortune that gives clericalism great power to disturb the peace of families and societies.

But if it is false that there are Latin race interests that merit sacrificing the independence or the peace of each nation occupied by that race—for otherwise, separate nationalities would not have formed—it is equally false that history proves the existence of a desire for and a practice of unifying the peoples of the Latin race for the good of the imaginary interests of that imaginary race.

History teaches us that as soon as two nations, Spain and France, were first constituted upon their emergence from feudalism, they found themselves hating each other for two hundred years and filling the world with ruin, scandal, blood, and all the waste of their vices and all the superstitions of their madness. Their younger sister, Italy, the **Cinderella** of the family, was so intimately united by feelings of blood that Venice hated Genoa most of all, Genoa detested Pisa, and Pisa abhorred Venice, Genoa, and Milan, which loathed all the Italian states, including the Papal ones. This situation lasted from the fall of the Roman Empire until the year 1870, when Italian unity was completed with the occupation of Rome, after more than a thousand years of deep hatred, violent anarchy, vengeance, and splendid, thundering, overwhelming disorders.

Out of racial sympathy, France devoured Belgium and oppressed it; Spain conquered Portugal, ruined it, degraded it, destroyed it. Francis I, the most Christian king of France, allied himself with the Sultan of Turkey, an appalling act in the sixteenth century, to fight another Christian monarch, Carlos V. He, in turn, concluded an alliance with a Protestant, Anglo-Saxon king to lay waste to the Latin race of France. In America, we see the Latin sisters Argentina and Brazil leap like vultures onto their little sister, Paraguay, already conquered and dead, and peck at her stomach. We see Guatemala and El Salvador bite each other with more fury than the sons of Oedipus in their cradle, and Chile robbing Peru and Bolivia. We see Uruguay cudgeled by its strong neighbors and holding onto its independence in a state of problematic difficulty; finally, the affliction between Mexico and Guatemala has lasted more than a half century, and Latin Guatemala has tried to obtain, by every means possible, an alliance with the Anglo Saxons in order to declare war on Mexico in the Arab way, with green flag of the prophet and the Koranic verse: "**God prohibits man in a just war from giving or begging quarter.**"

And if, in addition to these moral abysses, topographically exposed by history, which are insurmountable because no suspension bridge has ever yet been constructed across the gap between literary ideals and humanity's problems of hunger and thirst, we add the abysses of the Andes that impede all continental strategic mobilization, how is it possible to think seriously of confederations? The history, the annals, the interests of each nation are opposed to Bolívar's idea. Latinism currently has no political interests to defend. Better said, any Latin politics that implies the slavery of the individual under the omnipotence of the State is no ideal for the civilized world.

Alcides Arguedas
(Bolivia)

Alcides Arguedas Díaz (1879–1946) is one of the most important Bolivian writers—a novelist, essayist, journalist, sociologist, and historian. He focused his attention on the social, political, and economic problems that he believed were keeping Bolivians from fulfilling their human potential. His aim was to change the realities of Bolivian life. Arguedas's works recognized the problems of a servile indigenous population and a difficult geography and were a reaction against the romantic idealization of the Indian.

Arguedas was born in La Paz, Bolivia, the firstborn of three sons of Fructuoso Arguedas Fabre and Sabina Díaz Mas, wealthy hacienda owners of Spanish heritage. In 1910, he married Laura Tapia Carrie, with whom he had three daughters. After he received his bachelor's degree from the Colegio Nacional Ayacucho de La Paz, in 1898, he joined the military as a volunteer and newspaper correspondent during the first months of the federal revolution. Afterwards, he returned to his studies, pursuing a law degree at the Universidad de La Paz. He had no particular inclination to practice law, but his father had offered him a trip to Europe if he finished the degree. Upon completing the degree in 1903, he left for Europe. The Old World fascinated him, and he returned there a number of times under circumstances ranging from self-imposed exile (1905; 1906–1909) to diplomatic roles in France, London, and Spain (1910–1912; 1913; 1919). In 1922, he was named consul general for Bolivia in Paris; during that appointment, he bought property in nearby Couilly, which became his primary residence for more than twenty years. Arguedas led an idyllic life at his home in Couilly, as he described it in letters, rising early, writing for several hours every morning, gardening in the afternoon, writing again in the early evening, reading until it was time to go to bed. From time to time he left for other assignments, such as his appointment as special envoy and minister plenipotentiary for Bolivia in Colombia in 1929, an appointment he had to resign because of political changes in Bolivia and differences with the government of Dr. Hernando Siles Reyes (1882–1942). Later, in 1930, he was again named consul general in Paris by the military junta that had assumed control in Bolivia after the overthrow of Siles. Differences with the government of Daniel Salamanca Urey over the Chaco war with Paraguay led Arguedas, a pacifist, to resign that position. His final diplomatic post was as minister plenipotentiary for Bolivia in Venezuela in 1942.

Arguedas also had a career in Bolivian politics, albeit brief. He entered political life in 1916 as an elected deputy to the legislature from La Paz. Many years later, in 1937, he petitioned, from Paris, for a seat representing La Paz, but his name was not seriously considered by the political parties. In 1940, he tried again, this time as a senatorial candidate from the Liberal Party, and he was successful. While he was fulfilling his role as a senator and leader in the Liberal

Party, he was named minister of agriculture in the first cabinet of President Enrique Peñaranda Castillo in 1940.

Arguedas was a disciplined writer, both with his time and with his assessment of evidence. In his style and approach to writing, he was particularly inspired by Emile Zola's naturalism and Hyppolite Taine's deterministic approach to history. As a young man, he wrote for both national and foreign publications like *El Comercio* and *El Diario*. In 1915, he became an editor of the periodical, *Los Debates*. In 1919, he was named correspondent for *La Nación* in Buenos Aires. In 1937, Arguedas represented Bolivia in the Second International Congress of American History in Buenos Aires. In 1945, he was invited to speak in Buenos Aires in a series of lectures in the Faculdad de Filosofía y Letras on the subject of Bolivian history. Arguedas's fictional works were considered among the first of the Latin American "Indianist" novels, which portrayed the realistic and unhappy life of the indigenous peoples. His best known works are *Pisagua* (1903), *Wuata Wuara* (1904), *Vida criolla* (1905; 1912), and *Raza de bronce* (1919). The selection that follows is from the first (1909) edition of his great sociological study, *Pueblo enfermo* (translated as *The Sick People*). He also wrote a five-volume *Historia general de Bolivia* (1922–1929) and published his memoirs in 1934, a work he called *La danza de las sombras*.

Further Reading

Albarracín Millán, Juan. *Alcides Arguedas: La conciencia crítica de una época.* La Paz: Edic. Réplica, 1979.

Arguedas, Alcides. *Obras completas.* 2 vols. Edited by Luis Alberto Sánchez. Mexico, D.F.: Aguilar, 1959–1960.

Aronna, Michael. *'Pueblos enfermos': The Discourse of Illness in the Turn-of-the Century Spanish and Latin American Essay.* Chapel Hill, N.C.: University of North Carolina Press, 1999.

Díaz Arguedas, Julio. *Alcides Arguedas, el incomprendido.* La Paz: Ediciones Isla, 1978.

Medinaceli, Carlos. *La inactualidad de Alcides Arguedas y otros estudios biográficos.* La Paz: Editorial "Los Amigos del Libro," 1972.

Paz Soldán, Edmundo. *Alcides Arguedas y la narrativa de la nación enferma.* La Paz: Plural, 2003.

The Sick People (1909)

The Ethnic Problem in Bolivia

I. "The ethnic distribution of the Bolivian population," say the authors of the latest census, taken in 1900, "can be grouped into four principal races:

1. The *indigenous,*
2. The *white,* descending from foreigners, principally Spanish,
3. The *mestizo,* the product of the two previous, and
4. The *black,* whose proportion is quite small."

The term *race,* used in so categorical a manner to describe the slight variations that exist among population groups on Bolivian soil, seems out of place, and even more so if one takes into account the restrictions and reservations that its use raises today, given that science does not recognize it as having categorical value, nor is its scope believed to be concretely determined; for, according to Novikow, "no one has ever been able to say which features set the characteristics of a race."[1]

In Bolivia, for example, setting aside the extraordinary insight of the authors of the aforementioned census, no one would be able to specify, or even delimit, the differences that exist between the so-called "white race" and the "mestizo race." Physically they resemble each other, or better stated, are one. A *cholo* (mestizo race) is called "sir" the moment he leaves his environment and, therefore, belongs to the white race. One cannot discern the difference even by color, because color seems to depend solely on climate. The mestizos of the regions with lower temperatures (La Paz, Oruro, Potosí) are brown, perhaps copper-colored, and the "whites" are the same color, except for rarities that are the exception; those from high temperature regions (Sucre, Cochabamba, Tarija, etc.) are white. But this fact does not keep those of a certain *social* category from beginning to make up part of the "mestizo" race—that is, an individual's ethnic quality[2] is determined there only by how society regards him. The class that predominates over all others is the mestizo, and the mestizos do not encounter much opposition when they encroach on the arbitrary and conventional circle created by a small group that considers itself superior in blood, not because the quality of the latter is different from that of the intruding group, but rather because of their naming rights—the only distinguishing feature that seems to characterize the difference in what one claims to see here in the indigenous Bolivian population. For example, if the X family or the Z family rises from the lower classes and, through a series of political or economic circumstances, mixes with one that is deemed prestigious, it will come to create a special place for itself and, in effect, begin to join the upper social classes, and its descendents will actually belong to the "nobility" and will never cease to boast of it, inasmuch as Bolivia has received a very small influx of foreign blood, perhaps less than any other people. Its land-locked nature was the reason for its not interbreeding, and Onésime

---

1. Jacques Novicow [Arguedas's note. Iakov Aleksandrovich Novicow (1849–1912), a Russian social scientist, was the author of *L'avenir de la race blanche: Critique du pessimism contemporain* (*The Future of the White Race: A Critique of Contemporary Pessimism*), Paris, 1897.]

2. "Quality" (*calidad*) is a colonial-era Spanish term that covered roughly the same range of distinctions as the later term "race" (*raza*).

Reclus[3] is quite right when he asserts that "a large portion of this people speaks of itself as descending from the Spanish, even when it is at base indigenous in origin, with little or almost no 'blue blood' flowing through its veins; *Latin* blood does not predominate anywhere other than in the town of Tarija. . . ."

To prove the truth of this claim, one need not refer to our insubstantial and quite arbitrary statistics, but rather to our collective mode of being—abnormal, interesting, odd. Had indigenous blood not predominated here, the country would have been able to give conscious direction to its life from the beginning, adopting all manner of improvements in the material and moral order, and would today be at the same level of development as many peoples more favored by streams of immigrants from the old continent. This fact is easy to observe not only in Bolivia, where a large part of the population has retained its main ethnological features almost intact, but also, and more obviously, among the peoples that have been exposed, whether through geographical proximity or trade or whatever other causes, to the influx of others with a different psychological makeup, which, in sum and according to the beliefs of the majority of modern sociologists, seems to be the primary distinguishing feature of races. In such peoples, although many of the characteristics proper to the original population continue to manifest themselves in the moral order, these characteristics are more coherent and better directed. Examples: Chile, Argentina, Mexico.

The races, on the other hand, as Novicow, Lacombe, Colajanni, Finot, and others have noted, were able to exist, "pure," in prehistoric times; today, whether by peaceful advance, by conquest, or whatever other causes, the races have merged, become one so to speak, and there remain only remnants in places as yet uninvaded by the activity of colonizing peoples, and their culture is something less than rudimentary. The obvious proof of this fact among us, for example, is the cultural state of the two peoples that attained the highest level of development among the many populations in this part of the continent: the Quechua and the Aymara. Not only have both failed to preserve the very advanced civilization they had at the time of the conquest, but they have actually utterly lost it; and, although this loss may be explained by easily established reasons, it never ceases to amaze that today they remain resistant to contact with other peoples and do not retain even the most remote notion of their institutions.

It is, then, only on this condition—that is to say, on the condition of considering the "races" only from the *psychological* point of view, and for greater expository ease—that, with minor variations, I accept the classification established by the authors of the census. Consequently, and rearranging the usual order, it is necessary to speak at some length about the indigenous race, pure and mother race, and less about the others, especially the black and the white; for the black race, because of its low numbers, plays no active role in the whole, while the white race, save in details of moral order, can be perfectly incorporated into the mestizo. . . .

---

3. Onésime Reclus (1837–1916), French geographer.

III.[4] In the region called *Inter-Andean,* the Aymara has languished from time immemorial, savage and skittish as a forest beast, given over to his heathen rites and to cultivating the sterile soil on which his race will, without a doubt, soon end.

The pampa and the Indian form a single entity. The pampa cannot be understood without the Indian, just as this latter would feel homesick in any region other than the pampa.

In this region—as has been said before—nothing invites either relaxation or joy. The soul is constricted within itself, seeking refuge for its desires and aspirations within its own elements. The union between the intense blue of the sky and the muddy gray of the soil inspires neither dreams nor poetry. One necessarily seeks the hearth, communion with people, yearns for the timbre of the human voice. The sky, pure and clear in the summer months when the aridity and desolation of the plain are terrible, is filled with low and formless clouds in spring when parts of the plain reveal here and there the pleasant touch of green—a sullen, perverse seasonal exchange—and one might say that this region had been purposely created to offer a perpetually devastating vision. Here the only beauty is the sky, but not in solar clarity, but rather at night when the fire in indigenous homes is lighted and the stars burst into brightness in the firmament. They acquire an extraordinary brilliance and display themselves in such number that the eyes, eager to contemplate them, feel possessed by vertigo. As Mr. Dereims says, only the intense, luminous, pure sky of Africa is comparable to the sky of this region.[5] It has a blue that shocks and wounds; at night a profound and "velvety" darkness, and the stars burst forth in it clear, vibrant, sparkling intensely.

Man in this region feels abandoned by all the powers, alone amidst a harsh climate and soil; and this feeling, everywhere else generating habits of sociability and economy, here—I do not know why—separates and disconnects men, perhaps because in the thankless task of working the land one must invest great perseverance and immense energy to yield mean fruit, fruit that one must necessarily economize, consume sparingly if one wishes to avoid the tortuous famines that have been so frequent since time immemorial.

The physical aspect, the type of occupations available, and their monotony, have molded the spirit in a strange way. The man of the *altiplano* is noted for his hardness of character, the aridity of his emotions, his absolute lack of aesthetic inclinations. His spirit has strength for nothing but focusing on the persistence of misery. He arrives at a sinisterly pessimistic conception of life. Nothing exists but misery and struggle. All that is born of man is pure fiction. Man's natural condition is to be evil, as is nature's. God is harsh and vengeful; he takes pleasure in sending all types of calamity and misfortunes. . . .

---

4. In the intervening passages are census numbers regarding total population and racial distribution and a brief discussion of the black race.

5. Alfredo Dereims (b. 1862), *Geología nacional, excursiones científicas 1901–1904,* reprint, Cochabamba: Imprenta Universitaria, 1955.

Such is the ethics that emerges from such a region and among men who have lost the best of their qualities. For this reason, the constant obsession among these men is to placate the anger of God with curious practices, offering him sacrifices, trying to make him act more merciful, more generous. . . .

Before, when the great conquests of the Incas had not extended to those high and unmerciful zones, the inhabitants did not adore any God—according to Inca Garcilaso de la Vega[6]—and they lived like beasts, sheltered in caves with neither order nor polity. They killed each other without reason, and theirs was a life of perpetual battle, either with each other or with neighboring tribes. It was the Incas who gave them notions of divinity, and they came to accept easily all types of beliefs, for the coarseness of their life, their painful labors, the injustices that they often found themselves compelled to suffer, predisposed their spirit to accepting a ruling being or power that distributed rewards or punishments, and they fell into absolute fetishism, for they came to worship every manner of living or imaginary being, but always sustaining the primordial idea that death was a type of transition to another, more perfect state in which man would enjoy every type of property; this belief gave rise to their system of embalming, somewhat analogous to that of the Egyptians, and to their keen desire to provide the deceased with all sorts of utensils and things necessary for common use.

From this concept comes that complete absence of aspirations, the horrifying limitation of their spiritual sphere. They desire nothing; they aspire to nothing. At most, they yearn for full satisfaction of organic needs, of which the principal one, before love, is wine. Alcohol is a luxury among those men. Whoever has, drinks; this is logical. And, being men after all, the vanity of owning possessions is also a characteristic of theirs.

The passions do not reach maximum intensity. They love, they hate, they desire, but in moderation: they never arrive at passionate excitement. Their emotional language is scanty, poor, and cold: the woman charms, but not to the extreme of leading a man to make sacrifices.

Consequently, their art is not born viable, much less does it charm with its harmonious appearance. The plains give the sensation of the infinite, of the enormous, of the immeasurable. The straight line predominates, and thus there is no dazzling and consoling vision of diverse and communicative landscapes and, moreover, all attention is overcome by the serious problem of nutrition—the spirit remains indifferent, maybe cold, and never throbs nor gets excited enough to create the harmony of the curve or the resonant luxuriance of the sentence. Theirs is a rudimentary, unpolished art, in which proportions disappear and the straight and rigid line prevails—thus Tiahuanacu.[7] In the same way,

---

6. Born Gómez Suárez de Figueroa, "the Inca" Garcilaso (1539–1616) was a Spanish American writer and historian and the son of a conquistador related to the Spanish writer Garcilaso de la Vega (whose name he took) and an Indian woman from the royal house of the Incas.

7. Pre-Columbian culture of the Bolivian *altiplano,* near Lake Titicaca, known for its monumental, monolithic stone sculptures and architecture.

their music is always in the minor key, and it is unvarying, moaning, monotonous—an interminable sob.

The physical makeup of this rather disagreeable region has, I repeat,
imprinted hard features onto the character and constitution of the Indian.

Average in stature, perhaps more tall than short, markedly copper in color,
with rough and long matted hair, with eyes that gaze sidelong and unsociably,
and thick lips, the over-all ensemble of the Indian's face is not very appealing and
reveals neither intelligence nor kindness; to the contrary, although his face is
normally impassive and mute, it does not reveal everything that stirs in the interior of his soul. In that ensemble of rough lines, of clashing angularities, one
encounters sometimes, and in certain places, softer, purer lines and fairer com-
plexions as one begins to leave these high regions and enter better and balmier
climes. Down in the valleys, the same race acquires a kindly aspect; one sees
graceful, even pretty faces among the women.

The Indian's character has the hardness and aridity of the wasteland. He is
hard, embittered, egotistical, cruel, vengeful, and distrustful. He lacks willing-
ness, a persistent spirit, and feels a profound aversion for everything that is different from him. Therein lies his hatred of the white man.

His life is frugal and hard to an unbelievable degree. He knows neither comfort nor repose. He does not taste pleasures, does not know luxuries. For him,
owning an outfit covered in embroidery that he can wear to his village or parish
fiesta and getting as drunk as he is able and for the greatest time possible is the
height of happiness. A fiesta seems to him the more splendid the more days it
goes on. Dancing, drinking are his only satisfactions; he knows no others. He is
a social animal with others of his own species; outside of his center, he remains
reserved and sullen. In his house, absolute poverty, utter neglect. In the house of
the Indian there is nothing but filthiness, and his house is—according to an
anonymous note set down in the cited *Statistics*—"a miserable and tiny hovel
made of mud, stones, and with a roof of straw. An entire family lives inside this
gloomy and slovenly habitation, taking shelter there for the night, lying down
on the bare earth or on worm-eaten lambskins. All across the republic, far and
wide, one finds Indian settlements scattered through the countryside, through
the mountains, through the valleys and ravines, on land that belongs, for the
most part, to the lords of great estates."

• • • • •

IV. The mestizo race was born of the fusion of the white invader and the
Indian. The *cholo*, when he does not leave his natural environment, reveals,
despite the vices already inherent in him, excellent qualities of character—he
is proud, although inclined to robbery; valiant, but idle; timid, and at the
same time arrogant. Like the white man, he loathes exercising his will and
feels an aversion for everything that signifies effort. Intelligent, clever, he
acquires general ideas with little effort; but he has the defect of letting himself
be swept away by every intransigent and subjugating dogmatism. When he

acquires a certain level of culture, his dominating instincts are aroused, and he becomes ambitious for things that are vulgar and insignificant, a fan of the sparkling and the gaudy, disobedient, sarcastic, envious, aggressive, and intolerably sensitive.

Neither fervent admiration nor excited enthusiasm ever enlivens his spirit. He lacks the education to admire much; he lacks the understanding to feel enthusiasm.

If there is anything that can make him enthusiastic to the point of excitation and self-sacrifice for any reason, it is politicians, but this is not even because of the ideas they embody or the programs they defend, but "just because," for their likeability, because Bolivian politicians only know how to accommodate people through flattering their collective self-love, and the *cholo* is instinctively driven by his sheep-like spirit, as Nietzsche would say. A politician's moral qualities matter nothing to him: The proof of this is found in the bloody pages of the annals of the fatherland, wherein we can see that his idols were abnormal beings of violent passions—Belzu, Melgarejo, Morales, Daza.[8] In his admiration for this type of man, he rarely shows persistence in his affections and solidity in his character. No sooner does he raise them up than he knocks them down, and this with a surprising fickleness and even more surprising thoughtlessness. Changeable, inconstant, heedless—only his self-interest, what immediately concerns him, impassions him. If he has nothing, he will be a fanatic for the violent ideas of restoring social rights, and he will arrive at an intransigent and ferocious anarchism; just as, if he does possess something, he will be an intolerant, unyielding conservative. . . . Moreover, and this is what is strange in his character, once emancipated from ignorance, he is either naive to the point of foolishness or optimistic to the point of ferocity. Either he believes in everything, or he believes in nothing. And it is then that he becomes dangerous.

In the former case, he is a dreamer, rash, passionate; his faith in dogmas is uncontainable. He finds everything good and in a state of perfection. The social institutions, the laws of nature, phenomena of every natural and supernatural sort, life itself with its enormous load of brutal injustices and tremendous deformities, have for him a kindly aspect, and they correspond to a type of will disposed to the good and the beautiful—God. Nothing shocks his critical sense—in immoral actions, in criminal events he sees nothing but momentary and occasional deviations from the "morality innate in man." Life is good, and everything that belongs to it is equally good—he seems to proclaim this to be his emphasis in life, manifest in the least of his actions. . . . In the latter case, he is aggressive insecurity, taciturn sadness, the enormous egotism of unsociable beings. He falls in love with every ideal, but pursues none of them. Theoretically—or rather, superficially—he is a patriot, and his patriotism is

---

8. Manuel Isidro Belzu (1811–1865), Bolivian general and politician; Mariano Melgarejo (1818–1871), Bolivian general and politician who in 1864 created a military dictatorship; Agustín Morales (1836–1894), general who overthrew Melgarejo in 1871; Hilarión Daza (1840–1894), Bolivian general and politician.

limited by the most negligible of his interests; he says he is an altruist, and he is an egotist; he defends morality and knows no scruples whatsoever. He is a hypocrite of the first order, and one is prudent to distrust the majority of his statements.

Strong, bold, quick-tempered, his capabilities are heightened when he is among his own kind, just as they diminish or disappear in isolation; and he is a good soldier, but he does not function as a leader. That is to say, it is in the *cholo,* more than in any other being, that one observes—I repeat—that sheep-like tendency that has more defects than strengths. In this way, the strong or the bold always take possession of his will and guide it according to their aspirations, and he follows without putting up opposition, without protesting, and sometimes with manly enthusiasm, because—very curious to note—the popular classes in Bolivia, being barely conscious or not at all, become successively passionate over contradictory principles, over political strongmen who embody opposing tendencies—and this with uncontainable vigor, with faith, with self-denial. Always disposed to run behind anyone who proclaims the perpetually seductive dogmas of an illusory equality and fraternity, they never become tired of—or even less, disappointed by—their eternal failures. Forgetful and inattentive, in each new political strongman who comes along or starts an uprising they believe they have encountered the only one, the sole one, who, by tearing down prejudices and cleaning up the rubble accumulated by his predecessors, will make a new work of creation; and when they see that he does not fulfill the promises he made for the sole purpose of winning, that he neither creates nor changes anything, they feel oppressed and sad, but only for a short time. New figures appear, and they become passionate again with equal or greater intensity, as they have done perpetually, eternally, for more than eighty years, and all this tremendous doing and undoing comes from sheer disinterest, maybe from self-denial, because the popular classes never obtain any advantage from any political change, because these classes—a model of generosity—never ask for anything, yet they submit to everything, content with having added a little luster to the entities known as "parties," to which they feel honored to belong, ignorant though they may be of their parties' principles, for they have none, or if they do have any, they are violated by the very ones who proclaim them. . . .

Unfortunately, this is the country's dominant class; for that reason this country, slow in conquests of a practical—or better, economic—nature, has lost the fleeting superiority that it exercised in the first years of independence, when all the peoples that had risen up, with the help of a vigorous push from men of great character and much talent, gave themselves over to the immoderate exercise of a liberty won by heroic efforts and not a few sacrifices.

The National Character

I. These are the principal characteristic features of each of the peoples of Bolivia; but there are others common to the whole, equally characteristic of the rest of the peoples of Latin America, whose analysis has been perfectly set forth by the shrewd psychologist Bunge in his excellent work *Nuestra America*,[9] to which one must appeal if one wishes to know and understand the variations of that changeable character with its somewhat incoherent manifestations.

Bunge has argued with good reason—although he has not sufficiently substantiated his argument, which would be easy to do—that the characters of the Spanish American peoples vary according to the quantity and quality of indigenous blood predominating in each of them.

Bolivia, as we have seen—because of the special conditions of its geographic location, and because it had been the mold where were forged the Quechua and Aymara civilizations, today almost extinct despite the survival of the races that gave birth to them—has not received a large quota of European blood, and for that reason it shows in its characteristics a certain abnormality not at all common to the peoples of similar lineage and the same ancestry, which is why it will be necessary to specify briefly the particular features of its "national character," which we have already sketched, and occasionally even to push some of Bunge's obligatory and indispensable ideas, because we are examining similar collective phenomena but from different points of view.

Above all, what vigorously and visibly jumps out here, precisely because of the ethnic differences we have noted and the isolation in which these populations live from one other, is a certain spirit of intolerance—as Guyau[10] says—which, depending on the repeating cycle of political events and the degree of development attained by the various regional centers, degenerates into a frank and decided hatred, to the point of establishing itself as a general rule that, today, hatred is the dominant passion not only among peoples subjected to opposing meteorological currents and of contrary ethnic composition, but between regions in the same territory and groups isolated from it, and, oddest of all, even between regional and family members and groups.

Regional hatred is born of the absolute influence that each region wishes to exercise over the others, and ancestral differences also enter into it: the old animosities reappear that drew the Aymara and Quechua peoples into persistent struggle. The regions of the north and south of the republic live in perpetual antagonism, and as a pretext—to characterize it best—they seek the external progress that manifests itself in the liveliness of the streets in their capitals or in the facades of their monuments. They pretend that artifice can be the sole cause of material and moral progress, and the cities aspire—as if this were possible—to reach, in fact and by a given time, equal development and identical configurations. The eternal question on the capital of the republic, though it appears to be legally resolved, in practice has not even been posed yet, and this gives rise to the peevish ferment that makes the life of the country so agitated and puts into play all its excess energies, which overflow in uncontainable violence.

---

9. Carlos Octavio Bunge (1875–1918), Argentine social psychologist, *Nuestra America: Ensayo de psicología social,* Buenos Aires, multiple editions, first published in 1903.

10. Jean Marie Guyau (1854–1888), French sociologist.

As in Spain, two opposing currents also struggle here, and regional hatred is born not so much from questions of temperament as from economic interests, which inflame passions to the highest level. The cities, like organisms with their own functions, tend toward greater development depending, generally speaking, on small permanent factors or constant reiteration; and because the dominant view here holds that cities arise from the power of the State, they struggle to retain their development within determined districts, and they forget that a population is not just an artificial creation and that their progress does not depend on accidental factors such as the greater or lesser permanence of a college body, but rather (this is elementary, my God!) on location, on having good means of transportation, on the spirit of the race. To feel hatred toward a city simply because it has better streets and monuments, and because its commerce is more active and its municipal government wealthier, is lamentably naive; and it is abnormal to expect that an industrious region could restrain its upward movement and wait for the others, inactive or not well-favored in their physical environment, to reach its level.

Apart from this, modern population centers respond to needs of every order and are no longer founded by conquistadors but by settlers. Bolivia's cities were all founded by the former. Each one symbolizes a feat of arms, a victory, a disaster, or the discovery of a mine. A matter of the moment. Our old dominators, here, in the rugged recesses of the Inca Empire, did not bear in mind favorable location, terrain, climate, nor other factors necessary for siting a city. "Here, a battle was won against the rebels," or, "here there are signs of gold, and here a city will be founded," they said; and they laid the cities' foundations feverishly, seduced in advance by renown or fortune. Almost all our cities were created with the apparent intention that they last an instant, just enough time to exploit the riches of the environs and outskirts, and today they present a strange aspect—the original one—for the indolent, lazy residents never bothered to change it. There are also streets narrower than those of Seville or Córdoba, more sinuous than those of Toledo, through which traffic is made difficult, not responding to the needs of the new civilization. . . .

Among the current population centers, there may not be a single one capable of serving as capital, because none responds to the ends just indicated. If possible—this is an idea dear to the brilliant Saavedra and Bustamante[11]—a city should be founded solely for this purpose, on the banks of a navigable river or lake, facing vast horizons, and . . . thereby stifle the soporific hatred that separates us, because otherwise we will always suffer this peevish ferment, which will cause the accentuation of those differences in aspiration, which can only produce disorganization, since, for many people, a lack of cohesion often leads to a lack of energy, the indispensable condition for undertaking any project.

This regional hatred degenerates into local hatred for the same reasons—because one shabby little town, village, hamlet, undergoes more development

---

11. Juan Bautista Saavedra (1870–1939), Bolivian politician. Bustamente probably refers to Ricardo José Bustamente (1821–1886), Bolivian poet.

than another. Among tiny little towns, this creates eternal disputes. A deputy, for example, obtains some meager benefit from Congress for his municipality, and now the neighboring municipality, on threat of provoking serious disturbances, asks that it be favored with an equal benefit. A fountain is installed in the plaza of a town, or a bell in the crumbling tower of a church, and the neighboring town strives to surpass what it considers great progress, leading not merely to oversensitive peevishness, but to deep animosity, often sealed with blood. . . . The same thing happens in regional hatred! A public building, an office, a theater, a road is constructed in one city, and the other cities aspire to the same; but always—and this is the essential point—with the help of the State. It is the State that must construct, conceive, and provide the example of initiative and labor.

Caste hatred is different and has been going on since the conquest.[12] The conquistador, having despoiled the Indian of what belonged to him, believed not only that he could take over the Indian's goods and lands, but also, and especially, his person. And in fact, he did possess the Indian; he possessed his women, and from that brutal contact—brought about not by the love that animates the seed of beautiful qualities, but rather by uncontainable organic necessities—there arose the hybrid race, whose psychology I have tried to outline.

From the white man, the mestizo has a despotic arrogance before those he considers his inferiors; and, like the Indian, is submissive, humble, and servile, yet not at all generous, before his superiors. He is a partisan of the ostentatious, of the pompous, of gaudy colors, of everything that shines, thunders, or stuns. Perverse, vengeful, he does not know how to balance his passions, and he hates everything that is superior to him or that does not submit to his plans and designs. Examples: Daza, Melgarejo.[13]

In him, this hatred shuts out all other passions.

Terrible as an enemy, he hates all who excel or who are characterized by some merit.

The white man is nobler in his loathing. When the *cholo* has received an insult, he longs vehemently for vengeance. Skillful in hiding his antipathies, he is even more skillful in concocting means of retaliation, giving preference to those that wound pride and sensibilities, and he experiences singular pleasure in laying open the vulnerabilities of human frailty, the ones that are kept timidly and bashfully hidden, maybe because showing them means provoking people's scornful commiseration. If he cannot take proper revenge on the man he hates because he cannot discover any vulnerable points, then he adds the failings of his enemy's ancestors to his account and throws them brutally in his face, forgetting that, given human vulnerability, there is no social or family group, not even the smallest in size, that does not have some ugly event, or at least a misfortune, in its past.

---

12. *Casta* (caste) is another colonial-era Spanish term for "race."

13. See footnote 7 on page 349.

This is characteristic of barbaric groups and individuals. Mr. Bagehot says in this regard:

"No barbarian can bear to see one of his nation deviate from the old barbarous customs and usages of their tribe. [. . .] In modern times and in cultivated countries we regard each person as responsible only for his own actions, and do not believe, or think of believing, that the misconduct of others can bring guilt on [us]. Guilt to us is an individual taint consequent on choice and cleaving to the chooser. But in early ages the act of one member of the tribe is conceived to make all the tribe impious," etc., etc.[14]

Here, barbarism still prevails. Personal conduct is not judged independently from that of the family group. Ancestral misfortunes are suffered with harshness. For us, individual conduct is not the product of equally individual culture, education, and temperament, but rather of one's environment, and not even the social environment, but the family. . . .

This hatred finds outward expression in our mania for nicknames, and—although nicknames can just as well be seen as the outward expression of the malignity that fills all contemporary societies in general, and although their use is not restricted to small and uncultured social groups but is found even among the largest and most civilized societies—it should be noted that in small groups, where malignity grows for lack of artistic diversions, those who distribute the nicknames never seek out a spiritual and colorful descriptive term that expresses admiration for a man's condition, but rather one that, in itself, comprises defamation and is the product of imaginations trained in the avid search for everything harmful that language contains.

II. Another of the idiosyncrasies of the national character is the general propensity for obtaining everything through the help of the State. This peculiarity is common not only to the peoples of completely aboriginal composition, nor to those of Iberian origin, but to all the Latins, or people of Latin race, even the most civilized, as M. LeBon[15] has so palpably demonstrated to us.[16]

In Bolivia, it possesses particular traits.

Generally it is believed here, with perfect naiveté among a certain class of people, that the mission of the State is to obtain for everyone, without exception, the means of work and subsistence. An individual, whatever knowledge, aptitudes, and character he might have, must be employed in a government office. "Functionarianism" is a social danger, with the aggravating factor that every functionary, especially those in high positions, thinks that being irresponsible in the

---

14. Walter Bagehot (1826–1877), British economist, *Physics and Politics, Or Thoughts on the Application of the Principles of 'Natural Selection' and 'Inheritance' to Political Society* (London, 1872), chapter 3.

15. Gustav LeBon (1841–1931), French psychologist and sociologist, author of a number of works on social psychology in which he expounded theories of national traits and racial superiority.

16. *Psychologie du Socialisme* [Arguedas's note. Paris, 1898; trans., *The Psychology of Socialism*, New York: 1899].

management of the State's funds is an act revelatory of admirable speculative qualities.

Social morality, in this sense, has gone astray.

Administrative honesty is one of many clichés, or better, a convention like any other; the danger is that no one may dare attack it, because, in the first place, it is believed that publicizing to the four winds what is already an organic sickness is unpatriotic, and also because people demand "material" proof of the deed, as if it were not common among the violators to hide every trace that could bring their guilt to light.

One can scarcely have honesty here where it passes for axiomatic that "cheating the State means not cheating anybody." This is why, when political parties put overwhelming energy into their excited struggles, it is not to attain power as the pinnacle of their conscientious aspirations, but rather because, by attaining power, they can satisfy—as I will prove later—satisfactions of every kind and create positions in public affairs for a large portion of the social group.

This sort of impassioned job-mania—as it seems pointless to observe—is the prime cause and origin of the decline of commerce, of industry, of agriculture, of all the things that, in short, form the principal source of a nation's development, not to mention—on the contrary!—the well-being characteristic of active and enterprising peoples. Poverty is the natural condition of individuals here, so much so that one can be certain that in Bolivia there are no rich people in the true sense of the word, as there are in other nations. None of those who are considered rich here has an annual income of a million. Generally, a person who has 200,000 pesos of *capital* is considered—with the help of an imaginative phenomenon common among us—a "millionaire"; and we have none of those jarring contrasts that incite antipathy among the disinherited classes, who are quick to dream up means, generally draconian, of achieving equality. As a consequence, here there is not even the remotest hint of those conflicts over capital that are so difficult to resolve. Everyone who works, even the Indian, has something; and it would be easy to set up a list of ranks by following our clever and explanatory everyday language. It would be as follows:

Tycoons	8	to	10,000,000	pesos of capital
Millionaires	1	to	8,000,000	"
First-class rich people	100	to	500,000	"
Second-class " "	50	to	100,000	"
Third-class " "	20	to	50,000	"
With average fortunes	15	to	30,000	"
Without the means to live	8	to	15,000	"
The poor	2	to	5,000	"
The very poor			000	"

This semi-indigence arises from the fact that work continues to be considered a divine curse in Bolivia, and leisure the height of happiness. Laziness rules in an absolute, enslaving, terrible way, in its most repugnant aspect—immobility.

Everyone's vehement aspiration is to do nothing and to enjoy themselves the more. They await holidays with excessive impatience. Any effort causes grief. Intellectual and physical laziness both exist—and both to a superlative degree.

The first leads to the wandering rhetoric and clichés that characterize the great majority of those who hold higher degrees, including intellectuals. Most begin by composing verses in the plaintive style and end up delivering speeches in Congress or the municipal courthouse, but speeches without substance, like almost all those of our politicians. Physical laziness manifests itself in indolence and inactivity. He who thinks, digresses; he who works in the field takes long siestas; on top of a Sunday of repose, he who toils in the workshops takes Monday and Saturday off.

The calendar used here corresponds to our laziness. We are devoted to all the saints. There are national, departmental, and municipal fiestas, and between them, out of the three hundred sixty-five days of the year, three hundred are dedicated to inactivity. The ambient axiom is simple—there should be enough to eat today, no matter how much we might lack indispensable necessities tomorrow. Our way of thinking is much worse than that of the Andalusian in the story who sold his mattress to attend a bullfight. Here, hardly anyone even has a mattress to sell even in case of necessity; but we always eat and sleep, although not well. Because idleness predominates, everything that moves and stirs shocks the lymphatic temperament of the masses. For that reason, anyone who makes an effort is called a "hustler," in a contemptuous tone. Here, doing nothing is a matter of pride. "I live from my dividends" is a distinguished and high-toned answer. Suggestions for reform irritate collective self-love, because, yes indeed, we are extremely sensitive. Just let us enjoy ourselves, stop tormenting us . . . Must we work? No matter; we'll work. And if, for whatever reason, by any chance, there is no work, that doesn't matter either! God will provide. . . .

And that is the great question, the iron contraption of our logic. . . . God is our first and supreme refuge. A leaf does not move without his will. We put him in charge of making us happy. If he does not help us, we neither blaspheme, nor do our beliefs waver—we fall into a humble, resigned, sad conformity. . . . *God has willed it!*

We beg for God's intercession in all our business deals, easy or difficult; for it is worth noting that we Bolivians are fond of conceiving vast deals, gigantic projects—but only of conceiving them, never of carrying them out. We lack the one condition indispensable for completing any plan whatsoever—persistence of character.

Here, every last one of us consoles himself in his penury by sheltering his imagination in the bosom of the earth, where incalculable riches sleep. From the highest politicians to the humblest civil servants, all are at least shareholders in a mining claim or a rubber plantation, and all live cherishing the hope of a fabulous business deal that, in a magic stroke, will lift them from indigence to opulence.

Patient and orderly work neither tempts nor charms the Bolivian. If he works, it must be to get a truly fabulous reward for his labor; otherwise, he remains inactive, prowling around the corridors of government, casting about for a candidacy for deputy or town councilman, or both at once, and he is absolutely unaware of the healthy happiness of creating and undertaking. His laziness is a thousand times worse than the Muslim's, because the latter's is a product of fatalism, that is to say, a matter of belief; the other is laziness for the sake of laziness.

If we were to continue boring the reader with statistics (a remote science, unadaptable to this land), it would be seen that half or three-quarters of the mines, the source of our public and private wealth, do not belong to natives but rather to foreigners, who, in this and other matters, show true speculative talent. Almost all the companies in good economic condition today were founded by outsiders, and if a national company ever ventures to become involved in these business deals, it is not with the intention of establishing serious work and investing robust sums in it, but rather of using it to begin negotiations with some syndicate or company founded abroad and making a fat fortune from the deal. Each day, Bolivian nationals make thousands of petitions for mining claims or rubber plantations (in Potosí alone there were 378 in 1906), but few undertake work on the land they request; they limit themselves to paying the license fees, and then they fold their arms, expecting their syndicate savior to come bringing fistfuls of gold, simply for their having taken the trouble of presenting a document and paying the expenses for measuring and marking the boundaries. . . . The majority of commercial import and export houses is made up of foreign firms, and their prosperity grows to the extent that the prosperity of the national firms diminishes, and this prosperity is based on small factors. Thus, for example, there is an interesting contrast between a fabric store owned by a national and one owned by a foreigner. The national, first off, never ventures to order goods directly from the great manufacturers or through the normal channel of the customs agent; instead, he gets them from the foreign houses established in the country, so that when he sells them, he is forced to raise the price to compensate for his losses and make his profit. Then, when he sets up his business, he looks for a cheap location with no presence, and he furnishes it poorly, without resorting to the powerful aid of advertising, whose efficacy he feels rather unimportant, thinking thus the opposite of the "Yankees," who spend fabulous sums on commercials. As one critic says, these sums equal those that Russia, Germany, France, Austria, Spain invest in their armies ($500,000,000).[17]

Work? No. Here, work is an occasional affair, or better, secondary. In the store of a national, chatting goes on, opinions are exchanged, politics discussed, jokes made between the seller and buyer. The idea of doing business in a minute, with serious words, sincerely, is unknown here. The buyer needs to be talked to death, to be convinced, to be shown with his own eyes the value or usefulness of an object or piece of merchandise. Thus, if a manager or store owner should run into a client, he inquires about the health of the family, of the

---

17. *La Revue,* June 1906. [Aguedas's note.]

little ones, of the wife. The store of a national is always a center for agreeable and friendly get-togethers. Two or three friends come upon each other in the street, and, to "kill time," they go to the shopkeeper's store and pass the hours chatting and talking about the news from that morning's newspaper. In vain does the proprietor, alarmed by the drop in sales the day it occurs to his friends to come visit him, have a large placard placed in the store's most visible site, which reads, in black letters on a white background, "Chatting is harmful," or this other, more disturbing note: "Chatting prohibited." In vain. The friends continue coming as if nothing has happened, and when the business is a grocery store, they even play dice on the cashier's desk and serve themselves drinks on the sample case, thus keeping clientele from going there, because the Bolivian consumer is timid—he likes to bargain, to ask for his *yapa*,[18] and to do all these things he has to be alone with the seller, not in front of nosy people who will start gossiping as soon as he has turned his back.

The foreign merchant does the same, but using a different system. He well knows that everything has to have eye appeal, so he spreads out a range of colors and dazzles with the display. He sets himself up in a convenient, large space in a good location, and then he does not fold his arms and wait for the client, but rather calls him, searches for him, offers him credit, and even treats him politely. His entire shop is a showcase, and his shop assistants, carefully selected from people with lively spirits, only deal with putting before the eyes of the curious and the buyer whatever might attract their attention, while never huddling in small groups, much less letting the hint of a laugh be heard. And these trifles lead to the continual defeat of national retailers, who are obliged to give way to the more active and better experts in the field.

This kind of defeat for our nationals occurs not only in the strictly commercial field, but in all others as well. The few factories, the rare foundries, the breweries, the exploration for metals, and even agriculture, reserved exclusively for our nationals, are passing into the hands of foreigners. Mining is the field that has been most invaded. Large foreign companies begin to take, almost to grab, comfortable and easy possession of the best this country possesses. There is a highly significant fact worth noting here, one that gives clear proof of the shiftlessness I mentioned earlier—our neighbors, the Argentines and the Chileans, are the ones who have organized the most companies to exploit our region's precious metals, without there having been on the part of Bolivians the slightest movement to do the same. Studying the management staffs of commercial firms, it can be seen that foreign syndicates export a large part of Bolivian metal production—those organized by the Chileans are the most active.

And what happens is interesting.

All these classes of ruined industrialists and merchants develop an intense hatred of the "interlopers" who have come expressly to carry away the "silver that belongs to us," yet they do not notice that the increase in trade, domestic as well

---

18. *Yapa*, an Andean word for "a little something extra" given to a client.

as foreign, is solely due to the effort and initiative of those interlopers. Incapable of imitating them and making the same efforts, little by little the nationals lag behind, and it is not unreasonable to anticipate that shortly, economic movement will depend on the foreigners' energy, without any of our nationals taking part in it—and it will be fair and correct if this happens, for this, like everything issuing from relationships, is subject to laws of which it would be puerile to remind one.

III. But these woes, serious in themselves, would be trivial if it were not for another much more serious one, which, germinated in our political circles, was then passed contagiously to our industrial circles, and today is widespread throughout the system, even in its lowest levels—fraud.

Here no one dares undertake anything, because everyone is distrustful. Suspicion degenerates into fierce, intransigent egotism; and this is the close-minded egotism of the Indian, for whom everyone who approaches is a thief or a cheat. Surly, almost gloomy, our industrialists keep their money not under lock and key, but under dozens of locks and keys; our capitalists feel genuine panic when forming partnerships with other capitalists, and it would be easier for them to throw their money into the river than to deliver it into the hands of a national industrialist, toward whom they feel real terror, not unfounded, unfortunately. It has reached such a level of immorality that two nationals cannot work together as partners without one cheating the other. So long as a national is partners with a foreigner, he can embark on deals and enterprises; but when his partner is a fellow countryman, he generally fails. Fraudulent bankruptcies, illicit collusion, unreliability in keeping commitments, canceling and retracting contracts—all are commonplace. The tribunals of justice are crawling with plaintiffs—in 1900 alone the supreme court vacated 320 petitions, of which 249 were civil complaints, and every day the newspapers print invoices and payment notices in a special section, and threats are made to publish the names of those who have not fulfilled their economic commitments—everywhere measures of the degree of collective morality. The spirit of distrust dominates the majority of relationships, and business relationships are not freely made. People fear each other, to the point where it becomes difficult to find partners to undertake a business or run a factory.

Consequently, anyone who succeeds, in any sphere at all, engenders not only violent hatred in others, but uncontrollable envy—or rather, the envy generates the hate. People aspire to a complete, absolute leveling. Whoever excels, even by a hair, over a group with such a makeup, arouses aggressive irritability instead of affection.

Hatred and envy form a perfect and gloomy union in these small societies, accustomed to living focused exclusively on externals, far from the inspiring calm of reflection and generosity, the product of honorable souls and cultured spirits. Malicious, suspicious, distrustful, egotistical, miserly, they live in open struggle, never permitting anyone—except those who prosper in politics—to pull himself up; and anyone who has the misfortune of making it without being lowered to the sphere where evil passions are stirred up in larval convulsions, is left alone in his heights, in those heights where, if anything is felt among indigenous peoples, it is the infinite sadness of the person who has no one . . .

And this banal, merciless, sordid, implacable struggle increases the bitter sadness infused by the Indians through lack of hygiene; but the worst is that it is becoming chronic and is taking on a morbid appearance; the fault for this lies with alcohol, whose corrosiveness is now apparent. There is no desire to do anything for anything—quite the contrary. This leads to the passive, indifferent stillness that induces us towards anything except excitement, motion.

And if the sadness of a people can be measured by the preferred themes of the popular muse, we can certainly agree that ours is sad to the highest degree.

All, absolutely all of our popular songs speak of strong passions—love, loss, hatred, death. All of them mention lost illusions, happiness cut short, incomplete pleasures. The most rueful Spanish ballads find their adoptive homeland in Peru and Bolivia. Becquer[19] enchants—most of his verses have been set to music; and the stanzas of Espronceda,[20] those dedicated to Jarifa, are recited here from memory.

This kind of sickly sentimentality shows up not only in our poetry, but also in our customs, our private life, and, above all, our music.

You have only to hear it to be convinced.

A music of slow, rhythmical turns, always in a minor key, with variations on the same melancholy and monotonous theme. It never speaks of chaste joys, never suggests a tranquil idea of peace. Always displaying the horrors of suffering, a weariness of spirit, and a constant yearning to pass and disappear. It is a music composed of a strange and doleful union between the *Miserere* and the Andalusian *jipios*,[21] disturbing and dangerous music.

The evolution of music, of course, parallels physical evolution. The more complex an organism is, the more excited is its nervous agitation, and then it becomes imperative to interpret its aspirations in some way, and music is the easiest way of expressing that state. The ethnic groups comprising the country have not undergone any kind of agitation; to the contrary, they have descended in cultural level—hence their depression, a serious symptom of collective decline. Our popular music expresses this state; this is why it lacks the verve inherent in all sociable music. It is simple and sentimental—on a par with our poetry, designed, I insist, to show the fragility of emotions, an imbalance in telling of pains and pleasures, giving rise, as a corollary, to a pessimistic conception of life. . . . Picaresque themes do not charm us, and if we prefer any of them, it is the macabre

---

19. Gustavo Adolfo Becquer (1836–1870), Spanish poet; the most genuine representative of Spanish romanticism in its most intimate facet.

20. José de Espronceda (1808–1842), Spanish poet; the great exponent of romanticism in Spain, he wrote "A Jarifa en una Orgía," a very famous poem expressing disillusionment and lamentation with respect to lost pleasures.

21. The *Miserere* is a song composed from psalms that begin with the word "Miserere," a slow mournful part of the Latin Mass; the Andalusian *jipios* are songs sung in a semi-groan, close in style to Gypsy flamenco.

picaresque, the sort that toys with death or jests bitterly at life. Moaning, painful, impassioned romanticism is ours, and very much ours.

All social classes, when they give free outlet to their expansive spirits, once aroused by alcohol, are not happy, boisterous, fussy, but rather sullen, reserved, mute. Instead of shouting or loud laughter, we have the moaning lament—the Indians, *cholos,* and whites, drunk, do not sing; they weep. Their deepest concern comes out in their heartrending moans, which demand pity and consolation: pity for the thoughtlessness with which the natural forces work; consolation for the woes that disquiet our emotions; for life, so full of grief, so sad . . . .

The National Therapeutics

V. To remedy these ills readily and effectively, given our fatal custom of expecting everything to come from the aid and good will of the State, we must agree to let the State be the promoter of any movement toward reorganization; and, in order that its action be decisive and immediate, a program must be designed, and this is the opportune moment to do so, because shortly, in a few more months, we will celebrate the centennial of the first cry of independence raised by our forefathers [1810], and it would be a worthy commemoration if the conscientious governed and their governors, inspired just this once by genuine patriotism, would vow before the august altar of the youthful fatherland to try a new direction—for the mere act of trying would demonstrate that the illness is known and that we are trying to cure it. This is the moment to place milestones along the route by which we want to progress, and it would be a noble, legitimate source of pride for these conscientious governed and governors if, from now to the celebration of the centennial of the consolidation of independence, over the same fifteen years that our grandfathers fought to achieve their longed-for liberty, we ourselves would work to achieve something more than that liberty, not yet honored by persevering and judicious labor—a precise notion of our duties toward ourselves and toward the fatherland.

A program designed to realize this notion would have to embrace the following essential points:

Paying special attention to instruction and taking care that it be carried out by men who are current in the latest precepts of pedagogy, since our reorganization asks more of the teacher than of the soldier and the statesman;

Establishing normal schools with foreign teachers and complete sets of materials;

Centralizing the universities;

Building railroads, waterways, and horse paths;

Creating a character that, in sum, is nothing but the outcome of education;

Campaigning continuously against alcoholism and creating ways to prevent its progression;

Adopting widely a system of governmental conduct and progress and having this system followed unwaveringly by every governing person who rises to power and by every party (!) that wins election;

Sending new people abroad constantly, on any excuse whatsoever;

Facilitating immigration and creating special bodies in charge of sending in immigrants, pre-selected, from abroad;

Choosing civil servants for quality of characters, not for party preference;

Struggling perpetually against demagoguery;

Educating the indigenous race—a factor indispensable for our agricultural development;

Freedom of worship, not merely tolerance; and

Designating, definitively and courageously, the republic's capital, or creating a city to serve as such.

All this is indispensable, indeed necessary, and must be done at one stroke and not little by little as is the prevailing view among the immense majority. To achieve it, we must observe the procedure counseled by Don Joaquín Costa,[22] "the iron surgeon," as they call him in his country, whose remedies for his country's ills are identical to those for Bolivia, because there must be a reason for the deep emotional tie between the two countries, allowing it to be said that atavistically we suffer from woes whose cure is a matter of time and will.

Don Joaquín Costa says:

"Honor the laborer even more, if that is possible, than the soldier who returns from war, because it requires a greater hero's calling to carry out labor than to fight.

"What Spain (where he says Spain, read Bolivia) needs and must demand of the school is not necessarily men *who know how to read and write.* What it needs are *men*—and creating them requires educating the body as much as the spirit, and the will as much or more than the mind. Consciousness of duty, a spirit of initiative, confidence in oneself, individuality, character; and together with this, the restoration of the body, so worn down by lack of cleanliness, excess of work, and insufficient nourishment.

"Provide the Spanish brain with a solid education and abundant nutrition by supporting both the larder and the school; combat the contingencies of geography and race by working to redeem our inferiority in both regards through art, by approximating as far as possible the conditions of geography and race to those of central Europe, by increasing the productive power of the territory, and by elevating society's intellectual power and moral tone.

"The problem of the regeneration of Spain is pedagogical as much as, or more than, economic and financial, and it calls for a profound transformation of national education at all grade levels.

"Some universities should be eliminated and in their place: (1) support personal scientific research; (2) create regional and local schools for manual training—which is positive and indeed *practical*—in agriculture, in the arts and trades, and in commerce; and so forth, and so on.

---

22. Joaquín Costa (1846–1911), pioneering Spanish economist and social theorist. The passages cited are drawn from his *Reconstitución y europeización de España* (Madrid, 1901).

"We must improvise a nation, producing a revolution from the seat of power in the space of months, perhaps weeks; we need political *fakirs* who can reproduce the miracle of India, making the plant germinate and grow while the observer looks on, at the very instant it is sown in the earth, without waiting for the slow and painful evolutions of ordinary agriculture. We must break with the entire existing order, closing our eyes and ears to a whole lifetime of personal obligations; condense time, taking minutes for hours and hours for weeks; launch the country, without regard to the rashness of attempting too much or too little, not at great speed, but rather at a vertiginous speed, with the hope, however remote, of catching up to Europe in its race and giving consolation to the present generation during its few remaining years of life.

"The first concern of the republic should be to create men, to make men. There will never be a Spain other than the one that emerges from the brains of Spaniards. For this reason the republic must be a farmer, a cultivator of souls, and it must set to plowing with persistent effort and then sow the seed of the nation in every person's spirit."

Create men!

There, reduced to two words quite foreign to us, is our program. This, this is what Bolivia needs—men!

Men with directed wills and characters as firm as the granite of our mountains.

Practical, active, and honest men.

Thoughtful and good men.

There are those who embody an entire epoch—geniuses; others who prepare the means—talented men; others, finally, who have the gift of adding disparate activities to their own activity—men of character.

These last are the ones we need the most and the ones who appear most frequently.

Laziness, sadness, dirtiness are illnesses that can be cured. So at least believes Villazón,[23] the greatest of our contemporary statesmen. It is therefore necessary to establish our national pedagogy. And this is the exclusive work of men of character, whose activity always produces results. Arce,[24] despite his intolerance and his sectarian fanaticism, has the incontestable merit of having built our first railway, today in active service, and he well deserves the bronze statue that is to be raised in his honor. His adversaries can talk about his crimes, say that his corrupt administration was wicked; but there remain those rails, along which trains roll daily, bringing comfort to a hard-working people—though it is true that, when behavior contrary to order and liberty prevails, it remains like a bad seed and later produces serious, deep disturbances.

Even if the occasion is not appropriate, something has to be said. Often our legislators dread authorizing the implementation of some project for fear of the

---

23. Eliodoro Villazón (1849–1939), Bolivian politician, president of the republic (1909–1913).

24. Aniceto Arce (1824–1906), Bolivian politician, president of the republic (1888–1892).

dishonesty of those who govern. That does not matter. Let the funds be mismanaged, let there be waste, but let something be done.

Since we are fatally quick to tire in our behavior, let us stop thinking that we will be better off doing nothing. We must do things and undertake things, the only way to progress. Responsibility can be decided on later, when men no longer have any interest in misrepresenting events nor any fear of being sincere, and that is when, in the opinion of history, some governors will be called Linares[25] and others Daza, for example.

Create men!

If a man were to come along who was just, good, honorable, valiant, and great because of his virtues, it would be worth helping him to rise, working to place him in power, and then counseling him to govern at his discretion, without legislative houses, without parties, relying only on his own judgment and that of his collaborators, and then to make use of his muscles, of his character, to liberate us and root out this scrawny caste of petty politicians who find nothing in civil service but a means of showing off and making a living; and it is certain that such a man would make Bolivia a free, conscious, and modern people, making it acquire a consciousness of nationhood based on facts and results and not produced by a sickly imagination. We need men who will overthrow much of what is now on top and who will do the work of revolution, constructing anew, if it is possible, without compromises, without cowardice, strong in their labor and concerned, above all, with putting us to work, forcing us to move, and, when we are filled with faith and courage, implanting in our heads a lofty ideal, the only way of pursuing and attaining an end, a destiny; for as Tarde[26] says in *The Laws of Imitation,* "social peace, unanimous faith in the same ideal or the same hope, a unanimity that implies an assimilation of humanity each day more extensive and more profound—here is the end toward which all social revolutions flow, like it or not. Such is progress, which is to say, the advancement of the social world along logical pathways."

---

25. José María Linares (1810–1861), Bolivian attorney and politician. Member of the commission that formulated the laws of newly independent Bolivia.

26. Gabriel de Tarde (1843–1904), French sociologist, a founder of psychosociology.

GUIDE to THEMES

Education for Citizenship and Economic Development

Andrés Bello: "Speech Delivered at the Installation of the University of Chile, September 17, 1843"

Francisco Bilbao: "Chilean Sociability" (1844)

Domingo Faustino Sarmiento: *Facundo, or Civilization and Barbarism* (1845)

Juan Bautista Alberdi: *Foundations and Points of Departure for the Political Organization of the Republic of Argentina* (1853)

Juan Montalvo: *Seven Treatises:* Third Treatise: "Reply to a Pseudo-Catholic Sophist" (1882)

Eugenio María de Hostos: "The Purpose of the Normal School" (1884)

José Martí: "Our America" (1891)

Foreign Relations

Lucas Alamán: *The History of Mexico* (1849–1852)

Juan Bautista Alberdi: *Foundations and Points of Departure for the Political Organization of the Republic of Argentina* (1853)

José Victorino Lastarria: *America* (1865)

José Martí: "Our America" (1891)

Justo Sierra: "The Present Era," from *The Political Evolution of the Mexican People* (1900–1902)

Francisco Alonso de Bulnes: *The Future of the Latin American Nations* (1906)

History: Its Nature and Uses

José Victorino Lastarria: *Investigations Regarding the Social Influence of the Conquest and the Spanish Colonial System in Chile* (1844)

Andrés Bello: "Response to Lastarria on the Influence of the Conquest" (1844)

Lucas Alamán: *The History of Mexico* (1849–1852)

José Martí: "Our America" (1891)

Justo Sierra: "The Present Era," from *The Political Evolution of the Mexican People* (1900–1902)

Political Organization

Símon Bolívar: "Address to the Angostura Congress, February 15, 1819, the Day of Its Installation."

Domingo Faustino Sarmiento: *Facundo, or Civilization and Barbarism* (1845)

Esteban Echeverría: *The Socialist Doctrine of the Association of May* (1846)

Lucas Alamán: *The History of Mexico* (1849–1852)

Juan Bautista Alberdi: *Foundations and Points of Departure for the Political Organization of the Republic of Argentina* (1853)

José Martí: "Our America" (1891)

Justo Sierra: "The Present Era," from *The Political Evolution of the Mexican People* (1900–1902)

Race

Domingo Faustino Sarmiento: *Facundo, or Civilization and Barbarism* (1845)

Juan Bautista Alberdi: *Foundations and Points of Departure for the Political Organization of the Republic of Argentina* (1853)

José Martí: "Our America" (1891)

Euclides da Cunha: *Rebellion in the Backlands* (1902)

Alcides Arguedas: *The Sick People* (1909)

Religion

Simón Bolívar: "Address to the Constituent Congress of Bolivia" (1826)

José María Luis Mora: "On Ecclesiastical Wealth" (1831)

Francisco Bilbao: "Chilean Sociability" (1844)

Esteban Echeverría: *The Socialist Doctrine of the Association of May* (1846)

Lucas Alamán: *The History of Mexico* (1849–1852)

Juan Montalvo: *Seven Treatises:* Third Treatise: "Reply to a Pseudo-Catholic Sophist" (1882)

Francisco Alonso de Bulnes: *The Future of the Latin American Nations* (1906)

Women

Eugenio María de Hostos: "The Scientific Education of Women" (1873)

Soledad Acosta de Samper: "The Mission of the Woman Writer in Spanish America" (1895)

Clorinda Matto de Turner: "The Woman Worker and the Woman" (1904)